LEADING ISSUES IN
DEVELOPMENT ECONOMICS

LEADING ISSUES

IN

DEVELOPMENT ECONOMICS

SELECTED MATERIALS AND COMMENTARY

GERALD M. MEIER, *Stanford University*

New York / OXFORD UNIVERSITY PRESS / 1964

Printed in the United States of America

PREFACE

This is intended as a new kind of course book in economic development. It departs from the usual approaches of a text or book of readings. For the subject matter of economic development is now so wide-ranging and yet so lacking in received doctrine that it defies the compression and definitiveness of a textbook. Neither is the ordinary type of readings book able to do justice to the subject when it is limited to a small number of "classic" articles, each of which is simply left to stand alone. I have therefore wanted to organize this volume differently. I have distilled from the enormous literature on development a relatively few issues that have emerged to the forefront of the subject but which are still unsettled and in need of closer analysis; on each of these leading issues, I have then brought to bear a variety of materials that should be looked at together; and to ensure cohesion and direction, I have provided a substantive commentary through a series of connecting text Notes.

The following issues are explicated in successive chapters: (1) the validity of Rostow's analysis of the stages of growth, (2) the meaning and significance of dualism, (3) problems of capital accumulation, (4) effects of inflation on development, (5) criteria for allocating investment resources, (6) the relative emphasis to be given industrialization and agriculture in the development process, (7) the influence of international trade on development, (8) the scope for development planning, and (9) techniques of development planning. There are, of course, numerous other topics relevant to the subject. But the questions considered here are those that have become the main preoccupations of development economists.

An examination of the Table of Contents will make apparent the range of materials selected to illuminate these questions. The applied and policy materials emanating from governments, visiting missions, conferences and research groups within the newly developing countries are not easily available to students elsewhere. But it is just these materials that are needed to make the subject "come alive" for those who have not had firsthand experience with development problems. On the other side, in the poor countries, it is particularly unfortunate that the scarcity of books and periodicals thwarts the eagerness of a rising generation of economists to become grounded in the general propositions of development economics. I have therefore wanted to make readily accessible a substantial collection of theoretical, applied, and policy materials that would reflect the present state of development economics and that could be shared by students in rich and poor countries alike.

To provide an integral commentary and clarify problems raised by particular selections, I have also written a number of connecting text Notes. These supplement the other selections and suggest questions that might carry the reader on to further speculation. In some instances, a Note is designed to treat a subject more expeditiously than could be done through separate readings.

It should be stressed that more importance is to be attached to the set of readings on each issue—taken as a set—than to any one particular reading. Each selection should acquire added significance through its contextual position, and the materials should be enhanced by their very combination. By juxtaposing analytical arguments with a survey of experience and policy matters, a special effort has been made to give concreteness to some of the issues that are usually considered in only abstract terms. The materials have also been selected to convey a sense of diversity of possible approaches and variety of viewpoints on each issue.

I wish to express my appreciation to the authors and publishers who have granted permission to use excerpts from articles, books, and other publications in which American or foreign copyrights exist. Specific acknowledgement is given with each selection. Out of consideration for the limitations of space and the avoidance of repetition, I have omitted some parts of the original versions; tables and diagrams have been renumbered; some footnotes have been omitted, and others have been renumbered.

The work on this book has been greatly facilitated by association with the International Center for the Advancement of Management Education at Stanford University. Many of the materials were first tested in the economic development course at the Center. To the participants in that course—all of whom were from underdeveloped countries—I am especially grateful for sharing with me their practical experiences and their judgments about the major development problems of their own countries.

I am also indebted to John Adler, Werner Baer, Paul Clark, Gamani Corea, Torsten Gardlund, Joseph Grunwald, Derek T. Healey, Ursula Hicks, Hla Myint, Gustav Ranis, and Paul Streeten, who kindly reviewed a preliminary outline of contents and gave me good advice on the choice of materials.

I also wish to thank Miss Catherine E. Cooney, Mrs. Bernice Nesbitt, and Miss Marsha Huffman for their able secretarial assistance.

Palo Alto   G.M.M.
November 1963

SUMMARY OF CONTENTS

Preface v

Analytical Table of Contents ix

    I   Stages of Development 3

   II   Dualistic Development 48

  III   Capital Accumulation 90

  IV   Inflation 169

   V   Allocation of Investment Resources 229

  VI   Industrialization and Agriculture 285

 VII   The Export Sector 338

VIII   Scope of Development Planning 415

  IX   Techniques of Development Planning 464

       Index 569

ANALYTICAL TABLE OF CONTENTS

I STAGES OF DEVELOPMENT

Introductory Note 3
1 **The Rostow Doctrine**
   1.1 Trends in International Development—DEANE 5
   1.2 A Dynamic Theory of Production—ROSTOW 11
   1.3 The Traditional Society and the Preconditions for Take-off—ROSTOW .. 13
   1.4 The Take-off—ROSTOW 16
2 **Appraisals and Critiques**
   2.1 Rostow and Marx—Note 23
   2.2 Empirical Evidence on Rostow's Stages—KUZNETS 25
   2.3 Conditions of the Take-off—CAIRNCROSS 33
   2.4 A Critique of Rostow's *Stages*—HABAKKUK 36
   2.5 An Approach to European Industrialization—GERSCHENKRON ... 38
3 **Future Take-offs in Perspective—Note** 42
4 **Bibliographical Note** 47

II DUALISTIC DEVELOPMENT

Introductory Note 48
1 **Examples of Dual Economies**
   1.1 Dualism in African Economies—UNITED NATIONS 49
2 **Social Dualism**
   2.1 Dualistic Economics—BOEKE 53
   2.2 A Critique of Boeke's "Dualistic Theory"—HIGGINS 55
   2.3 The Plural Society—FURNIVALL 64
3 **Technological Dualism**
   3.1 Production Functions and Technological Dualism—Note 68
   3.2 The Genesis of the Employment Problem—ILO 71
4 **Underemployment**
   4.1 Labor Surplus on the Land—NURKSE 74
   4.2 Unemployment in Underdeveloped Countries—HABERLER 77
   4.3 The Concept of "Disguised Unemployment"—VINER 79
   4.4 Excess Supplies of Labor—Note 83
5 **Inter-Sectoral Relationships in a Dual Economy—Note** 85
6 **Bibliographical Note** 88

III CAPITAL ACCUMULATION

Introductory Note 90

1 The Role of Capital

1.1 Estimating Capital Requirements—ECAFE 92

1.2 The Cost of Capital Accumulation—LEWIS 95

1.3 The Supply of Capital and the Supply of Other Factors—ADLER AND

KRISHNASWAMY 98

1.4 Criticisms of the Capital-Output Ratio—Note 101

1.5 The Place of Capital in Economic Progress—CAIRNCROSS 104

1.6 Capital and Development—FRANKEL 110

2 Sources of Capital Formation—Note 112

3 The Government as Saver

3.1 Taxation in Underdeveloped Countries—HELLER 115

3.2 Taxation and Economic Surplus—CHELLIAH 119

3.3 Reconstruction of Tax Systems—GOODE 122

3.4 Taxation of Agriculture—Note 127

3.5 Taxation in India's Third Plan—NARASIMHAM 129

4 Foreign Aid

4.1 How Much Aid?—BENHAM 131

4.2 Estimates of Aid Requirements for Specific Purposes—UNITED NATIONS 136

4.3 Types and Conditions of Foreign Aid—MIKESELL AND ALLEN 138

4.4 External Financing for India's Third Plan—GATT 142

4.5 On Making Foreign Aid More Effective—Note 145

5 Private Foreign Investment

5.1 The Contribution of Private Foreign Investment—Note 149

5.2 Joint International Business Ventures—FRIEDMANN AND KALMANOFF 159

5.3 Foreign Capital in the Gold Coast—LEWIS 163

6 Bibliographical Note 166

IV INFLATION

Introductory Note 169

1 Inflation and Its Effects

1.1 Inflation and Capital Formation—ECAFE 170

1.2 Deficit Financing in Underdeveloped Countries—PATTERSON 174

1.3 Deficit Financing and Public Investment—SINGER 179

1.4 Effects of Inflation on Exports—LOVASY 183

1.5 The Control of Inflation—DORRANCE 184

1.6 Inflation and Monetary Policy—BLOOMFIELD 189

1.7 Organized and Unorganized Money Markets—TUN WAI 193

2 Inflation in Latin America

2.1 The Process of Inflation in Latin America—ECLA 203

2.2 Structural Vulnerability and Inflation—PREBISCH 207

2.3 The "Monetarist"-"Structuralist" Controversy—CAMPOS 210

2.4 Inflation in Chile—GRUNWALD 213

2.5   Stabilization Efforts in Chile—SCHOTT 219
2.6   Lessons from Latin American Experience—SEERS 224
3   **Bibliographical Note** 226

V   ALLOCATION OF INVESTMENT RESOURCES

Introductory Note 229
1   **Investment Criteria**
1.1   Survey of Criteria for Allocating Investment Resources—ECAFE 231
1.2   Social Productivity and Factor Intensity Criteria—ILO 235
1.3   Making an Optimal Choice of Technology—ECKAUS 243
1.4   Practical Conditions Facing Investment Choice—DOSSER 247
2   **Growth—Balanced or Unbalanced?**
2.1   Balanced Growth—NURKSE 250
2.2   Balanced Growth: A Critique—HIRSCHMAN 254
2.3   Balanced Growth versus Unbalanced Growth—STREETEN 259
2.4   A Balanced View of Balanced Growth—SINGER 263
3   **Manpower and Education**
3.1   Investment in Human Capital—Note 266
3.2   Human Resources Development—HARBISON 272
3.3   Role of Education—BOWMAN AND ANDERSON 276
3.4   Investment in Social Infrastructure—MYINT 280
4   **Bibliographical Note** 283

VI   INDUSTRIALIZATION AND AGRICULTURE

Introductory Note 285
1   **Emphasis on Industry**
1.1   Industrialization of Peripheral Countries—PREBISCH 286
2   **Emphasis on Agriculture**
2.1   Arguments for Development of Agriculture—PAPANEK 289
2.2   Agriculture's Contribution to Development—JOHNSTON AND MELLOR 291
3   **Import-Substitution and Industrial Protection—Note** 297
4   **Country Applications**
4.1   Role of Agriculture in Japan's Development—OHKAWA AND ROSOVSKY 304
4.2   Latin American Agricultural Policy—ECLA 315
4.3   Trends in Agricultural Development of Colombia—IBRD 318
4.4   Industrialization in the Gold Coast—LEWIS 322
4.5   Industrialization in the West Indies—LEWIS 325
4.6   Providing Employment in Ceylon—HICKS 327
4.7   Balance of Payments Implications: Asia and the Far East—ECAFE 332
5   **Bibliographical Note** 335

VII   THE EXPORT SECTOR

Introductory Note 338

1 **International Trade and International Inequality**
   1.1 Center and Periphery—PREBISCH 339
   1.2 International Inequalities—MYRDAL 344
   1.3 Development and Trade—HICKS 348
   1.4 Dynamic Benefits of Trade—HABERLER 352
   1.5 Patterns of Trade and Development—NURKSE 358
   1.6 Contribution of Trade to Development—CAIRNCROSS 363
   1.7 The 'Carry-over' Problem—Note 371
2 **Export Stimulation**
   2.1 Adjustments in Foreign Trade—LARY 376
   2.2 Exporting Manufactures—LEWIS 378
   2.3 Export Promotion in Pakistan's Second Plan—GATT 380
3 **Stabilization of Export Proceeds**
   3.1 Special Problems of Primary-Exporting Countries—SWERLING 385
   3.2 Fluctuations in Export Earnings—IMF 390
   3.3 Techniques of Stabilization—WALLICH 393
   3.4 Conclusions on International Compensatory Measures—UNITED NATIONS 399
   3.5 Compensatory Financing of Export Fluctuations—IMF 404
4 **Regional Integration and Development—Note** 408
5 **Bibliographical Note** 412

VIII SCOPE OF DEVELOPMENT PLANNING

Introductory Note 415
1 **Development Planning and the Price System**
   1.1 The Flaw in the Mechanism of Market Forces—ROSENSTEIN-RODAN 416
   1.2 On Planning in Backward Countries—LEWIS 418
   1.3 The Central Role of Planning—ECAFE 423
   1.4 The Market Mechanism as an Instrument of Development—JOHNSON .. 425
2 **The 'Big-Push' Argument**
   2.1 The Theory of the "Big Push"—ROSENSTEIN-RODAN 431
   2.2 A Critique—ELLIS 436
3 **Public Sector and Private Sector**
   3.1 Increasing Role of the Public Sector—ECAFE 440
   3.2 Physical Infrastructure vs. Directly Productive Activities—ECAFE 445
   3.3 Public Targets and Public Investment—ECA 448
   3.4 Investment in the Federal Development Program of Nigeria—FEDERAL
      GOVERNMENT OF NIGERIA 452
   3.5 Investment in the Public and Private Sectors of India—GOVERNMENT
      OF INDIA 456
   3.6 Investment in Ceylon's Ten-Year Plan—NATIONAL PLANNING COUNCIL
      OF CEYLON 460
4 **Bibliographical Note** 463

IX TECHNIQUES OF DEVELOPMENT PLANNING

Introductory Note 464

1 **Formulating a Development Plan**

1.1 Use of Models in Programming—UNITED NATIONS 465

1.2 Aims and Means of Programming—TINBERGEN AND BOS 476

1.3 The Framework of a Development Plan—SEERS 483

1.4 Planning Economic Development—LANGE 487

1.5 Problems of Development Planning—STOLPER 491

1.6 Designing a Practical Plan—MAYNE 496

2 **Allocating Development Resources**

2.1 The Budget and Public Expenditure Policy—ADLER 500

2.2 Choice of Policy Instruments—CHENERY 503

2.3 Sector Evaluation Using Accounting Prices—ECAFE 510

2.4 Project Evaluation—ECAFE 512

2.5 Capital Intensity in Industry—UNITED NATIONS 516

2.6 Programming Approach to Resource Allocation—CHENERY 520

3 **Development Planning in Practice**

3.1 On Assessing a Development Plan—LEWIS 523

3.2 Planning in African Countries—ECA 529

3.3 Industrial Planning in Asia and the Far East—ECAFE 532

3.4 Lessons from India's Industrial Growth—RAO 542

3.5 Indian Programming Techniques—LEWIS 547

3.6 The Strategy of Indian Planned Development—LITTLE 556

4 **The State of Development Planning—Note** 561

5 **Bibliographical Note** 565

Index 569

IX. TECHNIQUES OF DEVELOPMENT PLANNING 464

Introductory Note ....

1. Formulating a Development Plan
   1.1 Use of Models in Programming—TINBERGEN 465
   1.2 Aims and Means of Programming—FRISCH and DOS 470
   1.3 The Framework of a Development Plan—STONE 483
   1.4 Planning Economic Development—HANSEN 487
   1.5 Problems of Development Planning—STOLPER 491
   1.6 Designing a Practical Plan—MAYER 496

2. Allocating Development Resources
   2.1 The Budget and Public Expenditure Policy—LEWIS ... 500
   2.2 Choice of Techniques—DOBB 505
   2.3 Self-evaluation Using Accounting Prices—CHAKRAVARTY 510
   2.4 Project Evaluation—ECKAUS 512
   2.5 Capital Intensity in Industry—SEN 516
   2.6 Programming Approach to Resource Allocation—CHENERY 520

3. Development Planning in Practice
   3.1 On Assessing a Development Plan—LITTLE 525
   3.2 Planning in African Countries—... 530
   3.3 Industrial Planning in Asia and the Far East—... 535
   3.4 Lessons from India's Industrial Growth—... 541
   3.5 Indian Programming Techniques—RAJ 545
   3.6 The Strategy of Indian Planned Development—... ... 550

4. The State of Development Planning—Note 560

4. Bibliographical Note 565

Index 569

LEADING ISSUES IN
DEVELOPMENT ECONOMICS

STAGES OF DEVELOPMENT

H ISTORICAL PERSPECTIVE is one of the best safeguards against taking a superficial view of development problems. If we are to appreciate fully the variety, complexity, and pervasiveness of these problems, we must be aware of their historical dimension. This chapter therefore attempts to provide some historical understanding of the process of development.

It does so by focusing upon Professor Rostow's provocative application of a stage approach to the course of development. As a grand historical thesis, Rostow's analysis of stages of growth has generated unusually wide interest. Its appeal has been especially strong in the underdeveloped countries. But it has also received substantial criticism, and some of these critiques deserve equal attention for their concern with those historical factors neglected by Rostow.

After noting some long-term trends in world economic growth (1.1), the materials in the first part of this chapter set forth the essentials in Rostow's analysis of development as a sequence of stages. Basic to Rostow's analysis is his sketch of a dynamic theory of production which emphasizes the composition of investment and the growth of particular sectors in the economy (1.2). He believes that this theory of production allows the identification of certain "leading sectors," the growth of which is thought to be instrumental in propelling the economy forward. He also indicates that a sequence of optimum patterns of investment can be postulated from a set of optimum sectoral paths determined by the level of income and population, by technology, the quality of entrepreneurship, and by the empirical fact that deceleration is the normal optimum path of each sector. The actual course of investment, however, generally differs from these optima inasmuch as they are influenced not only by private choices, but also by the policies of governments and the impact of wars. Nonetheless, it is believed that, at any period of time, leading sectors can be identified, and the changing sequence of leading sectors plays an important role in Rostow's stages of growth. The sequence of stages suggests, in turn, that a succession of strategic choices is open to societies, and that political and social decisions about the allocation of resources are made in terms beyond the usual market processes.

Of Rostow's five stages of growth, the most relevant for presently poor countries are the first three—the "traditional society," the emergence of "the preconditions for take-off," and the "take-off" (1.3, 1.4). The take-off is meant to be the central notion in Rostow's schema, and it has received the most attention. Yet many poor countries are now still in a version of the preconditions process; we should therefore also consider carefully Rostow's attempt to explain the process, within a traditional society, by which the preconditions for take-off are created. From the discussion of these stages we want to distinguish the strategic factors that have been associated with the initiation of development in the past. A comparison might then be made between the present conditions in poor countries and the conditions under which the determinants of development have been forthcoming in historical cases of successful take-offs.

The second part of the chapter consists of materials that appraise the merit of Rostow's thesis. A comparison is first made with other stage approaches, particularly Marx's (2.1). The more critical assessments by Professors Kuznets, Cairncross, and Habakkuk (2.2, 2.3, 2.4) then indicate analytical weaknesses in Rostow's argument and its limitations in substantive evidence. These critiques point up several crucial questions: Is Rostow's dynamic theory of production an adequate underpinning for his argument? How significant analytically is the notion of leading sectors? Is there sufficient evidence to identify and determine the magnitude of the effects of a changing sequence of leading sectors? Does Rostow succeed in establishing empirically testable and distinctive characteristics for each of his stages of growth? Or, on the contrary, are the criteria for demarcating the different stages ambiguous and not easily identifiable? Does historical experience indicate periods of the take-off that are so decisive and so compressed in time as Rostow suggests? Does not the history of most countries show that the preconditions stage has actually overlapped the take-off stage? Does Rostow's pattern offer a mode of prognosis, or merely a new pattern of historical description and classification? And to what extent can the sequence of stages bear generalization?

Together with these questions, it is also instructive to compare Rostow's approach with Professor Gerschenkron's (2.5). Gerschenkron considers it important first to group countries along a scale of "degree of economic backwardness," and then to relate variations in the course and character of industrialization in different countries to the degree of economic backwardness on the eve of each country's industrialization.

Finally, we attempt to draw from Rostow's analysis some conclusions regarding the correspondence and variation between past and present take-offs (3). Special emphasis is placed upon the differences, and some of these give rise to problems that receive extensive consideration in subsequent chapters.

1. THE ROSTOW DOCTRINE

1.1 TRENDS IN INTERNATIONAL DEVELOPMENT *

Economic growth defined as a sustained secular increase in total national income, or in national income per head of population, is, like population growth, a fairly recent phenomenon in world history. Rapid economic growth—rapid enough to be reflected in perceptible improvements in average standards of living—has so far been confined to a relatively small proportion of the earth's population. It has been associated, wherever it has appeared, with the radical changes in productive techniques and organisation involved in the broad process which is usually described as an "industrial revolution."

...

The growth that began to gather momentum in Western Europe in the eighteenth century was totally without precedent. There had been economic growth before, here as elsewhere, but it had been precarious, readily reversible by famine, pestilence, war or simply by population pressure. In this crucial period covering the last quarter of the eighteenth and the first quarter of the nineteenth century, the British industrial revolution took shape and generated an economic expansion which continued to accelerate through an unprecedented rise in population, an unusual succession of bad harvests and a long and expensive war. The English example was imitated by Belgium, France,

Germany and by the overseas descendants of Europe in the United States, Australia and Canada. Sustained economic growth was achieved in the course of a generally slow, often socially painful, process of economic change which has been extraordinarily selective in its choice of location.

The result has been an increasing inequality of distribution of world incomes. In 1938, according to Professor Kuznets' calculations, about a quarter of the world's population, that is, Western Europe, its overseas descendants in America and Australasia, and the U.S.S.R., earned nearly two-thirds of the world's incomes.[1] By 1949 the income share of this group had risen above three quarters. Similar calculations based on the estimates contained in the 1959 United Nations *Yearbook of National Accounts Statistics* indicate that the international inequality is increasing and that it is appreciably greater than the intranational inequalities.[2] Table I illustrates the intercontinental distribution of world incomes.

The widening of the gap between high income and low income nations seems likely to continue for three reasons: (a) because even a small percentage increase (1 per cent or less) in the average incomes of the former is absolutely high in relation to the world average, (b) because the pro-

* From Phyllis Deane, "The Long Term Trends in World Economic Growth," *Malayan Economic Review,* October 1961, pp. 14, 16-22. Reprinted by permission.

1. Simon Kuznets, "Quantitative Aspects of the Economic Growth of Nations, I—Levels and Variability of Rates of Growth," *Economic Development and Cultural Change,* Vol. V, October 1956, p. 17.

2. Suphan Andic and Alan T. Peacock, "The International Distribution of Income, 1949 and 1957," *Journal of the Royal Statistical Society,* Vol. 124, Pt. 2, 1961.

TABLE I. DISTRIBUTION OF WORLD POPULATION AND INCOMES, 1938 AND 1961

	1938			1961		
	Percentage distribution		Average income as % of world average	Percentage distribution		Average income as % of world average
	Population	Income		Population	Income	
Overseas descendants of Western Europe	7.1	29.6	419	7.3	41.3	542
Europe	26.4	46.6	177	21.4	38.8	181
South and Central America	6.0	4.2	71	7.0	4.7	69
Asia	53.2	17.3	33	56.9	13.1	23
Africa	7.3	2.3	32	7.4	2.0	22

Sources: (a) 1938 figures from Kuznets, *op. cit.*, p. 17. These in their turn were largely based on estimates in W.S. and E.S. Woytinsky, *World Population and Production*, New York, 1953, p. 395.
(b) 1961 figures from P. N. Rosenstein-Rodan, "International Aid for Underdeveloped Countries," *Review of Economics and Statistics*, May 1961, p. 118.

ductivity of unindustrialised countries tends in any case to grow more slowly than the productivity of countries which have passed through an industrial revolution, and (c) because the populations of the undeveloped countries, already in a majority, are currently expanding at a greater rate than the populations of the developed countries.

It is evident then that the various regions of the world are growing at appreciably different rates and from markedly different levels—the differences in levels being wider than the differences in rates of growth. Can we say anything, on the basis of past experience, about the probable sustainable rates of growth in different kinds of regions, and by implication, for the world as a whole?

Definitive estimates of long term rates of growth demand a basis of national income data; more specifically they require average national incomes expressed at constant prices, over a period long enough to override the effects of temporary fluctuations in economic activity (war booms and cyclical disturbances, for example). Un-

fortunately such historical estimates of national income are available only for the advanced countries, that is, for a notably atypical sample of the world's economic units. For most of the unindustrialised countries the only consistent series available are estimates at annual prices for a few years in the 1950's.

Attempts to fill these vast lacunae in our knowledge of how the world has developed have been few and tentative. There are some isolated patches of uncertain light. Of these the most significant are those shed by the Indian inquiries. Dr. Mukherjee's critical review of Indian estimates of long term growth suggests a fluctuating experience over the past century, amounting in all to a long term rate of advance of under half of 1 per cent per annum.[3] Within the present century there

3. M. Mukherjee, "A Preliminary Study of the Growth of National Income in India, 1857-1957," Paper presented to the Asian conference of the International Association for Research in Income and Wealth, Hong Kong, 1960; and *idem* "A Review of Series Estimates of National Income in India, 1900–1958", Paper presented to the Second Indian Conference on Research in National Income, Delhi, 1960.

have been periods of expansion (1900-25 when the annual rate of growth in real incomes per head may have been in the region of 1 per cent), stagnation (1925-40), decline (1940-50), and of renewed growth (1950-60). Probably these are optimistic estimates of the growth achieved—at any rate for the period 1900-25. If we may hazard a guess concerning the other teeming areas of unindustrialised Asia, it seems probable that the Indian experience is near the upper limit of the conceivable rate of progress. Although there may have been small areas and brief periods of growth higher than that achieved in India during the first quarter of the twentieth century, the lot of the majority of the peoples of Asia outside Japan must have varied between stagnation, decline and very slow growth.

In smaller economic units more closely in contact with the growing nations of Western Europe and North America a moderate rate of growth could be achieved by developing an effective trading relationship with the expanding economies. Mrs. Eisner's estimates for Jamaica, for example, suggest an average annual increase in output per head of 0.2 per cent from 1870 to 1890, 0.5 per cent from 1890 to 1910 and 0.7 per cent from 1910 to 1930.[4] The development of an export sector, however, was not always an "open sesame" to sustained growth. In Egypt, after four or five decades of unsuccessful forced industrialisation, the economy began to grow in the second half of the nineteeth century on the strength of its exports. But it was advancing into a blind alley. The rest of the economy remained passive and when export markets collapsed and terms of trade turned against primary producers in the twentieth century Egyptian incomes lost ground almost as rapidly as they had gained it.[5] The overall rate of growth over the period from the 1880's to the 1950's was probably less than half of 1 per cent per annum.

Elsewhere in Africa high rates of growth were achieved by enclaves of European settlement and investment concentrated in areas of great mineral wealth. Within these enclaves the industrial revolution was complete and standard of living and technological advance were high by international standards. Beyond their confines techniques of production and levels of living remained primitive in the extreme. The Belgian Congo, where the rate of growth of gross domestic product is estimated to have averaged as much as 4½ per cent per annum over the period 1920-54 (in relation to a rate of population increase of perhaps only 1 per cent), was one example of this kind of restricted development.[6] The Union of South Africa with its substantial core of European settlers and capital, its migrant labour system and its deteriorating native reserves was another: national income per head seems to have grown at an average annual rate of about 2.1 per cent over the period 1911-51.[7] For most of the indigenous peoples of Africa, however, it is doubtful whether the twentieth century rate of progress was even as strong as the limping pace of Egyptian growth.

Economic growth in Latin America was similarly dependent on world markets for primary products and in the turbulent

4. G. Eisner, *Jamaica 1830–1930*, Manchester University Press, 1961.
5. Charles Issawi, "Egypt since 1800: A Study in Lop-sided Development," *Journal of Economic History*, March 1961. See for example, pp. 16-17, "The per capita income which had risen fairly rapidly till the First World War is today certainly lower than it was at that time. The level of living fell in the interwar period and today is not above the 1939 level."
6. "Quelques considérations sur le développement de l'économie congolaise de 1920 à 1954," *Bulletin de la Banque Centrale du Congo Belge et du Ruanda Urundi*, March 1956.
7. Based on estimates by Simon Kuznets, *op. cit.*, p. 89.

international conditions of the twentieth century fluctuated widely from year to year. Countries like Venezuela which possessed resources as valuable as petroleum enjoyed a long term trend in which the upswings counted for more than the downswings; though here, as in South Africa, development was largely confined to the export sector and to the urban enclave which it supported. For Latin America as a whole the ups and downs of the twentieth century, measured against the accelerating population increase, yielded a scarcely perceptible long term growth in product per head up to World War II. During the world wide shortage of raw materials which characterised the war, and more dramatically its aftermath, Latin American product per head surged. Growth rates reached an average of between 2 and 2½ per cent per annum over the period 1935-51.[8] They slackened markedly, how-

8. United Nations Department of Economic and Social Affairs, *Analyses and Projections of Economic Development,* Study prepared by the Economic Commission for Latin America, New York, 1955. For later rates of growth, see annual ECLA *Economic Survey of Latin America,* 1955 and later years.

ever, in the 1950's and over the whole period 1925-59 it is doubtful whether the Latin American rate of growth much exceeded 1 per cent per annum.

. . .

What it amounts to, then, is that evidence of secularly sustained growth in the nineteenth and twentieth centuries is confined to countries which have already achieved a certain measure of industrialisation, or are peopled by communities which have had an industrial revolution passed on to them as a heritage from their European ancestors. Elsewhere, in today's pre-industrial countries, annual rates of growth of around 1 per cent per annum have been achieved over periods of about a generation (rarely more) by regions which have been able to develop a profitable trading relationship with the industrial expanding areas. But such achievements have been precarious and readily reversible. For the majority of countries in which the mass of the population is tied down to agricultural or domestic pursuits the secular rate of expansion in real

TABLE II. RATES OF GROWTH IN NATIONAL PRODUCT PER MAN YEAR
IN SELECTED GROWING COUNTRIES

	Starting point of data	Annual per cent increase in product per man year		
		Up to 1913	1913-59	1950-59
Japan	1880	3.4	2.6	6.1
Sweden	1863	2.4	1.7	2.8
United States	1871	2.2	1.8	2.2
Canada	1872	1.9	1.5	2.0
Denmark	1872	2.1	1.2	1.8
Norway	1865	1.3	1.9	3.1
Germany	1853	1.5	1.4	4.5
France	1855	1.5	1.5	3.6
Italy	1863	0.7	1.7	4.7
United Kingdom	1857	1.6	0.8	1.7
Netherlands	1900	0.7	1.3	3.4

Source: D. C. Paige, F. T. Blackaby and S. Freund, "Economic Growth: the Last Hundred Years," *National Institute Economic Review,* July 1961.

incomes per head has probably averaged under half of 1 per cent per annum, if indeed it has been as high. At this rate incomes per head would take about 140 years to double.

So much then for the rates of growth which have been characteristic of the pre-industrial countries. At what kind of rate can the industrialised countries expand their real output per head and with it their standards of living? The evidence for the growing countries of the world—countries which have now passed through the crucial stages of their industrial revo-lution—has been examined recently by Deborah Paige. A summary of the calcu-lated rates of growth are shown in Table II. They are ranked in order of their estimated rate of growth over the whole period considered.

Here we have a wide range of growth rates. Long term rates of 1 per cent per annum and less were exhibited by Italy, which had barely started to industrialise at the beginning of the twentieth century, and by two of the three countries which had the longest history of relative affluence (the United Kingdom, France and the Netherlands). At the other end of the scale the fast growing countries were Japan (which led the field throughout), Sweden and the United States. The data for the Soviet Union have been the subject of much controversy, and it has not been possible to include comparable statistics in Table II. The evidence suggests, however, that there was moderate expansion averag-ing about 1 per cent per annum over the period 1860-1913,[9] a decline over the period of the First World War and the early turmoil of the Bolshevik revolution, and a sharp increase in the period of the first two Five Year Plans, and again after World War II. The volume of Soviet industrial output is estimated to have doubled in the decade ending in 1937 and to have more than doubled in the decade of the 1950's.[10] Nevertheless it is doubtful whether the Soviet economy as a whole grew faster than the Japanese in the 1950's and unlikely that it grew as fast over the long period 1913-59.

An interesting feature of the estimates in Table II is the universally faster rate of growth in the 1950's. Many of the undeveloped countries of the world also exhibited unprecedentedly high rates of growth in the 1950's. Does this represent a change of trend in world economic growth? The period which has elapsed since World War II is too short, of course, to provide a basis for conclusive answers to this kind of question. Insofar as the upward swing of the 1950's is a postwar phenomenon, a recovery phase, it may be a purely short term trend with little long term significance. There is evidence for some countries that the pace slackened in the second half of the decade. This was notably so for Germany, Norway, the Netherlands, France, Canada and Italy. The converse was true for Japan, Sweden and Denmark where the pace accelerated. There was little or no change of pace in Britain and the United Sates. Nevertheless, for all the countries in the table above, the 1954-59 rate of growth was also higher than the rate for the period 1913-59, though for Britain, the United States and Canada it did not differ appreciably from the rate for the period up to 1913.

There are at least two general reasons why we might expect world rates of growth to have been appreciably higher in the 1950's than in the period 1913-50. The first, of course, is the abnormality of the former period which includes two disas-

9. Raymond Goldsmith, "The Economic Growth of Russia 1860–1913," *Economic Develop-ment and Cultural Change,* Vol. IX, No. 3, April 1961.

10. N. M. Kaplan and R. H. Moorsteen, "An Index of Soviet Industrial Output," *American Economic Review,* June 1960.

trous world wars and a violent international depression. None of the growing countries sustained a steady rate of growth through these stormy years. Nor was this uncertain and depressed international environment one in which most of the pre-industrial countries could hope to find a means of escape from stagnation. The other reason to expect an upsurge in the 1950's and beyond is the fact that governments and international agencies have become much more aware of the needs and techniques of promoting growth. Economic plans deliberately designed to raise aggregate national output are no longer the exclusive preserves of dictatorships or the socialist countries and though governments vary enormously in the effectiveness and degree of dedication with which they pursue the carrot of growth, there seems little doubt that they are becoming collectively more experienced and more competent in matters of economic policy.

To some extent too, growth must be contagious. The rapidly growing countries may find themselves slowed down by the competition of the late starters, but countries which are looking for openings, either to begin growing or to adapt to the pressures of competition, will find more opportunities when international markets are growing than when they are stagnant. The benefits of technological progress accrue not only to the innovator but to his customers and eventually to his rivals: the wider a country's range of international contacts and the closer its relationship with growing economies, the more likely it is to share in the progress that has its origins outside its own borders.

Can we draw any quantitative conclusions then concerning present and past rates of growth of world incomes? Without an adequate framework of national income estimates we can advance only the most tentative and approximative hypotheses concerning current rates of growth.

In an article published in 1960 Professor Everett Hagen [11] classified the countries of the world into areas which were (a) certainly growing, (b) very probably growing, (c) possibly growing and (d) not growing. There are enough data for most of the "certainly growing" group and some of the "very probably growing" to indicate their rates of growth in the recent past. If we generalise for the rest on the assumption that the other "very probably growing" countries are expanding their average incomes at rates varying from 1 to $1\frac{1}{2}$ per cent per annum and the "possibly growing" group at 0.8 per cent we arrive at an estimate for the world rate of growth in the 1950's of between 2 and $2\frac{1}{2}$ per cent per annum. On a similar calculation based on estimated 1913-59 rates of growth and on the assumption that the undocumented countries in the "probably" and "possibly" growing groups were experiencing rates of between half of 1 per cent and 1 per cent per annum, we get an annual long term rate of growth for world incomes taken as a whole of between 1 and $1\frac{1}{4}$ per cent.

There is no need to emphasise the approximate nature of calculations such as these. At best they suggest probable relative orders of magnitude. If the world as a whole was expanding its average incomes at a rate of 2 to $2\frac{1}{2}$ per cent per annum in the 1950's (that is, at a rate which implies a doubling of the standard of living in 30 to 35 years) this was probably more than twice as fast as it had grown in the preceding half century and almost certainly faster than it had ever grown before. Before the twentieth century the industrial revolution had barely started to spread beyond the borders of four or five countries and most of the world's economies must have been raising

11. Everett E. Hagen, "Some Facts about Income Levels and Economic Growth," *Review of Economics and Statistics*, February 1960.

their income levels at less than half of 1 per cent per annum. By the mid-twentieth century world industrial production was expanding at an annual rate of about 4½ per cent per annum, and world trade by about 3½ per cent. Meanwhile world population was growing at something less than 2 per cent per annum and world agricultural production at about the same rate.

1.2 A Dynamic Theory of Production *

This article summarizes a way of generalizing the sweep of modern economic history. The form of this generalization is a set of stages of growth, which can be designated as follows: the traditional society; the preconditions for take-off; the take-off; the drive to maturity; the age of high mass consumption. Beyond the age of high mass consumption lies the problems which are beginning to arise in a few societies, and which may arise generally when diminishing relative marginal utility sets in for real income itself.

These descriptive categories are rooted in certain dynamic propositions about supply, demand, and the pattern of production; and before indicating the historical content of the categories I shall briefly state the underlying propositions.

The classical theory of production is formulated under essentially static assumptions which freeze—or permit only once-over change—in the variables most relevant to the process of economic growth. As modern economists have sought to merge classical production theory with Keynesian income analysis they have introduced the dynamic variables: population, technology, entrepreneurship, etc. But they have tended to do so in forms so rigid and general that their models cannot grip the essential phenomena of growth, as they

appear to an economic historian. We require a dynamic theory of production which isolates not only the distribution of income between consumption, saving, and investment (and the balance of production betwen consumers and capital goods) but which focuses directly and in some detail on the composition of investment and on developments within particular sectors of the economy. The argument that follows is based on such a flexible, disaggregated theory of production.

When the conventional limits on the theory of production are widened, it is possible to define theoretical equilibrium positions not only for output, investment, and consumption as a whole, but for each sector of the economy.[1] Within the framework set by forces determining the total level of output, sectoral optimum positions are determined, on the side of demand, by the levels of income and of population, and by the character of tastes; on the side of supply, by the state of technology and the quality of entrepreneurship, as the latter determines the proportion of technically available and potentially profitable innovations actually incorporated in the capital stock.[2] In addition, one must introduce an extremely significant empirical hypothesis; namely, that deceleration is the normal optimum path of a sector, due to a variety of factors operating on it, from the side of both supply and demand.[3] The equilibria which emerge from the application of these criteria are a set of sectoral paths,

* From W. W. Rostow, "The Stages of Economic Growth," *Economic History Review,* August 1959, pp. 1-3. Reprinted by permission.

1. W. W. Rostow, *The Process of Economic Growth* (Oxford, 1953), especially Chapter IV. Also "Trends in the Allocation of Resources in Secular Growth," Chapter 15, *Economic Progress,* ed. Leon H. Dupriez, with the assistance of Douglas C. Hague (Louvain, 1955); also, "The Take-off into Self-Sustained Growth," *Economic Journal* (March 1956).
2. In a closed model, a dynamic theory of production must account for changing stocks of basic and applied science, as sectoral aspects of investment, which is done in *The Process of Economic Growth,* especially pp. 22-5.
3. *Ibid.,* pp. 96-103.

from which flows, as first derivatives, a sequence of optimum patterns of investment.

Historical patterns of investment did not, of course, exactly follow these optimum patterns. They were distorted by imperfections in the private investment process; by the policies of governments; and by the impact of wars. Wars temporarily altered the profitable directions of investment by setting up arbitrary demands and by changing the conditions of supply; they destroyed capital; and, occasionally, they accelerated the development of new technology relevant to the peacetime economy and shifted the political and social framework in ways conducive to peacetime growth.[4] The historical sequence of business cycles and trend periods results from these deviations of actual from optimal patterns; and such fluctuations, along with the impact of wars, yield historical paths of growth which differ from those which the optima, calculated before the event, would have yielded. Nevertheless, the economic history of growing societies takes a part of its rude shape from the effort of societies to approximate the optimum sectoral paths.

At any period of time, the rate of growth in the sectors will vary greatly; and it is possible to isolate empirically certain leadings sectors, at early stages of their evolution, whose rapid rate of expansion plays an essential direct and indirect role in maintaining the overall momentum of the economy.[5] For some purposes it is useful to characterize an economy in terms of its leading sectors; and a part of the technical basis for the stages of growth lies in the changing sequence of leading sectors. In essence it

4. *Ibid.*, Chapter VII, especially pp. 164-7.
5. For a discussion of the leading sectors, their direct and indirect consequences, and the diverse routes of their impact, see "Trends in the Allocation of Resources in Secular Growth," *op. cit.*

is the fact that sectors tend to have a rapid growth phase, early in their life, that makes it possible and useful to regard economic history as a sequence of stages rather than merely as a continuum, within which nature never makes a jump.

The stages of growth also require, however, that elasticities of demand be taken into account, and that this familiar concept be widened; for these rapid growth phases in the sectors derive not merely from the discontinuity of production functions but also from high price or income elasticities of demand. Leading sectors are determined not merely by the changing flow of technology and the changing willingness of entrepreneurs to accept available innovations: they are also partially determined by those types of demand which have exhibited high elasticity with respect to price, income, or both.

The demand for resources has resulted, however, not merely from demands set up by private taste and choice, but also from social decisions and from the policies of governments—whether democratically responsive or not. It is necessary, therefore, to look at the choices made by societies in the disposition of their resources in terms which transcend conventional market processes. It is necessary to look at their welfare functions, in the widest sense, including the non-economic processes which determine them.

The course of birth rates, for example, represents one form of welfare choice made by societies, as income has changed; and population curves reflect (in addition to changing death rates) how the calculus about family size was made in the various stages; from the usual (but not universal) decline in birth rates, during or soon after the take-off, as urbanization took hold and progress became a palpable possibility, to the recent rise, as Americans (and others in societies marked by high mass consumption) have appeared to seek in larger families, values beyond those afforded by economic security and by an ample supply of durable consumers goods and services.

And there are other decisions as well that societies have made as the choices open to them have been altered by the unfolding process of economic growth; and these broad collective decisions, determined by many factors—deep in history, culture, and the active political process—outside the market place, have interplayed with the dynamics of market demand, risk-taking, technology and entrepreneurship, to determine the specific content of the stages of growth for each society.

How, for example, should the traditional society react to the intrusion of a more advanced power: with cohesion, promptness, and vigour, like the Japanese; by making a virtue of fecklessness, like the oppressed Irish of the eighteenth century; by slowly and reluctantly altering the traditional society, like the Chinese? When independent modern nationhood was achieved, how should the national energies be disposed: in external aggression, to right old wrongs or to exploit newly created or perceived possibilities for enlarged national power; in completing and refining the political victory of the new national government over old regional interests; or in modernizing the economy?

Once growth is under way, with the take-off, to what extent should the requirements of diffusing modern technology and maximizing the rate of growth be moderated by the desire to increase consumption *per capita* and to increase welfare?

When technological maturity is reached, and the nation has at its command a modernized and differentiated industrial machine, to what ends should it be put, and in what proportions: to increase social security, through the welfare state; to expand mass consumption into the range of durable consumers goods and services; to increase the nation's stature and power

on the world scene; or to increase leisure? And then the further question, where history offers us only fragments: what to do when the increase in real income itself loses its charm? Babies; boredom; three-day weekends; the moon; or the creation of new inner, human frontiers in substitution for the imperatives of scarcity?

In surveying now the broad contours of each stage of growth, we are examining, then, not merely the sectoral structure of economies, as they transformed themselves for growth, and grew; we are also examining a succession of strategic choices made by various societies concerning the disposition of their resources, which include but transcend the income and price elasticities of demand.

1.3 THE TRADITIONAL SOCIETY AND THE PRECONDITIONS FOR TAKE-OFF *

A traditional society is one whose structure is developed within limited production functions, based on pre-Newtonian science and technology, and on pre-Newtonian attitudes towards the physical world. Newton is here used as a symbol for that watershed in history when men came widely to believe that the external world was subject to a few knowable laws, and was systematically capable of productive manipulation.

The conception of the traditional society is, however, in no sense static; and it would not exclude increases in output. Acreage could be expanded; some *ad hoc* technical innovations, often highly productive innovations, could be introduced in trade, industry and agriculture; productivity could rise with, for example, the improvement of irrigation works or the discovery and diffusion of a new crop. But the central fact about the traditional society was that a ceiling existed on the level of

* From W. W. Rostow, *The Stages of Economic Growth*, Cambridge University Press, 1960, pp. 4-7, 18-19. Reprinted by permission.

attainable output per head. This ceiling resulted from the fact that the potentialities which flow from modern science and technology were either not available or not regularly and systematically applied.

Both in the longer past and in recent times the story of traditional societies was thus a story of endless change. The area and volume of trade within them and between them fluctuated, for example, with the degree of political and social turbulence, the efficiency of central rule, the upkeep of the roads. Population—and, within limits, the level of life—rose and fell not only with the sequence of the harvests, but with the incidence of war and of plague. Varying degrees of manufacture developed; but, as in agriculture, the level of productivity was limited by the inaccessibility of modern science, its applications, and its frame of mind.

Generally speaking, these societies, because of the limitation on productivity, had to devote a very high proportion of their resources to agriculture; and flowing from the agricultural system there was an hierarchical social structure, with relatively narrow scope—but some scope—for vertical mobility. Family and clan connexions played a large role in social organization. The value system of these societies was generally geared to what might be called a long-run fatalism; that is, the assumption that the range of possibilities open to one's grandchildren would be just about what it had been for one's grandparents. But this long-run fatalism by no means excluded the short-run option that, within a considerable range, it was possible and legitimate for the individual to strive to improve his lot, within his lifetime. In Chinese villages, for example, there was an endless struggle to acquire or to avoid losing land, yielding a situation where land rarely remained within the same family for a century.

Although central political rule—in one form or another—often existed in traditional societies, transcending the relatively self-sufficient regions, the centre of gravity of political power generally lay in the regions, in the hands of those who owned or controlled the land. The landowner maintained fluctuating but usually profound influence over such central political power as existed, backed by its entourage of civil servants and soldiers, imbued with attitudes and controlled by interests transcending the regions.

In terms of history then, with the phrase "traditional society" we are grouping the whole pre-Newtonian world: the dynasties in China; the civilization of the Middle East and the Mediterranean; the world of medieval Europe. And to them we add the post-Newtonian societies which, for a time, remained untouched or unmoved by man's new capability for regularly manipulating his environment to his economic advantage.

To place these infinitely various, changing societies in a single category, on the ground that they all shared a ceiling on the productivity of their economic techniques, is to say very little indeed. But we are, after all, merely clearing the way in order to get at the subject of this book; that is, the post-traditional societies, in which each of the major characteristics of the traditional society was altered in such ways as to permit regular growth: its politics, social structure, and (to a degree) its values, as well as its economy.

The second stage of growth embraces societies in the process of transition; that is, the period when the preconditions for take-off are developed; for it takes time to transform a traditional society in the ways necessary for it to exploit the fruits of modern science, to fend off diminishing returns, and thus to enjoy the blessings and choices opened up by the march of compound interest.

The preconditions for take-off were initially developed, in a clearly marked way, in Western Europe of the late seventeenth and early eighteenth centuries as the insights of modern science began to be translated into new production functions in both agriculture and industry, in a setting given dynamism by the lateral expansion of world markets and the international competition for them. But all that lies behind the break-up of the Middle Ages is relevant to the creation of the preconditions for take-off in Western Europe. Among the Western European states, Britain, favoured by geography, natural resources, trading possibilities, social and political structure, was the first to develop fully the preconditions for take-off.

The more general case in modern history, however, saw the stage of preconditions arise not endogenously but from some external intrusion by more advanced societies. These invasions—literal or figurative—shocked the traditional society and began or hastened its undoing; but they also set in motion ideas and sentiments which initiated the process by which a modern alternative to the traditional society was constructed out of the old culture.

The idea spreads not merely that economic progress is possible, but that economic progress is a necessary condition for some other purpose, judged to be good: be it national dignity, private profit, the general welfare, or a better life for the children. Education, for some at least, broadens and changes to suit the needs of modern economic activity. New types of enterprising men come forward—in the private economy, in government, or both —willing to mobilize savings and to take risks in pursuit of profit or modernization.

Banks and other institutions for mobilizing capital appear. Investment increases, notably in transport, communications, and in raw materials in which other nations may have an economic interest. The scope of commerce, internal and external, widens. And, here and there, modern manufacturing enterprise appears, using the new methods. But all this activity proceeds at a limited pace within an economy and a society still mainly characterized by traditional low-productivity methods, by the old social structure and values, and by the regionally based political institutions that developed in conjunction with them.

In many recent cases, for example, the traditional society persisted side by side with modern economic activities, conducted for limited economic purposes by a colonial or quasi-colonial power.

Although the period of transition— between the traditional society and the take-off—saw major changes in both the economy itself and in the balance of social values, a decisive feature was often political. Politically, the building of an effective national state—on the basis of coalitions touched with a new nationalism, in opposition to the traditional landed regional interests, the colonial power, or both, was a decisive aspect of the preconditions period; and it was, almost universally, a necessary condition for take-off.

. . .

The transition we are examining has, evidently, many dimensions. A society predominantly agricultural—with, in fact, usually 75 per cent or more of its working force in agriculture—must shift to a predominance for industry, communications, trade and services.

A society whose economic, social and political arrangements are built around the life of relatively small—mainly self-sufficient—regions must orient its commerce and its thought to the nation and to a still larger international setting.

The view towards the having of children—initially the residual blessing and affirmation of immortality in a hard life, of relatively fixed horizons—must change in ways which ultimately yield a decline in the birth-rate, as the possibility of progress and the decline in the need for unskilled farm labor create a new calculus.

The income above minimum levels of consumption, largely concentrated in the hands of those who own land, must be shifted into the hands of those who will spend it on roads and railroads, schools and factories rather than on country houses and servants, personal ornaments and temples.

Men must come to be valued in the society not for their connection with clan or class, or, even, their guild; but for their individual ability to perform certain specific, increasingly specialized functions.

And, above all, the concept must be spread that man need not regard his physical environment as virtually a factor given by nature and providence, but as an ordered world which, if rationally understood, can be manipulated in ways which yield productive change and, in one dimension at least, progress.

All of this—and more—is involved in the passage of a traditional to a modern growing society.

1.4 THE TAKE-OFF *

The beginning of take-off can usually be traced to a particular sharp stimulus. The stimulus may take the form of a political revolution which affects directly the balance of social power and effective values, the character of economic institutions, the distribution of income, the pattern of investment outlays and the proportion of

* From W. W. Rostow, *The Stages of Economic Growth,* Cambridge University Press, 1960, pp. 36-40, 46-50, 52-3, 57. Reprinted by permission.

potential innovations actually applied. Such was the case, for example, with the German revolution of 1848, the Meiji restoration in Japan of 1868, and the more recent achievement of Indian independence and the Communist victory in China. It may come about through a technological (including transport) innovation, which sets in motion a chain of secondary expansion in modern sectors and has powerful external economy effects which the society exploits. It may take the form of a newly favourable international environment, such as the opening of British and French markets to Swedish timber in the 1860's or a sharp relative rise in export prices and/or large new capital imports, as in the case of the United States from the late 1840's, Canada and Russia from the mid-1890's; but it may also come as a challenge posed by an unfavourable shift in the international environment, such as a sharp fall in the terms of trade (or a wartime blockage of foreign trade) requiring the rapid development of manufactured import substitutes, as with the Argentine and Australia from 1930 to 1945.

What is essential here is not the form of stimulus but the fact that the prior development of the society and its economy result in a positive, sustained, and self-reinforcing response to it: the result is not a once-over change in production functions or in the volume of investment, but a higher proportion of potential innovations accepted in a more or less regular flow, and a higher rate of investment.

The use of aggregative national-income terms evidently reveals little of the process which is occurring. It is nevertheless useful to regard as a necessary but not sufficient condition for the take-off the fact that the proportion of net investment to national income (or net national product) rises from, say, 5% to over 10%, definitely outstripping the likely population pressure (since under the assumed take-off circumstances the capital/output ratio is low),[1] and yielding a distinct rise in real ouput *per capita*. Whether real consumption *per capita* rises depends on the pattern of income distribution and population pressure, as well as on the magnitude, character and productivity of investment itself.

As indicated in the accompanying table, we believe it possible to identify at least tentatively such take-off periods for a number of countries which have passed into the stage of growth.

The take-off is such a decisive transition in a society's history that it is important to examine the nature of our definition and the inner mechanism of take-off somewhat more closely.

There are several problems of choice involved in defining the take-off with precision. We might begin with one arbitrary definition and consider briefly the two major alternatives.

For the present purposes the take-off

is defined as requiring all three of the following related conditions:

(1) a rise in the rate of productive investment from, say, 5% or less to over 10% of national income (or net national product [NNP]);

(2) the development of one or more substantial manufacturing[2] sectors, with a high rate of growth;

(3) the existence or quick emergence of a political, social and institutional framework which exploits the impulses to expansion in the modern sector and the potential external economy effects of the take-off and gives to growth an on-going character.

The third condition implies a considerable capability to mobilize capital from domestic sources. Some take-offs have occurred with virtually no capital imports, for example, Britain and Japan. Some take-offs have had a high component of foreign capital, for example, the United States, Russia and Canada. But some countries have imported large quantities of foreign capital for long periods, which undoubtedly contributed to creating the preconditions for take-off without actually initiating take-off, for example the Argentine before 1914, Venezuela down to recent years, the Belgian Congo currently.

In short, whatever the role of capital imports, the preconditions for take-off include an initial ability to mobilize domestic savings productively, as well as a structure which subsequently permits a high marginal rate of savings.

This definition is designed to isolate the early stage when industrialization takes

---

1. Capital/output ratio is the amount by which a given increase in investment increases the volume of output: a rough—very rough—measure of the productivity of capital investment; but since the arithmetic of economic growth requires some such concept, implicitly or explicitly, we had better refine the tool rather than abandon it. In the early stages of economic development two contrary forces operate on the capital/output ratio. On the one hand there is a vast requirement of basic overhead capital in transport, power, education, etc. Here, due mainly to the long period over which investment yields its return, the apparent (short-run) capital/output ratio is high. On the other hand, there are generally large unexploited backlogs of known techniques and available natural resources to be put to work; and these back-logs make for a low capital/output ratio. We can assume formally a low capital/output ratio for the take-off period because we are assuming that the preconditions have been created, including a good deal of social overhead capital. In fact, the aggregate marginal capital/output ratio is likely to be kept up during the take-off by the requirement of continuing large outlays for overhead items which yield their returns only over long periods. Nevertheless, a ratio of 3:1 or 3.5:1 for the incremental capital/output ratio seems realistic as a rough bench-mark until we have learned more about capital/output ratios on a sectoral basis.

2. In this context "manufacturing" is taken to include the processing of agricultural products or raw materials by modern methods: for example, timber in Sweden, meat in Australia, dairy products in Denmark. The dual requirement of a "manufacturing" sector is that its processes set in motion a chain of further modern sector requirements and that its expansion provides the potentiality of external economy effects, industrial in character.

TABLE I. SOME TENTATIVE, APPROXIMATE TAKE-OFF DATES

Country	Take-off	Country	Take-off
Great Britain	1783—1802	Russia	1890—1914
France	1830—60	Canada	1896—1914
Belgium	1833—60	Argentina‡	1935—
United States*	1843—60	Turkey§	1937—
Germany	1850—73	India‖	1952—
Sweden	1868—90	China‖	1952—
Japan†	1878—1900		

* The American take-off is here viewed as the upshot of two different periods of expansion: the first, that of the 1840's, marked by railway and manufacturing development, mainly confined to the East—this occurred while the West and South digested the extensive agricultural expansion of the previous decade; the second the great railway push into the Middle West during the 1850's marked by a heavy inflow of foreign capital. By the opening of the Civil War the American economy of North and West, with real momentum in its heavy-industry sector, is judged to have taken off.

† Lacking adequate data, there is some question about the timing of the Japanese take-off. Some part of the post-1868 period was certainly, by the present set of definitions, devoted to firming up the pre-conditions for take-off. By 1914 the Japanese economy had certainly taken off. The question is whether the period from about 1878 to the Sino-Japanese War in the mid-1890's is to be regarded as the completion of the preconditions or as take-off. On present evidence we incline to the latter view.

‡ In one sense the Argentine economy began its take-off during the First World War. But by and large, down to the pit of the post-1929 depression, the growth of its modern sector, stimulated during the war, tended to slacken; and, like a good part of the Western world, the Argentine sought during the 1920's to return to a pre-1914 normalcy. It was not until the mid-1930's that a sustained take-off was inaugurated, which by and large can now be judged to have been successful despite the structural vicissitudes of that economy.

§ Against the background of industrialization measures inaugurated in the mid-1930's the Turkish economy has exhibited remarkable momentum in the past five years founded in the increase in agricultural income and productivity. It still remains to be seen whether these two surges, conducted under quite different national policies, will constitute a transition to self-sustaining growth, and whether Turkey can overcome its current structural problems.

‖ As noted in the text it is still too soon to judge either the present Indian or Chinese Communist take-off efforts successful.

hold rather than the later stage when industrialization becomes a more massive and statistically more impressive phenomenon. In Britain, for example, there is no doubt that it was between 1815 and 1850 that industrialization fully took hold. If the criterion chosen for take-off was the period of most rapid overall industrial growth, or the period when large-scale industry matured, all our take-off dates would have to be set later; Britain, for example, 1819–48; the United States, to 1868–93; Sweden, to 1890–1920; Japan, to 1900–20; Russia, to 1928–40. The earlier dating is chosen here because it is believed that the decisive transformations (including a decisive shift in the investment-rate)

occur in the first industrial phases; and later industrial maturity can be directly traced back to foundations laid in these first phases.

This definition is also designed to rule out from the take-off the quite substantial economic progress which can occur in an economy before a truly self-reinforcing growth process gets under way. Consider, for example, British economic expansion between, say, 1750 and 1783; Russian economic expansion between, say, 1861 and 1890, Canadian economic expansion between 1867 and the mid-1890's. Such periods—for which there is an equivalent in the economic history of almost every growing economy—were marked by extremely important, even decisive, developments. The transport network expanded, and with it both internal and external commerce; a revolution in agricultural productivity was, at least, begun; new institutions for mobilizing savings were developed; a class of commercial and even industrial entrepreneurs began to emerge; industrial enterprise on a limited scale (or in limited sectors) grew. And yet, however essential these pre-take-off periods were for later development, their scale and momentum were insufficient to transform the economy radically or, in some cases, to outstrip population growth and to yield an increase in *per capita* output.

With a sense of the considerable violence done to economic history, we are here seeking to isolate a period when the scale of productive economic activity reaches a critical level and produces changes which lead to a massive and progressive structural transformation in economies and the societies of which they are a part, better viewed as changes in kind than merely in degree.

...

Whatever the importance and virtue of viewing the take-off in aggregative terms —embracing national output, the proportion of output invested, and an aggregate marginal capital/output ratio—that approach tells us relatively little of what actually happens and of the causal processes at work in a take-off; nor is the investment-rate criterion conclusive.

Following the definition of take-off, we must consider not merely how a rise in the investment-rate is brought about, from both supply and demand perspectives, but how rapidly growing manufacturing sectors emerged and imparted their primary and secondary growth impulses to the economy.

Perhaps the most important thing to be said about the behaviour of these variables

in historical cases of take-off is that they have assumed many different forms. There is no single pattern. The rate and productivity of investment can rise, and the consequences of this rise can be diffused into a self-reinforcing general growth process by many different technical and economic routes, under the aegis of many different political, social and cultural settings, driven along by a wide variety of human motivations.

The purpose of the following paragraphs is to suggest briefly, and by way of illustration only, certain elements of both uniformity and variety in the variables whose movement has determined the inner structure of the take-off.

By and large, the loanable funds required to finance the take-off have come from two types of source: from shifts in the control of income flows, including income-distribution changes and capital imports; and from the plough-back of profits in rapidly expanding particular sectors.

The notion of economic development occurring as a result of income shifts from those who will spend (hoard[3] or lend) less productively to those who will spend (or lend) more productively is one of the oldest and most fundamental notions in economics. It is basic, for example, to the *Wealth of Nations.*[4]

Historically, income shifts conducive to economic development have assumed

3. Hoarding can, of course, be helpful in the growth process by depressing consumption and freeing resources for investment, if, in fact, non-hoarding persons or institutions acquire the resources and possess the will to expand productive investment. A direct transfer of income is evidently not required.

4. See, especially, Smith's observations on the "perversion" of wealth by "prodigality"—that is, unproductive consumption expenditures—and on the virtues of "parsimony" which transfers income to those who will increase "the fund which is destined for the maintenance of productive hands." Routledge edition, (London, 1890), pp. 259-60.

many forms. In Meiji Japan and also in Czarist Russia the substitution of government bonds for the great landholders' claims on the flow of rent payments led to a highly Smithian redistribution of income into the hands of those in the modern sector. In both cases the real value of the government bonds exchanged for land depreciated; and, in general, the feudal landlords emerged with a less attractive arrangement than had first appeared to be offered. Aside from the confiscation effect, two positive impulses arose from land reform: the State itself used the flow of payments from peasants, now diverted from landlords' hands, for activity which encouraged economic development; and a certain number of the more enterprising former landlords directly invested in commerce and industry. In contemporary India and China we can observe quite different degrees of income transfer by this route. India is relying to only a very limited extent on the elimination of large incomes unproductively spent by large landlords; although this element figures in a small way in its programme. Communist China has systematically transferred all non-governmental pools of capital into the hands of the State, in a series of undisguised or barely disguised capital levies; and it is drawing heavily for capital resources on the mass of middle and poor peasants who remain.[5]

In addition to confiscatory and taxation devices, which can operate effectively when the State is spending more productively than the taxed individuals, inflation has been important to several take-offs. In Britain of the late 1790's, the United States of the 1850's, Japan of the 1870's there is no doubt that capital formation was aided by price inflation, which shifted resources away from consumption to profits.

The shift of income flows into more productive hands has, of course, been aided historically not only by government fiscal measures but also by banks and capital markets. Virtually without exception, the take-off periods have been marked by the extension of banking institutions which expanded the supply of working capital; and in most cases also by an expansion in the range of long-range financing done by a central, formally organized, capital market.

Although these familiar capital-supply functions of the State and private institutions have been important to the take-off, it is likely to prove the case, on close examination, that a necessary condition for take-off was the existence of one or more rapidly growing sectors whose entrepreneurs (private or public) ploughed back into new capacity a very high proportion of profits. Put another way, the demand side of the investment process, rather than the supply of loanable funds, may be the decisive element in the take-off, as opposed to the period of creating the preconditions, or of sustaining growth once it is under way. The distinction is, historically, sometimes difficult to make, notably when the State simultaneously acts both to mobilize supplies of finance and to undertake major entrepreneurial acts. There are, nevertheless, periods in economic history when quite substantial improvements in the machinery of capital supply do not, in themselves, initiate a take-off, but fall within the period when the preconditions are created: for example, British banking developments in the century before 1783 and Russian banking developments before 1890.

One extremely important version of the plough-back process has taken place through foreign trade. Developing economies have created from their natural resources major export industries; and the rapid expansion in exports has been used

5. W. W. Rostow et al., Prospects for Communist China, (New York and London, 1954), Part 4.

to finance the import of capital equipment and to service the foreign debt during the take-off. United States, Russian and Canadian grain fulfilled this function, Swedish timber and pulp, Japanese silk, etc. Currently Chinese exports to the Communist bloc, wrung at great administrative and human cost from the agricultural sector, play this decisive role. It should be noted that the development of such export sectors has not in itself guaranteed accelerated capital formation. Enlarged foreign-exchange proceeds have been used in many familiar cases to finance hoards (as in the famous case of Indian bullion imports) or unproductive consumption outlays.

One possible mechanism for inducing a high rate of plough-back into productive investment is a rapid expansion in the effective demand for domestically manufactured consumers' goods, which would direct into the hands of vigorous entrepreneurs an increasing proportion of income flows under circumstances which would lead them to expand their own capacity and to increase their requirements for industrial raw materials, semi-manufactured products and manufactured components.

A final element in the supply of loanable funds is, of course, capital imports. Foreign capital has played a major role in the take-off stage of many economies: for example the United States, Russia, Sweden, Canada. The case of Britain and Japan indicate, however, that it cannot be regarded as an essential condition. Foreign capital was notably useful when the construction of railways or other large overhead capital items with a long period of gestation played an important role in the take-off or the late preconditions period. Whatever its strategic role, the proportion of investment required for growth which goes into industry is relatively small compared to that required for utilities, transport and the housing of enlarged urban populations. And foreign capital can be mightily useful in helping carry the burden of these overhead items either directly or indirectly.

What can we say, in general, then, about the supply of finance during the take-off period? First, as a precondition, it appears necessary that the community's surplus above the mass-consumption level does not flow into the hands of those who will sterilize it by hoarding, luxury consumption or low-productivity investment outlays. Second, as a precondition, it appears necessary that institutions be developed which provide cheap and adequate working capital. Third, as a necessary condition, it appears that one or more sectors of the community must grow rapidly, inducing a more general industrialization process; and that the entrepreneurs in such sectors plough back a substantial proportion of their profits in further productive investment, one possible and recurrent version of the plough-back process being the investment of proceeds from a rapidly growing export sector.

The devices, confiscatory and fiscal, for ensuring the first and second preconditions have been historically various. And, as indicated below, the types of leading manufacturing sectors which have served to initiate the take-off have varied greatly. Finally, foreign capital flows have, in significant cases, proved extremely important to the take-off, notably when lumpy overhead capital construction of long gestation period was required; but take-offs have also occurred based almost wholly on domestic sources of finance.

...the overall rate of growth of an economy must be regarded in the first instance as the consequence of differing growth rates in particular sectors of the economy, such sectoral growth-rates being in part derived from certain overall demand factors (for example population, consumers' income, tastes, etc.); in part, from the primary and secondary effects of changing supply factors, when these are effectively exploited.

On this view the sectors of an economy may be grouped in three categories:

(1) Primary growth sectors, where possibilities for innovation or for the exploitation of newly profitable or hitherto unexplored resources yield a high growth-rate and set in motion expansionary forces elsewhere in the economy.

(2) Supplementary growth sectors, where rapid advance occurs in direct response to—or as a requirement of—advance in the primary growth sectors; for example coal, iron and engineering in relation to railroads. These sectors may have to be tracked many stages back into the economy.

(3) Derived-growth sectors, where advance occurs in some fairly steady relation to the growth of total real income, population, industrial production or some other overall, modestly increasing variable. Food output in relation to population and housing in relation to family formation are classic derived relations of this order.

In the earlier stages of growth, primary and supplementary growth sectors derive their momentum essentially from the introduction and diffusion of changes in the cost—supply environment (in turn, of course, partially influenced by demand changes); while the derived-growth sectors are linked essentially to changes in demand (while subject also to continuing changes in production functions of a less dramatic character)....

At any period of time it appears to be true even in a mature and growing economy that forward momentum is maintained as the result of rapid expansion in a limited number of primary sectors, whose expansion has significant external economy and other secondary effects. From this perspective the behaviour of sectors during the take-off is merely a special version of the growth process in general; or, put another

way, growth proceeds by repeating endlessly, in different patterns, with different leading sectors, the experience of the take-off. Like the take-off, long-term growth requires that the society not only generate vast quantities of capital for depreciation and maintenance, for housing and for a balanced complement of utilities and other overheads, but also a sequence of highly productive primary sectors, growing rapidly, based on new production functions. Only thus has the aggregate marginal capital/output ratio been kept low.

Once again history is full of variety: a considerable array of sectors appears to have played this key role in the take-off process.

...

What can we say, then, in general about these leading sectors? Historically, they have ranged from cotton textiles, through heavy-industry complexes based on railroads and military end-products, to timber, pulp, dairy products and finally a wide variety of consumers' goods. There is, clearly, no one sectoral sequence for take-off, no single sector which constitutes the magic key. There is no need for a growing society to recapitulate, for example, the structural sequence and pattern of Britain, the United States or Russia. Four basic factors must be present:

(1) There must be enlarged effective demand for the product or products of sectors which yield a foundation for a rapid rate of growth in output. Historically this has been brought about initially by the transfer of income from consumption or hoarding to productive investment; by capital imports; by a sharp increase in the productivity of current investment inputs, yielding an increase in consumers' real income expended on domestic manufactures; or by a combination of these routes.

(2) There must be an introduction into

these sectors of new production functions as well as an expansion of capacity.

(3) The society must be capable of generating capital initially required to detonate the take-off in these key sectors; and especially there must be a high rate of plough-back by the (private or state) entrepreneurs controlling capacity and technique in these sectors and in the sup-

plementary growth sectors they stimulated to expand.

(4) Finally, the leading sector or sectors must be such that their expansion and technical transformation induce a chain of requirements for increased capacity and the potentiality for new production functions in other sectors, to which the society, in fact, progressively responds.

2. APPRAISALS AND CRITIQUES

2.1 ROSTOW AND MARX—NOTE

Professor Rostow's analysis represents only the most recent of numerous attempts to reduce the sweep of economic history to an orderly sequence of stages. Tempted by the search for regularities in history, many writers have interpreted the course of development in terms of some pattern of stages. Of the earlier proponents of stages, only Marx commands Rostow's explicit attention. Indeed, Rostow presents his analysis as an alternative to Marx's theory of modern history. Describing his system as "A Non-Communist Manifesto," Rostow poses his five stages of growth against Marx's stages of feudalism, bourgeois capitalism, socialism, and communism.

We can recognize some broad similarities between Rostow's analysis and Marx's sequence. Both are audacious attempts to interpret the evolution of whole societies, primarily from an economic perspective; both are "explorations of the problems and consequences for whole societies of building compound interest into their habits and institutions"; [1] and both recognize that economic change has social, political, and cultural consequences.

From other viewpoints, however, there are fundamental differences. The basic Marxian problems of class conflicts, exploitation, and inherent stresses within the

capitalist process find no place in Rostow's analysis. Nor does Rostow reduce the complexities of man to a single economic dimension, as does Marx. Rostow recognizes that, in terms of human motivation, many of the most profound economic changes must be viewed as the consequence of non-economic human motives and aspirations. Instead of limiting human behavior to simply an act of maximization, Rostow interprets net human behavior "as an act of balancing alternative and often conflicting human objectives in the face of the range of choices men perceive to be open to them." [2] By allowing for the different facets of human beings, and interpreting the total performance of societies as an act of balance in the patterns of choice made by individuals within the framework permitted by the changing setting of society, Rostow avoids the Marxian assertion that the behavior of societies is uniquely determined by economic considerations. Rostow insists that although his "stages-of-growth are an economic way of looking at whole societies, they in no sense imply that the worlds of politics, social organization, and of culture are a mere superstructure built upon and derived uniquely from the economy." [3] On the contrary, what most concerns Rostow is how societies go about making their

---

1. W. W. Rostow, *The Stages of Economic Growth,* Cambridge University Press, 1960, p. 148.

2. *Ibid.,* p. 149.
3. *Ibid.,* p. 2.

choices and balances: "the central phenom- enon of the world of post-traditional soci- eties is not the economy—and whether it is capitalist or not—it is the total proce- dure by which choices are made." [4] Marx's assumption that a society's decisions are merely a function of who owns prop- erty is therefore rejected as inaccurate; instead it is maintained that "one must look directly at the full mechanism of choice among alternative policies, includ- ing the political process—and, indeed, the social and religious processes—as inde- pendent arenas for making decisions and choices." [5]

The implications of this broader view of human motivation become especially significant when Rostow's interpretation of post-traditional societies is contrasted with Marx's account of the post-feudal phase. Thus, Rostow concludes that his account of the break-up of traditional societies is

based on the convergence of motives of pri- vate profit in the modern sectors with a new sense of affronted nationhood. And other forces play their part as well, for example the simple perception that children need not die so young or live their lives in illiteracy: a sense of enlarged human horizons, independent of both profit and national dignity. And when independence or modern nationhood are at last attained, there is no simple, automatic switch to a dominance of the profit motive and economic and social progress. On the contrary there is a searching choice and problem of bal- ance among the three directions policy might go: external assertion; the further concentra- tion of power in the centre as opposed to the regions; and economic growth.[6]

This approach may have more immedi- ate relevance for the problems now con- fronting many underdeveloped countries than Marx's narrower view that political behavior is dependent on economic advan-

4. *Ibid.*, p. 150.
5. *Ibid.*
6. *Ibid.*, p. 152.

tage, and that the decisions of capitalist societies are made simply in terms of the free-market mechanism and private advan- tage.

Moreover, as Rostow observes, the Marx- ian sequence suffers by basing its categories on only one historical case: the case of the British take-off and drive to maturity. Ros- tow reminds us that Marx had presented his whole system before any other society except Britain had experienced the take- off, and instead of revising his categories so as to be more applicable to other cases, Marx merely generalized and projected his interpretation of the British case. A concen- tration on the British case, however, misses the variety of experience in the evolution of different societies, and makes the Marx- ian analysis of the "march of history" unduly rigid and artificial. If for no other reason than that it draws upon a far wider range of historical knowledge, and is thereby more comprehensive and less doc- trinaire, Rostow's analysis can claim to be a superior alternative to the Marxian sequence.

Nonetheless, if Rostow's thesis is to assert with a high degree of generality that it is able to trace a structure of history in the form of a sequence of stages, then it must also answer a number of criticisms that have commonly been levied against stage- theorists. "Stage-making" approaches are misleading when they succumb to a linear conception of history and imply that all economies tend to pass through the same series of stages. Although a particular sequence may correspond broadly to the historical experience of some economies, no single sequence fits the history of all countries. To maintain that every economy always follows the same course of develop- ment with a common past and the same future is to overschematize the complex forces of development, and to give the sequence of stages a generality that is unwarranted. A country may attain a later stage of development without first having passed through an earlier stage, as stages may be skipped, and different types of economy do not have to succeed or evolve from one another. The sequence is also blurred inasmuch as frequently the stages are not mutually exclusive, and characteristics of earlier stages often become mixed with characteristics of later stages. Anyone who attempts to impose upon economic history a one-way course of economic evolution is bound to be challenged, since it is difficult to accept one unique schema as the only real framework in which alone the facts truly lie; the same facts can be arranged in many patterns and seen from many perspectives.[7] What matters, therefore, is how suggestive and useful Rostow's pattern is in providing answers to our questions as we attempt to make sense out of the past and make the future more predictable. This comes down to the question of the adequacy of Rostow's pattern in helping us isolate the strategic factors which make for change, especially those factors that constitute the necessary and sufficient conditions for determining the transition of an economy from a preceding stage to a succeeding stage.

In this respect, Rostow's efforts are more substantial than those by other proponents of stages. Recognizing how important the search for strategic factors is, Rostow adopts an approach that is more analytical and related to a wider range of issues than any of the approaches of his predecessors. His argument abounds with terms such as "forces," "process," "net result," "inner logic"—all indicative of his desire to present an analytical, not merely a descriptive, set of stages. According to Rostow, the "analytic back-bone" of his argument is

"rooted in a dynamic theory of production," and he believes that his set of stages reveals a "succession of strategic choices" that confront a country as it moves forward through the development process. On this basis, perhaps the most illumination can be gained from Rostow's analysis by interpreting each stage as posing a particular type of problem, so that the sequence of stages is equivalent to a series of problems that confront a country in the course of its development. Rostow's ultimate objective, however, has been to present through his set of stages a theory about economic growth and a means of uncovering both the uniformities and the uniqueness of each nation's experience. To be in a better position to judge how successful Rostow has actually been in fulfilling these claims, we should now consider the following appraisals and critiques of his analysis.

2.2 EMPIRICAL EVIDENCE ON ROSTOW'S STAGES *

The very ease with which separate segments can be distinguished in the historical movement from non-modern to modern economic growth and within the long span of the latter should warn us that any sequence of stages, even if offered as a suggestive rather than a substantive scheme, must meet some minimum requirements—if it is to be taken seriously.

The following requirements are relevant:

(a) A given stage must display empirically testable characteristics, common to all or to an important group of units experiencing modern economic growth. This means the specification of modern economic growth; identification of the units that have manifested such growth; and establishment of empirically testable char-

7. Although Rostow gives little attention to the problem, his analysis raises many questions related to basic social theory. In this connection, it is illuminating to consult Isaiah Berlin, *Historical Inevitability*, London, 1954, especially sections II, VIII.

* From Simon Kuznets, "Notes on the Take-off," paper presented at the International Economic Association's Conference at Konstanz in September 1960, on "The Economics of Take-off into Sustained Growth." Reprinted by permission

acteristics claimed to be common to these units at the given stage.

(b) The characteristics of a given stage must be distinctive in that, not necessarily singly but in combination, they are unique to that stage. Mere precedence (or succession) in time does not suffice: given the unidirectional character of growth (by definition), any period is necessarily characterized by larger economic magnitudes than earlier ones and by the structural shifts that accompany such larger magnitudes (particularly a rise in per capita income). Stages are presumably something more than successive ordinates in the steadily climbing curve of growth. They are segments of that curve, with properties so distinct that separate study of each segment seems warranted.

(c) The analytical relation to the preceding stage must be indicated. This naturally involves more than saying that the preceding stage is one of preparation for the given. More meaningfully, we need identification (again in empirically testable terms) of the major processes in the preceding stage that complete it and, with the usual qualifications for exogenous factors, make the next (our given) stage highly probable. Optimally, this would permit us to diagnose the preceding stage *before* the given stage is upon us, and thus would impart predictive value to the whole sequence. But even short of this difficult aim, it means specifying the minimum that must happen in the preceding stage to allow the given stage to emerge.

(d) The analytical relation to the succeeding stage must be indicated. Here too a clear notion (again in empirically testable terms) must be given of the occurrences in the given stage that bring it to a close—aside from mere passage of time. Optimally, such knowledge would permit us to predict, *before* the given stage is finished, how long it still has to run. But even short of such precision, we should know

the essentials that occur during a given stage to bring about its end and clear the ground for the next stage.

(e) These four requirements relate to the common and distinctive characteristics of a given stage, viewed as one in an analytical (and chronological) sequence that links successive stages. However, these common and distinctive characteristics may differ among important groups of units undergoing modern economic growth. Consequently, the fifth requirement is for a clear indication of the universe for which the generality of common and distinctive characteristics is claimed; and for which the analytical relations of a given stage with the preceding and succeeding ones are being formulated.

Against the background of the requirements just stated, we may consider Professor Rostow's discussion of the common and distinctive characteristics of the take-off stage, and the relations between it and the contiguous stages.

. . .

How distinctive are these characteristics? Do they occur in combination only in the take-off stage and not in any other stage—particularly the preceding transition or preconditions stage and the succeeding self-sustained growth or drive to maturity stage? Professor Rostow is not explicit on this point. Presumably the transition stage does not see a rise in the investment proportion from 5 to 10 per cent or more. Yet much of what Professor Rostow would attribute to the take-off has already occurred in the pre-condition stage.[1] Thus, the agricultural revolution assigned to the pre-condition stage "must supply expanded food, expanded markets, and an expanded supply of loanable funds to the modern sector" (Rostow, p. 24); much of social

1. W. W. Rostow, *The Stages of Economic Growth,* Cambridge University Press, 1960, Chap. 3, pp. 17-35.

overhead capital is already invested in transport and other outlays—in the pre-conditions stage (*ibid.*, p. 24); and, in general, "the essence of the transition can be described legitimately as a rise in the rate of investment to a level which regularly, substantially and perceptibly outstrips population growth" (*ibid.*, p. 21). In short, one wonders whether the three specifically stated characteristics of take-off could not be found in the pre-conditions—unless explicit qualifications are attached, e. g., that the investment proportion in that earlier stage must stay below 5 per cent; that the marked agricultural revolution does not immediately call for, and in fact is possible without, a contemporaneous rapid growth in some manufacturing sector; and that investment in overhead capital in transport, etc., is not necessarily accompanied by a rapid growth of one or more modern manufacturing sectors. Finally, one should note that [a] characteristic of the take-off mentions both the *existence* and the *quick emergence* of the political, social, and institutional framework favorable to exploiting "the impulses to expansion in the modern sector" as admissible alternatives. But if that framework already exists at the beginning of the take-off, its emergence must be assigned to the pre-conditions stage. How then does the latter differ from the take-off in which the framework emerges?

The line of division between the take-off and the following stage of self-sustained growth or drive to maturity is also blurred. Presumably the latter stage is marked by the existence of the proper social and institutional framework—which also exists during the take-off. Presumably this later stage also witnesses the rapid growth of one or more modern manufacturing sectors. Indeed, the only characteristics that are distinctly appropriate to the take-off and not to the next stage are the rise in the rate of productive investment to over 10 per cent of national income or net national product; and the implicit rise in the rate of growth of total and per capita income. But are we to assume that both the rate of investment and the rate of growth of product (total and per capita) level off at the high values attained at the end of the take-off stage? And is it this leveling off, the cessation of the rise in the rate of investment and in the rate of growth, that terminates the take-off stage? No explicit statement is made by Professor Rostow; Rostow, Chapter 5, contains a list of dates when "maturity" was reached in a number of countries but little discussion of what took place between the end of the take-off stage and the terminal point of the next stage.

Given this fuzziness in delimiting the take-off stage and in formulating its distinctive characteristics; given the distinctiveness only in the statistical level of the rate of productive investment (and the implicit rate of growth), there is no solid ground upon which to discuss Professor Rostow's view of the analytical relation between the take-off stage and the preceding and succeeding stages. At any rate, the brief comments that can be made within the scope of this paper will follow the review of the empirical evidence.

To what universe do the common characteristics claimed for the take-off period apply? In his most recent presentation, Professor Rostow distinguishes the "general" case of a traditional society from that of the small group of nations (the United States, Australia, New Zealand, Canada, and "perhaps a few others") "born free" (Rostow, pp. 6 and 17-18). The distinction is particularly important in the analysis of the pre-conditions stage, and Professor Rostow does not indicate whether the characteristics of the take-off stage in the originally traditional societies are different from those in the countries "born free." The distinction made in the discussion of pre-conditions is not repeated in the discussion of the take-off; unless the qualification about the rates of investment higher than 5 per cent in some countries (Canada and Argentina) before the take-off stage (necessitated by heavy overhead social capital needs, see Rostow, p. 8) can be interpreted as such. But this qualification does not stress the distinction between traditional and free-born countries; social overhead capital needs were presumably heavy in Russia and for that matter, on a relative scale, in Switzerland. We may therefore infer that Professor Rostow, who includes the dates of the take-off period for both types of economy in the same list, assumes that the characteristics of the take-off are broadly the same for all countries undergoing modern economic growth.

...

I do not know what "a political, social and institutional framework which exploits the impulses to expansion in the modern sector, etc." is; or how to identify such a framework except by hindsight and conjecture; or how to specify the empirical evidence that would have to be brought to bear to ascertain whether such a framework is in "existence or in quick emergence." It seems to me that the passage just cited defines these social phenomena as a complex that produces the effect Professor Rostow wishes to explain; and then he treats this definition as if it were a meaningful identification.

It is easier to define the characteristic that specifies "the development of one or more substantial manufacturing sectors with a high rate of growth" once "high" is explained. But a review of empirical evidence on this point holds little interest if I am correct in assuming that the major distinctive characteristic of the take-off is a marked rise in the rate of growth of per capita and hence of total income. If the rate of growth does accelerate, some sec-

tors are bound to grow more rapidly than others, as has been demonstrated in Arthur F. Burns' and my own work on production trends—partly in response to the differential impact of technological opportunities (including raw material supplies), and partly in response to the different income elasticities of the demand for various goods. Under these conditions, one or more manufacturing sectors, and one or more sectors of agriculture, transportation, services, etc. are bound to show high rates of growth. The pertinent question is why manufacturing—rather than agriculture, transport, or any other rapidly growing industry—should be specified as the leading sector.

In considering this question, the two constitutive characteristics of a leading sector must be kept in mind. First, sector A leads, rather than follows, if it moves not in response to sectors B, C, D, etc. within the country, but under the impact of factors which, relative to the given national economy, may be considered autonomous. These may be technological changes embodying some new inventions; changes in the resource base resulting from new discoveries; changes in foreign demand, which, being external to the given economy, may be considered autonomous; and breaks in social structure (political revolution, agrarian reform, and the like), which could be viewed as changes exogenous to economic processes proper. The point to be noted is that the autonomous nature of this characteristic, relative to the given national economy, rests upon the origin of the stimulus, not upon the scope of the response. The latter may depend largely upon many other factors besides the stimulus, factors that are part and parcel of a given economy and society.

This brings us to the second constitutive characteristic of a leading sector, the magnitude of its effects; or more specifically, the magnitude of its contribution to a country's economic growth. Sector A may be leading in the sense of responding to an autonomous stimulus, but unless its contribution to the country's economic growth is substantial, it does not "lead" the country's economic growth—no matter how high its own rate of growth. After all, a thousandfold rise in the production of plastic hula hoops over a decade does not make it a leading industry.

How to set the lower limit to a significant contribution is a question that can be answered only in terms of empirical, quantitative analysis. We must distinguish the direct contribution—what the autonomous growth of sector A, the result of its weight in the economy multiplied by its percentage rate of growth, adds to the growth of the economy, total and per capita; from what sector A contributes indirectly, through the effects of backward and forward linkages with sectors B, C, D, ... ; and, finally, from what it may contribute, again indirectly, through its effects on social structure and qualities of the population (e. g., urbanization, organizational form of the economic unit, education, and the like), which in turn affect a country's economic growth in a variety of ways. The magnitude and particularly the timing of these direct and indirect effects differ ....

The establishment of these leadership characteristics of sectors—both in terms of the autonomous character of the impulse and the timing and magnitude of their direct and indirect contributions to a country's economic growth—is thus a task that involves intensive study, not merely of the leading sectors proper but also of those affected by them, extending into the quantitative framework of the whole economy. Leadership of sectors, or any other element in the acceleration of the rate of growth can be established only after careful analysis of the particular circumstances preceding and during the period of acceleration—country by country, and by the application of sta-

tistical, theoretical, and other tools to the historical evidence.

. . .

The failure of aggregative data to reveal the characteristics claimed by Professor Rostow as common to the take-off stage, at least in countries that did not experience the drastic and forced transformation associated with Communist revolutions, is disturbing. It casts serious doubt on the validity of the definition of the take-off as a generally occurring stage of modern economic growth, distinct from what Professor Rostow calls the "pre-conditions" or "transition" stage preceding it and the "self-sustained" growth stage following it. The doubt is only reinforced by some more general questions concerning Professor Rostow's overall scheme. These questions can be discussed under three heads: (a) the meaning of pre-conditions; (b) effects of the wide diversity of historical heritage of pre-modern economies on the characteristics of their transition to modern economic growth; (c) the meaning of self-sustained growth.

(a) Professor Rostow's discussion of the pre-conditions stage treats it, and indeed much of the sequence, as analogous to a mechanical, or more specifically, an aeronautical process—despite his several references to economic growth as essentially "biological." The picture suggested is that of the sequence involved in putting an aeroplane (or a glider) into flight. First there is the checking and fueling—providing the pre-conditions; then there is the relatively brief take-off, during which the driving force is accelerated to produce the upward movement; and finally there is the leveling-off into self-sustained flight. This analogy, perhaps unfair to Professor Rostow's stage sequence, is useful because it pinpoints the basic question in connection with the whole pre-conditions stage: can such pre-conditions be created without *at the same time* producing changes through-out the economy that, in and of them-selves, initiate modern economic growth—a higher rate of increase of total product, a higher rate of capital formation, growth of one or several modern productive sec-tors, and so on? To put it differently, is it realistic to talk of the pre-conditions cre-ated in one time span and of the initiation of modern economic growth in another span chronologically distinct?

The answer to this question depends upon what the pre-conditions are. Since the modern developed economies make effective use of a wide variety of techni-cal and social inventions, many of which date back to a time far earlier than the initiation of modern economic growth, pre-conditions whose creation is chrono-logically distinct from the early periods of modern economic growth can easily be found. Thus many current commercial instruments, maritime laws, and monetary practices originated, in much their modern form, long before the second half of the 18th century, which may be taken as the date of the beginning of modern economic growth. But for the pre-conditions that Professor Rostow emphasizes in his dis-cussion (Rostow, Chapter 3)—transforma-tion of agriculture and overhead capital investments—the answer is, to my mind, quite different. I do not see how, particu-larly in the "general" traditional society not "born free," a major change in agri-cultural productivity that provides more food per capita and more savings can be effected without a rapid growth of some manufacturing and other sectors which provide not only employment for the dis-placed agricultural population but also the producer and consumer goods required for the higher agricultural productivity and by the people who share in its benefits. And the production relations associated with increased overhead capital invest-ments should bring about similar con-comitant changes. Indeed much of what Professor Rostow says in Chapter 4 about income shifts and income flows in the process of take-off (particularly about agri-cultural incomes in Rostow, pp. 46-7) is equally relevant to the discussion of pre-conditions in Chapter 3.

Perhaps by further specification one could distinguish clearly, and in chrono-logical sequence, some phases of the agri-cultural revolution and of increased capital investments that precede the distinctive changes that can be established for the take-off stage; but I doubt that this is pos-sible. For any significant transformation of agriculture in the crowded traditional soci-eties and any marked rise in overhead capital investment are, to my mind, already part and parcel of modern economic growth; and, given the technological, eco-nomic, and social interrelations within the economy, can hardly occur unless they are *accompanied* by the changes that Professor Rostow assigns to the take-off stage. In short, the case for separation between the rather vaguely defined "pre-conditions" stage and the apparently more sharply defined take-off stage presented in Profes-sor Rostow's discussion, seems to me ex-tremely weak. And Professor Rostow's casual reference to the duration of the pre-conditions stage—"a long period up to a century or, conceivably, more" (Rostow, p. 27)—does not make the case stronger.

(b) In his recent book, Professor Ros-tow treats "traditional" economy as a single stage in a sequence of five stages; and, as already indicated, draws only one relevant distinction, that between the small group of nations "born free" and all others—the latter being a single category of traditional economies. Thus, it includes the Western European countries, whose civilization was in many ways the cradle of modern eco-nomic society, and which, during the epoch of merchant capitalism, were on the "tak-ing" side vis-à-vis much of the rest of the world. It also includes the old Asian countries with their different history and endowments, the African societies with their specific heritage and culture, and many countries in the Western Hemisphere which are not among the "free born." Disregarding for the present a major question as to the legitimacy of characterizing all pre-modern economies as a *stage,* we are forced to conclude that such treatment implies that the stages of pre-conditions and take-off are presumably characterized by basically the same important features in all these countries.

To say that this is a heroic oversimplification is not to condemn the scheme out of hand. After all, modern economic growth, when and where it occurs, does have distinctive characteristics—not merely by definition, but because it draws upon a transnational stock of useful knowledge and of social invention, and is powered by human views and desires that have many similar features the world over. Yet it is fair to argue that the stocks of knowledge and social inventions themselves change over time; and that the modern economic growth of different countries is a process of combining the different complexes of historical heritage with the common requirements of the modern "industrial system." The parameters of the combination are likely, therefore, to differ from country to country, depending upon their specific historical heritage; upon the time when they enter modern economic growth; and upon their relations with other countries, particularly those already developed. The proper analysis of the process of modern economic growth in individual countries requires, therefore, a far more meaningful typology of "traditionalism" (or, to use another term, "underdevelopment") than is provided by Professor Rostow. Nor can we disregard the *timing* of the process in relation to other countries, an aspect that plays such an important role in Professor

Gerschenkron's intriguing hypothesis of the increasing "strain of backwardness" and the association between the degree of backwardness and the characteristics of the transition to modern economic growth ...

The point of the comment is that it is in the *early* phase of a country's modern economic growth particularly that these distinct peculiarities of historical heritage, position in the sequence of spread of the industrial system, and relation to other already developed countries put their impress upon a country's growth. After 70 to 100 years of modern economic growth, one developed country would conceivably be similar in its characteristics to others—despite differences in initial position. (Even this comment has limited validity: compare Japan today, after eight decades of rapid economic growth, with say Germany or France after a century of it.) However, in the early phase the differences in pattern of growth are likely to stand out most clearly, for at that point the diverse historical heritages have not yet been overlaid with the similarities imposed by sustained modern economic growth. And since the take-off stage, which to my mind overlaps with much of the pre-conditions stage, is an early phase of modern economic growth, the differences among countries in the parameters of the take-off are likely to be more notable than those in growth at later stages. An adequate stage theory or any other analytical scheme for studying economic growth, should point out not only the similarities but also the major differences—the latter associated with observable differences in historical antecedents, timing of entry into the process of economic growth, and other relevant factors. Professor Rostow's disregard of the major sources of differences in the early phases of modern economic growth among the developed "traditional" countries imposes severe limits on his claims to generality.

(c) The "self-sustained" growth that is

supposed to occur in the stage following take-off is somewhat of a puzzle. Is it self-sustained in a sense in which it is *not* during the take-off and/or any earlier phase? If the reference is to the higher level of per capita income attained at the end of the take-off, which permits higher levels of savings and capital formation, which, in turn, permit higher rates of growth (assuming the marginal capital-output ratio is constant), then one can argue that the same automatic mechanism operates during the take-off—once a significant increase in per capita income occurs, which presumably happens at the beginning of the take-off stage. If the reference is to the existence of favorable social institutions, these must also have existed through most of the take-off stage. Furthermore, many institutional changes are gradual, and if they have continually improved during take-off or earlier, their effects on the rate of growth should have been continuous. Consequently, since both income increases and institutional improvements abounded, it is difficult to accept the suggestion that growth was not self-sustained before the end of the take-off stage, but acquired that property only during the succeeding stage.

Obviously, the term is an analogy rather than a clearly specified property or characteristic; and for this reason alone should be avoided. In one sense any growth is self-sustained: it means an irreversible rise to a higher level of economic performance that may make it easier to find reserves for further growth—whether these are funds for capital investment, greater efficiency of the labor force supplied with more consumption goods, economies of large scale, etc. In another sense any growth is self-limiting: the rise to a higher level may mean a reduction in incentive, pressure upon scarce irreproducible resources, and, perhaps most important, the strengthening of entrenched interests that

are likely to resist growth in competing sectors. And, indeed, the analysis of any widely and broadly conceived process of economic growth must reveal these and many more self-sustaining and self-limiting impacts of growth. If then Professor Rostow characterizes one stage of growth as "self-sustained" and others, by inference, as not, he must mean that in the latter stages the obstacles generated by past and current growth outweigh the self-sustaining impacts; whereas in the former stage the self-sustaining impacts outweigh the self-limiting ones. Obviously, both sets of impacts need documentation, both need to be weighed in terms of empirical evidence —far more than Professor Rostow provides in his casual characterization. Given the two sets of impacts of economic growth just suggested, the outcome is uncertain; and the process can never be *purely* self-sustained, since it always generates *some* self-limiting effects. In this sense, economic growth is always a struggle; and it is misleading to convey an impression of easy automaticity, a kind of soaring euphoria of self-sustained flight to higher economic levels.

The gist of the discussion in this paper can be summarized in a few brief propositions.

(a) Leadership of a sector depends upon the origin of its growth in an autonomous impulse, not in response to other sectors in the country; and upon the magnitude of its direct and indirect contributions to the country's economic growth. The autonomous impulse and the various types of contribution to growth differ in timing; and the identification and chronology of leading sectors require specification and evidence lacking in Professor Rostow's discussion.

(b) The doubling of capital investment proportions and the implicit sharp acceleration in the rate of growth of national product, claimed by Professor Rostow as characterizing his "take-off" periods, are not confirmed by the statistical evidence for those countries on his list for which we have data.

(c) There is no clear distinction between the "pre-conditions" and the "take-off" stages. On the contrary, given the pre-conditions emphasized by Professor Rostow, viz., transformation of agriculture and overhead capital investments, there is a *prima facie* case for expecting the "pre-conditions" and the "take-off" stages to overlap.

(d) The analysis of the take-off and pre-conditions stages neglects the effect of historical heritage, time of entry into the process of modern economic growth, degree of backwardness, and other relevant factors on the characteristics of the early phases of modern economic growth in the different "traditional" countries.

(e) The concept (and stage) of "self-sustained" growth is a misleading over-simplification. No growth is purely self-sustaining or purely self-limiting. The characterization of one stage of growth as self-sustained, and of others, by implication, as lacking that property, requires substantive evidence and analysis not provided in Professor Rostow's discussion.

A few additional comments may help to put these conclusions into proper perspective.

First, the evidence used to test Professor Rostow's scheme is not conclusive. Some non-Communist countries for which we have no data may have experienced a period of growth conforming with Professor Rostow's take-off stage. Also, his scheme may fit the Communist "take-offs," but my knowledge of them is inadequate for checking. All that is claimed here is that aggregative data for a number of countries do not support Professor Rostow's distinction and characterization of the take-off stage. On the other hand, the fact that the evidence is confined to aggre-

gative data does not limit their bearing. Economic growth is an aggregative process; sectoral changes are interrelated with aggregative changes, and can be properly weighted only after they have been incorporated into the aggregative framework; and the absence of required aggregative changes severely limits the likelihood of the implicit strategic sectoral changes.

Second, although we concentrated on the "take-off" stage, and the two contiguous stages—"pre-conditions" and "self-sustained growth"— much of what was said applies by inference to other stages in Professor Rostow's scheme. Moreover, the characterization of the "traditional" economy as a stage raises numerous questions. But an explicit discussion of the rest of the scheme would take us too far afield.

Third, my disagreement with Professor Rostow is *not* on the value and legitimacy of an attempt to suggest some pattern of order in the modern economic growth experience of different countries. On the contrary, I fully share what I take to be his view on the need to go beyond qualitative and quantitative description to the use of the evidence for a large number of countries and long periods, in combination with analytical tools and imaginative hypotheses, to suggest and explain not only some common patterns but also, I would add, the major deviations from them. However, for reasons clearly indicated above, I disagree with the sequence of stages he suggests.

2.3 CONDITIONS OF THE TAKE-OFF *

The stage that has struck the public mind most forcibly is undoubtedly that of the take-off: largely, no doubt, because the aeronautical metaphor—prolonged in the phrase "into self-sustained growth"—

* From A. K. Cairncross, "Essays in Bibliography and Criticism, XLV: *The Stages of Economic Growth,*" in *Economic History Review,* April 1961, pp. 454, 455-8. Reprinted by permission.

suggests at once an effortlessness and a finality congenial to modern thought. The reactions of historians and economists have been less favourable. They have grown accustomed to emphasizing the continuity of historical change, to tracing back to a previous age the forces producing a social explosion, and to explaining away the apparent leaps in economic development. They are inclined, therefore, to regard Rostow as a latter-day Toynbee, stressing a discontinuity that is no more than symptomatic of the underlying forces at work and making the symptoms more decisive (if, indeed, symptoms can be said to be decisive) than they really were. Is there a genuine discontinuity rather than a simple acceleration of growth? If so, in what form does the discontinuity show itself? In what sense does the discontinuity herald a decisive break with the past? And is it conceivable that this discontinuity is of such a character that it can be identified with a precise span of time, normally twenty years?

...

Even if one limits the argument to Britain, one has to take a long view in order to explain the burst of innovations that set off what may still be thought of as the industrial revolution. No one doubts —least of all Rostow—that innovation is a social process and that its acceleration in the eighteenth century was associated with what he calls for short "Newtonian science" (it has, in fact, very little to do with Newton and is not simply a matter of science): a new way of looking at the world and a new ambition to change it. The self-sustaining character of development derives from this outlook and ambition, which issue in a continuous effort of technological improvement. But if so, why deflect attention to the *stage* at which this effort bears sudden fruit rather than concentrate on the effort itself: on the change

in ideas and the ways in which these ideas took hold of economic activity?

The same point can be expressed differently by asking how one is expected to distinguish between the pre-conditions and the conditions of economic growth. Rostow traces the beginning of take-off in most countries to a "particular sharp stimulus" (p. 36). One may question some of the examples he gives—the German revolution of 1848, for example. One may also observe that the rest of his examples either involve a sudden change in market opportunities due to events abroad or attribute a special importance to deliberate government policies. But the market opportunities that result from agricultural improvement have earlier been relegated to the stage of pre-conditions; and government policies directed to the creation of social overhead capital are also assigned to the same stage. What distinguishes the stimuli that introduce a take-off and the stimuli that do no more than usher in the stage of pre-conditions?

Pre-conditions are, after all, a logical rather than a chronological concept. Must all of them ante-date the take-off? There is no reason to suppose that agriculture has ever completely fulfilled its required rôle *in advance* of the spurt in growth that Rostow calls take-off or that social overhead capital has to reach some definite stage *before* take-off. On the contrary, the experience of most countries has been that whether agricultural expansion started earlier or not, it continued into the period of industrialization and constituted a large proportion of total growth. Similarly, social overhead capital is needed more than ever as industrialization proceeds. How could one ever suppose otherwise if railways have been one of the most frequent "leading sectors" in the take-off?

But if the various stages overlap, what then is the meaning of a "stage"? The less tidy the chronology the more one is driven back to logic: to the isolation of the decisive factors that initiate growth and give it its "on-going character". When we enquire what these factors are we are offered three.

The first is "a rise in the rate of productive investment from, say, 5 per cent or less to over 10 per cent of national income" (p. 39). This is a view that has been expressed by other economists, notably Arthur Lewis, although no one else, of course, has associated it with the period of take-off. Rostow introduces the idea into his analysis of the stage of pre-conditions as well as of take-off so that one is left a little in doubt whether savings habits are assumed to alter before or during take-off. I suspect that, like many economists who have embraced the idea from first principles rather than after empirical investigation, he has found his initial enthusiasm for it evaporating on further reflection and that he now lays more stress on the other conditions that he gives. However that may be, it is abundantly clear, in spite of the limitations of the statistical data, that the periods during which he supposes economies to have taken-off did not witness a decisive break in savings or investment ratios, that in some countries at least the evidence tells against any antecedent rise, and that the normal experience has been a gradual increase in the ratio of savings and domestic investment to income as development proceeded. There is nothing in the historical record to justify the quite exceptional emphasis laid on a sharp increase in this ratio, however measured, at the outset of rapid growth.

The second condition is the emergence of leading sectors in manufacturing. On the importance of the idea of leading sectors Rostow insists again and again. It is the "analytic bone-structure" (p. 13) of his stages of growth. "It is the fact that sectors tend to have a rapid growth-phase, early in their life," he argues, "that makes it useful to regard economic history as a sequence of stages" (p. 14). Or again, "growth proceeds by repeating endlessly, in different patterns, with different leading sectors, the experience of the take-off" (p. 53).

Rostow's conception of leading sectors is not unlike what the Scandinavian economists have called "development blocks." The growth of any one industry is linked in various ways with the growth of other industries on which its activities impinge: so that if its costs fall sharply or the demand for its products accelerates, the effects ramify over a wide sector. Of these ramifications Rostow provides many interesting examples. They are undoubtedly relevant to a dynamic theory of production; but what is their precise relevance to the take-off? Does it really matter whether one industry leaps ahead or drags along behind it or whether a large group of industries advance on a broad front under impulses peculiar to each?

To this, if I understand him, Rostow's reply is that the historical experience has been otherwise: that at any one time there has been a particular industry that has provided the real momentum of economic development. It has varied widely in the early stages of growth in different countries; and in any one country there has been a succession of leading sectors after take-off, the power to generate fresh leading sectors being the acid test of self-sustained growth. It would seem, too, that Rostow would admit to the category of leading sectors only an extremely limited group—not more, perhaps, than one in each generation. In Britain this would mean accepting the cotton textile industry at one end of industrialization, the motor car industry at the other, and not more than three or four between—railways, steel, and electricity, for example.

If this is a correct interpretation, it seems to me highly misleading. The growth of productivity in an economy neither has been nor is governed by the development of leading sectors in this sense. The cotton textile industry was not big enough to dominate the growth of output in Britain in the eighteenth century nor is the motor car industry today, even when one takes account of all the changes that flow from the use of motor cars. Of course there are major breakthroughs in each generation and one can single these out and call the group of industries affected a leading sector. But the cumulative effect of unspectacular improvements in technique across the whole industrial field may well be of much greater importance.

Even if industrial change does take the form of a series of leading sectors, how does this help us to understand the take-off? We are given no basis on which to recognize a leading sector *ex ante*. What connection is there between the conception and later stages? Merely that there must have been two or more leading sectors before maturity is reached and that a particular leading sector—the motor car industry—characterized the age of high mass consumption? Or is the significance of leading sectors no more than that this is the *modus operandi* of sustained growth irrespective of the stages through which such growth subsequently moves? And why must leading sectors be in manufacturing? If railway-building can qualify, why not retail distribution or agriculture? One may sympathize with Rostow's insistence on the need to dig below the aggregate in order to uncover the real forces at work in the economy; one may accept his emphasis on industrial linkages and on the far-reaching consequences of a few major developments; but one may still question whether this provides the analytic bone-structure that he claims.

Rostow's third condition for take-off is "the existence or quick emergence of a political social and institutional framework which...gives to growth an ongoing

character" (p. 39). This is the most baffling condition of the three. How it differs from a pre-condition is hard to understand, and understanding is not assisted when two paragraphs later it seems to have been transformed into a pre-condition. The framework indispensable to take-off is defined in terms of its success not of any antecedent properties except perhaps the "capacity to mobilize capital from domestic sources" (which takes us back to the first condition). But a definition in these terms tells us nothing about the factors at work since we can only deduce their existence from the fact of take-off, never the likelihood of take-off from the ascertained fact of their existence.

In the light of all this, does Rostow's approach help us to understand what went on in any individual case of industrialization or make it easier to see what a country seeking to industrialize itself should do? It would be absurd to answer these questions with a blank negative; a great deal of what Rostow says is undoubtedly helpful. But this is so, in my view, in spite of, rather than because of, the stage approach which he adopts.

2.4 A CRITIQUE OF ROSTOW'S STAGES *

This book belongs to the honourable genre of literature, of which in economics Malthus's *Essay on Population* is the most eminent example, which attempts to sweep wide tracts of human experience into a few central categories. Professor Rostow's categories are now well known: traditional society, the preconditions for take-off, the take-off, the drive to maturity and the age of high mass-consumption. "These stages," writes the author, "are not merely descriptive . . . They have an analytic bone structure, rooted in a dynamic theory of

* From a review by H. J. Habakkuk of Rostow's *Stages of Economic Growth, Economic Journal,* September 1961, pp. 601-4. Reprinted by permission.

production." This is a mistaken view. The book contains some ideas on how one stage proceeds to the next, but they do not cohere into anything which could reasonably be dignified as a theory of production. The work is essentially an essay in classification.

The notion that there are similarities between the process of growth in different countries and periods is, of course, a familiar one. We know that certain conditions were more favourable to growth than others, that growth started in limited sectors and then proceeded on a broader front, and that as incomes per head rose there were changes in the relative importance of different types of economic activity. What Professor Rostow has done is to systematise such similarities, link them with certain political and social choices, and dramatise them. Though the criteria by reference to which his stages are derived are not easily identifiable, most people can easily recognise a traditional society and an age of mass consumption. But the three intervening stages are less self-evident. At the centre of the argument is the assertion that there is one short interval in the history of a society in which changes take place which ensure that growth becomes the normal condition of that society. "In a decade or two changes take place which ensure that henceforth both the basic structure of the economy and the social and political structure of the society are transformed in such a way that a steady rate of growth can be thereafter regularly sustained." Whether there were periods so critical and so precisely compressed in time is a question of fact, and I can only say that I do not believe that the European experience conforms to this pattern. Growth has been more rapid in some periods than in others, and some innovations, for example the railways, have had much more profound effects than others; but I see no evidence that there has

been one, and only one, decisive phase in the history of each growing economy.

The preconditions also present difficulties. The first requirement of a precondition is surely that it should occur first in time. But in England the principal changes in transport and in agriculture took place during rather than before the period of accelerated growth; in Russia the relevant agricultural dvelopments occurred late in the decade after the take-off had got under way, and in China they are occurring in the middle of the period to which Professor Rostow assigns her take-off. In many cases the increase of agricultural output and the creation of overhead social capital are not conditions whose pre-existence explains the acceleration of growth; they are part of the acceleration which needs to be explained.

And what meaning is to be attached to maturity, the stage that lies on the other side of the take-off? This is defined as "the period when a society has effectively applied the range of (then) modern technology to the bulk of its resources." This is an imprecise definition, for, except in a purely geological sense which does not seem to be what is intended, the "bulk of a country's resources" has no clear meaning independent of the level of technology; and, except in the purely engineering sense, one cannot define "modern" without reference to the factor endowment of the economy. But in a rough-and-ready way one can see what the author means. What is surprising is that he should extend this already protean definition to cover societies which he acknowledges contain large technologically backward sectors. Such an extension is apparently legitimate where the backward sector is geographically concentrated (the southern states in the United States) or is due to rapid population increase (Japan) or results from political decisions (the U.S.S.R.). Britain arrives at maturity about 1850 without the aid of any such exegesis, though very large sections of the economy were then technologically backward, however this term is defined. Moreover, while as a general rule the drive to maturity comes before and leads into the age of mass-consumption, Canada and Australia have entered the stage of mass consumption before reaching maturity. Is a stage which needs so much bullying really worth having?

The attempt to relate the stages of growth to political developments leads to further stretching of categories and straining of facts. Thus among the wars of regional aggression, which arise "out of the dilemmas and opportunities of men, risen to power on the banners of independence, trained as politicians and soldiers, but now facing responsibility for a turbulent transitional society," Rostow includes, *inter alia,* Bismarck's wars of 1864, 1866 and 1870, the Russo-Japanese War of 1904–5, and the wars of the French Revolution ... Moreover, though these wars of regional aggression are said to have arisen "directly from the dynamics of the preconditions period," two of them in fact fall about the middle of the take-off period.

But this book is aimed at the future, not the past. The power of its system lies in the metaphors with which it is expounded. There are continual references to "societies building compound interest into their habits and institutions," to "the onward march of compound interest," a shorthand way, the author explains, of suggesting that "growth normally proceeds by geometric progression." Taken literally, this appears to mean that growth has normally taken place at a constant rate which is not true; if it is not to be taken literally it is merely a misleading way of dressing up the platitude that growing societies grow. There are also references to "self-sustaining," "self-reinforcing" and "on-going" growth. This is not, so far as I can see, anything more than growth of the plain

straight-forward variety; but the adjectives seem to offer an assurance that once one or two critical decades are over a society can rely on automatic growth to carry it forward into the age of motor-cars and television sets. On many occasions, it is true, Professor Rostow is at pains to insist that he is not describing a single rigid pattern of growth; but none of his reservations blur the impression, sanctioned by the vivid and categorical chart which prefaces the book, that, after the take-off, the coming of the age of universal mass-consumption is as inevitable as the victory of the proletariat was in Marx (though as in Marx we shall have to work hard to ensure that the inevitable actually happens). And this is the impression the author clearly means to give; "in the end," he concludes, "the lesson of all this is that the tricks of growth are not all that difficult." This may be so, but it can be presented as the verdict of history only by concentrating on the success stories: there have been bump downs and even crash landings. After reading this book we are no better able to judge whether in any particular case the "tricks of growth" are going to work successfully. Though in the text the approximate date of the Turkish take-off is given as 1937, a footnote declares that—almost a quarter of a century later— it still remains to be seen whether Turkey has made the transition to self-sustaining growth. The take-offs can only be confidently identified retrospectively; one can only tell if growth is going to be self-sustaining if in fact it has been sustained for a long period.

2.5. AN APPROACH TO EUROPEAN INDUSTRIALIZATION *

The map of Europe in the nineteenth century showed a motley picture of coun-

* From Alexander Gerschenkron, *Economic Backwardness in Historical Perspective,* The Belknap Press of Harvard University Press, copyright, 1962, by The President and Fellows of Harvard College, pp. 353-9. Reprinted by permission.

tries varying with regard to the degree of their economic backwardness. At the same time, processes of rapid industrialization started in several of those countries from very different levels of economic backwardness. Those differences in points—or planes—of departure were of crucial significance for the nature of the subsequent development. Depending on a given country's degree of economic backwardness on the eve of its industrialization, the course and character of the latter tended to vary in a number of important respects. Those variations can be readily compressed into the shorthand of six propositions.

1. The more backward a country's economy, the more likely was its industrialization to start discontinuously as a sudden great spurt proceeding at a relatively high rate of growth of manufacturing output.[1]

2. The more backward a country's economy, the more pronounced was the stress in its industrialization on bigness of both plant and enterprise.

3. The more backward a country's economy, the greater was the stress upon producers' goods as against consumers' goods.

4. The more backward a country's economy, the heavier was the pressure upon the levels of consumption of the population.

5. The more backward a country's economy, the greater was the part played by special institutional factors designed to increase supply of capital to the nascent industries and, in addition, to provide them with less decentralized and better informed entrepreneurial guidance; the more backward the country, the more pronounced was the coerciveness and comprehensiveness of those factors.

6. The more backward a country, the less likely was its agriculture to play any active role by offering to the growing industries the advantages of an expanding industrial market based in turn on the rising productivity of agricultural labor.

. . . the differences in the level of economic advance among the individual European countries or groups of countries in the last century were sufficiently large to make it possible to array those countries, or group of countries, along a scale of increasing degrees of backwardness and thus to render the latter an operationally usable concept. Cutting two notches into that scale yields three groups of countries which may be roughly described as advanced, moderately backward, and very backward. To the extent that certain of the variations in our six propositions can also be conceived as discrete rather than continuous, the pattern assumes the form of a series of stage constructs. Understandably enough, this result obtains most naturally with regard to factors referred to in proposition 5, where quantitative differences are associated with qualitative, that is, institutional, variations.

. . .

Such an attempt to view the course of industrialization as a schematic stagelike process differs essentially from the various efforts in "stage making," the common feature of which was the assumption that all economies were supposed regularly to pass through the same individual stages as they moved along the road of economic progress. The regularity may have been frankly presented as an inescapable "law" of economic development.[2] Alternatively,

---

1. The "great spurt" is closely related to W. W. Rostow's "take-off" (*The Stages of Economic Growth*, Cambridge University Press, 1960, Chap. 4). Both concepts stress the element of specific discontinuity in economic development; great spurts, however, are confined to the area of manufacturing and mining, whereas take-offs refer to national output. Unfortunately, in the present state of our statistical information on long-term growth of national income, there is hardly any way of establishing, let alone testing, the take-off hypotheses.

2. See, for example, Bruno Hildebrand, *Die Nationalökonomie der Gegenwart und Zukunft und andere gesammelte Schriften*, 1, Jena, 1922, p. 357.

the element of necessity may have been
somewhat disguised by well-meant, even
though fairly meaningless, remarks about
the choices that were open to society.[3] But
all those schemes were dominated by the
idea of uniformity. Thus, Rostow was at
pains to assert that the process of industrialization repeated itself from country to
country lumbering through his pentamet-
ric rhythm . . . .

The point, however, is not simply that
these were important occurrences which
have just claims on the historian's attention. What matters in the present connection is that observing the individual
methods of financing industrial growth
helps us to understand the crucial problem
of prerequisites for industrial development.

The common opinion on the subject has
been well stated by Rostow. There is said
to be a number of certain general pre-
conditions or prerequisites for industrial
growth, without which it could not begin.
Abolition of an archaic framework in
agricultural organization or an increase in
the productivity of agriculture; creation
of an influential modern elite which is
materially or ideally interested in economic
change; provision of what is called social-
overhead capital in physical form—all
these are viewed as "necessary preconditions," except that some reference to the
multifarious forms in which the prerequisites are fulfilled in the individual
areas are designd to take care of the
"unique" factors in development. Similarly, the existence of a value system
favoring economic progress and the availability of effective entrepreneurial groups
basking in the sun of social approval have
been regarded as essential preconditions of
industrial growth.

These positions are part and parcel of an

undifferentiated approach to industrial history. But their conceptual and empirical
deficiencies are very considerable, even
though it is by no means easy to bid
farewell to this highly simplified way of
viewing the processes of industrialization.
It took the present writer several years
before he succeeded in reformulating the
concept of prerequisites so that it could
be fit into the general approach premised
upon the notion of relative backwardness.

. . .

There should be a fine on the use of
words such as "necessary" or "necessity"
in historical writings. As one takes a closer
look at the concept of necessity as it is
appended to prerequisites of industrial
development, it becomes clear that, whenever the concept is not entirely destitute
of meaning, it is likely to be purely defini-
tional: industrialization is defined in terms
of certain conditions which then, by an
imperceptible shift of the writer's wrist,
are metamorphosed into historical preconditions.[4]

The recourse to tautologies and dexter-
ous manipulations has been produced by,
or at any rate served to disguise, very real
empirical difficulties. After having satisfied
oneself that in England certain factors could
be reasonably regarded as having precon-
ditioned the industrialization of the country, the tendency was, and still is, to elevate
them to the rank of ubiquitous prerequisites of all European industrializations.
Unfortunately, the attempt was inconsistent with two empirical observations: (1)
some of the factors that had served as prerequisites in England either were not
present in less advanced countries or at
best were present to a very small extent;

3. See Rostow, *The Stages of Economic
Growth,* pp. 118f.

4. It is not surprising, therefore, to see Rostow
at one point (p. 49) mix conditions and preconditions of industrial development very freely.

(2) the big spurt of industrial development occurred in those countries despite the lack of such prerequisites.

If these observations are not ignored or shrugged away, as is usually done, they quite naturally direct research toward a new question: in what way and through the use of what devices did backward countries *substitute* for the missing prerequisites? ... It appears, on the one hand, that some of the alleged prerequisites were not needed in industrializations proceeding under different conditions. On the other hand, once the question has been asked, whole series of various substitutions become visible which could be readily organized in a meaningful pattern according to the degree of economic backwardness.... [I]t is easy to conceive of the capital supplied to the early factories in an advanced country as stemming from previously accumulated wealth or from gradually plowed-back profits; at the same time, actions by banks and governments in less advanced countries are regarded as successful attempts to create *in the course* of industrialization conditions which had not been created in the "preindustrial" periods precisely because of the economic backwardness of the areas concerned....

... the area of capital supply is only one instance of substitutions for missing prerequisites. As one looks at the various patterns of substitution in the individual countries, taking proper account of the effects of gradually diminishing backwardness, one is tempted to formulate still another general proposition. The more backward was a country on the eve of its great spurt of industrial development, the more likely were the processes of its industrialization to present a rich and complex picture—thus providing a curious contrast with its own preindustrial history that most often was found to have been relatively barren. In an advanced country, on the other hand, the very richness of its economic history in the preindustrial periods rendered possible a relatively simple and straightforward course in its modern industrial history.

Thus, the concept of prerequisites must be regarded as an integral part of this writer's general approach to the industrial history of Europe. At the same time, it is important to keep in mind the heuristic nature of the concept. There is no intention to suggest that backward countries necessarily engaged in deliberate acts of "substitution" for something that had been in evidence in more advanced countries. Men in a less developed country may have simply groped for and found solutions that were consonant with the existing conditions of backwardness. In fact, one could conceivably start the study of European industrializations in the east rather than in the west of the Continent and view some elements in English industrial history as substitutions for the German or the Russian way of doing things. This would not be a very good way to proceed. It would make mockery of chronology and would be glaringly artificial. True, some artificiality also inheres in the opposite approach. It is arbitrary to select England as the seat of prerequisites. Yet this is the arbitrariness of the process of cognition and should be judged by its fruits.

The main advantage of viewing European history as patterns of substitutions governed by the prevailing—and changing—degree of backwardness lies, perhaps paradoxically, in its offering a set of predictabilities while at the same time placing limitations upon our ability to predict. To predict is not to prophesy. Prediction in historical research means addressing intelligent, that is, sufficiently specific, questions as new materials are approached.

3. FUTURE TAKE-OFFS IN PERSPECTIVE—NOTE

"The historian is a prophet looking backwards"—this dictum is apt for much of Rostow's analysis. For it presumes that the choices now confronting the poor countries may be revealed in the light of the stages of preconditions and take-off that the currently rich countries experienced in earlier centuries, and that historical perspective may contribute to the formulation of development policy. From this viewpoint, Rostow's analysis may be most instructive for many countries that have not yet passed successfully through the take-off stage: it may point up the similarities and differences between past and present take-offs, and suggest what policy implications flow from the differences.

With respect to the role of particular sectors of the economy, Rostow observes many problems and patterns familiar from the past. He submits that present take-offs depend, as in the past, on the allocation of resources

to building up and modernizing the three non-industrial sectors required as the matrix for industrial growth: social overhead capital; agriculture; and foreign-exchange-earning sectors, rooted in the improved exploitation of natural resources. In addition, they must begin to find areas of modern processing or manufacture where the application of modern technique (combined with high income- or price-elasticities of demand) are likely to permit rapid growth-rates, with a high rate of plow-back of profits.[1]

It will be instructive to reconsider these conclusions after reading Chapters V and VI below, where questions not recognized by Rostow are raised regarding the allocation of investment resources and the role of industrialization.

Further, Rostow believes that for the presently underdeveloped nations, the inner mechanics of the take-off involve problems of capital formation, just as in the past. If their take-offs are to succeed, the underdeveloped countries "must seek ways to tap off into the modern sector income above consumption levels hitherto sterilized by the arrangements controlling traditional agriculture. They must seek to shift men of enterprise from trade and money-lending to industry. And to these ends patterns of fiscal, monetary, and other policies (including education policies) must be applied, similar to those developed and applied in the past."[2]

Again, this interpretation of the take-off should be critically re-examined after reading Chapter III, below, where a case is made against assigning as much importance to the role of capital accumulation as Rostow does. Rostow also notes some political and sociocultural similarities between past and present take-offs. As in the past, political interest groups range from defenders of the *status quo* to those prepared to force the pace of modernization at whatever cost; there exists the balance between external expression of nationalism in almost every case; above all, "there is continuity in the role of reactive nationalism, as an engine of modernization, linked effectively to or at cross-purposes with other motives for remaking traditionalist society."[3]

Historical cases of successful take-offs also indicate a contemporary catalogue of necessary social change:

how to persuade the peasant to change his methods and shift to producing for wider markets; how to build up a corps of technicians, capable of manipulating the new techniques; how to create a corps of entrepreneurs, ori-

1. Rostow, *The Stages of Economic Growth*, Cambridge, 1960, p. 139.

2. *Ibid.*
3. *Ibid.*, p. 140.

ented not towards large profit margins at existing levels of output and technique, but to expanded output, under a regime of regular technological change and obsolescence; how to create a modern professional civil and military service, reasonably content with their salaries, oriented to the welfare of the nation and to standards of efficient performance, rather than to graft and to ties of family, clan, or region.[4]

On the basis of the foregoing similarities, Rostow regards the process of development now going forward in Asia, the Middle East, Africa and Latin America as analogues to the stages of preconditions and take-off of other societies in earlier centuries. But there are also differences—by way of different kinds of problems now confronting poor countries, and in the manner in which some problems, although similar in kind to those of the past, are now expressed in different degrees of intensity and complexity. These differences are extremely important, and they deserve more attention than Rostow gives them. For insofar as most of these differences aggravate the problems of the take-off, they warn against letting the success-stories of past take-offs lull us into too easy an interpretation of the development task. The hard core of underdevelopment that now exists in the world economy poses some refractory problems that were absent in earlier take-offs. If we recognize these differences, we may hesitate to join Rostow in concluding that in the end the lesson of history is that "the tricks of growth are not all that difficult."[5]

In the first place, poor countries are attempting to accelerate their development from a lower economic level than was true for the presently rich countries at the time of their take-offs. Considering the evidence for currently advanced countries during the decade just prior to those which

Rostow characterizes as the take-off, Professor Kuznets concludes that the levels of per capita income in these countries before their take-off were already much higher than those now prevailing in the underdeveloped countries, by at least two or three times in most cases.[6] Not only do poor countries now confront the take-off stage from an absolutely lower level of per capita income than did the presently developed countries, but their relative positions are also inferior compared with other countries, unlike the position of the early comers to development that entered the industrialization process from a position of superior per capita income relative to other countries. The implications of attempting to develop rapidly from a lower level of per capita income, and from a relative position that entails more pressures of backwardness, should receive a fuller treatment than Rostow's analysis provides.

Professor Gerschenkron's suggestive analysis, outlined above, can provide a more profound understanding of these implications. We should examine, as does Gerschenkron, the processes of industrial development in relation to the degree of backwardness of the areas concerned on the eve of their great spurts of industrialization. Gerschenkron's approach has distinct advantages over Rostow's in maintaining that it is only by comparing industrialization processes in several countries at various levels of backwardness that we can hope to separate what is accidental in a given industrial evolution from what can be attributed to the historical lags in a country's development, and that it is only because a developing country is part

4. *Ibid.*
5. *Ibid.*, p. 166.

6. Simon Kuznets, "Present Underdeveloped Countries and Past Growth Patterns," in *Economic Growth,* edited by Eastin Nelson, Austin, 1960, p. 18; Kuznets, "Quantitative Aspects of the Economic Growth of Nations, I—Levels and Variability of Rates of Growth," *Economic Development and Cultural Change,* October 1956, pp. 16-25.

of a larger area which comprises more advanced countries that the historical lags are likely to be overcome in a specifically intelligible fashion.[7]

Another fundamental difference is that many of the poor countries have not yet experienced any significant degree of agricultural improvement as a basis for industrialization. The failure to have yet undergone an agricultural revolution makes the present problem of the take-off far more difficult than it was for the now developed countries when they entered upon their industrial revolutions. It is fairly conclusive that productivity is lower in the agricultural sector of underdeveloped countries than it was in the pre-industrialization phase of the presently developed countries.[8] Although direct evidence of this is unavailable, it is indirectly confirmed by data suggesting that the supply of agricultural land per capita is much lower in most underdeveloped countries today than it was in presently developed countries during their take-off, and that there is a wider difference between per worker income in agricultural and nonagricultural sectors in the underdeveloped countries today than there was in the pre-industrial phase of presently developed countries.

The more severe population pressures in the underdeveloped areas constitute another essential difference. Rates of population increase in these areas are higher than those that generally obtained during the take-off decades of the past.[9] Even though not all the poor countries are now densely populated, the rate of population growth is, or gives indications of soon becoming,

a serious problem for most of them. And, unlike the earlier cases in which population growth was induced by, or at least paralleled, a higher rate of development, the present growth in population is simply due to the introduction of public health measures that lower death rates. This acts as an autonomous factor, quite unrelated to the rate of internal development. Moreover, unlike the European industrial countries that began lowering their birth rates before their sharpest declines in mortality, the poor countries now will not do so until long after their mortality has reached a modern low level.[10] Given the fact that many poor countries are already experiencing population pressures more severe than those that confronted the currently rich nations when they were in their early phases of development, and that other poor countries may face a population problem in a relatively short time, the need to attain increases in production sufficient to outstrip potential increases in population is now more acute than it ever was in Western countries at the beginning of their industrialization.

Sociocultural and political differences also account for some obstacles to development that are now more formidable than in the past. Unlike the social heritage with which Western countries entered the take-off stage, the social structure and value pattern in many poor countries are still inimical to development.[11] The structure of social relations tends to be hierarchical, social cleavages remain pronounced, and mobility among groups is limited. Instead

7. Alexander Gerschenkron, *Economic Backwardness in Historical Perspective*, Cambridge, 1962, p. 42. For the application of this general conception of a system of gradations of backwardness to particular countries, see Chapters 1, 4, 7, 8.

8. Kuznets, "Present Underdeveloped Countries and Past Growth Patterns," *op. cit.*, pp. 18-19.

9. The relevant evidence is summarized in G. M. Meier and R. E. Baldwin, *Economic Development*, New York, 1957, pp. 281-90.

10. Kingsley Davis, "The Unpredicted Pattern of Population Change," *The Annals*, May 1956, pp. 56-7.

11. Illuminating discussions of the social, cultural, and psychological barriers to economic change can be found in D. C. McClelland, *The Achieving Society*, Princeton, 1961; E. E. Hagen, *On the Theory of Social Change*, Homewood, 1962; G. M. Foster, *Traditional Cultures and the Impact of Technological Change*, New York, 1962.

of allowing an individual to achieve status by his own efforts and performance, his status may be simply ascribed to him, according to his position in a system of social classification—by age, lineage, clan, or caste. A value system that remains "tradition-oriented" also tends to minimize the importance of economic incentives, material rewards, independence, and rational calculation. When the emphasis is on an established pattern of economic life, family obligations, and traditional religious beliefs, the individual may simply adopt the attitude of accepting what happens to exist, rather than attempting to alter it—an attitude of resignation rather than innovation. Within an extended family system or a village community, the individual may resign himself to accepting group loyalties and personal relationships which remain in a stable and tradition-dominated pattern, assigning little importance to material accomplishments and change. Even though they may have latent abilities, individuals may lack the motivations and stimulations to introduce change; there may not be sufficiently large groups in the society who are "achievement-oriented," concerned with the future, and believers in the rational mastery of nature. The positive value which the traditional way of life still holds for many of the people in a poor country inhibits the necessary orientation toward the future, and change is either resisted or, if accepted, is restricted to fringe areas.

In short, the cultural context in many poor countries may not yet be as favorable to economic achievement as it was in Western countries before their take-off. This is not, of course, to assume simply that, because the West is developed, Western values and institutions are therefore necessary for the attainment of the take-off, and that Western cultural patterns must be imported into the poor countries. Many Western values and institutions may be only accidentally associated with Western development, and many values and institutions in poor countries are not obstacles to development. But though the West need not be imitated, some institutional changes and modifications in the value structure are necessary if the inhibiting institutions and values are to be removed. To allow poor countries to enter into their take-off with as favorable a cultural framework as did the currently developed nations, there must be changes in their cultures so that new wants, new beliefs, new motivations, and new institutions may be created. Until these cultural changes are forthcoming, present take-offs will be more difficult to achieve than were those of the past.

If the degree of sociocultural development has been less than what occurred before the take-offs of the past, so too has there been a difference in political development. In many poor countries, the political foundations for developmental efforts are not yet as firm as they were in Western development. Whereas the currently developed countries had already enjoyed a long period of political independence and a stable political framework before their take-off, most of the currently poor countries have only recently acquired a real measure of political independence. Political instability, undifferentiated and diffuse political structures, and inefficient governments are still only too prevalent. In some countries, government leadership has yet to be exercised by groups that do not have vested interests in preserving the *status quo;* in others, there is still a wide gap between the traditional mass and a modern elite which controls the central structures of government and is the main locus of political activity.[12]

Although these several differences now

12. For a discussion of the difference between Western and non-Western political systems, see G. A. Almond and J. S. Coleman, eds., *The Politics of the Developing Areas,* Princeton, 1960.

intensify the problem of the take-off, there are some dissimilarities which, on the other side, make the problem less difficult. Some advantages may accrue to presently poor countries from their position of being late-comers to development. Most helpful now may be the ability of the poor countries to draw upon the accumulated stock of knowledge in countries that have already developed. Not only may improved pro-ductive techniques and equipment be de-rived from these countries; more generally, they may benefit from the transference of ideas in the realm of social techniques and social innovation as well as technological. How valuable this imitative ability might be, however, is debatable, since it is still necessary to modify and adapt—not simply imitate—the technological and social inno-vations within the context of the borrow-ing country's environment. This problem receives fuller treatment in Chapter V, below. And aside from the requirements of re-adaptation, there also remains the ultimate difficulty of having change ac-cepted and integrated into the recipient society. We should not, therefore, accept too readily the view that by drawing upon the lessons and experiences of countries that have developed earlier, the latecomers are in a position to telescope the early stages of development.

The existence of many advanced coun-tries that have already reached a high level of development, which was not the case when these same countries undertook their take-off, may now, however, help to ease the take-off of poor countries by providing a flow of resources from the rich to the poor countries. Never in the past has there been so much international concern with the desirability of increasing trade, techni-cal assistance, private foreign investment, and the flow of public funds as objectives of development policy. But how effective foreign economic assistance may actually prove to be is, of course, another matter.

Some judgment on this may be had from Chapter III, below.

Finally, there is now a strong conscious desire for development on the part of national leaders in many countries that have not yet had a successful take-off. The national interest in deliberate and rapid development, the willingness of national authorities to assume responsibility for directing the country's economic develop-ment, and the knowledge of a variety of policies that a government can utilize to accelerate development—all these give new dimensions to the role that the State may play in the development of emerging nations. Through governmental action, to a degree unknown in Western develop-ment, a more favorable environment for a take-off might be created. Nonetheless, as a reading of Chapters VIII and IX, below, will indicate, the mere act of development planning cannot be expected to remove the difficult choices and decisions that must be made to accelerate development.

Depending on how much importance we attach to each of the various differences between past and present conditions, we may reach contrasting conclusions as to whether present conditions are more or less favorable than in the past for the take-off. But in the final analysis, what will decide whether the take-off of a poor country will succeed is whether its government can implement effectively the possible policies that might make the country's develop-ment potential realizable, and whether its people are prepared to bear the costs that accelerated development will necessarily entail. Regardless of whether we interpret conditions in the currently poor countries as being on balance more or less favorable for the take-off, we must not expect these countries to follow simply the historical patterns of presently developed countries. We must still give due weight to the sever-ity of the particular problems confronting these countries. And we must determine what policies might now be most effective in removing the barriers to development. With the benefit of historical perspective, however, we should be better able to appraise the significance of these present-day development problems and their various policy implications. In the following chapters, we undertake such an appraisal.

4. BIBLIOGRAPHICAL NOTE

1. As a background to the Rostow doctrine, it is useful to consult the following discussions of the methodology of economic stages: Walter Eucken, *The Foundations of Economics,* Chicago, 1951 (English translation), pp. 64-102; C. R. Fay, "Stages in Economic History," in *English Economic History,* Cambridge, 1940; Herbert Giersch, "Stages and Spurts of Economic Development," in *Economic Progress,* edited by L. H. Dupriez, Louvain, 1955; N. S. B. Gras, "Stages in Economic History," *Journal of Economic and Business History,* II, 1930; B. F. Hoselitz, "Theories of Stages of Economic Growth," in *Theories of Economic Growth,* edited by B. F. Hoselitz, Glencoe, 1960; Arthur Spiethoff, "Pure Theory and Economic Gestalt Theory: Ideal Types and Real Types," in *Enterprise and Secular Change,* edited by F. C. Lane and J. C. Riemersma, Homewood, 1955.

2. For a more detailed exposition of some elements in Rostow's general thesis, see the additional writings by Rostow: *The Process of Economic Growth,* second edition, New York, 1962, especially Chapter IV; "The Take-off into Self-sustained Growth," *Economic Journal,* March 1956; "Trends in the Allocation of Resources in Secular Growth," in *Economic Progress,* edited by L. H. Dupriez, Louvain, 1955; "Some General Reflections on Capital Formation and Economic Growth," in *Capital Formation and Economic Growth,* National Bureau of Economic Research Conference, Princeton, 1955; "Industrialization and Economic Growth," in *Contributions and Communications to the First International Conference of Economic History,* Stockholm, 1960.

The International Economic Association organized a conference at Konstanz in September 1960, on "The Economics of Take-off into Sustained Growth." Papers presented at this conference are to appear in a forthcoming volume, edited by Rostow, to be published by Macmillan & Co., Ltd., London.

3. In addition to the critiques presented in Section 2, above, the following appraisals of the Rostow doctrine also deserve attention: P. Baran and E. Hobsbawm, "The Stages of Economic Growth," *Kyklos,* XIV, No. 2, 1961; P. T. Bauer and Charles Wilson, "The Stages of Growth," *Economica,* May 1962; S. G. Checkland, "Theories of Economic and Social Evolution: the Rostow Challenge," *Scottish Journal of Political Economy,* November 1960; E. E. Hagen, *On the Theory of Social Change,* Homewood, 1962, Appendix II; D. C. North, "A Note on Professor Rostow's 'Take-off' into Self-sustained Economic Growth," *The Manchester School,* January 1958; Goran Ohlin, "Reflections on the Rostow Doctrine," *Economic Development and Cultural Change,* July 1961; G. L. S. Shackle, "The Stages of Economic Growth," *Political Studies,* February 1962.

II

DUALISTIC DEVELOPMENT

ALTHOUGH MOST OF THE POOR COUNTRIES have not yet experienced a take-off into self-sustained growth, they do exhibit some elements of modernization or industrialization in one sector or in parts of their economies. In many countries, a modern money economy has developed alongside a traditional indigenous economy, resulting in what is termed a "dual economy." The contrast in economic organization between the advanced exchange economy and the backward indigenous economy is one of the most striking—and puzzling—characteristics of a poor country. Since the country's future development necessarily entails the spread of the modern money economy, any effort to accelerate the country's rate of development must deal with the problem of dualism.

It is therefore essential to have an understanding of the features and implications of dualism. What conditions have given rise to a dual economy? Why does dualism persist? Does the existence of dualism necessarily create tensons that impede the economy's development; or, on the contrary, might it serve as a "growing point"? How can the absorption of the indigenous economy into an expanding modern money economy be brought about?

This chapter focuses on these questions. At the outset, it illustrates the nature of dualism in some African economies (1.1). The discussion then attempts to explain how dualism has arisen. One explanation, propounded principally by J. H. Boeke and other Dutch economists in their studies of Indonesian development, emphasizes the differing social organizations and cultural contrasts that result in "social dualism" (2.1). More recent analyses have challenged this explanation, as indicated in B. H. Higgins's criticisms of Boeke's thesis (2.2).

The attention to dualism now centers less upon its sociocultural aspects, and more upon its purely economic features, especially in terms of the effects of a dual economy on the pattern of development. Underemployment is commonly believed to be a dominant feature of densely populated underdeveloped countries, and the labor force is continually increasing with population growth. It is therefore important to consider how dualism is related

48

to the problem of providing adequate employment opportunities for the currently underemployed workers and for the increase in the labor force.

In this connection, one version of dualism looks to resource endowments and differences in the production functions in the two sectors as the basis of a "technological dualism" which, in turn, has resulted in an inadequate number of openings for productive employment. The Note on "Production Functions and Technological Dualism" sets forth this argument (3.1); and the International Labour Office's report on the employment problem (3.2) introduces some additional considerations.

Some of the effects of a dualistic structure on employment are clarified by the materials in section 4, which examines the phenomenon of underemployment. Professor Nurkse offers a careful formulation of the meaning of "disguised unemployment" and makes a plausible case for its existence (4.1). But Nurkse's analysis must still be questioned in the light of discussions by Professors Haberler and Viner, who concentrate on the ambiguousness of disguised unemployment, and who argue that the claims by the proponents of a theory of widespread disguised unemployment are highly overstated (4.2, 4.3). In distinguishing various types of surplus labor and their different causes, the Note on "Excess Supplies of Labor" (4.4) discusses further some distinctions suggested by Professor Viner.

Finally, in section 5, the Note presents a model of the interaction between the advanced sector and indigenous sector in a developing economy. As a summary of Professor W. Arthur Lewis's celebrated analysis of "Development with Unlimited Supplies of Labour," this model emphasizes how resources can be drawn into the modern exchange system through capital accumulation and a growing capitalist sector.

The issues raised in this chapter cannot be resolved without confronting empirical evidence. So far only slight attention has been given to the kinds of data that must be adduced to specify directly the production functions actually used in different sectors, and to measure the extent of disguised unemployment. Although the necessary empirical investigations have not yet been made, this chapter furnishes some relevant questions that should be asked in an empirical inquiry.

1. EXAMPLES OF DUAL ECONOMIES

1.1 DUALISM IN AFRICAN ECONOMIES *

The most significant economic development in Africa since the beginning of this

* From United Nations, Department of Economic Affairs, *Structure and Growth of Selected African Economies,* New York, 1958, pp. 1-5.

century has been the enlargement of the money economy involving the shift of resources from subsistence production to production for sale. Initially the traditional economies of the continent were basically organized for the needs and with the resources of self-contained rural communities. Such subsistence economies may be characterized by three related features:

(i) Lack of specialization on a significant scale. Although areas of specialized activity in non-agricultural fields, notably handicrafts, have long existed in urban centres of North Africa and northern Nigeria, both total urban population and the number of persons in specialized occupations were probably small.

(ii) Lack of regular production of a surplus with a view to sale. Even within the framework of a subsistence economy surplus may be achieved. Exchange, chiefly barter, may take place, for example, on a village level—between communities producing different goods, in particular between urban centres and nearby agricultural communities and between agricultural communities producing different crops—and between communities having access to the sea and overseas countries. The significant point, however, is that in a subsistence economy, exchange is marginal and incidental, depending upon the availability of a marketable surplus, and not the primary objective of economic activity.

(iii) Stationary technology. That is to say, production is carried on by means of simple techniques and implements which have not undergone any substantial change over many generations.

The three features mentioned above are of course structurally related; thus, specialization is a prerequisite for exchange as well as for the development of skills and technological advance; on the other hand, in the absence of such advance, expansion of output and consequently of marketable surplus will eventually reach its technological limit; finally, in the absence of a market, there will be no incentive for producing a surplus and no scope for specialization. Under certain conditions, however, it is possible, even without any change in technology, to expand output with a view to achieving a marketable surplus; this happened in many instances in Africa.

The combination of these three features composes a pattern of static economy which almost all African economies at the turn of the preceding century exemplified with relatively inconsequential differences among them. The vicious circle of stagnancy in which the traditional economies were caught has been broken by the rise of exchange activity, the main impetus to which has come from outside through foreign business enterprise and government administrations which have provided the means and incentives to bring certain of the products of Africa within reach of world markets.

The growth of exchange activity, which involves the shift of productive resources of the traditional economy from mainly subsistence activities to production for exchange, may take place in a number of ways. It is possible, however, to distinguish two main threads. On the one hand, some producers in the traditional economy may be transferred into producers for market. When this takes place, it is usually by small-scale agricultural producers taking up the cultivation of cash crops for export, the initial impulse for this change coming, and continuing to be fed, from the outside, and fostered by government action. This form of production does not require heavy capital investment (except for transport facilities provided by the government) or advanced technology and is, therefore, within the reach of the traditional agriculturalist. When, on the other hand, the lure of the export market is for products requiring heavy capital investment and advanced technology, as in the case of a considerable amount of mineral production and some plantation agriculture, the development of the exchange economy may be dominated by large-scale foreign enterprise whose chief economic need from the traditional economy is, in the first instance, for unskilled labour. A similar set of conditions may arise in cases where immigrant settlers from advanced economic backgrounds establish themselves as producers for export in the midst of a traditional economy. When the growth of an exchange economy takes these latter forms, it draws away part of the labour resources of the traditional economy into wage-earning employment. Some members of the traditional economy may be drawn away permanently, while others may temporarily take on work as wage earners. In the former case, there is a permanent loss of labour resources by the indigenous economy. In the latter case, although labour resources of the economy become commercialized in so far as they are separated from it, the loss of productive labour may set up conditions for cumulative decline of the traditional economy.

Three factors appear to have played a crucial role in determining the dominant trend of the exchange economy: first, whether or not the country is endowed with natural resources and tolerable climatic conditions which may prove sufficiently attractive to foreign enterprise and settlement; second, whether or not government policy has been conducive to the development of such enterprise and such settlement on any substantial scale; finally, whether or not, owing to favourable natural and market conditions and government policy, the production of cash crops offers a profitable alternative to wage-earning opportunities.

The first two factors have an important bearing on the scope of non-indigenous enterprise, and consequently on employment opportunities outside the traditional economy; the latter factor bears on money incentives which partly determine the flow of workers seeking employment outside the traditional economy. It is the conjunction of the three factors, rather than any single factor, that has a determining influence on the pattern of growth of the exchange economy.

While the growth of exchange activity has been the source of some of the major problems facing the peoples and governments of Africa, no considerable economic development is possible without further growth in the same direction. Such a process, involving changes in the use of resources and in patterns of production, will ultimately lead to the disappearance of the traditional economy. It must be borne in mind, however, that at the present stage of their development the economies of African countries are heterogeneous economies; therefore, in analysing their significant structures and relations it would be misleading to deal with them as if they were homogeneous modern money economies. In a number of cases it may be more profitable to break down the domestic economy into more homogeneous component systems rather than to consider it as a unit. The mutual transactions of the component systems may be recorded in a statement of balance of payments, similar to that encompassing the transactions between two foreign economies. Heterogeneous analytical models may be devised for the various countries, taking into consideration their respective peculiarities.

The evidence of this and other studies suggests that most African economies may be represented by some form of model, the basic feature of which is a distinction between a traditional economic system and a modern exchange system. The effect of economic development which springs from the exchange economy is to encroach upon the traditional economy, drawing part of its productive resources into the orbit of the exchange economy. The manner in which this erosion of the traditional economy takes place varies from country to country, but it tends to follow certain basic patterns. It is the purpose of the models to elucidate this process of interrelationship between the traditional and exchange economies. The heart of the matter is in the manner in which the productive resources of the traditional economy are drawn into the exchange economy, and the models suggested here concentrate upon this aspect. To simplify the analysis to the greatest extent possible consistent with the realities of the situation, two models may be constructed which represent opposite extremes between which most African economies lie and towards one or other of which each of them inclines. In these models the domestic economy, which embraces all the economic activities within a given territory, is considered to comprise two economic systems—an exchange economy and a traditional economy.

Prototype 1

(a) Commercialization has been brought about chiefly by the transformation of part or parts of the traditional economy, usually by peasant agricultural producers of crops for export.

(b) There is relatively little foreign investment in large-scale enterprises.

(c) The outflow of workers from the traditional economy as wage earners to the exchange economy is relatively small.

Prototype 2

(a) The exchange economy has been brought about largely by foreign capital and enterprise, mainly in mining, by foreign settlement or by both. It is highly capitalized and its techniques are advanced.

(b) The exchange economy depends heavily upon foreign capital.

(c) There is a relatively large outflow of workers as wage earners from the traditional economy to the exchange economy.

These points represent the basic elements for the construction of more elaborate models appropriate for the analysis of the significant features of the economic struc-

ture and growth of specific territories. Within such framework, it would be possible to study the structural aspects including such questions as the nationality of the factors of production—capital, entrepreneurship, skill and labour on the one hand, and on the other, the pattern of production, income, distribution and expenditure, distinguishing between their monetized component and subsistence component. It would then be possible to undertake a more dynamic study in which the strategic factors which control the expansion and contraction of exchange activity would be taken into account. Such an analysis of economic growth would of course be concerned with the trends of significant economic variables generally considered in analysis of modern money economies—output, income, expenditure, capital formation—but it would focus particularly on the shift of resources from the traditional to the exchange economy.

The present study is concerned with the structure and growth of economic activity in three countries of Africa: the Federation of Rhodesia and Nyasaland, Morocco and the Sudan. Although the individual country studies do not closely follow a common pattern, the data and conclusions contained in them lend themselves to a comparative summary.

Of the three countries under consideration, the Federation lies closest to the models of the second type outlined above. The Sudan lies close to the first type. Morocco, though lying closer to the second type than to the first, exhibits elements of both.

In the Federation the exchange economy is highly developed and is based principally upon large-scale mining and agriculture for export, and also upon domestic industry established and operated generally by immigrant settlers from developed economies. The complement of unskilled and semi-skilled labour is drawn from the traditional economy and represents numerically a large proportion of the total gainfully occupied population in the exchange economy, as well as a large proportion of the labour resources of the traditional economy. The number actually involved in wage earning is, in effect, greater than that indicated by the available labour statistics, which relate to the level of employment at a given point of time and therefore do not take into account the high turnover implied by the system of migrant labour. The traditional economy, in which agriculture and handicraft are primitive and largely undifferentiated, is thus losing ground to the exchange economy.

The exchange economy in Morocco, as in the case of the Federation, is highly developed and in large measure has been organized with immigrant capital, entrepreneurship and skill. Production for export, though important, is less significant than in the Federation. A fairly large part of the activities of the exchange economy is accounted for by indigenous resources derived from the traditional economy not only in the form of unskilled and semi-skilled labour, but also in the form of entrepreneurship, capital and commodities. The traditional economy in Morocco is characterized by agricultural techniques and handicraft production which are considerably more advanced than those of the traditional economy in the Federation.

In the Sudan, the exchange economy, though based almost entirely on production for export, has not been brought about by large-scale foreign enterprise or immigrant settlers. Although assisted by capital and skill imported from abroad, the major part of the activities of the exchange economy depends upon a type of peasant agriculture brought into existence by a transformation of part of the traditional economy. In its present stage, the exchange economy is less complex and technologically less advanced than in the case of the two other countries under study. The flow of workers from the traditional economy to become wage earners in the exchange economy is relatively insignificant. The traditional economy is dominated by production for subsistence.

2. SOCIAL DUALISM

2.1 DUALISTIC ECONOMICS *

It is possible to characterize a society, in the economic sense, by the social spirit, the organizational forms and the technique dominating it. These three aspects are interdependent and in this connection typify a society, in this way that a prevailing social spirit and the prevailing forms of organization and of technique give the society its style, its appearance, so that in their interrelation they may be called the social system, the social style or the social atmosphere of that society.

It is not necessary that a society be exclusively dominated by one social system. Where this is the case or where, at least, one social style prevails, the society in question may be called homogeneous; where, on the contrary, simultaneously two or more social systems appear, clearly distinct the one from the other, and each dominate a part of the society, there we have to do with a dual or plural society. It is, however, advisable to qualify the term dual society by reserving it for societies showing a distinct cleavage of two synchronic and full grown social styles which in the normal, historical evolution of homogeneous societies are separated from each other by transitional forms, as, for instance, precapitalism and high capitalism by early

* From J. H. Boeke, *Economics and Economic Policy of Dual Societies,* New York, 1953, pp. 3-5. Reprinted by permission.

capitalism, and which there do not coincide as contemporary dominating features. Without this qualification it would be impossible to distinguish between homogeneous and dual societies, because every society, in its progression, will show, beside the prevailing social system, the remains of the preceding and the beginnings of its future social style. But, exactly when and where this is a process of endogenic social progression, of evolution, ultimately homogeneity will appear because one system, be it a mixture, penetrates through all the strata of society. By this qualification it becomes self-evident that a society maintains its homogeneous character when its late-capitalistic social system is gradually superseded by a socialistic system that has grown up internally, even when this process of supersession momentarily stirs up the most violent disturbance, war or revolution, in short gives clear proofs of a *temporary* social dualism. In a dual society, on the other hand, one of the two prevailing social systems, as a matter of fact always the most advanced, will have been *imported from abroad* and have gained its existence in the new environment without being able to oust or to assimilate the divergent social system that has grown up there, with the result that neither of them becomes general and characteristic for that society as a whole. Without doubt the most frequent form of social dualism is to be found there where an imported western capitalism has penetrated into a precapitalistic agrarian community and where the original social system—be it not undamaged—has been able to hold its own or, expressed in opposite terms, has not been able to adopt the capitalistic principles and put them into full practice. When stated in these general terms the case of social dualism is widespread. Therefore, although in this treatise most of the data are drawn from Indonesia, this should not be interpreted to mean that social dualism is an

Indonesian specialty. Far from it: rather it may be found to exist in the largest part of the world, and if most of the arguments relate to Indonesia, the explanation is that originally this book treated of Indonesia only, that the author is most familiar with that country, and that no other country illustrates more clearly the characteristics of a dual society.

On the basis of the foregoing argument we now come to the following definition: Social dualism is the clashing of an imported social system with an indigenous social system of another style. Most frequently the imported social system is high capitalism. But it may be socialism or communism just as well, or a blending of them. Nevertheless even in that case it remains advisable to keep the term social dualism because this emphasizes the fact that the essence of social dualism is the clash between an imported and an indigenous social system of divergent character.

Every social system has its own economic theory. A social economic theory is always the theory of a special social system. Even if it announces itself as a general theory still it is historically determined. Therefore the economic theory of a dualistic, heterogeneous, society is itself dualistic. It has to describe and to explain the economic interactions of two clashing social systems. Indeed it will be realistic and not pure theory in so far as it has to be based on historical facts, generalizing them in an "ideal-typical" (Max Weber) way. In so far it even will have to be three economic theories combined into one: the economic theory of a precapitalistic society, usually called primitive economics, the economic theory of a developed capitalistic or socialistic society, usually termed general economic theory or summarily social economic theory, and the economic theory of the interactions of two distinct social systems within the borders of one society, which might be called dualistic economics, if this term had not better been reserved for the combined economic theory of a dual society as a whole.

2.2 A Critique of Boeke's "Dualistic Theory" *

The economist who is trying to provide a systematic analysis of the development of underdeveloped areas has two choices before him. He may integrate orthodox economic and social theory, as it exists in advanced western countries, and choose assumptions appropriate to the institutional framework of underdeveloped areas; or he may endeavor to develop a distinctive theory which is applicable only in underdeveloped areas. Perhaps the leading exponent of the latter approach is Dr. J. H. Boeke, who has recently restated and elaborated his special theory of underdeveloped areas.[1] Dr. Boeke's "dualistic theory" is of special interest and importance because of his years of reflection as Professor of Eastern Economics at Leiden University. While his theory is based largely on Indonesian experience, Boeke feels that it has general applications. The reason for his choice of title for his recent book, which is mainly an amalgamation of two earlier studies of the Indonesian economy, Dr. Boeke says, is his

...conviction that the economic problems of Indonesia are typical for a large and impor-

tant part of the world, that therefore an analysis of these problems may be illuminating for many similar countries and that the experience gained in several decades of economic colonial policy may serve as a guide to the host of inexperienced planners for the well-being of that part of the world that has not yet conformed to their western ideals.[2]

An analysis based largely on Indonesian experience may prove to have less general application than Boeke believes; meanwhile, as one of the few attempts at a general theory of economic and social development of underdeveloped areas, Boeke's theory enjoys considerable vogue. Also, to the degree that Boeke reflects attitudes of the former Netherlands East Indies Government, his ideas are of considerable historical interest.[3]

Dr. Boeke gives the following formal definition of a dual society:

Social dualism is the clashing of an imported social system with an indigenous social system of another style. Most frequently the imported social system is high capitalism. But it may be socialism or communism just as well, or a blending of them.[4]

This dualism, he says, is a "form of disintegration, [which] came into existence with the appearance of capitalism in precapitalistic countries." [5] The invading force is capitalism, but it is not colonialism. Colonialism is a "dust-bin term"; both it and "the antithesis native-foreign" are "objectionable," and

...it is to be hoped that with the obtaining of national sovereignty the true character of economic dualism will be acknowledged sincerely and logically, for its negation is decidedly not to the interest of the small man.[6]

* From Benjamin Higgins, "The Dualistic Theory of Underdeveloped Areas," *Economic Development and Cultural Change,* January 1956, pp. 99-108, 111-12. Reprinted by permission.

1. J. H. Boeke, *Economics and Economic Policy of Dual Societies,* New York, 1953 (hereinafter referred to as Boeke, *Economics . . .*); "Three Forms of Distintegration in Dual Societies," lecture given in the course on Cooperative Education of the International Labour Office, Asian Cooperative Field Mission, October 1953, and published in *Indonesië,* Vol. 7, No. 4, April 1954, hereinafter referred to as Boeke, "Three Forms...."; and "Western Influence on the Growth of Eastern Population," *Economia Internazionale,* Vol. 7, No. 2, May 1954, hereinafter referred to as Boeke, "Western Influence...."

2. Boeke, *Economics . . . , op. cit.,* p. vi.
3. For evidence that the whole structure of government in the Netherlands Indies rested on a theory of "dualism," see Rupert Emerson, *Malaysia,* New York, 1937, esp. pp. 420-25.
4. Boeke, *Economics . . . , op. cit.,* p. 4.
5. Boeke, "Three Forms . . . ," *op. cit.,* p. 282.
6. Boeke, *Economics . . . , op. cit.,* p. 20.

On the other hand, dualism is for Boeke virtually synonymous with "Eastern." Dualism arises from a clash between "East" and "West" in the sense in which these terms are used in Rudyard Kipling's famous phrase, "East is East and West is West and never the twain shall meet." While cautioning that "the only true and really cogent antithesis is represented by the words *capitalistic* and *non-* or *pre-capitalistic*," Dr. Boeke contends that "we may use the term 'eastern economics' instead of 'dualistic economics' because both terms cover the same situation, to wit, the situation that is typical for the countries in South and East Asia." [7]

The pre-capitalistic or eastern sector of a dualistic economy has several characteristic features. One of these is "limited needs," in sharp contrast with the "unlimited needs" of a western society. Accordingly,

. . . anyone expecting western reactions will meet with frequent surprises. When the price of coconut is high, the chances are that less of the commodities will be offered for sale; when wages are raised the manager of the estate risks that less work will be done; if three acres are enough to supply the needs of the household a cultivator will not till six; when rubber prices fall the owner of a grove may decide to tap more intensively, whereas high prices may mean that he leaves a larger or smaller portion of tapable trees untapped.[8]

In short, in the familiar terminology of western economics, the pre-capitalistic sector of the eastern economy, in contrast to the "homogeneous" western economy, is characterized by backward-sloping supply curves of effort and risk-taking.

Such needs as there are in eastern societies are social rather than economic. It is what the community thinks of commodities that gives them their value.

If the Madurese values his bull ten times as

much as his cow, this is not because the former is ten times as useful to him in his business as the latter, but because the bull increases his prestige at the bull races.[9]

A closely related feature, in Boeke's view, is the almost complete absence of profit-seeking in an eastern society. Speculative profits are attractive to the Oriental, but "these profits lack every element of that regularity and continuity which characterizes the idea of income." [10] Similarly, there is no professional trading in the eastern village community. Eastern industry is characterized by "aversion to capital" in the sense of "conscious dislike of investing capital and of the risks attending this," only slight interest in finish and accuracy, lack of business qualities, failure to come up to even the minimum requirements of standard and sample, lack of elasticity of supply, lack of organization and of discipline, and corrective local specialization. All this is said to be in sharp contrast to the industry of the westernized, capitalistic sector of underdeveloped areas. The Oriental is, unfortunately, totally lacking in organizing power where modern western enterprises are concerned. Where western industry is dominated by common sense reason, eastern society is molded by "fatalism and resignation." [11]

Because of these great differences between eastern and western economies, western economic theory is totally inapplicable to underdeveloped areas. "We shall do well," Dr. Boeke sternly admonishes, "not to try to transplant the tender, delicate hot-house plants of western theory to tropical soil, where an early death awaits them." [12] Western economic theory, he says, is based on unlimited wants, a money economy, and many-sided corporative organizations, none of which exists in the

---

7. *Ibid.*, p. 12.
8. *Ibid.*, p. 40.

9. *Ibid.*, pp. 37-8.
10. Boeke, *Economics . . .*, p. 41.
11. *Ibid.*, pp. 101-2 and 106.
12. *Ibid.*, p. 143.

rural sector of eastern societies. Western theory is designed to explain capitalistic society, whereas the eastern village is pre-capitalistic. He is particularly critical of any effort to explain the allocation of resources or the distribution of income in terms of marginal productivity theory, mainly because of the great immobility of resources in an eastern society.

This picture of the nature of underdeveloped areas leads Professor Boeke to pessimistic views on the chances for success of recent efforts to develop them, economically and socially, along western lines. At best, these efforts are likely to be abortive; at worst, they may hasten retrogression and decay. Perhaps Boeke's strongest statement of this conclusion is his most recent. We cannot reverse the process of social disintegration in dual societies, he says, "because it is not possible to transform the operating forces into the opposite of what they are. The contrast is too all-inclusive, it goes too deep. We shall have to accept dualism as an irretrievable fact." [13] The acceptance of social and economic dualism leads to two policy conclusions: "First, that as a rule one policy for the whole country is not possible, and second that what is beneficial for one section of society may be harmful for the other." [14]

Even in agriculture, efforts to bring about improvement in methods may cause retrogression instead, especially if "mental attitudes" of farmers are not changed in the process. For "capitalism can only be realized by capitalist minded individuals," and if the foreign experts "try to attain their objectives merely by technical, outside means... only one result can be expected: an accelerated increase in population which... makes the problem more insoluble than ever." Worse, if the innovation is a technical or economic failure, "the

result will be increased indebtedness." Meanwhile, the culture of the village community is "perfectly adapted to the environment"; and the methods of eastern agriculture "could hardly be improved upon." [15] The existing agricultural system is a result of adaptation, and is not at a low stage of development.

Dr. Boeke doubts whether the Javanese cultivator can turn to new crops. Nor does he think that Indonesians could

assume part of the work of the western enterprises, the agricultural part, so as to allow entrepreneurs to devote their energies exclusively to the industrial aspect of the business. This would mean that what is now one united concern, one business, what is being nursed and developed in serried areas, uniformly raised, scientifically guarded and improved, qualified on the basis of the knowledge of market requirements, promoted by means of cheap and plentiful capital, brought into immediate contact with industrial processing, would begin to disintegrate and retrogress at all these points. The present organization of these enterprises is the product of a long history, and handing over cultivation of these products to the petty native peasant would mean a return to an arrangement in the main abandoned as inefficient. [16]

As for industry, "Eastern business will always present a very different appearance from western, even in cases where the two are concerned in the production of the same commodity." Technological progress along western lines is impossible. "There is no question of the eastern producer adapting himself to the western example technologically, economically or socially." Indeed, if eastern enterprises endeavor to

13. Boeke, "Three Forms...," *op. cit.*, p. 289.
14. *Ibid.*, p. 289.

15. Boeke, *Economics...*, *op. cit.*, p. 31; and "Three Forms...," *op. cit.*, p. 292. These remarks apply to Indonesia. "Eastern agriculture in some other countries provides plenty of room for improvement, and even in Java agricultural experts can suggest ways of raising productivity significantly."
16. Boeke, *Economics...*, *op. cit.*, pp. 193-4.

imitate western methods, they will merely lose their competitive qualities.[17] Efforts to industrialize Indonesia, along western mechanized lines, have left Indonesia "further from self-sufficiency than it was a century ago," while its national small industry "has for the most part been ruined in the course of modern development."[18]

Similarly, Dr. Boeke does not believe that there is anything government can do about unemployment of underdeveloped areas. He distinguishes five kinds of unemployment: seasonal, casual, unemployment of regular laborers, unemployment of urban white collar workers, and unemployment among Eurasians (he does not specifically mention disguised unemployment). All five kinds of unemployment, Dr. Boeke says, "are beyond the reach of government help," because dealing with them "would entail a financial burden far beyond the government's means."[19]

Economic development of any kind is hampered by limited wants and still more limited purchasing power. Either an increase in supply of foodstuffs, or industrialization, will lead to a glutting of markets, a fall in prices, and havoc. Even the transmigration programme, on which the Indonesian government has placed so much hope for economic development, is of little use, according to Boeke. It only transplants Java's population problem to the Outer Islands, while Java itself is worse off than before.[20]

Any effort on the part of the West to improve these harassing conditions by educating Indonesian leaders in the western tradition can only hasten decay.

In my opinion, here the western influence tends to divert the attention of the leading classes from their own society to the new and promising western power. The masses, however, unable to follow their leaders on their western way, thus lose the dynamic, developing element in their culture. Eastern culture in this way comes to a standstill, and stagnation means decline.[21]

Again, "the penetration of the West... has deprived the villages ... of their leaders in a social and cultural respect."[22]

In the field of international relations as well, the outlook for the underdeveloped area is dismal. For

after the Second World War disintegrating forces have asserted themselves and binding forces have grown weaker in the international field as well. I am alluding to the formation of new sovereign nations and to the decline of the uniting influence of colonial and imperial powers on all the dual countries.[23]

Dr. Boeke has little to suggest by way of positive policy, as a substitute for the "technical- and capital-assistance" approach which he deplores. However, his idea seems to be that any industrialization or agricultural improvement must be "a slow process," small-scale, and adapted to a "dualistic" framework. "The conclusion to which these arguments about industrialization as well as about agricultural reforms lead us can be no other than the one already expressed, to wit, that social-economic dualism, far from being considered as a passing phase the termination of which may be hastened considerably by a western policy of integration, must be accepted as a permanent characteristic of a large number of important countries, permanent at least within a measurable distance of time." We must have a

17. *Ibid.*, p. 103. See also p. 217, where Boeke argues that "native industry," because it has "practically no organization," is "without capital, ignorant of the market," and "technically helpless," cannot compete with western enterprise, and will suffer trying to do so.

18. *Ibid.*, p. 227.

19. *Ibid.*, p. 318-19.

20. Boeke, *Economics ...*, *op. cit.*, p. 187, 182-3.

21. *Ibid.*, p. 39.

22. Boeke, "Western Influence ...," *op. cit.*, p. 367.

23. Boeke, "Three Forms ...," *op. cit.*, p. 294.

"dichotomy of social-economic policy, which is fundamentally different according to the social groups at which it is aimed."[24]

What this policy means in concrete terms is not spelled out. "I will expose no plans," says Dr. Boeke, except to stress the need for "village restoration." This restoration will not take place through a revival of the rural gentry, but must "follow more democratic ways." New leaders must spring from "the small folk themselves," and must be accompanied by "a strong feeling of local social responsibility in the people themselves." Just how all this is to be accomplished Professor Boeke does not say; but the sphere of action must be small, the time slow, and the goal won by "faith, charity, and patience, angelic patience."[25]

In examining this discouraging analysis of the prospects for underdeveloped areas, I wish first to record certain differences between Dr. Boeke's impressions of eastern society and my own. Let us return to Dr. Boeke's emphasis on "limited wants," or backward-sloping supply curves of effort and risk-taking. There is an all-important difference between saying that the people of underdeveloped countries really cannot envisage a standard of living higher than their own, or that they could think of no satisfactory way of spending increases in income, and saying that they see no simple way of raising their standard of living by their own efforts or enterprise. The last of these statements is to some extent true, and the reasons for it receive attention below. The first two are definitely not true, especially in Indonesia. There, both the marginal propensity to consume and the marginal propensity to import are high. Wants of the villagers, far from being limited, are so many and varied that any "windfall,"

occuring initially through increased exports, is quickly spent on imported semi-luxuries unless rigorous import and exchange controls are applied to prevent it. Far up the great rivers of Kalimantan (Borneo), hundreds of miles into the jungle, good rubber prices result in a spate of orders for bicycles, mattresses, watches, fountain pens, and the like. Sampans in the remotest canals are loaded with Australian tinned milk and American tinned soup. The same is true of the other islands as well. Indeed, the limitless wants of the Indonesian people confront the authorities concerned with import and foreign exchange controls with their major problem. To turn these wants into a wellspring of economic growth, the people must be shown the connection between satisfaction of their wants and their own willingness to work, save, and take risks—a difficult but not impossible task.[26]

Dr. Boeke himself recognizes the high income elasticity of demand for semi-luxuries, largely imported.[27] Why, then, does he attach such importance to "limited needs," contending that in "diametric opposition" to western economies with their "limitless needs," the economic motive does not work continuously" in eastern society, calling for a distinct "theory of values"?[28]

Having seen enterprises efficiently organized and operated by Orientals, along western lines, I do not share Dr. Boeke's pessimism regarding possibilities of technological progress in eastern industry. Dr. Boeke's characterization of the Oriental casual worker as "unorganized, passive, silent, casual"—a kind of behavior which, he says, "is characteristic of the Easterner" —seems inconsistent with the growing strength of organized labor in Indonesia,

24. *Ibid.*, p. 293.
25. Boeke, "Western Influence . . . ," *op. cit.*, pp. 366-9.

26. This point is made, in different terms, by Professor D. H. Burger, "Boeke's Dualisme," *Indonesië*, Vol. VII, No. 3, January 1954.
27. Boeke, *Economics . . . , op. cit.*, p. 249.
28. *Ibid.*, p. 39.

India, and elsewhere.[29] Similarly, it is hard
to reconcile Dr. Boeke's isolation of "repug-
nance to alienation from the village community" with the continued growth of the
large cities in Indonesia. This movement
can no longer be explained in terms of rural
insecurity; nor are employment opportunities better in the cities. It would seem
that the life of the larger cities, with their
cinemas, cafes, shops, libraries, and sports
events, has proved attractive to villagers
who get a taste of it; the result is conges-
tion, inadequate community facilities, and
unemployment in the larger cities. It is also
hard to reconcile Dr. Boeke's argument
that native agriculture cannot compete
with western, with the postwar growth of
small-holders rubber exports, which has
recently constituted the larger share of
rubber exports of Indonesia, despite an
increase in total exports.

Again, Dr. Boeke's insistence on the
difficulty of persuading Javanese people to
leave their villages, in order to move to
the Outer Islands, conflicts with the existence, in the files of the Department of
Transmigration in Indonesia, of two million applications for removal under the
transmigration schemes.

At times, Dr. Boeke's facts seem to conflict with each other. For example, at one
point he lays great stress on the immobility
of labor in native agriculture. Yet, at
another point he states that wages cannot
be raised by industrialization, because

as soon as, for instance, a new mill is opened
or an irrigation work is constructed, from all
sides wage labourers, colonists, traders, and

partisans rush in, if need be from hundreds of
miles away, to seize this opportunity to supplement their scanty means of living.[30]

The latter of these two contrasting pic-
tures seems more accurate to the present
writer. In periods of rising prices, plantation owners complain of the difficulty of
maintaining a labor force, in the light of
an infinitesimal increase in wage rates on
neighboring plantations or in neighboring
factories. The drain of trained Chinese
workers from the bauxite and tin mines—
communist and non-communist alike—in
response to more attractive wage offers
from Red China, has become a major problem. Even landowners in Java sometimes
sharecrop their farms and move their families many miles away, in response to higher
wage offers. Obviously, in eastern society
as in our own, other factors than income
incentive influence the degree of mobility
of particular individuals and groups; but
I see no evidence that Oriental labor is
intrinsically more immobile than western
labor.

Again, at one point Dr. Boeke explains
the impossibility of significant expansion
of smallholder agriculture.[31] Yet earlier,
he complains of the Netherlands East
Indies Government's difficulty in forcing
smallholders to grow less rubber during
the 1930's; imposition of what "penal"
export duties resulted instead in an increase in productivity of native smallholders.[32] This experience seems to suggest that expansion of smallholders' agriculture is a matter of finding the right
incentive system.

Such discrepancies between Dr. Boeke's
description of eastern economies and the
impressions of other observers illustrates
the need for much more extensive and
intensive fact-gathering, before generali-

29. *Ibid.,* p. 145. At one point (p. 144), Dr.
Boeke seems even to deny the possibility of
growth of labor organizations. Because of the
nature of agricultural enterprises, which are scattered and more likely to support each other in
their common interests than to compete, every
effort at organization could be nullified, Dr.
Boeke argues. The fact is, however, that it is precisely in plantation agriculture that the Indonesian
trade union movement is strongest.

30. Boeke, *Economics . . . , op. cit.,* p. 177.
31. *Ibid.,* pp. 216-17.
32. *Ibid.,* pp. 124-6.

zations can be made, especially as a basis for policy.

Some degree of "dualism" certainly exists in underdeveloped areas. In most of them, it is possible to discern two major sectors; one which is largely native, in which levels of technique, and levels of economic and social welfare are relatively low; and another, usually under western leadership and influence, in which techniques are advanced, and average levels of economic and social welfare are relatively high.

There is then no denying the existence of this "dualism," although it is perhaps less sharp than Dr. Boeke suggests, seems to be becoming still less sharp and does not prove by its mere existence that it is immutable. But is this dualism a special feature of "eastern" countries? Merely to raise the question is to answer it. Dr. Boeke himself suggests at one point that dualism exists in other underdeveloped areas, including those of Latin America and Africa, as well as those of the Orient. But there is perhaps no country in which "dualism" is more striking than in Italy, with its industrialized and progressive North, and its agricultural and stagnant South. Indeed, one could go further, and argue that some degree of dualism exists in virtually every economy. Even the most advanced countries, such as Canada and the United States, have areas in which techniques lag behind those of the most advanced sectors, and in which standards of economic and social welfare are correspondingly low... Most economies can be divided into distinct regions, with different degrees of technological advance.

Dr. Boeke does say that the term "dual society" should be reserved for "societies showing a distinct cleavage between two cynchronic and full grown social styles." [33]

33. Boeke, *Economics ... , op. cit.,* p. 3.

But does this qualification help? What is "full grown"? Where does one find a "full grown" capitalism side-by-side with a "full grown" pre-capitalistic society, with nothing in between? And, if such countries could be found, would it be helpful to classify all other countries as "homogeneous"? It seems more realistic to rank countries on a more or less continuous scale of homogeneity, perhaps with Dr. Boeke's native Holland at the upper end, as a country exhibiting an extraordinary degree of homogeneity.

Many of the specific characteristics of the "eastern" society described by Dr. Boeke, seem to the present writer to be attributable to western societies as well. The preference for speculative profit over long-term investment in productive enterprise appears wherever chronic inflation exists or threatens. Such attitudes prevail in Greece today, in Germany, France, Austria, and Italy after World War I. And surely the "conscious dislike of investing capital and of the risk attending this" prevails everywhere. A famous American financier has said, "nothing is so shy as a million dollars"; western economists have recently developed a whole field of analysis relating to "liquidity-preference" and "safety-preference," to take account of the reluctance of investors the world over to accept risk or illiquidity, and their strong preference for keeping their capital in safe and liquid form. Only the prospect of large and fairly safe profits has called forth the large volume of investment that has resulted in the rapid development of the now advanced countries. Growth breeds growth, stagnation breeds stagnation, in any economy. As for valuing goods according to prestige conferred, rather than direct use-value, what western society is free from such behavior? Veblen made such behavior a vital aspect of his analysis of American society, and gave it his famous label, "conspicuous consumption."

Similarly, Dr. Boeke's distinction between eastern societies, especially Indonesia, where "export is the great objective," and western countries, where export "is only the means which makes import possible"—a distinction which Dr. Boeke regards of "essential importance"—is hard to understand in view of the popularity of protectionist policies in most countries in recent decades. Dr. Boeke also speaks of absenteeism of regular laborers as "undoubtedly in part an expression of the very general pre-capitalistic phenomenon of desiring a large number of holidays." But employers in the United States or Canada in the early part of World War II, or in Australia since the War, would be quick to deny that absenteeism is no problem in the capitalist world. The same is true of the "backward-sloping supply curve of effort," which was all too evident in Australia during the post-war period, and which began to appear in certain industries such as coal mining, in the United States in recent years. It is the present writer's contention that this "backward-sloping supply curve" is not exclusively a feature of eastern societies, but appears in any society which stagnates (or slows down) long enough to weaken the "demonstration effect," provided by people moving from one standard of living to another, as a result of their own extra effort, directed specifically towards earning additional income.

Again, Dr. Boeke's contrast between colonization in the Western World, where "people on their own initiative and at their own cost leave their country for abroad to better their living conditions" and eastern migration policy which "means propagating migration from overcrowded regions with financial help from the government" seems to overlook the very large role that private and public assistance played in the migration from Europe to the New World. Dr. Boeke also remarks that in Indonesia "when recruiting new colonists, the attraction exerted by the large, well-known colonies was needed, where relations and friends from the village awaited the newcomer." Surely immigrants always needed some pressures at home to make them move, and surely migrants always preferred to move to places where they could join their own kin; hence the concentration of Scandinavians and Germans in the States of Wisconsin and Minnesota, and of Dutchmen in New York. Also, internal migration in western countries as well as eastern may require active government intervention....

Similarly, Boeke's contrast between urban growth in western and in eastern societies does not ring true in the ears of the present writer. In dual societies, Boeke contends, urban development proceeds at the cost of rural life. In East and West alike, so far as one can judge from available data, urbanization is accompanied by an absolute growth, but relative decline, in the rural population; although in countries where the birth rate has not fallen, the relative fall in rural population and income may not stick. If Dr. Boeke means that urbanization has yet to bring true economic progress in eastern countries, he is of course right; but that is because urbanization in the East has not brought the same degree of industrialization, nor the same decline in birth rates. In short, "urban growth" has not been "urban development."

In sum, it seems to the present writer that Dr. Boeke exaggerates the degree of "dualism" in such countries as Indonesia; the contrast between the advanced and underdeveloped sectors appears to me to be less sharp than Boeke contends, and to be diminishing. Nor can I see that such dualism is specifically eastern. Contrasts between the levels of technique and of economic and social welfare, and even contrasts in economic and social behavior, can be found among different sectors of many western economies. To my mind, it is Dr. Boeke's "homogeneous" societies that are rare.

...

Professor Boeke stresses the need for a distinctive economic and social theory for underdeveloped countries, but he does not really provide one. His "theory" consists in description of eastern society, and demonstration that it lacks those features of western society which have resulted in the economic and social development of the West. Since eastern society is so different, it follows, in Professor Boeke's mind, that such economic and social development on western lines is impossible for the East. My own belief is that an explanation of the relative stagnation of the underdeveloped areas can be found, by applying familiar tools of economic and social analysis, within a model defined by appropriate institutional assumptions. It is my further belief that given such an explanation of underdevelopment the solution to the problem will suggest itself.

I do not deny that some existing social and cultural institutions of underdeveloped countries differ from those of the West in a manner constituting a barrier to economic development. Institutions, however, can be changed, as they were changed in Europe and in the New World during the periods of rapid economic and social advance in those areas. The time has not yet arrived for a definitive analysis of the sociological factors in economic development of underdeveloped areas, and certainly this is not the place for such an analysis. Elsewhere, [34] however, I have indicated four kinds of sociological barriers to economic development. First is the dilution of incentives to save, invest, work,

34. Benjamin Higgins, "Economic Development of Underdeveloped Areas: Past and Present," *Ekonomi dan Keuangan Indonesia,* December 1954.

and restrict family size in an undivided family system. In contrast to a society in which the single family is the basic unit, a society organized around the undivided family—which can become almost coterminous with the village—does not guarantee to a man's immediate family all the benefits, if he works harder, saves more, accepts greater investment risk, or practices birth control. Any gains resulting from such decisions are divided among a group so large that the relation of a particular family's standard of living to its own decisions is a very loose one. Second is the limited scope of entrepreneurial spirit in underdeveloped areas. In many of these countries a feudal attitude towards commerce and industry still prevails, among educated people. There, as in Europe generations ago, "the gentleman does not sully his hands in trade." Innovation in the economic sense is accorded little reward or respect. Yet development of the capitalist type cannot take place without capitalists. Third is what has been referred to above as the "backward-sloping supply curve" of effort and risk-taking. To have an incentive to work harder or better, or to take additional risk with one's capital, one must have a clear picture of the more ample life which additional income will bring. A strong spirit of emulation, or a high "demonstration effect," occurs only where some people are currently demonstrating the effects of additional effort or risk-taking. If life in the villages has been much the same for generations, and no one in the village has before him the picture of people moving to ever higher standards of living through their own efforts or their own willingness to risk capital, the expenditure of additional effort, or the acceptance of additional risk, will seem rather absurd. In many Oriental villages, there are virtually only two classes: rich and poor. Nothing approaching the more or less continuous gradation of modes of life found in the West exists in such villages. There is no lower-middle, middle-middle, and upper-middle class through which to move, and a single jump from lower to upper class occurs very rarely, and is hard to imagine, apart from political upheavals.

The fourth sociological problem might be termed the "population multiplier." Boeke points out that industrial investment in Indonesia led to no decline in the proportion of the labor force engaged in agriculture, and implies that the occupational structure is essentially immutable in underdeveloped countries—"traffic in these densely populated regions has to remain within limited bounds, otherwise it creates havoc." I believe that the explanation of stable occupational structure is quite different. In the absence of any control of population growth, industrialization, by producing an initial rise in *per capita* income, permits a more rapid increase in the native population. If the bulk of industrial investment goes into export industries (such as plantations, mining, and petroleum), or into production for the limited western market (automobiles, tires), as it did in Indonesia, rather than production for the home market combined with measures to generate domestic demand for manufactured goods, most of the increase in population *must* find employment in agriculture, or remain unemployed.

Such institutional factors are indeed obstacles to economic development. They must be taken into account in any complete analysis, and still more in any recommendations for policy. But they are not immutable; the recent experience of Japan, and some recent anthropological studies of primitive cultures subjected to the "shock" of occupation by American armed forces and similar cases, suggest that cultures can change with astonishing rapidity, and apparently with little pain, if the right formula is found.

2.3 THE PLURAL SOCIETY *

All tropical dependencies, and indeed all tropical countries, so far as they have been brought within the modern world, have in common certain distinctive characters in their social structure. In Dutch colonial literature they are often said to present a dual economy, comprising two distinct economic systems, capitalist and pre-capitalist, with a western superstructure of business and administration rising above the native world in which the people, so far as they are left alone, lead their own life in their own way according to a traditional scale of values in which economic values rank so low as to be negligible. It is unquestionably true that there is a wide difference between the social standards of tropical peoples and those of the modern West, that the natives are slow to assimilate western values, and that over native life there is a western superstructure representing an outpost of Europe and not rooted in the soil. Yet the Dutch picture of a native world, in which economic values are disregarded, seems, so far as it is based on facts, to be drawn from Java, where for some two hundred years employers secured labour through compulsion rather than by appealing to the desire of gain. In Africa likewise... a popular belief in the native disregard of economic values has been held to justify compulsion as a means of securing labour. But everywhere experience has shown that the desire of gain can easily be stimulated or, rather, liberated from the control of custom. In British colonies under indirect rule, interpreted according to the British tradition of the rule of law, economic forces soon permeate the native world and, in colonies under direct rule, it is just in the economic world that all men meet, if not on equal, yet on the same terms. Even in

* From J. S. Furnivall, *Colonial Policy and Practice,* Cambridge University Press, 1948, pp. 303-6, 308-12. Reprinted by permission.

respect of Dutch dependencies some of their own writers vehemently dispute the theory of a dual economy.[1] Yet in all tropical dependencies the western super-structure over native life is a prominent feature in the economic landscape.

But the western superstructure is only one aspect of a distinctive character, common to all tropical dependencies, that cannot fail to impress even the most casual observer; the many-coloured pattern of the population. In Burma, as in Java, probably the first thing that strikes the visitor is the medley of peoples—European, Chinese, Indian and native. It is in the strictest sense a medley, for they mix but do not combine. Each group holds by its own religion, its own culture and language, its own ideas and ways. As individuals they meet, but only in the market-place, in buying and selling. There is a plural society, with different sections of the community living side by side, but separately, within the same political unit. Even in the economic sphere there is a division of labour along racial lines. Natives, Chinese, Indians and Europeans all have different functions, and within each major group subsections have particular occupations. There is, as it were, a caste system, but without the religious basis that incorporates caste in social life in India. One finds similar conditions all over the Tropical Far East—under Spanish, Portuguese, Dutch, British, French or American rule; among Filipinos, Javanese, Malays, Burmans and Annamese; whether the objective of the colonial power has been tribute, trade or material resources; under direct rule and under indirect. The obvious and outstanding result of contact between East and West has been the evolution of a plural society; in the Federated Malay States the indigenous inhabitants number barely a quarter of the total population. The same thing

has happened in the South Pacific. The Fiji chieftains invited British protection, and one result has been that half the inhabitants are immigrants from India. In African dependencies there are Indian immigrants in East Africa and Syrians in West Africa, and in some regions the "coloured," or Eurafrican, population forms a separate caste. Sometimes a section of the native population is westernized: "there are some territories, of which those in West Africa are perhaps most typical, in which sections of the population most closely in contact with European influences have attained a development out of all relation to the rest of the population ... which is often still living in primitive conditions and has interests different from those of an urban or industrial society."[2] One finds much the same thing in Java, and in all tropical dependencies "westernized" natives are more or less cut off from the people, and form a separate group or caste. The plural society has a great variety of forms, but in some form or other it is the distinctive character of modern tropical economy.

Outside the tropics society may have plural features, notably in South Africa, Canada and the United States, and also in lands where the Jew has not been fully assimilated into social life; in other countries also there are mixed populations with particularist tendencies. But in general these mixed populations have at least a common tradition of western culture, and, despite racial origins, they meet on equal terms and their relations are not confined solely to the economic sphere. There is a society with plural features, but not a plural society. It is significant that, in Canada and the United States, and also in Australia, when the influx of alien elements threatened national life and common social standards, barriers were raised

---

1. J. W. Meijer Ranneft, *Koloniale Studiën*, 1928, p. 151.

2. *Britain and Her Dependencies*, pp. 34, 44; L. W. B. Teeling, p. 126.

against free immigration. In tropical dependencies there was no common social will to set a bar to immigration, which has been left to the play of economic forces. The plural society arises where economic forces are exempt from control by social will. It is general in the modern tropics because everywhere and always the social order seems to have had plural features. In Burma under native rule the people were not organized territorially but on quasi-feudal lines by race and occupation, and that is the normal character of tropical society based on personal authority. But in such lands, apart from minor backward groups, there is a common cultural tradition; there is a society with plural features but not a plural society. Again, in the great fairs held annually in medieval times in ports and market towns, each company of merchants was governed by its own heads according to its own customs. But the concourse did not form a plural society, because it lasted no longer than the fair. All that happened was that, during the fair, the town was transformed into a bazaar. In the modern tropics the bazaar lasts throughout the year, and the whole country is converted into a shop or factory; from a social organism into a business concern. Despite certain plural features, tropical society was distinct from the plural society which has been created by economic forces. This is a modern invention because, only in modern times, have economic forces been set free to remould the social order. The result is a social structure quite distinct in its political and economic properties from the homogeneous unitary society of western lands and, for a solution of colonial problems, it is essential that its properties should be clearly understood.

. . .

The political aspect of the plural society is reflected in its economic aspect. A plural society is no ordinary business partnership.

In form it is also a political society and is, or should be, organized for "the good life," the welfare of the people enabling them to live as well as possible. As a business partnership its function is solely economic, to produce goods as profitably as possible. But as a social institution also it has an economic aspect, and is concerned with both production and consumption, supply and demand. It is in the interest of a society that its members shall get what is best and not merely what is cheapest; by custom or law it must regulate demand. It is also in the interest of society that in the supply of goods, production for profit shall be regulated by custom or law on behalf of social welfare. In a plural society both supply and demand take on a special character.

Let us first consider the matter of demand. In buying goods it is only common sense to pay no more than necessary. But purchasers are not always guided solely by common sense. Some will pay a higher price for home products than for foreign products, or for goods untainted by sweated labour. In such cases there is a social demand for home manufacturers, or for a higher standard of wages. In this matter there is a difference between the plural society and the homogeneous society. When the recent depression flooded Java with cheap cottons from Japan, European merchants tried to boycott Japanese goods; but the boycott collapsed because Chinese merchants bought them and seemed likely to capture all the trade. When Britain annexed Upper Burma the British Government contemplated retaining the Burmese prohibition of trade in opium and alcohol, but this was impossible because the demand of the Chinese and Indians had to be met. In a plural society the feebleness of social will is reflected in the weakness of social demand, which is the economic aspect of social will. Economists deal in great detail with problems of aggregate demand but, partly it may be because they take a homogeneous society for granted, they have not given social demand so much attention as it deserves. If any town or village in the western world wants better sanitation, it can spend more on conservancy. There is a collective demand which may conflict with individual demand, and at periodical elections people can choose between better conservancy and having more money in their pockets. Economists can measure this collective demand with their supply and demand curves and schedules, but collective demand is only one form of a social demand that, in general, defies measurement. The monastic schools in Burma were a response to social demand, but no one could estimate their cost, or balance it against their value. In tropical countries social demand usually takes effect through custom. Sometimes a patch of scrub jungle round a village is reserved as a public convenience and is closed to fuel cutting. People could get their fuel with less trouble, more cheaply, by cutting timber there, but social demand, taking effect through village custom, prevails over individual demand. So long as custom retains its force, no one would thing of cutting down the scrub. But we have noticed that in Rangoon Indian immigrants saw a way to make easy money, and cleared the scrub to sell fuel in the market. Individual demand for private gain prevailed over the social demand for common welfare, and prevailed the more readily because society was no longer homogeneous. Even in the West social demand is most effective when it requires no stronger support than custom, because no one thinks of encroaching on it. In London rickshaws might be cheaper than taxis, but we would walk rather than use them. The individual demand for cheaper transport is overborne by the social demand for human dignity. And because we resist the temptation of cheapness we finally attain better, and probably cheaper, transport in tubes and motor-buses. During the present century Rangoon, in common with most eastern towns, has been flooded with rickshaws. In Batavia the Dutch refused to sanction them; they disliked seeing Javanese between the shafts and already had too many Chinese. Now motor transport in the towns of Java is probably better and cheaper than in any country in the tropics. Social demand can take effect only through organic social will, as embodied in the social structure, and, in default of social will, individual demand prevails over social demand. A villager in Burma may wish to spend money on schooling for his children, but the maintenance of a school is conditional on the existence of social demand and, if there is no village school, he may spend his money on giving them new clothes, or on furniture that he does not use, or even on English books that he cannot read.[3] If he cannot satisfy those wants which he has as a member of society, he will satisfy his individual wants; he must take what he can get.

Here is one of the distinctions between a homogeneous society and a plural society. A plural society is broken up into groups of isolated individuals, and the disintegration of social will is reflected in a corresponding disorganization of social demand. Even in a matter so vital to the whole community as defense against aggression, the people are reluctant to pay the necessary price. In religion and the arts, in the graces and ornaments of social life, there are no standards common to all sections of the community, and standards deteriorate to such a level as all have in common. And because each section is merely an aggregate of individuals, those social wants that men can satisfy only as members of a community remain unsatisfied. Just as the life of an individual in a

3. Furnivall, *Economic Review*, 1912, pp. 380 ff.

plural society is incomplete, so his demand tends to be frustrated. Civilization is the process of learning to live a common social life, but in a plural society men are decivilized. All wants that all men want in common are those which they share in common with the animal creation; on a comprehensive survey of mankind from China to Peru these material wants, essential to the sustenance of life, represent the highest common factor of demand. In the plural society the highest common factor is the economic factor, and the only test that all apply in common is the test of cheapness. In such a society the disorganization of social demand allows the economic process of natural selection by the survival of the cheapest to prevail.

If, again, we examine plural economy from the standpoint of production or supply, we find a similar predominance of economic forces. In selling goods it is common sense to charge as much as one can.

All those engaged in production have in common, in greater or less degree, the desire for gain, to get as much as possible while giving as little as possible. But, in a plural society, that is almost all they have in common. Everywhere, in all forms of society, the working of economic forces makes for tension between groups with competing or conflicting interests; between town and country, industry and agriculture, capital and labour. In a homogeneous society the tension is alleviated by their common citizenship, but in a plural society there is a corresponding cleavage along racial lines. The foreign elements live in the towns, the natives in rural areas; commerce and industry are in foreign hands and the natives are mainly occupied in agriculture; foreign capital employs native labour or imported coolies. The various peoples meet only in the market, as competitors or as opponents, as buyers and sellers.

3. TECHNOLOGICAL DUALISM

3.1 PRODUCTION FUNCTIONS AND TECHNOLOGICAL DUALISM—NOTE

One of the most important effects of dualistic development is its influence on the pattern of employment. Several writers have suggested that the labor employment problems of a poor country are due to the existence of "technological dualism"—that is, to the use of different production functions in the advanced sector and the traditional sector.[1] In this interpretation,

1. As an alternative to Boeke's sociological theory of dualism, the theory of technological dualism has been emphasized by Benjamin Higgins, *Economic Development*, New York, 1959, pp. 325-33. The theory of technological dualism incorporates the "factor proportions problem," as discussed by R. S. Eckaus, "The Factor Proportions Problem in Underdeveloped Areas," *American Economic Review*, September 1955. Earlier references include Joan Robinson, *The Rate of Interest and Other Essays*, London, 1952, pp. 110-11; M. Fukuoka, "Full Employment and Constant Coefficients of Production," *Quarterly Journal of Economics*, February 1955.

dualism is associated with "structural unemployment" or "technological unemployment"—a situation in which productive employment opportunities are limited, not because of lack of effective demand, but because of resource and technological restraints in the two sectors.

The traditional rural sector is said to have the following characteristics: it is engaged in peasant agriculture and handicrafts or very small industries; the products can be produced with a wide range of techniques and alternative combinations of labor and capital (improved land)— that is, the sector has variable technical coefficients of production; and the factor endowment is such that labor is the relatively abundant factor, so that techniques of production are labor-intensive (in the sense that relatively large amounts of labor and relatively small amounts of capital are used).

In contrast, the modern sector is composed of plantations, mines, oil fields, or large-scale industry; there is either in fact, or entrepreneurs believe there is, only a very limited degree of technical substitutability of factors, so that production is characterized by fixed technical coefficients; and the production processes in this sector are relatively capital-intensive. This situation can be represented by a production function as in Figure II.1, where the points a, b, c, etc., denote the fixed combinations of factors—capital (K) and labor (L)—that would be used to produce the outputs q_1, q_2, q_3, etc., irrespective of what the relative factor prices might be.[2] The line OE joining the points a, b, c, etc., represents the expansion path of this sector, and its slope is equal to a constant, relatively capital-intensive factor ratio.

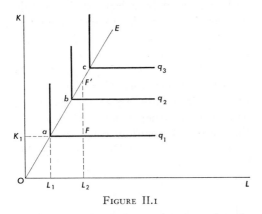

FIGURE II.1

Only when capital and labor are actually available in proportions equal to the fixed capital-labor ratio is it possible that both factors can be fully utilized simultane-

ously. If the actual factor endowment is to the right of line OE—say, at point F—there must then be some unemployment of labor in this sector. To produce an output of q_1, the sector will use OK_1 units of capital and OL_1 units of labor; even though OL_2 units of labor are available, the excess supply of labor will have no effect on production techniques and L_1L_2 units of labor will remain in excess supply, regardless of the relative factor prices of capital and labor. Only if the capital stock were to increase in the amount indicated by the length of the dashed line FF′ could the redundant labor be absorbed in this sector. Failing a sufficient accumulation of capital, the excess labor supply will simply remain unemployed, or must seek employment in the traditional sector.[3]

Having in mind the different production functions in the two sectors, we may now summarize the argument that technological dualism has intensified the problem of employment in dual economies. In many countries, the advanced sector was initially developed by an inflow of foreign capital. As foreign enterprises operated under efficient management with modern production techniques, output in this sector expanded. At the same time, however, population was growing—in some cases at a rate considerably in excess of the rate at which capital was accumulating in the advanced sector. And since production processes in this sector were capital-intensive, and fixed technical coefficients were used, this sector did not have the capacity

2. Units of capital (K) are measured on the vertical axis, and units of labor (L) on the horizontal axis. The curve q_1 is an isoquant representing a certain level of output; as drawn, the output q_1 can be produced only with the unique combination of factors at point a (OK_1 of capital and OL_1 of labor). The curves q_2, q_3, etc., represent different levels of output, with output increasing along the expansion line OE. Output can be increased, however, only by increasing the use of K and L in the constant proportions given by the slope of OE.

3. It is interesting to note that Marx had a similar view of the problem of unemployment: according to Marx, the amount of employment offered by capitalists depends upon the amount of capital in existence, and there is unemployment because there is insufficient capital to employ all the potentially available labor. If A represents the total labor available, and N the amount of employment required to work the existing stock of capital at its normal capacity, then A − N is Marx's "reserve army of unemployed labor." Cf. Robinson, *op. cit.,* pp. 110-11, n.2.

to create employment opportunities at a rate sufficient to absorb the greater labor force. While investment and output expanded in the advanced sector, capital accumulation was nonetheless slow relative to population growth, and labor became a redundant factor in this sector. Entry into the traditional rural sector was then the only alternative open to surplus labor.

As the labor supply increased in the traditional sector, it may have been possible initially to bring more land under cultivation, but eventually land became relatively scarce. Labor increasingly became the relatively abundant factor, and since technical coefficients were variable in this sector, the production process became ever more labor-intensive in the traditional sector. Finally, all available land became cultivated by highly labor-intensive techniques, and the marginal productivity of labor fell to zero or even below: "disguised unemployment" began to appear.[4] Thus, with continuing population growth, the limited availability of capital caused a surplus of labor to arise in the traditional rural sector. Given the labor surplus, there was no incentive in the traditional sector to move along the production function toward higher capital-labor ratios and thereby achieve an increase in output per man.

Further, it is contended that, over the longer run, technological progress did not ease this situation. For in the modern sector technological progress favored more capital-intensive techniques, so that it was all the more difficult to increase employment opportunities in this sector as investment and output expanded. At the same time, there was no incentive in the rural sector to introduce labor-saving innovations (even if it were assumed that the technical possibilities were known and the necessary capital was available).

It has also been suggested that the locus

of technological progress is such that a capital-intensive invention affects the choice of technique in only those cases in which the cost of labor to capital is high, but not when it is low as in the traditional sector. As Professor Leibenstein argues,[5] this is because the gradual type of technological progress, which, through redesign and general improvement, increases the effectiveness of given types of machines and tools, is more likely to cause a shift of points on the production function in the region of high rather than low capital-labor ratios, such as in the shift from q to q′ in Figure II.2. In the traditional sector, where the capital-labor ratio is low, there is less likelihood of recognizing opportunities for gradual inventions and improvements, the scale of operations may not be sufficient to support any new equipment, and there may be a lack of the complementary inputs needed to adopt some type of new capital good. Accordingly, it is maintained that there is little tendency for the isoquants to shift at points with low capital-labor ratios. If the expenditures line EE′ in Figure II.2 represents the existing ratio of labor cost to capital cost (in this case: relatively low wage rates, as reflected in the slope of EE′), then the shift

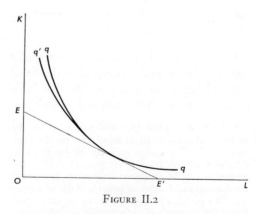

FIGURE II.2

5. Harvey Leibenstein, "Technical Progress, the Production Function and Dualism," *Banca Nazionale del Lavoro Quarterly Review*, December 1960, pp. 13-15.

4. Higgins, *op. cit.*, p. 330.

in the capital-intensive portion of the iso-quant has no effect on the choice of technique in the traditional labor-intensive sector.

Although the theory of technological dualism indicates why factor endowment and the differences in production functions have resulted historically in the rise of underemployment of labor in the traditional sector, its empirical relevancy can certainly be questioned. Has production in the advanced sector actually been carried on with fixed coefficients? Even if an advanced, capital-intensive process was initially imported, was there subsequently no adaptation to the abundant labor supply? Was technical progress actually labor-saving in the advanced sector? These questions call for empirical studies beyond the highly impressionistic statements contained in the foregoing summary of the theory of technological dualism.

Finally, greater clarity is needed on the nature of the unemployment or underemployment in the traditional sector. Ambiguity surrounds the concept of excess labor supply. And the actual extent of "disguised unemployment" may be considerably less than might be inferred from the foregoing analysis. This issue will be examined in section 4, below.

The question of empirical evidence should be kept in mind when reading the next selection which offers a more detailed account of the evolution of the modern and traditional sectors.

3.2 THE GENESIS OF THE EMPLOYMENT PROBLEM *

The problem confronting less developed countries may be described in its historical setting as a problem of slow or arrested growth of the modern sector in the face of continuous growth of population in the

* From International Labour Office, *Employment Objectives in Economic Development,* report of a meeting of experts, Geneva, 1961, pp. 28-32.

traditional sector, which did not provide a corresponding increase in employment opportunities and in which income per head remained low or even fell.

We shall not enter into a discussion of the reasons for, and explanation of, underdevelopment in terms of basic resource endowment, entrepreneurial traditions, technological inheritance, and the other factors which are well covered in the literature on the subject, but shall confine ourselves to pointing out the main reasons for the emergence of the dualistic society in underdeveloped countries, a feature which is particularly relevant for the analysis of the employment problems. Given the technologies that were chosen and the composition of output ("product-mix") that was considered desirable in the modern sector, the rate of investment in that sector has not been high enough to prevent population in many countries from pressing increasingly heavily on the means of subsistence in the traditional sector. In many of these countries the evolution of the modern sector appears to have the following characteristic features:

(*a*) The rate of capital accumulation in the modern sector over the past several decades has been slow—slower than the rate of population growth in the traditional sector. A large part of such stock of physical capital as has been formed in the modern sector has been created chiefly by foreign investment for the production of mineral and agricultural products for export markets. A large part of the export earnings returned to the capital exporting countries in the form of withdrawal of profits and other incomes, and was therefore not spent in the capital receiving countries.

(*b*) The growth of the modern sector did not increase significantly the demand for output of the traditional sector. Unlike the investment activities in most of the present advanced industrial countries, therefore, the investment activities hitherto undertaken in the modern sector in a number of less developed countries did not produce on the domestic economy any significant "linkage" effect—that is, the stimulation, mainly through increased demand for related products, which the rise of investment in one industry may provide to the development and expansion of other industries in the modern sector. As the history of these countries has shown, the linkage effect mostly leaked abroad through increased induced imports. The increased demand both for capital equipment and intermediate goods needed for investment in mining and plantations and for consumers' goods such as textiles—in certain cases food as well—induced by expanded employment in these fields of investment were met, in the main, by imports. The increased demand for technical and managerial personnel induced by these investments was likewise met primarily from abroad rather than by expansion of domestic training programmes. Moreover, even where growth of the modern sector did lead to a demand for labour or products from the traditional sector, the social and political barriers to change in the traditional sector diminished and delayed its response to this demand. This lack of an internal linkage effect appears to be another important factor responsible for the arrested growth of the modern sector in many of these countries.

(c) The technologies adopted in the modern sector, and especially those applied to mining, processing of mineral and plantation products for export and large-scale manufacturing, were predominantly capital-intensive. Employment directly generated by expanded activities in these fields was therefore also relatively small. One historical reason for this is that the choice of techniques on the part of foreign enterprises was governed to a large extent by the availability of capital in foreign capital markets and the scarcity of skilled operatives in less developed countries. Even domestic capital, where it existed, was provided to the modern sector at lower interest rates than prevailed in the traditional sector. For some major operations it was therefore found more profitable to substitute machines for labour, although for many other major operations on the plantations and in the mines low wages were still a decisive factor which made labour-intensive techniques highly profitable. The costs and risks of training unskilled workers, to permit use of techniques calling for relatively intensive use of skilled labour, were considered to be high and in some instances they were certainly exaggerated. Also relevant is the fact that much existing capital equipment has been designed for use in countries where capital is relatively plentiful and labour relatively scarce. Finally, at least in some fields of production, the sad fact seems to be that techniques with low capital-labour ratios have also a low output per unit of capital. As private enterprises, of course, the productive organisations in the modern sector were more interested in maximising profits than in maximising either output or employment.

Turning to the evolution of the traditional sector, in which peasant agriculture is the predominant component, certain of its characteristic features can also be briefly described:

(a) The proportion of savings going into productive investment particularly in peasant agriculture was small in certain areas; possibly smaller than was required to maintain the level of productivity. In many of these countries this was due not so much to the shortage of savings inside the traditional sector as to the unproductive uses to which savings were put, for sizable amounts of savings often existed inside the traditional sector as a result of the great inequality in the distribution of agricultural income. The savings in the modern sector also seldom flowed into peasant agriculture for purposes of productive investment. As good land became scarce and labour redundant, the incentive to introduce labour-saving improvements was destroyed. In some countries the pattern of land holding also discouraged investment and technological progress in the traditional sector. This chronic lack of productive investment, combined with the lack of incentives as well as technical education on the part of peasants, kept productivity and incomes in peasant agriculture at a low level.

(b) In certain areas the traditional sector not only remained stagnant but deteriorated for either or both of the following two reasons. First, a number of handicraft industries, notably handlooms, were ruined by competition from cheaper machine-made goods either imported from abroad or manufactured at home. Secondly, with the extension of commercial agriculture and of the land area under large estates or plantations (the latter often associated with extensive methods of cultivation and non-diversified agriculture), a process of alienation of land from smallholders frequently took place. As a result a large number of peasants became landless agricultural labourers, and many others were forced to settle on small tracts of less productive or unproductive land. The latter phenomenon often occurred in countries where there was plentiful potentially fertile virgin land which was, however, not readily accessible to the peasants because no capital was invested in the development of such land. In these circumstances the growth of the modern sector *per se* created underemployment and reduced the level of income in the traditional sector.

(c) As time moved on, population in the traditional sector was increasing—at first very slowly because of the excessively high mortality rate and, later on, more rapidly owning to the fall in mortality rates brought about by the introduction of modern medical science. The slow growth of the modern sector made it impossible to absorb the increased peasant population in this sector and the difficulty was enhanced by the use of highly capital-intensive techniques in many fields of economic activity in the modern sector. For lack of alternative employment opportunities, the bulk of the increased rural population had no choice but to remain in the traditional sector. The deficiency in productive investment made it even difficult to raise the productivity of the existing traditional sector or, in some areas with potential fertile land, to widen the size of this sector by, for instance, large-scale land settlement.

The parallel evolution of the modern and the traditional sectors described above brought about a steady rise in under-employment in the traditional sector. This was made possible by the household form of production organisation. So long as the average product and income distributed among the members of the household enterprise are considered tolerable, it can always afford to take on additional labour. It matters little whether underemployment takes the form of work-sharing, part-time work or other work of very low productivity. Members of households will seek wage-earning employment when the average income becomes intolerably low or when they believe better employment opportunities are available in the modern sector. This description, however, does not apply to the landless agricultural workers, because they are obliged to seek other wage-earning employment when the wages they earn individually as farm hands prove too low to support their families.

The continuous absorption of additional labour has also been made easier by the flexibility of technical coefficients of production in peasant agriculture. Along with the successive diminution in the size of holdings as a result of subdivision and fragmentation of land as the population has increased, there have also been corresponding adaptations in the intensity and organisation of work, in the use of implements and draught animals, in the system of cropping and in other aspects of agricultural production—all in the direction of organising work at a lower level of productive efficiency. Thus more work has been created on land for surplus labour

but the additional work yields little or no additional output.

The above is of course a highly simplified account of the genesis of the employment problem. It may exclude other elements in the process. Nevertheless, it does draw attention to the essential characteristics of underdevelopment which lie at the roots of the present employment problem in a number of the less developed economies in Asia, the Middle East, Latin America and Africa.

4. UNDEREMPLOYMENT

4.1 LABOR SURPLUS ON THE LAND *

The concept of surplus farm labor has attracted increasing attention in the underdeveloped countries, especially in Asia. The simplest definition of it implies that some labor could be withdrawn from subsistence farming without reducing the volume of farm output. In technical terms, the marginal productivity of labor is believed to be zero. If this is true, it has some far-reaching implications. But is it true? Is it even conceivable? Some economists have had serious doubts on this score. It must be admitted that the idea of "disguised unemployment," as it is usually called, has sometimes been carelessly formulated and inadequately substantiated.

The subject must be viewed in relation to the general population problem. The crucial fact is that world population has doubled in the last hundred years. About two-thirds of the increase has taken place in the underdeveloped areas, chiefly in Asia, largely through a fall in death-rates. This has been part of the uneven impact of Western civilization on the rest of the

world. Now in the poorer countries as a rule the majority of the population works in agriculture to start with, for basic and obvious reasons. Just as food is the major item of consumption in low-income communities, so the struggle for food takes up most of their time and resources. In such countries rapid population growth naturally leads, and in some has already led, to excess population on the land.

Consider for a moment the effects of population growth in a community of peasant cultivators. Numbers are increasing while land, capital and techniques remain unchanged. Alternative employment opportunities may be lacking because of the rigid social structure, and may actually be decreasing because of the decline of traditional handicraft industries due to the competition of imported manufactures.

With the growing pressure of people on the land, farms become smaller and smaller. What is more, farms are divided and subdivided into tiny strips and plots. Accordingly it seems to me that agricultural unemployment in densely populated peasant communities may be said to take at least two basic forms: (1) underemployment of peasant cultivators due to

* From Ragnar Nurkse, "Excess Population and Capital Construction," *Malayan Economic Review,* October 1957, pp. 1, 3-5. Reprinted by permission.

the small size of farms; (2) unemployment disguised through fragmentation of the individual holding.

...

To the extent that the labor surplus is absorbed—and concealed—through fragmentation, it cannot be withdrawn without bad effects on output unless the fragmentation is reversed and the holdings are consolidated. Over a limited range the marginal productivity of labor might be zero without any such reorganization. It could be zero over a much wider range if the remaining factors of production were appropriately reorganized, which would require for one thing a consolidation of plots. Appropriate reorganization of the other factors of production is clearly a necessary and a reasonable pre-requisite for purposes of policy as well as analysis.

There are a number of empirical studies that tend to confirm this general picture. The evidence can never be entirely satisfactory in a matter such as this where some things, including the weather, would have to be held constant and others subjected to a reorganization which may necessitate a revolutionary change in rural life, bringing inevitably other changes with it. Nevertheless the connection between over-population and fragmentation goes a long way to make the existence of surplus farm labor plausible.

On a theoretical view of the matter it is clear that excess population can be so great in relation to land and capital that the marginal productivity of labor is reduced to zero. There are, however, two reasons why some economists have found this idea difficult to accept. First, anyone trained in Western economics would have to ask: Who would employ these people if their product is zero? Or else one might ask: How can these marginal people live, what do they eat, if they really produce nothing?

The answer to the first question is that in many countries the wage-labor system, which Western economists are apt to take for granted, hardly exists. The prevailing condition in subsistence farming is one of peasant family labor.

The answer to the second question—how can they live?—is that they live by sharing more or less equally in the total product of the farm, which includes the product of intra-marginal labor and of any land and capital goods the peasants may own. The product from these factors goes into the same pot and the members of the household eat out of that same pot. These institutional arrangements are foreign to the economics of business enterprise, and so the conditions which they make possible may seem paradoxical.

If this sharing of food is considered a little further the ultimate limit to the multiplication of people on the farms becomes starkly plain.[1] If the average total product per person falls below the physical level of subsistence, the outcome is the Malthusian state of starvation cutting down numbers or at least checking their further increase. At the point where this average product equals the physical subsistence level, the marginal product of labor may well be zero or even negative.[2] Still, it need not be as low as zero. Conversely, if and when labor's marginal product is zero, the average product need not be as low as the physical subsistence level; it may be a little above that level.

In any case, excess population neces-

1. The analysis concentrates on the subsistence farm sector. The reader should bear in mind that even the most backward economy usually contains other sectors also, including export production, commerce, government and even some industrial activity.

2. Professor J. E. Meade has shown this very clearly in his book, *The Theory of International Economic Policy;* Vol. II, *Trade and Welfare,* issued under the auspices of the Royal Institute of International Affairs, London: Oxford University Press, 1955, Chapter 6 and Appendix 1.

sarily implies that the marginal product is less than the average. In this state of affairs further population growth brings down the average level of consumption. Why? Because the additional labor contributes less than the average worker previously, and so it pulls down the average product per head. If the average product is as low as we know it to be, it does not seem far-fetched to suppose that in some cases the marginal product of labor may be zero. The upshot of the argument does not, of course, depend on its being exactly zero, although this is a convenient case on which to concentrate the analysis. The essential point is that the marginal workers live, in effect, on a subsidy if their own contribution to output is less than their intake of food and other necessities.

The relationship between total product and total population is illustrated in the accompanying diagram (II.3). Average product per head is reflected in the slope of the vector from the origin to any point on the curve. The marginal product is reflected in the slope of the curve itself at any given point. The average product per head reaches a maximum at A (where the angle AOL is largest) and declines thereafter as population increases further. The marginal product becomes zero at B (where the average product measured by the angle BOM may still be substantial). If population increases beyond M, the marginal

product becomes negative and the average product continues to fall. If we suppose that the average product at N represents the absolute physical minimum of subsistence, then population cannot increase beyond N. This supposition is of course purely arbitrary and illustrative. Actually the physical subsistence level of average product per head may lie, not in the range of negative marginal product, but conceivably at B or somewhere between A and B where marginal product is still positive. The diagram merely illustrates the possibilities and does not, of course, tell us what actually happens.

It must be conceded that this view of the matter is essentially that of "optimum population" theory (in the diagram the optimum size of population is OL). Now this theory has sometimes been criticized as being an unrealistic exercise in comparative statics. It assumes that nothing changes except the number of people—and, in response thereto, the volume of total product. It abstracts from, and ignores, any connections that may exist between population size on the one hand and, say, the state of techniques or the volume of capital on the other hand. It holds all other things constant. Is this not bound to lead to a distorted view of reality?

The criticism may be perfectly valid with regard to population trends in the Western world. But if we consider Asia over the last hundred years, I am not sure that the objection has much force. I began by saying that the population explosion in Asia, due largely to the fall in death-rates, reflects the *uneven* impact of Western civilization. The point is precisely that while population has doubled, other things such as techniques, capital supplies and cultivable land have remained *too much the same.* Therein lies the whole problem. Of course, there has been some advance in these other things too, but not nearly at the same rate as in population. In Asia there has been

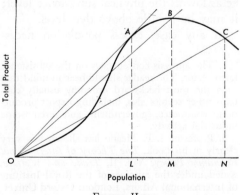

FIGURE II.3

nothing like the advance that accompanied population growth in the West. In this state of affairs it seems to me that the "optimum population" approach, questionable though it may be in the West, has a good deal of validity in the East. The economic problem of the East has been largely a consequence of dynamic population growth in an otherwise relatively static environment.

"Optimum population" theory directs attention chiefly to the variation of *average* product as the size of population varies. We have found it at least equally important to consider the *marginal* product. The question might be asked: Why this obsession with the margin? Why not stress the obvious fact of a low general level of productivity? The answer is that the marginal approach is useful here because of the need to take away some labor from current production for work on capital construction.

4.2 UNEMPLOYMENT IN UNDER-
DEVELOPED COUNTRIES *

In the literature before the Great Depression unemployment was usually regarded as a temporary maladjustment of demand and supply of labor. It was explained in terms of cyclical or other shifts in demand, low mobility of labor and sluggish price and wage adjustment.

The Great Depression and the Great Keynesian Simplification (of economics) born of the depression experience has made the world employment conscious. Underemployment equilibrium (with or without competition) is regarded as the rule and full employment the rare exception. According to the predominant simpler versions of the new doctrine there is practically always some slack in the econ-

omy and this slack is always due to insufficiency of effective demand. The unemployment is either open or disguised. The phrase "disguised unemployment" was coined by Mrs. Robinson and used to designate workers, who having lost well paid positions in industry to which their skill and training entitles them, are doing odd jobs, raking leaves or selling apples to eke out a miserable living.

Keynesian unemployment, open or disguised, was thought to exist only in rich industrial countries. Poor and underdeveloped countries are spared this particular scourge, because they still have plenty of investment opportunities and their poverty keeps the rate of saving low.

According to ultra modern i.e. Post Keynesian theory, disguised unemployment exists also in underdeveloped countries, typically and chronically (but by no means exclusively) in agriculture. Disguised unemployment is said to be present if a part of the labor force, say 5%, can be removed from the farms without reducing aggregate output; in fact aggregate output may even increase when the input of labor is reduced. It is, in other words, a case of zero (or negative) marginal productivity of labor.

The term "disguised unemployment" is surely not a good one, because most of the writers who believe that such conditions are widespread in the underdeveloped world (e.g. Arthur Lewis, Ragnar Nurkse, P.N. Rosenstein-Rodan) do not wish to suggest that disguised unemployment in underdeveloped countries is curable by the same easy methods as disguised and open cyclical or secular unemployment in industrial countries. A mere strengthening of effective demand by means of easy money policy and deficit spending is not only insufficient but positively harmful.

The modern theory of disguised unemployment can be regarded as an extreme version of the well known theory of pro-

* From Gottfried Haberler, "Critical Observations on Some Current Notions in the Theory of Economic Development," *L'Industria*, No. 2, 1957, pp. 3-5. Reprinted by permission.

tection associated with the name Mihail Manoilesco and the theory is, in fact, being utilized for the justification of import restrictions.[1] While Manoilesco only claimed that the marginal productivity of labor in agriculture was low compared with other branches of the economy, the modern theory of disguised unemployment goes the whole hog and maintains that it is zero or possibly negative.

To my mind, the claims of the proponents of the theory of widespread disguised unemployment are tremendously exaggerated. I can perhaps better explain what I think is wrong with the theory of disguised unemployment by stating positively what in my opinion is actually true in varying degrees in various countries, not only in underdeveloped but in developed countries as well: If it were possible to improve methods of production in agriculture; *if* the skill of farm laborers is increased; *if* social habits could be changed, a new spirit implanted and the resistance to moving to and living in cities and to working in factories could be overcome; *if* technology in industry could be changed so as to employ unskilled rural workers; *if* capital and other cooperating factors (entrepreneurs, managers, skilled foremen, etc.) could be provided in larger quantities and better quality; *if* and to the extent that all these things happen or are done, agriculture can release a lot of labor without loss of output

1. For example, in numerous publications of ECLA. See esp. *International Co-operation in a Latin American Development Policy,* United Nations, 1954, It is interesting to note that the originators of the idea (Nurkse and Rosenstein-Rodan) are careful to point out that conditions in the sparsely populated countries of Latin America are not the ones where one would expect disguised chronic unemployment. They refer specifically to old thickly populated countries such as Egypt, India and South East Europe. This has not prevented ECLA from embracing the idea wholeheartedly and to make it a corner stone of its highly protectionist and interventionist policy recommendations.

and industrial output be stepped up at the same time.

Now there is no doubt that all these things gradually do happen and did happen all the time in developed as well as underdeveloped countries. In fact, economic development largely consists of these changes. Furthermore, few would deny that many of these changes and improvements can be speeded up by appropriate policies (although, if the measures taken are inappropriate or the dosage incorrect the result will be a slow-down rather than a speed-up) and that for some of these changes to happen Government action is indispensable. But it is very misleading to speak of disguised unemployment. In that sense there always was disguised unemployment in developed as well as underdeveloped countries and practically everybody is a disguised unemployed. even in the most highly developed countries, because each of us will produce more ten years hence when technology has made further progress, skill and training have been further improved, the capital stock increased, etc.

The cases where after removal of a part of the labor force output remains unchanged (or even rises) without capital having been increased, technology improved, social habits changed, etc., or where such changes can be expected to be the automatic and immediate consequence of a prior reduction in labor input, must be comparatively rare and inconsequential compared with the increase in output due to the gradual introduction of all those changes and improvements.

The theory of disguised unemployment is often associated with the proposition that the capital-labor proportion is fixed—forgetting conveniently other productive agents. In other words production functions (isoquants) are said to have rectangular (or at least angular) shape. In some modern highly mechanized industries one may sometimes find situations faintly approaching this case. But the assumption that this should be the case in more primitive economies (agriculture) and should be a chronic situation seems to me preposterous.

4.3 The Concept of "Disguised Unemployment"*

The term "disguised unemployment" is commonly used to designate a situation in which the removal from a working combination of factors of some units of labor, nothing else of consequence or worth mentioning being changed, will leave the aggregate product of the working combination undiminished, and may even increase it. To say that there is "disguised unemployment" is therefore equivalent to saying that in that working combination the marginal productivity of labor is zero or almost zero and may even be a negative quantity. The "unemployment" may be only metaphorical, since there may be hard work even at the margin, when "unemployed" must mean "unproductively employed." But sometimes it is intended to be realistically descriptive, as when it is used to include seasonal unemployment; in such cases, I do not know what the adjective "disguised" is supposed to mean. I will in this note treat "seasonal unemployment" as a distinct phenomenon not obviously presenting a serious problem and not obviously having any peculiar relationship to agriculture in underdeveloped countries. As I look at the agricultural world with my inexpert eye, it seems to me that agricultural employment is most seasonal, is least continuous, in the temperate zones where agriculture is most "de-

veloped" and yields the highest levels of average and marginal product per labor-year.

As an intermittent phenomenon, resulting from the vagaries of weather and human error zero marginal productivity of labor in agriculture is a commonplace concept. But how can a priori the possibility of zero marginal productivity of employed labor, as a chronic phenomenon, be plausibly established? One way that has been suggested is on the assumption that the (average and marginal) technical coefficients of production are constant, so that the addition to a working combination of more units of labor will add nothing to the aggregate product unless additions are made also to the quantities used of all (or of some) of the other factors of production—Pareto's "fixed coefficients," or Frisch's "limitational factors."

I am not aware that anyone has ever given a convincing illustration of a technical coefficient which is "fixed" in a valid economic sense. The plausibility of the idea has resulted, I believe, from the confusion of chemical ingredients of a product, or actual engineering elements in a productive process, with potential economic input-items in a productive process. If iron ore, or coal, were as expensive per ton as gold I am sure that the steel industry would find ways of appreciably reducing the amounts of iron ore, or of coal, it uses to produce a ton of steel of given specific character, even though the chemical constituency of the steel were invariant, and, moreover, it would readily find ways of changing the chemical constituency of a ton of "steel" without reducing its suitability for its ordinary uses, and this not only in the long run but in the very short run. As far as agriculture is concerned, I find it impossible to conceive of a farm of any kind on which, other factors of production being held constant in quantity,

* From Jacob Viner, "Some Reflections on the Concept of 'Disguised Unemployment,'" in *Contribuicoes à Análise do Desenvolvimento Econô mico*, Livraria Agir Editôra, Rio de Janeiro, 1957. Reprinted by permission.

and even in form as well, it would not be possible, by known methods, to obtain some addition to the crop by using additional labor in more careful selection and planting of the seed, more intensive weeding, cultivation, thinning, and mulching, more painstaking harvesting, gleaning, and cleaning of the crop. Even supposing that there were such a farm, on which every product had technically and economically fixed ingredients, labor would still have positive marginal productivity unless there were not only fixed technical coefficients of production for all the economically relevant potential products of the farm, but the proportions between the technical coefficients were uniform for all of these products. For if these proportions are different as between different products, then it will always be possible by appropriate change in the product-mix, in the direction of more production of those products whose labor technical coefficients are relatively high, to absorb productively any increment of labor.

Unless one assumes non-economic motivation on the part of employers, there is difficulty also in conceiving why they should hire at any wage-rate additional units of labor beyond the point at which they know the labor will add less in value to the product than the wage-cost, to say nothing of the case where the labor will add nothing to and may even subtract from the product. The employer may, of course, be ignorant as to the facts, but I know of no experience to persuade me that the speculative economist is on such matters better informed than the experienced farmer in immediate touch with reality. This is probably what W. A. Lewis has in mind, although I cannot find that he anywhere explicitly says so, when he concedes that in agriculture "disguised unemployment" occurs only for peasant or self-employed labor, and not for plantation

labor.[1] Since there is a good deal of plantation agriculture in underdeveloped countries, this is an important limitation of the applicability of the concept of "disguised unemployment." But it raises its own difficulties. In Brazil, for instance, I take it that agriculture is even in the same localities a mixture of hired labor on plantations, of self-employed labor on owned (or rented?) small farms, and of squatter labor. Should there not be a tendency for equalization of the marginal productivity of labor in all agrarian uses where labor can fairly readily move from one type of use to another? Where there is labor-mobility, marginal productivity of labor must rise substantially above zero in peasant or squatter agriculture or sink to zero or near-zero on the plantations. This would especially be the case, for a reason to be explained later, if a member of a peasant or squatter family would not lose access to the family supply of food by taking employment on a nearby plantation. When I was in Brazil, I heard of complaints by plantation owners in districts in which there was also peasant and squatter agriculture of "shortage of hands" (*falta de mao*). I don't see how this can be reconciled with the prevalence of zero marginal productivity of labor, whether on the plantations of for self-employed agricultural labor.

...

W. A. Lewis has suggested, as an explanation of "disguised unemployment" in agriculture that, when "there are too many persons on too little land" the farmer cannot afford to keep cattle, so that the land gets no manure and land is put under the

1. *The Theory of Economic Growth*, Homewood, 1955, pp. 326-7. In "Economic Development with Unlimited Supplies of Labour," *The Manchester School*, May 1954, pp. 141-2, the presence of "disguised unemployment" is claimed for hired agricultural labour also, although in lesser degree than for self-employed labour.

plough which ought to be left in forest or in fallow; arid land is overcropped, so that fertility is destroyed.[2] ... Given the situation as Lewis describes it, the *long run* marginal productivity of labor could be zero or negative, but it would be in the long run interest of the owner of the crowded farm not to over-work it. Genuine unemployment on the farm, or employment of the "surplus" labor only on such tasks as would not impair fertility, would in the long run be more profitable than full employment, but the shortsightedness of the owner, or the hunger of his family, might nevertheless trap him into exploiting the short-run marginal productivity of labor, which I would expect to be always positive in a situation such as here described. Lewis concedes that this phenomenon of impairment of soil-fertility through over-crowding would be present only in "over-populated areas," and lists China, India, Japan, Java, Egypt, some countries in the Middle East, Kenya, and some small islands as the only countries in this category. Latin America and Eastern Europe, which many writers have regarded as subject to "disguised unemployment," are thus excluded by Lewis, and, as we have seen, he would exclude also the plantation agriculture of any country.

Ragnar Nurkse has suggested that where "disguised unemployment" prevails in agriculture, it would be desirable to transfer the surplus labor off the farms to produce capital goods, while keeping the consumption of food by the population as a whole constant through taxation or direct controls.[3] This would be relevant for Lewis's type of zero or negative marginal productivity of agricultural labor resulting from loss of fertility of soil through over-crowd-

ing and over-cropping. But as I have pointed out, it would not be a solution in the short run, for in the short run transferring labor out of agriculture would, or might, reduce the total output. N. Koestner has objected against Nurkse's argument that it fails to take account of the fact that the urban working-man needs more calories than the idle rural inhabitant.[4] But for Lewis the "disguised unemployed" of agriculture may be working as hard as anyone else, and may in fact need more calories for farm-work than they would need for factory-work. They are "idle" in the sense only that their work is unproductive. On the other hand, Nurkse, does not mention the inevitable and possibly appreciable loss of food involved in deterioration, spoilage, and spillage when the food is consumed in the city instead of on or near the farm where it is produced.

Still another kind—or source—of zero or less marginal productivity of agricultural—or urban—labor can be conceived of, and may even be important in practice, although I have not encountered it in the literature, and it would not be a simple matter, even if it existed, to demonstrate the fact. Suppose that given the "quality" of the labor force and the supplies of other productive resources, the marginal productivity function of labor could be represented, in the familiar manner, by a slowly-descending curve which within the range of observation remains substantially above the zero-productivity level. Suppose,

2. *The Theory of Economic Growth, op. cit.,* pp. 327-8.
3. *Problems of Capital Formation in Underdeveloped Countries,* Oxford, 1953, pp. 36 ff.

4. "Some Comments on Prof. Nurkse's Capital Accumulation in Underdeveloped Countries," *L'Egypte contemporaine,* XLIV, April 1953, p. 9. Nurkse, however, as far as I can see, has made a more than adequate concession on this point. See his original discussion in *Some Aspects of Capital Accumulation in Underdeveloped Countries,* Cairo, 1952, p. 25, (repeated in substance in his *Problems of Capital Formation,* p. 39): "A food deficit may arise also from the investment workers, the previous unemployed in disguise, having to eat a little more than before because they are now, perhaps, more actively at work."

however, that the quantity of food available for the farm family depends wholly on the output of the farm, that the food is shared by all members of the family, and that when it falls below a certain quantity per capita the energy and productive will and capacity of the worker-members of the family decline. It then becomes conceivable that if some of the members of the family, including working-members, were removed from the farm, (or if the whole family were removed from the farm, and the farm joined to a similar adjoining farm) and if those removed could no longer draw on the food-resources of the farm, the labor remaining on the farm would acquire a sufficiently higher marginal productivity curve, so that the farm would produce more than it did before when the number of workers was greater. In such a case, much of what has been said about "disguised unemployment" and about appropriate remedies for it would be relevant. Not so, however, Nurkse's proposal of removal of some of the workers off the farms without termination of their dependence, direct or indirect, on the farm for their food. Unless the per capita food consumption on the farm was increased, there would in this case be a reduction in the total food output of the farm if any of its workers were removed.

Let me now, as my last illustration, suggest the possibility of a special kind of unemployment which is not "disguised" or "hidden," but is open and voluntary. This is the kind of unemployment which would result from a rise in productivity, or in income per time-unit of labor, when the supply curve of labor was of the kind to which many years ago I gave the label of a "rising-backward supply curve." When income per time-unit of labor and aggregate income per laborer both rise, the laborer's relative valuation of marginal units of leisure and of wages per unit of labor may so change as to make a shorter working-day, week, or year attractive even at the cost of a smaller increase in the size of the pay envelope. (For labor paid on a piece-rate basis and for self-employed labor a similar adjustment may occur through reduction in the intensity rather than in the duration of the labor). The English mercantilists of the eighteenth century thought that this was the usual pattern of behavior of labor, and therefore believed in the inexpediency of high wages. There is no reason why such behavior should be peculiar to agricultural labor, but it may be that it is more likely to be prevalent for habit-ridden rural populations, as an initial response to the availability of choice between higher income or less—or less intensive—labor.

Lewis claims that "disguised unemployment" is not confined to agriculture, but is in underdeveloped countries common also in cities in the form of over-staffed retinues of domestic servants and of over-crowded service occupations where self-employment is the rule.[5] To make plausible the argument that maintenance of a large retinue of domestic servants is a symptom of "disguised unemployment" any more in the city of an underdeveloped country than it would be in London or Paris, one must assume, as Lewis does, that provision of employment for persons who otherwise would be openly unemployed is a major motive of the employers in the underdeveloped countries. Nurkse has claimed that the attractiveness of the consumers' goods of advanced countries to the population of underdeveloped countries operates as a serious barrier both to the development of their own industries and to capital formation.[6] Since industrialization in underdeveloped countries, when not directed otherwise by government, tends to concentrate on consumers' goods of advanced-

5. *The Manchester School,* May 1954, pp. 141-2.
6. *Problems of Capital Formation, op. cit.,* Chap. 3.

country types, a shift of taste away from Lewis's type of domestic service to tangible consumers' goods should promote instead of retarding industrialization, although I do not venture to guess whether it would promote or work against "economic welfare."

I refrain from discussing here the appropriateness of the application of the term "underemployment" to agriculture, even to American agriculture, merely to signify either allegedly low-productivity employment or considerable seasonal unemployment, in the absence of convincing evidence that the employment is not reasonably "productive" when everything relevant to "real income" and to available alternatives is taken into account or that we know how to grow spring wheat or cabbages in an American winter.[7] If we must do without the spring wheat or the cabbages if we are to escape the seasonal unemployment, perhaps it is sensible to reconcile ourselves to its persistence. I find it unhappy semantic usage also to label as "underemployment" and as "disguised unemployment" labor which would be "unnecessary" to maintain product undiminished if "intensity of work per hour" were raised,[8] since this would lead to the conclusion that there was "underemployment" and "disguised unemployment" in the most prosperous American urban industries even when overtime work was common.

4.4 Excess Supplies of Labor—Note

The preceding selections have queried the precise meaning of disguised unemployment. We should also carefully distinguish various other types of underemployment.

The strict interpretation of disguised unemployment is that the marginal productivity of labor, over a wide range, is zero, so that labor can be withdrawn without any loss of output even if no change in production techniques or use of other productive resources occurs. But, as A. K. Sen observes,[1] it is pertinent to distinguish between the amount of labor and number of laborers. For it may be asked why would labor be applied beyond the point where the marginal productivity of labor becomes zero? Sen suggests that the correct answer is "not that too much labour is being spent in the production process, but that too many labourers are spending it."[2] It is *laborers* who are abundant; *labor-time* is employed only up to the point where its marginal product is zero. In this situation, disguised unemployment takes the form of a smaller than "normal" number of working hours per head per year: although the marginal productivity of labor is just equal to zero at the margin, the marginal productivity of the laborer is zero over a wide range. If each laborer is working a number of hours that is less than the "normal" hours of work per laborer, then the same total product could be produced by fewer laborers working normal hours. Part of the labor is surplus. Although each laborer must work more hours if the smaller number of laborers is to produce the same output as did the larger number, this does not entail a reorganization of production through a change in production techniques or an increased supply of another factor; it does, of course, involve some sacrifice of leisure.

It has already been stated that it is unreasonable to interpret seasonal underemployment as disguised unemployment

7. Cf. Arthur Moore, "Underemployment in American Agriculture," National Planning Association, Planning Pamphlets No. 7, Jan. 1952; *Underemployment of Rural Families*, Materials Prepared for the Joint Commission on the Economic Report, February 1951.

8. Chiang Hsieh, "Underemployment in Asia," *International Labour Review*, LXVI, June 1952, p. 709.

1. A. K. Sen, *Choice of Techniques*, Oxford, 1960, pp. 13-15.

2. *Ibid.*, p. 15.

(4.3). Similarly, we should distinguish another type of underemployment that might be termed "traditional" underemployment. This arises when sociocultural determinants of the division of labor between men and women in the traditional sector leave the men underemployed. In some African economies, for instance, it is common practice for the men to clear and prepare the land for cultivation while the women do the routine work of sowing and cultivating. The men are left in surplus supply in agriculture, but they then frequently become migrant laborers in the exchange sector. As temporary immigrants from the traditional sector, they might work in industry or mining on a seasonal basis, or even for a year or two, and then return to their peasant farms.[3] The migration of labor for short periods might have only a negligible effect on agricultural output, but several studies have shown that adult manpower cannot be spared from the traditional system of agriculture for more than two or three years without reducing output.[4] This special situation of temporary labor migration does not conform to a precise interpretation of disguised unemployment. It is more enlightening to analyze the labor supply as a case of joint supply whereby workers are being supplied jointly to the advanced sector and the traditional sector over a period of time. An important part of this problem is to determine whether and for how long an individual will offer his labor for wage employment in the wage sector.[5]

Another special type of unemployment —the unemployment of "school leavers"— has recently appeared in the towns and cities of a number of countries, especially in Africa.[6] This type of urban unemployment involves young men from rural areas who leave school after receiving a certain minimum of education, or who cannot find a secondary school place as a result of the overexpansion of primary education relative to the facilities for secondary education. They then seek "white-collar" work, such as clerical jobs, instead of returning to the rural sector, which they now view with disdain. Having been established at a time when very few had the necessary minimum educational qualifications, and when there was a need to rely on expatriates, the wage and salary structure has not been scaled down sufficiently to reflect the larger supply of applicants now available. The result in many urban areas is the presence of a large number of school leavers who are attracted by the prospects of a relatively high salary and who prefer to remain unemployed in the town, awaiting an opening, rather than revert to a peasant life. And where the society supports an extended family system in agriculture, a similar arrangement tends to emerge in the towns, with an employed family member supporting other relatives. As educational programs expand, the problem of school leavers is likely to become increasingly acute.

The particular features of these different

---

3. Informative discussions of migrant labor are presented by Guy Hunter, *The New Societies of Tropical Africa,* Oxford, 1962, pp. 93-101, 191-203; W. J. Barber, *The Economy of British Central Africa,* Stanford, 1961, pp. 71-3; W. Elkan, "Migrant Labor in Africa: An Economist's Approach," *American Economic Review, Papers and Proceedings,* May 1959, pp. 188-97; W. Watson, *Tribal Cohesion in a Money Economy,* Manchester, 1959.

4. Barber, *op. cit.,* pp. 72-3, and other references listed.

5. See E. J. Berg, "Backward-Sloping Supply Functions in Dual Economies—The African Case," *Quarterly Journal of Economics,* August 1961, pp. 468-92.

6. See A. C. Callaway, "Unemployment Among African School Leavers," *Journal of Modern African Studies,* September 1963, pp. 351-71; International Labour Office, "Unemployed Youth: An African Symposium," *International Labour Review,* March 1963, pp. 183-205.

types of underemployment and unemployment deserve closer consideration than they have received in the literature on development—not only to distinguish them from the case of disguised unemployment, but also so that different policies might be formulated for their appropriate solutions.

5. INTER-SECTORAL RELATIONSHIPS IN A DUAL ECONOMY—NOTE

When a dual economy exists the ultimate question for the country's future development is how the modern exchange sector is to expand while the indigenous sector contracts. This requires an analysis of the interrelationships between the two sectors. Professor W. Arthur Lewis has offered a perceptive analysis of this problem.[1] This note summarizes Lewis's model and assesses its relevance for contemporary problems of development.

Lewis analyzes the process of economic expansion in a dual economy composed of a "capitalist" sector and a "subsistence" sector. The capitalist sector is defined as that part of the economy which uses reproducible capital, pays capitalists for the use thereof, and employs labor for wages for profit-making purposes (in mines, plantations, factories). The subsistence sector is that part of the economy which does not use reproducible capital (the indigenous traditional sector). In this sector, output per head is much lower than in the capitalist sector, and with the available techniques, the marginal productivity of labor in agricultural production may be zero or negative—constituting a case of disguised unemployment.

A fundamental relationship between the two sectors is that when the capitalist sector expands, it draws upon labor from the subsistence sector. For countries that have experienced high rates of population growth and are densely populated, it is assumed that the supply of unskilled labor to the capitalist sector is unlimited. A large component of the unlimited supply of labor is composed of those who are in disguised unemployment in agriculture, and in other over-manned occupations such as domestic service, casual odd jobs, or petty retail trading; other sources of labor are women who transfer from the household to commercial employment, and the growth in the labor force due to population increase. The large pool of unskilled labor enables new industries to be created or old industries to expand in the capitalist sector without encountering any shortage of unskilled labor.

The wage which the growing capitalist sector has to pay is determined in Lewis's model by what labor earns in the subsistence sector. Peasant farmers will not leave the family farm for wage employment unless the real wage is at least equal to the average product on the land.[2] Capitalist wages, as a rule, will have to be somewhat higher than subsistence earnings in order to compensate labor for the cost of transferring and to induce labor to leave the traditional life of the subsistence sector (Lewis observes that there is usually a gap of 30 per cent or more between capitalist

1. "Economic Development with Unlimited Supplies of Labour," *The Manchester School*, May 1954, pp. 139-91; also, Lewis, "Unlimited Labour: Further Notes," *ibid.*, January 1958, pp. 1-32. The analysis has also been extended in some respects by Professors Gustav Ranis and J. C. H. Fei, "A Theory of Economic Development," *American Economic Review*, September 1961, pp. 533-65; "Innovation, Capital Accumulation, and Economic Development," *ibid.*, June 1963, pp. 283-313.

2. As noted in 4.1, above, even though the marginal product of labor is zero in disguised unemployment, a member of the extended family shares in the total product and receives approximately the average product.

wages and subsistence earnings). At the existing capitalist wage, however, the supply of labor is considered to be perfectly elastic.

This situation is illustrated in Figure II.4, where OA represents subsistence earnings, OW the real wage rate in the capitalistic sector, and WS the perfectly elastic supply of labor. Given a fixed amount of capital at the outset, the demand for labor is initially represented by the marginal productivity schedule of labor, N_1D_1 in Figure II.4. If we assume profit maximization, capital will then be applied up to the point where the current wage equals the marginal productivity of labor. If OW is the current wage, the amount of labor employed in the capitalistic sector is OL; beyond L, workers earn whatever they can in the subsistence sector. The total product N_1PLO in the capitalist sector will then be divided between wages in the amount OWPL and the capitalists' surplus or profits in the amount WPN_1.

In tracing the process of economic expansion, Lewis emphasizes that the key to the process is the use which is made of the capitalist surplus. The driving force in the system is generated by the reinvestment of the capitalist surplus in creating new capital. As the capitalist sector expands, labor withdraws from the subsistence sector into wage employment, the surplus then becomes even larger, there is still more reinvestment of profits, and the process continues on progressively absorbing surplus labor from the subsistence sector.

Figure II.4 illustrates this process by the outward shift of the demand for labor, from N_1D_1 to N_3D_3 over time. When some of the initial surplus WPN_1 is reinvested, the amount of fixed capital increases, and the schedule of the marginal productivity of labor is then raised to the level of say, N_2D_2. Both the capitalist surplus and capitalist employment are now

larger. Further investment then raises the marginal productivity of labor to say, N_3D_3. And so the process continues.

The growth in capitalist profits is crucial in this process. As the capitalist sector expands, the share of profits in the national income increases; and since the major source of savings is profits, savings and capital formation also increase as a proportion of the national income.

Barring a hitch in the process, the capitalist sector can expand until the absorption of surplus labor is complete, and the supply function of labor becomes less than perfectly elastic. Capital accumulation has then caught up with the excess supply of labor; beyond this point real wages no longer remain constant but instead rise as capital formation occurs, so that the share of profits in the national income will not necessarily continue to increase, and investment will no longer necessarily grow relatively to the national income.[3]

The expansion process might be cut short, however, by a rise in real wages and a reduction in profits that halts capital accumulation before the excess labor supply is completely absorbed. This may be due to a rise in average product in the subsistence sector because the absolute number of people in this sector is being reduced without a fall in total output, or labor pro-

3. In the Ranis-Fei model, disguised unemployment is considered to exist when the marginal product of labor is less than its average product; when labor has a marginal product of zero, it is termed "redundant labor."

The horizontal supply curve to the capitalist sector is then considered to end when the redundant labor force in the agricultural sector is taken up and a relative shortage of agricultural goods appears, so that the terms of trade turn against the capitalist sector. This upward trend in the labor supply curve is later accentuated by a rise in the agricultural real wage traceable to the removal of disguised unemployment and the commercialization of agriculture (so that real wages are determined by competitive market forces, not by the non-market institutional average product). Ranis and Fei, "A Theory of Economic Development," op. cit., pp. 539-40.

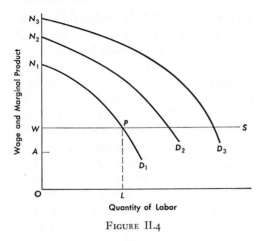

FIGURE II.4

ductivity happens to increase in the subsistence sector, or the terms of trade turn against the capitalist sector.[4]

Although the Lewis model highlights some basic relationships in dualistic development, we should be aware that its applicability is circumscribed by certain special conditions. The assumption of an unlimited supply of labor is unrealistic for many poor countries—certainly for some African and Latin American countries which are sparsely populated. In light of the previous critical comments on disguised unemployment (4.2, 4.3), we should also be skeptical about Lewis's reliance on this concept. But the existence of disguised unemployment is not strictly necessary for the expansionary process that Lewis describes; all that is

4. If, for instance, the capitalist sector produces no food, and the demand for food rises as the capitalist sector expands, then the price of food will rise in terms of capitalist products—that is, the terms of trade turn against the capitalist sector. In order to keep the real income of workers constant, capitalists then have to pay out to labor a larger part of their product as wages, thereby reducing their profits.

The possibility that industrialization can be inhibited by a deterioration in the terms of trade for the industrial sector points up the extreme importance of providing an agricultural surplus for consumption in the expanding industrial sector. This is one of several reasons why agricultural output must expand along with industrial development. This problem, together with other relationships between industry and agriculture, will be discussed more fully in Chapter VI, below.

required is that labor productivity be relatively low in the subsistence sector, and that the supply of labor to the capitalist sector be greater than the demand for labor. The case of a migrant labor force, however, poses special problems (4.4) that cannot be adequtely analyzed in Lewis's model. To make it more relevant for this type of situation, the Lewis model has been modified by Professor Barber in his analysis of the interaction between the indigenous economy and the expanding money economy in British Central Africa.[5]

Even if an unlimited supply of unskilled labor is assumed to exist, it is nonetheless generally true that in poor countries skilled labor is in very short supply. Lewis recognizes this problem, but discounts its importance by considering it to be only a temporary bottleneck which can be removed by providing the facilities for training more skilled labor. This will, however, at best involve a time lag, and recent experience in developing countries indicates that the problems of skill formation are not quickly overcome for uneducated and untrained manpower.

A more serious limitation of the Lewis model is that it simply takes for granted the demand side of the investment process. Can we assume, as Lewis does, that a capitalist class already exists? A major obstacle to development in many countries still may be the absence of a capitalist class with the necessary ability and motivation to undertake long-term productive investment. We must confront the problem of how a class of private capitalists is to emerge, or else we must rely at the outset on the presence of foreign capitalists or a class of state capitalists. The analysis of the behavior in the capitalist sector may then have to be modified, according to which type of capitalist class exists.

Further, it is assumed that whatever the

5. Barber, *The Economy of British Central Africa*, Stanford, 1961, pp. 180-88.

capitalist sector produces, it can sell; no allowance is made for a problem of aggregate demand. But why should this be true if the output is to be sold within the capitalist sector itself, or if the product is an export good? The remaining alternative—that the capitalist sector sells to the non-capitalist sector—presents a special difficulty. For then productivity must rise in the non-capitalist sector in order to ensure an adequate market for the output of the capitalist sector. But if real wages rise in the non-capitalist sector, the supply-price of labor to the capitalist sector will then be higher, profits will be reduced, and the expansionary process may stop before all the surplus labor is absorbed.

Despite these restrictions on its direct applicability, the Lewis model retains high analytical value for its insights into the role of capital accumulation in the development process. What is clearly of prime significance is the way investment becomes a rising proportion of national income. With this emphasis on the strategic importance of capital, we should now turn to the next chapter which examines some special problems of capital accumulation.

6. BIBLIOGRAPHICAL NOTE

1. The major study of social dualism is J. H. Boeke's *Economics and Economic Policy of Dual Societies,* New York, 1953. This is a revised version of two earlier books: *The Structure of the Netherlands Indian Economy,* New York, 1942, and *The Evolution of the Netherlands Indies Economy,* New York, 1946. An excellent discussion of special aspects of Boeke's thesis is provided by Royal Tropical Institute, *Indonesian Economics,* The Hague, 1961. The collection of essays in this volume examines the fundamentals of dualism and the applicability of the concept. Also instructive is J. S. Furnivall, *Netherlands India. A Study of Plural Economy,* Cambridge, 1939.

An illuminating survey of various interpretations of dualism is provided by Howard S. Ellis, "Dual Economies and Progress," *Revista de Economia Latinoamericana,* 1962. Problems of a dual wage level are discussed by Vera C. Lutz, "The Growth Process in a 'Dual' Economic System," *Banca Nazionale del Lavoro Quarterly Review,* September 1958; A. O. Hirschman, "Investment Policies and Dualism in Underdeveloped Countries,"

American Economic Review, September 1957. An interesting article that relates economic dualism to the nature of technical progress is Harvey Leibenstein's "Technical Progress, the Production Function and Dualism," *Banca Nazionale del Lavoro Quarterly Review,* December 1960.

2. The phenomenon of disguised unemployment is analyzed by A. Navarrete and I. M. Navarrete, "Underemployment in Underdeveloped Countries," *International Economic Papers,* No. 3, 1953; Harvey Leibenstein, "The Theory of Unemployment in Backward Economies," *Journal of Political Economy,* April 1957; Harry Oshima, "Underemployment in Backward Economies—An Empirical Comment," *Journal of Political Economy,* June 1958; K. N. Raj, *Employment Aspects of Planning in Underdeveloped Economies,* Cairo, 1957; K. N. Raj, "Employment and Unemployment in the Indian Economy," *Economic Development and Cultural Change,* April 1959; Simon Rottenberg, "The Meaning of 'Excess Supplies of Labour,'" *Scottish Journal of Political Economy,* February 1961; N. K. Sarkar, "A Method of

Estimating Surplus Labour in Peasant Agriculture in Over-Populated Under-Developed Countries," *Journal of Royal Statistical Society*, Vol. 120, Pt. 2, 1957; T. R. Sundaram, "Utilization of Idle Man-power in India's Economic Development," *Pacific Affairs*, Summer 1961; P. Wonnacott, "Disguised and Overt Unemployment in Underdeveloped Economies," *Quarterly Journal of Economics*, May 1962.

III

CAPITAL ACCUMULATION

MANY ECONOMISTS EMPHASIZE capital accumulation as the major factor governing the rate of development. Professor Rostow, for example, explicitly specifies a rise in the rate of productive investment to over 10 per cent of national income as a necessary requirement for a country's take-off (Chapter I, 1.4, above). Similarly, in presenting his model of a dual economy (summarized in Chapter II, section 5, above), Professor Lewis contends that

The central problem in the theory of economic development is to understand the process by which a community which was previously saving and investing 4 or 5 per cent of its national income or less, converts itself into an economy where voluntary saving is running at about 12 to 15 per cent of national income or more. This is the central problem because the central fact of economic development is rapid capital accumulation (including knowledge and skills with capital).[1]

The discussion of technological dualism (Chapter II, 3.1) also implied that development requires primarily large amounts of capital investment, especially in the underdeveloped sector.

Certainly there has been no tendency among development economists to underestimate the importance of capital. On the contrary, it has been stressed so much that a reaction has set in, and there is emerging a strong minority view that the role of capital has received excessive attention to the neglect of other essential components of the development process. The materials in section 1 present opposing views on the legitimacy of emphasizing capital as the key variable determining the rate of development. The statements by the Economic Commission for Asia and the Far East and Professor Lewis (1.1, 1.2) attribute a strategic role to capital, while J. H. Adler and K. S. Krishnaswamy, Professor Cairncross, and Professor Frankel argue against excessive concentration on capital (1.3, 1.5, 1.6). Since capital-output ratios have figured prominently in the discussion of capital accumulation, the Note on capital-output ratios clarifies various interpretations of the capital-output ratio, and at the same time levies a number of criticisms that restrict the use of a capital-output ratio in practice (1.4).

1. W. Arthur Lewis, "Economic Development with Unlimited Supplies of Labour," *The Manchester School*, May 1954.

To the extent that an increase in the rate of investment is necessary or desired, a developing country must mobilize the necessary savings. The Note in section 2 focuses on this issue by outlining the various sources of capital formation (excluding the process of inflation which is to receive particular attention in the next chapter).

The remaining sections examine three of the more important sources of capital formation—taxation, foreign aid, and private foreign investment. The discussion in section 3 emphasizes that the financing of government's share in economic development should be considered from two basic points of view. First, an adequate amount of taxation is needed to provide the government with a non-inflationary means for purchasing investment goods out of revenue. Second, in re-orienting tax policy to the tasks of development, it is necessary to recognize the peculiar characteristics of underdeveloped countries and to give particular attention to the probable effects of different kinds of taxes on private incentives to work, save, and invest. Considering the general problems of tax policy that characterize many underdeveloped countries, the materials in section 3 provide some notions on what might be the most desirable characteristics of the revenue structure and what role might be assigned to various taxes.

Since recourse to foreign economic aid is now perforce an essential element of international development, section 4 is concerned with the problem of making capital assistance more effective. To this end, it reviews the objectives and magnitude of foreign aid and appraises the different types and conditions of aid.

Section 5 attempts to pose some questions concerning the potential contribution of private foreign capital. These concern the benefits and costs of various forms of private foreign investment, viewed within the context of the recipient country's development plan. While the Note (5.1) establishes some general principles, the other materials in this section relate to specific illustrations and applications.

In examining the various sources of capital formation, we should consider not merely the aggregate amount of capital that might be supplied from each internal or external source. Most important is an assessment of each source of capital formation from the wider standpoint of how its contribution to the flow of resources for developmental purposes can be intensified.

1. THE ROLE OF CAPITAL

1.1 ESTIMATING CAPITAL REQUIREMENTS *

The general rate of development is always limited by shortage of productive factors. If any one scarce factor associated with under-development should be singled out, it would be capital. The final goal of development programming is, therefore, to find the best way of breaking the vicious circle between capital shortage and under-development and to design the most efficient and optimum rate of capital accumulation.

It would be an over-simplification, of course, to regard economic development as a matter of capital accumulation alone. Other things are needed in addition, such as entrepreneurship and training of workers and public administrators. Yet these are seldom possible without some increase in the stock of capital. Therefore capital accumulation may very well be regarded as the core process by which all other aspects of growth are made possible.

Capital increases by investment, and more investment necessitates more savings or foreign assistance. Foreign assistance, if not in the form of grants, means some burden in the future. The extent to which foreign loans can be serviced and repaid will ultimately depend on what can be saved at home in the future. Domestic savings are, therefore, the more reliable source of investment to break the vicious circle of poverty and under-development. But domestic savings can be increased only by a sacrifice in consumption which has to be compared with the future increases in consumption it promises. Investment, moreover, yields different results, depending on the industries in which it is made. In order, therefore, for the government of an under-developed country to design an appropriate plan for development, it must be informed of the quantitative aspects of savings and investment, and their effects on production and consumption.

These quantitative aspects are of crucial importance in determining the most desirable rate of development. It is important, for one thing, particularly when population is growing rapidly, to estimate the rate of development that would be needed to bring about an improvement in *per capita* income or a high rate of employment for the growing work force. Another element which may play a role in estimating a minimum rate of development is the necessity to give a certain minimum size to some projects in order that they are at all economically sound. In some industries where so-called "indivisibilities" play a role, there are such minimum sizes of projects. For the country as a whole, this may mean that only a "big push," as it has been called, can really help to start the process of development. Although this may produce results which appear ambitious in the light of current efforts, it provides a fair indication of the tasks involved in the planning effort.

Whatever the initial approach, there are some useful concepts which should be borne in mind in planning the rate of development. These concepts may conveniently be described in terms of investment. There is, first, the concept of a *minimum rate of investment*, which measures the rate needed to prevent *per capita* income from falling in the face of population growth. A rate of investment somewhat above this minimum is the lowest target at which any plan should aim, even though this may involve a heavy effort when population is growing rapidly. For some countries this may be a rate that can be easily attained on the basis of an effort which does not require any fundamental policy

* From United Nations, ECAFE, *Programming Techniques for Economic Development,* Report of the First Group of Experts on Programming Techniques, Bangkok, 1960, pp. 8-13.

decisions, any changes in attitudes or be-haviour patterns, or any improvements in techniques, skills and methods of business or public administration. For these coun-tries, the minimum rate of investment is clearly too low, and is useful only for reference.

A second concept of use in this context is that of a *practical maximum rate of invest-ment*. In theory a maximum rate of invest-ment may refer to a level of capital accumu-lation which involves saving and investing at least all income above, say, a subsistence level. Clearly, such a maximum is of no practical significance. A practicable maxi-mum may, therefore, be determined differ-ently in the light of the extent to which the population would be willing to accept austerity now, so as to enjoy a higher stand-ard of living in the future. The planner must form his best judgement as to what this practical maximum would be. The rate just defined above is the one to be deter-mined by an evaluation of people's poten-tial propensity to save.

A third concept is that of the highest rate of investment consistent with *absorptive capacity*. Absorptive capacity depends on natural resources, taxes, the labour supply, the level of labour, technical and manage-rial skills, entrepreneurial capacity, the efficiency of public administration, the extent of "technology-mindedness" of the population, and so on. Such capacity sets a limit to the amount of efficient investment physically possible, and although it can itself be increased through further invest-ment, it does effectively limit the rate of development possible, particularly in the short run. Maximum absorptive capacity may, of course, permit of a higher rate of investment than that allowed by the ability of the population to save. In this case, it would be the role of an ideal international policy to fill the gap and to raise invest-ment to the highest level consistent with absorptive capacity. On the other hand,

where absorptive capacity is below the practicable rate of savings, both national and international policies should be direct-ed towards raising such capacity. These policies would then constitute the initial phase of a long-term plan.

Thus, one of the logical ways to start planning the general rate of economic development is first to estimate the amount of domestic savings and capital imports that could be expected with no change in economic policies; then to calculate the rate of growth that this level of savings and investment would provide; and finally to compare it with the desired rate of growth. Usually, the ratio of saving to income is fairly stable over long periods of time, and these saving-income ratios are lower in under-developed countries (under 10 per cent) than in higher advanced countries (about 15 per cent). Any empirical esti-mation of this ratio must start with the observation of the rates of savings experi-enced by the country in the recent past. The estimates may be based on data for incomes and the savings of households, business and government, or domestic investment *minus* capital imports. It may also be possible to base the estimates on the experiences of comparable countries, keep-ing in mind the differences in income levels.

After estimating the current rate of sav-ings, the crucial question will be what amount of net national output may be expected from the investment to be made on the basis of the estimated savings. A number of studies have been made on the amount of capital required to increase out-put by one unit per annum in each sector of the economy and for a national economy as a whole. This amount is called the "capital-output ratio," or "capital coeffi-cient."

Available data clearly show that for a number of countries, e.g. the Federal Republic of Germany, Japan, Norway, the

United Kingdom and the United States, the capital-output ratio for a national economy as a whole remains stable over somewhat longer periods at a level of 3 to 4. This fact may well be explained by complementarities of industrial activities, or it may be that the increases in the capital-output ratios in some manufacturing industries are compensated by decreases elsewhere, possibly by external economies due to better transport or organization of the economy. Even though there are variations, it is perhaps one of the most useful parameters with a fair degree of stability. For post-war years the coefficient was found to be 2.6 for Ceylon, 2.3 for India, 4.7 for Japan, 2.3 for Malaya, etc. A better use of already existing idle capacity may have been responsible for the low values found for Ceylon, India and Malaya. These values can be expected somewhat to rise in the future. Since, moreover, the capital coefficients differ so much from one industry to another, and, in some cases, from one technique to another, it is conceivable that capital-output ratios will change in the future, depending upon the industrial structure of the economy and on the techniques to be chosen. Nevertheless, fairly reliable estimates of capital-output ratio can be made for most countries.[1] If exact estimates are difficult, the maximum and minimum values of possible estimates may be taken, and some alternative rates of development calculated.

This capital-output ratio may be considered, at this stage of our programming,

1. One may wonder if it is safe to assume that national output is proportional to (or a linear function of) capital only. In general, national output would be technically related to the employment of labour and capital, and this relation would change through time. To base the projection of national output mainly on the capital-output ratio implies a certain type of technical change in the relevant future. There are some other econometric models, such as the Douglas function, which may be usefully applied to some countries. Details of this type of possible formulations are omitted from the text here.

as a tentative figure, and may be adjusted later as improved information, based on detailed sectoral studies, becomes available.

Although the capital-output ratio is usually calculated as the "average" capital-output ratio, what really matters is the "marginal" or "incremental" capital-output ratio: we need information on the capital required to *increase* the national output. If we want to increase output by 20 and estimate the capital-output ratio as 4, then the required addition to the capital stock, to be provided by new investment, is 80. Evidently the figure 4 in this example stands for the "incremental capital-output ratio."

Given estimates of the current rate of savings and the capital-output ratio, the rate of economic growth, in terms of national output, could be projected in the following way. If the current level of national output is 1,000, and the saving ratio is 0.06, domestic savings would be 60, which may be invested to generate the increased national output. With a capital-output ratio of 4, this amount of savings and investment could generate an increase in national output of 15, not more. An increase in national output of, say, 20 will not be possible, because the amount of investment required for this purpose is 80, which exceeds the current savings of 60. Hence, the increase in output warranted by the savings of 60 is $60 \div 4 = 15$, which gives the growth rate of 1.5 per cent in national output. The rate of growth in national output can thus be calculated by dividing the saving ratio by the capital-output ratio.

This method of projecting the future level of national output can be checked by other ways of forecasting, e.g. extrapolation of past figures. If the projected national income shows a lower growth rate than actual income did in the past, it may be that the saving ratio has been underestimated or the capital-output ratio over-

TABLE I. RATE OF ECONOMIC GROWTH IN TERMS OF NATIONAL OUTPUT

National output (1)	Saving ratio (2)	Saving (3)		Investment (4)	Capital-output ratio (5)	Increase in national output (6)
1,000	0.06	60	=	60	4	15

$$\text{Growth rate } (G) = \frac{(6)}{(1)} = \frac{15}{1,000} = \frac{(2)}{(5)} = \frac{0.06}{4} = 0.015$$

estimated. If the ratios are right, a slowing down of economic growth must be expected. Another check would be to divide the projected national output by the numbers in the active labour force, to obtain an index of the average productivity of labour in the future. If this index does not rise as much as the past trend, the estimates of parameters should again be reconsidered. If they are correct, inefficiency or unemployment must be expected in the future, unless measures are taken to prevent them.

The rate of growth of an economy will be somewhat less than shown by the preceding calculations, if the gestation period of the investment envisaged is large. The calculation above tacitly assumes that capital created by the investment in one period can be used productively in the following period. If, however, the gestation period of some investment project is longer than one year, say three years, then capital available for productive use will not increase before three years. At that time, the level of national income will be higher, and hence the rise in production, as a percentage of total national income, is somewhat less. This means that the extension of the gestation period has the same effect as the decline in the saving ratio, or the increase in the value of the capital-output ratio. If this is the case, then the rate of economic growth computed in the preceding way must be adjusted downward. Needless to say, a lengthening of this time lag has further adverse effects, owing to the additional postponement of the fruits of investment.

If such projections of current trends show no significant rise in the people's standard of living, there is a definite need to increase the growth rate of national output. Suppose that the expected population increase is 1.5 per cent a year, the saving ratio 6 per cent, and the capital-output ratio 4. This will leave the standard of living unchanged, and represents the minimum rate of investment as defined [above]. If the *per capita* national income must increase by, say, 2 per cent a year, the national income must increase by 1.5 + 2.0 = 3.5 per cent every year. This means that, with the same capital-output ratio, the savings ratio must be increased from 0.06 to 0.14, requiring a considerable adjustment in policy measures. If such a sudden rise in the saving ratio is difficult to achieve, the targets for improvements in living standard must be lowered to what was called... the practical maximum rate of investment.

1.2 THE COST OF CAPITAL ACCUMULATION *

If the ambition is to grow as rapidly as the countries of Europe and North America have grown during the past century,

* From W. Arthur Lewis, "Some Reflections on Economic Development," *Economic Digest,* Institute of Development Economics, Karachi, Vol. 3, No. 4, Winter 1960, pp. 3-5. Reprinted by permission.

the desired growth rate is about 2 per cent per head per annum. Allowing for population growth, this in most of the poorer countries means that national output should grow by about 4 per cent per annum. Higher rates than this are stated as objectives in some development plans, but 4 per cent is so difficult to attain that it is really quite an ambitious target.

Economic growth at about 4 per cent per annum requires that a country withhold from personal consumption about a quarter of the national output. One half of this or about 12 per cent of national output, is needed to provide an adequate framework of public services, the other half is required for capital formation. The need for capital formation, or investment, is familiar; a word should be said about the framework of public services.

The governments of these countries ought to spend every year about 3 per cent of national income on education, 2 per cent on public health, 3 per cent on economic services such as communications, agriculture, and geology; and about 4 per cent on general administration and welfare. This cost, aggregating 12 per cent of national income, is somewhat higher than in the more developed countries, who can provide the same range of public services more intensively for 10 per cent of national income. This is mainly because the average public servant is paid more in relation to average national income in a poor than in a rich country—a fact which mainly reflects the shortage of educated persons. Expenditure on the public services is just as necessary to growth as capital investment. Law and order, education, agricultural extension, geological survey, public health and such services are foundations of economic growth.

As for capital investment, no catalogue is necessary. The most urgent need of most developing countries is for better transport, especially roads and harbours. The next priority is water—its conservation for agricultural, industrial and domestic purposes. Then there is the tremendous need for capital for housing in all our rapidly expanding cities. Many people think of capital primarily in terms of manufacturing industry and electric power, but even in the most advanced countries less than one-third of capital investment is in factories. Public services, utilities and housing are the great eaters up of capital investment, without which other productive activities could not take place.

Nowadays in most underdeveloped countries people know what economic growth requires; the difficulty is to make available the quarter of the national income which it costs. Personal consumption, which should only be 75 per cent of the national income, is nearer 85 per cent, leaving for the public services and for capital formation together only about 15 per cent instead of the 25 per cent they need. How is this transition to be effected?

The problem is not new. The countries which are now developed have all had to make this transition during their "industrial revolutions" or "take-off periods." In the Soviet Union the transition has been achieved in effect by taxation which is a form of compulsory saving. Elsewhere it came automatically, over a fairly long period, as a by-product of the rise of a capitalist class to dominance in the economic system.

Capitalists are distinguished from other dominant classes by their passion for saving and for productive investment. Earlier dominant classes had different ambitions. Priestly classes saved, but they invested their wealth more usually in monuments and churches than in factories and farms. Landowners saved, but in their heyday they used their savings to buy more land, rather than to invest in improving land, and the persons from whom they bought were usually selling in distress to finance consumption. Nowadays landowners in developed countries have learned to behave like capitalists, but elsewhere landowners are still not prone to productive investment. The capitalist was the first dominant type to make saving and productive investment into a religion of life.

As capitalism develops within a backward economy, the proportion of the national income accruing as capitalist profits increases all the time, and so the share of the national income saved and invested grows automatically all the time, until the economy is fully converted to capitalism, when the share of profits in the national income is stabilised. All the countries now developed have gone through this process, except the U.S.S.R.; and the countries now in line for development can tread the same path if they so desire.

For the most part they do not so desire. This is not primarily because of anticapitalist ideology. Most of the leaders of new states proclaim some sort of socialist leaning, but within a year or two of taking office their desire for development proves stronger than their antipathy to capitalism; and they adopt programmes for stimulating private capital investment; for stimulating even indeed the foreign private capital investment which they have hitherto denounced. Their main objection to relying solely on the growth of private capitalism is that it is so slow. By this method it may take anything up to a century to raise the rate of domestic saving from 5 to 10 per cent. Most political leaders want quicker results than this.

Taxation provides a more rapid alternative. If 20 per cent of national income is raised in taxes, of which 12 per cent is spent on government services, the other 8 per cent, added to 5 per cent of private saving, makes a respectable level of capital formation. Countries which have followed this path in recent years include Ghana, Burma, Ceylon and China.

This relatively high level of saving out of taxes, 8 per cent of national income, accords very well with the modern pattern of demand for capital. For nowadays half of investment is done by public agencies anyway, in electric power, communications, water supplies, schools and other public services; so there is no longer need to rely on private savings for financing investment of this kind. In addition, many private investors look to public agencies for finance, whether for private housing, for agricultural credit, or for manufacturing industry. So it is quite appropriate for the major part of saving to be done on public account.

Neither can it be said that 20 per cent is too much of the national income to take in taxes. Developed countries take 30 per cent or more. In Asia and Latin America the distribution of income is even more uneven than it is in Europe and North America. The top 10 per cent of the population gets 40 per cent of the national income; landlords think nothing of taking half the peasants' produce as rent. There is a large surplus over and above what the masses of the people receive for their consumption, and it is not too much to ask that some of this surplus be mobilised for economic development. Admittedly it cannot be done all at once. But there is no technical obstacle in the way of raising the share of taxes in the national income from 10 to 20 per cent over a period of ten years.

This can be done even in egalitarian countries, such as we find in West Africa, where land is plentiful, and where there are very few rich persons. Output is growing in these countries anyway; so it is possible to raise the proportionate share of taxes in national income over a period of time without actually reducing the absolute level of consumption per head.

What is lacking in most of these countries is not the means but the will.

1.3 THE SUPPLY OF CAPITAL AND THE SUPPLY OF OTHER FACTORS *

Given the diversity of development aims and the structural changes required to attain them, what can we say, in general terms, about the rôle of capital formation in the development process? We may start from two limiting positions. At the Santa Margherita meeting of the International Economic Association, Professor Cairncross expressed, and elaborated, the view that in the light of the experience of the Victorian era, capital formation was a concomitant phenomenon of the process of economic growth and not a causal impelling factor. The driving forces of growth were technological innovations on the supply side and steadily widening markets on the demand side, which resulted in large business profits, which in turn financed capital formation. Professor Cairncross concluded, or, at any rate, came close to the conclusion, that the level of aggregate capital formation was not the key variable, perhaps not even one of the key variables determining the rate of economic growth, but that changes in productive efficiency, the compounded result of technological change, the growth of markets, and entrepreneurial ingenuity and daring, were responsible for the economic development of the period.

On the opposite extreme of the spectrum of views is the proposition that the rate of economic growth and development is uniquely determined by the level of new investment. It is not surprising that this view is expressed, with a frequency that

makes it monotonous, at international political conferences and meetings, in the debates of the United Nations and the Organization of American States, and in the various documents prepared for such conferences and debates. But it is surprising that in technical discussions and writings, in analytical models as well as in policy papers, the relationship between capital formation and economic development is stressed to the exclusion of all other causal factors and relations.

We submit that two issues must be distinguished—and kept apart. One is the problem of capital formation, to which we shall return later; the other is the meaning of the capital-output ratio. Professor Rosenstein-Rodan has pointed out that the marginal productivity of capital is a partial derivative, the supply of all factors other than capital remaining constant, while the marginal capital-output ratio is a full derivative, the supply of all factors other than capital being variable. In other words, the increase in total output associated with an addition to the stock of capital is determined not only by the amount of additional capital but also by additions of some other units—labour, land, technical skill, management. Only if it is assumed that the supply of these other factors is infinitely elastic, is the increase in output determined solely by the amount of additional capital. If we do not make this assumption—which gives us an analytical description of a limiting case—we become immediately concerned with the elasticity of supply of other factors or, more generally, with the responsiveness of other factors to economic incentives.

In recent years, a great deal of attention has been given to the supply of entrepreneurship as the strategic factor which, aside from capital, determines the rate of growth and development. Without in any way denying the importance of entrepreneurship, we suggest that the emphasis on

---

* From J. H. Adler and K. S. Krishnaswamy, "Comments on Professor Byé's Paper," in *Economic Development for Latin America*, Proceedings of a conference held by the International Economic Association, edited by H. S. Ellis, St. Martin's Press, New York, 1961, pp. 126-30. Reprinted by permission.

this single factor has led to a neglect of the analysis of the supply conditions of other factors. How does the subsistence farmer, whom we usually do not include in the entrepreneurial class, respond to higher prices of commodities which he *could* produce for the market? How does entrepreneurship enter into the picture if a large proportion of total saving accumulates in the hands of the government? Or conversely, what is the rôle of entrepreneurship if the most important factor limiting the development of a region is the lack of transportation facilities and the government does not have enough funds (capital) to build highways? Can entrepreneurship make up for lack of technical knowledge and productive skills?

These questions suggest that for an understanding of the process of development it is insufficient to concentrate on an analysis of entrepreneurship. It is essential to broaden the analysis into a more general enquiry into economic incentives and the response of various factors to them. It is equally necessary to determine—perhaps in general terms and perhaps case by case—under what institutional arrangements and under what economic and social conditions the supply of capital and entrepreneurship and technical skill can best be matched. There are numerous examples of economies where capital is held idle—for example, in the form of foreign balances—by a group of capitalists while entrepreneurial talent and technical skill go begging. There are cases in which capital and entrepreneurship are available but technical skills are lacking, or are so expensive as to make production unprofitable. Finally, there are instances in which both entrepreneurship and technical skills are available but capital is lacking.

Thus, the conceptual link between the marginal productivity of capital and the capital-output ratio is the fact that the magnitude of both depends on the supply of all other factors of production; the greater the supply, the higher the marginal productivity and the lower the capital-output ratio.

Limitations on the supply of factors other than capital explain, at least in part, a phenomenon which is characteristic of under-developed economies. On the one hand, we find that the return on capital in established enterprises is remarkably high —rates of return of 30 or even 50 per cent are frequently mentioned as typical of some economies. On the other hand, we find that the expected return on new ventures is low, or even negative. This apparent paradox can be explained only by the difference in the supply conditions of factors other than capital. Old enterprises have solved their supply problem. Knowledgeable management knows the conditions in the input and the output markets, it has been able to acquire the necessary labour skills, and it has found the right technology which permits that combination of inputs which corresponds to the price relations among inputs. All or most of these conditions are absent when it comes to the setting up of new enterprises. Management lacks experience and knowledge of the market, skilled labour is expensive or simply not available and therefore has to be trained, and the technology appropriate for the size of the market and for the supply conditions of the non-capital inputs is untried or has not even been invented. In technical terms, we could say that we are faced with a steeply down-sloping marginal productivity curve of capital, or a pronounced discontinuity. But the technical terms do not give an indication of the fact that this sharp drop in the productivity curve is due to the limitations on the supply of factors other than capital.

How does the argument so far developed affect the magnitudes of the marginal capital-output ratio? When we turn from the concept of marginal productivity to the capital-output ratio, we have to drop the assumption that the supply of all other factors is given and have to think in terms of a flow. As long as the rate of capital formation remains constant and the distribution of capital among its various uses remains the same, and there is a steady automatic growth in the supply of all other factors, we should expect the capital-output ratio to remain unchanged, or, if external economies make themselves felt, to decline gradually. If, however, the supply of capital expands suddenly—for instance, as an indirect result of a drastic improvement in the terms of trade, or because of a sudden increase in government revenues such as oil revenues—while the rate of supply of all other factors remains constant, the capital-output ratio is likely to increase because the efficiency of utilizing additional capital is bound to decline. Some capital is poorly used, or goes to waste, or remains idle, accumulating in the form of bank deposits or foreign balances.

If, on the other hand, the supply of factors other than capital increases more rapidly than the stock of capital, we should expect an improvement in the efficiency of the utilization of capital, and a decrease in the capital-output ratio. With management improving, labour becoming more efficient, and technical skills increasing, capital "goes further." Since the existing stock of capital is committed to particular uses, and is combined with other factors in rather inflexible proportions, an improvement in the supply conditions of the non-capital factors will be reflected primarily in the marginal capital-output ratio, the relation of new, additional capital to additional output. But there may be some improvement in the use of existing capital as well. As in the case of a sudden spurt in the supply of capital, an at least temporary oversupply of non-capital factors may occur. Entrepreneurship may be frustrated, and labour skills may go to waste.

The relationship between new capital and additional output is a complex relationship since it depends not only on the composition of investment, which may change over time and cause an increase or decrease in the capital-output ratio, but also on the supply of all non-capital factors. Given a certain rate of capital formation and, we may add, a certain state of technology, there is an appropriate, or optimum, flow in the supply of all non-capital factors of production which corresponds to it.

The preceding observations modify, but do not destroy, the emphasis which much of the literature has put on the rôle of the rate of capital formation as determining the rate of growth of total output. For it may still be argued that conditions in most under-developed countries today are such that the supply of non-capital factors is adequate to take care of a considerable increase in the rate of capital formation; or that an increase in the rate of capital formation is more difficult to bring about than an increase in the supply of the non-capital factors and therefore deserves most attention; or—and this seems to us to be the most pertinent argument—that we are dealing in reality with conditions of joint supply of capital and non-capital factors. Professor Cairncross has emphasized the fact that in the nineteenth century entrepreneurship provided its own capital by ploughing entrepreneurial income back into the economy. But just as entrepreneurship creates its own capital, the availability of additional capital permits the exploitation of economies of scale in larger productive units and the use of technological improvements. It also creates new markets for technical skills and managerial talent, and provides new opportunities for skilled and unskilled labour. An increase in the supply of one factor of production sets in motion a complex rearrangement of the flow of all other factors and brings about an increase in their supply.

This increase in the supply of non-capital factors is not automatic in the sense that economic policy can be concerned only with the rate of capital formation and that the supply of non-capital factors will take care of itself. But it is automatic in the sense in which the term is used in economic theory. An increase in the supply of capital brings into play new incentives and new market forces changing the demand for non-capital factors of production. It depends on the speed and intensity of the response on the supply side whether the flow of non-capital factors can be left alone, or whether some form of intervention is called for. It is impossible to generalize on this point. The conditions as to the responsiveness of the non-capital factors to economic incentives (that is, higher rewards or more demand at the existing level of rewards) differ from econonmy to economy, and, within each economy, from factor to factor. Where the response is spotty and sluggish, as, for instance, in societies in which the attractiveness of leisure is greater than the attractiveness of higher income, or where mobility is impeded by social and cultural institutions, intervention—in the form of measures to eliminate those impediments and to reinforce incentives—is called for. But whatever the specific shortage—of particular skills, of technical knowledge, of institutions to bring capital and entrepreneurial talent together—its elimination will in most instances result in an increase of output only if it is accompanied by an increased availability of capital.

1.4 CRITICISMS OF THE CAPITAL-OUTPUT RATIO—NOTE

A capital-output ratio is frequently employed to estimate the amount of investment needed to achieve a certain rate of growth in income. This was done explicitly in ECAFE's calculations of capital requirements (1.1) and implicitly by Professor Lewis (1.2). A definite causal relationship between the growth of capital and of output, however, cannot be as readily assumed as the foregoing selections would imply. And it is misleading to suppose that the whole of any increase in output is simply due to capital accumulation.

Many conceptual difficulties and statistical pitfalls surround the derivation and use of capital-output ratios. Even after it is decided which of the several possible definitions of "capital" and "output" are best to use, and some solution to the problem of valuation is accepted, there still remain ambiguities. It is first necessary to distinguish between the average and the marginal capital-output ratio. The average ratio is the value of the total stock of capital divided by total annual income; the marginal—or incremental—ratio for the entire economy is the value of the addition to capital (net investment) divided by the addition to income (net national income). The marginal ratio need not, of course, equal the average ratio, and even though any change in the average ratio may be expected to be slow, the marginal ratio can vary a great deal more.

In framing a development plan, it is common practice to calculate the amount of additional capital required to produce a one unit increase in annual output at the margin. For this purpose, a marginal capital-output ratio is used. Net investment is estimated over the plan-period; the increase in net output (or income) is estimated between the year before the plan-period and the last year of the plan. All measurements are made at the same price level. The use of a marginal capital-output ratio in this fashion has been inspired to a large extent by the Harrod-Domar theory of growth, which relates a country's rate of growth of income to its savings-income ratio and marginal capital-output ratio.[1] The Harrod-Domar analysis, however, relates to an advanced economy, and it seeks an answer to the question of how much national income would have to grow to induce sufficient investment to maintain this rate of growth in income. For a poor country, the relevant problem is not that of sustaining a certain rate of growth, but rather the prior task of initiating or generating a higher growth rate in the first place.

Moreover, it is important to be clear whether all other productive factors that must co-operate with capital are also assumed to increase when capital increases. In an advanced economy an adequate supply of co-operant factors is likely to exist. The institutional, political, and social prerequisites for development also already exist. When using the marginal capital-output ratio under these conditions, it is reasonable to make a *mutatis mutandis* assumption that the supply of other necessary factors is forthcoming. But in a poor country where the co-operant factors tend to be in short supply, and the other prerequisites for development may not yet exist, it is not legitimate to consider an increase in capital as a sufficient condition for an expansion in output. Even though investment may be a necessary condition, an increase in output may still not be produced unless other conditions are also fulfilled along with the increase in capital supply. Since an expansion in output depends on many factors of which capital

formation is only one, greater output may require changes in other factors along with an increase in capital. Or output may even increase independently of investment. Even if we accept the assumption that there is a fixed relationship between capital and output as determined by technical factors, it does not follow that we can infer from this relationship that only capital is needed to increase output. We must also consider explicitly the effect of other variables on output—for example, the supply of trained manpower, entrepreneurship, institutional arrangements, attitudes, etc. To ignore these other variables or simply to assume that accommodating changes occur, and then to attribute all of the output-increment to investment, is to take a too mechanical—and too easy—view of the changes that are necessary for an increase in output.

On the other hand, exclusive attention to a capital-output ratio may exaggerate the need for investment, in so far as output may be increased by changes in other factors without requiring a sizeable amount of investment, or even any additional capital. If, for instance, unutilized capacity exists, it is possible to raise output with the fuller utilization of the existing capital stock or without requiring much more capital. Or there may be considerable opportunity to raise output by applying better methods of production to existing plant. To avoid taking either an over-optimistic view of what can be accomplished by capital accumulation alone, or an over-pessimistic view of how much investment is needed, we should guard against a too simple use of capital-output ratios.

For the purpose of clearly recognizing the changing circumstances that may occur when additions to the capital stock are made, it is helpful to distinguish between the "net marginal capital-output ratio" and the "adjusted marginal capital-

1. Evsey Domar, "Expansion and Employment," *American Economic Review*, March 1947, pp. 34-5; "The Problem of Capital Formation," *American Economic Review*, December 1948, pp. 777-94; "Economic Growth: An Econometric Approach," *American Economic Review, Papers and Proceedings*, May 1952, pp. 479-95; R. F. Harrod, "An Essay in Dynamic Theory," *Economic Journal*, March 1939, pp. 14-33; *Towards a Dynamic Economics*, London, 1948; W. J. Baumol, *Economic Dynamics*, New York, 1951, Chap. 4.

output ratio."[2] The net ratio interprets the marginal capital-output ratio as net of any changes in other factors; it considers the capital-output ratio with a *ceteris paribus* assumption—the supplies of all other factors are held constant. The adjusted ratio, however, refers to what the capital-output ratio would be if it were adjusted to a given specific increase in the supply of other factors; it assumes that investment is accompanied by changes in other output-yielding variables. For a given increment in output, the net marginal capital-output ratio is higher than the adjusted marginal capital-output ratio. Capital requirements will therefore be underestimated if they are initially based on an adjusted marginal capital-output ratio, but the other output-yielding factors do not actually accommodate themselves to the growth of capital as expected.

In calculating capital requirements, a development plan usually concentrates on an overall or global capital-output ratio for the entire economy. But this ratio depends on capital-output ratios in the various sectors of the economy, with the overall ratio being an average of the sectoral ratios, weighted by the increases in sectoral outputs. Since the over-all ratio will be affected by the changing composition of output and investment among the several sectors, it is essential to analyze the capital-output relationships at the sectoral level.

Recognizing the problems raised above, W. B. Reddaway has offered a summary of what needs clarification when considering a marginal capital-output ratio for a sector. He states that it would be desirable to divide the increase in output for a sector between two dates into these components:[3]

Output

i. Increase due to better methods applied to old plant, involving little or no net capital expenditure (called P for progress).

ii. Changes due to fuller (or lower) utilization of old plant, as a reflection of changes in demand (called D).

iii. Changes due to introduction of double-shifts, etc. (S).

iv. Changes due to better weather (W).

v. Changes of the kind for which a certain relationship between capital and output may reasonably be assumed as "given" by technical factors—at least if we assume a fixed number of shifts, fairly full utilization, and no shortage of labour; the bringing into use of new steel mills is a good example. If the capital cost of these is x and the capital-output ratio in a new mill is r, then the increase in annual output $= x/r$.

Investment

Investment in the period will consist of x, plus any capital expenditure designed to save labour without increasing output (M for "modernization") and plus (or minus) an adjustment for the difference between expenditure on construction in the period and completion (L for "lag").

Observed Capital-Output Ratio

If we work from historical statistics (or from figures for future years included in a plan) the traditional marginal capital-output ratio for a sector is then equal to

$$\frac{x + M + L}{\dfrac{x}{r} + P + D + S + W}$$

If we consider only the first term in the numerator and the first term in the denominator—ignoring changes in M, L, P, D, S, and W—we are then using the capital-output ratio in an oversimplified way. Only if these other changes are small relatively to x and x/r can the marginal capital-output ratio be considered approximately equal to r. But this is to treat the ratio as if it were simply a technical relationship applicable to a new plant; in

2. Such a distinction is suggested by Harvey Leibenstein, *Economic Backwardness and Economic Growth*, New York, 1957, p. 178.

3. W. B. Reddaway, *The Development of the Indian Economy*, Homewood, 1962, pp. 207-8.

practice, the actual ratio is likely to differ from r, depending on the values of the other terms in the above ratio.[4] Although M, D, S, and W may be relatively small, P will not be insignificant if there are large opportunities for increasing output by methods which involve negligible amounts of investment, and L will not be small if much of the period's investment goes into projects that are not completed during the period. When P is significant, the observed marginal capital-output ratio will be lower than if simply r is estimated; and when L is significant, because new investment projects take a long time to complete and considerable construction is started in the period, then the observed ratio will be higher than simply r. These considerations caution us against assuming that the marginal capital-output ratio is constant, even at the sectoral level.

At the aggregate level, the difficulties are compounded. Even in the simplest (but most special) of cases—namely, production coefficients fixed in all sectors and relatively small values for all the other variables that might affect output—the over-all marginal capital-output ratio will still not be fixed, since sectoral output may vary with changes in demand. More generally, the over-all ratio will vary according to a number of conditions, some of which may allow only a small additional income to be generated when more capital is accumulated, while others may contribute to a large increment in output. Thus, the following conditions will tend to make the capital-output ratio high: the sectoral pattern of investment is biased toward heavy users of capital, such as public utilities, public works, housing, industry rather than agriculture, and heavy industry rather than light industry; there is excess capacity in the utilization of capital; other resources are limited, and capital is substi-

tuted for these limitational factors; capital is long-lived; the rate of technological and organizational progress is low; and investment is for completely new units of production rather than simply for extensions of existing plant.

In contrast, the marginal capital-output ratio will be lower when the composition of output is biased toward labor-intensive commodities, the average life of capital is shorter, the rate of technological and organizational progress is high, and when some capital expenditure allows fuller use of previously unutilized capacity, increases the productivity of labor, allows capital-saving innovations, opens up new natural resources, or permits the realization of economies of scale.

From such considerations, we must conclude that the marginal capital-output ratio is unlikely to be constant over time. A projected ratio must be estimated over the period for which investment requirements are being calculated, and it may then turn out that there is a wide discrepancy between the actual ratio and the projected ratio.

1.5 THE PLACE OF CAPITAL IN ECONOMIC PROGRESS *

Capital occupies a position so dominant in the economic theory of production and distribution that it is natural to assume that it should occupy an equally important place in the theory of economic growth. In most of the recent writings of economists, whether they approach the subject historically (e.g. in an attempt to explain how the industrial revolution started) or analytically (e.g. in models of an expand-

4. *Ibid.*, pp. 208-9.

* From A. K. Cairncross, "The Place of Capital in Economic Progress," in *Economic Progress,* edited by L. H. Dupriez, Papers and Proceedings of a Round Table held by the International Economic Association, Louvain, 1955, pp. 235, 236-7, 245-8; Cairncross, *Factors in Economic Development,* George Allen and Unwin, London, 1962, pp. 111-14. Reprinted by permission.

ing economy) or from the side of policy (e.g. in the hope of accelerating the development of backward countries), it is the process of capital accumulation that occupies the front of the stage. There is an unstated assumption that growth hinges on capital accumulation, and that additional capital would either provoke or facilitate a more rapid rate of economic development even in circumstances which no one would describe as involving a shortage of capital.

Yet there seems no reason to suppose that capital accumulation does by itself exercise so predominant an influence on economic development. In most industrialized communities the rate of capital accumulation out of savings is equal to about 10 per cent of income. If one were to assume that innovation came to a standstill and that additional investment could nevertheless yield an average return of 5 per cent, the consequential rate of increase in the national income would normally be no more than ½ per cent per annum. We are told that the national income has in fact been rising in such communities at a rate of 2–3 per cent per annum. On this showing, capital accumulation could account for, at most, one-quarter of the recorded rate of economic "progress." Nor were things very different in the nineteenth century. . . .

Even this way of putting things exaggerates the rôle of capital in economic development. For the yield on additional capital would rarely be as high as 5 per cent if there were not a discrepancy between the existing stock of capital and the stock appropriate to the existing state of technique. If innovation in the broadest sense of the term were at a standstill, accumulation would continue until the rate of interest fell to a point at which saving ceased. The sole object of accumulation in those circumstances would be to take advantage of the progressive cheapening of

capital in order to introduce more roundabout methods of production, not to keep pace with current developments in technique. Ordinary observation suggests, however, that the scope for investment *in industry* to take advantage merely of lower rates of interest, once the long-term rate is below 5 per cent, is extremely limited, although there may be a good deal more scope in other directions where capital charges form an unusually high proportion of the final cost (e.g. in the erection of dwelling-houses, public buildings and the like).

The contribution of capital to economic progress is not, however, confined to the usufruct of additional capital assets, similar to those already in existence. It embraces three distinct processes. First, a greater abundance of capital permits the introduction of more roundabout methods of production or, to be more precise, of a more roundabout pattern of consumption. This covers the freer use of capital instruments in the production of a given product, the use of more durable instruments, and a change in the pattern of consumption in favour of goods and services with relatively high capital charges per unit cost. Secondly, the accumulation of capital is a normal feature of economic expansion, however originating. This is the process normally referred to as widening, as opposed to deepening, the structure of production. It may accompany industrialization, or any change in the balance between industries that makes additional demands on capital; or it may accompany an extension of the market associated with population growth, more favourable terms of trade, or the discovery of additional natural resources. Thirdly, additional capital may be required to allow technical progress to take place. It may either finance the discovery of what was not known before or more commonly, the adaptation of existing knowledge so as to allow of its commercial exploitation through some innovation in product, process or material.

Now of these three, the first is generally of subordinate importance; it is unusual for capital accumulation, unassisted by other factors, to bring about a rapid increase in income. The second, which also abstracts from any change in technology, accounts for nearly all the capital accumulation that has taken place in the past; forces making for rapid increase in income may be largely nullified unless they are reinforced by a parallel increase in capital. It is to the third, however, that one must usually look—at least in an advanced industrial country—for the main influences governing the rate of growth of real income per head. Whatever may have been true in the past, it is now technical innovation—the introduction of new and cheaper ways of doing things—that dominates economic progress. Whether technical innovation, in the sectors of the economy in which it occurs, makes large demands on capital is, however, very doubtful. Many innovations can be given effect to in the course of capital replacement out of depreciation allowances, which, in an expanding economy, may be fully as large as net savings. Others may actually reduce the stock of capital required. Existing buildings and existing machines can often be modified so as to allow most of the advantages of the new techniques to be gained. It is economic expansion, far more than technological change, that is costly in capital.

...

Given that the national income is increasing, whether under the influence of technical progress, population growth, or some other factor, there is good reason to expect that additional capital will be required in some important sectors on a comparable scale. Habits of thrift—a phrase that must now be stretched to include not only the practices of corporations in adding to reserves but the propensities of Finance Ministers—appear to admit of capital accumulation at a rate of about 2½ per cent per annum, and this has in recent years been close to the rate of growth of income. Provided, therefore, that the capital requirements of industry—the main sector left out of account—are also increasing at this rate, the capital-income ratio will remain constant and the whole of the country's thrift will be effectively mobilized. There can be no guarantee however, that industry's requirements will in fact mount at this rate, even in the long run. In the short run, for reasons that are familiar, the whole process of capital accumulation may be thrown out of gear.

Now the significant feature of this argument is that it hinges far more on the indirect than on the direct demand for capital. It assumes that technical progress operates largely in independence of capital accumulation and that capital is needed, not in order to allow innovations to be made but in order to consolidate the improvements in income that innovation brings about. Moreover, it implies that if, at any time, the process of innovation creates a bulge in the demand for capital, it should be possible to adapt the pattern of investment so as to accommodate the high-yielding requirements of industry by displacing part of the larger, but less remunerative, requirements of house-building, stock-building, and so forth.

It is hardly necessary to show that this implication may be mistaken. Public policy may maintain the demand for capital in the sectors capable of compression or the capital market may be so organized that industry is unable to draw capital from the sources that finance other forms of accumulation. But unless the bulge is a very large and consistent one it is doubtful whether innovation need suffer greatly.

The effect of technical progress is generally to widen the divergence between the actual stock of capital and the stock consistent with the full exploitation of current worker opportunities. Some part of the additional capital will be needed to finance the innovations in the sectors of the economy in which they arise; some will be linked with the innovations directly, either because associated industries are offered a wider market or because social capital has to be provided in an area where it has become insufficient; some will be linked indirectly, in the way already outlined, because the increased expenditure of consumers will give rise to a derived demand for capital. Now it is common to find that, particularly with a major advance in technique, the influence which it exerts on the scope for eventual capital accumulation is far more profound than its immediate impact on the current flow of capital formation. There is generally a chain reaction, strung out through time, one physical asset being wanted only after another has been created. Although the full consequences may be entirely foreseeable, development does not work up to its full momentum until a whole series of changes have occurred: an extension of capacity here, an application of the new technique there; a shift of location in one industry, a building up of new attitudes in another. The introduction of the steam engine, for example, brought into existence a large reservoir of projects that trickled out into capital formation all through the nineteenth century: the stock of capital appropriate to existing technique was far above the existing stock both because the steam engine was capable of wide application and because many industries that themselves made no use of it (such as bridge-building) were transformed in scale or (like agriculture and many pursuits ancillary to it) in location.

Moreover, because the chain reaction takes time and the innovation is, *ex hypothesi*, a profitable one, the process is to a large extent self-financing. If there is a spate of such innovations, interest and profits are likely to show some response and a corresponding shift in the ratio of savings to income will ease the heavier burden of finance. It may happen, however, that the situation is not regulated in this way: interest rates may be sticky upwards as well as downwards. The probable outcome will then be a series of spurts in investment, followed by periods of indigestion....

A variant of this situation is one in which there has been a considerable lag behind the known opportunities for the fruitful use of capital at existing rates of interest. A country may fail to make use of technical knowledge available elsewhere and suddenly become alive to the possibilities of applying that knowledge. At that stage its capital requirements will increase discontinuously and the additional capital which it requires before bumping up against the limits of technical advance may be very large. It appears to be this situation that is in the minds of those who assume that the injection of additional capital into a country's economy will almost automatically speed up its economic progress. Sometimes the argument is framed more specifically in terms of a shift of employment from agriculture to industry, with a large net gain in productivity from the shift, and the large capital investment needed to accomplish it operating as a brake.

This is a complex situation and it may exist in some underdeveloped countries. But it is by no means obvious that additional capital, whether borrowed from abroad or accumulated through the exertions of surplus labour in the countryside, would by itself suffice to start off a cycle of industrialization. The problem is often one of organization quite as much as of capital creation: of training managements and men; of creating new attitudes towards industrial employment; of taking advantage of innovations that need little capital and using the resulting gains to finance investment elsewhere.

On the whole, there is a greater danger that the importance of capital in relation to economic progress will be exaggerated than that it will be underrated. How many successful firms, looking back over their history, would single out difficulty of access to new capital as the major obstacle, not to their growth, but to the adoption of the most up-to-date technique? How many countries in the van of technical progress have found themselves obliged to borrow abroad? It is where there has been a lag, where technical progress has been too slow, that capital is called upon to put matters right. No doubt where capital is plentiful, more risks can be taken and development is speeded up, so that rapid development and rapid capital accumulation go together. But the most powerful influence governing development, even now, is not the rate of interest or the abundance of capital; and the most powerful influence governing capital accumulation, even now, is not technical progress.

...

There is general agreement that, in all countries, the process of economic growth and capital accumulation are closely interconnected. It was in terms of this interconnection that the earliest theories of economic development were formulated; and in the work of modern economists, output is still assumed to be limited by capital, whether there is abundant labour or not. A high rate of capital formation usually accompanies a rapid growth in productivity and income; but the causal relationship between the two is complex and does not permit of any facile assumption that more capital formation will of itself bring about a corresponding acceleration in the growth of production.

In industrial countries this is only too obvious. Capital formation may assume forms, such as house-building or an addition to liquid stocks, that are unlikely to add very perceptibly to productivity although they may yield a sufficient return to make them worth while. If all capital formation were of this character, or represented an enlargement of the capital stock with assets broadly similar to those already in existence, it would be hard to account for the rates of growth actually recorded. A moment's reflection will show that even an average return of 10 per cent to capital in a country saving 10 per cent of its income annually would raise income by no more than 1 per cent per annum.[1] Similarly, efforts to impute the recorded expansion in industrial production to the additional labour and capital contributing to it invariably leave a large unexplained residue.[2] It is necessary, therefore, to take account of other influences, such as technical progress and improvements in social and economic organization, which may operate through investment, or independently of it, so as to raise the level of production. These influences, if they take effect uniformly throughout the economy in competitive conditions, will tend to swell the national income without raising the average return to capital, the extra output slipping through to the consumer, the wage-earner or the government.

How far it is correct to attribute an expansion in output to high investment, when high investment is only one of the

1. This point is developed in my "Reflections on the Growth of Capital and Income" (*Scottish Journal of Political Economy*, June 1959). See also the comments by E. Lundberg, "The Profitability of Investment" (*Economic Journal*, December 1959).

2. See, for example, W. B. Reddaway and A. D. Smith, "Progress in British Manufacturing Industries in the Period 1948-54" (*Economic Journal*, March 1960) and O. Aukrust, "Investment and Economic Growth," *Productivity Measurement Review*, February 1959.

factors at work is necessarily debatable. It would certainly be legitimate if capital formation was lagging behind, and finance could be identified as a bottleneck in the process of expansion. It might also happen that the rate of technical advance was itself controlled by the scale of investment, not merely because capital formation was the means by which new techniques were adopted but also because high investment created an atmosphere favourable to experimentation and innovation. There is undoubtedly some tendency for all the symptoms of rapid growth to show themselves simultaneously. But there is no invariable dependence of growth on a high rate of capital formation and it is easy to imagine circumstances in which efforts to increase capital formation may actually slow down the progress of the economy.[3]

Moreover there is some justification for turning the causal relationship the other way round. If income is growing fast, investment opportunities are likely to be expanding correspondingly fast, so that the growth in income draws capital accumulation along behind it. The biggest single influence on capital formation is market opportunity, and many types of capital accumulation are likely to be embarked upon only when income is booming. If capital formation does not respond, its failure to do so will certainly act as a drag on the expansion in output. But there is no reason why it should bring it to a halt, and, given a re-arrangement of the investment pattern, income might grow a long way before the shortage of capital became acute. In the meantime the rapid growth in income, particularly if it were accompanied by high profits, would be likely to generate additional savings and so mitigate any symptoms of capital shortage that manifested themselves.

3. The ground-nuts scheme in Tanganyika is an extreme example.

All this presupposes that a spurt in income could precede an acceleration of investment, and that capital formation is subordinate to other elements in the process of growth. These suppositions are not altogether extravagant. Technical progress does not always involve high net investment: indeed it may permit of a *reduction* in the stock of capital or an expansion in output without any comparable investment. A change in the pattern of investment could also, by enforcing the continued use or overloading of old types of plant, make possible a far more rapid construction of those newer types which bear the fruits of technical progress in greatest abundance.

Attempts are sometimes made to settle the issue by citing the apparent constancy of the capital-income ratio and deducing from this the "neutrality" of technical progress. But the capital-income ratio is affected by many things other than technical progress: the distribution of consumers' expenditure between capital-intensive and labour-intensive products; indivisibilities in past investment—for example, in the transport and communication network; changes in the pattern of trade; investment in social assets such as roads, schools, and hospitals to which no income is imputed; and so on. Even if these influences, too, are neutral and if the capital-income ratio does remain constant—and neither of these assumptions seems well-founded—the fact that capital and income grow at the same rate tells us nothing about the causes of growth in either. There is no reason at all why one should rule out the suggestion that the same circumstances that favour rapid growth of income are also favourable to a rapid growth of investment.

This may seem a rather arid and irrelevant issue: arid, because if capital requirements must keep pace with the growth of income that is all we need to know for practical purposes; irrelevant, because the issue relates to experiences in industrial rather than pre-industrial countries. But when it is so commonly urged that countries will be able to take-off if only they are provided with sufficient capital from outside, the issue seems neither arid nor irrelevant. For this thesis assumes the very causal relationship that is in dispute.

1.6 CAPITAL AND DEVELOPMENT *

To regard the investment of capital as leading automatically to that net increase in the value of the capital which increase can be detached as "income," is a common fallacy. The symbolism of accounting is a device to assist the making of choices; but no amount of calculation guarantees the result.

The accumulation of capital was never regarded in the nineteenth century, as it now frequently is, as the necessary consequence merely of an "investment" decision. The accumulation of capital was not regarded as necessarily consequent upon, and as automatically resulting from the exercise of individual or social *will*. On the contrary, as the common tongue of enterprise clearly shows, the success of "venture" capital was regarded, and rightly regarded, as having much to do with "good fortune," "wise-choices," the correct "embarking" of capital in the "right" directions, at the "right" time. It was seen to be a matter of "patience," "waiting," "flexibility," "adaptability," "experience," "growth," and as dependent upon the "character" of the entrepreneur, his "intuition" and "experience," his "connexions," "goodwill," his courage in meeting "unforeseen circumstances," and his "foresight" in being able to ally himself with the new opportunities, innovations and resources which would yield the "quasi-rents" of new endeavours.

* From S. Herbert Frankel, *The Economic Impact of Under-Developed Societies*, Basil Blackwell, Oxford, 1953, pp. 67, 69, 76-9. Reprinted by permission.

Much confusion has resulted from the fact that the large volume of fixed-interest bearing securities issued by modern governments (mainly for purposes of war finance) led to the belief that investment was something which automatically yielded income. Thus it became fashionable to speak as if (and for some apparently even to believe that) capital *necessarily generates* income of itself; both "capital" and "income" came to be regarded as "abstract," functionally related, entities....

Capital, it cannot be emphasized too strongly, is, apart from the symbolism of accounting, always "concrete" in the sense that it is embedded in, and attuned to, the particular purposes and state of knowledge which led to its "creation." It is but temporarily incorporated in ever changing forms and patterns suited to the evanescent ends for which it is designed. It is a social heritage dependent upon the institutions and habit-patterns of thought and action of individuals in society. In the last resort, it dissolves always into its basic element: the action of man's labour upon the natural environment. That is why capital cannot be "stored-up" for long; nor can it be "transferred" from one situation to another without the individuals who will re-adapt and "re-fashion" it for use in a new pattern of activity. For no two situations, no two regions, no two societies, no two problems of choice, in time, or place, are alike. In this sense capital is like technical "know-how," which also does not exist in the abstract ready to be applied to any new situation. To transfer "know-how" is not to apply something which is known. It is to apply new ways of thinking to find out what is not known: as when research is undertaken to develop new crops; discover the nature of soils; prospect for minerals; adapt old aptitudes to new skills; and perfect machines for new tasks. It is because existing forms in which knowledge i. e. capital, is incorporated are no longer suitable that the old has constantly to be re-fashioned anew in attempts to meet the future. Capital is, as has been said repeatedly, a means of saving time; but it is only possible to save time if one can discover the purpose to which one will devote it. . . .

It is because in the last resort the misuse of capital resources is always a loss of alternative opportunities that action which wastes the scarce capital resources of the world is eventually harmful for lenders and borrowers alike.

The problems of the borrowers are not solved by the receipt of capital which leads to the adoption of an economic pattern which is not income-creating or is incapable of relatively permanent integration into the economic structure into which it is imported. Such injections of capital disrupt the existing but do not rebuild new and continuing patterns of economic behavior. Such capital imports may in certain cases only postpone the need for meeting the real problem of the economy as long as the capital lasts. The problems of the lending countries can also not be solved by perpetuating patterns of behavior which are socially, psychologically and economically so unstable that the *raison d'être* for the supply of capital comes to consist in little more than the distribution of unearned largesse to others. There is no limit to the demands for "capital" which will be made by the recipients or prospective recipients of it on these terms; whereas the amount of capital which can be created by any society, however productive, is not similarly infinite.

I can conceive of no more dangerous illusion at the present conjuncture of world affairs than the facile belief that we have "solved" the problem of capital accumulation, and that the problem is now not how to produce capital but to whom to give it. The truth is that capital is relatively scarcer and "time" more pressing

than perhaps ever before in the context of the world changes with which we are confronted. The uncertainty engendered by the present international disruption and tension; the heavy demands on the world's resources for coping with the aftermath of two world wars; and the cost of defence to ward off the third world war, all reduce the relative amount of capital available for continuous economic growth. Moreover we are experiencing a period of great technical and scientific transition which threatens a large portion of the capital resources and "social heritage" of both the developed and under-developed areas of the world with obsolescence. The advance in public hygiene and social medicine by lowering death rates is engendering a vast increase in the population of many regions which, in relation to their existing patterns of economic and social action, are already over-populated. This further intensifies the demand for capital for new forms and techniques of production.

All these changes expose to view the inadequate amount of administrative experience and skill necessary to cope with the new challenge to man's individual and social ingenuity. It leads to the feeling that "time" is "running out"; that it is insufficient to cope with all these problems by "waiting" for new institutions, new aptitudes, new skills to *grow*. In the last resort this may lead to counsels of despair such as those which urge "catastrophic" solutions for these problems; which wish to take "time by the forelock" by "spending" capital recklessly to stem the tide; and which are even prepared, if capital in material terms is not available, to expend human lives without mercy to "create" it, quite overlooking that so to degrade man is not a means consistent with the alleged use of capital to uplift him.

Neither the mere "expenditure" of capital nor the application of force can solve the real problems of our time. We are faced not with problems of "spending" capital; but of "investing" it in those multitudinous personal and social forms which can grow only in conjunction with the always unique social heritage of different individuals and societies.

The problem is, indeed as it always has been, how to "husband" resources in the widest sense of the word. It is how to invest those limited supplies of the world's capital so as to ensure that the "borrower" of it will put it to use in such directions as will most readily and in the *relatively least period of time* release new capital resources for coping with the problems arising out of the overall scarcity.

The real problem confronting the "under-developed" countries of the world is therefore not only how to economize in the use of foreign capital, but how to utilize all capital—the very social indigenous heritage itself—to achieve new goals of social action with the *least* unnecessary or premature social disintegration and disharmony.

There is, as I have already suggested, an alternative to such strict social economy concerned to foster the irritatingly slow but relatively more harmonious changes involved in the *growth* of new human aptitudes, experiences and purposes. It is the alternative which involves the sacrifice of men and women to-day in order to construct rapidly that which it is *hoped*, or *alleged*, will ease the life of *others* to-morrow. The line between "capital" as the servant and as the idol of the fuller life is narrower than we are apt to think.

It is the realization that true economic growth is a many-sided individual and social process which I believe is the most important lesson of past attempts to link under-developed territories and peoples into a wider world economy. It consists in the re-fashioning of aptitudes, and beliefs of individuals to give them new freedom in their multitudinous daily tasks—many of them not assessable in accounting or financial terms. Once this is realized we will perhaps hear less of attempts to reduce "consumption," increase "saving" and force home and foreign "investment" in under-developed societies. The real task is not to force change but to induce it in a manner which will be meaningful to the members of the societies it affects.

2. SOURCES OF CAPITAL FORMATION—NOTE

The process of capital formation involves three steps: (1) an increase in the volume of real savings, so that resources can be released for investment purposes; (2) the channeling of savings through a finance and credit mechanism, so that investible funds can be collected from a wide range of different sources and claimed by investors; and (3) the act of investment itself, by which resources are used for increasing the capital stock.

The first requirement—an increase in the volume of real savings—is of fundamental importance if a higher rate of investment is to be achieved without generating inflation. This crucial step of mobilizing savings should not be confused, however, with the monetary financing of investment. The significance of financial institutions lies in their making available the means to utilize savings. As one study of the role of financial institutions concludes:

However poor an economy may be there will be a need for institutions which allow such savings as are currently forthcoming to be invested conveniently and safely, and which ensure that they are channelled into the most useful purposes. The poorer a country is, in fact, the greater is the need for agencies to collect and invest the savings of the broad mass of persons and institutions within its borders. Such agencies will not only permit small amounts of savings to be handled and invested conveniently but will allow the owners of savings to retain liquidity individually but finance long-term investment collectively.[1]

Although the existence of a more developed capital market and financial intermediaries will aid in the collection and distribution of investible funds, they in no way lessen the need for real saving. The rate of investment which it is physically possible to carry out is limited by saving, and a "shortage of capital"—in the sense of a shortage of real resources available for investment purposes—cannot be solved merely by increasing the supply of finance. Indeed, it is comparatively easy to introduce institutional arrangements to increase the supply of finance, and a lack of finance need not persist as a serious bottleneck. Once a sizeable class of savers and borrowers come into being, financial intermediaries are likely to appear, and lending institutions are readily created. But the creation of new financial institutions is no substitute for the necessary performance of real saving.

It is therefore important to be clear on the various sources from which the necessary savings can be mobilized to provide the wherewithal for capital expenditure. From internal sources, an increase of savings may be generated voluntarily through a reduction in consumption; involuntarily

through additional taxation, compulsory lending to the government, or inflation; or, finally, by the absorption of underemployed labor into productive work. From external sources, the financing of development may be met by the investment of foreign capital, restriction of consumption imports, or an improvement in the country's terms of trade.

An increase in voluntary saving through a self-imposed cut in current consumption is unlikely when the average income is so low. At best, it can be hoped that when income rises, the marginal rate of saving may be greater than the average rate. Instead of relying on voluntary saving, the government will normally have to resort to "forced" saving through taxation, compulsory lending, or credit expansion. The efficacy of credit expansion and its resultant inflationary consequences are discussed in the next chapter. As for taxation, the country's "taxation potential" depends upon a variety of conditions—the level of per capita real income, the degree of inequality in the distribution of income, the structure of the economy, the political leadership and administrative powers of the government. It is generally true in underdeveloped countries that the actual ratio of tax revenue to national income is at present less than the tax potential. The potential can be more fully exploited, especially if the increase in taxation is undertaken gradually over a number of years. The saving that is forced by additional taxation, however, is likely to be less than the aditional tax revenue, since there may be a reduction in private voluntary saving instead of a fall in consumption by the full amount of the tax. Nonetheless, an increase in taxation remains the most expeditious way of meeting a rise in capital expenditure. There is only narrow scope in a poor country for the practice of compulsory saving through the practice of compulsory purchase of non-negotiable govern-

1. Edward Nevin, *Capital Funds in Underdeveloped Countries*, London, 1961, p. 75. For a more thorough discussion of the role of financial institutions, see United Nations, *Methods of Financing Economic Development in Underdeveloped Countries*, New York, 1949; W. Diamond, *Development Banks*, Baltimore, 1957; Shirley Boskey, *Problems and Practices of Development Banks*, Baltimore, 1959; United Nations, ECAFE, "Mobilisation of Domestic Resources for Economic Development and the Financial Institutions in the ECAFE Region," *Economic Bulletin for Asia and the Far East*, August 1950.

ment bonds. Of greater practical significance may be the operation of state marketing boards which have a statutory monopoly over export crops. These boards may
compel native producers to save by purchasing the native's produce at prices below
world prices.

Finally, another internal source of saving is represented by the "investible surplus" of underemployed labor. If this
"investible surplus" is utilized in productive activity, the national output would be
increased, and the required savings might
be generated from the additional output.
It should also be noted that the direct formation of capital through the use of underemployed labor can be obtained by what
is termed the "unit multiplier" method.[2]
If labor does have zero productivity in
agriculture, it can be withdrawn and put
to work on investment projects (construction, irrigation works, road building, etc.)
without a drop in agricultural output.
Most of the payment of the additional
wages will be directed towards foodstuffs,
and agricultural income will rise. The
higher income may then be taxed, and the
tax revenue can finance the investment
project. If taxes are levied in an amount
equivalent to the additional wage-bill,
there will be no change in consumption but
income will have risen by the amount of
the investment. When the investment projects are completed there will be an
increase in output, and some of this
increase in income may also be captured
through taxation. How much scope there
is for this method of direct investment in
kind depends upon the ease with which
labor can be attracted to investment projects, the degree to which labor can form
capital directly without requiring additional investment expenditure, the absence

of an adverse effect on agricultural output,
and the capacity to offset the investment
with taxation. We shall consider more
thoroughly the general problem of taxation in section 3 of this chapter.

When we look to external sources of
financing development, the capital assistance provided by foreign economic aid and
the private investment of foreign capital
are of most importance. Section 4 of this
chapter examines the contribution of foreign aid, and section 5 focuses on private
foreign investment. Some contribution
may also come from a restriction of consumption imports. Provided that there is
not simply a switch in expenditure from
imports to domestic consumption, the level
of savings will then rise. Imports of capital
goods can then be increased, and this will
represent a genuine addition to the rate of
capital formation: the increase in the flow
of investment goods imported is, in this
case, matched by an increase in the flow of
domestic income saved. If, however, consumers increase their domestic spending
when they can not import, then resources
will be diverted from domestic capital production in favor of the increased domestic
consumer spending, and the increase in
imports of investment goods will be offset
by reduced domestic investment. An increase in saving is therefore necessary if
the restriction of consumption imports is
to result in an increase in total net capital
formation.[3]

A similar analysis applies to changes in
the terms of trade. When export prices
rise, the improvement in the country's
commodity terms of trade makes it possible
for the country to import larger quantities
of capital goods. But again, this source of
capital formation will not be fully exploited unless the increment in domestic money
income due to the increase in export pro-

2. James S. Duesenberry, "Some Aspects of the
Theory of Economic Development," *Explorations
in Entrepreneurial History*, Vol. III, No. 2, pp.
65-7.

3. Cf. Ragnar Nurske, *Problems of Capital Formation in Underdeveloped Countries*, Oxford,
1953, pp. 111-16.

ceeds is saved. If the extra income merely increases consumer spending on home produced or imported goods, the opportunity for new saving is lost. The extra resources made available by the improvement in the terms of trade must be withheld from consumption and directed into investment.[4] Either a corresponding increase in voluntary saving or in taxation is necessary to give the country a command over additional imports of investment goods.

4. *Ibid.*, pp. 97-103.

3. THE GOVERNMENT AS SAVER

3.1 TAXATION IN UNDERDEVELOPED COUNTRIES *

The problem of capital formation in the underdeveloped economies, as it confronts public finance, breaks down into three main parts. The first concerns the financing of social overhead investment which must be undertaken directly by government. The second deals with an intermediate zone in which the actual investment projects are in private hands but the funds are made available through government finance. The third deals with the necessary incentives to private investment, both domestic and foreign, as they are influenced by taxation and other fiscal measures. In all three categories, government effort is directed toward maximizing savings, mobilizing them for productive investment, and canalizing them so as to serve the purposes of a balanced development program.

. . .

The pressing need for large government outlays for economic development strongly influences the approach to the problem of determining the appropriate level of taxation in an underdeveloped country. In a highly developed economy, tax policy tends to accept the level of expenditures as its revenue goal (modified,

* From Walter W. Heller, "Fiscal Policies for Underdeveloped Economies," in *Conference on Agricultural Taxation and Economic Development,* edited by Haskell P. Wald, International Program in Taxation, Harvard Law School, Cambridge, 1954, pp. 63-4, 66-8, 81-5. Reprinted by permission.

of course, by considerations relating to the levels of employment, prices, and economic activity). The sequence of decision tends to run from expenditures to taxes. But in underdeveloped countries the level of expenditures depends much more heavily on the ability of the tax system to place the required revenues at the disposal of the government. By the same token, the size of the government's development program depends in large part on the economic and administrative capacity of its tax system to marshal the necessary resources. In this sense, the sequence of decision tends to run from taxation to expenditures.

Recognizing the strategic importance of an adequate flow of tax revenue—and the inadequacy of their own revenues—the governments of many developing countries have sought to increase the proportion of national income collected in taxes. Much of the increased demand for technical assistance in fiscal matters since World War II apparently grows out of this desire for a more productive tax system. Underdeveloped countries are under no illusion that they can—or should—push their tax ratios of 10 to 15 per cent of national income to the 30 to 40 per cent levels reached in such advanced countries as Austria, Belgium, France, Germany, the Netherlands, Norway, the United Kingdom, and the United States. But they are aware that even a modest increase in taxation may be able to finance a large percentage increase in a government's contribution to the development program. A country in which the share of the government sector in the gross national product is 12 per cent may be taken as fairly typical of low-income countries. If one assumes that not more than one-third of the government's share is devoted to economic development, an increase of only 2 percentage points in the ratio of taxes to national income (to 14 per cent) would enable the government to increase its contribution to development expenditures by 50 per cent.

Does experience or informed judgment provide any reliable guide as to what level of taxation is appropriate for an underdeveloped economy? Experience shows, first, that the less advanced the economy of a country, generally, the lower the ratio of tax payments to national income. It shows, second, that through intensive administrative and legislative efforts (and in some cases, aided by favorable international market conditions or by foreign aid), quite a few less advanced countries have considerably increased their ratios in post-war years....

The judgment of technical assistance experts in public finance, as reflected in their mission reports and other writings, appears to be that most underdeveloped countries could increase the proportion of their national income taken by taxation without unduly disturbing the economy and perhaps even with positive gains in the face of inflationary pressures. Yet where the optimum level lies permits of no doctrinaire answer. It will differ from country to country depending on the preferences of citizens, the administrative competence in government, the relative importance of existing tax levels on one hand and undeveloped external economies on the other as barriers to private investment, and many other factors. As regards taxation, one of the key factors is whether additional taxes can be so levied as to tap funds that otherwise would have gone into such channels

as luxury consumption or socially unproductive investment or foreign exchange hoarding, or whether they woud simply displace private productive investment and essential consumption. No categorical answer can be given then, to this question: How far and how fast can taxes be raised? Only through a careful enquiry into economic characteristics, social and cultural institutions, and prevailing standards of tax administration and compliance can an intelligent approximation be provided for any given country.

. . .

The tax systems of the underdeveloped economies differ most noticeably from the pattern in advanced countries in their heavy emphasis on commodity taxation and the taxation of exports and imports. The dominance of *in rem* as against personal taxes is particularly marked in Latin American countries. Reflecting in part their Spanish origins, the tax systems of these countries have traditionally relied on stamp taxes and commodity taxes. They also stressed the schedular rather than the global approach to income taxation (though several countries have in recent years superimposed a global income tax or even substituted it for the schedular tax). The net impact of this influence has been toward regressivity and retarded growth of progressive instruments of taxation. In those underdeveloped countries to which the British system has in part or in whole been exported, the tendency is to rely somewhat more heavily on income taxation as, for example, in India and Israel.

In analyses of the tax problems of underdeveloped economies, the traditional objectives of progressivity and equity in taxation, reinforced by the modern economic objectives of taxation, have pointed strongly to more aggressive use of net income and wealth taxation. Particularly before World War II, public finance missions seldom failed to urge the adoption of fuller use of net income taxes. Frequently, these recommendations seemed to reflect the ideological precepts of the technical advisers rather than an appreciation of the institutional setting of the country in which the recommendations were to be put into practice.

Fortunately, in recent years, there has been a growing sensitivity to the institutional framework within which technical assistance efforts are to be applied. There is a growing realization that conditions within which the most modern, equitable and flexible instruments of taxation thrive do not yet prevail in many of the underdeveloped countries and that substantial modifications of the fiscal techniques applicable in developed countries are necessary to adapt them to the underdeveloped economy. To translate this point into specific terms, Richard Goode, a member of the United Nations Technical Assistance Mission to Bolivia, set forth the conditions for successful use of income taxation side by side with the conditions actually found in underdeveloped countries. Problems involved in modernizing the tax systems of underdeveloped countries are brought out so effectively in his analysis that it is quoted here at some length.[1]

1. The first condition is the existence of a predominantly money economy. The subsistence farmer cannot be satisfactorily reached by an income tax, not so much because he does not have money to pay—that may mean that he cannot pay a tax of any kind—as because the greater part of his real income cannot be satisfactorily assessed. Even highly skilled administrators have made little progress toward including the value of home-produced and consumed foods in the taxable income of farmers. In many underdeveloped countries these

1. See the address by Dr. Richard Goode before the Forty-fourth Annual Conference of the National Tax Association, 1951 (Proceedings of that Conference, pp. 213-15). [See other excerpts in 3.3, below.]

products and others obtained by barter make up a major fraction of the total real income of large segments of the population. Admittedly these groups are usually the poorest in the society, and failure to subject them to direct taxation may not be seriously objectionable from the equity point of view. It does, however, encourage use of other taxes.

2. Another condition that may not be strictly necessary but is very helpful is a high standard of literacy among taxpayers. In many underdeveloped countries the majority of the population is illiterate. For example, among the eleven Latin American republics for which data are readily available, seven have illiteracy ratios higher than 50 per cent. In many regions of Asia and Africa the figure is higher, as it probably also is for several Latin American countries for which data are not available. Illiteracy, like exclusion from the money economy, is most characteristic of the poorest farmers, but often wage earners, independent craftsmen, and small shopkeepers cannot read and write well enough to fill out the simplest income tax return with the guidance of printed instructions. Wage earners may be covered by withholding, but in any refined system they must be able to file claims for exemptions and refunds.

3. Prevalence of accounting records honestly and reliably maintained is another prosaic but important condition for satisfactory income taxation. In most underdeveloped countries many businessmen keep no books at all; others maintain two or more sets. Vigorous tax administration can do much to improve accounting standards if combined with an educational campaign, but more trained personnel and office equipment are essential.

4. A fourth requirement for satisfactory income taxation is a large degree of voluntary compliance on the part of taxpayers. The best administrative organization cannot satisfactorily collect income taxes from the self-employed when, as in many countries, evasion is generally attempted and incurs little or no moral disapproval from the public. The roots of a tradition of voluntary compliance with tax laws are not easy to trace, but it is fairly clear that such a spirit does not grow up over night. Although something can be done in the short

run, a long period of popular education and efficient and equitable administration of those taxes that can actually be enforced seems necessary to establish firmly the habit of general voluntary acceptance of the fiscal responsibilities of citizenship. Adoption of elaborate measures that will not be uniformly applied delays improvement in taxpayer morale.

5. The political conditions for development of income taxes into a major revenue source, like the voluntary compliance, are intangible and hard to explain. The environment most favorable to progressive taxation seems to be one of free political democracy. In many underdeveloped countries wealth groups have enough political power to block tax measures that they consider threats to their positions. Until the popular will is stronger and more united or until the rich are ready to accept the ability-to-pay principle—whether from altruism or a sense of guilt or fear—steeply progressive taxes will not be collected.

6. Honest and efficient administration is needed for any tax, but minimum acceptable standards appear to be higher for income taxes than for many other levies. Difficult as the task of establishing a satisfactory administration may be, it is probably the condition for successful income taxation that can be met most quickly. The expert, nevertheless, must guard against the assumption that a tidy organization chart and non-political staffing assure good administration. Nor can he be confident that the best obtainable administration will eliminate obstacles to heavy reliance on income taxes.

A recitation of such limitations is, of course, a counsel of caution, not of despair. It suggests the lines along which action must be taken to remove the barriers listed and underscores again the necessity of improving administration and compliance to the limits possible within the framework of existing social institutions. At the same time, it calls for ingenuity in adapting and modifying advanced fiscal instruments to the conditions existing in economically underdeveloped countries. In the case of the income tax, for example, the difficulties encountered in many countries do not rule out the income tax entirely but strongly suggest that it not be used as a mass tax.... A personal income tax with a narrow base but high rates on large incomes, buttressed by administrative efforts concentrated on this area, may be a suitable instrument for achieving some of the ends of economic policy and distributive justice.

The types of limitations encountered in the underdeveloped economy may also suggest modification in the approach taken to taxation of wealth. A relatively refined form of wealth tax may be found in the net worth taxes of the Netherlands, Germany, and the Scandinavian countries. However, this requires skilled administration and conditions of compliance which generally are lacking in the underdeveloped countries. The appropriate action may be, not to abandon the attempt to tax wealth, but to determine whether a simpler tax on such outstanding sources of wealth as real property, or business assets, might yield a fairly good approximation to the refined net worth tax. If the correlation between real property holdings and net worth is reasonably close, and if the enforcement of a tax against the real property base is feasible, the indicated ends of tax policy may be served by a rough-hewn counterpart of the tax technique of the advanced country.

It is also worthy of note that the institutional limitations strike different types of taxes with substantially different force. Taxation of land, for example, is closely linked to systems of land tenure and to the agrarian structure as a whole. Consequently, techniques in land taxation are difficult to transfer from one country to another. In contrast, transferability of techniques applicable to corporations is considerably greater. In this case, the financial institution itself—the corporate method of doing business—has been transferred to, and taken root in, the underdeveloped country in much the same form as in the developed country. By the same token, the common use of the corporate form may permit the imposition of substantially the same type of tax on agricultural corporations operating, e.g., large-scale and rubber plantations, as is levied on corporations engaged in manufacturing or mineral extraction; here a considerable part of the corporation tax experience of advanced countries may be directly transferable to the less advanced countries.

In connection with institutional barriers to the application of modern fiscal policy, it should not be forgotten that taxation is itself an instrument of social change. It does not need to wait passively until restrictive and binding social institutions are changed but can itself help hasten the change. For example, a tax reform which changes the relationship between landlords and tenants can be the beginning of an overall land reform. Effective progressive taxes also can have significant distributive effects which will influence not only financial relationships but the social structure as such.

Some will argue that no matter how clearly the fiscal course toward economic development and stability may be charted, those in control of the governments in underdeveloped countries will not follow this course if it conflicts with their own interests. But in answer to this pessimistic appraisal, one may cite the concrete evidence of widespread willingness to entertain new ideas and advice as exemplified in the technical assistance programs. One may also surmise that the pressure generated by growing aspirations of the peoples of the less advanced areas of the world and the growing realization on the part of the governing groups that their enlightened self-interest for the longer run lies in the direction of economic development, have engendered a new receptivity to fiscal

improvements and change. It may be concluded, then, that though the barriers are high, the portents are hopeful.

3.2 TAXATION AND ECONOMIC SURPLUS *

Writers on underdeveloped areas point generally to the low level of savings in these areas. This level must be raised; but, according to many economists, such cannot be done to any significant extent because of the low level of *per capita* income which is said to be the cause of the low level of savings and investment. From this follows the concept of the vicious circle of poverty. It is doubtful, however, if the rate of savings in an economy, or at least the potential savings in an economy, can be related directly to the level of *per capita* income as such. The share of the national income going to the upper income groups and the share of property income in total income are probably more important determinants of the potential rate of savings.

Certain rough computations made by Mr. S. J. Patel indicate that the share of property incomes in India and the United States is not very different. Mr. Patel worked out the distribution of the national income of India for 1950–51.[1] From this he has drawn the following conclusions: (a) more than half of the national income is accounted for by the income of the self-employed; (b) wages and salaries represent nearly 23 per cent of the total, which is much smaller than the share going to wage and salary earners in the United States; (c) gross income associated with property ownership in India amounts to a little more than 23 per cent of the total.[2] The last conclusion is significant for our purposes. In broad terms, the income from

* From R. J. Chelliah, *Fiscal Policy in Underdeveloped Countries,* George Allen and Unwin, London, 1960, pp. 63-7. Reprinted by permission.

1. S. J. Patel, "The Distribution of the National Income of India, 1950-51," *The Indian Economic Review,* Vol. III, No. 1, February 1956, p. 8.

2. *Ibid.,* p. 9.

property in the United Kingdom and the United States has varied from 20 to 25 per cent of the total over the last ten years or so. But whereas in the United States the groups which receive this share of the income save a considerable part of it, their counterparts in India fail to do so. As regards the distribution of income in India by groups of income receivers, Mr. Kuznets' calculations show that the top quintile gets about 55 per cent of the national income. The same situation exists in other countries of the region. A comparative study of income distribution in the United States, Ceylon, Japan, and the Philippines, made by ECAFE, showed that the degree of inequality was more or less the same in the countries covered.[3] It was also seen that in Ceylon 10.6 per cent of income receivers received 37.0 per cent of the income, and that in the Philippines 10 per cent received 33.3 per cent of the income.[4] In the light of these data, it is difficult to accept the argument that these countries cannot afford to save and invest a higher proportion of their income than a mere 5 per cent.

It is clear that in these countries the potential rate of savings is higher than the actual rate of savings. A plausible explanation for the marked divergence between the two is given by Mr. Patel:

Although *per capita* income in India is low, the *possible rate* of savings does not have to be significantly lower than in the developed countries, for the proportion of the saving-generating income, or gross property income, in both cases is approximately the same. The low rate of productive investment in India may, therefore, be explained, not by a reference to the low average income, but the preponderance of 'feudal' income (in property income), which in the main is sterile at present for furthering economic development.[5]

In all pre-industrial societies, agriculture contributes more than half of the national output, and a significant part of this accrues to what we may call "feudal" proprietors and intermediaries. Economic development can be accelerated if the larger part of this "surplus" can be made available for productive investment. Such surplus may exist in other sectors of the economy, too. One of the central tasks of fiscal policy is to mobilize such surplus for purposes of economic development.

Accordingly, the starting point for any realistic theory of public finance for underdeveloped countries must be the concept of the economic surplus generated in the economy. Though the concept of economic surplus is somewhat tricky, it is a valid and useful one for our purposes. Civilization is made possible for any society or nation when its economic system begins to generate a surplus over essential consumption.[6] Following Professor Baran, we may distinguish between actual economic surplus and potential economic surplus.[7] Actual economic surplus is the difference between actual current output and actual current consumption. It is thus identical with actual accumulation of various assets. Potential economic surplus is "the difference between the output that could be produced in a given natural and technological environment with the help of employable productive resources, and what might be regarded as essential consumption."[8] Part of this surplus may not actually materialize because of waste of resources in idleness

6. It is of course impossible to define precisely the term "essential consumption." It is not fixed for all time, nor is it the same for all countries and groups; nevertheless, for a given society, at a given time, it is possible to have a rough idea of the essential consumption required in its quantitative and qualitative aspects. Other concepts are used in economics which cannot be defined rigorously: for instance, depreciation.

7. Paul A. Baran, *The Political Economy of Growth,* Monthly Review Press, New York, 1957, pp. 22-3.

8. *Ibid.,* p. 23.

3. *Economic Bulletin for Asia and Far East,* Vol. III, Nos. 1-2, November 1952, p. 23.

4. *Ibid.,* p. 22.

5. S. J. Patel, *op. cit.,* p. 11. Italics in the original.

and mis-employment. The rest of the surplus is utilized for various purposes. The character of a civilization and its future progress depend on the purposes for which and the manner in which this surplus is utilized. The surplus can be used for what the classical writers called "unproductive consumption," or for "unproductive investment" (palaces and pyramids), or for productive investment. Economic progress requires that, in the initial stages at any rate, a high proportion of this surplus be channelled into productive investment. In an agrarian country like India, a great part of the surplus originates in the agricultural sector and is appropriated by landowners, moneylenders, and merchants who usually do not possess the habit of productive investment. According to a number of observers, India can invest 15 per cent of her income without any reduction of *mass* consumption.[9] What is required for this purpose is a comprehensive mobilization of the economic surplus currently generated in the economy. The communists attempt to do this by socialization of industry and collectivization of agriculture. In a democratic society, the alternatives are voluntary saving and, in its absence, taxation. The task of tax policy for economic development, accordingly, is to mobilize this surplus, direct it into productive channels, and continually to enlarge its size.

Granted the above, what should be the fundamental principle underlying the tax structure? It should be the principle of the mobilization of the economic surplus. Taxation must mop up a great part of the surplus which at present is not being used for productive investment. The problem is to discover the surplus and channel it into investment without, in the process, destroying or gravely restricting its occurrence.

The second canon is that each person should be made to contribute to taxation in accordance with his unused capacity or

9. Mentioned in *ibid.,* p. 225

ability to contribute to economic development. This ability can be measured in terms of that part of the economic surplus (or the claim to it) accruing to him which he is not already, on his own, utilizing for productive investment. A person's income can be said to contain a surplus if it is above the level needed to maintain the minimum consumption necessary for efficiency and for incentives. This minimum will obviously differ in different countries and for different classes of the population.

Taxation also must mobilize the increases in the surplus that arise as a result of initial developmental efforts. This is the same thing as increasing the incremental saving ratio. Hence the third canon of taxation is that it must be so fashioned as to prevent consumption from increasing proportionately with income in the earlier stages of development. As will be shown later, commodity taxation can be used effectively for this purpose.

The fourth important canon of taxation for India is the canon of income-elasticity of taxation. As incomes rise the share of taxation in total incomes must rise. At present all the governmental units in India together take in taxation only around 7 per cent of the national income. Even if it is not possible immediately to raise the share of the government, it is imperative to do so as national income begins to register significant increases. As will be seen readily, this requires built-in flexibility in the tax system. To impart the needed flexibility to the tax system, it is necessary to tax goods that have a high income-elasticity of demand and also adopt a progressive scale of income taxation. Since the marginal rate will be higher than the average rate, the share of the government will increase more than proportionately as income increases.

Last, but not least, there is the canon of equity. Since taxation is to be used as a tool to promote economic development, the rule of equity demands that the burdens involved in rapid economic development be distributed equitably among the different sections of the population. This is exactly what is done when a great part of the surplus in the economy is channelled into investment. If the poorer classes are prevented from increasing their consumption to the full extent of the rise in their incomes, the richer classes are prevented from using their surplus for excess consumption. Sacrifices in consumption are shared alike by all members of the society. A corollary from this general rule, one that often is forgotten, is the rule of horizontal equity. That is to say, people in similar circumstances and behaving in the same manner (in terms of their utilization of the surplus) must be treated equally for tax purposes. This is an unambiguous rule of equity and yet it is one that the Indian tax system does not satisfy.

3.3 RECONSTRUCTION OF TAX SYSTEMS *

The mission or individual expert who conscientiously undertakes to prepare a plan for reconstruction of a foreign tax system faces a difficult task. Even to understand how the existing tax system actually operates requires considerable knowledge of the local social organization, legal institutions, administrative practices, and economic system. Most of us find it hard to say what results can be expected from a new tax law or administrative reorganization in our own country and will find it still harder to do so in an unfamiliar setting.

The outside expert, nevertheless, does enjoy some advantages. He is more likely to subject to critical examination local preconceptions with respect to economic and social consequences of taxation and to question accepted procedures. He brings

* From Richard Goode, "Reconstruction of Foreign Tax Systems," in *Proceedings of the Forty-fourth Annual Conference of the National Tax Association,* 1951, pp. 212-13, 215-22. Reprinted by permission.

with him some acquaintance with other, and presumably more advanced, revenue systems.

Ordinarily the country to be studied is economically underdeveloped with a relatively low income per head. Agriculture or extractive industries will usually account for a large fraction of total production. Often there is a large group of virtually self-sufficient farmers and at the other extreme a section of the economy heavily dependent on export of a few crops, forest products, or minerals. The export industries and complementary activity will be subject to wide fluctuations originating in the outside world, whereas the subsistence farmers may participate only indirectly in these movements. Usually the government's budget will represent a larger share of national income than it did in industrialized countries at a similar stage in their development, because of public investment programs, modern ideas about the welfare state, and military expenditures. In many countries unbalanced budgets have been partly responsible for an inflation that has also been fed from other internal and external sources.

The following remarks are addressed mainly to the fiscal problems of an underdeveloped primary-producing country of the type just described.

. . .

A basic economic issue concerns the wisdom of progressive taxation in a capital-poor country. Income taxes, of course, need not be highly progressive, but they are virtually always somewhat so, and their heavy use opens the way for steep progressivity. Critics of progressive taxation warn that it will absorb private savings, dull initiative and enterprise, and perhaps stimulate capital flight. They assert also that high income taxes will discourage foreign investment. They argue that the industrialized countries built up their capital stock and acquired a great comparative advantage at a time when the income tax was low or non-existent. The suggested conclusion is that the underdeveloped countries should wait until they have accumulated more capital and passed through at least the first stages of industrialization before attempting heavy income taxation.

These objections call for fuller examination than they can be given here, but I do want to raise some opposing considerations. In the first place, the picture of a frugal class of wealthy persons who invest their savings in capital equipment is more appropriate for an expanding capitalist system than for most underdeveloped countries. Lavish consumption appears to be more characteristic in many of these societies. Savings when made often go into land holdings and construction of elaborate residences. Lack of capital markets and savings institutions impedes the flow of savings from both the wealthy and the middle classes into productive domestic investment.

High tax rates, to be sure, may discourage enterprise; but, again, the more serious difficulty is usually the absence of a spirit of enterprise and a low social evaluation of business as compared with the liberal professions and gentlemanly agriculture.

Capital flight seems to be motivated more often by fear of political instability, expropriation, or currency devaluation and by lack of suitable local financial institutions than by tax avoidance. In the long run the problem can be resolved only by elimination of its causes. Short of a basic solution, exchange controls may be fairly effective in checking undesirable capital movements.

The foreign capitalist will undoubtedly look at income tax rates, along with many other factors, in deciding whether to invest in a country. High tax rates in his home country, however, may prepare him for considerably more severe income taxation than exists in many underdeveloped countries. . . .

Perhaps the most significant point is that most underdeveloped countries have long refrained from heavy income taxation and still have not realized in large measure the benefits attributed to this policy. Other factors must be retarding economic progress.

These considerations weaken the argument that higher income taxes are incompatible with economic development. But I do not believe that they wholly destroy the case. The country that succeeds in moving toward a higher level of development must somehow greatly increase the flow of domestic savings into productive investment. One approach is to try to encourage private savings and investment. Avoidance of high and progressive income taxes will not in itself assure success, but the outside expert should not be too critical of a government that deliberately adopts a policy of moderate income taxation along with other more positive measures to stimulate private capital formation. The alternative is for the state itself to mobilize the resources. This course may sometimes be appropriate, but the wise planning and skillful administration necessary for its success call for a level of competence on the part of the civil service that is extremely difficult to achieve in any country.

Taxation of business profits presents special problems in all fiscal systems. Many underdeveloped countries tax the unincorporated firm as a unit, separate from its owners. This practice is dictated partly by administrative convenience and seems also to reflect a preference for schedular income taxes which many countries took over from France. The results often seem rather arbitrary, especially when the business income tax is at graduated rates and is not integrated with the global personal income tax.

The corporation income tax, of course, also raises the issue of the desirability of integration with the individual income tax. The corporate tax, however, often is in good part a levy on large-scale foreign-owned enterprises. Since the local government does not have jurisdiction over foreign shareholders, it cannot reach them by an individual income tax. This consideration and the administrative complications of a refined integration plan are arguments in favor of an independent corporation income tax. On the other hand, caution is advisable in order not to discourage adoption of an efficient form of business organization.

The excess-profits-tax principle has considerable appeal in the underdeveloped, as in the developed, countries. But the problem of establishing a reasonable base is usually even graver in the underdeveloped countries because of lack of adequate accounting and statistical records and trained personnel. Where inflation is more or less chronic, both the invested-capital and the base-period-earnings methods may yield harsh results. The visiting expert and local officials will be well advised to be cautious in recommending an excess-profits tax. If the principle is adopted, they should bear in mind that special risks and the capital shortage justify profit rates that may seem very high in comparison with those prevailing in industrialized countries.

Most underdeveloped countries are not ready for major reliance on income taxes. Under existing circumstances, these taxes may lack the distinctive advantages that we usually associate with them. There are, undoubtedly, a good many countries in which substantially increased income tax yields are feasible and desirable. Greatly improved administration and compliance, however, are essential in most instances to prepare the way for the larger role that income taxes may appropriately fill at a later stage of development.

Export Taxes Export taxes, being barred by the U. S. Constitution (Art. I,

secs. 9 and 10), have received little attention in this country. These duties are important sources of revenue in certain mining countries and are used to a somewhat lesser extent by agricultural countries. Since the mineral-producing countries consume only a negligible part of their own output, their export taxes are roughly equivalent to production or severance taxes. They take the form of export duties mainly because the border is a convenient control point.

Often the economic equivalent of an export tax is obtained through foreign exchange controls. Exporters are required to surrender all or part of their foreign exchange receipts to the government and are compensated in local currency at a rate that overvalues the local currency. The difference between the true value to the exporter of the local currency and the compulsory delivery rate is, in effect, a tax on gross proceeds from exports. The following discussion draws no distinction between this type of arrangement and an outright export tax.

The popularity of export duties on minerals is partly attributable to the almost universal feeling that the area in which mineral deposits are found should share in the gains from exploiting these wasting resources. The largest mining companies are often foreign-owned, and the export duties are an easy way of taxing these businesses. Sometimes the taxes are partly at the expense of foreign consumers. Another attraction of export taxes, especially when they are specific rather than ad valorem, is that they are comparatively simple to administer.

In order to analyze the economic effects of export duties, let us first consider a country whose exports of a taxed mineral are only a small part of the world total. Domestic producers will be faced by a world price determined largely by external demand and supply. They can sell their whole output at the world price but cannot obtain a higher price. The export duty may be viewed either as a reduction in net proceeds from exports or as an additional cost of exporting. With any given price and cost conditions the duty makes it unprofitable to mine some ore that would otherwise yield a net return above costs, and production will fall. To some extent this contraction will be brought about by closing marginal mines, and may occur slowly. But for many types of minerals a prompt first adjustment will be made by changing the grade of ore extracted in almost all mines. Suppose, for example, that the price of the mineral is $1 a pound at the mill and the cost of extracting and milling a (short) ton of ore is $60. The pay limit will then be an ore of 3 percent fine metal content. It will be profitable to extract all ore of 3 percent or higher grade, but no firm will deliberately mine a lower grade. Now suppose that an export tax of 25 cents per pound of fine metal is imposed. Costs and the world price will remain approximately the same, but the pay limit will be raised to ore with 4 percent metallic content. This shift may forfeit a large fraction of economically available deposits. When selective mining processes are used, low-grade ores may be permanently lost unless drastic price increases or cost reductions occur at a later date. The foregoing is a highly simplified but broadly accurate description of the operation of Bolivia's taxes on tin exports.

The export tax is likely both to hasten the day of exhaustion of the country's mineral resources and to reduce current exports. The available supply of foreign exchange will decline, and imports of both consumer and capital goods must be curtailed. Sometimes it is argued that the immediate decline in output is desirable because the life of the industry is prolonged. Presumably this contention is based on the assumption that export taxes

will be reduced in the future or cost-price relations will improve. One objection to this argument has already been stated. The low-grade deposits left by selective mining can usually be recovered only at costs higher than would have been incurred had they been extracted along with the high-grade ores. Another consideration is the fact that an underdeveloped country has a high time preference for imports and can reasonably subject prospective future receipts to a substantial discount. Finally, postponement of extraction incurs the risk that substitutes will be introduced.

The situation will be less dark when the taxing country accounts for a large fraction of the world supply. In this case, contraction of its output will raise the world price, and part of the tax will be passed on to foreign consumers. Nevertheless, the higher price will encourage development of substitutes and economy in use of the taxed commodity. The history of the Chilean nitrate industry is instructive. Chile has the only commercial deposits of natural nitrates, and prior to World War I the government and the industry took advantage of this situation to levy a high export tax and to establish a cartel and price-maintenance arrangement. During World War I, however, a synthetic nitrate industry was established in Europe and America. The synthetic industry has grown until at the present time natural nitrates account for only a minor fraction of world consumption. Since 1930, Chilean production has remained below the 1910–13 level. Of course, we cannot assume that Chile could have prevented the rise of synthetics, but it does seem reasonable to suppose that the new industry would have developed much less rapidly had the Chilean government and nitrate industry followed tax and production policies that allowed lower prices for natural nitrates.

It appears that a policy of high export taxes may be shortsighted. Yet the fiscal expert must recognize the force of the sentiment in favor of special taxation of the extractive industries and also the difficulty of finding substitute revenue sources. It seems to me that a special tax on net profits of the mining industry, supplemented perhaps by a modest royalty on production or gross receipts, is the best compromise. The profits tax will not change the pay limit or affect production with existing plant and equipment. To be sure, it may discourage investment and thus over time curtail production. But the injurious effects are much less immediate and direct and probably smaller in the long run.

The foregoing argument is much abbreviated, but it is, I think, a useful example of a type of problem that will be encountered in many underdeveloped countries.

Consumption Taxes Consumption taxes are the backbone of the revenue system in many underdeveloped countries. They raise the familiar issues of equity and possible unintended distortion of production patterns. Where a large fraction of the population is desperately poor, heavy taxes on neccessities and on so-called luxuries of mass consumption will impose a cruel burden and may also impair health and productive efficiency.

But government is a necessity and must be supported. Hardly any underdeveloped country is in a position to forego substantial consumption taxes. Considerable revenue can often be obtained from taxes on commodities consumed mainly by middle- and high-income groups. It may be possible to select many excises that are mildly progressive over a fairly wide income range in a society where there is a sharp distinction between consumption habits of rich and poor. Much nonessential consumption is in the form of imported goods, and the taxes can often be most simply collected as customs duties with supplementary excises on any domestic production.

As a means of raising the remainder of consumption tax revenue, much can be said for a tax of broad coverage and comparatively low uniform rate in preference to a large number of special excises that usually reflect no clear social or economic policy. The general tax will be less discriminatory among consumers and producers and will often be simpler to administer. The tax can usually be collected more effectively at the point of importation or from wholesalers or manufacturers than from retailers in countries where retail trade is largely carried on by small shopkeepers and itinerant vendors. A good economic case can be made for exempting capital equipment. Administrative expediency may suggest exempting much handicraft production. Caution is advisable, however, to avoid uneconomic discrimination against larger and more mechanized producers.

The broad consumption tax will undoubtedly be regressive. Where the poorest section of the population is composed of largely self-sufficient farmers, however, regressivity will be less pronounced than in a country in which a larger fraction of output passes through the money economy. Furthermore, the alternative to the consumption tax is often greater inflation, which is even more regressive in impact.

Real Estate Taxes To the North American expert, taxes on land and buildings will appear to be an obvious revenue source in a predominantly agricultural community. Throughout most of Latin America, however, extremely low rates and assessment ratios make the true property tax almost minuscule.

Intensive use of the property tax is blocked in most Latin American countries by a small but politically powerful group of large land-owners. Even the low property tax rates in existence are rendered almost meaningless by original undervaluation, omitted properties, obsolete assessments, and widespread delinquency. Assessments twenty to twenty-five years old are common, even in countries that have experienced many years of inflation. New construction is often not added to the rolls, and when it is the unfortunate owner usually finds his assessment ratio far out of line with that of his neighbors.

...

Real estate taxes are not merely a promising source of revenue. They have positive economic advantages. A grave social and economic problem in many Latin American countries is the practice of holding large tracts of good farm land completely idle for speculative or prestige reasons or of using the land as pasture. A property tax based on a realistic assessment of the land's value in its most productive use would put a carrying charge on idle or underutilized land and would tend to break up large holdings or force them into higher and more economic uses. In the cities, another problem arises from the popularity of real estate as a hedge against inflation. Substantial taxes on urban land and buildings would help drive capital into socially more productive uses than construction of luxury residences, hotels, and office buildings. These taxes would also put a charge on a favorite form of conspicuous consumption.

Formidable political and administrative obstacles stand in the way of effective property taxation in the underdeveloped countries. Improvement of real estate taxes, nevertheless, seems to me to be one of the key problems on which the visiting fiscal expert and the local government should concentrate their energies.

A useful tax survey is much more than a listing of Adam Smith's four canons or some modern variant of them, an outline of the existing revenue system, and a facile prescription for rewriting the tax laws and reorganizing the administrative machinery. If the standard textbooks and treatises are not already available in the country seeking advice, they can be sent at far less expense than a foreign mission. The visiting expert must make a real effort to understand the local situation, to appraise the economic effects of the tax system, and to foresee the consequences of his recommendations. The kind of skill that is required is a scarce commodity even in the most advanced countries, but fortunately the supply does not diminish by being shared with others. In carefully studying a foreign system the expert will gain by being forced to re-examine some of his own ideas. It is often easier to concentrate on economic and administrative essentials in a new environment.

3.4 Taxation of Agriculture—Note

Some reference has already been made to the taxation of agriculture, but since it can play so critical a role in accelerating development it merits special attention. Although a large proportion of the population is still engaged in subsistence agriculture, and a high proportion of the national output comes from this sector, the tax system in most of the newly developing countries has tended to place the main burden of taxation on the monetized or market sector. Taxes levied on the subsistence sector are undoubtedly more difficult to assess and collect, and they are bound to be politically unpopular. When, however, a disproportionate share of taxation falls on the market sector, it may adversely affect the country's rate of development by reducing both the sources and incentives to saving. And unless the agricultural sector is taxed in order to expand the "agricultural surplus," the growth of the non-agricultural sector may be retarded. As development proceeds, the proportion of the working population engaged in non-food production increases; to make this possible, the marketable surplus from agriculture must also rise—that is, the proportion of food produced in the agricultural sector which is not consumed by the food producers must increase and be transferred to the non-agricultural sector. To accomplish this requires either taxes in money which impel greater deliveries to market, taxes in kind or compulsory sales to the government, or a deterioration in the terms of trade of the agricultural sector vis-à-vis the non-agricultural sector.[1]

Taxation of the agricultural sector may also serve as an important policy instrument in underdeveloped countries: the incentive and distributional use of taxation may be utilized to redirect agricultural production, encourage the more efficient use of the land, accomplish changes in land tenure, promote new productive investment in agriculture, and stimulate movement of redundant labor from agriculture to non-agricultural employment.

Various types of taxes on land, agricultural produce or agricultural incomes are possible. One of the oldest forms of taxation is an annual tax on land. Such a tax, expressed for instance as a percentage of the value of the produce per acre, may be objected to as being regressive in its incidence, but the tax could be made progressive on the owners of larger size holdings. If it were based on the potential productivity of the land, a land tax might also be used to promote improved methods of cultivation. The adoption of a progressive land tax is, however, unlikely since it is only practicable for a system of individual land tenure, is strongly resisted by land-owning classes, and it is not administratively feasible to undertake a periodic reassessment of each individual holding.

If the marketing system is controlled by the government, another possibility is to levy produce taxes. When the government buys an agricultural crop and sells it through official markets at fixed prices, it can pay the seller the price net of tax, and collect the actual tax later from the buyer (a wholesaler or other intermediary). This type of tax, however, is difficult to administer when prices are not controlled; nor can it readily make allowances for differences in family status or for costs of production, or be levied at other than proportional rates.

In general, the taxation of agriculture is easier when plantation agriculture prevails or native farmers are producing cash crops for export. Where a large proportion of total produce is exported, the government can tax agriculturalists through export levies, or can force savings through the operation of a state agricultural marketing board that pays the producers less than the international prices received by the board. A serious drawback of export taxation, as noted in 3.3, is the possible disincentive effect on export production, and the taxation may cause a shift of productive effort from exports to production for the home market.

In the absence of a land tax or income tax, the rural sector can be taxed indirectly through consumption taxes on commodities from the non-agricultural sector. By turning the terms of trade against farmers, these taxes may tend to increase the marketed surplus of agricultural products. Again, however, the scope for this type of taxation is still limited in most developing countries.

Considering the obstacles connected with a land tax or produce taxes, some economists have suggested that the most practicable way to tax income arising in agriculture is to develop a form of personal tax or "simple" income tax.[2] This may

---

1. This is the same problem that we discussed previously in connection with the Lewis model (Chap. II, 5, above): the growth of the demand for labor in the non-agricultural sector is dependent upon an increase in the supply of food which goes to the market. In Chap. VI, below, we shall return to the problem of how industrialization may be promoted by forcing the necessary savings from agriculture via taxation.

2. Cf. David Walker, "Taxation and Taxable Capacity in Underdeveloped Countries," Nyasaland Economic Symposium, July 1962 (unpublished paper).

prove useful for taxing people with incomes below the exemption level of a proper income tax and for reaching subsistence agriculture and the production of output for the domestic market.

Such a tax has been effectively utilized in Uganda. Known as the graduated tax, the Uganda tax is administered as follows. Local tax authorities first draw up a list of the main sources of income and wealth in the area (crops, cattle, trading, transport, wages, salaries, etc.). Calculations are then made of the taxable capacity of different types of income or income yielding assets. In the case of a crop such as coffee, for instance, each tree is assumed to yield a certain income for the year. This yield may be placed somewhat below the level that could be achieved by an average farmer on average land so as to encourage output. Corresponding values are placed on the other sources of income or potential income, so that the income of individual taxpayers can be aggregated. Rates of tax are then imposed, and these may be graduated for broad income categories.

This sort of tax has several distinctive features: it provides direct taxation on individuals who are too poor and illiterate to be taxed through a proper income tax; it can be based on a measure of the individual's taxable capacity rather than on only his money income; it can take account of factors that influence taxable capacity such as the possession of assets and the consumption of unmarketed produce; its revenue is more stable than would be a tax that is assessed wholly on agricultural produce; it can provide incentives to make farming improvements (through the setting of standard unit rates of return above which all production is tax free); and its assessment does not require the taxpayer to make out a complicated tax declaration but can be levied simply and inexpensively by local assessment committees.

No one of the foregoing taxes is free of administrative and political problems. It is clear that if the government is to succeed in mobilizing the surplus from agriculture, more consideration must be given to the reform of agricultural taxation. There remains a vital need to devise a workable system of agricultural taxation that will be more adequate in terms of yield and more conducive to development in terms of long-run economic effects.

3.5 TAXATION IN INDIA'S THIRD PLAN *

The amount of financial resources to be mobilized [in India's Third Plan] by means of additional taxation—either through the levy of new taxes or the stepping up of rates on existing taxes and increasing the surpluses from public enterprises, including the railways—is estimated at Rs 17.1 billion; this is nearly one third of the domestic financing effort. In the Second Plan, the total yields from additional taxation introduced during the period of the Plan are now estimated at more than Rs 10.5 billion, which is 25 per cent higher than the original target (including in the target Rs 4 billion referred to as the "uncovered gap").

The role of taxation in mobilizing resources for the Plan is considered crucial in India. The intention is to divert an increasing proportion of additional incomes generated during the phase of development to saving. In the view of the Indian authorities, taxation is an instrument not only for mobilizing but for allocating domestic resources in accordance with the given investment program. It is, therefore, not only the amount but also the distribution of the tax-take that is important. The various taxes on personal income, such as capital gains tax, wealth tax, gift tax, are designed to curtail consumption; similarly,

* From M. Narasimham, "India's Third Five-Year Plan," *IMF Staff Papers,* November 1962, pp. 410-12.

the tax incentives and concessions in respect of corporate taxation are designed to contribute to increased private investment in the priority sectors. Taxation in India has another function in keeping with the objectives of the Plan and the constitutional directives to the State, viz., to aim at a redistribution of income with a view to achieving a more equitable distribution of income and wealth.

In view of the concentration of the largest number of people in the lowest income brackets, the limited possibilities for enlarging, to any considerable extent, receipts from direct taxation have led to increasing emphasis on indirect taxation, especially commodity taxation in the form largely of excise duties and sales taxes. The aim is to cover a wide range of consumer goods, with particularly high duties on luxuries and semiluxuries, and thus introduce an element of progression in the indirect tax structure; but it cannot be denied that to be revenue yielding the indirect taxes have to be wide and to fall on the poorer sections of the community.[1] The importance of indirect taxation is also related to the relative inelasticity of land revenue. While the rural sector has maintained its dominant position in national economic life, its contribution to the exchequer has been falling as a proportion of the total. Although, according to one estimate,[2] this sector accounts for nearly 70 per cent of the national income, only a little over two fifths of the tax revenues originate in this sector. To make the agricultural sector yield larger revenues for purposes of investment, apart from raising directly taxes in that sector, reliance has to be placed on taxes on articles consumed in that sector.

The choice between different forms of taxation obviously depends upon the likely incidence and effects of further increases in each direction. The relative merits of direct and indirect taxation are determined on the basis of individual taxes. The Third Plan states, "The crucial point is to locate the surpluses as they are being generated in consequence of development so that additional taxation could be directed appropriately. The details of tax measures to be adopted during the Third Plan will have to be decided upon in the light of the economic situation as it emerges from year to year."[3] At the end of the Second Five Year Plan, the proportion of tax revenues to national income was only 8.9 per cent. It is proposed that this be increased, by the end of the Third Plan, to 11.4 per cent, which will still be lower than in neighboring countries, like Ceylon and Burma.

The prospects for raising this additional taxation are good, especially with the increasing consumption (and production in India) of a wide range of semiluxuries. The marginal ratio of tax receipts to national income that the tax target assumes has been calculated at 15 per cent, which is less than was in fact realized in the Second Plan.

Of the total of Rs 17.1 billion, Rs 11 billion is to come from the Central Government and Rs 6.1 billion from the States. A good start has been made in the first two years with regard to Central taxation; taxation so far levied is expected to yield Rs 8.5 billion over the five years; the States have also stepped up tax rates in the current year, and the prospects for their attaining targeted levels appear reasonable.

1. "There is however, no escape from the fact that, in a country like India where the bulk of the people are poor, resources on an adequate scale cannot be raised without calling for a measure of sacrifice from all classes of the people" (Government of India, Planning Commission, *Third Five Year Plan*, New Delhi, 1961, p. 104).

2. *Reserve Bank of India Bulletin,* September 1961, p. 1400. The figure here relates to income originating in the entire rural sector and is thus wider than the income from agriculture proper.

3. Government of India, Planning Commission, *op. cit.,* p. 103.

4. FOREIGN AID

4.1 How Much Aid? *

From the standpoint of the under-developed countries, the amount of economic aid received is small in relation to their needs. A considerable share of the total has been going to a few countries: those in which the United States has special military interests (notably South Korea, South Vietnam, and Taiwan) or which she is especially concerned to prevent from turning Communist (such as Cambodia and Laos, Bolivia, and Guatemala); French territories in Africa, especially Algeria; and Israel. Most of the others have been receiving comparatively little.

The United Nations report (E/3131) to the twenty-sixth session of the Economic and Social Council in 1958 lists twenty countries with per caput incomes of less than $100. Together they received net economic aid of $1,004 million in 1956–7. Of this total, $336 million went to South Korea, $246 million to South Vietnam, $41 million to Cambodia, $49 million to Laos, and $34 million to Libya. The remaining fifteen countries, with a combined population of over 670 million, received only $400 million, about 60 cents a head. India received only 10 cents a head.

Eighteen countries with per caput incomes between $100 and $200 received net economic aid of $464 million. Of this total, $111 million went to Taiwan, $24 million to Bolivia, $26 million to Guatemala, $79 million to Morocco, and $50 million to Tunisia. The remaining thirteen countries, with a combined population of 175 million, received $174 million, about $1.00 a head.

The amount of aid received by most underdeveloped countries was equivalent

to some 1 per cent, or less, of their national incomes—hardly enough to have a very significant effect in stimulating their economic growth.

It is true that the amount of net economic aid now being provided is greater, perhaps by a quarter, than in 1956–7. But populations have grown, and prices have risen; fundamentally the situation is much the same as it was then.

How much aid is needed? The combined population of non-Communist under-developed countries is over 1,200 million and their average income per head is about $130 a year. In order to raise their incomes forthwith to substantially higher levels, say an average of $200 a year per head, something over $85 milliard [billion] a year would be needed. This is obviously quite out of the question. Nor do most of the underdeveloped countries seek continuous large-scale charity. What they want is external aid sufficient to give their own economies a dynamic upward trend.

Further increases in wealth are easier for a nation, as for an individual, when it has already travelled a certain distance along this road. Higher incomes make possible not only a larger amount of saving and investment but also a larger proportion than incomes which are so low that they afford little margin for saving after providing for subsistence needs. The development of an adequate "infrastructure" of roads and other transport facilities, supplies of electric power, educated and trained workers makes it much easier to raise output per worker in all fields of economic activity. Economic growth in various fields provides better facilities ("external economies") to both existing and new establishments and expands the purchasing-power of the home market.

This phenomenon has been called "the take-off into self-sustained growth"; and

---

* From Frederic Benham, *Economic Aid to Underdeveloped Countries,* Oxford University Press, London, 1961, pp. 37–42, 112–18. Reprinted by permission.

it is often urged that economic aid should be of an amount and nature which will eventually enable the recipient country to go ahead under its own steam.

This seems sensible. I disagree, however, with the implications of the view, which is at present fashionable, that what a country needs to reach the "take-off" stage is an annual investment equal to a certain percentage, say 15 per cent, of its national income.

One reason for my disagreement is that the real national incomes per head of underdeveloped countries differ widely. Those of the richer countries of Asia, Africa, and Latin America are three, four, or five times as high as those of their poorest neighbours. Yet the costs of particular capital assets—a certain mileage of roads, a power-station of given capacity, school buildings for so many children—are much the same in all these countries. Hence the same percentage of national income invested provides a much greater amount of capital assets in a richer country than it does in a poorer one. If a richer country and a poorer country both manage to save the same percentage (say 10 per cent) of their national incomes, then the external aid needed to bring this percentage up to the "take-off" level (say 15 per cent) would be several times greater, relatively to its population, for the former. This seems absurd. On the whole, a poorer country needs more external aid per head than a richer country, and not only one-third or one-quarter as much.

I disagree with this view itself, apart from its implications. Economic growth does not only depend on the amount (or percentage) of investment. It depends on the character and abilities of the people, especially on their capacity to learn and apply improved methods of production; and on the numbers and qualities of their entrepreneurs. It depends on the provision of adequate incentives to effort and invest-

ment (including land reform, where needed); on general economic and social policy; on the ability and honesty of Ministers and civil servants; on social customs; and, over a period, the fortunes of some countries may be considerably affected by marked favourable or adverse movements in their terms of trade.

All this seems very obvious, and no doubt those who stress the importance of investment would say that they are merely simplifying by assuming other factors to be more or less equal. But in fact they are not equal. For example, in some countries large increases in output have been brought about at relatively little cost by discovering and planting higher-yielding crop varieties, by better breeding and feeding of animals, by stamping out plant and animal diseases, by the use of powered vessels for fishing and by turning fish into fish-meal for export, by technical training, and so forth. In some countries a great deal could be done on these and similar lines. On the other hand, some investment (for example, in certain large-scale irrigation schemes, in some steel mills, in the East African groundnuts scheme) has yielded little return.

One has only to look around the world to see that the attainment of a certain level of income per head, or of a certain level of investment, is no guarantee whatever of sustained economic growth. India is striving hard to raise her income per head from about £25 to £30 a year. What about Ceylon, which has been stagnating on an income of some £40 a head per year? Why should India necessarily do any better? What about Argentina, which Professor Rostow thought had "taken off" around 1935? During most of the post-war period Argentina made very little progress, owing to President Perón's attempt to speed up industrialization at the expense of agriculture, and to other factors such as adverse terms of trade. If the percentage of income invested is the chief criterion, what about Laos, a country which has been receiving grants equal to over 20 per cent of its income during recent years? No doubt it will be said that for economic growth other conditions also must be present. That is precisely what I am urging.

It may be that many people in under-developed countries would prefer to take life as easily as they can rather than to work harder and save more in order, eventually, to raise their standards of living. Nobody can blame them if they do. But a country is not likely to make rapid economic progress unless the mass of the people have a strong desire, an enthusiasm, to bring it about.

If this enthusiasm can be aroused—and this may need a lot of propaganda—there are hundreds of things that people can do to help themselves. They can improve their homes, their diet, their appearance, by learning such arts as carpentry, cookery, dressmaking; they can even learn to build themselves new and better houses. The underemployed labour can be transformed into a national asset by inducing people to give their labour freely (under expert supervision) for the benefit of their village communities in projects such as making or improving local roads, putting up schools and other communal buildings, sinking tube-wells, and digging irrigation trenches. Those who can read and write can teach others to do so. Those farmers who have tried out improved methods can convert others to adopt them. A whole village can become alive and dynamic instead of squalid and dead.

Whatever may be the relative stress laid on different factors, however, it seems clear that most countries have been and are receiving too little economic aid to make possible a continued and progressive increase in their output per head. Apart from a few favoured countries, which I have mentioned, external aid has amounted to only one to two dollars a year (or less) per head of their populations—around 1 per cent or less of their national incomes. It is not enough, as is shown by the relatively small rise in the real incomes per head of most underdeveloped countries during recent years compared with the relatively large rise in most of the more advanced countries.

...

If it is agreed that economic aid is necessary and desirable, the question then arises of how much. On what principles should the annual amount be determined? One method of approach to this question is to estimate how much aid would be required to raise the real incomes per head of under-developed countries by a certain percentage each year. Thus a group of experts reporting to the United Nations estimated that "a 2 per cent increase in the per capita national incomes cannot be brought about without an annual capital import well in excess of $10 billion." [1] That was in 1951; their estimate of $10 billion would be substantially higher today, owing to the rise in prices since 1951.

Mr. Hoffman uses the same method of approach.[2] He takes the average income per head of his "hundred countries" at $100 a year and assumes that it is increasing at the average rate of 1 per cent a year. He estimates that in order to raise this 1 per cent to 2 per cent additional economic aid (over and above some $4 billion "overseas investment" which is being provided already) of about $3 billion a year would be needed.

1. U.N. Dept. of Economic Affairs, *Measures for the Economic Development of Under-Developed Countries,* Sales No. 1951.II.B2. (N.Y. 1951, p. 79.) For a criticism of this report see "United Nations Primer for Development" by Professor S. H. Frankel in his book *The Economic Impact on Under-developed Societies* (Oxford, Blackwell, 1953), pp. 82-110.
2. Paul G. Hoffman, *One Hundred Countries,* Washington, 1960, pp. 45-7.

One reason for the higher estimate of the United Nations Committee is that they believe that "the most urgent problem of these countries is industrialization"; they therefore provide for "an annual transfer out of agriculture of 1 per cent of the total working population into employment other than agriculture" and estimate that this would require a capital of $2,500 for each person absorbed into non-agricultural employment.

The first point to be noted about this type of estimate is that even if the proposed objective were achieved, the gulf between standards of living in the industrial countries (or, more accurately, the richer countries) and the less developed countries would continue to widen.

Incomes in the former are so much higher than in the latter that for them the same percentage increase means a much greater absolute increase. The industrial countries are increasing their own incomes per head by at least 2 per cent a year; some (for example, France, West Germany, and Italy) by much more. In the United States an increase of 2 per cent per head is equal to over $40 a year, in the United Kingdom to over $20 a year, in the underdeveloped countries to only $2 to $3 a year.

The second point is that some underdeveloped countries are much poorer than others. If aid were provided solely to relieve poverty, they would need considerably larger amounts per head than the others; their incomes per head should be raised by much more than the average percentage of 2 (or whatever it may be). On the other hand, as Mr. Hoffman says,[3] it is possible that, say, "ten or fifteen or more key countries will make the most of the opportunities offered, plan and build wisely, attract a disproportionate amount of outside investment, and achieve real breakthroughs towards self-propelling,

self-generating economies with enormous increases in living standards." I think it is optimistic to suppose that "ten or fifteen or more" countries may do this, on their share of an extra $3 milliard a year. But there may well be an argument for providing a larger proportion of aid, as time goes on, to those countries which use it most fruitfully, rather than to those which are poorest.

The third point is that, in my view, as I have urged earlier, aid is best provided mainly in the form of grants, supplemented by public and private investment. The United Nations Committee and Mr. Hoffman equate aid with capital investment. Moreover their estimates (like other estimates of this type) assume a fixed average capital-output ratio. Thus Mr. Hoffman assumes an average capital-output ratio of three to one: "$3 billion in capital is needed to yield $1 billion in income." (The Indian Planning Commission assumes for the Third Five-Year Plan a capital-output ratio of 2.53 to 1.) I have no confidence whatever in the assumption of a fixed capital-output ratio as an instrument of planning; on this point I agree entirely with the criticisms of Professor Bauer.[4]

Personally, therefore, in estimating the amount of economic aid required I would reject any method which attempts to calculate how much would be needed to raise incomes per head in the underdeveloped countries by such-and-such a percentage a year. The fact is that most countries need all they can get, and far more than they are likely to get. The real question is how much the industrial countries can be persuaded to provide.

In this connexion, I should perhaps mention an argument which has been put forward by some industrial countries. They

3. *One Hundred Countries*, p. 45.

4. P. T. Bauer, *United States Aid and Indian Economic Development*, Washington, 1959, pp. 35-40. Compare also my remarks on the relation between investment and economic growth above.

say that it would be unwise for them to provide much, if any, increase in their economic aid, at any rate for some time, since they must first strengthen their own economies. On the same reasoning, a wealthy man might tell his poor relative that in order to provide more adequate help later on he must first plough back his profits to expand his business. Meanwhile, his relative may be starving, or unable to pay for the tools or the training which would enable him to earn a better living. It is true that in order to provide external aid (other than by direct gifts of commodities) a country must develop an export surplus. But this can always be achieved, given the will to achieve it, by suitable monetary and public-finance measures which increase saving relatively to consumption.

Another argument sometimes put forward for restricting the amount of external aid is that a number of underdeveloped countries have only a limited capacity for absorbing it. It is true that in the past some countries were not able to utilize all the aid available to them. This was because aid was offered to them before they had drawn up their development plans and had arranged to obtain the equipment, and the administrators, engineers, and other skilled personnel required to carry them out.

If mistakes are to be avoided, a public development plan should be carefully drawn up in the light of the resources likely to be available, both locally and from external aid. This takes some considerable time. Although a development plan should be flexible, and subject to revision from time to time owing to changes in relevant circumstances, it requires a great deal of thought and investigation. A number of things may seem urgently needed, but resources are limited, so that priorities must be decided on. A Government should not embark on a project unless it is sure not only that it will serve a useful purpose

but also that the resources which it will absorb could not be better used in some alternative way. The technical aspects of each project should be examined; to give just one example, it is futile and wasteful to provide an area with irrigation canals if the water is going to leak through and bring salt to the surface. A project should be properly "phased." A large expansion of education, for instance, may require a number of additional schools, but it is useless to build the schools without providing the teachers for them; one of the first measures must be teacher-training.

If a country is prepared to accept outside help, virtually everything it needs for a project could be imported. . . . Resources may be limited, but not "absorptive capacity."

A somewhat similar device (which was followed, for example, by Burma) is for a country to employ one or more foreign firms of consultants to assist in planning its development and in placing contracts for various projects with other foreign firms, who provide the skilled personnel and any special equipment required. Another possibility is for a country to facilitate direct investment by foreign companies; this may include the establishment of "joint ventures" in which its Government is a partner.

At the moment, there are a number of newly independent countries, especially in Africa, and some of them have been faced with an outflow of skilled foreign personnel. They need to borrow administrators, experts, and technicians, while their own people are being trained. A major source from which they can borrow is the United Nations, which is taking emergency measures to recruit additional personnel, to expand its present "pool" of experts, in order to meet their requests.

However, although "limited absorptive capacity" is a myth, in so far as any number of projects can be carried out with sufficient outside help, it remains true that a country will not "take off" into self-sustaining economic growth unless it has the will to do so, and the appropriate social conditions (including incentives).

I return to the key question of how much more the industrial countries might be willing to provide in economic aid—as distinct from military aid, export credits, and private capital. A figure which has often been suggested is 1 per cent of their national incomes. This would amount to a total of some $10 milliard a year, of which nearly half would come from the United States. It is not a large enough sum to achieve any miracles, but it is about three times the amount provided at present.

I propose, therefore, that the more-developed countries should undertake to provide a minimum of $10 milliard a year for the next ten years for economic aid as defined by the United Nations. This would consist mainly of grants (including grants for technical assistance) and I should hope that a considerable proportion of it would be channelled through the United Nations, including especially SUNFED, which should be established as soon as possible with a guaranteed income of at least $1,000 million a year.

At present, the general practice is for each country to decide annually how much (if anything) it will contribute to each United Nations organization (such as United Nations Technical Assistance or the United Nations Special Fund) for the coming year. This makes it impossible for these United Nations organizations to plan their expenditure on a firm long-term basis. Contributions would be more valuable if they were promised in advance, at the rate of so much a year, for several years ahead.

The same applies to bilateral economic aid, but here there is a complication. Some countries may make excellent use of their economic aid, so that aid-giving countries might wish to increase the annual amounts

provided for them. Other countries, for one reason or another, might not make good use of it and might spend the amounts provided somewhat wastefully, merely for the sake of spending them. Aid-giving countries might therefore reserve the right, in such circumstances, to reduce the annual sums which they had provisionally guaranteed to such countries, and to give the amount of the reduction to the United Nations or to other countries.

The proposed contributions should be increased if prices rise, in order to prevent their real value from falling. Economic aid from the Soviet Union and other Communist countries would be additional to the $10 milliard, and should be welcomed.

It must be remembered that real incomes per head in most industrial countries are rising at the rate of at least 2 per cent a year. The proposed contributions would not stop this upward trend, but they would make it somewhat flatter.

4.2 ESTIMATES OF AID REQUIREMENTS FOR SPECIFIC PURPOSES *

The studies summarized above have covered global capital requirements of under-developed countries. There is, in addition, a large number of estimates covering capital requirements for more limited purposes. These consist of estimates of total capital and of foreign aid needed for the development of particular under-developed regions and countries and for specific economic and social projects. In order to shed additional light on the magnitude of the problem of foreign aid it may be useful to review briefly a small sample of these limited estimates made in recent years.

A recent example of regional estimates of external capital requirements of under-

* From United Nations, Department of Economic and Social Affairs, *The Capital Development Needs of the Less Developed Countries,* New York, 1962, pp. 15-19.

developed countries is contained in the Charter of Punta del Este. It is estimated that Latin American countries would require a "minimum" of $20 billion of external resources over the next ten years for the purpose of achieving a "substantial and sustained growth of per capita incomes at a rate designed to attain, at the earliest possible date, levels of income capable of assuring self-sustaining development." To reach this objective it is considered that "the rate of economic growth in any country of Latin America should be not less than 2.5 per cent per capita per year."

According to the Charter, the United States is to provide, principally in public funds, a major part of the estimated external resources required. As an immediate contribution to the Alliance it has undertaken to provide from public funds more than $1 billion during the year ending March 1962. It is, furthermore, envisaged that the United States assistance, "where appropriate will take the form of grants or loans on flexible terms and conditions." The loans are to be provided on a long-term basis, "where appropriate running up to fifty years at very low or zero rates of interest."

As shown later in this report, the average net inflow of foreign capital into Latin America during 1956–1959 was about $1.4 billion per annum. If allowance were made for exceptional payments made to Venezuela for petroleum leases during that period the net annual inflow of capital would be closer to $1 billion per annum. The gross flow of capital from the United States public funds to Latin America, excluding military grants in 1959 and 1960 amounted to about $560 million and $400 million respectively.[1] The estimate of

foreign capital requirements contained in the Charter of Punta del Este, which amounts to a minimum of $2 billion per year, of which a large part is to be in the form of United States public loans and grants, would therefore imply an appreciable rise in the total volume of capital inflow and especially in the flow of public loans and grants over the next decade.

A good example of estimates of foreign aid needs of under-developed countries for a specific development programme is contained in the documents published by the Conference of African States on the Development of Education in Africa, held in Addis Ababa in May 1961.[2] The general purpose of the education plan as stated in these documents is to provide for each African state "a full and balanced educational programme," with a view to enabling "every individual, male and female, to make the maximum contribution to society which his mental endowments and physical conditions will permit."

On the basis of the inventories of education needs of each African country covered by the plan a programme is prepared for increasing school enrolments at the various levels of education during the years 1961 to 1980. The education programme is to be achieved in two phases. The first phase is reflected in a short-term plan and covers the years 1961 to 1965. It emphasizes the expansion of second-level education, which will produce a substantial rise in the level of specialized manpower required for economic development and of suitable cadres for higher education and for teaching primary schools. The long-term plan (1961–1980), which includes the short-term priority action mentioned above, is designed to enable the African States to achieve a desirable educational pyramid.

1. The net flow of capital amounted to $340 million in 1959 and to $184 million in 1960. Military grants in two years, not included in the above figures, were about $60 million and $70 million, respectively.

2. ECA and UNESCO, *Outline of a Plan for African Educational Development* (Unesco/ED/180); and *Final Report* (Unesco/ED/181).

...the plan aims at providing universal primary education within two decades. It also provides for an eight- to ten-fold increase in the percentage of age groups enrolled in second-level and higher education during that period.

The total cost of the above education plan is expected to increase steadily from $590 million in the first year of the programme to $1,150 million in 1965, $1,880 million in 1970 and $2,600 million in 1980. To estimate the domestic resources available for education, projections are made of national income of the African States for the period covered by the plan. It is further assumed that the share of national income devoted to education will rise from 3 to 4 per cent between 1961 and 1965, and thereafter will increase further, reaching 6 per cent of national income by 1980. The difference between total costs and domestic resources allocated to education represents a deficit in resources which should be covered by foreign aid.

. . . the estimates of foreign aid requirements under the African education plan rise from $140 million in the first year of the plan to $450 million in 1965 and to about $1 billion in 1970. On the assumption of a pronounced acceleration in the rate of growth of the national income of Africa in the nineteen-seventies,[3] a larger share of education would, according to the plan, be defrayed from domestic resources, and it is estimated that the amount of foreign aid required for the programme will decline to $400 million by 1980.

The need for a significant rise in the present level of foreign aid to meet the requirements of the education plan mentioned above is presented in the following passage extracted from the plan: "In the present stage of its educational develop-

ment, Africa needs assistance in the form of cash grants and materials, services of essential personnel, and provision of training facilities abroad. It is true that this help is being given now to an appreciable extent. But the size of the problem is so immense that the extent of the existing external aid will have to be more than doubled during the next five years and almost quadrupled between 1966 and 1970."

The above sample of . . . estimates of aid requirements for specific purposes is too small to provide a reliable basis for estimating total foreign capital needs of the under-developed countries; it covers only a small fraction of such needs. The limited estimates covered by the sample, nevertheless, suggest that estimates of the additional foreign capital requirements of the under-developed countries of about $3 billion per annum . . . are conservative rather than extreme.

4.3 Types and Conditions of Foreign Aid *

Various types of financial and technical assistance have been made available to developing countries, including stabilization assistance, loans, and grants for economic and social projects, surplus agricultural commodities, and the provision of professional and technical personnel for education, industrial and agricultural training, resource surveys, etc. Each type may have its place in the context of a long-range program in which there is a continuous relationship between the donors and the recipient countries, and a continuous review of the economic and social progress of the recipient countries. However, the

---

3. It is assumed that the national income of Africa will rise by about 50 percent from 1960 to 1970, and by about 70 percent from 1970 to 1980.

* From Joint Economic Committee, Congress of the United States, *Economic Policies Toward Less Developed Countries,* Studies prepared by R. F. Mikesell and R. L. Allen, U.S. Government Printing Office, Washington, D.C., 1961, pp. 11-12, 26-7, 29-30.

several types of external assistance currently made available by various agencies should be integrated, and directed toward the achievement of long-range economic, social, and political objectives for these countries. There has been far too much piecemeal and discontinuous assistance provided by a multitude of agencies without coordination at the country level and without any clear idea of what the overall impact of their activities may be.

Although there may be times when stabilization assistance in the form of external debt refinancing or general purpose loans may be necessary in order to assist a country in building a foundation of financial stability for sound development planning, this type of assistance should be used sparingly and with adequate safeguards. The most desirable type of development assistance is financial and technical help in the formulation and implementation of specific projects for economic and social development. Ordinarily such projects should be undertaken within the framework of long-range plans formulated by the developing country in consultation with, and perhaps with the help of, external assistance agencies. Although funds should ordinarily be allocated only as required for use in specific projects, there can and should be commitments of funds for financing a portion of a country's long-run development program over a period of several years, subject, of course, to the preparation of sound projects and the carrying out of agreed self-help measures. This approach to development assistance requires not only a continuous relationship and involvement in the development programs and policies of the recipient countries, but the closest coordination of the activities of various national and multilateral agencies operating in the country. Failure to establish a system of coordination of assistance activities at the country level constitutes perhaps the greatest

weakness in our foreign-aid programs at the present time.

We have rejected any mechanical relationship between the volume of economic assistance and the rate of economic growth of developing countries. Foreign aid is basically a means of helping countries to help themselves, but in saying this we recognize that external agencies can have an important influence on the policies and programs of the host countries. In a sense, therefore, foreign aid, both financial and technical, should be regarded as a mechanism for influencing the policies of developing countries for achieving economic and social progress as well as a supplement to their resources.

Involvement by external agencies in development policies and programs which are concerned with monetary, fiscal, investment, and administrative policies of sovereign states is a delicate matter and the greatest care must be taken in order to avoid charges of political interference. This is one of the reasons why we have suggested that serious consideration be given to making available the bulk of our development assistance through regional and international institutions. For example, it is believed that the Inter-American Development Bank, or such agencies as the Economic and Social Council of the OAS and the U.N. Economic Commission for Latin America are in a better position to bring pressure on Latin American governments to adopt sound financial policies and social reforms than is the U.S. Government acting unilaterally. The creation of the International Development Association and the channeling of a large portion of our assistance to Latin America through the Inter-American Development Bank constitute significant moves toward multilateralizing our development assistance. However, we believe it would be desirable to move much further in this direction over the next few years, perhaps by channeling more of our aid dollars through IDA. This recommendation also reflects the view that as the relative economic position of the United States declines, we must exercise our leadership role more through multilateral organizations in which both the economic burden and the responsibility for achieving free world goals are shared, rather than through unilateral action.

. . .

A major issue in the field of development assistance has been that between financial assistance specifically designed for individual projects, and general purpose loans for financing a broad range of commodities for use in a number of investment projects either in a particular sector of the economy or for development projects generally. For example, a loan might be made to cover the direct foreign exchange costs involved in building a particular steel mill or a section of a highway; or a development loan may be made to finance highway development in general. Alternatively, a country may obtain a loan to finance imports of capital goods for a wide variety of investment projects set forth only in the most general terms in the loan agreement. From an examination of hundreds of loans made by our public lending agencies, the distinction between specific project loans and general purpose development loans is often unclear and many loans seem to fall someplace in between the two concepts. Moreover, a "project" itself is not well defined; it may be anything from a few locomotives or a dozen tractors for a tractor pool, to a gigantic hydroelectric dam and irrigation system.

What is fundamentally significant in this whole field is the relationship of the lending (or granting) authority to the overall development programs and policies of the recipient country. It is much more important for our development assistance agencies to influence, and maintain a continuous review of, the development plans and economic and social progress of a country, sector by sector, than it is to make sure that a certain proportion of funds allocated for a particular section of a highway is spent for bulldozers or shovels which meet agreed specifications.

Project type loans are frequently favored because it is said that only in this way can we be sure that external funds are used for productive projects. But of course what is really important is how a country allocates its total investment expenditures, whether derived from internal or external sources. On the other hand, the project approach to development assistance does have a very definite advantage in that it provides the lending or granting authority an opportunity to review in detail proposed projects in relation to alternative uses of capital and for its officials to involve themselves more deeply in the development plans for particular sectors of the economy. It is for this reason that we tend to favor the project approach to development assistance, not so much with the idea of making sure of what is happening to every dollar made available, but rather as an administrative mechanism for achieving a greater degree of involvement in the development process of a country. Although individual projects should not be considered in isolation and out of context with the general pattern of a country's development, it is not enough in most cases simply to make large general purpose development loans on the basis of a broad development plan, no matter how well conceived. A review of the engineering, accounting, and economic aspects accompanying an application for a specific project loan will often have an educational value for the officials of the developing country, which will carry over to projects financed by the country out of its own resources. Also, any close examination of an individual project requires a detailed examination of related projects which are to be financed from other sources, and more broadly, a review of plans for the entire economic sector into which the project fits as well as the relationship of that sector and its projects to other sectors of the economy.

In the past the tendency on the part of development assistance institutions to concentrate on projects rather than on long-range development programs has been criticized because it is impossible for countries to undertake long-range planning unless they know where the financing of individual projects is going to come from over a period of time. Thus it is argued that individual development institutions or a consortium of institutions should make large general purpose development loans to assure the availability of funds over a period of several years. This is a valid consideration, but a commitment to provide financing up to a certain level for a long-range development program is not inconsistent with the project approach. The development assistance agency can agree in advance to make available a certain amount of aid over a period of years by agreeing to financing individual projects as they are formulated by the country and reviewed by the assistance agency. In addition, the development agency should be in a position to offer technical assistance in the formulation of projects suitable for external financing so as to provide a continuous flow of development assistance in accordance with agreed long-range plans and commitments of funds. The implementation of this approach, of course, requires considerable flexibility with respect to the timing of the actual allocation of funds and therefore argues for the availability of funds over a period of years rather than dependence upon annual appropriations. Dependence of development assistance agencies on annual appropriations not only makes it difficult for

them to promote rational development planning by a long-range commitment of funds, but in addition, it puts aid agencies under pressure to make allocations of funds before the end of a given fiscal year. This not only may mean waste as a consequence of misdirection of investment, but also weakens the position of the development assistance agency in influencing the policies and programs of the recipient countries.

· · ·

The terms on which development assistance is made available may be determined on the basis of either the type of assistance provided or on the basis of the capacity of the recipient country to service foreign obligations. The terms on which U.S. and multilateral development assistance has been made available to various countries constitutes a hopeless hodgepodge which, by and large, defies any rational explanation. Some countries are receiving hard loans (repayable in dollars at $5\frac{3}{4}$ percent from the Export-Import Bank or the World Bank), loans repayable in local currencies from the DLF, agricultural commodities in exchange for local currencies under Public Law 480, and, in addition, loans from the private capital markets of the world. The International Development Association has recently made several loans repayable over a 50-year period in foreign exchange, but without interest. The loans to be made by the new Agency for International Development (AID) are to be repayable in dollars, but on much more generous terms than loans from the Export-Import Bank, the World Bank, or the hard-loan window of the Inter-American Development Bank. Some countries receiving hard loans are also recipients of grants for certain purposes. In some cases there are perhaps administrative reasons for providing grants rather than loans. For

example, certain types of technical assistance projects in which the personnel is
provided directly by the U.S. Government
or an international agency might involve
special problems if undertaken on the basis
of a loan agreement. On the other hand,
technical assistance in the form of contracts
with private groups in which the recipient
country has some voice in the selection of
the private agencies might well be financed
on a loan basis.

Except where the nature of the technical
assistance creates special problems for loan
financing, it seems desirable to base the
terms of financing of development assistance on a judgment regarding a country's
capacity to service foreign obligations.
Moreover, there are strong reasons for
preferring loans—however generous the
terms—over grants in nearly all cases. Also
there appears little justification for differentiating between grants and loans on the
basis of whether the project constitutes
economic development or social development. It might be argued, of course, that
some developing countries would refuse to
enter into loan contracts for social development programs or that they would be
less willing to undertake basic self-help
or reform measures if the assistance were
to be made available in the form of a loan
rather than as a grant. In addition, there
may be cases where grants would be appropriate for nonprofit private organizations
abroad such as American schools or hospitals. All of these factors need to be considered. However, in the case of governmental projects which must eventually be
financed and expanded from public revenues, a distinction between grants and
loans based on whether the investment
adds to the "social" capital or "economic"
capital of a country does not appear to be
a very sound one, since quite obviously a
country requires different types of capital,
all of which contribute to the expansion
of the social value product.

4.4 EXTERNAL FINANCING FOR INDIA'S THIRD PLAN *

Basic objectives Progress towards increasing per capita incomes and a further
advance towards self-sustaining growth
are the basic objectives of the Third Five-
Year Plan, running from April 1961 to
March 1966. The Third Plan aims at securing an increase in national income of over
5 per cent per annum so that over the
fifteen years 1951–66, the total increase in
national income will be of the order of 80
per cent, national income having increased
by about 42 per cent over the period of the
First and Second Plans. Taking account of
anticipated population growth at a rate of
2 per cent per year, per capita income is
envisaged to increase annually by about 3
per cent from its present low level equivalent to about $63 a year.

Investment To achieve these aims it is
planned to step up investment by about 50
per cent as compared to the Second Plan,
with total investments, net of replacements,
amounting to approximately Rs.102,000
million [1] over the period 1961–66. This
requires that net investment be increased
from an assumed 11 per cent of the
national income in 1960 to 14 per cent in
1965. The allocation of investment between the different sectors of the economy
is as follows [in Table I].

This allocation of resources continues the
general pattern of investment found in the
Second Plan. However, in the public sector
there is greater emphasis on agriculture,
industry and power and on certain aspects
of social services.[2] Industry, minerals,
transport and power, when taken together,

* From *GATT Programme for Expansion of
International Trade, Trade of Less-Developed
Countries,* Special Report of Committee III,
Development Plans: Study of the Third Five-Year
Plan of India, Geneva, 1962, pp. 28-33.

1. Rs. 4.76190 = US $1.
2. The difference in distribution of plan outlays
is set out in Table 3 on page 27 of the *Draft Outline of the Indian Third Five-Year Plan.*

account for about 60 per cent of the proposed total fixed investment and for almost 90 per cent of the direct foreign exchange component of the Plan.

International resources for the achievement of the Plan Compared to the Second Plan the Third Plan calls for a large additional effort in mobilizing domestic resources. Domestic savings for financing the implementation of the Third Plan are to be stepped up from Rs.47,000 million in the Second Plan to Rs.75,000 million. Additional taxation is relied upon to provide almost one third of the internal finance for all public expenditures under the Third Plan. Surpluses of the railways and other public enterprises are to contribute approximately one sixth of the internal finance for the Plan. Small savings are expected to increase by about 45 per cent over the Second Plan.

The rate of savings in the economy which is at present approximately 8 per cent of national income is to be raised to about 11 per cent by the end of the Third Plan. Since the successful implementation of the Plan requires that net investment towards the end of the Plan period should amount to 14 per cent of national income, additional resources will have to be found. Over one quarter of investment will have to be financed out of external resources.

Recognizing the difficulty of forecasting trends in import prices and export earnings, as related to domestic requirements and availabilities over a five-year period, and basing themselves on a study of recent trends and conjecture about world market conditions, the planning authorities have assessed India's external trade and payments situation over the Plan period as outlined in the following paragraphs.

TABLE I. OUTLAY, INVESTMENT AND FOREIGN EXCHANGE COMPONENTS
OF INVESTMENT IN THE THIRD PLAN

(In million rupees)

	Public sector			Private investment	Total investment	Foreign exchange component
	Total	Current outlays	Investment			
1. Agriculture, minor irrigation and community development	10,250	3,500	6,750	8,000	14,750	750
2. Major and medium irrigation	6,500	100	6,400	—	6,400	
3. Power	9,250	—	9,250	500	9,750	2,700
4. Village and small industries	2,500	900	1,600	2,750	4,350	11,900
5. Industry and minerals	15,000	—	15,000	10,000	25,000	
6. Transport and communications	14,500	—	14,500	2,000	16,500	3,000
7. Social services	12,500	6,000	6,500	10,750	17,250	800
8. Inventories	2,000	—	2,000	6,000	8,000	
Total	72,500	10,500	62,000	40,000	102,000	19,150

Imports On the assumption of a policy of continuing import austerity, import requirements for the five-year period (including surplus commodity aid) are estimated to come to Rs.62,930 million. This is an increase in total import outlays over those of the Second Plan of about 16 per cent. While the advance in production in a number of important industries has made it possible to some extent to substitute imports by domestically produced goods, import requirements of certain raw materials, non-ferrous metals, specialized equipment and mineral oils and fuels have gone up. The projected increase in import requirements is almost fully attributable to an increase in expenditures for maintenance imports, such as essential materials, components, certain semi-manufactures, and fuels, from Rs.28,900 million in the Second Plan to Rs.37,700 million in the Third Plan. On the other hand, the progress made by India in the preceding Plan periods in expanding production of essential products and in improving the infrastructure on which development is to proceed, has made it possible to provide for a reduction in the direct foreign exchange component of investment from about 30 per cent in the Second Plan to about 20 per cent in the Third.

Export earnings Total export earnings for the Third Plan period as a whole are estimated to come to Rs.34,500 million, an average of Rs.6,900 million per year. This compares with anticipated total export earnings for the whole of the Second Plan of about Rs.30,500 million. The estimated total value of exports during the Third Plan is thus only 11–12 per cent higher than the total expected to be realized over the preceding five-year period. The modest increase in expected export earnings during the Third Plan is primarily based on the assumption of continuing difficulties to expand sales of a number of important

export commodities in overseas markets in the face of import restrictions and other measures affecting those major Indian export commodities for which there exists sufficient installed capacity or for which additional capacity could be made available within a short time-span and with but little extra effort.

Invisibles Net receipts from invisibles have in recent years shown a downward trend partly as a result of a rapid increase in payments of interest abroad on both the public and private debt and partly because of the decline in sterling balances. Net earnings from invisibles are expected to decline from Rs.4,000 million for the whole of the Second Plan period to not more than Rs.1,200 million for the whole of the Third Plan period.

Repayment obligations Repayments to be made over the years 1961–66 on obligations incurred by the end of the Second Plan will come to about Rs.4,200 million. The outstanding total foreign debt by the end of 1960 (including World Bank) in dollar equivalents amounted to more than $1,400 million. Net disbursements on capital account during the Third Plan period are estimated to come to approximately Rs.5,000 million. This estimate allows for some repayments which might fall due in respect of loans to be obtained in the Third Plan, and also takes into account certain other capital transactions, mainly on private account.

Foreign exchange reserves Unlike at the beginning of the First and Second Five-Year Plans, India will not be able to draw significantly on its foreign exchange reserves to cover part of the balance-of-payments deficit under the Third Plan. Official net holdings of foreign exchange and gold have fallen from Rs.9,130 million in 1950–51 and Rs.5,830 million at the end of 1956–57, to approximately Rs.2,740 million at end of June 1960. This is sufficient to pay for only about three months' imports under the present austere import policy.

Balance-of-payments prospects If one deducts disbursements on capital account and expenditures for financing essential maintenance imports from total export earnings, there is a deficit of Rs.5,000 million to be met before coming to the development import requirements for the implementation of the Plan of about Rs.21,000 million. The relatively largest part of the deficit is expected to arise in the initial years of the Plan when heavy repayments fall due. The deficit is expected to narrow thereafter as larger domestic outputs in steel, machine building, drugs and chemicals, etc., become available.

External assistance required for the Third Plan Total requirements of external assistance for implementing the Third Plan (including Rs.6,080 million assistance provided under the agreement with the United States for the supply of foodstuffs under United States Public Law 480) amount to Rs.32,000 million. Of that amount, Rs.5,000 million are required to cover the excess of payments over receipts as shown . . . above. Approximately Rs.19,000 million are required for financing imports of machinery and equipment for projects in the Third Plan and Rs.2,000 million are required for components, intermediate products, etc., for increasing the production of capital goods not directly related to specific Plan projects. This is about two-and-one-half times the amount of actual disbursements of external assistance during the Second Plan.

External assistance available for financing the Plan The carry-over of aid from the Second Plan and aid which has already been negotiated for utilization during the Third Plan (exclusive of aid under PL 480) is estimated to amount to approximately Rs.4,000 million. If the assistance provided under the agreement with the United States for the supply of 17 million tons of foodgrains under PL 480, valued at Rs.6,080 million, is taken into account, total external assistance committed so far for use during the Third Plan amounts to over Rs.10,000 million. The foreign exchange gap which remains to be covered by additional external assistance amounts to approximately Rs.22,000 million.[3]

Prospects for balancing the external account It is generally recognized that it is not unusual for less-developed countries in the process of rapid economic development to experience balance-of-payments difficulties. The imbalance on external account characterizing the Indian economy at present is thus not a temporary or fortuitous phenomenon. At the same time the Indian authorities, as stated in paragraph 40 of the Draft Outline, are aware of the importance of aiming at a progressive reduction in the imbalance, so as to eliminate it within a foreseeable period. It is hoped that such a balance, which would reduce and eventually dispense with the need for the country to rely on special foreign aid programmes, can be achieved within a period of ten years or so.

4.5 ON MAKING FOREIGN AID MORE EFFECTIVE — NOTE

In relation to the national incomes of contributing countries, the magnitude of foreign economic aid is not impressive— less than 0.5 per cent of their combined gross national products.[1] Nor is the picture different when we consider the amount of aid received on a per capita basis: of 45 underdeveloped countries receiving aid in the period 1957/58–1958/59, more than a

3. This figure does not make allowance for inflows of private foreign capital. Such inflows have unofficially been estimated to amount to not less than Rs.1,000 million over the five-year period.

1. United Nations, Department of Economic and Social Affairs, *International Economic Assistance to the Less Developed Countries,* New York, 1961, p. 2.

quarter of the countries received during this period less than one dollar per head, while another quarter received only between one and two dollars per head.[2]

When economic assistance is related, however, to other important elements of the development process—such as export earnings, investment, or savings—the strategic value of aid becomes more pronounced. For example, the amount of public economic assistance as a ratio of export proceeds for 49 underdeveloped countries rose from 9 per cent to 16 per cent between 1953/54–1955/56 and 1957/58–1958/59. For Asia and Africa the ratio in 1957/58–1958/59 amounted to as much as 19 per cent and 18 per cent, respectively; in one-third of the countries the ratio was 20 per cent or more.[3] In a considerable number of countries the net flow of foreign funds has grown at a higher rate than export earnings, and the share of foreign capital assistance in the total supply of foreign exchange has been sizeable. The ratio of public aid to domestic investment has also risen substantially over this period. If the assumption can be made that all of the net receipts of public capital for underdeveloped countries went, directly or indirectly, into additional investment, over one-fifth of the total new capital formation in recipient countries would be due to the component of public foreign capital.[4] Moreover, during the decade of the 1950's it was mainly the enlarged flow of foreign saving that made it possible to raise or maintain the total supply of saving in a majority of the underdeveloped countries. For in a considerable number of countries the ratio of net domestic saving to gross domestic product actually declined during the 1950's, and it was only the increase in foreign aid to these countries that allowed the ratio of total net saving to gross domestic product to rise at all or to be maintained.[5]

Despite the increased importance of foreign aid during the past decade, its accomplishments still leave much to be desired. In many instances, the experience with aid has been disappointing from the standpoint of project performance; more broadly, the initial expectations of what foreign aid could do to accelerate development have not been realized. It is now widely recognized that a greater effort must be made to achieve more effective utilization of the assistance rendered. Measures designed to improve the use of aid may now be even more valuable than efforts to raise the magnitude of assistance. Specific recommendations for the better utilization of aid must be devised with regard to the particular arrangements and circumstances of individual countries. Some relevant principles, however, might be suggested for making aid a more effective component of development programming.

What matters for securing the effective use of aid is not so much its specific form or the terms on which it is rendered, but rather the extent to which aid is successfully integrated into development plans and priorities. Clarity on the objectives of foreign assistance is the necessary first step in determining how much aid is needed by a recipient country. The essence of capital assistance is the provision of additional economic resources, but external assistance should add to—not substitute for—the developing country's own efforts. If financial assistance from abroad is to result in a higher rate of domestic investment, it must be prevented from simply replacing domestic sources of financing investment, and it

2. *Ibid.*, pp. 44-5.
3. *Ibid.*, pp. 45-6.
4. *Ibid.*, pp. 1, 46-7.

5. For statistical evidence on the rate of domestic saving and the contribution made by foreign saving, see United Nations, *World Economic Survey* 1960, New York, 1961, Chap. 2; *International Flow of Long-Term Capital and Official Donations* 1951-1959, New York, 1961, pp. 30-31.

should not be dissipated in supporting higher personal consumption or an increase in non-developmental current expenditure by the government.

Even when the objectives are clearly defined, however, it is still extremely difficult to calculate the magnitude of external assistance required to attain these objectives. The usual type of calculation begins by establishing a target for the increase in per capita real income over a given time period, and then, on the basis of estimates of population growth per annum and the economy's marginal capital-output ratio, it is concluded that a certain percentage of national income must be saved and invested to attain the per capita income target. If domestic saving is expected to be less than this amount, then the balance must be sought from external sources. To the extent that private foreign investment or foreign exchange reserves do not fill the gap, public funds from abroad are required. But, as we already noted in previous materials (section I), this is a highly over-simplified way to determine capital requirements. A superficial and narrow interpretation of the development process is adopted when aid is calculated merely on the basis of the relationships between a capital-output ratio, a savings ratio, and population growth. Other strategic factors besides investment must be considered, and a more comprehensive analysis of the role of foreign capital is needed to appreciate the full implications of external assistance.

It has become increasingly evident that not every poor country is immediately able to employ considerable amounts of capital productively, in the sense of having the investment cover its costs and also yield a reasonable increase in income. At least in the short run, the country's capital absorptive capacity may be low—that is, the country may not have the capacity to absorb a large amount of real productive capital. This is because complementary factors are in short supply, knowledge and skills are limited, and well-conceived projects are not readily forthcoming. The deficiencies in managerial, technical, supervisory, and skilled manpower seriously restrain absorptive capacity. For this reason, the productive use of capital assistance may depend heavily upon the effectiveness of technical assistance, since the contribution of technical aid is essentially to raise absorptive capacity. Once the pace of development gains momentum, the absorptive capacity will be higher, and foreign capital can then be utilized more effectively.

When foreign aid is available on a general purpose basis, the allocation of the foreign capital is decisive in determining whether it contributes as much as possible to raising the growth-potential of the recipient country. The efficient allocation of investment resources then depends upon the application of investment criteria in terms of the country's entire development program, [6] and domestic policy measures must be adopted to supplement the use of foreign assistance. Regardless of the amount of aid received, the formation of capital depends, in the last resort, on domestic action.

It is appropriate therefore to emphasize the necessity of self-help measures: unless recipient governments adopt policies to mobilize fully their own resources and to implement their plans, the maximum potential benefits from aid will not be realized. As the record of foreign assistance in several countries shows, external aid may be incapable of yielding significant results unless it is accompanied by complementary domestic measures such as basic reforms in land tenure systems, additional taxation, investment in human capital, and more efficient government administration.

Insofar as the effective use of foreign aid may depend on domestic social and

6. Cf. Chap. V, below.

political reforms, more systematic attention needs to be given to the sociocultural and political aspects of foreign assistance. This should serve to correct the overemphasis on capital productivity and technical productivity at the expense of noneconomic variables that may be more controlling in determining the success of aid.

Just as the absence of complementary domestic policies may limit the effectiveness of aid, so too may its impact be neutralized by changes in the other components of the total flow of resources from rich to poor countries. The total flow is affected by private foreign investment, export earnings, and the terms of trade, as well as foreign aid. It is therefore essential to recognize the relationships between capital assistance, private foreign investment, and international trade. The contribution of international assistance will be greater if public loans and grants are not competitive with, but instead stimulate, private foreign investment. Public aid for economic overhead facilities can create opportunities for private investment, and the private investment can, in turn, ensure fuller use of these facilities and raise their financial and economic return. Similarly, policies should be pursued that will bolster export earnings so that the inflow of development capital will be able to do more than simply offset a weak trend of export earnings or a deterioration in the recipient country's terms of trade. Of particular concern now is the need for policies that stabilize the poor countries' foreign exchange earnings; this problem is examined in Chapter VII, section 3, below.

While the dependence on external aid may have to be large at the outset of a development program, most plans aim for a progressive reduction in aid and the eventual realization of a self-financing plan. To achieve this, the emphasis must be placed on a high marginal rate of saving: the proportion of income that is saved out of an increase in output must be much higher than the average savings ratio at the plan's beginning. The reliance on foreign aid will also diminish if, as development proceeds, the composition of investment alters toward projects with a lower import content, the production of import-substitutes increases, export revenue expands, and total domestic output grows without inflationary financing.

Finally, attention should be given to ways of minimizing the burden of debt service payments. When the return flow of interest and amortization payments exceeds the inflow of new capital assistance, the country confronts a transfer problem and must generate an export surplus. If the country is to accomplish this without having to endure the costs of internal and external controls, or currency depreciation, its development program must give due consideration to the country's debt servicing capacity.

This becomes part of the problem of selecting appropriate investment criteria. To provide for adequate servicing of the foreign debt, the inflow of capital should increase productivity sufficiently to yield an increase in real income greater than the interest and amortization charges. If this is done, the economy will have the capacity to raise the necessary funds—either through a direct commercial return or greater taxable capacity. Moreover, to provide a sufficient surplus of foreign exchange to avoid a transfer problem, the capital should be utilized in such a way as to generate a surplus in the other items of the balance of payments equal to the transfer payments abroad. This does not mean that a project financed by foreign aid must itself make a direct contribution to the balance of payments, for the ability to create a sufficiently large export surplus depends on the operation of all industries together, not only on the use made of foreign investment. The basic test for the allocation of capital aid is not simply a narrow balance of payments criterion, but rather the more general criterion that capital should be invested in the form that yields the highest social marginal product. As long as capital is distributed according to its most productive use and the excess spending associated with inflation is avoided, the necessary export surplus can be created indirectly. The allocation of foreign aid according to the criterion of productivity will also be the most favorable for debt servicing, since it maximizes the increase in income from a given amount of capital, thereby contributing to the growth of foreign exchange availabilities.

The problem of debt-servicing will also be eased for the aid-receiving country when capital assistance is offered at lower interest, for longer terms and with more continuity, and when the creditor country follows a more expansionary domestic policy and a more liberal commercial policy. These considerations are becoming critical for many countries that have already reached a point at which an increasing share of their current earnings of foreign exchange is being required for amortization and interest payments.[7] The rate of development would certainly be adversely affected if, in order to meet its external obligations, a developing country had to adjust its balance of payments by reducing its imports of strategic capital goods. To ease this problem of adjustment, it would be helpful if a larger proportion of aid took the form of grants or loans at very long term and at very low interest.

7. United Nations, *International Flow of Long-term Capital and Official Donations 1951-1959, op. cit.,* p. 32; *International Economic Assistance to the Less Developed Countries, op. cit.,* p. 47.

5. PRIVATE FOREIGN INVESTMENT

5.7 THE CONTRIBUTION OF PRIVATE FOREIGN CAPITAL — NOTE

Although public foreign capital has been the dominant source of international financing of development, increasing attention is now focused on the contribution that might come from foreign private sources. The American government, in particular, has emphasized the desirability of an increase in private foreign investment. President Truman's original Point Four program envisaged governmentally financed assistance in public health, education, and agriculture, but for other activities it relied on private capital as a complement to public technical assistance. So far, however, only a small amount of private capital, relative to government loans and grants, has flowed to poor countries: in recent years, an average of about $2 billion a year.[1] The bulk of the capital has come from the United States, but outflows have also been significant from the United Kingdom, Federal Republic of Germany, France, and the Netherlands. More than half of the total private foreign investments in the past few years have been in Latin America, particularly Argentina, Brazil, Cuba, Mexico, Venezuela, and the West Indies. Africa has attracted between one-fifth and one-third of the total long-term private capital inflow—less than Latin America but considerably more than Asia. The major part of foreign direct investment in Latin America has come from United States companies and has gone

1. IMF, *Balance of Payments Yearbook,* annual. This estimate includes reinvested profits of subsidiaries, and also the inflow to the franc area and United Kingdom territories.

mainly into mineral extraction, the petroleum industry, manufacturing, and mining. Investments in Africa are concentrated in petroleum, mining, and agricultural enterprises. Foreign direct investments in Asia, apart from investments in the petroleum industry, are concentrated in mines and plantations, with investments in manufacturing significant only in India, Israel, some Middle Eastern countries, and the Philippines.

Despite the dominance of public capital, there is still a widespread belief that capital from official sources is only a transitional arrangement and that foreign economic aid should be gradually replaced by private foreign investment. To this end, considerable interest is being shown in measures that might promote private foreign investment and allow it to make a greater contribution to the development of the recipient countries. In an attempt to promote a larger flow of private capital to developing nations, several capital-exporting countries have adopted a range of measures that include tax incentives, investment guarantees, and financial assistance to private investors. International institutions are also encouraging the international flow of private capital; the International Finance Corporation, for instance, cooperates directly with private investors in financing new or expanded ventures.

Of far greater influence, however, than the measures adopted by capital-exporting nations or international organizations are the policies of the capital-recipient countries themselves. Controls exercised by the host country over the conditions of entry of foreign capital, regulations of the operation of foreign capital, and restrictions on the remittance of profits and the repatriation of capital are far more decisive in determining the flow of foreign capital than any policy undertaken by the capital-exporting country.

Policies of the host country are now being adopted in the context of development planning, and their rationale and effects have taken on new dimensions in this light. No longer is it simply a matter of private investors dismissing investment prospects with the complaint that a "favorable climate" does not exist; nor need host countries contend that an inflow of private capital entails nothing but "foreign domination." The meaning of a "favorable climate" calls for reinterpretation in terms of development planning, and the effects of foreign investment in countries that are newly independent should not be analyzed as if the undesirable features in the history of colonialism need be repeated. The central problem now is for the recipient country to devise policies that will succeed in both encouraging a greater inflow of private foreign capital and ensuring that it makes the maximum contribution feasible toward the achievement of the country's development objectives.

The practice of development planning need not in itself be inimical to the promotion of a larger inflow of private capital. If a development plan reserves some areas of investment for the public sector, there is at least, on the other side, a clear statement of policy regarding areas in which private investment is desired. For a development plan may expressly define the particular role assigned to the private sector, indicate more clearly the existence of investment opportunities, facilitate advance calculation, and reduce the foreign investor's uncertainties regarding his position vis-à-vis the domestic private and public industrial sectors.

Although the prevalence of national development plans does not necessarily limit the scope for private activity and may actually promote more attractive business opportunities, it does mean that private investors must share with the government a common interest in accelerating development. The tasks of development require both more effective governmental activity and more investment on the part of international private enterprise. But the private investor must be aware of the developmental objectives and priorities of the host country and understand how his investment fits into the country's development strategy. The contribution of private foreign capital has to be interpreted in terms beyond private profit. At the same time, the government must recognize that if risks are too high or the return on investment is too low, international private investment will be inhibited from making any contribution at all. Development planning now requires the government to influence the performance of private foreign investment, but in doing this, the government should appreciate fully the potential contribution of this investment, and it should devise policies that will meet the mutual interests of private investor and host country. This calls for more intensive analysis of the consequences of private foreign investment and for more thought and ingenuity in devising new approaches that favor the mobilization of private foreign capital while ensuring its most effective "planned performance" in terms of the country's development program.

At present, the policies taken by the developing countries reveal a mixed picture of restrictions and incentives. On the one hand, the foreign investor's freedom of action may be restricted by a variety of governmental regulations that exclude private foreign investment from certain "key" sectors of the economy, impose limitations on the extent of foreign participation in ownership or management, specify conditions for the employment of domestic and foreign labor, limit the amount of profits, and impose exchange controls on the remission of profits and the repatriation of capital.

On the other hand, a progressive liber-

alization of policy towards private foreign capital has occurred during recent years. Many countries now recognize that an inflow of private capital may offer some special advantages over public capital, and a number of investment incentive measures have been recently adopted or are under consideration. These incentive devices include assistance in securing information on investment opportunities, the provision of supplementary finance, establishment of economic overhead facilities such as in industrial estates, protective tariffs on commodities that compete with those produced by foreign investors, exemptions from import duties on necessary equipment and materials, the granting of exchange guarantees or privileges, tax concession schemes for the encouragement of desired new investments, and special legislation for the protection of foreign investments.

To remove the ambivalence that characterizes these policies, it is desirable to reexamine the role of private foreign capital more systematically by appraising the prospective benefits and costs of private foreign investment. Such an appraisal may then provide a more rational basis for determining what type of policy is most appropriate for securing the maximum contribution from private foreign investment.

From the standpoint of national economic benefit, the essence of the case for encouraging an inflow of capital is that the increase in real income resulting from the act of investment is greater than the resultant increase in the income of the investor.[2] If the value added to output by

2. Much of the following analysis is based on Sir Donald MacDougall, "The Benefits and Costs of Private Investment from Abroad: A Theoretical Approach," *Economic Record,* March 1960, pp. 13-35; Paul Streeten, *Economic Integration,* Leyden, 1961, Chap. 4; G. M. Meier, *International Trade and Development,* New York, 1963, pp. 92-9.

the foreign capital is greater than the amount appropriated by the investor, social returns exceed private returns. As long as foreign investment raises productivity, and this increase is not wholly appropriated by the investor, the greater product must be shared with others, and there must be some direct benefits to other income groups. These benefits can accrue to (a) domestic labor in the form of higher real wages, (b) consumers by way of lower prices, and (c) the government through higher tax revenue. Beyond this, and most importantly in many cases, there are likely to be (d) indirect gains through the realization of external economies.

An increase in total real wages may be one of the major direct benefits from an inflow of foreign capital. This can be recognized in Figure III.1 where the line EG illustrates the marginal productivity of capital in the capital-recipient country, given the amount of labor. If initially the domestically owned capital stock is AB, total output is ABCE. We shall assume that profits per unit of capital equal the marginal product of capital, and that total profits on domestic capital are ABCD, and total real wages are CDE. Let there now be an inflow of foreign capital in the amount BF. Total output then increases by the amount BFGC, and the profits on

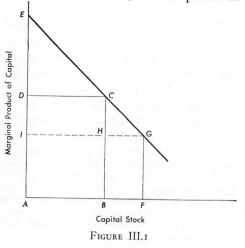

Figure III.1

foreign capital are BFGH of this amount. Since the profit rate on total capital has fallen, profits on domestic capital are reduced to ABHI. But the total real wages of labor are now GIE, with the increase in real wages amounting to DCGI. Although in this case, with a given marginal productivity of capital schedule, most of labor's gain—the amount DCHI—is merely a redistribution from domestic capitalists, there is still a net increase in the real incomes of domestic factors, represented by the rise in real wages in the amount CGH.

For a developing country, the inflow of foreign capital may not only be significant in raising the productivity of a given amount of labor but may also allow a larger labor force to be employed. If, as was contended in the discussion of dualistic development in Chapter II, a shortage of capital in heavily populated poor countries limits the employment of labor from the rural sector in the advanced sector where wages are higher, an inflow of foreign capital may then make it possible to employ more labor in the advanced sector. The international flow of capital can thus be interpreted as an alternative to labor migration from the poor country: when outlets for the emigration of labor are restricted, the substitution of domestic migration of labor into the advanced sector becomes the most feasible solution. The social benefit from the foreign investment in the advanced sector is then greater than the profits on this investment, for the wages received by the newly employed exceed their former real wage in the rural sector, and this excess should be added as a national gain.

Domestic consumers may also benefit from direct foreign investment. When the investment is cost-reducing in a particular industry, consumers of the product may gain through lower product prices. If the investment is product-improving or product-innovating, consumers benefit from better quality products or new products.

In order that labor and consumers might enjoy part of the benefit from the higher productivity in enterprises established by foreign investors, the overseas withdrawal by the investors must be less than the increase in output. But even if the entire increase in productivity accrues as foreign profits, this requirement may still be fulfilled when the government taxes foreign profits. For many countries, taxes on foreign profits or royalties from concession agreements constitute a large proportion of total government revenue. The fiscal benefit derived from foreign investment is evident from the fact that the share of government revenue in the national product of countries that have received substantial foreign investment (Iraq, Venezuela, Peru, Ceylon, Costa Rica, Guatemala) is considerably higher than in most of the other low income countries.

The most significant contribution of foreign investment is likely to come from external economies. Direct foreign investment brings to the recipient country not only capital and foreign exchange but also managerial ability, technical personnel, technological knowledge, administrative organization, and innovations in products and production techniques—all of which are in short supply. This ensures in the first instance that a project involving private foreign investment will be adequately formulated and implemented, unlike the situation that has frequently confronted public economic aid when the recipient country has not had the talent or inclination to undertake adequate feasibility studies and formulate projects that might qualify for public capital. For many countries, the principal limitation on the inflow of public foreign capital has not been on the supply side, but rather the lack of soundly formulated projects that can be presented as ready for financing. The pre-

investment survey, act of investment, and operation of the investment project are all ensured in private foreign investment.

Beyond this, however, the "private technical assistance" and the demonstration effects that are integral features of private foreign investment are of benefit elsewhere in the economy. The rate of technological advance in a poor country is highly dependent on the rate of capital inflow. New techniques accompany the inflow of private capital, and by the example they set, foreign firms promote the diffusion of technological advance in the economy. This benefit is highly important in a developing country, for while domestic enterprises might not be adept in the practice of innovating, they may make up for this deficiency by imitating the advanced techniques that are being demonstrated by foreign firms. In addition, foreign investment may lead to the training of labor in new skills, and the knowledge gained by these workers can be transmitted to other members of the labor force, or these workers might be employed later by local firms.

Private foreign investment may also serve as a stimulus to additional domestic investment in the recipient country. This is especially likely through the creation of external pecuniary economies.[3] If the foreign capital is used to develop the country's infrastructure, it may directly facilitate more investment. Even if the foreign investment is in one industry, it may still encourage domestic investment by reducing costs or creating demand in other industries. Profits may then rise and lead to expansion in these other industries.

Since there are so many specific scarcities in a poor country, it is common for invest-

3. The various meanings of "external economies" are clarified by T. Scitovsky, "Two Concepts of External Economies" *Journal of Political Economy,* April 1954; H. W. Arndt, "External Economies in Economic Growth," *Economic Record,* November 1955.

ment to be of a cost-reducing character by breaking bottlenecks in production. This stimulates expansion by raising profits on all underutilized productive capacity and by now allowing the exploitation of economies of scale that had previously been restricted. When the foreign investment in an industry makes its product cheaper, another industry that uses this product benefits from the lower price. This creates profits and stimulates an expansion in the second industry.

There is also considerable scope for the initial foreign investment to produce external investment incentives through demand creation in other industries. The foreign investment in the first industry can give rise to profits in industries that supply inputs to the first industry, in industries that produce complementary products, and in industries that produce goods bought by the factor-owners who now have higher real incomes. Similar effects may also follow from investment that is product-improving or product-innovating. A whole series of domestic investments may thus be linked to the foreign investment.

Against these benefits must be set the costs of foreign investment to the host country. These costs may arise from special concessions offered by the host country, adverse effects on domestic saving, deterioration in the terms of trade, and problems of balance of payments adjustment.

To encourage foreign enterprise, the government of the host country may have to provide special facilities, undertake additional public services, extend financial assistance, or subsidize inputs. These have a cost in absorbing governmental resources that could be used elsewhere. Tax concessions may also have to be offered, and these may have to be extended to domestic investment since the government may not be able to discriminate, for administrative and political reasons, in favor of only the foreign investor. Moreover, when several

countries compete among themselves in offering inducements to foreign capital, each may offer more by way of inducement than is necessary: the investment may be of a type that would go to one country or another, regardless of inducements, but the foreign enterprise may "shop around" and secure extra concessions. Without some form of collective agreement among capital-receiving countries regarding the maximum concessions that will be made, the cost of "over-encouraging" certain types of foreign investment may be considerable.

Once foreign investment has been attracted, it should be expected to have an income effect that will lead to a higher level of domestic savings. This effect may be offset, however, by a redistribution of income away from capital if the foreign investment reduces profits in domestic industries. The consequent reduction in home savings would then be another indirect cost of foreign investment. But it is unlikely to be of much consequence in practice, for it would require that foreign investment be highly competitive with home investment. In a poor country, it is more probable that foreign capital will complement domestic investment and will give rise to higher incomes and profits in other industries, as already noted.

Foreign investment might also affect the recipient country's commodity terms of trade through structural changes associated with the pattern of development that results from the capital inflow. If the inflow of capital leads to an increase in the country's rate of development without any change in the terms of trade, the country's growth of real income will then be the same as its growth of output. If, however, the terms of trade deteriorate, the rise in real income will be less than that in output, and the worsening terms of trade may be considered another indirect cost of the foreign investment. Whether the terms of trade will turn against the capital-receiving country is problematical depending on various possible changes at home and abroad in the supply and demand for exports, import-substitutes, and domestic commodities. It is unlikely, however, that private foreign investment would cause any substantial deterioration in the terms of trade. For if an unfavorable shift resulted from a rising demand for imports on the side of consumption, it would probably be controlled through import restriction. And if it resulted, on the side of production, from a rising supply of exports due to private direct investment in the export sector, the inflow of foreign capital would diminish as export prices fell, thereby limiting the deterioration in the terms of trade. Moreover, if the deterioration comes through an export bias in production, it is still possible that the factoral and the income terms of trade might improve even though the commodity terms of trade worsen, since the capital inflow may result in a sufficiently large increase in productivity in the export sector.

Of greater seriousness than the foregoing costs are those associated with balance of payments adjustment. Pressure on the balance of payments may become acute when the foreign debt has to be serviced. If the amount of foreign exchange required to service the debt becomes larger than the amount of foreign exchange being supplied by new foreign investments, the transfer mechanism will then have to create a surplus on current account equal to the debit items on account of the payment of interest, dividends, profits, and amortization on the foreign borrowings.[4] When a net outflow of capital occurs, a reallocation of resources becomes necessary in order to expand exports or replace imports. To accomplish this, the country may have to endure internal and external controls or experience currency depreciation. The adverse effects of these measures of balance of payments adjustment must then be considered as indirect costs of foreign investment, to be added to the direct costs of the foreign payments.

The direct costs in themselves need not be a matter of great concern. For even though part of the increased production from the use of foreign capital has to be paid abroad in profits or interest—and this is a deduction that would not be necessary if the savings were provided at home —this is merely to say that the country must not expect to get an income from savings if it does not make the savings.[5] What is fundamental is that the country does have additional investment, and the benefits from this may exceed the direct costs of the foreign savings that made possible the capital formation.

The indirect costs, however, are rightly a cause of concern, insofar as the capital-receiving country may be unable or unwilling to endure a loss of international reserves and does not want to impose measures of balance of payments adjustment in order to find sufficient foreign exchange for the remittance of the external service payments. External measures such as import quotas, tariffs, and exchange restrictions may suppress the demand for imports, but they do so at the expense of productivity and efficiency. Internal measures of higher taxation and credit tightness involve the costs of reduced consumption and investment. And the alternative of currency devaluation may cause the country to incur the costs of a possible deterioration in its terms of trade, changes in income distribution, and necessary

4. The length of time which elapses before this occurs will depend on the growth in new foreign investment, rate of interest and dividend earnings, and the amortization rate. Cf. E. D. Domar, "The Effect of Foreign Investment on the Balance of Payments," *American Economic Review*, December 1950, pp. 805-26.

5. Cf. J. R. Hicks, *Essays in World Economics*, Oxford, 1959, p. 191.

shifts of resources. To avoid, or at least minimize, these indirect costs, the role of private foreign investment must be related to the debt servicing capacity of the host country. And this depends on the country's development program as a whole, since the ability to create a sufficiently large export surplus rests on the operation of all industries together, not simply on the use made of foreign investment alone.

In the past there has been a general tendency for poor countries to overestimate the costs of foreign investment and to discount the benefits, especially the indirect benefits. Now, however, there is wider appreciation that within the context of a development program and with a careful appraisal of the prospective benefits and costs of foreign investment, policies may be devised to secure a greater contribution from the inflow of private capital. Instead of discouraging investment from abroad simply because it involves some costs, the newly developing countries are increasingly recognizing that they should attempt to devise policies that will minimize the costs and maximize the benefits. Although the formulation of specific policies must depend on particular conditions in each country, we may at least suggest some of the principal considerations that might shape these policies.

In general, the attraction of private foreign investment now depends less on fiscal action, upon which most countries have concentrated, and more on other conditions and measures that guarantee protection of the investment and provide wider opportunities for the foreign investor. If private foreign investment is to be encouraged, it is necessary to allay the investor's concern over the possibilities of discriminatory legislation, exchange controls, and the threat of expropriation. Investment guarantees may be utilized more effectively to lessen the investor's apprehension of non-business risks. Either unilaterally or

through bilateral treaties, governments can offer some assurances designed to reduce the likelihood of expropriation or of impairments of investors' rights and to assure investors of an adequate recourse if such impairment should occur.[6] While progress can still be made through the bilateral approach, various proposals are also being made to negotiate multilateral charters for the protection of foreign investment, on a regional or world-wide basis. Such a charter would codify the basic guarantees under which private foreign investments could operate: in particular, the charter would establish fundamental rules relating to respect for contracts and agreements, and would guarantee non-discrimination and payment of full and transferable compensation in case of a taking of the investor's property. It is, however, extremely difficult to achieve multilateral agreement on a single set of rules and to secure treaty commitment by many governments.

Short of requiring agreement on a uniform set of substantive rules, as in a multilateral investment charter, it is still possible to establish some form of international machinery—either an investment tribunal or arbitral body—that would allow disputes arising between the foreign investor and the host government to be submitted for settlement. There is now wide interest in the potentialities of international arbitration and conciliation for settling disputes and strengthening foreign investments.[7]

6. For a detailed review of the various measures that might be adopted, see United Nations, Economic and Social Council, *The Promotion of the International Flow of Private Capital: Further Report by the Secretary-General,* Document E/3492, Geneva, 1961, Chap. III.

7. For a survey of various proposals, see Earl Snyder, "Foreign Investment Protection: A Reasoned Approach," *Michigan Law Review,* April 1963, pp. 1087-124; *The Encouragement and Protection of Investment in Developing Countries, International and Comparative Law Quarterly,* Supplementary Publication No. 3, 1962.

Finally, along with assurances against the occurrence of risk and measures for the adjustment of investment disputes, considerable attention is being given to the possibilities of providing guarantees under which the investor will be compensated for any loss he may suffer from other than normal business causes. Although such a guarantee is something of a measure of last resort, it does help to minimize the investor's risk and gives some advance assurance of a reliable "safety margin." Some capital-supplying nations have provided insurance coverage, but the insurance of investments in developing countries might be made more effective through the establishment of a multilateral investment insurance program as opposed to participation in a number of bilateral programs. Among the various international investment insurance proposals put forward by public and private agencies, the most promising may be an international guarantee fund that would be established and managed as an affiliate of the World Bank. Whether an international insurance fund can be established depends upon the settlement of a number of technical problems: agreement by the participating countries on "the rights and duties" of investors and borrowers, the willingness and ability of governments of both capital-exporting and importing countries to provide the necessary financial subscription, the willingness of capital-exporting countries to support investors of other countries, the readiness of capital-importing countries to pool their widely varying investment risks, the exact definitions of the risks to be covered, and the resolution of international legal questions relating to the specific provisions of an international guarantee fund.[8]

8. The several advantages and disadvantages of a multilateral investment insurance program are outlined in International Bank for Reconstruction and Development, *Multilateral Investment Insurance,* A Staff Report, Washington, D.C., March 1962.

While investment guarantees may help in removing "disincentives" to foreign investment, the attraction of private capital depends even more on positive inducements in the form of greater opportunities for profit-making. The private investor's first concern is whether his costs will be covered and a profit earned. Many developing countries now offer special tax concessions that provide a tax holiday or reduce the rate of tax on profits, but these measures are not effective unless the investment yields a profit. The foreign investor is likely to be less interested in receiving an exemption after a profit is made than he is in being sure of a profit in the first instance. It is therefore most important to raise his profit expectations. To do this, it may be necessary to undertake additional public expenditures, especially in developing the country's infrastructure and in ensuring a supply of trained labor. Yet rarely is a government willing to undertake expenditures expressly for the purpose of attracting foreign investment; instead of incurring the present cost of additional expenditures, most governments prefer to assist foreign investors through a future sacrifice in revenue. Though more politically feasible, tax concessions are not likely to be the most powerful inducements that the host country can offer to encourage a flow of investment.

Newly developing nations are now mainly interested in having foreign enterprises contribute to their industrialization, rather than following the historical pattern of being directed to agriculture or mining. In most cases, however, the size of the domestic market has remained too small to offer much attraction. As a development program proceeds, domestic markets may widen, and this limitation will be reduced. Much can also be done to widen markets and establish a more substantial base for industry by promoting regional markets through arrangements for a common market or a free trade association. The general problem of regional integration is examined in Chapter VII, but it should be noted here that the establishment of a customs union or free trade area may have considerable potential for attracting investment to the development of manufacturing industry.

In considering measures to encourage foreign investment, a developing country does not want, of course, to seek foreign capital indiscriminately. The objective is to ensure that the investment supports activities from which the recipient nation may derive maximum national economic gain, as assessed through benefits and costs. To achieve the most effective utilization of foreign investment in terms of its entire development program, the country may have to adopt policies, such as preferential tax treatment or other incentives, that will attract private capital into activities where it will have the maximum catalytic effect of mobilizing additional effort. From this standpoint, it is especially important that policies affecting the allocation of foreign capital be based on an awareness of the external economies that can be realized from different patterns of investment. Beyond a consideration of the direct increase in income resulting from the investment and other short-term criteria, it is important to look to the more indirect and longer-run possibilities—from the widening of investment opportunities to even the instigating of social and cultural transformations.

Finally, the recipient country may be well advised to emphasize a partnership arrangement between foreign and domestic enterprise. Joint international business ventures that involve collaboration between private foreign capital and local private or public capital are among the most promising devices for encouraging and protecting private international investment, integrating foreign investment within a development program, and stimulating domestic investment. Selection 5.2, below, discusses some relevant aspects of joint ventures.

Foreign enterprise may also become a partner in the host country's development efforts through various contractual arrangements for the transfer of technical and managerial skills. License agreements, technical services agreements, engineering and construction contracts, or management contracts can prove of considerable benefit to a developing country. By negotiating such contractual arrangements, the developing country is able to gain the equivalent of the "technical assistance" component of direct foreign investment without necessarily having to grant its supplier a controlling or even any equity participation in the recipient enterprise. And the foreign enterprise can participate in the profits of the local enterprise without having to incur any capital risk or make the substantial commitments needed for a direct equity investment. While the necessary technical or managerial services are secured from a foreign firm, financial aid may be provided from foreign public sources of capital, either directly or indirectly through a development bank or development corporation. The potentialities for thus combining local public or private ownership with technical assistance from private foreign enterprise and capital assistance from public sources can be of considerable practical importance. This approach can be particularly efficacious when activities are reserved for public ownership or for majority-ownership by local nationals, but there is still a need for seeking technical information or managerial services from abroad. This combination of interests also provides a significant alternative to the contention that government must assume the responsibility for directly producing goods and services whenever local private enterprise lacks the necessary technical competence to do so. In many cases it may be unwarranted to believe that the government can acquire the technical competence and undertake the entrepreneurial function any more readily than can a private firm. The superior alternative may therefore be simply to have the government assist in attracting the missing technical and managerial skills from abroad to co-operate with local private producers. Not only does this allow local enterprise to draw from the stock of accumulated knowledge abroad, but it also facilitates access to continuing know-how and improvements as they occur. In general, since these contractual arrangements are extremely flexible devices, they may be adapted to widely diverse circumstances, and their utility in meeting a variety of objectives is becoming increasingly appreciated.

With the foregoing broad considerations in mind, we should now turn to a closer examination of some specific terms under which private foreign investment might make the maximum contribution to local income.

5.2 Joint International Business Ventures *

Joint international business ventures in the less developed countries have become an important phenomenon of the postwar period. In these countries the attainment of political independence, or the desire to develop a purely agricultural or single commodity economy into a more diversified and potentially richer economic system, has almost everywhere, led to ambitious plans for industrialization.

. . .

At the same time, ambition has often

* From Wolfgang G. Friedmann and George Kalmanoff (eds.), *Joint International Business Ventures,* Columbia University Press, New York, 1961, pp. 3-6, 261-5. Reprinted by permission.

had the better of sober planning. Scarce foreign exchange has been expended for the importation of modern machinery, which has remained unused or has rapidly worn out because of lack of sufficiently trained personnel or the absence of a domestic market. Gradually, an increasing number of the industrially underdeveloped countries have come to modify—though certainly not to abandon—their goals or at least the methods by which to reach these goals. They have come to see that cooperation with industrially developed countries for the use of their capital, their resources, and their skill and experience is a more economic, and ultimately a quicker way of achieving industrialization than to "go it alone." On the other hand, these countries have not abandoned the basic ambition to attain national sovereignty, not only political but also economic. This implies keeping control, or at least general direction, over basic industries and, if possible, over the entire field of foreign investment. The result of these divergent desires and problems has been an increasing interest in some form of partnership association which permits the foreign investor to invest his capital, his know-how, and his managerial and technical skills, in a local enterprise, in association with national—public or private—interests.

There has been a corresponding evolution—more often by necessity than by desire—in the capital-exporting and industrially developed countries. Reluctantly in most cases, willingly in some, governments and entrepreneurs have come to realize that the days are gone or are rapidly passing when a United States or British or French corporation could direct its foreign operations (for example, in manufacturing abroad) without regard to the desires and interests of the host country. It is increasingly recognized that operating through local branches or even wholly owned subsidiaries does not give sufficient play for the development of true partnership. Every year brings more examples of enterprises, originally wholly owned by American, British, or French interests, converting to joint ownership with national interests. At the same time, many new enterprises being established in economically underdeveloped countries are, from the beginning, jointly owned.

. . .

The central concept in the joint international business venture is that of partnership. Partnership has two sides—technical and emotional. On the technical side, it is a joining of contributions; on the emotional side, it is a feeling of united or cooperative effort. In either sense of the word, it is possible to achieve some degree of international partnership in any form of enterprise, however owned or controlled. The creation of local sources of supply, the training and employment of local labor and managerial staff, and the stimulation of "demonstration effects" on the business community at large are a few examples of the possible ways of achieving partnership. . . .

In the widest sense, the "joint venture" comprises any form of association which implies collaboration for more than a very transitory period. It excludes pure trading operations. Associations that do imply a degree of partnership may range from a long-term construction job, in which the industrialized country supplies the machinery, the leading personnel, technical assistance, and, in some cases, long-term loans (often backed by government guarantees), and the recipient country supplies the land, the labor, some of the materials, and the administrative conditions for the development of the enterprise, to equity partnerships in the narrower sense. Such partnerships show a great variety of patterns. There may be "50-50" partnerships, in which the local

investor—public or private—holds one-half of the shares, and the foreign investor, the other half. There may be equity associations in which one partner holds a majority (though often only 51 percent of the shares) and the other partner the minority. An existing enterprise may be transformed into a joint venture with the foreign investor retaining a controlling interest, while the minority shares are held by the local government or a government-controlled development corporation, a small group of local capitalists, or the public. National investment laws or policies, especially in the field of basic raw materials, public utilities, and basic industries sometimes will hold the foreign investor to a minority participation.

. . .

The joint capital venture still remains the principal symbol of partnership. The reasons . . . may be summed up in the following general propositions.

1. In a significant proportion of cases, there is an immediate business advantage in the association of local capital with the enterprise. The foreign investor may be short of capital, or he may be unwilling to bear the entire risk alone.

2. Closely allied are cases in which availability of the best local entrepreneurial or managerial talent is linked with local participation.

3. The acceptance of a joint venture is sometimes the only alternative to desisting from or abandoning an existing enterprise by a foreign investor. A joint venture may be "forced" upon a foreign investor, either through legislative requirements for local participation, or by administrative measures which make the granting of the necessary licenses and currency allocations contingent upon jointness. Such forced ventures are generally disliked by the foreign investor because they hamper his freedom of decision and movement. It is all the

more important for the foreign investor to appreciate the noneconomic factors which, in the great majority of the less developed countries, create the psychological pressure for jointness. Such understanding will eliminate the less desirable alternative of a forced joint venture.

4. To many of the governments and peoples of the less developed countries, partnership in the full sense, that is, jointness in ownership, control, and responsibility, is a symbol of equality.

5. Such symbols are important, regardless of the immediate business aspects because they help to reduce deeply ingrained suspicions of foreign economic domination. Whether such suspicions are justified in a particular case or not, they are a real and an important aspect of that national sensitiveness which characterizes many emancipated peoples who were formerly held in a state of political or economic dependency.

6. Overwhelmingly, the new nations want economic development. In the world of today, they will get support from either the Western or the Communist world. The joint venture is a vehicle, though not the only one, for helping these aspirations and for influencing the course they will take.

Is the joint venture likely to be a permanent or a transient phenomenon in the economic evolution of the less developed countries, and in the transformation of their relationships with the industrially developed countries of the Western world?

From the point of view of the less developed countries, the joint venture serves three essential purposes: 1) It stimulates the engagement of responsible local capital in productive enterprises; 2) it helps to develop a nucleus of experienced managerial personnel in the public and in the private sectors, in proportion to the participation of public authorities and private capital in joint ventures; 3) it helps to advance the training of native labor and technicians.

. . .

To say that the proportion of joint ventures appears to be on the increase is not to imply that the joint venture either does or should form the normal pattern of foreign investment in the less developed countries. A number of investors from the developed countries tend to favor one or the other of two extremes: On the one hand—like General Motors—they insist on wholly-owned subsidiaries, even though they may be quite ready to substitute local for foreign personnel up to the managerial level. On the other hand, they may find it preferable to abstain or withdraw from equity investment and to confine their participation to licensing and technical assistance arrangements. The decision to insist on full ownership may stem from the desire to maximize the dividends coming to the original shareholders, or sometimes from old-fashioned ideas of management. Solid business reasons may also militate against joint ventures. The major oil companies of the Western world resist joint venturing mainly for two reasons: 1) because oil exploration is a risky business attended by many failures which a large organization with world-wide affiliations and capital reserves can sustain better than local interests concentrated on one venture only; and 2) because the requirements of established world-wide operations and markets cannot be taken into account in joint ventures in individual, less developed countries.

Another important factor is the nature of the product or service involved. Generally, the establishment of a separate and continuing enterprise with shared equities and responsibilities is appropriate to a standardized product with a continuous market, rather than to a nonrecurring project. There are many joint ventures in the manufacture of such products as chemicals, drugs, plastics, bicycle tubes, diesel trucks, and radio equipment. The construction of a dam or a steel mill, while involving a prolonged period of close collaboration in matters of finance, technical services, and equipment, does not lend itself to the establishment of a legally and financially separate enterprise.

Quite often the question of joint venturing will be decided by the nature of a previous relationship between the parties concerned and the degree of intimacy to be achieved in continuing collaboration. . . .

Political and psychological conditions sometimes militate against joint ventures. Where difficult and unstable conditions prevail in a country, the association of a foreign investor with local interests may increase the precariousness of the situation. Pressure on the foreign firm may be increased through the local interests involved. The chosen partner may fall out of favor with a new government and prove to be a liability rather than an asset. Conditions of this kind generally would jeopardize the foreign enterprise altogether, regardless of the form of its operation. It is doubtful, for example, whether jointness —even with minority participation—would have provided effective protection for United States industry in the revolutionary conditions prevailing in Cuba. Some of the enterprises expropriated in Cuba, such as the Cuban Telephone Company, were partly owned by Cubans.

Perhaps the most unanimous and widespread argument against joint ventures is a disparity of outlook between the foreign investor and the local partners. In joint ventures between industrially developed countries, such as the United States, Britain, West Germany, the Netherlands, Italy, or Sweden, there is a certain community not only of tradition and of scientific, technical, and legal standards, but there has also been more experience with respon-

sible investment practices and legal supervision, although such standards have often evolved only after disastrous experiences with unscrupulous speculators. In many of the less developed countries, this stage has not yet been reached in the business environment. Power and wealth are often concentrated in relatively few hands, and they are not matched by a corresponding sense of responsibility. The partner from the industrialized country, usually a large corporation with world-wide interests and long experience, generally takes a long-term view of profits, placing the development of the enterprise before quick dividends. Tax considerations may provide an additional incentive to reinvest in a developing foreign enterprise.

Inflationary conditions may produce the reverse situation. The local partner will want to leave his investment in the enterprise where it is relatively inflation-proof, while the foreign investor will be anxious to take out his earnings before devaluation decimates them. The relevant investigations of our study tend to show that the conflict of interest between foreign and local investors is not nearly so frequent as often assumed.

The most ubiquitous and essential criteria are flexibility of mind and attitude, and the ability to appraise the elements inherent in a particular country, a particular situation, and for a particular product or service.

The joint venture is an important symbol of the changing relationship between the developed and the less developed countries, but it cannot be regarded as a panacea. It is a device to be adopted, rejected, or modified after a sober consideration of the many legal, psychological, and technical factors prevailing in a given situation. Confidence between the partners will overcome the most difficult obstacles; lack of confidence will destroy the most perfect devices.

5.3 FOREIGN CAPITAL IN THE GOLD COAST (GHANA)*

In any country the early stages of industrialization are usually the work of foreigners, because usually only they have the knowledge and the capital. This was true of the industrialization of Britain from the fifteenth century to the seventeenth, when the foundations of later greatness were being laid, and it is true of every modern industrial country since that time, except the U.S.S.R. The U.S.S.R. relied on foreigners for knowledge, but supplied the capital herself, by squeezing it out of her farmers. Japan used both foreign knowledge and foreign capital, but the very unequal distribution of income in the country enabled her wealthy classes to supply a much greater proportion of the required capital than is possible in more egalitarian countries.

There is no question that industrialization is impossible in the Gold Coast without bringing in the knowledge of expatriates; the question is only on what terms they come in, and how much of their own capital they may invest.

Whatever the foreigner's faults may be, the fact remains that the Gold Coast needs him more than he needs the Gold Coast. Foreign capital does not need the Gold Coast. If all the foreign capital now in the Gold Coast were driven out, it would have little difficulty in being absorbed elsewhere, for the simple reason that the Gold Coast is a very small place relatively to the world as a whole. There are many places within the sterling area crying out for capital—England herself, not to mention Australia, the Rhodesias, Ceylon and elsewhere. The Gold Coast cannot gain by creating an atmosphere towards foreign

capital which makes foreigners reluctant to invest in the Gold Coast.

Terms must be reached which are acceptable to both sides. The Government should decide on what terms foreign capital will be acceptable, should announce these terms definitely, and should abide by them.

The issues which have to be decided are (I) from what industries foreign capital will be excluded altogether, (II) whether foreign capitalists will be required to have African partners, (III) what rules are to regulate employment, (IV) whether profits or prices are to be regulated, (V) whether capital and profits can be freely transferred, and (VI) what is to be the procedure on nationalization.

(I) *Exclusion.* Certain countries have excluded foreign capital altogether from certain sectors of the economy. Ownership of land or of mineral rights is a common exclusion, not only in West Africa, but also in Asia and in Latin America. Our interest, however, is only in factory industries. Here there are two possible classes of exclusion, industries which are reserved to the government, and those which are reserved to African enterprise.

Most governments now reserve "public utilities" exclusively for public operation. The definition of a public utility is based upon two concurrent characteristics. The industry must be one whose products are consumed by very wide sections of the community. And it must be one which is most economically conducted as a monopoly, or at any rate on a scale of production so large that the producer would have power to exploit the consumer. There are obvious candidates for inclusion in this category, such as electricity or railway transport. Other borderline candidates remain subject to dispute—such as steel or cement.

Since the Gold Coast market is very small, several industries fit into this category which would not fit in larger coun-

* From W. Arthur Lewis, *Report on Industrialization and the Gold Coast,* Government Printing Department, Accra, 1953, pp. 8, 9-11.

tries. For there are many industries which would have a monopoly of the local market which would elsewhere be competitive. In many of these cases the government will not really want to reserve production to itself, if only because it has not enough money to undertake all the industries that may have a local monopoly. But, if the industry could be left to private enterprise, is there any economic reason for distinguishing between foreign and domestic capital? In the absence of private domestic capital, a Government may well be tempted to operate an industry itself, to keep the industry out of foreign hands, whereas, had domestic capital been available, the Government might well have been content to leave the industry in the hands of domestic private enterprise. But there is really no *economic* justification for this distinction. If a monopoly is to be left to private enterprise, it may be that it must be subjected to price and profit controls, in order to protect the consumer. If this is so, these controls are desirable whether the industry is owned abroad or at home. However, even though there is no economic justification, for psychological or political reasons a Government may decide that certain important industries are not to be open to foreign ownership. If so, it should decide which these industries are, and settle the issue by an announcement.

Apart from major industries, which the Government decides in effect to run as public utilities, there may also be minor industries which the Government wishes to keep open for small African enterprise. For example, a Government might decide that no foreigner is to engage in retail trade. In the sphere of manufacturing the relevant industries would be those which can be conducted on a small scale, such as pottery, motor repairs, laundries, furniture or handicraft industries. Such a decision would not be wise. It is very desirable to have small scale industries, but it is also desirable that these industries should be stimulated by competition to adopt ever improving techniques. To keep foreigners out of such industries would be to deprive the Gold Coast consumer of improving service, and to condemn this sector of the economy to relative stagnation.

(II) *Partnership.* The Government of India has announced that it will look most favourably upon foreign capitalists when they propose to operate in partnership with Indian capital (private or public). This partnership may take the form merely that local capitalists, or the Government, are to participate in the capital, or it may take the form that local capitalists are also to participate managerially.

Managerial participation is most valuable to the country, since its nationals in this way gain the best experience, and are thus able to launch out on their own. It would, however, be very irksome to foreign capitalists to be told that they must always act in partnership with local capitalists. This would certainly drive some away, and prevent others from coming. To insist on participation in capital is less irksome, but is also less useful, and hardly worth embodying into an edict.

All the same, though it is undesirable to legislate on this subject, the idea of partnership should be given every encouragement. It appeals to some European firms in the Far East as a form of political insurance, since the firm is less likely to arouse hostility, or to be discriminated against, if it is known to be partly owned in the country, and if it has domestic capitalists to protect it. It ought similarly to appeal to some foreign companies in the Gold Coast. Moreover, apart from these political considerations, partnership has the real economic advantage of helping to train domestic capitalists, and therefore the Government should try to persuade as many foreign firms as possible to give the system a trial.

It is also surprising that more foreign firms do not make it easy for Gold Coast Africans to buy their shares. It is to the interest of foreign firms in the Gold Coast to do all that they can to identify African interests with their own, in order to diminish the suspicion which foreign enterprise everywhere attracts and the peculiar risks of discrimination which it therefore runs.

(III) *Employment*. Since the foreigner's greatest contribution is to train up domestic entrepreneurs, no foreigner should be allowed to operate in the country if his prejudices are such that he denies superior employment to the local people. Many countries have passed legislation to this effect, and the Gold Coast should do the same.

The law would apply to any industrial firm, within five years of the passing of the law, or five years of the firm coming into operation, whichever is later. It would apply to senior appointments, say to persons whose taxable income exceeds £600 a year. It would require that within five years one quarter of persons holding such appointments must be Gold Coast Africans. And it would apply to all firms employing fifty persons or more.

A period of grace is needed to enable the firms to select and train Africans for superior jobs. The percentage of Africans to be employed need not be set beyond a quarter, since this percentage is large enough to wither away reluctance to employ Africans which has been founded only on prejudice.

(IV) *Profit or price controls*. It is usual to regulate public utilities, whether owned at home or abroad.

In general, prices and profits of factories operating in the Gold Coast are regulated by the possible competition of imports. Further regulation is needed only if the factory has artificial or natural protection from imports.

By artifical protection we mean protection deliberately granted by the Government, in the form of tariffs or import licensing. Such protection carries with it an obligation to prevent abuse, and is usually accompanied by the Government fixing a maximum price for the product. Many industrialists will ask for such protection, at least in the initial stages of the industry, and they will most of them agree that price control is a proper adjunct to protection.

By natural protection we mean that which is afforded by having costs of production much lower than the costs of competing imports. This is likely to be confined to cases where the industry is based on some heavy raw material available locally. These cases are not numerous...

It should therefore be made clear that price controls may be applied to public utilities, to industries accorded protection, and to natural monopolies.

Industries manufacturing for export should not be price controlled. The way to prevent excessive profits in this case is to levy an appropriate royalty, excise duty, or export tax.

(V) *Transfers*. If industries are subjected to price control, whether by the Government or by potential competition from imports, this removes one of the motives which governments sometimes have for prohibiting the transfer abroad of profits or of capital, namely, dislike of excessive profits. There remain, however, three other motives for prohibiting such transfers: when foreign exchange is scarce, or to stop capital flight, or to encourage reinvestment in the country.

The first case, shortage of foreign exchange, does not arise in the Gold Coast, and is not likely to arise under the present currency arrangements.

The second case, capital flight, would

occur if the Government proceeded to persecute foreigners, to levy heavy taxes, or to threaten expropriation. It would be very foolish for the Government to frighten foreign capital away, at this stage of Gold Coast development, so the problem need not be discussed.

The third case similarly can hardly arise. If foreigners do not wish to reinvest their profits or capital in a country, attempts to force them to do so are more likely to prevent new capital from coming in than to secure any useful contribution from the capital which is forced in this way.

It is, nevertheless most important to encourage firms to reinvest their profits in the country—not necessarily in the same industry—because profits are the major source of saving in any economy. Industrial countries encourage reinvestment by taxing distributed profits more severely than they tax undistributed profits; but this does not work in dependent countries, partly because the effect of double taxation arrangements is to nullify tax exemptions, and partly because the distinction one wishes to make is not between distributed and undistributed profits, but between profits reinvested in the country and profits transferred abroad (whether distributed or reinvested abroad). It may be possible to create legal distinctions between profits transferred abroad, profits held idle in the country, e. g. in cash, and profits reinvested in the country, but it

would take much ingenuity to devise practicable distinctions. In any case, the attitude of the Government should be not to prohibit transfers, but merely to make reinvestment attractive.

So many countries restricted transfers during the nineteen-thirties, because of shortage of foreign exchange, that foreign capitalists have become wary of making investments unless the Government pledges itself not to restrict transfers. The Gold Coast Government should give this pledge.

(VI) *Nationalisation.* Every capitalist would like to have a guarantee that his firm will not be nationalised. In these days no government can usefully give a pledge that subsequent government will not nationalise an industry. What the Government can do, however, is to give an undertaking that if a firm is nationalised, it will be paid fair compensation...

When the Government has made its decisions on these six issues, it should announce them and should stick to them. One of the essential prerequisites of investment is confidence, and the prerequisite of this is knowledge. Lack of confidence at present holds up investment in the Gold Coast. The Government should do all it can to make plain its position, and to indicate that foreign capital is very welcome, on the terms indicated in its announcement.

6. BIBLIOGRAPHICAL NOTE

1. The following references are recommended to those who wish to pursue further the issue of the importance of capital in the development process: M. Bronfenbrenner, "The Appeal of Confiscation in Economic Development," *Economic Development and Cultural Change,* April 1955; A. K. Cairncross, "Reflections on the Growth of Capital and Income," *Scottish Journal of Political Economy,* June 1959; D. Furtado, "Capital Formation and Economic Development," *International Economic Papers,* No. 4; S. Kuznets, *Six Lectures on Economic Growth,* Glencoe, 1959, Lecture IV; W. Arthur Lewis, *The Theory of Economic Growth,*

Homewood, 1955, Chap. V; K. Martin, "Capital-Output Ratios in Economic Development," *Economic Development and Cultural Change*, October 1957; National Bureau of Economic Research, *Capital Formation and Economic Growth*, Princeton, 1955; W. B. Reddaway, "Some Observations on the Capital-Output Ratio," *Indian Economic Review*, February 1960; Joseph J. Spengler, "Capital Requirements and Population Growth in Underdeveloped Countries; Their Interrelations," *Economic Development and Cultural Change*, July 1956; T. W. Swan, "Economic Growth and Capital Accumulation," *Economic Record*, November 1956; United Nations, Department of Economic Affairs, *Domestic Financing of Economic Development*, New York, 1950; United Nations, ECAFE, "Financing of Economic Development," *Economic Bulletin for Asia and Far East*, December 1962.

2. Problems of taxation in underdeveloped countries are examined in the following: R. J. Chelliah, *Fiscal Policy in Underdeveloped Countries,* London, 1960; John F. Due, *Taxation and Economic Development in Tropical Africa,* Cambridge, 1963; Richard Goode, "Taxation of Saving and Consumption in Underdeveloped Countries," *National Tax Journal*, December 1961; U. K. Hicks, "The Search for Revenue in Underdeveloped Countries," *Revue de Science et de Legislation Financieres,* January and March, 1952; U. K. Hicks, *Development From Below*, London, 1961; Nicholas Kaldor, *Indian Tax Reform*, New Delhi, 1956; Nicholas Kaldor, "Will Underdeveloped Countries Learn to Tax?" *Foreign Affairs*, January 1963; A. M. Martin and W. A. Lewis, "Patterns of Public Revenue and Expenditure," *Manchester School of Economic and Social Studies*, September 1956; Paul A. M. van Philips, *Public Finance and Less Developed Economy*, The Hague, 1957; A. R. Prest, *Public Finance in Underdeveloped*

Countries, London, 1962; Carl S. Shoup, et al., *The Fiscal System of Venezuela: A Report*, Baltimore, 1959; U. Tan Wai, "Taxation Problems and Policies of Underdeveloped Countries," *IMF Staff Papers*, November 1962; Haskell P. Wald (ed.), *Papers and Proceedings of the Conference on Agricultural Taxation and Economic Development*, Cambridge, 1954; United Nations, *Taxes and Fiscal Policy in Underdeveloped Countries*, New York, 1955; United Nations, ECAFE, "Taxation and Economic Development in Asian Countries," *National Institute Economic Review, Far East*, November 1953; "Taxation and Development of Agriculture in Underdeveloped Countries," *Economic Bulletin for Asia and Far East*, June 1958; "Public Finance in African Countries," *Economic Bulletin for Africa*, June 1961. A comprehensive list of readings for individual countries is provided in *Bibliography on Taxation in Underdeveloped Countries*, Harvard Law School, International Program in Taxation, 1963.

3. The following may be consulted for further study of the means and objectives of foreign economic aid: Robert E. Asher, *Grants, Loans, and Local Currencies*, Washington, D. C., 1961; P. T. Bauer and J. B. Wood, "Foreign Aid: The Soft Option," *Banca Nazionale del Lavoro Quarterly Review*, December 1961; Eugene R. Black, *The Diplomacy of Economic Development*, Cambridge, 1960; A. K. Cairncross, *The International Bank for Reconstruction and Development*, Princeton, 1959; Milton Friedman, "Foreign Economic Aid: Means and Objectives," *Yale Review*, Summer 1958; J. K. Galbraith, "A Positive Approach to Economic Aid," *Foreign Affairs*, April 1961; B. H. Higgins, *United Nations and U.S. Foreign Economic Policy*, Homewood, 1962; R. L. Major, "Aid to Underdeveloped Countries," *National Institute Economic Review*, May 1961; Max F. Millikan and W. W.

Rostow, *A Proposal: Key to an Effective Foreign Policy*, New York, 1957; Millikan, "New and Old Criteria for Aid," *Proceedings of the Academy of Political Science*, January 1962; Alan D. Neale, *The Flow of Resources from Rich to Poor*, Center for International Affairs, Harvard University, November 1961; B. K. Nehru, "A Rational Approach to Foreign Assistance," *International Development Review*, October 1960; P. Rosenstein-Rodan, "International Aid for Underdeveloped Countries," *Review of Economics and Statistics*, May 1961; United Nations, FAO, *Development Through Food: A Strategy for Surplus Utilization*, Rome, May 1961; United Nations, *International Flow of Long-term Capital and Official Donations 1951–1959*, New York, 1961 (62.II.D.1); United Nations, *The Capital Development Needs of the Less Developed Countries*, New York, 1962 (62.II.D.3); Jacob Viner, "The Need for External Assistance of Underdeveloped Countries," *Confluence*, 1955; Charles Wolf, Jr., *Foreign Aid: Theory and Practice in Southern Asia*, Princeton, 1960.

4. Problems of private foreign investment in underdeveloped countries are examined in the following: E. R. Barlow and I. T. Wender, *Foreign Investment and Taxation*, New York, 1955; J. N. Behrman, "Promoting Development Through Private Direct Investment," *American Economic Review, Papers and Proceedings*, May 1960; Roy Blough, "Joint International Business Ventures in Less Developed Countries," *Institute of Private Investment Abroad*, Vol. 2; A. A. Fatouros, *Government Gaurantees to Foreign Investors*, New York, 1962; R. N. Gardner, "International Measures for the Promotion and Protection of Foreign Investment," *American Society International Law Proceedings*, 1959; J. Frank Gaston, *Obstacles to Direct Foreign Investment*, New York, 1951; John M. Hunter, "Long-term Foreign Investment in Underdeveloped Countries," *Journal of Political Economy*, February 1953; R. F. Mikesell (editor), *U.S. Private and Government Investment Abroad,* Eugene, 1962; Ragnar Nurkse, "The Problem of International Investment Today in the Light of Nineteenth Century Experience," *Economic Journal*, December 1954; Samuel Pizer and Frederick Cutler, "Expansion of U.S. Investments Abroad," *Survey of Current Business*, August 1962; United Nations, *Financing of Economic Development—Recent Governmental Measures Affecting the International Flow of Private Capital*, New York, 1955; "Laws and Regulations Affecting Foreign Investment in Asia and the Far East," *Economic Bulletin for Asia and Far East*, May 1957; United Nations, Economic and Social Council, *The Promotion of the International Flow of Private Capital*, February 26, 1960 (E/3325); *Further Report by the Secretary-General*, May 18, 1961 (E/3492).

INFLATION

A<small>LTHOUGH WE OUTLINED</small> in the preceding chapter various ways of mobilizing resources for developmental expenditures without causing inflation, many countries have in practice desired a higher rate of investment than could be maintained by noninflationary sources of finance, and recourse to the substitute method of monetary expansion and credit creation has become common. Increased spending of an inflationary sort is therefore an important issue of development policy. On this issue, however, there are marked differences of opinion regarding the causes and consequences of inflation. We want in this chapter to sort out these differences and reach some assessment of the effects of inflation in newly developing economies.

To do this, the chapter begins with materials of a general nature that examine in analytical terms the main forces and consequences of inflation. A central question is whether deficit financing can be an effective way of increasing capital formation (1.1, 1.2, 1.3). Other consequences of inflation are also clarified (1.4, 1.5). And policy implications are considered—especially the role of monetary policy (1.6). In connection with the possibilities of monetary and credit policy, the characteristics of the "organized" and "unorganized" money markets of underdeveloped countries are also examined (1.7).

Against the background of this general analysis, the materials in section 2 give specific attention to the problem of inflation in Latin America. While section 1 identifies a number of contributing factors to inflation, section 2 draws the issue sharply—in terms of Latin American experience—between the traditional "monetarist" view of inflation and the contrasting "structuralist" view. The "structuralist" arguments dominate the discussion in section 2, but a critique of the structuralist position is implicit in section 1, and the more general inflationary factors associated with monetary and income expansion should be kept in mind when considering the reasoning about inflation in Latin America.

Different interpretations of the causes of inflation lead naturally to divergent conclusions on policies for curbing inflation. Section 1 emphasizes the orthodox prescription of restraining demand by the exercise of monetary and fiscal discipline. This policy is criticized, however, in some of the selections in section 2 as being concerned with only the "propagating" factors of inflation or the "symptoms" instead of the underlying real structural causes. In contrast, the structuralist position looks to the supply side of the problem and stresses the need for social and economic reforms to correct basic structural imbalances.

There is no denying that underdeveloped countries are especially prone to inflationary pressures, and that the policies available to an underdeveloped country for effectively controlling inflation are more limited than those in an advanced country. What remains controversial, however, is whether these inflationary pressures encourage or inhibit development. This issue pervades this chapter, with arguments presented both in favor of and against the method of development through inflation.

Besides the usual points advanced in favor of inflation, consideration is given to the following special contentions: inflation permits the employment of underemployed workers; monetary or credit expansion is necessary to allow the "development authorities" to bid resources away from consumption; in the early stages of inflation, the "money illusion" may induce factors of production to work more intensively; the period of inflation may be short since it will increase investment which, in turn, will expand total output, and a large portion of the increment in output may then be saved and taxed to offset the rise in investment; and none of the alternative methods of financing a rise in investment is any less free of hardships.

As for the case against inflation, the following arguments are especially persuasive: inflation has harmful effects on the efficient allocation of resources, being particularly detrimental in creating distortions in investment patterns; balance of payments pressures result from the adverse impact on exports, the spill-over into imports, and the discouragement of foreign investment; the volume of resources available for domestic investment may actually fall as voluntary savings decline and incentives are diminished; and the government lacks the power to constrain the inflation and prevent the pressures from becoming progressively severe.

1. INFLATION AND ITS EFFECTS

1.1 INFLATION AND CAPITAL FORMATION *

The general case for inflationary financ-

* From United Nations, ECAFE, "Inflation and the Mobilization of Domestic Capital in Underdeveloped Countries of Asia," *Economic Bulletin for Asia and the Far East,* Vol. II, No. 3, 1951, pp. 22-5.

ing of capital expenditure may be summarized briefly as follows.

Given the need for capital formation on a certain scale and given the importance of public investment in capital formation, the resources needed for such investment have to be directed to the government somehow. This cannot be done merely by mobilizing the genuine voluntary savings of the people since in a poor country such savings are very low. The relevant issue, therefore, is the choice of means whereby sacrifices are compulsorily elicited from the people. This can be done by: (a) Making people work harder or longer without giving them more money income; (b) Taking away more of the people's income through taxation or compulsory lending; (c) Curtailing less desirable private investment; (d) Forced savings through inflation.

There are limits beyond which, for political or administrative reasons, the first three courses cannot be pursued.

Thus, governments wedded to a free economic system cannot, beyond a certain point, make people work harder or longer without giving them more money income. The same is true of compulsory lending as is shown by the experience of countries like India. The limits to taxation is a large subject ... But a few tentative remarks may be offered here. In countries where entrepreneurial capacity is scarce, high taxation imposed upon the few rich people who are mainly responsible for such saving and investment as take place, may provoke a virtual non-cooperation from these classes and result in a general paralysis in the economic system. Direct taxation of the myriads of small incomes is not feasible administratively nor, perhaps, politically. If indirect taxes are levied on an extensive scale, it is arguable that their effect may not be very different from that of a rise in the price-level induced by inflation. And inflation has at least this advantage over indirect taxes: it requires no administrative skill or machinery to engineer an inflation. As regards the curtailment of less desirable private investment by direct or monetary controls, it is arguable that if underdeveloped countries are capable of administering such controls well, they need not fight shy

of inflation very much, for in that event, they will also have the capacity to control some of the excesses of inflation.

The argument presented so far merely states that the desired rate of public investment may not be attained if there is rigid insistence on orthodox financing principles. But it does not follow that by inflationary financing of capital expenditures the required capital formation would necessarily be assured. It may be that there are limits to what even an inflation can achieve by way of forced savings; or, that inflation, if prolonged, may impair productive capacity and thus be detrimental to capital formation over a period of years. The advocates of inflationary financing of developmental expenditure are thus also obliged to argue that, at least in an underdeveloped economy, the inflation resulting from deficit financing need not last long or develop into severe inflation with its attendant evils.

It is arguable that, as the development projects are completed, they would have the effect of increasing production, and, unless the marginal propensity to save and the marginal tax yield are both zero, finance for development plans in the next period would therefore be available from increased savings or the proceeds of increased taxation. Assuming that the government's investment for developmental purposes remains the same from year to year (in real terms), the proportion which was deficit-financed would very soon start to decline, and in a few years all the finance required might be non-inflationary. Since the inflation need not last very long or become very severe, it need not destroy the incentive to save on the part of private individuals as much as is sometimes supposed. Insofar as inflation redistributes national income in favour of the richer sections of the community, it may actually have salutary effects on private saving and investment. Again, decisions to save are closely related to the profitability of available investments. As development plans are completed, they would eliminate some of the bottlenecks which hamper production and thus create new investment opportunities. These new opportunities would in themselves be an inducement to higher savings. It may be that inflation engendered by the government's development programme encourages speculative and unproductive private investment, which may prolong the inflation and make it wasteful. But it should be possible to control private investment to some extent. The inflationary pressures released by budget deficits might be suppressed by controls if a cumulative price-wage spiral threatened to develop.

In brief, deficit financing may lead to inflation, but at the end of it all we would have the dams and the irrigation canals and the roads which could not have been started in the first place if rigid insistence on sound financing was maintained. Admittedly, inflation will impose hardships; but this may be inevitable—the real issue is about the means of enforcing sacrifices. Inflation need not have serious untoward consequences because it need not last long and its adverse effect can be suppressed to some extent.

In the foregoing paragraphs, the case for inflation is presented in its most favourable form, and in general terms. In any concrete situation, however, it cannot be taken for granted that the consequences of inflationary financing would be as favourable as might be imagined in the abstract. Some weaknesses in the argument just presented are examined below.

Assuming that, for political or administrative reasons, capital formation on the required scale cannot be undertaken by orthodox financial measures, it must also be recognized that the very simplicity and convenience of deficit financing creates a danger of extravagance and ineptitude in spending money and of neglect of the possibilities that even in an underdeveloped country exists for tapping savings or collecting higher taxes. The choice between deficit financing on the one hand and taxation and borrowing on the other is never an exclusive choice, and there is always a danger of excessive reliance on the course that seems likely to provoke the least resistance.

Even, however, if it could be assumed that the administration of deficit financing would be highly efficient, one cannot be too complacent about the duration and extent of the inflation induced by it. Given a certain rate of real investment by the government from year to year, and assuming no untoward effects on private investment, total productive capacity would no doubt soon be increased. This, after all, is the justification of development expenditure, and short of complete mishandling of the investments, some increase in production must result. But if the government is to reduce the proportion of its investment which is "deficit financed," it must by conscious policy divert a part of the increased output itself. It is not enough to say that more output means more savings and taxes for the government. Even if people save more, they can invest these savings in private investment, and there may be nothing to offset the continuing real investment undertaken by the government. Inflation may continue despite higher production and higher savings because private investment absorbs the new savings. The political and administrative difficulties which initially necessitated deficit financing will eventually have to be overcome if the resulting inflation is to be short-lived.

In an underdeveloped country, we cannot even be sure that much of the increased production would in fact be saved. If the increased production accrues to the poorer sections of the community, it may go almost entirely to increase consumption. In underdeveloped countries inflation does not necessarily redistribute income in favour of the rich or investing classes. The class to gain by inflation is the entrepreneurial class; but in predominantly agrarian societies, the entrepreneurial class consists to a large extent of poor peasants and merchants. A redistribution of income in favour of the peasants is not conducive to greater savings; and the merchants seldom invest in productive ventures.

The great inelasticity of the tax system is also likely in many countries to keep down the yield of taxes as real production increases. Indeed, since prices would be probably rising in response to budget deficits, there is a danger that the government's command over real resources through taxation may actually decline as inflation proceeds apace in spite of a higher aggregate productivity. Many taxes, such as land revenue, are not easy to revise upwards in money terms as prices rise; and it cannot be taken for granted, therefore, that given a certain growth in real production and a certain rate of government expenditure in real terms, the part of this expenditure in money terms that is deficit financed will decline progressively ...

Again, if conditions in underdeveloped countries are such that the initial capital investment needed is of a long-term character (e.g., irrigation canals rather than wells), production may increase only after a considerable time has elapsed. But in view of a high propensity to consume and the absence of a broad-based industrial structure which makes short-run supply conditions very inelastic, the inflationary impact on an underdeveloped country is likely to be very disturbing in the short run. It would be urgent for such countries, therefore, to try to suppress the inflationary pressures for a while. Whether poor

countries with a scarcity of administrative skill are in a position to undertake effective control measures is a moot question to be discussed later. Attempts to control private consumption and investment may indeed be as unpalatable as higher taxation or compulsory savings. The original justification for deficit financing, viz., that it is simple and encounters less opposition, may well be illusory. This is all the more likely since the danger of inflation in many underdeveloped countries does not arise currently only from attempts to promote economic development; the legacy of inflation in the past, the boom in raw material prices, etc., are also factors in the total situation which make the dangers of deficit financing more serious than they would be if we started from a position of firm monetary equilibrium.

Lastly, it cannot be taken for granted that inflationary financing of capital expenditure will necessarily elicit the sacrifices required from the people. In the ultimate analysis, some group has to suffer a decline in its standard of living through higher prices. But in democratic countries with powerful pressure groups having considerable influence on the government, there are limits beyond which a redistribution of income woud be politically intolerable. In predominantly agricultural countries, the classes, which cannot raise their incomes at least as fast as prices, are not very numerous. The peasants, merchants and a few rich entrepreneurs do not suffer any decline in real income through rising prices. There are not many rich people who live on interest payments made in money terms—the village money lenders in many cases collect their dues in kind. The only classes to provide forced savings, therefore, are the small class of professional men, government employees, and the industrial proletariat. It is difficult to justify a method of enforcing savings which hurts only a few people on the ground that voluntary savings are small and the need for capital formation is very urgent. Apart from this, economic development does not depend on supply of capital alone but also on the inventiveness, organizational ability and integrity of the people. The growth of all these factors depends very much on the vitality of the two classes—professional and the urban proletariat—most likely to be hurt by inflation. This is the reason why many governments initiate an inflation under duress, and then go on to neutralize its effects by cost-of-living allowances, price controls, compulsory requisition of foodstuffs, etc. The result is that nearly everybody's income increases *pari passu* with rising prices, and there is very little forced savings, but a maze of administrative problems. Or worse still, the few who suffer may be the most essential but the least powerful or vociferous elements in the society. Inflation on the scale required to attain the necessary capital formation may, therefore, be self-frustrating.

What is the upshot of this discussion of the role of inflationary financing in the mobilization of domestic capital? It may be conceded that, in certain circumstances, inflationary financing of capital expenditure may expedite capital formation. This course, however, has many pitfalls, and, unless moderately and wisely used, may do more harm than good. In any event, inflation promises no relief from the difficult and unpalatable measures of control or taxation or compulsory savings which also have to be adopted. The only course for an underdeveloped country is one of trial and error—a course in which higher taxation, mobilization of voluntary savings, exhortations for more work without pay, deficit financing, controls of various sorts, etc., will all have to be adopted in varying degrees from time to time, depending on the situation as it develops.

1.2 Deficit Financing in Underdeveloped Countries *

Following Professor Nurkse's pioneering work, [1] it has become fashionable for less discerning observers than he to regard the underemployed workers of the underdeveloped countries as a huge reservoir easily tapped for the capital formation so urgently desired. That there is much such underemployment by western standards in these areas is evident; the question before us, however, is to what extent deficit financing is a feasible method for bringing these resources into use in the sense of increasing total net production.

At the outset, let us explicitly recognize that not all types of labor are likely to be unemployed in these countries. Indeed, skilled labor of all kinds—and especially those skills most needed for economic development purposes—are almost always scarce and therefore the most we can hope for from a policy of deficit financing with respect to these resources is to bid them away from their present occupations into more productive ones. There seems likely to be some net general inflationary effects in such bidding but the amount will probably be so small as to be uninteresting from our point of view. Much more serious are the severe limitations of the bottleneck variety which the shortage of engineers, managers, entrepreneurs, foremen, operators of complex equipment, etc., place on the efficient use of unskilled workers, whether in the new government projects or in the private projects from which the skilled workers have been enticed. In the absence of appropriate numbers and kinds of skilled workers the gross output of the unskilled labor transferred to new jobs

* From Gardner Patterson, "Impact of Deficit Financing in Underdeveloped Countries: Some Neglected Aspects," *Journal of Finance*, Vol. XII, No. 2, May 1957, pp. 179-89. Reprinted by permission.

1. Ragnar Nurkse, *Capital Formation in Underdeveloped Countries*, Oxford, 1953.

may be exceedingly small; and the danger of inflation from their employment correspondingly large. The underdeveloped countries can increase their supply of skilled labor, perhaps using deficit financing for this purpose, but this is a long process normally and, on the basis of recent history, perhaps it can be safely assumed that the program of economic development fired by deficit financing will not be postponed until adequate additional supplies of such skills are available.

With respect to unskilled labor, the situation seems to be quite different. By offering high enough money wages, a substantial amount of such labor, especially from the rural areas, probably can be obtained without directly reducing the production of the sector of the economy from which these people are drawn. But an aspect of this that is sometimes given inadequate attention is that the value of the goods and services these additional labor resources are creating must be offset, for some time and in no small part, by the additional consumption this transfer of occupation entails. Not all of the expanded production is net. In most underdeveloped areas such a change in occupation will involve a great many changes in area of residence, more particularly from villages to urban areas or to new dam sites, new highways, etc. Such changes will often bring about a welcome relief from crowded housing conditions in the villages, but it will also necessitate some additional housing in the new areas of residence. Simple, rudimentary, and primitive as such housing may be, it can represent a substantial offset for a time to the value of the new output of the previously underemployed workers. Probably a much larger offset will be the value of the additional consumption—food, clothing, entertainment—which these workers will demand as a price for leaving their former work and homes. In almost all cases the *quality* of consumption, and the real cost of producing it, tends to be greater for workers who are physically uprooted than it was during the previous period. In assessing the importance of this, it must also be remembered that while the economic planner may find what he regards as a huge amount of underemployment in these countries and, indeed, may find that the marginal productivity of a significant proportion of the labor force is zero, or possibly in extreme cases even negative, this is not the way the individual worker sees it. As an individual he does work, he does produce something, and what the outsider may regard as underemployment has probably held through all living memory and any change therefore is likely to have a cost in the improvement of that particular individual's economic well-being. Furthermore, the fact that those remaining in the village will have more spacious housing, fewer mouths to feed out of a given food supply, etc., is no more likely in an underdeveloped country than in ours to be regarded as important compensation by the member of the household who leaves. Nor is it possible for the departing member to take with him any significant proportion of the goods which he might have consumed had he remained. It seems to follow that whereas deficit financing can doubtless bring some underemployed unskilled labor resources into net additional and productive employment, that is, can increase gross production, there are for a time large direct and immediate offsets. Moreover, the offsetting goods themselves are often in short supply and likely to be so for some time inasmuch as the immediate object of making use of the unemployed labor resources is assumed here to be the creation of productive capital goods rather than consumer goods, durable or otherwise. These offsets, it must be noted, are not included in any increase in demand occasioned in the economy as a whole as a consequence of the higher monetary incomes growing out of the deficit financing.

...

In sum, the possibility of deficit financing bringing unemployed resources into new production seems likely to be limited largely to unskilled workers in the underdeveloped countries and, unfortunately, even here the net increase in production for capital formation purposes may be relatively small for a not inconsiderable period because of the increase in consumption such employment entails. On top of this are the bottleneck limitations imposed by the fact there are usually few, or no, unemployed skilled workers, tools, machinery, and, often, raw materials, needed to complement the unskilled workers' efforts.

Let us now turn to the question of the extent to which increased savings can be induced or forced by deficit financing practices. That is, whether deficit financing yields some net increase in current production or not, is the net additional purchasing power the government can create an effective device for transferring real resources from consumption to investment in the underdeveloped countries?

In those underdeveloped countries a large part of which has not yet been monetized there may well exist a large untapped savings potential. During the period the barter aspects of economy (usually involving especially the rural areas) are being replaced by monetary exchanges, even very poor people apparently are willing to build up relatively large stocks of cash. If, as is typical, the rural areas constitute a large part of the economy, the total savings, and so the total new investment which can initially be made without inflation, may be impressive. Indeed, it is possible that it may be enough, provided the choice of investments and their execution have been inspired, to result in a sufficient increase

in the total product to permit a taxing away in one form or another of a sufficient amount of the *subsequent* increase in total production to carry out further investment and still provide some increases in consumption. Thus might the vicious circle of poverty begetting poverty be broken.

If this chance to save during the monetization process has been missed and deficit financing is continued after cash stocks have been built up as much as the people voluntarily want them to be, then what? [2] Once monetized, the money-income ratio in underdeveloped countries tends to be low; that is, the economies are very sensitive to deficit financing. In other words, the continued even moderate deficit financing tends to be inflationary and so the question becomes: Is inflation a feasible way of increasing (i.e., forcing) savings in these areas? To this no a priori answer can be given. It depends very much on the structure and organization of the particular economy, on the social and political conditions then ruling, on whether the crops during this period have been especially good or bad or just average, etc. Here we can look at only one or two of what seem to be rather interesting and sometimes neglected aspects of all this.

So long as the deficit-finance-inspired inflation is relatively mild, the price rises may well, as Professor Lewis has so eloquently argued,[3] serve to increase the profits of the industrial and mercantile classes and by so doing increase their savings. Indeed, if the entrepreneurs now hoard

2. Even after the economy has been monetized, some savings might be garnered via deficit financing and without inflation if the increase in money in circulation is limited to something less than the increases in productivity; but to so gear the new cash creation is very likely beyond the administrative capabilities and to so limit it beyond the firmly held desires of the bureaucracy of most underdeveloped countries.

3. W. Arthur Lewis, *The Theory of Economic Growth,* Homewood, Ill.: Richard D. Irwin, Inc., 1955.

this cash, or pay off past bank loans, or buy government bonds, the inflation tends to taper off very quickly and the inflation has induced the required savings for the planned investments. This is a relatively happy state of affairs. But if, as is at least equally likely, this group now spends their funds, they will feed the inflation. In either event, this situation does, of course, involve, indeed it is made possible by, a redistribution of income against other sectors of the economy, particularly wage-earners and farmers. Nonetheless, if the entrepreneurial classes and/or the government make appropriate investments with the new funds, in the longer run labor productivity will presumably increase and real wages improve. Clearly there are some possibilities for economic development here.

But the possibilities are limited ones. In the first place, the redistribution of income initially involved may run counter to the economic welfare objectives of the government and thus be unacceptable and so offset by the government. If the general inflation resulting from the deficit financing becomes more serious it may lead the manufacturing and merchandising sectors of the economy to hoard their output—engage in inventory accumulation in general—in anticipation of further price increases. While this is a form of saving induced by inflation, it is not normally of the sort which facilitates the nation's economic development program. Quite the contrary, such action not only tends to reduce the physical capabilities of other sectors of the economy to produce — and so makes genuine saving, as distinct from non-consumption by others, more difficult—but also, once known, tends to increase tensions among the various groups of the society, some such tensions already being the inevitable price of rapid and drastic change of the economic structure of the nation. If the savings of the mercantile group made possible by inflation take the still-not-rare form of jewels, gold, and other precious but in many respects economically barren forms, then added difficulties are created for the economic development program since foreign exchange is frequently one of the limiting factors of planned investments. Still and all, if the inflationary effects of deficit financing can be kept relatively mild, there may be a significant increase in the useful savings of this group.

But this is not the end of the story. There is more to be said of the reactions by the labor and farmer groups to inflation bred by deficit financing. If the labor force is unorganized, wages tend to be rigid and deficit-finance-induced inflation can well result in reduced consumption from current income, as has been assumed above. However, this will not necessarily result in an equivalent amount of forced savings. Any encroachment on the already low consumption standards of these people is likely to be offset in part through disinvestments, such disinvestment taking many forms, among them failing to maintain workers' houses and other durable personal property, and less investment in the training and education and health of themselves and their children.

But if labor is well organized, and this is increasingly the case inasmuch as frequently one of the objectives sought under a program of economic development is strong labor unions, the response to inflation is likely to be quick and strong demands for wage increases. Such increases probably will tend to lag behind price increases, but the lags have a way of becoming shorter now that the notion of escalator clauses is widely known and greatly admired. These high wages will of course hinder the transfer of real resources to the government deficit-financed investment projects inasmuch as wage earners in countries where per capita incomes are very low tend to have a high income-elasticity of demand and a low price-elasticity of demand. Moreover, from the savings that might be forced out of the labor groups in the process must be subtracted not only the disinvestment noted above in the case of unorganized workers but also the goods and services not produced during the strikes, slow-downs, and general impairment of labor's efficiency which so often accompany these efforts of organized labor to maintain their real incomes in the face of inflation. And, as already noted, in many of the underdeveloped countries, governments are not prepared for the reasons of general welfare and political expediency to let real wages decline significantly. In many of the underdeveloped countries the numbers in the wage class are relatively small and so, even if wages are rigid, only relatively small amounts of resources can be transferred to the government's projects. All an all, for both economic and political reasons there seems little prospect for inducing any large amount of forced savings from wage earners via inflation.

In most underdeveloped countries the peasants constitute by far the largest occupational group. What are the prospects of forcing them to increase their savings by deficit financing and inflation? The answer depends, in the first instance, upon an important question of fact. If general inflation distributes incomes in favor of the peasants via higher prices for agricultural products than for other goods and services, and if this group has a higher propensity to save than the other groups from whom the income has been transferred, then inflation may increase the voluntary savings of the peasants and the total savings of the economy. But it is, I suspect, more often the case in the underdeveloped countries, especially those who export agricultural products, that inflation resulting from deficit-financed economic development makes itself felt much more rapidly and intensely on the goods the peasants buy than on those they sell. In this event, in the first

instance at least, the inflation redistributes incomes away from the peasants. Now this, too, may result in some forced savings in the form of reduced consumption. But the savings may take other forms too, and perhaps less happy ones from the point of view of economic development. Farmers have shown, in times past, that they have their own ways of meeting an inflationary squeeze: hoarding of their produce. This is a form of savings of course, but it rarely contributes to increased production, its effect tending to be to raise the price of the hoarded produce which in turn permits the peasants to evade the forced savings while pushing the entire economy on to a higher inflationary level. These are not ideal circumstances for transferring real resources to the government's investment program and, moreover, in its efforts to meet some of these problems the government may take recourse to large imports of foodstuffs and other agricultural produce. This is surely a most wasteful expedient— though it may well be unavoidable in the circumstances—and if pursued very far constitutes a large offset to the value of the hoped-for investment for which the deficit financing was employed.

An attempt to force savings from the peasants by inflation may have other undesirable and, in part, self-defeating consequences. The farmer, as well as the urban laborer, may be expected to attempt to maintain consumption by dissaving. These dissavings, frequently ignored or underestimated by those urging deficit financing, may quickly reach large dimensions. If, as is frequently the case, the farmers have been the recent recipients of some economic development efforts in the form of new machinery, improved irrigation systems, new land improvement schemes, etc., the disinvestment can easily and rapidly become a multiple of the savings the farmer is trying to avoid....

From this, I conclude that the amount

of increased *net* savings which can be forced or induced by inflation among the labor and farm groups, who constitute a very large proportion of the population of underdeveloped countries, is likely to be small, once the economy has been monetized and inflation has gone on long enough to be apparent to most people.

...

In the long run, of course, it is always hoped that inflation generated by deficit-financed economic development in underdeveloped countries will be self-limiting as the additional goods and services flow from the investments, and that these investments will result in substantially higher per capita real incomes. This may prove a justified hope, provided the inflation does not in the meantime reach such proportions as to result in tremendous amounts of misinvestment, waste, and acute social and political tensions.

The reservations expressed here as to the effectiveness of deficit financing in underdeveloped countries as a means of encouraging economic development stem not from the fear that it will fail at first—indeed it can be a powerful and helpful tool, especially in the very beginning of the program when much of the economy has still to be monetized. Nor are the reservations serious if deficit financing is restrained to amounts less than the increase in productivity each year, and if it is restricted to fields where returns are quick and which have a large output-capital ratio: one thinks of pest control, seed improvement, improved animal care, community projects, cottage industries, etc. Its major shortcomings are rather that those using it will seriously overestimate the unemployed resources that can thus be brought into work, overestimate the net increase in production that will result from whatever unemployed or underemployed factors of production can be put to work,

underestimate the cost of inflation in terms of disinvestment elsewhere in the economy, and underestimate the adverse impact of inflation on the willingness of the peoples in the underdeveloped countries to embrace economic change.

1.3 DEFICIT FINANCING AND PUBLIC INVESTMENT *

The difficulty of transforming latent resources into actual output in under-developed countries is ... deeply rooted. Different analysts have differed about what these other root causes are—and indeed they may be different as between different under-developed countries. Lack of entrepreneurship or technical knowledge, the lack of an adequate framework of public services, lack of incentives for increased effort, ignorance, lack of a market or credit organization, lack of communications, immobility of resources, absence of adequate economic institutions have all been cited with different degrees of emphasis. A common factor of all these cited obstacles is that they relate to deficiencies of effective supply rather than of effective demand.

Insofar as a lack of essential public services and of communications is among these obstacles, public capital formation assumes particular importance in creating the preconditions for an expansion of output, and this may add to the importance of public investment, financed, if necessary, by deficits. Again, however, the analogy with the case for public investment and compensatory public finance in more developed countries during periods of depression is more superficial than real. The purpose of the public expenditure is different in the two cases. In the depression case, it is to increase incomes and create the demand and price incentives for resumed production; the greater the multi-

* From H. W. Singer, "Deficit Financing of Public Capital Formation," *Social and Economic Studies,* September 1958, Special Number, pp. 91-6. Reprinted by permission.

plier the greater the effect. The public capital formation is justified by its monetary and secondary effects. That is why it might even consist of building pyramids or burying gold or bank notes in disused coal mines. In under-developed countries, public investment could be economically justified only for its impact on productivity, for lowering cost curves and increasing the elasticity of supply curves—not for raising demand curves. Hence, the monetary income effects of deficits incurred to finance public investment are not the main purpose, but an unintended by-product. If output can not be expanded under the impact of rising demand, the case for deficit-financed public investment is obviously greatly weakened. It is, in fact, reduced to an argument of *pis aller*, or of political or administrative expediency. The expansion of public services is essential— and better ways of doing this may be barred for political or administrative reasons. The income effects of a deficit will normally be at best a helpful accessory. The redistribution of income in favour of profits, as well as the broadening of demand, may possibly serve to assist in the movement towards the main objective, e.g. by adding a further inducement to private investors to take advantage of the opportunities presented by lower cost as a result of the provision of better public services. But the lowering of real cost curves remains the chief objective.

Marginal rates of savings and taxation in under-developed countries are often— but not necessarily or universally—very low. This can be attributed to the low level of incomes, the nature of tax systems, the difficulties of effective tax administration, the lack of savings institutions and facilities, a high propensity to consume even in the face of a redistribution of incomes towards profits, etc. Whatever the reasons, the multiplier must in under-developed countries often be assumed to be

quite high. To this should be added that often there are no surplus foreign exchange reserves so that the capacity to run an import surplus is small, while the marginal propensity to import may be high. Where foreign exchange, and especially accretions of foreign exchange, are largely reserved for producers' goods, and there is little or no home production of these producers' goods—both being the case in many under-developed countries—the availability of imports becomes a determinant of investment. Thus an increase in the import surplus may be in fact associated with inflationary pressures.

The marginal rate of savings or taxation may be particularly low where the increase in incomes associated with the act of deficit-financed public investment will accrue partly in kind. For instance, where previously unemployed or under-employed farmers are drawn from the countryside as a result of deficit-financed public works or construction of urban public utilities, the real per capita income of those remaining on the land is increased. But this increase may take the form, not of higher money incomes through additional sales, but of increased consumption in kind. Since the persons drawn from the countryside will in their turn also have a high propensity to consume, and specifically also to consume food, the multiplier may become *pro tanto* very high, and the inflationary gap may express itself sharply in terms of food shortages.

Thus, while the multiplier is likely to be high in under-developed countries, the response of supplies to price increases and pressure of demand is likely to be small. Where the factors reducing productivity or lowering elasticity of supply are simultaneously tackled, there may, of course, be an expansion of supplies hand in hand with the deficit-financed public investment; alternatively the public investment may itself be specifically directed towards removing some of the obstacles. In the first case the combined result need not be inflationary; in the second case, while the immediate effects would be inflationary, the longer-term effects would be beneficial, and the inflation would be self-correcting after a time if it is not allowed to become cumulative in the earlier stages. Productive public investment directed towards reducing obstacles to increased supply in the more immediate future, or simultaneously with an attack on these obstacles by other means, provide the classical case in defence of deficit financing.

Added to low productivity and to low elasticity of supply when confronted with increased demand, there is a third related, yet distinct characteristic. This is resource immobility, i.e. a low capacity of shifting resources from one use to another, or from one sector to another. While resource immobility obviously contributes to inelasticity of supply, the distinction is of analytic and practical value. Super-imposed upon the difficulty of increasing supplies of given sectors from the resources already committed to it, there is the further difficulty of augmenting the resources committed to one sector by reducing the resources committed to another. In a developed, especially an industrial, economy with a large stock of capital, resource mobility is to some extent provided by the depreciation of capital. This continuously sets free resources in one branch which are then available for use elsewhere. In a growing economy, resource mobility is facilitated by the fact that it is easier to change the allocation of new resources than to change the distribution of resources already committed; it is easier to have differential rates of growth in different sectors of the economy than to have some absolutely declining. An under-developed country has neither much capital to depreciate nor a large volume of fresh resources from growth. Fundamen-

tally, however, the greater ability to shift resources observed in more developed economies must be treated as a concomitant of technical progress, technical ability and a high level of skill and training in the population. That is to say, the same forces which are fundamental to a high level of income are also fundamental to resource mobility. The two tend to go hand in hand.

Resource immobility has an important implication. To set free resources to the extent of, say, 5 per cent of national income in order to augment investment by that amount, it is not sufficient that the same amount of resources should be taken away from consumption or private investment or current public expenditure. This is a necessary, but not sufficient, condition. If the resources set free by the reduction in consumption or other expenditure can not be transformed into the resources required for additional investment, the sacrifice will *pro tanto* have been made in vain. It is not difficult to conceive of situations where an increase in investment by 5 per cent of national income may involve curtailments in other directions of perhaps 8 or 10 per cent of national income. This situation has some resemblance to the multiplier effect involved in curtailing domestic incomes in order to achieve certain required reductions in total import demand.

The comparative immobility of resources between sectors in under-developed countries, combined with a greater inelasticity of supply within each sector, has consequences which can be expressed in various ways. First, in under-developed countries global pressure of demand on resources is more dangerous and more liable to lead to inflation; hence, to maintain stability, under-developed countries may have to forgo, at least partially, the use of one of the instruments which might otherwise be conducive to economic growth. Second, in under-developed countries measures to increase the mobility of resources as between sectors are a precondition for raising the degree of pressure of total demand on resources, since a pressure of total demand will inevitably require adjustments in the allocation of resources between sectors. Third, in the under-developed countries the burden of adjustment which will be thrown on imports will tend to be correspondingly greater; the difficulties of achieving an expanded balance of supplies from domestic production lead to an increased need to add to supplies, especially in the bottleneck sectors, through imports from outside.

If a combination of high multipliers, low elasticities of supply and resource immobility is typical of under-developed countries, it follows that deficit financing of public investment is particularly dangerous, at least until these three characteristics have been modified prior to, or simultaneously with, the deficit-financed expenditure. These warnings could be fortified by reference to other characteristics of under-developed countries. Where habits of monetary exchange and use of monetary institutions are still in their infancy and have to be carefully nursed, it may be especially dangerous to have the value of money depreciate. Where the discipline of reconciling ambitions with limited resources has to be developed, the requirement of a balanced budget should not be easily abandoned. Where shifts to profits may easily result in increased speculation, high-level consumption or capital flight, the mechanism of inflation loses much of its purpose. Where administrative controls are particularly difficult, inflation may more easily get out of hand. This is indeed a formidable array of warning signals to those thinking of applying the technique of deficit financing in under-

developed countries, even as the counterpart of productive public investment. The warnings look serious enough to cause acute apprehension in regard to deficit-finance proposals in most, or nearly all, actual combinations of circumstances that are likely to be encountered in under-developed countries.

But there remains the exceptional combination of circumstances. There remains the case where perhaps there is a special opportunity to increase production of food and other consumer goods conspicuously and rapidly with the aid of public works, and bridge the interval by drawing on a previously accumulated surplus of foreign exchange. There is perhaps the case of the under-developed country with very high marginal rates of savings or taxation. There is the case of underlying deflationary tendencies offering scope for public deficits.

There is, finally, the case where better alternatives to deficit financing, such as increased taxation, are politically or administratively impossible, or where its broader economic effects are especially harmful, and where yet some forms of productive public investment are an absolute precondition of economic progress, and where economic progress in turn is an absolute precondition for political and social stability. But even where deficit financing leads to increased capital formation the dangers of deficit financing must still be weighed against the dangers of economic stagnation or deterioration; and it is often far from clear that the non-existence of better alternatives should be accepted as a genuine premise of debate. Where the need for public investment over and above what present revenues permit is so crucial and imperative, it is difficult to see why the effort to overcome the obstacles obstructing the use of less dangerous methods of financing could not also be made. A determination to achieve the end would seem to presuppose a determination to make possible the best means. So that even if the discussion is restricted, as it is in this paper, to the financing of productive investment, it would appear that the circumstances justifying deficit financing as a deliberate choice would be rather special and the justified doses closely circumscribed.

1.4 EFFECTS OF INFLATION ON EXPORTS*

The expansion and diversification of exports is of paramount importance to primary producing countries seeking to develop their economies. Though foreign loans and grants are helpful in supplementing foreign exchange receipts, exports are, as a rule, the main source of the means required to secure imports essential in the process of development. Moreover, the intended rise in national income may generate additional demands for imports and make a corresponding expansion of exports desirable. Diversification of exports is sought in order to reduce dependence on a few commodities, and thus to mitigate the sharp fluctuations in export receipts arising from oscillations in demand for, or supply of, individual export goods.

The contention of this paper is that inflation tends to hamper the expansion of exports and to retard their diversification. The initial effect arises from increased domestic demand, and from the resulting rise in prices relative to those in competing or importing countries. Competition for goods or factors of production will induce diversion of products from the export to the domestic market. But even if there is no such diversion, inflationary price increases tend to spread to the export sector, mainly through adjustment of

wages to a higher cost of living; increases in costs will then discourage exports. As inflation progresses, the economy becomes structurally oriented toward meeting domestic demand. Speculative investment in building and the development of high-cost industries (the latter often enhanced by import restrictions) are familiar phenomena in countries with protracted inflation. Measures taken to limit price increases in essential cost of living items may lead to scarcities both for domestic consumption and for exports.

On the other hand, the effects of inflation on exports may be partly or wholly offset by measures promoting exports through exchange rate adjustments and other devices.

The initial effect of inflation is an increase in prices on the domestic market, which makes selling on that market more profitable than exporting. Returns from the latter will not move in line with domestic prices; export prices are practically "given" for most primary producing countries and cannot be significantly altered in response to rising costs of production. Where a country's share in world exports of a particular commodity is large enough to enable it, by a change in volume, to influence international prices, inflationary cost increases will tend to encourage such a change with a view to raising the price of the commodity and maintaining it at a high level. But sooner or later this will invite an expansion of output in competing countries or the creation of substitutes which, in turn, will adversely affect the country's exports.

For the majority of export goods, however, changes in supply from individual exporting countries have little effect on world prices. Differences between world and domestic prices will affect exports through the diversion of either goods or factors of production to the domestic market; even if no such diversion takes place,

* From Gertrude Lovasy, "Inflation and Exports in Primary Producing Countries," *International Monetary Fund Staff Papers*, March 1962, pp. 38-40.

exports will be affected through cost increases and the reduction or elimination of profits on export sales. The effects will vary for different commodities; they will be most pronounced and most immediate on commodities for which domestic demand responds strongly to increases in money income, and on those whose supply cannot be readily expanded, so that increased demand is met at the expense of exports rather than by an expansion of output. "Major" export commodities of primary producing countries are not often affected by direct competition from the home market, since they consist largely of raw materials or basic foodstuffs, often produced mainly for export and with comparatively small domestic consumption and low income elasticity. Competition from the home market is most likely to affect certain "minor" exports, partly or largely produced for consumption in the exporting country; diversion of at least part of these exports to the domestic market is likely even if production is expanded.

Competition between industries for factors of production may affect the supply even of export goods for which domestic demand is limited or nonexistent. Labor may shift as wages offered in other occupations become more attractive, and land may be diverted to the cultivation of crops for which domestic demand is rising.

Wage increases in response to the rising cost of living may raise the cost of exports even if industries supplying the home market offer no alternative employment to labor employed in the export sector. Such increases are likely to be more pronounced in mining and processing than in agriculture, where the share of paid labor receiving money wages tends to be relatively small. Rising costs of material and equipment will reduce or even eliminate profits on exports. The decline or cessation of exports may then result in an accumula-

tion of inventories and ultimately in a reduction of output.

1.5 THE CONTROL OF INFLATION *

In many of the less highly developed countries, incomes are not rising as rapidly as the desires of the community. In these countries, personal savings are low, so that only limited resources are released for the expansion of the community's capital. At the same time, the tax systems provide only enough revenue to meet part of the community's desires for government services, with very small surpluses available to finance development. Under these circumstances, inflation may appear to be an easy method of providing finance to expand investment and hence to be an easy way of obtaining capital for a more rapid expansion of output. If a government can persuade the central bank to create money to finance a development program, or if the banking system freely makes loans to private investors for the finance of physical investment, the problem of expanding the community's real assets may appear to be easily solvable. Consequently, it is sometimes argued that "a case could be made for making inflation an instrument of (development) policy, rather than the control of inflation an object of policy." [1]

There is no doubt that, on occasion, a monetary expansion somewhat greater than the current increase in real output will introduce an element of flexibility in an economy, and lead to some "forced saving" releasing resources for development.

* From Graeme S. Dorrance, "The Effect of Inflation on Economic Development," *International Monetary Fund Staff Papers*, March 1963, pp. 1-4, 25, 27-31.

1. H. J. Bruton, *Inflation in a Growing Economy* (Annual Lectures by Visiting Professor of Monetary Economics, 1960-1961, University of Bombay, Bombay), p. 57; parentheses added.

However, there are strict limits to the amount of development which may be fostered in this way. Admittedly, the available simple evidence on the relation between inflation and growth is difficult to interpret. The difficulty is common in analyses of the effects of pervasive influences, like the degree of inflation, on phenomena which are also subject to other, complex, forces.

Table 1 presents summary data gathered from three sources. This evidence varies from the inconclusive simple comparison of average rates of growth for the years 1954–60 as derived from the UN national account statistics, to the rather more persuasive conclusions obtained from a recording of the data relating to specific periods of rather constant price change identified by U Tun Wai.[2] The rates of growth in the simpler comparisons are based on one observation per country; hence each observation reflects not only the effect of inflation but also the effects of the available natural resources and their stage of exploitation, and the general political atmosphere and other influences, such as the general social attitudes, in each country. The separation of shorter periods for individual countries when different rates of price increase prevailed, based on Tun Wai's observations, tends to strengthen the influence of the rate of inflation, as distinct from other forces, in the last three comparisons in Table 1. These latter data suggest that in the postwar years the less highly developed countries have, on the average, enjoyed annual increases in per capita output of approximately 4 per cent during those periods when they maintained monetary stability. During periods of mild inflation the increase in output in these countries was only half as great. During periods of strong inflation, the increases in output tended to be even smaller.

It is true that individual units of investment financed by bank credit are likely to be created even in inflationary conditions. It is not the immediate products of monetary expansion which are in question; rather it is the over-all effect on progress which deserves consideration. An expansion of the monetary system's assets involves an equal expansion of its liabilities. Unless members of the community are

2. "The Relation Between Inflation and Economic Development: A Statistical Inductive Study," *Staff Papers*, Vol. VII (1959-60), pp. 302-17.

TABLE 1. RELATIONSHIP OF RATES OF INFLATION TO ECONOMIC GROWTH
IN RECENT YEARS

	Annual Rates of Growth Per Capita (per cent)		
	Stable countries	Mild inflation countries	Strong inflation countries
Sample based on UN data	2	2	2
ECLA sample	3	—	2
U Tun Wai samples, based on			
Per capita national income			
Unadjusted	6	2	3
Adjusted for terms of trade	4	1	1
Per capita social product	4	3	—

willing to increase the real value of their money balances by an amount equal to the increase in bank credit, and thereby indirectly to provide finance for the new investment, either prices will rise, or imports will be so encouraged and exports discouraged that there will be a fall in the community's capital held in the form of exchange reserves, i.e., a disinvestment in reserves offsetting the newly financed domestic investment. If prices rise, the real value of any increase in money holdings will be eroded. This fall in the real value of money may be considered as a tax on money holders. Inflationary policies, or policies which lead a government to be weak in resisting inflationary pressures, may be assessed by criteria similar to those used in assessing alternative taxation proposals.

The efficiency of any tax is largely dependent on the degree to which it cannot be evaded. The degree to which a tax "cannot be evaded" is, in turn, largely a function of the degree to which it does not lead to incentives encouraging evasion. A mild inflation may well encourage little, or no, evasion of the "inflation tax." On the other hand, a strong inflation, and frequently a mild one also, will lead to community reactions which have effects similar to those of widespread tax evasion.

A development policy may have wider aims than the encouragement of a high level of investment. It may be directed to the encouragement of types of investment different from those which would emerge in an economy in which all economic decisions are made by individual economic units acting without positive inducements by the government. If an attempt be made to foster development through an "inflation tax," the types of economic incentive induced by inflation are also relevant to its effectiveness. A strong inflation creates distortions in the economy, which may be regarded as comparable to the undesirable incentives induced by unsatisfactory forms of taxation.

It must be recognized that rapid economic development, by evoking supply shortages in certain specific fields, frequently leads to increases in the prices of certain commodities. The number of these may be fairly large. Under these circumstances, some rise in the average level of prices may frequently be an unavoidable companion of economic progress. This observation does not, however, lead to the conclusion that inflation aids development, or that its control should not have a high priority among the targets for economic policy.

It is often alleged that, even though inflation may be undesirable, a cure by means of a stabilization program may be worse than the disease of inflation. Those who favor monetary reform are accused of placing a higher value on price stability than on economic growth. If the analysis presented in this paper is valid, an economy experiencing inflation must be one where development is proceeding less rapidly than it would if the economy were stable, all other conditions being similar. It does not follow, however, that a change in the climate will immediately ease an inflating economy's difficulties. In particular, it does not follow that a stabilization program will bring an immediate increase in output.

The desirable reshuffling of the economy, resulting from stabilization, may lead directly to a temporary decline in the demand for physical investment. There is an inevitable lag between the decision to create physical capital and the actual consumption of resources in capital production. On the other hand, investment already in progress may be abandoned rather quickly. One of the effects of inflation is the encouragement of industries which would be uneconomic in a noninflationary world. Stabilization may bring a quick cutoff in the development of these industries, leading to a decline in the demand for investment resources. While a stable environment will make alternative industries appear to be profitable fields for investment, it takes some time for entrepreneurs to convert their investment desires into consumption of resources. Hence, the period immediately after the start of a stabilization program may well be marked by a lag in the consumption of investment resources, with a consequent decline in the production of capital goods.

It might be thought that, as inflation is a situation of generalized excess demand for goods and services, a reduction in demand might do no more than eliminate the excess. But the situation which develops in an inflation is that the supply of goods and services, which necessarily cannot be less than effective expenditure, includes types of commodities and services for which demand will exist only so long as inflation continues. The reduction of this demand caused by the cessation of inflation, and its replacement by expenditure appropriate to stable conditions, involves a corresponding readjustment of supply. It would be utopian to expect that all phases of this readjustment process would be closely synchronized. There are particular difficulties in the smooth adjustment of investment expenditures, which follow from the effects of inflation discussed above. In the first place, inflation induces an accumulation of inventories in excess of those which would have been built up in stable conditions. Necessarily, therefore, the cessation of inflation will lead to disinvestment in inventories, reversing this part of the flow of demand. Secondly, investment in industries during the inflation is likely to have been directed to those enjoying a high degree of pro-

tection. Insofar as the exchange rate is unified or changed to a more realistic one, or insofar as stabilization by strengthening the balance of payments (e.g., by reducing purchases of imports for addition to inventories), enables exchange restrictions to be eased, the protection afforded these industries will be diminished, and their attractiveness for investment will decline. Thirdly, the increasing attractiveness of physical assets during an inflation may be expected to lead also to a rise in the demand for owner-occupied housing. Once stabilization is under way, the existing supply of this type of house, together with the rising demand for financial assets, can be expected to lead to a reduction of investment of this kind. And even if stabilization and the easing of rent control make rental housing a desirable form of investment, it takes time to convert desires to invest into orders for bricks and mortar.

Thus the flow of resources evoked by an inflation will be not only in excess of, but also partially inappropriate to, the flow of demand in stabilized conditions. The severity of the consequential adjustment problems, and the time required to solve them, will depend, in part at least, on the degree to which the economic system has been distorted. This degree of distortion will in turn depend largely on the duration and rate of the inflation which is being brought to an end. When the inflation has not been too severe, and in its current bout has lasted no more than about two years, as in Peru at the time of the adoption of its 1959 stabilization program, the problem is not too serious. When inflation has been rampant for decades, as in Argentina by 1958, the problem will have become very serious.

It should be emphasized that the depressive influences discussed above are temporary, rather than fundamental. After a relatively short period, they should evaporate. If the stabilization program is effective, the period of uncertainty must pass, and a new set of expectations should enable investors to make plans for future capital creation, with a consequent rise in their demands for resources. The decline in investment arising from the lag between the end of development of protected industries and the expansion of more economic (from a long-range view) alternative investment, is by definition a temporary cutback in investment. Likewise, by definition, disinvestment in inventories must also be temporary. The general adjustment which should accompany stabilization (including the elimination of controls, such as ceilings on rents) may be expected to revive the demand for investment in rental housing to replace the decline in the demand for owner-occupied residences. The general flight from real assets to financial assets, which is one of the healthy signs of stabilization even though it may exert depressing effects on investment, should also be temporary. After a short period of adjustment, individual economic units may be expected to desire additions to their stocks of both physical and financial assets. At the same time, the capital flight resulting from inflation should stop. The switch in the flow of saving from foreign to domestic investment, and the repatriation of earlier accumulations of foreign assets, will lead to an increase in the demand for domestic resources.

A government which decides to eliminate the distortions created by inflation will be faced with a host of problems while the economy is readjusting to a condition of monetary equilibrium. There is no doubt that the difficulties facing the community will be dependent on the imagination exercised by the government. A stabilization program which relies on monetary instruments alone will involve more stresses in the economy than one which includes fiscal and broader economic improvement measures as well. If a stabilization program can be quickly associated with measures for the development of previously neglected facilities (e.g., the rehabilitation of obsolescent railway systems and the development of public utilities), the stresses will be eased. Foreign assistance (e.g., drawings on the International Monetary Fund to make more rapid elimination of exchange restrictions possible, and loans from the International Bank for Reconstruction and Development to facilitate the redeployment of resources for development) will make the elimination of distortions in production easier. However, no cleaning-up process is pleasant. Stabilizing an inflating economy is one of the least pleasant of the operations facing a responsible government.

If an abrupt ending of an inflation is likely to bring a temporary decline in output, is not some alternative possible? Might not a tapering-off policy be adopted? Might not the rate of inflation be brought to an end slowly? The answer to these questions is that a gradual approach is fraught with more danger than sudden stabilization.

Among the real damages done by inflation is the distortion created in the economy. There is need to reorient the system. Drastic changes must be made in the community's expectations. These changes are not likely to occur if the community believes that the government may be lukewarm in its attack on inflation. If individuals see little change in the economic climate, they will be under very few effective pressures to change their views. The fundamental changes which are required will not take place.

The persistence of expectations as to the movements of prices is a particular problem to be faced in introducing a stabilization program. In the early stages of an inflation, individuals may continue to believe that prices will soon stop increasing. But once inflation is established, they will expect prices to go on rising; and even if they believe that the inflation has been halted, and that prices will be stabilized, they will not expect stabilization to take place immediately. Moreover, they will always be conscious of the possibility that the program may fail. Even, therefore, when money and financial assets begin once more to appear attractive, the acquisition of such assets may be deterred by a lingering fear that they may again decline in real value. By contrast, the continued holding of inventories offers protection, even if the program succeeds, against any loss except that of the potential income from financial investments; and the holder of foreign financial assets risks the loss only of the possibly excessive returns on domestic financial assets over the return on foreign ones. If the program fails, such holders stand to gain much more. Thus, to enable a stabilization program to succeed, it is above all necessary for the government to convince the community that the value of money will henceforth be maintained.

In short, an attempt to slow down an inflation will take a long time to be effective and its final result will be uncertain. The restrictions on credit necessary to bring some stabilization will deter borrowers from investing, but the inflation-induced distortions of the economy are likely to persist. The continued rise in prices (even though it be slower than before) will deter the accumulation of financial assets and continue to act as a brake on the flow of resources to investment. Unless the authorities are firm in their attack, the atmosphere of financial stability necessary to induce a revival of output to levels higher than those which would have prevailed under inflation will not emerge.

1.6 INFLATION AND MONETARY POLICY *

The problem of increasing and mobilizing real resources and of channeling them into expenditures serving the needs of balanced development—as well as the implementation of other measures designed to promote development—are primarily a responsibility of the government through its tax, expenditure, debt and other financial and economic policies. The formulation of the over-all development program itself is also primarily a government responsibility. The major objective and responsibility of the central bank should be to strive to achieve and maintain reasonable internal financial stability through control of the availability and cost of money. To the extent that the central bank is able, with the cooperation of the government, to achieve this objective, it will not only prevent the inequities and misuse of resources associated with inflation (or deflation), but also provide a necessary, though not sufficient, condition for increased saving, for attracting foreign investment and for promoting more balanced economic growth. As we shall see, the central bank can also contribute in other ways, within the framework of a policy aimed at stability, to encourage development. The maintenance of internal financial stability, it need hardly be added, would also help to foster, though not necessarily to assure, the maintenance of external payments stability as well. External payments stability would in turn tend to facilitate the process of economic development.

. . .

Obviously, the central bank alone cannot assure such stability. At best its role can be only a contributory one, however

* From Arthur I. Bloomfield, "Monetary Policy in Underdeveloped Countries," in *Public Policy*, Vol. VII, edited by C. J. Friedrich and S. E. Harris, Harvard University Press, 1956, pp. 244-7, 250-61, 267-72. Reprinted by permission.

strategic that role might be. The financial policies of the government must carry a large part of the load. There must in any case be the closest possible coordination between the policies of the central bank and the government if there is to be hope of a job well done. For example, an irresponsible fiscal policy could easily upset the efforts of the central bank to maintain internal and external stability, just as an ill-advised monetary policy could counteract the effects of a prudent fiscal policy. Besides, trade, payments and exchange policies must be closely integrated with both, especially in the face of large and persisting imbalances in international payments.

While the achievement and maintenance of monetary stability is the dominant contribution that the central bank can make to balanced economic development in underdeveloped countries, it can also promote this objective in other ways. Within the framework of a policy aimed at stability, it can seek to influence the flow of bank credit, and indeed of savings, in directions more in keeping with development ends. Thus, through selective credit controls applied to the banking system, through help in establishing and supporting special credit institutions and through influence over the lending policies of such institutions and of other institutional investors, it can help to some degree to rechannel real resources in desired directions, both between the public and the private sector, on the one hand, and within the private sector itself, on the other. The central bank can also play a useful role in increasing and mobilizing savings by helping to develop a market in government securities, by helping to establish special savings institutions, by encouraging a spread of banking facilities and of the banking habit, by promoting the liquidity and solvency of the banking system and by other related measures.

In its attempt to maintain monetary stability, the central bank must constantly strive, despite the limitations to which it is subject, to adjust the aggregate money supply to the demands of the public for money balances at constant prices. These demands grow as the economy grows, thereby making possible a certain, though in most cases limited, rate of growth in the money supply without inflationary consequences. If the money supply is allowed to grow at a rate in excess of the public's demand for money at constant prices, there will be an upward pressure on prices; if it grows at a slower rate, there will be deflationary pressures and some retardation of production. In its attempt to keep the money supply growing at the "right" rate, however, the authorities will have to take account of undesirable developments that might occur in the balance of payments. If the pursuit of this goal involves large and persisting drains on exchange reserves, the authorities might have to slow up the rate of credit expansion; if it involves a large and persisting payments surplus, they might perhaps want to increase it.

Although the growth of real income is the major factor determining the public's demand for money, the rate of expansion in the money supply consistent with internal financial stability will not, of course, be exactly equal to the rate of growth of income. For one thing, the shrinkage of the non-monetary sector as the economy grows will in itself involve an increasing demand for money at constant prices. Moreover, the demand for money is likely to be stimulated by such factors as the growing differentiation of production, the spread of banking habits and the relative expansion of purely financial transactions. All these factors, which make for a decline in the income-velocity of money over time, would enable an expansion in the money supply at a rate somewhat greater than that of real income without inflationary consequences. On the other hand, when the public has little confidence that monetary stability can be maintained, there will be a move to economize on money holdings and the income-velocity of money will rise.

...

Although the experience of underdeveloped countries...provides many illustrations of resort to various measures of general and selective credit control, it must be emphasized that the central banks in most of these countries, especially in the Middle East and in Asia and the Far East, have made in general relatively limited use of the various instruments of control at their disposal. This should not necessarily be regarded as to the discredit of the central banks concerned. The overall potentialities of many of these instruments are narrowly limited . . . by institutional factors, and it is not self-evident that more vigorous measures of credit restraint would in most cases have significantly altered the course of events. Some of these instruments, despite the intentions of the drafters of the statutes, are not too well adapted to the financial structures and administrative capacities of the countries concerned and are in fact of so complex and novel a character as to justify scepticism regarding their use. Some, moreover, were designed to meet special or emergency situations of a sort that have not as yet emerged in many of these countries.

Despite all this, there is reason to believe that on certain occasions...there was in at least some cases scope for more aggressive measures of credit restraint than were actually undertaken. There were a number of reasons for this hesitancy. Measures of credit restraint are never popular and most central banks were under strong pressures from the business community and often from the government itself to avoid restrictive measures. Since many of these banks are relatively new and have yet to establish the degree of standing and prestige necessary to make their views and their leadership in monetary matters appropriately felt in the community—or in fact to make their legal position secure—it was often understandably difficult to resist such pressures. In some cases, as intimated above, there was undoubtedly uncertainty as to what instruments to use, how to use them or how effective they might be. But perhaps of greatest importance was the fear by many central bank officials that restrictive monetary measures might hamper the progress of economic development itself. In countries where growth is the primary objective of national economic policy, such a fear tends to be all too deeply rooted. In some countries, moreover, the "old-fashioned" notion still prevails that so long as bank loans are made for "productive" purposes and to meet the "needs of trade" there cannot even be a danger of inflation.

It is impossible here to attempt any over-all evaluation of the effectiveness of such credit-control measures as have actually been undertaken in underdeveloped countries in recent years. Experience has naturally varied widely from country to country according to the particular circumstances. Most of the central banks concerned seem in the main to have been groping their way and cautiously experimenting with various credit-control techniques in an effort to determine their relative effectiveness and suitability under differing conditions and to test their adaptability to the local environment. In these respects they have received and can expect to receive only relatively little guidance from the lessons, experiences and philosophy of central banking in the more developed countries.

Despite the impressive array of instruments at its disposal, and the seemingly wide range of tasks that it might perform, monetary policy in the great majority of underdeveloped countries has been, and of necessity must be, relatively limited in role, scope, and effectiveness in view of the many institutional obstacles which it faces. Even in developed countries, monetary policy is subject to many limitations; in underdeveloped countries the limitations are multiplied many times over. Effective control by the central bank over the money supply tends to be impeded by wide externally generated swings in the balance of payments and, at times, by the difficulty of resisting excessively large demands for central bank credit by the government and its instrumentalities; some of the tools of monetary control, even over that (often relatively small) segment of the money supply most directly susceptible to central bank influence, are subject to technical limitations; the response to monetary-policy measures is often likely to be relatively slow and uncertain; and some parts of the economy are in fact virtually outside the reach of central bank action. Besides, fiscal policy, which needs to be so closely coordinated with monetary policy, is itself subject in most underdeveloped countries to severe limitations, which are likewise inherent in the economic backwardness of these countries.

On the other hand, there is a danger of underestimating the potentialities of monetary policy in underdeveloped countries. As this paper has tried to show, there is still a constructive role for monetary policy to perform in the majority of these countries in helping to maintain internal and external stability, to promote economic development, and to lay the basis for a more effective application of its tools in the future. Indeed, there is reason to believe that most of these countries have not as yet fully utilized the potentialities of monetary policy, however limited they might now be.

A key problem in the formulation and implementation of appropriate monetary policies lies in the nature of the relationship between the central bank and the government. All too often in the past, such policies have been hampered or thwarted in underdeveloped countries by excessive political interference in the operations and policies of the central bank and by undue government recourse to central bank credit. These problems cannot be solved merely by legislation or by formal administrative arrangements. A heavy responsibility devolves upon the government. It goes without saying that the government must try to order its fiscal affairs so as to keep its resort to within the appropriate limits. Although the government and the central bank must of necessity be in close and continuous consultation on a wide range of matters, effective monetary policy also requires that the central bank should exercise, and be encouraged by the government to exercise, a wide measure of freedom in policy-making, in operations, and in independently developing and expounding its own point of view on the basis of its objective appraisal of the situation at hand, freed from short-run political pressures which may often conflict with the long-run welfare of the economy. The central bank should also have the maximum degree of freedom to comment upon and to criticize the government's fiscal and over-all economic policies and objectives and to try to the best of its ability to convince the government of its views. Such freedom would also help to promote the bank's prestige in the community and its position of leadership in monetary matters, so necessary to make its policies effective.

The argument has been raised that the establishment of central banks in some of the more underdeveloped countries was premature and that it would have been better if the previously existing monetary arrangements, which permitted little or no scope for monetary policy, had been left unaltered. It is difficult to accept this view. Apart from the fact that political considerations invariably made the establishment of a central bank inevitable in such instances, all of the countries in question have reached a stage of economic development—including a degree of monetization of the economy and of growth of the domestically oriented sector—where there is at least some scope for constructive central bank action.

Perhaps a more valid criticism is that many of the central bank statutes in underdeveloped countries are unduly complicated and contain too many "fancy gimmicks" of a sort not too well adapted, despite the intentions of the drafters of the statutes, to the financial structures and especially to the administrative capacities of the countries concerned. Admittedly, simpler statutes would in most cases have been preferable, and some of the more recent statutes are in fact of this kind. In any case, there is no necessary obligation imposed upon the central bank to use all of these more complicated provisions, some of which were actually designed for "emergency" or more distant situations.

Another criticism has centered on the danger of misuse of the powers inherent in the establishment of central banks in underdeveloped countries, especially that of government access to central bank credit. In some cases, admittedly, the central bank has served on balance as little more than an engine of inflation. But this risk is in general much more than outweighed by the stabilizing influence, developmental contribution and other benefits that such an institution, under wise management and with appropriate cooperation from the government, should be able to bring to the countries in question. Most of the newer central banks have in fact

already demonstrated their ability and potentialities in this respect, despite the many limitations and obstacles which they, and indeed central banks in underdeveloped countries in general, face and will continue to face for some time to come.

1.7 ORGANIZED AND UNORGANIZED MONEY MARKETS *

The size of an organized money market in any country may be indicated by either or both of the following ratios, although neither measurement is perfect: the ratio of deposit money to money supply and the ratio of the banking system's claims (mostly loans, advances, and bills discounted) on the private sector to national income....

The ratio of deposit money to money supply actually measures banking development rather than the development of the money market. However, to the extent that the development of commercial banking is synonymous with the development of the money market, this ratio may be used an an indicator of the growth of a money market. In most underdeveloped countries, there are hardly any lending agencies of importance other than commercial banks. There are no discount houses or acceptance houses, and savings institutions (including life insurance companies) are in the early stages of development....

Both ratios might be expected to be low in an underdeveloped country and high in a developed one. The ratio of deposit money to money supply should be higher in a more developed country because, with economic development, there is also development of the banking system....

As an economy develops, the size of the

* From U Tun Wai, "Interest Rates in the Organized Money Markets of Underdeveloped Countries," *International Monetary Fund Staff Papers,* Vol. V, No. 2, August 1956, pp. 249-50, 252-3, 255, 258, 276-8; "Interest Rates Outside the Organized Money Markets of Underdeveloped Countries," *ibid.,* Vol. VI, No. 1, November 1957, pp. 80-83, 94-7, 107-9, 119-25.

typical business and industrial unit is likely to expand; the amount of self-financing tends to decline, and greater use is made of the money market to finance business operations. The net result is that the claims (loans, advances, and investments) of the banking system on the private sector tend to increase more rapidly than national income; thus the second ratio is also likely to increase. . . .

A comparison, for a number of developed and underdeveloped countries, of the two ratios for a period of years broadly confirms the expectations noted above. For estimating the size of the money market, however, use of the ratio of deposit money to money supply by itself may be misleading. For example, this ratio is almost as high in some of the Latin American countries as in the most highly developed countries. A possible explanation may be that, while the money markets are fairly large in some Latin American countries, they may not be functioning as efficiently as in the more developed countries.

Judging by the first ratio, the money markets in Brazil, Chile, Colombia, and Peru are relatively the largest in Latin America; the only substantial markets in Asia are in Ceylon, Malaya, and Japan. According to the second criterion, the size of the money market is significant in Chile, Colombia, Cuba, and Peru in Latin America, and only in Japan in Asia. Only in Japan do both ratios approximate those prevailing in developed countries. In relation to the whole economy, money markets are quite small in Burma, India, Indonesia, Pakistan, and Thailand among the Asian countries and in Bolivia, the Dominican Republic, Guatemala, and Honduras in Latin America.

. . .

The structure of interest rates in the organized money markets of underdeveloped countries is usually more or less the same as in the developed ones. The short-term rate of interest is generally much below the long-term rate, as indicated by the spread between the government treasury bill rate and the government bond yield; the rate at which bills of exchange are discounted is also lower than the rate at which loans and advances are granted.

The lowest market rates are usually the call loan rates between commercial banks. The next lowest are those paid by commercial banks on short-term deposits, followed by the government treasury bill rate. Then come the rates at which commercial banks discount commercial paper, varying according to the type of security and the date of maturity. In most countries, especially in Asia, the government bond yield comes next, followed by the lending rates of commercial banks.

. . .

In general, the level of interest rates in underdeveloped countries, even in organized money markets, is higher than in the more developed countries. The more notable difference between the two groups of countries, however, is that the range of interest rates is generally much wider in underdeveloped countries. The volume of loans granted at relatively low rates in an underdeveloped country is not very important, as only limited amounts of financial assets are available to serve as collateral for lending at low rates. It is usually the foreign business firms with longer experience and larger capital which are able to borrow at the lower rates. Most of the indigenous firms have to pay the higher rates; this is especially true where foreign banks occupy an important position in the banking system.

. . .

Central banks have been established in most underdeveloped countries; in Latin America for the most part they were established in the twenties and thirties, whereas in Asia, except in India, Japan, and Thailand, they are of postwar origin. The statutes of a number of central banks in Asia (for example, Burma and Ceylon) have granted them wide powers including that of control over the rates at which commercial banks may grant loans, but these powers have not so far been exercised. Where central bank lending to commercial banks is substantial, one would naturally expect changes in the bank rate to be reflected immediately in market rates. Where such lending is nominal, the influence would be felt directly only if marginal lending should influence the market rate.

In most underdeveloped countries, central bank lending to commercial banks is not of any great consequence. In nine countries, Bolivia, Burma, Ceylon, India, Indonesia, Israel, Mexico, Panama, and Thailand, there has been practically no lending; and in nine others, Brazil, Cuba, Egypt, Honduras, Japan, Pakistan, the Philippines, Uruguay, and Venezuela, it has been equal to about 10 per cent or less of the claims which commercial banks have on the private sector. In some Latin American countries and Turkey, central bank lending to commercial banks has been of great importance; in Chile, Colombia, Ecuador (development banks), and Turkey it has been equal to about one fourth, and in Costa Rica, El Salvador, Guatemala, and Nicaragua to about one third to one half, of the claims which commercial banks have on the private sector....

In spite of the small direct dependence of commercial banks on the central banks for funds, the latter are able to influence market rates by changes in the bank rate because of their economic, and at times their legal, position in the domestic money market, with wide powers for selective credit control, open market operations, and moral pressures.

The general expectation is that the long-term trend of interest rates in underdeveloped countries, at least in the organized markets, should be downward. Generally speaking, in these countries the banking systems and with them the money markets are likely to develop at a faster rate than the other sectors of the economy. The long-term supply of loanable funds therefore tends to increase more rapidly than the long-term demand. Where, for one reason or another, the growth of banking has been restricted or the banking system subjected by law to many restrictions, including controls on interest rates and of the purposes for which loans may be granted (as in a number of countries in Latin America), the long-term trend of interest rates may, however, not be downward.

In some countries in Asia, a comparison between interest rates before and after the great depression (1929–34) and the rates prevailing today show in fact a definite downward trend. This is true especially in Burma, Ceylon, and India....

Long-term data for Latin America are not available. But judging from the generally inflationary conditions prevailing there and also from limited information on Brazil and Chile, it seems that the long-term trend of interest rates has not been downward. In Chile, the weighted average rate of interest on loans granted by commercial banks was 8.67 per cent during 1929–34. The average was lower during the depression, but in the war and postwar years it has again been high. During 1949–54 it averaged as much as 11.67 per cent. In Brazil, the government bond yield on 5 per cent bonds and obligations averaged 6.33 per cent during 1929–34 but was 7.05 per cent during 1949–53....

Apart from any movement in the interest rate on loans against a specific type of collateral, the weighted average rate will tend to fall as the economy develops and business units hold larger quantities of financial assets, such as government bonds, which are more attractive to bankers as collateral. The loans against such collateral will tend to grow in importance at the expense of loans granted against less attractive collateral, such as land and houses. Since the rate on the former type of collateral is lower than on the latter type, the weighted average rate will fall.

The average level of interest rates in the organized money markets of underdeveloped countries can thus be lowered by encouraging the development of the banking system. Closer connections between these markets and world money markets, such as London, would also help in reducing interest rates. Statutory control of interest rates, though necessary at times, usually does not lead to a lowering of the effective rate; all it ensures is that the nominal rate is within the law as ways and means are found to circumvent the law through higher minimum deposit requirements, better types of collateral, etc. Where banking development is slow, government may consider lending money at low rates of interest in competition with private lending and thus attempt to bring down interest rates. Government lending is already of some significance in some underdeveloped countries, such as Burma, Japan, and Pakistan in Asia, and Mexico in Latin America. The solution of the problem of high interest rates, however, is not simple. Where government lending is financed by the printing press and not from budgetary surpluses, there is a great likelihood of inflation and of a cyclical rise of interest rates. However, if government lending is financed by tax receipts and borrowing from the public (i.e., genuine savings), and if the quantity of such lending is significant, then in the long run interest rates must fall.

In [the above] examination...of the interest rate structure and the lending practices of organized money markets in underdeveloped countries,... it was shown that these differed much less than might have been expected from those prevailing in most developed countries. In underdeveloped countries, however, unorganized money markets also play a very important role, and any study of credit conditions in these countries that is to be adequate must be extended to cover the unorganized as well as the organized markets. Efforts have often been made to repair the deficiencies of the unorganized markets by government action designed to stimulate the development of cooperative credit or to provide credit through agricultural banks, etc.; it is convenient to include these government-sponsored institutions in a study of unorganized money markets in general.

Interest rates in the unorganized money markets of underdeveloped countries are generally very high in relation both to those in the organized money markets and to what is needed for rapid economic development. These high interest rates are caused by a disproportionately large demand for loanable funds coupled with a generally inelastic and limited supply of funds. The large demand stems from the special social and economic factors prevalent in the rural areas of underdeveloped countries. The low level of income leaves little surplus for saving and for the accumulation of capital for self-financing of agricultural and handicraft production. The uncertainty of the weather, which affects crop yields and incomes, causes an additional need for outside funds in bad years. A significant portion of the demand for loanable funds in rural areas is for financing consumption at levels much higher than are warranted by the low income of the peasant....

The supply of loanable funds in the

unorganized money markets is very limited and inelastic because the major source is the moneylender, and only very small quantities are supplied by indigenous bankers and organized institutions, such as cooperative credit societies and land mortgage banks. The moneylender in most cases is also a merchant or a landlord and therefore is willing to lend only at rates comparable with what he could earn by employing his capital in alternative uses which are often highly profitable. The lenders in the unorganized money markets do not have the facilities for mobilizing liquid funds available to commercial banks in organized markets and therefore the supply of funds is rather inflexible. Since the unorganized money markets are generally not closely connected with the organized money markets, there is little possibility of increasing the supply of loanable funds beyond the savings of the lending sector of the unorganized money markets. The limited supply of loanable funds indeed reflects the general shortage of capital in underdeveloped countries.

The disadvantages of the high rates of interest in the unorganized money markets are well known and include such important effects as "dead-weight" agricultural indebtedness, alienation of land from agriculturists to moneylenders and the agrarian unrest that is thus engendered, and a general slowing down of economic development. . . .

The organized money markets in underdeveloped countries are less fully integrated than the money markets in developed countries. The unorganized money markets in underdeveloped countries are even more imperfect, and indeed it is questionable whether the existing arrangements should be referred to as "markets." They are much less homogeneous than the organized markets and are generally scattered over the rural sector. There is very little contact between the lenders and borrowers in different localities. The usual textbook conditions for a perfect market are completely nonexistent: lenders and borrowers do not know the rates at which loans are being transacted in other parts of the country; the relationship between borrower and lender is not only that of a debtor and creditor but is also an integral part of a much wider socioeconomic pattern of village life and rural conditions.

In unorganized money markets, moreover, loans are often contracted and paid for not in money but in commodities; and the size of the average loan is very much smaller than in the organized money markets. Both borrowers and lenders in the two markets are often of quite different types. In the organized money markets, the borrowers are mainly traders (wholesale and retail) operating in the large cities and, to a less extent, manufacturers. Agriculturalists rarely account for a significant portion of demand except in those underdeveloped countries where export agriculture has been developed through plantations or estates. In the unorganized money markets, the borrowers are small agriculturalists, cottage industry workers, and some retail shopkeepers. The lenders in the organized money markets consist almost exclusively of commercial banks. In the unorganized markets, the suppliers of credit consist of a few financial institutions, such as cooperatives, private and government-sponsored agricultural banks, indigenous bankers, professional moneylenders, large traders, landlords, shopkeepers, relatives, and friends. Proper records of loans granted or repaid are usually not kept, and uniform accounting procedures are not adopted by the different lenders. Loans are granted more on a personal basis than in the organized money markets, and most of the loans granted by the moneylenders and by other noninstitutional sources are unsecured beyond the verbal promise of the borrower to repay.

The unorganized money market may be divided into three major parts: (1) a part in which the supply is dominated by indigenous bankers, cooperatives, and other institutions, and the demand by rural traders and medium-sized landlords; (2) a part in which the demand originates mainly from small agriculturists with good credit ratings, who are able to obtain a large portion of their funds from respectable moneylenders, traders, and landlords at high but reasonable rates of interest, i.e., rates that are high in relation to those prevailing in the organized money market but not exorbitant by the standards of the unorganized money market; (3) a part in which the demand originates from borrowers who are not good credit risks, who do not have suitable collateral, and who in consequence are driven to shady marginal lenders who charge exorbitant rates of interest.

The general belief is that there is little connection between the unorganized and the organized money markets in underdeveloped countries. It is, however, quite uncertain whether the connection is so slight as to be negligible. Some of the missing statistics which would be helpful in determining the exact degree of connection are the volume of loans granted by lenders in the organized money markets to borrowers from the unorganized markets and the amount of relending which borrowers from the organized markets carry out in the unorganized markets.

The extent to which commercial banks operating in the organized money markets have financed directly or indirectly the agricultural sector of the economy is one indication of the closeness of the connection between the two markets....

Commercial bank loans to agriculture are less than 10 per cent of the banks' total loans in most underdeveloped countries, except in some Latin American countries, such as Colombia, Cuba, Peru, and Paraguay, and in Indonesia and the Philippines. Thus, according to this criterion, the link between the two money markets is rather slight.

Another way of determining the degree of connection between the organized and unorganized money markets is to measure the relative importance of institutional credit in the unorganized money market, i.e., the relative importance of credit supplied to that market by such institutions as commercial banks, cooperative credit societies, land mortgage banks, private agricultural banks, and agricultural credit institutions financed by the government. These institutions, except the commercial banks, lend money mainly in the unorganized money market, but a significant portion of their working capital (subscribed capital, deposits, and borrowings) is derived from the organized money market. To show the relative importance of institutional credit in the unorganized money market, and thus of the link between the organized and unorganized money markets, the outstanding agricultural loans of such institutions have been compared with national income originating in the agricultural sector and with the currency in circulation. From these comparisons, it would seem that, according to this criterion, the link is negligible in most underdeveloped countries, except a few Latin American countries, such as Costa Rica, the Dominican Republic, El Salvador, Mexico, and Nicaragua.

In addition to these quantitative indicators, there is some scattered information on the amount of finance which moneylenders obtain from commercial banks and on the extent of credit which traders in agricultural commodities give to agriculturists. Commercial bank lending to moneylenders does not seem to be important, except in Southeast Asia in prewar years....

The link between the two money markets afforded by exporters and traders in agricultural commodities borrowing from commercial banks and making advances to agriculturists, either directly or through smaller merchants, seems to be fairly common in underdeveloped countries with a large export sector. Exporters make advances to agriculturists in order to ensure an adequate supply of agricultural produce at favorable prices....

Where marketing boards have been established, these financial links are not severed, for the buying agents of these boards continue giving credit to the smaller traders who in turn give credit to the agriculturists. Thus, in Nigeria a substantial source of seasonal credit is available from these buying agents who have obtained much of their funds from the commercial banks. It is believed, however, that the small middlemen who receive loans from the buying agents frequently use the funds in other businesses before utilizing it for the purchase of the crop.

In some underdeveloped countries, a link between the two markets is also provided by importers who extend credit to wholesalers who in turn extend credit to village retailers....

So far this discussion has dealt mainly with the extent to which the volume of credit in the unorganized money market is affected by operations in the organized market. Some attention should be paid, however, to the significance of the relation between the two markets for the general direction of monetary policy. The link between the markets is much more effective in countries where it is provided mainly through commercial banks granting credit to agriculture, either directly or through cooperative societies and special agricultural credit institutions, than in countries where it is provided either by exporters of

agricultural commodities making loans to agriculturists or by importers financing the distribution of imports. In most underdeveloped countries, except a few in Latin America, the general situation is that commercial bank loans to agriculture are not so important as the financial assistance that percolates down through the large dealers to the agriculturists. As a rule, the proportion of credit made available in the unorganized market that is in fact supplied by the organized market is larger than is generally supposed; but, except in a few countries, the unorganized market is not much affected by changes in credit conditions in the organized market.

Many explanations have been offered for the high interest rates that generally prevail in unorganized money markets. One theory is that interest rates are high there because they are determined by custom and have always been high. This might be called the theory of the customary rate of interest....

The theory of customary rates is not satisfactory, however, because it does not explain how or why the custom of high rates developed. The true explanation has to be found in the economic and social conditions of underdeveloped countries, which cause the demand for loanable funds to be large in relation to the available supply. Some writers tend to explain the high rates of interest in terms of demand factors while others emphasize supply.

The demand for funds, in relation to the supply, is large because the average borrower in the unorganized money market has a very low income and therefore has no surplus funds to finance his business operations. The majority of the cultivating tenants—one of the most important groups of potential borrowers—have to borrow money not only for investment in land, cattle, etc., and for working capital to make purchases of seeds and fertilizers, but also for their minimum basic necessities of food, shelter, and clothing.

On the supply side, there is a general shortage of capital in underdeveloped countries and an inadequate level of domestic savings. Also, the small amount of domestic savings is not channeled effectively into the unorganized money market because of the absence of proper financial and credit institutions which not only would integrate the organized and unorganized money markets but also would facilitate the mobilization of savings in the rural areas. . . .

The difference in the levels of interest rates between the organized and unorganized money markets stems partly from the basic differences between the sources of supply of funds in the two markets. In an organized money market, facilities for the expansion of credit are open to the commercial banks, which have the use of funds belonging to depositors. These banks are therefore able to charge relatively low rates of interest and yet make satisfactory profits for the shareholders. On the other hand, moneylenders in an unorganized money market have little influence on the supply of funds at their disposal and, furthermore, their supply price tends to be influenced by the alternative uses to which their funds can be put.

A number of institutional factors are also responsible for high rates of interest in unorganized money markets. The size of the loan is usually small and thus the fixed handling charges are relatively high. Defaults also tend to be larger in unorganized money markets. These higher defaults are due not so much to a lower standard of morality and willingness to repay debts as to the fluctuations in prices and incomes derived from agricultural products, which reduce the ability of the agriculturists to repay debts at inopportune times. . . .

Another general factor causing high rates of interest is experience in regard to inflation. While this is probably of importance in many Latin American countries, it hardly seems relevant for prewar colonial territories which, by their rigid currency exchange standards, had maintained fairly stable conditions but still had high interest rates in the unorganized money markets. The large development programs in most underdeveloped countries, however, constitute possible inflationary pressures and may be considered as a factor in maintaining high rates of interest.

The list of causes of high interest rates could be extended to include other social and economic factors in underdeveloped countries—even to fairly remote factors, such as the system of land tenure which prevents land from being used as collateral. A general statement, however, is that interest rates in the unorganized money markets of underdeveloped countries are high because the economy is underdeveloped and the money market unorganized.

Any program to bring down interest rates in unorganized money markets must be comprehensive and should be guided by the principle that interest rates can be lowered only by reducing the demand for loanable funds as well as by increasing the supply. The demand for loanable funds for financing consumer expenditures can be reduced by changing social habits and concepts of acceptable standards of well-being. India has passed a law limiting the amount of expenditures which may be incurred for religious and social occasions. Such laws will not prevent people who are bent on spending money for such purposes from doing so; but it is believed that the masses, who are forced by custom to maintain levels of expenditures much above their income, will welcome this law and use it as an excuse to cut unnecessary consumption expenditure.

A reduction in borrowing for productive purposes may not be desirable, especially as the amount of self-financing which can take its place is negligible. Such borrowing can be reduced in the long run only through an increase in savings from higher agricultural output and income. It is not sufficient that the ability of the farmer to save be increased. The willingness to save must also be created. The problem of cheap agricultural credit is inseparable from the whole problem of agricultural development, including such measures as increasing the use of fertilizers and proper seeds; making available adequate marketing facilities, including proper grading, transportation, and storage of crops; and providing an efficient agricultural extension service.

There is no question that merely increasing the supply of loanable funds without reducing or limiting the demand will not solve the problem of high rates of interest. Experience in many underdeveloped countries, especially in Southeast Asia, indicates that an increase in supply merely stimulates demand (mainly for financing consumption) and does not lower the general level of interest rates.

Even if it is true that the cure for high rates of interest is to be found more on the demand side than on the supply side, the supply of credit should also be increased. Supply should be increased in such a way that legitimate credit needs are met at cheaper rates without encouraging borrowing for consumption. This can be achieved by increasing the supply of institutional credit while at the same time taking steps to discourage borrowing from noninstitutional lenders. In this connection, it could be argued that legislation regarding moneylenders which has had the effect of drying up noninstitutional credit may be a blessing in disguise—although in a manner different from that intended by legislators.

Increasing the supply of institutional credit is a difficult problem, but the efforts of governments have had a fair degree of success. One problem is that of getting the commercial banks to lend more to agriculture. This problem cannot be solved merely by opening more branches, because even at present agriculturists who are fairly close to the big cities are as isolated from the organized money market as others living some distance away from the cities. The opening of more bank branches is desirable, but the branches' business will as likely as not be confined to financing local retail and wholesale trade.

One way of inducing the organized financial institutions to lend more to agriculture is by making agriculturists more creditworthy and generally reducing the risks of lending by lessening the impact of some of the natural calamities (floods, plant and animal diseases); improving the human factor, i.e., reducing carelessness and increasing honesty; reducing the uncertainties of the market through crop insurance, stabilized agricultural prices, etc. The lenders might also take certain steps, such as spreading loans between different types of borrower and region and supervising the use of loans for productive purposes.

Summary The unorganized money market is generally larger than the organized money market. Its nature and working are quite different from that of the organized money market. Noninstitutional sources of supply, such as moneylenders, landlords, shopkeepers, relatives, and friends, are more important than credit institutions and thus business is carried on in a personal way and not subjected to standardized procedures.

The direct connection between the two money markets is rather poor and is less close than the connection between the organized money markets in underdeveloped countries and world money markets. The organized and unorganized money markets are, however, loosely connected through large exporters, wholesalers, and landlords who borrow in the organized market and carry out some relending in the unorganized market.

Interest rates in the unorganized money market range from fairly low rates charged by the cooperative credit societies to the very high and exorbitant rates charged by loan sharks to borrowers with poor credit ratings or to those in urgent need of funds. The major portion of the loans, however, are granted at rates in between these two extremes. It is estimated that in the majority of countries the weighted average rate of interest in the unorganized money market must lie between 24 per cent and 36 per cent per annum.

The high rates of interest prevailing in the unorganized money market have been a heavy burden to the agriculturists. Annual interest payments have been fairly large in relation to the net income of the farmer, thus reducing his ability to make improvements on the land.

The high rates of interest are due to both demand and supply factors and stem from the economic and social conditions prevailing in underdeveloped countries. The need for funds by agriculturists is more urgent than the need of borrowers in the organized money market, because the low level of agricultural income makes it practically impossible for the farmer to set aside funds for self-financing. The supply is small because of the low savings, even of those in the upper income brackets, and the lack of institutional arrangements to mobilize and channel the available savings into the unorganized money market. It seems, however, that the exorbitant rates

of interest charged by loan sharks and unscrupulous moneylenders are due mainly to the semimonopolistic position occupied by them.

Generally speaking, there are no seasonal and cyclical fluctuations in interest rates, such as occur in the organized money market. The rates charged by moneylenders and by credit institutions do not vary with the cycle. The quantities lent, however, have varied, with the supply from credit institutions expanding more rapidly in the boom and contracting much faster in the slump. Since the rate charged by credit institutions is much lower than the rate charged by the moneylenders, the weighted average rate of interest in the unorganized money market has fallen in the boom and risen in the slump; this is the opposite of the movements in the organized money market.

Governments have attempted to influence the cost and availability of credit in the unorganized money market through direct lending to the agriculturists and by controlling the rate of interest and the conditions of moneylending. Although some success has been achieved, these measures, generally speaking, have not as yet lowered rates of interest, partly because of inflationary pressures created by deficit financing for such lending and other expenditures and partly because controls have been evaded.

In view of the fact that the unorganized money market is larger than the organized money market, and since the two markets have not been closely connected, the use of orthodox monetary policy as an instrument of economic policy has very limited possibilities in underdeveloped countries. The cost and availability of credit in the unorganized money market can be influenced by the central bank either by improving the link between the two money markets or by having a large amount of credit supplied by it directly or indirectly through credit institutions and even through moneylenders. There are inflationary dangers in the latter approach, but the art of central banking in underdeveloped countries is to be able to steer the monetary system into a position of dependence on the central bank without inflation, so that when inflationary pressures arise, the authorities can cut credit not only in the organized money market but also in the unorganized money market.

2. INFLATION IN LATIN AMERICA

2.1 THE PROCESS OF INFLATION IN LATIN AMERICA*

There is no simple and self-evident causal nexus between development, on the one hand, and inflation, on the other, in either direction. Yet they are obviously not completely unconnected phenomena either. An under-developed country that attempts to change and to grow rapidly faces certain tensions which may result in inflation. Whether this happens or not depends on the following factors: (*a*) the pace at which economic change occurs; (*b*) whether external developments are favourable or otherwise; (*c*) the flexibility of the internal economy (reflecting not merely the productive structure but also a wide range of institutional, social and cultural characteristics); (*d*) the extent to which the policies followed by Governments ease or aggravate the process of transformation.

(*a*) Suppose, for example, that the national product is growing quickly, as it may have to if the rate of increase of the population is high. This implies a fast expansion in demand, especially for some types of goods and services, because, *inter alia*, growth will be accompanied by urbanization. Examples of items of consumption which typically expand quickly in a growing economy are consumer durables, household electricity and passenger transport.

(*b*) For under-developed economies such as those in Latin America, these rises in demand may create problems. Of course they can be accommodated, if exports are rising fast enough. Foreign exchange supplies will then permit imports of durables—to continue with the previous examples—to increase, and also allow equipment for electricity generation and for transport services to be purchased overseas. It will similarly be possible to ease other shortages that arise during the inevitably somewhat uneven process of growth.

It should be borne in mind that imports will have to grow at least as quickly as income if this room to manœuvre is to be maintained. If, however, export markets are weak, the domestic economy will itself have to satisfy these types of expanding demand. Some sectors, such as the engineering industry, will have to grow particularly fast. The agricultural sector will also have to expand its output because of the increasing need for food to feed city populations. Not only industries producing "final" products will be affected but also—and more especially—those producing "intermediate" goods and services, such as steel, energy of various kinds, and freight transport.

(*c*) Those brought up in the classical tradition of economics might expect that declines in the sales of export products would induce labour and capital to shift readily into secondary industries of their own accord, because of the more attractive wages and profits to be found there. For this to happen, two conditions must be fulfilled. In the first place, prices must act as signals to show what changes in the channelling of resources are necessary. Secondly,

* From United Nations, Economic Commission for Latin America, "Inflation and Growth: A Summary of Experience in Latin America," *Economic Bulletin for Latin America*, February 1962, pp. 26-8.

factors of production must move readily and easily in response to such signals.

The first conditions will be met if there are no monopolistic elements which affect the levels of wages or of profits in particular industries, or trends of prices. More important, prices need to be such that profits reflect the social benefit to the economy as a whole of acts of investment.

The second condition is that labour must be mobile enough in all senses (geographically, industrially and occupationally) to flow in response to wage changes, and that capital should also move into the most profitable openings irrespective of where it arises. ("Profitable" here refers of course to the long term.) This mobility is greatest if the export sector can sell its surplus output in the home market, or if its resources can be used where they are, without much adaptation, to produce other goods. In addition, and perhaps more crucially, entrepreneurs must emerge to take advantage of the possibilities of profits and to combine labour and capital efficiently.

There are certain financial corollaries of this physical transformation. The flow of saving has to be high enough to finance the capital requirements, and has to increase when a rising yield signals that import substitution has to be accelerated. This problem is easier to solve to the extent that capital is available from overseas, and conversely more difficult to the extent that capital is absorbed in the purchase of foreign securities, United States dollars, or gold.

Apart from the physical and financial conditions for dynamic equilibrium, there are also social ones. The purpose of economic growth is, in the final analysis, to solve social problems by providing better nourishment, housing, etc. This implies that it is more successful to the extent that inequalities of income are reduced. Indeed, since the manufacturing industries mostly require large markets, increasing equality could in any case hardly be avoided in the long run.

(d) Merely to state these conditions indicates that economic transformation may not come about automatically, through the normal interplay of economic forces. Yet dynamic equilibrium can still be achieved if Government policy is far-sighted and firm enough to ensure that the necessary substitutes for imports are produced and also to curb inessential consumption and investment by fiscal and monetary policy. This in turn implies the need for efficient and honest public servants.

These last two conditions—(c) and (d) —are of course themselves interrelated. Structural obstacles to growth also affect the distribution of political power and the context within which it is wielded.

The question of whether inflation is inevitable in the process of rapid development therefore resolves itself into three subsidiary questions: are markets for the country's exports buoyant?; is the internal economy flexible?; and is government policy efficient?

If exports rise rapidly enough, as they did in Venezuela for many years, the economy can grow quickly without serious danger of inflation, even though labour and capital are immobile, enterprise is deficient, and the Government lacks an adequate development policy. In that case, however, the economy will *grow* rather than *develop*: it will not achieve enough import substitution to enable it to weather comfortably a subsequent weakening of export markets. On the other hand, if exports are stagnant, or even more if they fall back, then the pace of price rises will depend on structural factors and on Government policy. The greater is the weakness in exports and the more intractable are structural obstacles to development, the less easy is it for a Government to avoid inflation and still to maintain a satisfactory economic expansion.

This brief review of ideal conditions points to the ways in which inflation can emerge and propagate itself—the plural is used because there are, in theory at least, several possible processes of inflation. For the sake of exposition, let us suppose that an economy has been growing in dynamic equilibrium, as has been defined above, and that something happens to divert it from this path.

A convenient first hypothesis is that the rise in exports slows down or stops. If growth is to continue undiminished, this must mean an acceleration of the rate of import substitution, i.e. of industrialization. Some local industries will have to expand particularly quickly. Imports of capital equipment, and of raw materials unavailable locally, will not fall. They will increase, because of the very need for industrialization, so imports of consumer goods will tend to be reduced, probably sharply.

This need to expand certain industries rapidly will have a direct impact on the price level, because goods produced for the first time domestically will almost certainly be more expensive than the imports they replace. Otherwise they would have been produced before. The new substitutes will be produced under the protection of tariffs or import controls; they will be marketed in monopolistic conditions; they will usually be manufactured in rather small quantities because of the limited size of local markets, and in any case the techniques used may be relatively inefficient.

But what is of greater significance for the economy is that the expansion of these industries means a big increase in the demand for certain inputs. To attract workers into the new industries, for example—especially skilled workers—higher wages have to be offered. This creates shortages of certain types of workers elsewhere, raising costs in other industries,

and it affects the general wage level. The increased demand for electricity aggravates problems of lack of energy that exist, and the increased need for transport facilities will add to the strain on that sector. The accelerated pace of urbanization associated with this economic development implies that passenger transport facilities, urban social services and food supplies will also have to grow more quickly.

Import substitution thus changes consumption functions throughout the economy. It requires from the productive sectors a flexible response which is difficult to achieve in an economy where the markets for labour and capital are imperfect. Failure to make the needed spurt in output means rising prices. Moreover, to the extent that the economic transformation is not adequate, the pressure of demand for imports will not be relieved. The exchange rate will thus be devalued, which will also raise costs. Once prices rise, for whatever reason, this affects the levels of living of various sections of the community, and leads to attempts to raise wages and other forms of income—attempts which are more or less successful according to the power of the sections concerned. Then, in time, thrift is discouraged, and capital is diverted away from the types of long-term investment which are needed. So inflation gains momentum. Moreover, as prices rise deficits appear in government accounts because of the inflexibility of taxes.

An alternative possibility is that the growth rate of population may accelerate, making it necessary for that of national income to accelerate too. The rate of growth of exports, although previously satisfactory, will then prove too slow, and the same problem of an import "bottleneck" will arise.

So far it has been assumed that the pressure of excess demand appears because imports of some types cannot keep climbing fast enough. It may also make itself felt if supply lags for different reasons. For example, agricultural output may cease to expand at a satisfactory pace. This will mean rising food prices, or, alternatively, increasing imports of food, a state of affairs which aggravates any foreign exchange shortage. And, moreover, it immediately stimulates pressure for wage increases. On the other hand, failure of the output of steel or of petroleum to grow in line with demand will create the need for rapid import substitution in other sectors, even if exports are rising reasonably fast.

The acceleration of demand for particular goods will pose formally similar problems. This might happen as the result of "autonomous" changes in the pace of urbanization, or in the distribution of income, or in the coverage of consumer credit, or in taste (for example, as a result of the "demonstration effect"). In any of these ways a price inflation can develop, and, once it starts, it develops cumulative features.

Apart from long-term models, such as have been outlined here, inflation might emerge because of fluctuations in exports, even if these fluctuations were to take place around a rising trend. Over the short run, capacity to produce substitutes for imports cannot be increased, so there is an immediate danger of devaluation if the growth of income (and the demand for imports) continues while exports fall back. This is especially likely to occur if there is a chronic long-term tendency to inflation.

Moreover, when exports recover, the process is not necessarily reversed. By that time rises in internal prices and incomes will have occurred, and it will seem unrealistic to consider going back to the old exchange rate. Incomes will also be rising in the export sector, and so will prices of imported manufactures (particularly if the recovery of the country's exports is part of a world boom). So both in a slump and

in a boom prices tend to move upward, and the long-term pace of inflation depends in part on the violence and frequency of short-term fluctuations in commodity markets.

Similarly, a budget deficit might grow because of the decline in revenue from exports, or indeed for any other reason, such as quite irresponsible increases in public outlays. Then again, demand may rise because an expansion of monetary policy causes private investment to outrun private savings. Whatever the cause, an excess of total demand means rising prices. This discourages exports, while it stimulates imports, thus inducing devaluation, and causing a shortage of foreign exchange for certain types of imports.

Again, wage rises may be greater than productivity increases. This at once results in rising prices, especially if the organization of industry is monopolistic. It also unbalances the budget, and increases the costs of basic activities such as electricity production and transport. Either their prices will be adjusted, in which case the upward trend in prices is strengthened, or they will be held constant, in which case the enterprises will lack short-term financing for investment. Since consumption will at the same time be stimulated, familiar problems of shortage of capacity will appear.

While, therefore, there are many ways in which the process may begin, it will in time, however it started, show certain predictable symptoms, including a strained foreign balance, and shortages of particular types of goods.

It should be noted that a different theory is required to explain inflation in semi-industrialized countries like Brazil or Chile and in fully developed countries. In the former case, the model has to allow for the changing patterns of demand, due to urbanization, for the high share of food in workers' expenditure, for hindrances to the mobility of labour and of capital, for the general impossibility of selling export products in the home markets, for the chronic shortage of productive capacity, for the lack of certain industries (notably those producing capital equipment), for the inflexibility of the fiscal mechanism and so on. These are features which do not have to be given the same weight (or, in some cases, any weight at all) in the analysis of inflation in developed economies.

Besides, a general theoretical explanation of Latin American experience has to take account of dynamic factors such as population growth. This compels government initiative in providing social and economic capital, and in creating employment opportunities if these do not emerge. Analysis of trends in this region also has to allow for adverse secular trends in markets for primary commodities, and an income-elasticity of demand for imports greater than unity.

The process which has been described cannot be classified as one of "cost" inflation or of "demand" inflation, in the manner customary in professional discussion in Western Europe and North America. It has elements of both, but also structural features and trends which are peculiar to less developed economies.

The importance of various aspects of this process varies from country to country, according to the rate at which each grows, its experience with foreign trade, its economic and social structure, and the policies which its Government puts into effect. In some cases the external and internal obstacles to growth make it difficult for Governments intent on economic development to avoid inflation, at least in the short run (i.e. until they can make structural improvements). In others, due advantage may not be taken of a favourable structural situation and possibilities of expanding trade. Perhaps the need to develop basic sectors is ignored, or export markets are lost because of ill-conceived policies in the spheres of public investment, or irresponsible fiscal, monetary or wages policy. Developments in Argentina in the years after the last war illustrate these points.

2.2 STRUCTURAL VULNERABILITY AND INFLATION *

The economists of ECLA are often thought of as having a certain leaning towards inflation, as being prompted by the belief that this phenomenon is inevitable in the economic development of Latin America. Nothing could be further from our thoughts....

Two facts largely explain why our thinking is wrongly judged. We reject the theory, which is so current, that inflation is caused solely by the financial disorder and lack of monetary restraint of the Latin American countries, not because we deny the existence of these patent aberrations but because there are extremely powerful structural factors in Latin America which lead to inflation and against which monetary policy is powerless. This is the first fact.

The second is the critical position we have adopted towards certain measures aimed at monetary stabilization. We all agree that a supreme effort must be made to arrest inflation and to achieve stability on sound bases. But we are seriously worried about achieving this at the expense of a decline in over-all income, of its stagnation or of a slowing-down in its rate of development.

Those who profess this type of anti-inflationary policy—both those who suggest it from outside and those who live in the midst of this harsh and hazardous reality of Latin America—sometimes entertain the esoteric notion that sin can be

* From Raúl Prebisch, "Economic Development or Monetary Stability: The False Dilemma," *Economic Bulletin for Latin America*, Vol. VI, No. 1, March 1961, pp. 1, 23-4.

redeemed by sacrifice. The evil of inflation must be atoned for by retrenchment. But very often the conventional punishment is not visited upon those who unleashed inflation or who thrived on it, but on the broad masses of the people who were suffering its consequences.

The general mistake persists of considering inflation as a purely monetary phenomenon to be combated as such. Inflation cannot be explained as something divorced from the economic and social maladjustments and stresses to which the economic development of our countries gives rise. Nor can serious thought be given to an autonomous anti-inflationary policy, as if only monetary considerations were involved; it must be an integral part of development policy.

Economic development calls for constant changes in the form of production, in the economic and social structure and in patterns of income distribution. Failure to make these changes in time or to undertake them partially and completely leads to these maladjustments and stresses which release the ever-latent and extremely powerful inflationary forces in the Latin American economy.

This should not be construed as meaning that inflation is inevitable in our countries. Far from it. To avoid inflation, however, there must be a rational and far-sighted policy of economic development and social betterment, in other words, an essentially new approach in which an answer other than inflation is sought to these maladjustments and stresses arising from development.

...

Steady and intensive economic development calls for a series of reforms in the pattern of production, in economic and social structure and in income distribution. These reforms will enable the economy to grow faster than primary exports and to cushion the internal impact of fluctuations in these latter, while at the same time removing local obstacles to development. If such reforms are effected only in part, or inadequately, or not at all, maladjustments and tensions arise which will call into play or stimulate the inflationary forces latent in the Latin American economy....

Rightly considered, it is *change* in economic conditions that favours the action of these inflationary forces. If an energetic economic development policy were to promote the steady growth of the economy, if *per capita* income were to increase persistently enough and on a satisfactory scale, without the fluctuations registered at present, and if income distribution were modified not regressively but progressively —if all this were carried out with a reasonable degree of efficacy—the maximum degree of resistance to the action of inflationary forces would be ensured, whereby to maintain monetary stability.

There are also cases, not so much of resistance to inflationary forces, as of weakness on the part of these forces themselves. In reality, it is not usually difficult to maintain monetary stability in situations of relative economic and social stagnation based on an out-dated system of land tenure and income distribution, with little social mobility. But sooner or later social pressures emerge to militate against this precarious equilibrium, spurring on inflationary forces which quickly put an end to monetary stability.

These forces are not always associated with adverse circumstances. They are also intimately allied to prosperity. A favourable change in economic conditions opens up new opportunities for consumption or investment which, when they exceed the genuine resources available, precipitate inflationary expansion.

True, inflation is not a purely economic phenomenon, and a thorough understand-

ing of its nature and significance calls for
sociological research of a kind in which
Latin America is behind the times. If the
stagnation or slow progress of the economy provokes those social pressures which
degenerate into inflation in default of an
enlightened development policy, rapid
growth also brings about conditions favourable to the increased mobility of dynamic
elements, to changes in the existing social
complex, likely to stimulate the action of
inflationary forces.

New social groups force their way into
politics and economic affairs—in close combination—and resort to inflation to establish and consolidate their power, altering
income distribution in their own favour.
History has afforded examples of other
highly efficacious ways of redistributing
income, among them that concentration of
land ownership which is still widely prevalent in the Latin American countries. But
inflation perhaps outdoes them all in its
flexibility and the far-reaching scope of its
consequences.

Thus, inflation is a manifestation of
economic and social change, an essentially
dynamic phenomenon. Consequently, cam-
paigns to prevent or combat it cannot be
waged through autonomous monetary
measures, but must form part of a vast
and deliberate effort to channel economic
and social forces towards the attainment
of clearly-defined objectives.

Hence the irremediable fallacy of the
orthodox position. It heedlessly ignores
the phenomena of economic development.
Whether a Latin American country is
enjoying a boom or suffering a slump in
its exports, whether it is growing at a
rapid rate or barely developing at all, the
formula is the same; inflationary forces
must be combatted by means of a firm
credit restriction policy and certain other
expedients which, as a general rule, do not
venture beyond the monetary sphere.

But does this mean that orthodox mone-

tary policy is indifferent to a country's
economic development? Does it set up
monetary stability as a primary objective,
for the sake of which such development
must be curbed or smothered? This would
be an unjust assumption. The difficulty is
not lack of interest in economic development, but a concept that is perhaps even
more serious: the implicit negation of the
need for a development policy, of the need
for reforms in the pattern of production,
in economic and social structure and in
income distribution—of the need, that is,
for a conscious and deliberate endeavour
to influence economic and social forces.

Deliberate action of this kind is unnecessary because economic development is a
spontaneous phenomenon. Herein lies the
basic error—in the belief or the supposition
that, once monetary stability is assured and
the economy relieved of any kind of State
intervention, the free interaction of its
forces will suffice to bring about maximum
efficiency in the utilization of the factors
of production.

The orthodox application of anti-inflationary policy generally implies economic
contraction and social distress; it is the
present price that must be paid for a welfare shortly to be enjoyed, the indispensable sacrifice whereby to earn the remission of our economic sins and the grace
of foreign private capital. Emanating at
times from profound conviction, and at
others from the impression that without
it external contributions to help control
inflation will be unobtainable, a policy of
this type demands qualities of energy and
firmness which—however admirable in
themselves—end by foundering amid the
tensions, antagonisms and resistances of
every kind which the contraction or relative stagnation of the economy brings in
its train.

All of this is much to be regretted, for
such qualities are highly necessary in any
campaign against inflationary forces. But

monetary policy should not be expected to yield results which it cannot produce alone. It is impossible to combat inflation or prevent its reappearance by purely monetary measures; they must be incorporated in the framework of an energetic economic development policy which ensures the structural equilibrium of the economy. Only then can monetary policy be required to give what it is capable of achieving, namely, stability, an essential requisite for economic development, but not the only one.

Structural equilibrium is not static, but dynamic; that is, it must perpetually adapt itself to the new demands of economic development. In the Latin American countries this means a continuous transformation of the structure of production and the composition of imports so that the rate of growth of the economy may exceed that of exports. These changes cannot result from the spontaneous interaction of economic forces, but must be the outcome of measures which forestall the claims of future events. Nor should they be the consequence of successive devaluations of the currency; this is a fantastic theory, which purports to show that if the exchange rate is left to find its own level through the machinery of free interplay, the readjustments referred to will be achieved without the necessity of deliberate action.

In this whole field there is a deplorable confusion, resulting from the static reasoning on which the orthodox conception of monetary matters is based, and which fails to reckon with the dynamic process of development. Of course, the main objective of a sound monetary policy—to which I unconditionally subscribe—is to stabilize the external equilibrium of the economy; not, however, its structural equilibrium, but the deviations from this which take place in the course of the operation of the economy.

Structural equilibrium is not a matter for monetary policy, nor is the remedying of external vulnerability. For such purposes structural reforms are indispensable, and without them the risk of inflation will continue to be very great. A tax policy planned to provide incentives to investment, and measures which actively promote capital formation on the part of the broad masses of the population, will give monetary and financial leaders a more stable base from which to operate against the inflationary expansion of credit.

Nevertheless, this concerns only one aspect of inflation. Not all inflationary pressures originate in credit. The inflation of costs must also be guarded against. It is expedient to do so by means of measures which equitably distribute the social burden of heavier costs. But the fundamental solution lies in changes in the pattern of production which will obviate such increased costs or permit their absorption.

2.3 The "Monetarist"—"Structuralist" Controversy *

In several Latin American countries now facing problems of acute inflation, there is a sharp theoretical and policy clash between two groups which, for want of better terms, I shall call the "monetarists" and the "structuralists."

To the "monetarists," views are ascribed that are close to those imputed to the International Monetary Fund, even though several of them dissent from the IMF in many respects. The "structuralists," on the other hand, claim to have support for their views in the studies of the Economic Commission of Latin America, even though official ECLA reports do not show the fatalistic view of the inflationary process in Latin America nor the degree of scepticism toward monetary and fiscal poli-

* From Roberto de Oliveira Campos, "Two Views on Inflation in Latin America," *Latin American Issues*, edited by A. O. Hirschman, Twentieth Century Fund, New York, 1961, pp. 69-73. Reprinted by permission.

cies that is implied in the "structuralist" view.

In a heroic oversimplification, the views of the two contending schools of thought—at least as expressed in Brazil—can be summarized as follows:

The "monetarists" hold that:

(a) Inflation has ceased to promote development and in fact has become incompatible with it; even those countries that managed to have inflation and development are now facing an acceleration of inflation and a deceleration of development;

(b) Inflation must be stopped quickly, before it degenerates into explosive tensions, and the only effective method seems to be the curbing of excess demand through a prudent combination of monetary and fiscal policies supplemented by international financial assistance;

(c) Most of the alleged supply inelasticities and bottlenecks are not autonomous or structural, but are caused by price and exchange rate distortions generated during the course of the inflationary process itself.

The "structuralists," on the other hand, hold that:

(a) Inflation is a natural accompaniment of growth;

(b) Inflation cannot be curbed through monetary and fiscal means without provoking unemployment or stagnation of growth because of supply rigidities;

(c) The instability of export proceeds, generating a capacity-to-import bottleneck as well as supply inelasticities inherent in the growth process, renders it impossible to curb inflation in the short run; it in fact renders desirable a *gradual* attack on inflation, except to the extent that foreign assistance becomes available to render the supply of imports more elastic.

To a certain extent the two contending views are less different than they might seem, the divergences being more of method and emphasis than of substance.

There is, however, a *hard core* of dispute which centers mainly on the usefulness of monetary and fiscal policy as well as on the relationship between structural factors and the inflationary process itself.

An implicit assumption of the "structuralist" view is that a sharp distinction exists between the inflationary behavior and policies of less developed countries taken *as a group,* on the one side, and the developed countries as a group, on the other; and accordingly a separate theory is needed to account for such discrepant behavior.

This approach ... tends to overestimate differences *between* the two groups and slur differences *within* the groups. For instance, *within* the less developed group Brazil followed expansionist monetary policies and is suffering from acute inflation. Mexico pursued more prudent monetary and fiscal policies and has had only a moderate rate of inflation. *Within* the industrialized group, France, until the recent stabilization program, followed inflationary monetary policies while Germany adhered to a conservative approach. It may be said, in this respect, that there is (or was until recently) a greater similarity of behavior between Brazil and France than between Brazil and Mexico.

In short, countries in similar stages of development and achieving comparable rates of growth had varying degrees of inflation and varying monetary experiences, depending on the set of monetary and fiscal policies they chose to adopt.

Is a new or modified theory of inflation, emphasizing supply inelasticities or bottleneck factors which are judged to be inadequately covered by the "demand-pull" or "cost-push" theory, in fact needed for the understanding of inflation in Latin America? Is there room for a "structural" theory of inflation, which would regard changes in money supply as merely passive adjustments to irresistible autonomous pressures generated by bottlenecks in the import capacity, or inelastic food supplies or institutional arrangements?

On the ground of the data and comments I have seen, this effort at theorizing would seem an exercise in "unnecessary" originality; but I am of course open to persuasion.

To naïve and unsophisticated minds like my own, a number of questions would occur immediately: Why not undertake a statistical effort to detect such correlation as may exist for different countries in Latin America, between (a) expansion of the effective money supply, indicating a passive behavior of the monetary authorities, (b) rate of price inflation, (c) rate of growth in real product?

A few things would undoubtedly stand out.

(a) In the heavy inflated countries the rate of expansion in the money supply has been of such an order of magnitude (20 to 30 per cent per year) as to outstrip any realistic possibility of growth of the supply (via increases in the real domestic product plus net imports); at that rate of monetary expansion no economy, even though highly developed and presumably exempted from major inelasticity or supply bottlenecks, would fail to have inflation.

(b) No clear relationship appears to exist (if anything the correlation is negative) between the rate of inflation and the rate of development. The highly inflated countries (Argentina, Chile, Bolivia) tended to stagnate; some of the low-inflation countries (Mexico, Venezuela, El Salvador, Ecuador) seem to be developing fast. For the others there is a mixed picture but it may be said tentatively that (1) where inflation coincided with rapid development, the latter can best be explained by other factors (absorption of foreign resources, improvement in the terms of trade) than by the full utilization of capacity supposedly brought about by inflation,

(2) in recent periods the acceleration of inflation has coincided with a deceleration of development.

(c) The above data would give a *first hint* that the behavior of inflation in Latin America would seem to conform pretty much to what might be expected in the light of old-fashioned theories.

It might of course be argued that the above investigation would merely represent a *tautological* illustration of the inflationary process. The relevant question then would be: Why is it that the monetary authorities in Latin America find it so peculiarly difficult to behave actively and usually confine themselves to register on the liability side (money supply) all of the asset creation plans of the government sector, private sectors and net foreign balance? Several answers might suggest themselves:

(1) *Those pressures are irresistible in the process of growth.* This answer would *prima facie* be unsatisfactory as (a) some of the Latin American countries achieved high rates of growth without inflation or with moderate inflation, (b) even the overinflated countries (Brazil, Argentina) have achieved, in discontinuous periods of their history, rapid growth with nothing like their present inflation, (c) given demand pressures for governmental or private investment in development programs, it does not follow that the money supply must be passively adjusted to ratify those programs; after all, investment programs can be financed by taxes, by foreign loans, by physical rationing of consumption, by shifts in the composition of investment, etc.

(2) *Supply inelasticities, institutional rigidities and the capacity-to-import (pressures from the real or income side) are the active factors and monetary expansion a residual.* This line of argument would encounter the same difficulties mentioned above, namely, (a) some countries managed at times to control inflation despite

bottlenecks and (b) there is no intrinsic organic reason why bottlenecks and inelasticities should be greater in Brazil and Argentina, for instance, than in Mexico or Ecuador. Again it is very difficult to resort to bottlenecks and inelasticities to explain the Argentine inflation at the beginning of the Peronist era.

The upshot of this initial statistical effort would be to bring out clearly, to my mind, that the role of old-fashioned monetary and fiscal policy is vitally important. Money factors are not residual but at the very core of the process. The inflated countries are those that choose incompatible targets.

2.4 INFLATION IN CHILE *

Fragmentary and incomplete data suggest that *per capita* gross national product [in Chile] has increased at an average annual rate of about one per cent since the beginning of the century. Since 1940, the first year for which fairly reliable national income statistics are available, gross national product has increased by an average of 5 per cent annually up to 1953 but only by about one per cent annually between 1953 and 1959. Because population has been increasing at the rate of 2.5 per cent per annum in recent years this means that 1959 *per capita* income was below the 1953 level.

Between 1953 and 1959 *per capita* consumption levels were maintained only at the expense of investment. Since 1940, gross investment rarely has exceeded 12 per cent of gross national product in Chile, but in the last three years it even has fallen below 10 per cent. While this permitted average consumption per person to hold steady in the face of a rapidly increasing population and slowly growing GNP, it is probable that consumption of lower income groups

* From Joseph Grunwald, "The 'Structuralist' School on Price Stabilization and Economic Development: The Chilean Case," *Latin American Issues,* edited by A. O. Hirschman, Twentieth Century Fund, New York, 1961, pp. 97-9, 108-14, 117-21. Reprinted by permission.

has fallen because of the adverse effects of inflation on the distribution of income.

The structure of the economy has changed considerably in the last two decades. Income generated in agriculture declined from 20 to 15 per cent of total national income since 1940, while the manufacturing industry share increased from 12 to about 20 per cent of the total. About 28 per cent of the labor force is now employed in agriculture as compared with 36 per cent in 1940. Manufacturing industry now employs about one fifth of the labor force as compared with 16 per cent in 1940. There also has been an increase in the proportion of the working population in commerce and services, whose relative contribution to national income has remained unchanged. On the other hand, employment in mining has decreased as productivity has risen.

In this over-all picture the outstanding impression is a relatively slow growth of agricultural production, which has barely been able to keep up with the population increase. Chile not only was nearly self-sufficient in agriculture some twenty years ago, but in some products even had an export surplus. Yet now the country is spending close to one fifth of its import budget on imports of foodstuffs.

...

It is not surprising that the long history of fiascos in the stabilization policies led to a deep division in the thinking on approaches to the country's economic problems. The growing young intellectual community became impatient with the lack of dynamism which had characterized the Chilean economy during recent years and which was aggravated by the policies of the stabilization program. The inability of these policies to attain price stability, of course, sharpened the dissent.

Traditional monetary policies were challenged already in the 1940's but the issues on how to fight inflation did not become seriously defined until the 1950's and particularly after the advent of the Klein-Saks mission in Chile. The greater role of the International Monetary Fund in the lending policies of the international agencies and of the United States government from 1957 onward has brought the debate to the fore in other Latin American countries also. There is no question but that those who doubt the efficacy of orthodox methods in fighting inflation have become an ever increasing group.

In all fairness, it must be stated that the dividing line between "monetarists" and "structuralists" is perhaps not as sharp as drawn here. Some "structuralists" have exaggerated their differences with the "monetarists" for political reasons. It is obvious that the "monetarists" would agree with much of what the "structuralists" say and vice versa. If one examines the complete program of the Kein-Saks mission, which came under such strong fire by the "structuralists," one will probably find one of the most "structural" programs that was ever proposed in Chile on a practical level. It was the International Monetary Fund which helped draw the lines of battle.

The challenge to the purely monetary approach was based on the belief that monetary policies attack only the symptoms of the sickness but provide no cure for it. Basic structural factors are seen as underlying the inflation and are distinguished sharply from circumstantial, cumulative or propagation factors. The "basic" factors are the causal forces of inflation. The propagation factors might also be important once an inflation is under way, but gearing policy only toward them, according to this view, will not eliminate inflationary pressures because the fundamental maladjustments will persist.

The "basic" or structural factors underlying inflation essentially are connected with the alleged inelasticity of supply and with the rigidity in the public financial apparatus. In other words, the structural factors are closely related to the state of underdevelopment of the economy.

"Inelastic" Supply A great many things go into the concept of "inelastic" supply.[1] This means roughly that the supply of goods and services does not expand and its composition does not adjust sufficiently fast to meet not only a rising demand but also a change in the pattern of demand without serious price pressures. Rigidity is particularly pronounced in the infrastructure of the economy, which in turn induces a lack of flexibility in production, particularly in agriculture where flexibility is low anyway because of the existing institutional arrangements. Obviously, an integral part of this picture is an inefficient labor and capital market or, to put it in other words, a low mobility of resources.

The inelasticity of the capacity to import or its sharp fluctuations in the short run are a chapter of the same story and so is the low saving rate with the accompanying low capital formation. Another factor is a monopolistic development in industry and in the distribution system, fostered principally by the small size of the domestic market. And one must not forget the personal income distribution, which, because of its high degree of inequality in lesser developed areas, plays an important role in this concept of "inelasticity" according to the "structuralists."

1. *Agriculture.* One explanation runs in the following terms: the increase in urbanization which accompanies economic growth signifies that an increasing share of the population depends upon commercially distributed agricultural products. Many of the people who are now in the

1. The "structuralists" seldom specify which concept of elasticity is meant. Sometimes price and often income elasticity are used under the general heading "elasticity."

city obtained a large part of their food requirements directly from the farm on which they worked before they migrated. This additional demand for commercial food products plus the change in the composition of demand due to urbanization plus the demand generated by the rapidly increasing population, can only be satisfied if the agricultural production system is sufficiently elastic to respond rapidly to the demand increases. This, however, is not the case for various reasons of which backward institutional arrangements are the most important.

According to this school of thought, the *latifundio* system and the existing land tenure relations constitute an effective brake on the growth in agricultural production. If ownership of the land is several stages removed from those who actually work the land, incentives for improvements in methods, use of modern inputs and conservation will necessarily be weak. It must be remembered also that the holding of land is an efficient defense against inflation, and it is not surprising that substantial tracts of expensive and good farm land (particularly around the large cities) are held by persons in businesses and professions other than farming.

In addition, the possibility of having effective price stimuli for agricultural production is greatly reduced by the highly unequal income distribution. Large sectors of the community whose incomes are close to the subsistence level must be protected by repressing inflation in essential goods and services. This means that some farm products will be subjected to price controls, which in turn constitute a disincentive for agricultural output.

2. *Capacity to import.* The other important items in this category of the "basic" or structural factors are, first, the low level of the capacity to import and, second, its instability. On the export side, the culprit

is a monoproduct (or "few-product") export system (copper in the case of Chile). The exports involved are usually primary products and therefore subject to great price fluctuations. The dependence on one or a few exports thus induces a great instability in the foreign exchange earnings and also in the public finances, whose revenues are based upon such exports to a large extent.

On the other hand, export diversification is hindered by orthodox monetary methods because of the vast disparity in the productivity of the principal exports and the rest of the economy. For example, if the productivity levels of copper are a multiple of those existing in other productive activities, it is argued that a free rate of exchange, uniform for all exports, even with a minimum of import restrictions will not be sufficiently high to give the necessary incentive for the development of other export industries.[2]

On the import side, the "structuralist" school maintains that economic development as such implies disequilibrium of the balance of payments because the income elasticity of imports is higher for the less developed countries than for the more advanced nations. In the 19th century the then developing countries had a relatively high import elasticity for primary products which permitted the less developed

2. This argument implies, first, that the community for certain reasons prefers export diversification even if it means a lower national income than might be obtained through the expansion of the traditional raw material exports. One wonders, though, if this preference would still hold in Chile were the large copper companies not in the hands of foreigners but owned by the Chilean government. Another implicit assumption might be that the demand for the raw material exports is highly inelastic. (But if this is so then the productivity difference is not very relevant.) In the case of Chile, the demand for copper seems to have been much more elastic than was thought considering the fact that the country lost a substantial part of the world market by not encouraging copper exports between 1946 and 1954.

areas to share in the economic growth of the industrializing countries. This is no longer true today. In fact, today's advanced countries show a relatively low elasticity of imports for primary products, while the import elasticity in general of today's less developed areas is very high. This squeeze may introduce a chronic inmbalance in the foreign trade of the now developing countries, at least to the extent of limiting their capacity to import needed capital goods. This adds to the rigidity in the supply structure of the country and thus constitutes one of the "basic factors" underlying inflationary pressures.

In the face of these balance-of-payment rigidities it is natural that a tendency toward import substitution has developed. Import substitution as a policy has been justified on two grounds: first, that through it goods become available which otherwise could not be obtained at all because of foreign exchange shortage (or supply difficulties as during wartime); second, that import substitution investment brings with it further developmental effects which could not be obtained through imports. The basic premise of this position is that investment funds which are used in import substitution are not available for investment in other lines. The objective is to obtain a faster growth of gross national product than the slowly expanding capacity to import will permit.

Nevertheless, it was soon realized, even by the "structuralists," that often import substitution introduces other rigidities so that sometimes the net benefit of this policy has been difficult to assess. First of all, domestic production of what was previously imported does not always reduce dependence upon imports: raw materials, machinery and other capital goods and supplies will have to be imported for the new production. In some cases this sensitizes the economy even more than the

import of the finished product. Once a factory exists with substantial capital equipment and labor force it will be more difficult to let the plant and its employees become idle because of import problems than it would have been to reduce the importations of the finished product, particularly if it is not a basic necessity.

The second point of rigidity which import substitution might introduce is of course the need of protection for the new industry. If the new industry is "inefficient" from the point of view of the international division of labor, its productivity levels will be low, its prices necessarily high and permanent protection will be needed.

The third type of rigidity introduced by import substitution is the creation of monopoly structure since the productive plant for many of the substituted imports necessarily must be large relative to a restricted market such as Chile's.

3. *Distribution of income.* Another "structural" impediment for a more elastic supply of products is said to be the very unequal distribution of personal income. This income distribution in itself implies a certain composition of demand both domestically and for imports, which is not conducive to a high growth rate. Domestic production and imports would cater to the restricted higher income groups. Therefore, it is argued, investment and import substitution would be geared toward such production to the detriment of growth industries and investment in social overhead which could give greater flexibility to the economy. The negative effect of the unequal income distribution on the expansion of agricultural production through preventing a substantial betterment of relative prices in agriculture has already been mentioned.

In addition, the savings rate is exceedingly low not only because of low income levels in general but also because of a completely disproportionate propensity to consume of the upper income groups. Consumption habits of this group are said to be entirely out of line with those of equivalent income groups in more developed countries. Specifically it was claimed for Chile that if the upper income groups had the same consumption pattern as their counterparts in the more advanced countries, the savings rate could be doubled.

The other category of structural factors has to do with the instability of government revenues in the face of the rigidity of government expenditures. In a country where about one quarter of public income depends upon the exports of one product, it is clear that public finances will be affected severely by fluctuations in the price of that product. On the other hand, current expenditures are relatively rigid, consisting principally of salaries and social security contributions. If, for some reason, public employment cannot be reduced significantly, it is clear that when revenues drop due to lower copper income, the only item that can be effectively curtailed is public investments. In addition, deficit financing may become unavoidable....

While it is relatively easy to spell out the criticism by the "structuralist" school of orthodox stabilization policy, it is rather difficult to detail its positive policy proposals. The policy objectives are rather clear, but what is the concrete economic policy recommended by the "structuralist" school? It is not easy to find a satisfactory answer in its writings or pronouncements.[3]

Attacking the "structural" factors is a multi-faced problem and, in addition, it may take time for results to appear. The

"structuralists" do not wish to discard monetary policy altogether, but they believe that it must be subordinated to the objective of correcting the basic maladjustments. The picture given is that monetary policy should be used not only to hold the line until the longer-run policies can take effect but also to support the structural changes.

The result is that a rather vague picture of economic policies emerges from the "structural" line of thought. This writer is not aware of any concrete, well-defined policy proposal that "structuralists" might have put forth for the Chilean case. The lack of precision is undoubtedly due to the fact that the "structuralists" have not been in a policy-making position in that country and the formulation of a concrete program is usually relegated to a time when such a policy can be considered practically.

Nevertheless, a certain pattern of economic policies does arise from the "structuralist" position. Such a program would consist of both domestic and foreign economic policies.

In regard to the latter, the principal objective would be the lessening of the vulnerability of the economy to foreign trade. This refers both to the problem of the instability of foreign exchange income and to the fluctuations in public revenues. This vulnerability, as was pointed out before, is considered one of the basic generators of inflationary pressures.

The other measures would have to do more specifically with increasing the elasticity of supply, that is, making the supply respond faster to changes in the level and composition of demand—making resources more mobile.

A third body of policies would be directed toward protecting and, if possible, increasing the real income of the masses. The motivation for the redistributing measures, according to the "structuralists," would be based not only on social and

---

3. The difficulty is that there is no coherent "structuralist" theory. It is obvious that the primary concern of the "structuralists" is economic development, not inflation. But for the process of economic development it has not yet been possible to specify a body of internally consistent mechanisms.

political grounds, which certainly loom very importantly, but also on economic reasons: such measures are seen to stimulate an orientation of resources toward high-priority economic activities.

Probably the most important part of the program of the "structuralists" is, as has been indicated, the elimination of the obstacles toward greater flexibility in production. This aspect is directed principally toward agriculture.

Government investment in transportation, marketing facilities, irrigation and the provision of development credit and technical know-how are advocated as means to overcome the relative stagnation in agriculture. Price controls are also considered one of the factors contributing to the agricultural bottleneck, but the elimination of price controls in agriculture and a consequent improvement in the relative prices of agriculture depend upon a betterment in the distribution of income so that the purchasing power of the masses can be increased.

The present land tenure arrangements are seen as among the greatest obstacles to the growth in agricultural output. Agrarian reform, therefore, is an integral element in "structuralist" economic policy. It should not be ignored that land reform is also seen as a part of the policy designed to redistribute income and raise the purchasing power of the lower income groups.

The tax system too should be revised with the design to increase agricultural production. Such an objective would also be in line with the aim of making the tax system more progressive. In this respect the idea would be to diminish the proportion of indirect taxes in favor of increasing direct taxation. Nevertheless, in view of the administrative difficulties of increasing income in less developed areas, this would mean that property taxes should be increased. Obviously the emphasis would be on property taxes in agriculture in order

to force an expansion of production in the *latifundios*.

What the "structuralists" have in mind in regard to the group of measures designed to lessen the vulnerability of the economic system to foreign trade undoubtedly includes a foreign exchange rate structure designed to encourage other than traditional exports. This does not mean that a cumbersome multiple exchange rate system would be favored but it would signify a two- or three-rate system in economies where the productivity of the traditional export industries is vastly superior to their nearest competitors.

The giving of incentives alone, however, is not considered sufficient; the state must attack more vigorously the problem of establishing an adequate infrastructure to make the emerging of other industries possible. And if the building of roads and other transportation means and the providing of energy, etc., is not enough, then the government should intervene to build the necessary factories or undertake the needed agricultural cultivation. This kind of industrialization and agricultural development would work both ways, to increase and diversify exports and to reduce import requirements.

In regard to reducing the instability of fiscal revenues due to foreign trade fluctuations, several measures have been put forward. One would be that the government should establish a stabilization or contingency fund when foreign trade income is high. In the case of Chile for instance, if copper prices are above those foreseen in the government budget, the excess tax revenue would go into this special fund. In bad years the fund could be drawn upon in order to meet the necessary government expenses not covered by the lower tax revenues.

Because of lack of confidence in the fortitude of the public administration which is necessary for such a scheme to be successful, a stronger measure is sometimes proposed. The burden of stabilization would be shifted to the copper companies. A minimum tax on copper exports would be levied which would be based upon the average production and prices over, say, a given five-year period. When copper exports fell below this average, the companies would have to pay the minimum tax, but they could deduct the excess taxes paid in that year from the tax liability in years when their export value was above the average. The revenue received over the minimum would be used by the government for export diversification, economic development in general, or be destined for a stability and contingency reserve. Such schemes would be combined with measures to reduce the proportion of fiscal revenues deriving from foreign trade.

The Chilean "structuralists" with few exceptions ignore the question of foreign aid. This is probably a reaction to what they consider an excessive preoccupation of the last Chilean governments with outside financial help as a means to resolve all economic problems. Other "structuralists," however, recognize the need for foreign aid. . . .

Monetary policies and also fiscal policies are complementary in this program. They should be geared to create the conditions to obtain the desired changes in the structure of production, government finance and volume and direction of investment. One of the basic assumptions in this respect is that qualitative credit controls are possible and must be introduced.

Nevertheless, in this view the expansion of money must be kept passive, that is to say, in step with any increase in the cost of output. If money is completely passive, permanent inflation will result unless costs are being restrained. Credit controls in the private sector of the economy would have to be tightened whenever the government

sector was forced to increase its borrowing for necessary purposes.

Here it is interesting to point out that the "structuralists" do not necessarily favor massive cost-of-living wage and salary adjustments and in their pronouncements have frequently insisted on the desirability of restricting wage and salary increases, with the proviso, of course, that this would be politically feasible only if positive economic development measures were taken at the same time.

In general, the "structuralist" position is that the investment rate can and must be increased. Orthodox anti-inflation policy dictates that planned investments should be reduced to equal planned savings. Development policy, however, should have the opposite objective, that is, increasing the rate of savings. In the thinking of the "structuralists" this is possible because the unequal distribution of income means a great concentration of disposable income in the hands of the few, whose savings could be increased substantially. If ordinary incentives fail to raise the propensity of the rich to save (or invest), then the "structuralists" would certainly want the government to tax the upper income groups in order to finance an increase in public investment.

2.5 STABILIZATION EFFORTS IN CHILE *

Chile has long suffered from inflation. In fact, the country is frequently cited as the outstanding example of chronic inflation. Statistics going back to 1875—such as they are—show that in not more than perhaps 15 out of the last 80-odd years has the Chilean peso failed to depreciate substantially—in terms of its rates of exchange with the world's major currencies, in terms of its internal purchasing power, or in

* From Francis H. Schott, "Inflation and Stabilization Efforts in Chile, 1953-1958," *Inter-American Economic Affairs*, Winter 1959, pp. 4-14. Reprinted by permission.

terms of both. Yet, although inflation became intensified over the decades, that acceleration remained gradual until 1953. A cost of living index, first computed in 1928 and used until the end of 1957, showed annual increases averaging about 6 percent in 1931-35; 8 percent in 1936-40; 16 percent in 1941-45; 20 percent in 1946-50; and 22 percent in 1951-52, the last years of "normal" inflation. In 1953, the pace of inflation suddenly quickened. In that year the cost of living rose by 56 percent; in 1954 it climbed by 71 percent, and in 1955 it almost doubled in a single year, rising by 85 percent.

A number of immediate factors as well as more basic structural causes accounted for this change for the worse. There can be little doubt that the inflationary crisis of 1953-55 was generated by a sudden and substantial deterioration of the Government's financial position in 1952-53, which in turn was the combined consequence of legislation occasioning large new expenditures and of the revenue-reducing effects of a decline in copper prices and exports.

An election-minded Executive and Congress joined forces prior to the Presidential campaign of 1952 to enact several laws enormously raising salaries and pensions of Government workers and guaranteeing future annual adjustments of the remunerations by the full amount of, or even by more than, the preceding year's cost of living increase. This guarantee was extended later to all white-collar workers in private employment. While this legislation differed only in degree and not in kind from earlier laws dealing with the same matters, the difference in degree was substantial.

The proportion of the additional Government expenditures financed from noninflationary sources, moreover, was less than in earlier years. In particular the revenue estimates were artificially inflated by assuming a higher copper price—and consequently higher copper-tax income—than could reasonably be expected, and this un-realistic estimate served as the justification for a failure to vote new and higher taxes. (Copper taxes normally account for 15-25 percent of total Government revenues.)

The consequences of the financial legislation of 1952 did not become fully apparent until 1953. In that year, weakening copper prices and Chile's temporary unwillingness to export at these prices combined to reduce copper-tax revenues substantially. Moreover, the Government's budgetary problem was seriously aggravated by the occurrence and subsequent widening of a grievous split between the Executive and the Congress. . . .

Under the combined impact of heavy Government expenditure commitments, a weak copper market, and a lack of cooperation between the Executive and Congress in dealing with these problems, massive and increasing deficit financing of Government expenditures through the banking system occurred in the years 1953 to 1955. The fiscal deficit in turn generated an accelerating spiral of price rises, credit expansion, exchange rate depreciation, and wage increases, in which all of these factors finally came to make mutually-intensifying contributions to a still further acceleration of the inflation.

The initial inflationary impulse of a larger Government deficit was magnified in good part because the Government's budget itself was not "inflation-proof"—i.e., the rise in Government revenues to be expected in the course of inflation lagged behind the increase in expenditures caused by inflation. Thus, major groups of income-tax contributors were permitted to pay taxes accruing in one year in the course of the following year, which meant that a substantial part of the real value of these taxes was lost to the Government. In the cases of many other taxes—especially real estate taxes and custom duties—the tax base was not adjusted as rapidly as prices rose. On the expenditure side, the Government was attempting to hold down the rise of the cost of living by subsidies for basic import commodities and failed to raise these controlled prices promptly as inflation progressed. This failure made the subsidized commodities relatively less expensive than competing domestic and other imported goods, and stimulated their consumption at the same time that the cost of the subsidy per unit of the commodities was increasing. An initial start toward larger government deficits, therefore, almost inexorably resulted in still larger deficits as time went by.

Certain other links in the inflationary chain were of a more familiar type. Given the initial start toward accelerated inflation and the legal linking of the cost of living and wages, wholesale salary and wage adjustments became a massive cost-raising factor. They then became the occasion for progressively more frequent and larger price increases on the part of producers, who in turn were attempting more and more to anticipate future cost increases instead of only compensating actual ones. Successive rounds of depreciation of the various effective rates of the country's complex multiple exchange rate system—forced by the exigencies of the deteriorating balance of payments position—led to abrupt and partially anticipatory price increases for imported goods. The monetary authorities, finally, had virtually no choice but to permit a rising rate of expansion of bank credit and the money supply, both to finance growing Government deficits and to meet the increasing demand for money to finance transactions at higher cost levels.

More basic factors in Chile's socio-economic structure contributed to the long-term nature and the intensity of the inflation. The most important of these was what Chileans themselves often call the "struggle" or even "civil war" between the country's major economic interest groups. In essence, each of these groups utilized the particular instruments of economic policy that it could best manipulate in an attempt to secure for itself a larger share of the real national income. Salary earners... secured legislation guaranteeing annual salary increases in line with or in excess of the increase of the cost of living, sought to influence the method of computing the increases in the cost of living index, and demanded special bonuses over and above the compensatory increases. Wage earners made use of strikes, legislation aiming at larger social benefits, and Government subsidies for consumption staples. Businessmen found protection in their access to bank credit on easy terms and their ability to build monopolistic positions behind the wall of import restrictions. Farmers obtained guarantees of large and regular price increases for basic crops in line with increasing costs, as well as special credit facilities and preferential income tax treatment. Exporters and importers utilized preferential exchange rates and quotas. And far from being able to adjudicate these conflicting aims or to impose its will, the Government's main role had gradually become that of a participant in the struggle. Clearly, the financing of growing budget deficits through massive central bank credits could be viewed as an attempt by the fiscal authorities to secure and spend a larger share of the real national income than Chile's taxpayers could actually be forced to provide for Government purposes. The country's resistance expressed itself not only in the Government's inability to obtain adequate new tax legislation but also in the prevalence of large-scale tax evasion.

This chronic struggle became more bitter in 1953-55, primarily because the acceleration of the inflation itself increased the danger of substantial inroads on the real income of each special interest group. Consequently, certain groups refined and intensified the use of their economic weapons, which naturally called forth strong reactions on the part of groups that were temporarily left behind.

A second major structural factor contributing to the persistence and eventual acceleration of the inflation was the extremely slow long-term growth of the Chilean economy—a lag that made individual Chileans doubly aware of the importance of the "relative share" in the national income their particular interest group was able to secure.

Part of the explanation for the virtual stagnation of the Chilean economy over the last decades must be sought in the shattering blow dealt Chile by the collapse of its export markets for copper and nitrate in the 1930's—consequences of the Great Depression and the development of synthetic fertilizers substituting for Chile's nitrate. It is noteworthy, for example, that Chile's international terms of trade have never again been as favorable as they were in 1925-29. More important yet, however, inflation itself had gradually come to be the single most important factor impeding the growth of the economy. Thus, in a society that had traditionally placed great emphasis on high consumption levels rather than on saving and investing, inflation contributed to a further decline in saving and to a misdirection of investment into "inflation-proof" real estate and foreign exchange balances. The Government, moreover, was increasingly unable to maintain and expand its investment in the most important types of "social overhead" projects, such as railroads, ports, highways, and irrigation, since an ever-rising share of budgetary expenditures had to be diverted to the payment of salaries and pensions of a growing staff of Government workers. The expansion of Government employment, in turn, was occasioned by attempts to provide the social services of a modern welfare state, by the desire to broaden the industrial base through Government participation in new industries, and by the shortfalls of Government investment in basic public facilities, which made their maintenance a problem requiring increased manpower. The slow growth of employment opportunities in the private economy, moreover, reflected itself in heavy pressures to augment the Government payroll.

Chile's dependence on a few major exports for its exchange earnings and a substantial part of its budgetary revenue also was aggravated by and in turn partly caused the economy's slow growth. Ever since 1931 the country had employed exchange restrictions, which were characterized by a combination of multiple exchange rates and quantitative restrictions on imports and exports. The system as a whole had been manipulated to achieve social and political as well as economic objectives—including the subsidizing of food products and raw materials deemed essential, the curtailing of agricultural exports that were important items of domestic consumption, and the limiting or shutting out of imports that might have competed with the products of new and established industries. During the entire 25-year period ended in 1955, but especially during the years of accelerated inflation in 1953-55, the exchange system was subject to substantial lags in exchange rate adjustments behind the domestic inflationary spiral. This situation created an almost permanent cost squeeze on actual and potential exporters, thus discouraging foreign and domestic investments in export industries in general, and particularly in mining and agriculture (the sectors most hampered by the exchange system). The import licensing system, furthermore, was subject to pressures originating from excess demand for exchange so severe that the most arbitrary administrative devices had to be used to adjust imports to exchange availabilities. Thus Chile was losing the measuring rod of international prices for

the allocation of its own economic resources, and the growth of the country's
international trade and of its national
income was thereby retarded.

Perhaps the most basic factor contributing to the lag in economic progress, however, was the virtual abandonment of a
rational method for distributing Chile's
national income. Although, as already
noted, each major economic interest group
had developed its own defense mechanism
against inflation, there were actually wide
differences in the bargaining strength and
the effectiveness of the legal weapons available to each group. The relative gains and
losses of the various groups varied over
time, of course, and it is very difficult to
be categorical about the long-term redis-
tributive effect of the inflation.... In fact,
there is perhaps only one statement with
regard to the redistribution of real income
through the inflation that can be made
with complete assurance—the redistribution was utterly arbitrary, rewarding or
punishing large or small groups of people
according to the capricious actions of shifting Congressional coalitions, the ability to
obtain additional margins of bank credit
through regulations especially devised for
the group's benefit, the ability to obtain
export and import licenses, and other similar criteria.... Evidently, such a method
of income allocation was bound to be detrimental to genuine productive effort and
thus to the country's economic development. It proved in fact a profoundly
demoralizing influence on society as a
whole.

...

Toward the end of 1955, the Chilean
Government decided to institute a broad
remedial program. In developing and
implementing this stabilization program,
the government employed the services of
a group of United States economic and
financial advisers [Klein-Saks mission],
who aided in outlining the over-all requirements of stabilization, analyzed alternative
techniques, and recommended a wide
range of specific measures.

Since the outstanding characteristic of
Chile's inflation was the closely-connected
and mutually-intensifying contribution of
various underlying factors, the only program judged to have a chance of success
was a broad attack on many fronts, in
which all of the country's economic fac-
tions, through a retreat from their previous
extreme positions, would contribute to the
success of the stabilization effort. Furthermore, it appeared indispensable to apply
to all policy recommendations not only the
test of their anti-inflationary potential, but
also to take into account their likely effects
in aiding or hindering the gradual elimination of the structural distortions that had
resulted from long-term inflation. Without
applying this additional criterion to the
stabilization policies, no progress would
have been possible in putting Chile back
on the road of balanced economic development.

Five major areas of Government policy
appeared to be most in need of rapid and
far-reaching changes—the Government's
finances and the public administration,
credit policy, wage regulations, price controls and consumption subsidies, and the
foreign exchange system. Thus, it was evident from the beginning of the program
that the persistence of large Government
deficits had long been an important contributing factor in the inflation, and during
the years of the most rapid price increases
probably the principal one. Reducing the
Government deficit in turn implied the
necessity for drastic revisions in the control
of expenditures and the scaling-down of at
least some Government services, a far more
rigorous enforcement of existing taxes, and
the levying of new taxes with large yields.
The magnitude of the problem precluded
achievement of the objective by any single

one of these possible techniques. It also seemed indispensable to make an early beginning on a sustained program designed to rationalize the Government administration, with the aim of getting more Government service for a given level of expenditure and thereby put the Government on a basis that the country's taxpayers would be willing to support permanently.

As regards credit policy, it appeared essential to end the practices of using bank credit for import and inventory speculation and as a means of appropriating larger shares of the national income. There was an immediate need for strengthening the existing methods of limiting bank credit and money supply expansion, in order to make these controls tight enough to force a progressive reduction in the rate of price increases. With respect to wage policy, it was clear that massive Government-decreed wage and salary increases had become a major factor contributing to the increase of Government deficits and the over-all rate of inflation, but had nevertheless become more and more ineffectual in maintaining the real income received by wage and salary earners since each successive round of such increases appeared to call forth still more rapid price inflation. Thus, reductions in the rate of wage and salary increases had to be instituted along with other measures to curb budgetary deficits and credit expansion.

These general measures designed to reduce the rate of price increases had to be supplemented with more specific measures aimed at restoring normal consumption patterns and competitive and realistic pricing on the part of business. A gradual removal of the bulk of the existing subsidies was thus required, as well as an attack on the most damaging of the prevailing monopolistic practices in production and distribution. In this regard, a thorough reform of Chile's exchange sys-

tem to make the country's internal market subject to a greater degree of indirect price control through import competition was essential. It followed that the much-abused quantitative limitations on imports and on many exports also had to be removed, and that a realistic and flexible exchange rate system had to be instituted.

At the very beginning of the program, one basic decision was necessary—the choice between an attempt at ending the inflation suddenly through measures of whatever severity might be required, or an attempt to bring the inflation gradually under control through a series of somewhat less drastic measures aimed at the specific major areas of policy action outlined above. The adoption of the latter approach was and will continue to be the subject of much controversy in Chile and abroad. It should be realized, however, that under the concrete circumstances existing toward the end of 1955 a "crash program" —no matter how desirable—was virtually out of the question....

Yet, it must be acknowledged that the gradual approach actually chosen proved eventually to be one of the factors working against a greater degree of success of Chile's stabilization program, in good part because public enthusiasm and faith in the eventual success of the stabilization effort has been difficult to sustain....

2.6 LESSONS FROM LATIN AMERICAN EXPERIENCE *

What in brief occurred in Latin America was that the great depression, and subsequent vicissitudes in commodity markets, population trends, and political developments, set the countries of Latin America a task of adjustment, involving further industrialization and the creation of inte-

* From Dudley Seers, "A Theory of Inflation and Growth in Under-developed Countries Based on the Experience of Latin America," *Oxford Economic Papers,* June 1963, pp. 190-92. Reprinted by permission.

grated, diversified economies. For this task they were in every way unprepared—economically, politically, administratively, and socially. The inflations that developed in some countries are one symptom of the failure to carry out the needed adjustments; other symptoms are stagnation, chronic reliance on foreign aid, and increasingly frequent political upheavals.

We can now see why Latin America has suffered more in these ways than other regions. One reason is that the increase in its commodity exports has been slower, at least since 1950, than for other primary producing areas. This is partly because the region's exports consist largely of foodstuffs, for which the income-elasticity of demand is not high (coffee, sugar, bananas); but also partly because its exports are directed towards North America, and economic growth there has been slower than in western Europe; and partly because discrimination against Latin American products has been increasing with the start of the European Common Market and the increased protection of United States mineral producers (petroleum and non-ferrous metals). Secondly, its rate of population growth has risen to over 2½ per cent a year, which is the highest rate of any region in the world. Thirdly, economic aspirations are probably rising more quickly here: the "demonstration effect" is stimulated by the widespread exhibition of films, television programmes, radio programmes, etc., originating in the United States (as well as by reports of travellers), and recently the Cuban revolution has further accelerated the rise of expectations. In addition, several Latin American countries have now reached difficult stages of industrialization, particularly the creation of heavy industries, without as yet getting much benefit in the form of saving imports of capital goods or exporting manufacturers. Others are too small to be able to carry out much import substitution. Some might

add that Latin American administrations are particularly incompetent to face these problems because of their archaic social structures, though this is a matter of speculation (there is strong competition for the title of the least competent administration in the world!).

The most important lessons to be drawn from the experience of Latin America seem to me therefore as follows:

(1) *Methodology*. It is a mistake to treat underdeveloped economies as if they were developed when one is analyzing economic trends. It is particularly mistaken to apply "global" methods of analysis, whether monetary or income, devised for developed countries, or to omit social factors.

It is also not very helpful to attempt to attribute inflation in Latin America either to "cost" or to "demand" pressures; inflation can only be understood as a whole process which incorporates both aspects.

One has to distinguish analytically between countries which pursue orthodox monetary policies for long periods, and those with managed currencies. They operate in quite different ways.

(2) *Substance*. It is meaningless to set up a hypothesis that inflation helps or hinders growth. Growth and inflation are interrelated but not in any simple way. In Latin America there are examples of growth and inflation (Brazil), stagnation and inflation (Argentina), growth and stability (pre-1958 Venezuela), stagnation and stability (pre-1959 Cuba).

Inflation can continue for decades without ever developing into a galloping inflation like the classic twentieth-century inflations of Germany, Hungary, and China. Latin American experience implies that necessary conditions for galloping inflation are heavy physical damage and/or strong unions. (Latin American trade unions are relatively weak, by comparison with European unions, in resisting a decline in real wages.) While a long experience with inflation breeds distrust in the currency, it also breeds confidence that the inflation will not explode. Chile has had inflation for about a century, without it ever causing a complete financial collapse.

There is an inherent and ever-present risk of inflation in developing economies which export primary products, because of the active or potential need for structural change. So long as exports are booming it is possible to grow rapidly without inflation and without industrialization. But every commodity market weakens one day (even for petroleum), and if growth has to continue then, if only because of population increase, structural change has to occur. It is difficult to achieve this without inflation in an underdeveloped country. A suggestive parallel is with the structural changes needed in developed countries which have to convert themselves from a peace to a war economy, or vice versa (though one must also allow for the lack of administrative experience in an underdeveloped economy, the immobility of factors, etc.).

(3) *Policy*. Policy measures devised for developed economies are not necessarily, or usually, transferable to economies which are fundamentally different.

The essence of a fundamental stabilization policy is a long-term development programme to achieve the structural changes which are needed. Any other sort of stabilization policy is a palliative.

It is dangerous to insist, as the International Monetary Fund does, on indiscriminate policies of financial restraint. The result is a serious check to growth, and there is no reason to expect the resultant level and pattern of investment to be compatible with development needs. In addition, monopolistic tendencies are aggravated and the distribution of income is made more unequal (restricting the possibilities of further import substitution).

The proponents of *any* major economic policy measure in an underdeveloped economy are under an obligation to show how this measure will stimulate growth.

Even policies of restraint in the developed countries aggravate inflationary tensions overseas because they act as a brake on purchases of primary products.

Foreign borrowing will give a developing economy the room to manœuvre it requires to carry out structural change without great tensions. (Whether this is worthwhile, in view of the political strings which are always attached to loans, in one way or another, is outside the scope of this paper.)

3. BIBLIOGRAPHICAL NOTE

1. General aspects of the problem of inflation in less developed countries are examined in the following: J. H. Adler, "Deficit Spending and Supply Elasticities," *Indian Journal of Economics,* Vol. XXXVI; Adler, "Note on 'Spurt' Inflation and Economic Development," *Social and Economic Studies,* March 1961; S. H. Axilrod, "Inflation and the Development of Underdeveloped Areas," *Review of Economics and Statistics,* August 1954; W. Baer and I. Kerstenetzky (ed's.), *Inflation* *and Economic Growth* (Papers presented at a Conference on Inflation and Economic Growth, held in Rio de Janeiro, January 1963), New Haven, 1964; E. M. Bernstein and I. G. Patel, "Inflation in Relation to Economic Development," *IMF Staff Papers,* November 1952; M. Bronfenbrenner, "The High Cost of Economic Development," *Land Economics,* August 1953; Henry J. Bruton, *Inflation in a Growing Economy,* Bombay, 1961; Bent Hansen, *Inflation Problems in Small Countries,*

National Bank of Egypt, Cairo, 1960; Nicholas Kaldor, "Economic Growth and the Problem of Inflation," *Economica*, August 1959; W. Arthur Lewis, *Theory of Economic Growth*, Homewood, 1955, Chap. V; F. Pazos, "Economic Development and Financial Stability," *IMF Staff Papers*, October 1953; Richard C. Porter, "The Dangers of Monetary Policy in Agrarian Economies," *Pakistan Development Review*, Winter 1961; V.K.R.V. Rao, "Deficit Financing, Capital Formation and Price Behavior in an Underdeveloped Economy," *Indian Economic Review*, February 1953; A. S. Shaalan, "The Impact of Inflation on the Composition of Private Domestic Investment," *IMF Staff Papers*, July 1962; U Tun Wai, "The Relation Between Inflation and Economic Development," *IMF Staff Papers*, October 1959; United Nations, ECAFE, *Mobilization of Domestic Capital*, Bangkok 1952, and "Deficit Financing for Economic Development with Special Reference to ECAFE Countries," *Economic Bulletin for Asia and the Far East*, November 1954.

2. The over-all problems of credit supply and inflation can be supplemented by the following readings on the development of banking and financial institutions: J. Ahrensdorf, "Central Bank Policies and Inflation," *IMF Staff Papers*, October 1959; A. Ali, "Banking in the Middle East," *IMF Staff Papers*, November 1957; A. I. Bloomfield, "Central Banking in Underdeveloped Countries," *Journal of Finance*, May 1957; S. Boskey, *Problems and Practices of Development Banks*, Baltimore, 1959; A. K. Cairncross, "Banking in Developing Countries," in *The Future Organisation of Banking*, Institute of Bankers in Scotland, Edinburgh, 1958; L. V. Chandler, *Central Banking and Economic Development*, Bombay, 1962; W. Diamond, *Development Banks*, Baltimore, 1957; E. K. Hawkins, "The Growth of a Money Economy in Nigeria and Ghana," *Oxford Economic Papers*, October 1958; S. Kanesthan, "New Central Banks in the Sterling Area," *Indian Economic Journal*, October 1959; H. M. Knight, "A Monetary Budget," *IMF Staff Papers*, October 1959; E. Laso, "Financial Policies and Credit Control Techniques in Central America," *IMF Staff Papers*, November 1958; J. Marquez, "Financial Institutions and Economic Development," in *Economic Development for Latin America*, edited by H. S. Ellis, New York, 1961; Edward Nevin, *Capital Funds in Underdeveloped Countries*, London, 1961; I. G. Patel, "Selective Credit Controls in Underdeveloped Countries," *IMF Staff Papers*, September 1954; G. Rosen, "Capital Markets and Industrialization of Underdeveloped Countries," *Indian Economic Journal*, October 1958; R. S. Sayers, "Central Banking in Under-Developed Countries," in *Central Banking After Bagehot*, Oxford, 1957; S. N. Sen, *Central Banking in Under-Developed Money Markets*, 3rd ed., Calcutta, 1961.

3. An excellent guide to the literature on the "structuralist school" is contained in Dudley Seers, "A Theory of Inflation and Growth in Under-developed Countries Based on the Experience of Latin America," *Oxford Economic Papers*, June 1963, pp. 192-5. For additional readings on inflation in Latin America, the following may be consulted: Werner Baer, "Inflation and Economic Growth: An Interpretation of the Brazilian Case," *Economic Development and Cultural Change*, October 1962; David Felix, "Structural Imbalances, Social Conflict, and Inflation," *Economic Development and Cultural Change*, January 1960; Felix, "An Alternative View of the 'Monetarist'-'Structuralist' Controversy," in *Latin American Issues*, edited by A. O. Hirschman, New York, 1961; D. L. Grove, "The Role of the Banking System

in the Chilean Inflation," *IMF Staff Papers,* September 1951; Eugenio Gudin, "Inflation in Latin America," in *Inflation,* edited by D. C. Hague, London, 1962, Chap. 23; J. K. Horsefield, "Inflation in Latin America," *IMF Staff Papers,* September 1950; G. Maynard, "Inflation and Growth: Some Lessons To Be Drawn from Latin-American Experience," *Oxford Economic Papers,* June 1961.

ALLOCATION OF INVESTMENT RESOURCES

HAVING CONSIDERED THE OVER-ALL CONTRIBUTION of capital to development, and the various ways of financing a higher rate of investment,
we now turn to the remaining problem of how to determine the composition
of investment. When investment resources are as scarce as they are in a poor
country, the rational allocation of capital is of the greatest importance. If
public investment absorbs a large proportion of the total resources available, or the state attempts to influence the direction of private investment,
it becomes necessary to establish "investment criteria" for selecting the "best"
investment projects from among the many possible projects. This problem
is examined in section 1.

To determine the best utilization of investment resources, we must analyze
the allocation of capital among different sectors and the choice of optimum
techniques among the alternative techniques of production. As indicated in
section 1, several investment criteria have been propounded, but primary
attention should be given to the following: minimum capital intensity (minimum capital-output ratio), maximum social marginal productivity of capital,
maximum surplus over wages available for investment ("marginal reinvestment quotient"), and maximum employment absorption (1.1, 1.2, 1.3).

These criteria raise problems regarding not only their own precise formulation, but also possible conflicts among the criteria. For example, on the
basis of the existing relative scarcities of factors, it may appear sensible to
minimize the capital-output ratio and adopt less capital-intensive techniques
of production; however, to maximize the available investible surplus and
attain the maximum growth rate, the optimal technique may have to be
highly capital-intensive. Although the materials in this chapter set forth
the different investment criteria that have been formulated, we should not
examine them with the expectation of resolving their differences and determining from them a single definitive criterion. For the relevance of each
criterion depends on judgments about social objectives, designation of the
time period involved, and specification of various constraints. Since a number
of possible variables may be maximized (real national income, real per capita

income, per capita consumption, employment, etc.), and the maximization may occur over different periods of time, and various constraints may be introduced (income distribution, balance of payments, etc.), it should be apparent that different criteria are warranted for different sets of conditions. The disagreement over alternative investment criteria thus stems from the variety of conditions assumed. Nonetheless, even after the appropriate criterion is selected, there are still problems of practical application, as illustrated in selection 1.4.

Section 2 summarizes the present status of the much-discussed "balanced growth" versus "unbalanced growth" approaches to investment. By emphasizing that investment decisions are mutually reinforcing and that over-all supply "creates its own demand" (2.1), the balanced growth doctrine has considerable appeal as a means of initiating development. Critics of the doctrine argue, however, that a poor country does not have the capacity to attain balanced investment over a wide range of industries, and that, moreover, the method of balanced growth can not achieve as high a rate of development as can unbalanced growth. Instead of striving for balanced investment, proponents of unbalanced growth advocate the creation of strategic imbalances that will set up stimuli and pressures which are needed to induce investment decisions (2.2, 2.3).

From the discussion in section 2, we may also now recognize that the phrases "balanced growth" and "unbalanced growth" initially caught on too readily, and that each approach has been overdrawn. After much reconsideration, each approach has become so highly qualified that the controversy is essentially barren. Instead of seeking to generalize either approach, we should more appropriately look to the conditions under which each can claim some validity. It may be concluded that while a newly developing country should aim at balance as an investment criterion, this objective will be attained only by initially following in most cases a policy of unbalanced investment (2.3, 2.4). In operational terms, the crucial question is then how to determine what is the proper sequence of investment decisions in order to create the right amount of imbalance in the right activities.

In the final section we consider the desirability of allocating investment resources to the "social infrastructure"—to raising the level of education, research, and training. As the Note on investment in human capital (3.1) emphasizes, an improvement in the quality of human resources has a special significance, and it is essential to examine the basis for allocating resources between investment in both material capital and human capital. We conclude this chapter therefore by discussing a number of questions related to the role of education as a critical factor in development.

1. INVESTMENT CRITERIA

1.1 SURVEY OF CRITERIA FOR ALLOCATING INVESTMENT RESOURCES [*]

Economists have put forward a number of criteria and techniques for allocating investment resources to different sectors or projects in planning the development of underdeveloped economies. Although many of these criteria and techniques differ in their approach to the problem, some are closely connected. The differences in approach usually reflect different evaluations as regards the objectives of economic development, and this suggests a basis for determining the order in which the criteria may conveniently be studied.

The most general objective of economic development is to maximize the national income or the rate of economic growth. Accordingly, the criteria which are most appropriate for allocating the available investment resources in the pursuit of this objective will be considered together in this note, as a first group. Included are the capital-output ratio or rate of capital turnover, ... social product analysis, and the rate of savings and reinvestment.

...

The incremental capital-output ratio (or capital coefficient) seeks to represent the amount of additional investment required to produce an additional unit of output. The ratio is usually based on an analysis of past experience where possible, but may allow for anticipated changes in the future period. The over-all capital-output ratio can be used as a tool for estimating capital requirements for the whole economy, while capital-output ratios for individual sectors, industries or processes may be used to estimate capital requirements sector by sector or project by project.

This concept assumes a stable relationship between capital and output, which is more likely to be the case in the over-all economy. However, the sectoral capital-output ratios may vary widely with the stage of economic development, the pattern of investment, the relative importance of non-capital inputs, and the amount of investment in complementary sectors.

The capital-output ratio when applied as a priority criterion is synonymous with the capital-turnover criterion suggested by J. J. Polak.[1] It is maintained that, to maximize income, choice should be made of investment projects with a low capital-output ratio, i.e. a high rate of capital turnover. However, this criterion has some serious limitations. Firstly, the time element plays a key role, since quick maturing projects with a lower capital-output ratio in the short run do not necessarily have a lower ratio in the long run. Secondly, the supplementary benefits of an investment project to other economic activities are neglected. In view of project complementary, in fact, a project with a higher capital-output ratio should not necessarily be accorded a lower priority.[2] Thirdly, when applying this concept to agriculture in under-developed countries, it should be noted that the magnitude of fixed capital investment may be quite small in proportion to total inputs, e.g. of work-

[*] From United Nations, ECAFE, "Criteria for Allocating Investment Resources among Various Fields of Development in Underdeveloped Countries," *Economic Bulletin for Asia and the Far East*, June 1961, pp. 30-33.

1. Polak, J. J., "Balance of Payments Problems of Countries Reconstructing with the Help of Foreign Loans," *Quarterly Journal of Economics*, February 1943, pp. 208-40. Reprinted in American Economic Association, *Readings in the Theory of International Trade*, pp. 459-93.

2. United Nations, Economic Commission for Asia and the Far East, "Problems and Techniques of Economic Development Planning and Programming with Special Reference to ECAFE Countries," *Economic Bulletin for Asia and the Far East*, November 1955, pp. 25-62.

ing capital such as fertilizer, so that the fixed capital-output ratio may vary rather widely due to factors other than capital investment.[3]

...

Two main proposals for applying [the social product] criterion have been advanced. One is the *national product (or consumption)* test suggested by J. Tinbergen.[4] This is based on an assessment of the project's direct, indirect and secondary consequences, all values of which are reckoned at "accounting prices" as referred to later. "Indirect consequences are those to be expected in the absence of further changes in total national income," while "secondary consequences consist of the changes in production which are the consequence of the change in national income, both in the short and the longer run, connected with the new production."

The other proposal is the *social marginal productivity* (SMP) criterion which was first advanced by A. E. Kahn.[5] H. B. Chenery[6] attempts to quantify the SMP principle by applying it to a number of empirical situations in several countries. In allocating investment resources, one should take into account "the total net contribution of the marginal unit to national product, and not merely that portion of the contribution (or of its costs) which may accrue to the private investor." The efficient allocation is the one which maximizes the value of national product, and the

rule for achieving this is to allocate resources in such a way that the social marginal productivity of capital is approximately equal in the different uses.

As a rule, the SMP is not correlated with the rate of capital turnover referred to earlier. The results obtained from the two criteria will diverge, especially widely in the case of projects which create greater external economies. As a practical rule of thumb, nevertheless, Kahn admits that the capital-turnover criterion is useful where capital is relatively scarce and labour extremely plentiful, except that some investments which clearly relate to a bottleneck in development may be capital-intensive. In case the social opportunity cost of labour is very close to zero, the SMP criterion will in fact approximate the capital-turnover criterion. Chenery also considers that the rate of capital turnover is "particularly useful in choosing among projects within a given sector."

The SMP criterion is expressed in terms of once-for-all effect on the national income, and does not include the specific multiplier effect of investment on future income levels. In other words, it does not take account of what happens to the final products—this determines in part the investment rate in future which in turn determines the level of future incomes. Nor does it take account of changes in the nature and quality of the factors of production such as population and labour force that may, in part, be an indirect consequence of the current investment allocation.

From the criticisms mentioned above of the SMP criterion comes the argument by W. Galenson and H. Leibenstein[7] that the appropriate goal of development should be the maximization of *per capita* output, or

3. United Nations, Economic Commission for Asia and the Far East, *Report of the FAO/ECAFE Expert Group on Selected Aspects of Agricultural Planning,* Bangkok, 1961 (mimeographed).

4. Tinbergen, J., *The Design of Development,* Baltimore, 1958.

5. Kahn, A. E., "Investment Criteria in Development Programmes," *Quarterly Journal of Economics,* February 1951, pp. 38-61.

6. Chenery, H. B., "The Application of Investment Criteria," *Quarterly Journal of Economics,* February 1953, pp. 76-96.

7. Galenson, W. and Leibenstein, H., "Investment Criteria, Productivity and Economic Development," *Quarterly Journal of Economics,* August 1955, pp. 343-70.

average income, at some future point in time, rather than the maximization of national income now. Hence, the correct criterion for investment must be to maximize the rate of savings and thus of reinvestment, and to "choose for each unit of investment that alternative that will give each worker greater productive power than any other alternative." It is assumed that profits are largely saved for reinvestment and that wages are largely spent. The best allocation of investment resources is to be achieved, it is claimed, by distributing the available capital among the various alternative uses in such a way that "the marginal *per capita* reinvestment quotient" of capital is approximately equal in the various uses. Apart from human factors such as the quality of the labour force, it is the capital-labour ratio (or capital intensity) that determines output *per capita*. As a corollary, the reinvestment criterion favours capital-intensive projects even where capital is scarce....

However O. Eckstein [8] considers that it might be desirable to employ fiscal means to attain an income distribution which will yield sufficient savings, rather than to depend on planned investment based on the reinvestment criterion. Furthermore, "endless growth for its own sake does not make too much sense," or there may be circumstances in which the current consumption may be a more immediate concern. Consequently, at a later stage of development or even in the present in some instances, the reinvestment criterion may have to be tempered by the consideration of the value of current consumption to the community.

It is often argued that, since underdeveloped economies are generally characterized by massive underemployment along with scarcity of capital, one should select those investment projects that substitute abundant labour for scarce capital, or, in other words, mobilize the maximum amount of labour per unit of investment. The maximization of employment may also be a social and political objective. The employment absorption criterion has a family relationship with the case for low capital intensity, i.e. low capital-labour ratio.

The maximum labour absorption, however, does not necessarily lead to the maximization of the addition to total output. Adherence to capital-saving and labour-intensive investments may result in perpetuation of low labour productivity. Moreover, a course of maximizing the rate of investment may do more within the not so distant future to provide work for the underemployed than the capital-saving and labour-intensive use of the existing investment potential can do in the immediate future....

A variant of the employment absorption argument is found in a doctrine advanced by R. Nurkse.[9] He draws attention to the potential savings concealed in rural underemployment and proposes to mobilize the underemployed for capital formation. This proposal implies that the output of the formerly excess labour when productively employed less minimum maintenance costs of that labour, can be used entirely for the production of capital goods. This involves essentially a plan for forced savings out of the labour of the previously disguised unemployed. Although admitting that there may be circumstances under which it would be best to put into effect Nurkse's proposal, Leibenstein suspects that "there is no evidence to lead us to believe that the

8. Eckstein, O., "Investment Criteria for Economic Development and the Theory of Intertemporal Welfare Economics," *Quarterly Journal of Economics,* February 1957, pp. 56-85.

9. Nurkse, R., *Problems of Capital Formation in Underdeveloped Countries,* Oxford, 1953, pp. 36-47.

particular technique suggested by Nurkse is the best way of obtaining the forced savings, or that the amount so obtained is the optimum amount." [10]

Since foreign exchange, a factor which is vital to the development of an under-developed economy, is usually scarce in under-developed countries, the balance of payments effect assumes importance as a criterion for the allocation of investment resources and the determination of priorities. It is often advocated that priority should be given to those projects which minimize balance of payments deficit or, in other words, increase the supply of foreign exchange or economize the use of it.

The balance of payments effect has two different aspects, namely the effects during the investment phase which are always negative, and the operating effects. J. J. Polak [11] classifies investments into three types according to whether the operating effect is positive, neutral, or negative. Type I includes exports and substitutes for imports, Type II replacements for goods at present consumed, and Type III goods sold in the home market in excess of the demand resulting from increase in real incomes. He maintains that the amount of investments in Type I sectors must be sufficiently large for the resulting positive balance of payments effects to offset the negative effects of investments of Type III and of the investment phase of all types of projects. However, this is not a very operational approach, because the output of many commodities may fall into several categories. Moreover, it does not tell what changes should be made in the programme in case the criterion is not satisfied.

In quantifying the SMP principle, H. B.

Chenery [12] incorporates the balance of payments effect. He suggests that a premium should be attached to foreign exchange earning or saving. This premium mathematically "represents the amount of increase in national income which would be equivalent to an improvement of one unit in the balance of payments under specified conditions." It generally "measures the average over-valuation of the national currency at existing rates of exchange, taking into account the expected effect on imports and exports of the whole investment programme and also the balance-of-payments position at the beginning of the period."

The difficult foreign exchange situation currently prevailing might result in over-emphasis on balance of payments effects in investment allocations. This criterion, therefore, needs to be balanced by the consideration of comparative advantages in the long run.

Whatever the criteria for resource allocation, difficulties arise in the measurement of present and future benefits from a given project and of the costs that are incurred in obtaining such benefits. Market prices, particularly those of the factors of production, form a very imperfect guide to resource allocation in under-developed economies, because there exist fundamental disequilibria which are reflected in the existence of massive underemployment at present levels of wages, the deficiency of funds at prevailing interest rates and the shortage of foreign exchange at current rates of exchange. The equilibrium level of wage rates will be considerably lower than market wages, while equilibrium interest rates will probably be much higher than market rates.

If a criterion is to be based on the concept of social product, it will be essential

10. Leibenstein, H., *Economic Backwardness and Economic Growth,* New York, 1957, p. 261.

11. Polak, J. J., "Balance of Payments Problems of Countries Reconstructing with the Help of Foreign Loans," *Quarterly Journal of Economics,* February 1943, pp. 208-40.

12. Chenery, H. B., "The Application of Investment Criteria," *Quarterly Journal of Economics,* February 1953, pp. 76-96.

to remedy this defect. To do this, the use of "accounting prices" or "shadow prices" which truly reflect intrinsic values of factors of production is suggested by J. Tinbergen [13] and by H. B. Chenery and K. S. Kretschmer.[14]

In the application of this theory, however, a certain arbitrariness may enter into the assessment of these intrinsic values. Shifts in accounting prices which may arise from the realization of investment programmes are difficult to predict. Moreover, the application of accounting prices might result in favouring, more than long-term considerations would warrant, those projects which are labour-intensive, which create or save foreign exchange and which promise a quick yield on the capital employed.

The concept of accounting prices has to be made precise before it can be applied in the actual preparation of economic plans. A recent attempt at greater precision defines accounting prices as "the values of the marginal productivity of factors when a selection of techniques has been made which produces the maximum possible volume of output, given the availability of resources, the pattern of final demand and the technological possibilities of production." [15] It would then be for the government to calculate marginal productivity of factors and manipulate the system of sudsidy and taxation in such a way that the supply prices of factors to the producers became equal to the value of their marginal productivity. However, even apart from the difficulties in calculating the marginal productivity of the factors, the problem of producers' response to changes in taxes and subsidies would also have to be studied.

13. Tinbergen, J., *The Design of Development,* Baltimore, 1958.
14. Chenery, H. B., and Kretschmer, K. S., "Resources Allocation for Economic Development," *Econometrica,* October 1956, pp. 365-99.
15. Quayyum, A., *Theory and Policy of Accounting Prices,* Amsterdam, 1959.

1.2 SOCIAL PRODUCTIVITY AND FACTOR-INTENSITY CRITERIA *

Traditional economic analysis emphasizes the importance of the "marginal" principle (which is equally applicable to all kinds of scarce resources)—the principle, namely that capital (like other resources) should be so allocated between and within different sectors of the economy that the returns from, or net productivity of, the last or marginal unit employed in each of the different uses shall be as nearly as possible equal. If capital is allocated in any other way it would be possible to enlarge the national product by shifting some capital from uses in which its marginal productivity is low to other uses in which its marginal productivity is higher. This principle will imply that, in an underdeveloped economy in which capital is scarce and labour relatively abundant, capital investment in any one direction should be discontinued at a point at which the marginal productivity of capital is higher, and that of labour lower (because the labour will have less capital to help it in its work) than would be appropriate if the country had more capital and less labour. To this extent the principle will favour spreading capital rather widely and thinly throughout the economy and using labour-intensive rather than capital-intensive methods of production.

Some economists, however, have taken the view that if underdeveloped countries spread their capital widely and thinly and content themselves with labour-intensive techniques, new investment will not make a sufficient impact in any one sector of the economy to bring about any radical transformation in the economic structure or to achieve a "take-off into self-sustained

* From International Labour Office, "Some Aspects of Investment Policy in Underdeveloped Countries," *International Labour Review,* Vol. LXXVII, No. 5, May 1958, pp. 389-90, 393-7, 400-404, 411-15.

growth." In the view of these economists, whom we may call the "capital-intensive investment" school, it will be more advantageous to concentrate a large proportion of newly available capital on the establishment of industrial nuclei or islands of advanced and relatively capital-intensive technology, even at the cost of leaving the rest of the economy starved of capital, in the hope that these industrial nuclei or "development blocks," consisting of a number of mutually sustaining projects, will constitute strategic growing points from which the impulse towards growth will spread to the rest of the economy. Individual projects within such development blocks may of course be more or less capital-intensive; this approach will, however, call for a certain degree of concentration of capital in particular regions or sectors of the economy.

...

The Marginal Productivity Approach:
The basic reasoning underlying the marginal productivity approach is simple, and can be illustrated by means of a simple diagram. It rests upon the proposition that as more capital is employed in any project or any undertaking in combination with given amounts of labour and land, the increment of product attributable to the utilization of additional capital will after a time start to fall off. (As a factory, a farm or a mine becomes better equipped with capital, the need for yet more capital, after a point, becomes less urgent). This state of affairs is illustrated in the accompanying diagram [Figure V.1], in which the amount of capital invested in the various projects (measured in any convenient units, for example blocks of £100) is measured horizontally, and the productivity of successive increments of capital is measured vertically. The aggregate product of the three projects taken together will be greatest if capital is invested in each pro-

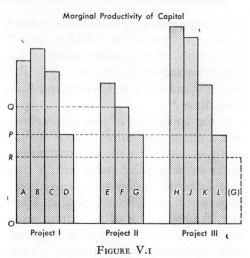

FIGURE V.1

ject up to the point at which its marginal productivity (the productivity of the last unit of capital employed) is as nearly as possible equal in each project. This situation is depicted in the diagram, the productivity of the last unit of capital invested in each project, D, G and L, being equal in each case to OP. If capital had been allocated between the projects in any other way the total product would have been less. If, for example, the marginal unit of capital invested in Project II had been invested instead in Project III, so that the marginal productivity of capital would have been OQ in Project II and OR in Project III, the community would have lost an amount of product worth OP in Project II and gained a smaller amount of product, worth OR, in Project III.

This simple proposition needs, however, a number of qualifications, which go a long way to destroy its simplicity and to cast doubt on its practical usefulness. In the first place it is necessary to say that the marginal productivity of capital should be as nearly as possible equal in all uses, and not exactly equal, because certain investments have to be made, if at all, on a certain minimum scale. A country with gold-bearing ore, for example, might not be able to mine it without a rather substantial investment. Where, instead of investing a little more or a little less in any particular direction it is necessary for technical reasons to invest much more or much less, it may be necessary either to desist from further investment in a particular direction at a point at which the marginal productivity of capital remains considerably higher than it is in other uses or to push on with investment in this particular direction to a point at which the marginal productivity is considerably lower than it is elsewhere in the economy.

Secondly, even in a situation in which there might be no advantage in a different allocation of small amounts of capital between different uses, it might be advantageous to devote large amounts of capital to particular sectors, industries or projects, if this would make possible the use of an entirely different and more productive technology. For example, while small amounts of additional capital invested in improving or increasing the number of handlooms in a country's cotton textile industry might have a low productivity, it is entirely conceivable that high returns might be obtained from investing enough capital in the industry to transform its structure from a handloom to a power-loom basis.[1]

Thirdly, there is the question of the time-period that we have in mind in evaluating marginal productivity. The productivity of resources in different uses will depend upon the relationship between costs of production and the prices of the products produced, and these in turn are matters of supply and demand. In the short run the aim may be to adjust the utilization of resources to prevailing conditions of supply and demand, but in the long run supply and demand will themselves be affected by investment decisions. An invest-

ment which enabled a new commodity or service to be placed on the market might have a low productivity so long as few people knew about or wanted the product; but the mere fact of its being placed on the market and being tried out in the first place by a few people might in time lead large numbers of others to desire it, and in the longer run the investment might be highly productive. Moveover, cost conditions also may change over a period of time, so that, as managements and workers acquire knowledge, skill and experience in a particular line of production it may become possible to produce at relatively low costs a commodity which, initially, could only be produced at high costs. This is the basis for the argument for temporary protection or other assistance for "infant" industries.

Another important set of qualifications to the marginal productivity doctrine arises from a distinction that is often drawn between private marginal productivity and social marginal productivity. The private marginal productivity of capital in any use is the rate of return on the last unit (say the last £100) of capital invested *to the entrepreneur who makes the investment.* This may be greater or less than the social marginal productivity, by which is meant the annual value of this investment to society. Many investments of incalculable value to society would not be undertaken at all, or would be undertaken on a totally inadequate scale, by private enterprise because the benefits are widely diffused and it would not be feasible to charge individual consumers a price for these benefits. In many cases the benefits are of such a nature that it is difficult or impossible to attach a monetary valuation to them—for example, the benefits resulting from public education and public health services. Other investments that are of a kind to attract private enterprise may, from a social point of view, be carried too far or not far

---

1. United Nations: *Measures for the Economic Development of Underdeveloped Countries* (New York, 1951), p. 49.

enough in the absence of state intervention because they incidentally yield disservices or services to persons other than the producers or consumers of the particular commodity concerned. . . . Conversely there will be cases where social marginal productivity exceeds private marginal productivity. This may be true, for example, of resources devoted to research, from which great practical benefits often follow of such a nature that they can neither be patented nor kept secret, and so benefit others besides the entrepreneur who employs the resources that have made them possible.

. . .

The notion that any business transaction may confer uncompensated benefits or impose uncompensated costs on third parties or on the community as a whole seems to have even wider implications for policy in underdeveloped than in advanced economies. Most writers who stress the importance of the marginal principle therefore take the view that the objective of policy should be defined in terms of an attempt to equate not the private but the social marginal productivity of capital in all uses.

To substitute the concept of social marginal productivity for that of private marginal productivity is, however, a big step to take, and opens the door to all sorts of difficulties of interpretation. If it is desired to bring the whole of a country's investment programme within the framework of marginal analysis it will be necessary to attach an arbitrary monetary valuation to the products of social investments in such things as education and public health services. Alternatively and more pragmatically it may be decided that the country's investment programme is to consist of a certain independently determined expenditure on things of this kind, plus such other projects of all kinds as may be considered to satisfy the social marginal productivity criterion. To apply this criterion it will be necessary

—wherever it is judged that the annual value to society of a particular project differs from the annual return it would yield to a private entrepreneur—to attach a "shadow" or "accounting" price to the product, reflecting the social value attributed to it. Wherever it is judged that the cost to society of a particular project differs from what it would cost a private entrepreneur to undertake it, it will be necessary to apply a shadow cost. And it will be these shadow prices and costs, and not the market prices and costs, if any, that should be used in ranking investment projects and determining which are worth undertaking and which are not.

. . .

Arguments for Capital-intensive Investments: One can distinguish several strands of thought in the arguments that have been put forward in favour of capital-intensive investments in underdeveloped countries.

. . . It may be argued that, for various political and administrative reasons, fewer resources than would be economically justified may go into capital-intensive projects. . . . Firstly, governments need support from all regions. It may be politically dangerous to foster a belief that one region within a country is being unduly favoured. Secondly, small projects need comparatively little engineering and planning talent. The preparation of large projects to a point at which they are ready for financing may need a great deal of both, and these are very scarce resources. Those who dispose of funds may not wish to commit themselves in advance to financing projects that, when thoroughly surveyed, may not appear attractive. But, equally, governments will not wish to devote scarce resources to thorough economic and engineering surveys of possible projects without some degree of assurance that if the survey is promising funds will be forthcoming. Thirdly, governments will not wish to raise expectations which they may find themselves unable to fulfill. The mere undertaking of an economic and engineering survey of an ambitious project in a particular region, however much the government may insist that this involves no commitment, is likely to raise expectations.

These are arguments for the view that, at least in the earlier stages of economic development, the scales are weighted against large-scale capital-intensive projects or the establishment of development blocks. It may be argued further that the deliberate establishment of development blocks will be the best way of achieving a "take-off into sustained growth." It is a familiar fact all over the world that a great proportion of new undertakings, large and small, tend to be established, and a great proportion of the growth that takes place in existing undertakings tends to occur, in or near large centres where an industrial nucleus already exists. Proximity to markets, dependence on other undertakings for materials or components, and availability of power, transport facilities, a more or less trained labour force accustomed to the discipline of industrial work, and various ancillary services such as repair services and banking and credit facilities, are among the reasons for this.[2] If these are the conditions in which growth occurs spontaneously, these are the conditions, it may be argued, that investment policy should seek deliberately to create in underdeveloped economies.

Another strand of thought in the case for a capital-intensive approach to investment planning in underdeveloped countries is the argument that this will make possible a more rapid rate of investment because it will not be necessary to distribute so much income to labour as under a more labour-intensive approach. If labour-intensive methods are adopted more workers will immediately be brought into employment from the pool of surplus labour that is found in so many of these countries. They will have to be paid wages, but it will be unrealistic to expect them to save. Consumption will expand by the full amount, or very nearly the full amount, paid out in additional wages, and there will be less left over for saving and investment, the importance of which, for sustained economic growth, can scarcely be exaggerated. Of course it is highly desirable to provide additional employment opportunities as soon as it is safe to do so, but to do this too soon (so the argument runs) is to risk disaster, whereas a policy of capital-intensive investments, and of reinvesting the income they generate, will make it possible within quite a few years to provide more new jobs with the new capital that is created than it would have been possible to provide with a labour-intensive investment policy.

One statement of this argument is contained in an article by W. Galenson and H. Leibenstein.[3] They do not entirely jettison the marginal approach, but their prescription for policy is that the policy-maker should try to equate not the marginal productivity of capital in all uses, but what

2. F. Perroux has reminded readers that the growth of an industry A may enhance the profits of an industry B which purchases resources produced by industry A, of an industry C whose products are complementary to (i.e. are demanded jointly with) the products of industry A, of an industry D whose product is a (presumably cheaper) substitute for productive resources used in industry A, and of an industry E whose products are consumed by the individuals whose incomes are increased by the growth of industry A. (François Perroux: "Note sur la notion de 'pôle de croissance,'" in *Economie appliquée* (Paris), Tome VIII, Nos. 1-2, Jan.-June 1955, p. 312, footnote 1.)

3. W. Galenson and H. Leibenstein: "Investment Criteria, Productivity and Economic Development," in *Quarterly Journal of Economics,* (Cambridge, Mass.), Vol. LXIX, No. 3, Aug. 1955, p. 343.

they call the "marginal per capita re-investment quotient," which seems to be defined as net productivity per worker minus consumption per worker. The article includes a table showing, on certain assumptions, the amount of employment provided over a period of time by an initial investment of 1,200 rupees in various types of cotton textile machinery. If this sum is invested in handlooms (cottage industry) it will initially provide, on these assumptions, employment for 35 people, but there will be no margin for reinvestment and after 25 years the number of jobs provided will still be 35. If on the other hand the same sum is invested in a large-scale modern mill, it will initially provide employment for five workers, but, thanks to reinvestment of a large proportion of the income generated, the additional employment will exceed 12,000 after 25 years. Among the assumptions on which this calculation rests are that every penny paid in wages is spent on consumption and that every penny not paid to labour is reinvested. Also, no allowance is made for capital depreciation. The authors do not discuss the problems of ensuring that the entire surplus over and above what is paid to labour is in fact reinvested. One may feel that they have left out of account a large part of the problem, and they would no doubt agree that their table greatly exaggerates the difference in employment creation over time that would in practice be likely to result from the different types of investment. Nevertheless even a small fraction of the difference shown in their table would be a very important matter.

This line of argument is supported by an appeal to Malthusian views. The authors argue that many underdeveloped countries do not have a choice between slow and relatively comfortable development on the one hand and rapid development achieved by means of rapid investment and re-stricted consumption on the other. They believe that the latter is the only road to development. They argue that there is a critical "minimum effort" hurdle that must be overcome early in the development process if development is to be self-sustaining, and that rapid population growth (which they believe will be stimulated by a labour-intensive pattern of investment) will very greatly reduce the chances of overcoming this hurdle because it will reduce the ratio of capital to labour, the "per capita output potential" and the "per capita re-investment quotient." . . .

Finally, the establishment of a certain number of modern capital-intensive plants may be advocated as a means of providing training and experience for management and labour in modern technologies and of helping to remedy the shortage of experienced and competent management and skilled labour in underdeveloped economies. Moreover, good managers being scarce, it may be desirable to ensure that they are employed in undertakings large enough to give full scope for their abilities. On the other hand it may be argued that the management of a large undertaking is much more difficult than that of a small undertaking, and that a country in which there are few persons capable of directing and managing large undertakings efficiently may yet contain a large number of persons capable of running small businesses well. Capital being scarce, concentration upon large-scale capital-intensive investments will reduce the amount of capital available for small businesses. But "the growth of an economy usually requires a large number of small changes, each taking advantage of local opportunities and availability of resources, and each in turn making further growth possible. Dispersal of savings and dispersal of entrepreneurship are important aspects of economic development even in countries in which the State has played an important part as provider of capital or as manager of business enterprises." An economy in which capital is available on reasonable terms for small businesses may provide opportunities for training and providing industrial experience for greater numbers of entrepreneurs, managers and skilled workers than an economy in which available capital is dispersed less widely.

. . .

Investment Criteria in Theory and Practice: This article may conclude with a few observations on the question whether either of the two approaches that have been discussed provide practically useful criteria for determining what use should actually be made of scarce capital.

The substitution of the notion of social marginal productivity for that of private marginal productivity seems necessary if the marginal principle, as a basis for investment policy, is to be defended as being conducive to economic and social welfare. If there were a general presumption that social and private productivity would more or less coincide in the majority of cases, one could use market prices, which are objective facts, for the purpose of calculating the social as well as the private marginal productivity of capital in all those cases where this general presumption held good, and it might not be unduly difficult to make reasonably satisfactory, albeit arbitrary, adjustments when dealing with special cases where the presumption did not hold good. It is very doubtful, however, whether there is any such presumption, particularly in underdeveloped countries where the pricing system has not yet permeated the whole economy, and where there are underemployed labour, overvalued currencies and other factors distorting the structure of prices. The more extensively one adjusts market prices upwards or

downwards to allow for social factors, i.e. the more one uses shadow or accounting prices in calculating social marginal productivity, the further one gets from the realm of objective facts and the more heavily one relies on subjective value judgments. It is arguable that by the time one has finished making all the adjustments to private marginal productivity that would be needed to convert it into social marginal productivity one will be left with a concept so tenuously related to anything that is objectively measurable that one might as well sever the connection altogether and admit that marginal analysis can provide no practical guidance to governments in taking investment decisions.

Not all writers would agree, however, that the substitution of social for private marginal productivity entirely destroys the practical usefulness of marginal analysis as a tool of investment policy. H. B. Chenery, in particular, has developed a formula for measuring social marginal productivity, and, to provide examples of how it might be used in practice to distinguish between investment projects that should, and others that should not, be included in investment programmes, has applied it for the purpose of ranking a number of industrial projects in Greece and agricultural projects in Southern Italy.[4] He has endeavoured to sketch out a general method for using data likely to be available in underdeveloped economies as approximate indicators of the difference between social and private marginal productivity.

Even if it is felt that ranking investment projects in accordance with a formula would be an unduly rigid and mechanical approach, and that attempts to "quantify" or measure social marginal productivity with any degree of precision are likely to

4. Hollis B. Chenery: "The Application of Investment Criteria," in *Quarterly Journal of Economics*, Vol. LXVII, No. 1, Feb. 1953, p. 76.

meet with little success, it is still arguable that the concept remains a useful one, enabling us to retain an analytical framework within which it is possible to fit, and to show the bearing of, the various considerations that should influence investment policy—an analytical framework, moreover, that compels those responsible for such policy to bring their value judgments out into the open and make them explicit so that they can be debated and discussed. This, it may be argued further, is likely to help in applying value judgments consistently—in drawing up a logically coherent investment programme, and avoiding one consisting of a job lot of projects each included because some pressure group wanted it included. If, for example, an investment programme includes a project whose inclusion can be justified, on the marginal principle, only if it is judged that the social cost of employing additional labour is much below the private cost of doing so, or that the country's currency is considerably overhauled, it may be difficult, once this has been made explicit, to exclude other projects that would have equal or superior claims on the basis of the same value judgments. The choice, it may be argued, is between an investment programme consisting of a number of projects each one of which has been selected on its merits (or supposed merits) but not necessarily in terms of a consistent set of criteria, and a programme comprising projects that can be justified by reference to a consistent and defendable scale of values. We have seen that a social marginal productivity approach without further definition will not give an unequivocal answer to the question what specific projects should be included in an investment programme, since the claims of different projects will depend upon the interpretation that is given to the concept and the value judgments underlying this interpretation. But

if the concept is given an interpretation that leads to the inclusion of a project X, it may be possible to argue forcibly that consistency demands that projects Y and Z should also be included, while projects W and V should be excluded.

So much by way of comment on the practical usefulness or otherwise of the marginal productivity approach to investment policy. What of the practical usefulness of the capital-intensive approach? It is not enough to say that governments should favour capital-intensive investments. What types of capital-intensive projects should they favour? How are they to identify strategic growing points? Since some of the writers who favour capital-intensive investments have reproached the marginal school with failing to provide specific guidance to governments in taking their investment decisions, one might expect that they would have some rather specific answers to give to these questions.

The literature bearing on these questions is, however, disappointing. Galenson and Leibenstein say—

> Too little attention has been paid to the *pattern* of industry which will facilitate, or indeed make possible, industrial development. It is not a matter of indifference whether capital is allocated, say, to the manufacture of iron and steel or to the manufacture of textiles. Development mission recommendations are all too prone to assume that funds invested in light industries based, for example, on local raw materials, will in some unexplained manner lead to economic development.[5]

They favour the establishment of heavy industries ("industries which are essential to the development of modern industry") on the grounds that the combination of much capital with little labour will give a large reinvestment quotient. Even if this is true of particular establishments using capital-intensive methods, it is necessary to

5. *Op. cit.,* p. 361.

ask what will be the effects of such a policy on the rest of the economy? Comparative cost conditions and the opportunities for international trade can scarcely be left out of consideration. If the establishment of heavy industries is expected in the present or the near future to provide a country with machines, tools or materials more cheaply than they could be imported, investment in such industries will presumably be included in an investment programme drawn up in accordance with marginal productivity criteria. But if the establishment of heavy industries is likely to mean protecting local industrialists, indefinitely or over an extended period of time, who produce inferior or more expensive machines, tools or materials, a government will have to set against the advantages of achieving a high reinvestment quotient in these particular industries the disadvantages of imposing needlessly high costs on industries using these products (whose growth it is presumably desirable to encourage), and presumably reducing their reinvestment quotients. There is also the problem of maintaining a balance between the rate of growth of capital-goods and consumer-goods industries. The establishment of heavy industries, even if they employ relatively little labour, will involve some increase in the community's wage bill, and if additional consumer goods to spend the additional wages on are not made available, inflationary pressure may be generated. It is generally agreed that a certain development of transport and power is necessary for other development. But over and above this, a general case for giving priority to the establishment of heavy industries does not appear to have been made out. Much will depend upon the resources of the country in question and upon what prospects it has of developing a national market large enough to support heavy industry on an economic

basis. Historical evidence does not appear to support the view that the leading role in the take-off phase of economic growth can be played only by heavy industry.

. . .

It may be felt that the many pages of economic journals and other literature devoted in recent years to controversy over investment criteria in underdeveloped countries yield disappointingly little in the way of practical guidance. It has never been claimed, however, that economic analysis can provide rules of thumb that can serve as a substitute for the judgments of governments and business men. Moreover, not all of the considerations on which sound investment decisions must be based are economic in character. There are important sociological and psychological considerations concerning which economic analysis, as such, can have little to say. There is here, as many writers have pointed out, an important field for "inter-disciplinary" studies.

1.3 MAKING AN OPTIMAL CHOICE OF TECHNOLOGY *

When alternative technologies require, for the same level of output, more of some productive factors but less of others, the economic issue arises: Which is the best technological process to use in a given situation? This is the problem of making the optimal choice of technology which was referred to previously. Though the problem need not be resolved here, it is important to pose it. As alternative processes are considered in discussing the transfer of technology to underdeveloped

* From R. S. Eckaus, "Technological Change in the Less Developed Areas," in *Development of the Emerging Countries. An Agenda for Research,* The Brookings Institution, Washington, D.C., 1962, pp. 126-31. Reprinted by permission.

areas, the criteria for choice must be kept clearly in mind.

The optimal allocation or combination of resources in production, which is equivalent to the choice of technology, is an old problem in economics and fully discussed in the context of a static economy. In such circumstances the rule for choice is, roughly, to use that combination of techniques in the various sectors which, over-all will employ productive factors in proportions as close as possible to the proportions in which the resources are available. This is entirely consistent with using factors in different intensities in different sectors, for optimal allocation requires that resources make the same *relative* contributions to output in the various types of production. Thus, capital-intensive methods in producing electric power in central stations and labor-intensive agricultural methods, for example, may both be optimal for particular countries. The criterion for optimal choice does not involve maximizing either the productivity of the employed labor force, the equipment used, or of any other particular resource input. Its objective is to maximize the total output that can be obtained from *all* the resources *available* to the country. Even with such an optimal allocation, the productivity of any one factor such as the labor employed in some particular line of production can be increased by choosing a different technology which is, say, more capital-intensive. That, however, will always involve a greater loss of output in other sectors. Of course, any costless method of increasing the productivity of labor or any other resource ought always to be seized, but such methods seldom exist. A criterion for choice of technology which is confined to increasing the productivity of the amount used of only one productive factor, such as labor or machines of particular types, is quite misleading.

The criteria for optimal choice of technique in developing economies start from the static criterion and consist of modifications of it that arise from the many problems involving time in an essential way, the statement of different goals, and the imposition of additional constraints. In a dynamic context, for example, differences in the gestation period of production processes and in their durability must also be taken into account in choosing the technology which in turn determines the relative intensity with which productive factors are used. As between processes with equal input requirements and equal outputs, the one with the quicker payoff is to be preferred. When a faster return requires having more inputs or getting less output, again an economic question arises.

If the goal is to increase the rate of growth, another set of influences related to but not purely technological must be taken into account. Different technologies which use different combinations of labor, capital plant and equipment and material will give rise to different distributions of incomes. Each income distribution will have its own savings characteristics and, therefore, will differ in the amounts of resources that will be made available for further investment and economic growth. In this way, there may be a specific savings and investment potential associated with each type of technology. The choice of technology in the context of a developing country must take this feature as well as the immediate contribution to output into account.

The choice of technology in developing economies involves other features not generally considered in a static context. Economies of scale, which do not fit easily into static economic analysis may be an essential feature in a developing country. One type of technology may have external effects, as in labor training, which tip the scales in its direction.

These issues may be illustrated and made more concrete by a few examples. The recent Chinese experiment with small iron ore smelting furnaces provides a frequently cited example of a technological revival supposedly more suited to their conditions than the methods now generally in use as it requires a great deal of the abundant labor which they have. However, the experiment appears to have been virtually dropped; it is likely that the process was simply physically inefficient. The small furnaces undoubtedly required more fuel per unit of output and possibly more capital also, as well as more labor.

On the other hand, it is not unusual to find plants embodying the most modern technologies in the less developed areas, using a good deal of equipment per worker and relatively little labor with a very high average productivity. This may be justified on several grounds. Sometimes it is argued that such methods are the only physically efficient ones, or, that, even at the low wages prevailing, they are economically more efficient than methods that use more of the abundant labor which is available. Both of these answers, if they were true, would be adequate reasons, but, as stated above, it would be wrong to justify a technology solely on the grounds that it increased the productivity of the workers in the plant. It is, after all, the productivity of the entire labor force and the output of the entire economy which is important for development.

To illustrate the impact of changes in technology on savings patterns, the possible implications of a land reform program can be cited. In some of the less developed areas of the world, land reform programs increase the labor intensity of cultivation by breaking up large landholdings and distributing them in parcels to individual families. This means that a change in technology as well as a change in property relationships is involved. The effect may

very well be in such cases to increase output per acre or per hectare and total output, though output per man would fall. A further effect might be that an increased proportion of the total output is consumed as the result of its wider distribution in the hands of the workers of the land, and that total saving is reduced. This in turn would tend to impede further over-all progress by reducing the total investment possible.

The problems of measurement are handled best in the context of investigation of the characteristics of particular technologies . . . On the the other hand, the principles of optimal choice of technology can be investigated and established before they need to be invested with facts and numbers. The logic of making optimal choices has by no means been completely explored in spite of the extensive literature cited above. More work is needed in order to integrate the rules for optimal choice into an overall programing framework. In the present state of knowledge the choice issue is usually analyzed for projects as if they are and could be considered separately from each other and independently of the overall growth pattern of a country.

There are analytical tools which, when given empirical content, can be used to establish the *consistency* of various projects in an over-all plan. These are best represented by the input-output approach first developed by Professor Wassily W. Leontief at Harvard University[1] and, perhaps most skillfully used in application to underdeveloped areas by Professor Chenery.[2] Where input-output methods cannot be applied, something equivalent has to be developed for the purpose of establishing

1. *Studies in the Structure of the American Economy, Theoretical and Empirical Explorations in Input-Output Analysis,* Harvard Economic Research Project (Oxford University Press, 1953).

2. For example, "The Role of Industrialization in Investment Programs," *American Economic Review, Papers and Proceedings,* Vol. 45 (May 1955), pp. 40-57.

over-all consistency in economic programing. The development of input-output type information must, therefore, be seriously considered in research plans for any underdeveloped area. However, it would be premature to put such research on the current agenda for every country. In many areas the economic programing currently required is not sufficiently complex or elaborate to require the full input-output apparatus to establish consistency. In these and other cases, the quality of the statistical data available may not warrant the empirical effort involved. Where the data make the project feasible, various methods of constructing input-output tables should be considered. These are by no means completely settled in themselves so that in this, as in other fields, alternative approaches should not be foreclosed by a premature commitment to a particular method.

The problem of optimality is logically and practically distinct from that of consistency. Though input-output tables will help establish the latter, more is required for the former problem. The theoretical framework necessary for forming policy has not yet been completed, though theoretical programing models exist which give useful insights and are of value as partial guides. Relevant work is going on, but much more needs to be done. Again, for some countries, the priorities are so obvious and the opportunities so limited that no highly sophisticated tests of optimality and consistency are necessary. For other areas, with greater scope for choice and action and better data availabilities, the problems of formulating a consistent and optimal development program are pressing ones.

. . .

The problem of optimal choice of technology can be treated with the full generality with which it needs to be treated only in the context of complete, consistent, and optimal programs. Though it will always

be necessary to make pragmatic compromises with inadequate methods and data, the nature of the inadequacies should be recognized.

This conclusion can be illustrated by another type of reference. One of the sectors in which the choice of technology is most important for underdeveloped areas is transportation. Transportation systems can be based on railroads and locomotives and rolling stock of various types, or highways and buses, trucks, and cars, or some combination of the two systems. The choice of methods is a choice of technology. Yet it is obviously not one that can be made in abstraction from the rest of the economy for the choice itself will determine how the rest of the economy develops. That is, it is not legitimate to ask "What is the optimal technology to move so many tonmiles of freight?" and then choose a technology of railroads or highways and buses, and leave it at that, because the answer to the question will change the way the question is formulated; specifically it will change the number of ton-miles which have to be transported to achieve the economic development specified.

Lacking a fully general way of treating the problem, partial solutions may have to be accepted, but that does not justify being permanently satisfied with second best. There should be a major effort to improve the ability of countries to take into account the full ramifications of technological choice: to have that choice fully sensitive to the targets specified, on the one hand, and to have the choice feed back and affect the targets to be chosen on the other hand. The analytical problems are among the most complex faced by economists. Research work in this area may seem far removed from the pressing issues of economic development because of its abstraction. Yet it is only by pursuing the abstractions that models can be formulated which, when given empirical content, will provide concrete guidance in particular circumstances.

1.4 PRACTICAL CONDITIONS FACING INVESTMENT CHOICE *

The conditions which face a development planning commission in its investment allocation will, of course, often include some of those implied in the criteria discussion. But often again, other features, not fully brought out in the discussion, might be overwhelmingly important. We might classify these factors as follows, subsequently to discuss each group in turn.

(i) Political inhibitions or political consequences surrounding some lines of investment.

(ii) The strategy of obtaining foreign or international capital.

(iii) The greater need for, and difficulty of, co-ordination of investment decisions.

(iv) The greater need for, and difficulty of, forecasting future demand.

Group (i), of course, is very wide and really reflects the whole political set-up of the country. However, some specific cases can be brought forward.

Take those less-developed countries still under the colonial administration of one or other of the Great Powers. Any inhibitions about public investment in some sectors which exist in the home-country tend to be reflected abroad. Indeed, in the British case in particular, they tend not merely to be reflected, but accentuated; compared with the considerable state intervention of various kinds in manufacturing industry in Britain, the inhibition against direct investment and operation in manufacturing in her colonies seems particularly strong (irrespective of any calcula-

tions of relative return from this against other investments, of course).

At the opposite pole, newly-independent countries (whether from colonial rule or a "traditional" régime) have their own inhibitions springing from nationalism. Investments which in any way assist (in their distribution of benefits) previously-ruling classes (e.g. landowners), foreign enterprises generally, or certain overseas countries in particular, may be discriminated against, even if calculated returns (on any of the criteria) are relatively high.

If we now change the emphasis slightly, though still in Group (i), to political consequences of certain investment choices, we come to a major consideration, the size and nature of the public sector that is politically acceptable to a country. Suppose we do use one or other of the special criteria that we have reviewed. It is more likely to lead to a proliferation of the tax system, with its administrative and disincentive disadvantages, than operating with a rate-of-profits rule, or with a rule specifically designed to minimise taxes. Why is this so? The reason lies in the operation of those public productive units making a product for sale. If projects are ranked by a rate-of-profit criterion and some number above the zero profit line are undertaken, then, of course, insofar as expectations are correct, there will be an addition to government revenues, which is "tax-relieving." But if, for example, the "social marginal product" rule is used for the allocation of the same sum of capital, the projects chosen will, with equally good (or bad) forecasting, yield smaller net revenue (except in the unlikely case that both rules choose the same projects). Indeed the "social marginal product" criterion may choose projects yielding a negative rate-of-profit,[1] so that the pro-

* From Douglas Dosser, "General Investment Criteria for Less Developed Countries: A Post-Mortem," *Scottish Journal of Political Economy,* Vol. IX, No. 2, June 1962, pp. 93-8. Reprinted by permission.

1. The reason being, of course, that the socially-adjusted prices may markedly differ from market prices; products normally cannot be sold at socially-adjusted prices!

ductive units require subsidies. So when this special criterion is used, a given demand for government revenue requires a greater tax collection, with its attendant disadvantages. Furthermore, use of the "social marginal product" may require yet greater extensions of the tax system, due to its distributional implication. This is most clearly seen when so many negative-profit-projects are chosen by the rule that the net contribution to the revenue is negative. The attendant subsidisation means a transfer of income from those most burdened by the structure of the tax system to consumers of the products of the subsidised enterprises. This might produce the "desired" income distribution of the society but it would be a capricious and uncertain way of achieving it. If we may assume that the budget is redistributing in a "conventional" way (progressive income tax, high profits tax, etc.), this is a disturbing influence, and requires a more complicated set of tax policies (e.g. varied according to expenditure patterns) to return the economy to the desired distributional position. Similar considerations apply to any other criterion which selects a list different from the most profitable (in the market price sense); even, in the short run, to the re-investment type (Eckstein, and Galenson and Leibenstein) though it might be argued that in the long-run they diminished taxation necessary for a given level of investment by promoting private saving.

The preceding sentence brings out the essential point: use of different criteria implies a different size of public sector, not just in the sense of how great a proportion of investment is public, but how extensive must the public finance system be in order to fulfill the major, accepted functions of the budget of redistribution and even stabilisation. And, in any one country, such a size for the public sector may or may not be acceptable.

Let us turn to group (ii), the problems facing a development authority in obtaining foreign capital. These do not arise where no foreign capital is desired, but it would be difficult to name such a country. Most less-developed nations have a keen interest in it, whether it be private foreign capital or aid or loans from one or other of the international agencies ... Reference to the international institutions emphasises that nationalist antipathy toward foreign (private) enterprises and an appetite for international capital are quite compatible, so both newly-independent and colonial territories will face this consideration in development planning.

The greater amount of foreign private capital will be obtained the greater the range of investment opportunities offering the necessary (high) rates of return (in a private profit sense). One would not think it necessary to make such a naïve statement, but the fact is that use of the special criteria obscures which developments would be undertaken by private foreign (or even private indigenous) capital. A special criterion will cut across private profitability, filling in some of the "needs" that private capital would have undertaken, and hence diminishing the total influx of foreign capital (which has alternatives in other countries or its own) and possibly lowering the incentive to save and invest within the country concerned. If projects are ranked by a special criterion, and then exceptions made where foreign private capital would undertake the development, we are virtually being guided by a rate-of-profit criterion. One might almost say that the special investment criteria were suited to cases where foreign private capital was prohibited or quite unlikely to flow in, but this would not be the case with a host of less-developed countries.

But even if private capital is discouraged, the development commission will very likely wish to make friends with the supra-national agencies providing "neutral" capital. There is little doubt that some "projects" are "eye-catchers," others not. The international agencies tend to prefer large-scale projects. To choose such projects or those where it can be argued that like countries have been favourably treated, might well be to obtain capital that would otherwise not be forthcoming. And "agency capital" is very acceptable capital for it usually carries no strings, and is either cheap or free. This must be a primary guide in choosing projects in less-developed countries,[2] irrespective of rates of return in terms of profit or any special criterion.[3]

One further distinction ought, however, to be made. What we have just said applies to investment choice from the point of view of an internal development board. If we are talking of rules for the agencies for the allocation among projects in different countries of international development aid, it clearly does not apply. Thus, quite consistently, different criteria of investment choice could be propounded for one and the same country, according as to whether the economic adviser concerned is working in the said country or in, say, the United Nations.

The third group of important problems in development planning concerns co-ordination of investment decisions, or co-ordination of parts of the plan. This has sometimes hardly been referred to in the "investment criteria" approach ...

Even in later discussion it has not been stressed that greater co-ordination is often necessary in less-developed economies (compared with other economies) due to the initial lack of interdependence between

sectors (before development). When a project is developed in isolation in high-income countries it can usually rely on the ability of supplying sectors to provide the additional producer goods. The new project will probably be small in relation to the existing supplying sectors, thus requiring but a marginal change in the latter. In low-income countries, this may not be so; furthermore, the supplying sectors may not exist at all. Where the supplying sector in mind is a particular kind of labour, the same remarks apply; a project in a developed country can rely on a supply of near-suitably-trained labour, but this is unlikely to be the case in a low-income country. Thus there is greater need for co-ordination, and greater difficulty, because new supplying sectors may have to be created rather than marginal adjustments assumed. Reference to "external economies" or "socially-adjusted" prices in later criteria does not completely cover this point. For the former concern benefits outside the project which come into existence when the project is in operation; and an adjusted-price for, say, a kind of labour not at present available is, to say the least, not a concept which can be easily operated.

The question of future demand, the fourth group of factors listed, is an important and difficult one. As noted in our review, the problem of future price trends, which enter into every type of calculation of return in some way or other, has frequently been glossed over. It might be argued that this is legitimate for one of three reasons. Firstly, "excess demand" is already present in the economy or will be occasioned by the development plan, so that all the new final goods produced can be easily disposed of at prices written into the calculation. Secondly, a sufficient degree of State intervention will occur in order to dispose of the new products, i.e. if prices have to be lowered below anticipated levels to run the projects at planned

2. This is definitely not a cynical comment on the actions of development boards; it follows from the rules for the distribution of aid followed by the international agencies themselves.

3. The projects are often so vast, e.g. the Aswan High Dam or the Indus Waters scheme, that any precise calculation of return in any sense is impossible.

outputs, State subsidies will be available to meet losses. Thirdly, prices are only used for accounting purposes, and the distribution of use of factors and products is entirely administered. We should say each of these was a rather special case; it could be answered that so is the situation we are about to present, namely one where foreign trade is important; but it would seem of wider generality.

Whilst some of the criteria have paid full attention to the importance of foreign trade in respect of scarcity of foreign exchange, another consequence of the dominance that exports exert on many less-developed countries has been less appreciated. This is the necessity of accepting exogenously-determined prices for a large proportion of one's products. Where this exists, it knocks out the first and third

arguments for the unimportance of actual price trends, and the second now carries the implication of the possible need for quite massive subsidies.

Many less-developed countries will therefore feel the need to estimate future price trends, at least for export crops, whichever form of criterion they might use, if only to estimate the size of subsidies required. And they frequently have the relatively great volatility of primary product prices to contend with.

If one or more of the four groups of factors we have discussed operate strongly in many less-developed countries, and the discussion of investment criteria has not given them full weight, this offers one explanation of the lack of any general adoption of one or other criterion by development planning boards.

2. GROWTH—BALANCED OR UNBALANCED?

2.1 BALANCED GROWTH *

It is no longer so certain that the less developed countries can rely on economic growth being induced from the outside through an expansion of world demand for their exports of primary commodities. In these circumstances reliance on induced expansion through international trade cannot provide a solution to the problem of economic development. It is not surprising therefore that countries should be looking for other solutions. It is important to keep these things in mind, because they form the background to the case for balanced growth which is now so much in vogue.

The circumstances indicated do not apply to all underdeveloped countries

* From Ragnar Nurkse, "The Conflict Between 'Balanced Growth' and International Specialization," *Lectures on Economic Development*, Faculty of Economics (Istanbul University) and Faculty of Political Sciences (Ankara University), Istanbul, 1958, pp. 170-76. Reprinted by permission.

today: Kuwait and perhaps Iraq have nothing to worry about. But in so far as these circumstances do exist in reality it is clear that the poorer countries, even if they are only to keep pace with the richer, to say nothing about catching up with them, must expand production for their own domestic markets or for each others markets. Now domestic markets are limited because of mass poverty due to low productivity. Private investment in any single industry considered by itself is discouraged by the smallness of the existing market.

The limits set by the small size of the local market for manufactured goods are so plainly visible to any individual businessman that we are fully justified in taking for granted conditions of imperfect competition, and not the pure atomistic competition which even in advanced economies does not exist to any significant degree, outside the economics textbooks.

The solution seems to be a balanced pattern of investment in a number of different industries, so that people working more productively, with more capital and improved techniques, become each others customers. In the absence of vigorous upward shifts in world demand for exports of primary products, a low income country through a process of diversified growth can seek to bring about upward shifts in domestic demand schedules by means of increased productivity and therefore increased real purchasing power. In this way, a pattern of mutually supporting investments in different lines of production can enlarge the size of the market and help to fill the vacuum in the domestic economy of low income areas. This, in brief, is the notion of balanced growth.

Isolated advance is not impossible. A solitary process of investment and increased productivity in one industry alone will certainly have favorable repercussions elsewhere in the economy. There is no denying that through the normal incentives of the price mechanism other industries will be induced to advance also. But this may be a snail's pace of progress. The price mechanism works but it may work too slowly. That is one reason for the frequently observed fact that foreign direct investments in extractive export industries have created high productivity islands in low income areas and have had little impact on the level of productivity in the domestic economy.

Within the domestic economy itself, advance in one direction, say in industry A, tends to induce advance in B as well. But if it is only a passive reaction to the stimulus coming from A, the induced advance of B may be slow and uncertain. And B's slowness and passiveness will in turn slow down and discourage the initial advance in A. The application of capital to one industry alone may therefore be subject to sharply diminishing returns. As

a way of escape from slowness if not from stagnation, the balanced growth principle envisages autonomous advance along a number of lines more or less simultaneously.

Viewed in this way, balanced growth is a means to accelerated growth. Some economists treat the problem of achieving balanced growth as quite separate from the problem of speeding up the rate of advance in a backward economy. I admit that this may be a convenient distinction to draw on other grounds. But in my view, balanced growth is first and foremost a means of getting out of the rut, a means of stepping up the rate of growth when the external forces of advance through trade expansion and foreign capital are sluggish or inoperative.

In the existing state of affairs in low income areas the introduction of capital using techniques of production in any single industry is inhibited by the small size of the market. Hence the weakness of private investment incentives in such areas. The balanced growth principle points to a way out of the deadlock. New enterprises set up in different industries create increased markets for each other, so that in each of them the installation of capital equipment becomes worth while. As Marshall said, "The efficiency of specialized machinery ... is but one condition of its economic use; the other is that sufficient work should be found to keep it well employed" (Principles, p. 264). The techniques that have been developed in production for mass markets in advanced countries are not well adapted and sometimes not adaptable at all to output on a more limited scale. It is easy to see that the relationship between the size of the market and the amount of investment required for efficient operation is of considerable importance for the theory of balanced growth.

Frequently the objection is made: But

why use machinery? Why adopt capital using methods in areas where labor is cheap and plentiful? Why not accordingly employ techniques that are labor-intensive instead of capital-intensive?

The answer is obvious. As an adaptation to existing circumstances, including the existing factor proportions, the pursuit of labor-intensive production methods with a view to economizing capital may be perfectly correct. But the study of economic development must concern itself with changing these circumstances, not accepting them as they are. What is wanted is progress, not simply adaptation to present conditions. And progress depends largely on the use of capital, which in turn depends on adequate and growing markets, which in the absence of a strongly rising world demand for the country's exports means a diversified output expansion for domestic use.

Reference has been made to the importance of autonomous advance in a number of mutually supporting lines of production. How is this achieved? Autonomous advance in different branches simultaneously may come about through the infectious influence of business psychology, through the multiplier effects of investment anywhere which can create increased money demand elsewhere, or through deliberate control and planning by public authorities. According to some writers the balanced growth argument implies that the market mechanism is eliminated and that investments must be effected according to a coordinated plan. This opinion, which is widely held, seems to me dubious. There are many important reasons for government planning, but this is not necessarily one of them. As a means of creating inducements to invest, balanced growth can be said to be relevant primarily to a private enterprise system. State investment can and often does go ahead without any market incentives. Planning

authorities can apply capital, if they have any, wherever they may choose, though if they depart too much from balance as dictated by income elasticities of demand they will end by creating white elephants and intolerable disproportionalities in the structure of production. It is private investment that is attracted by markets and that needs the inducement of growing markets. It is here that the element of mutual support is so useful and, for rapid growth, indispensable.

It is important to note that the doctrine under consideration is not itself concerned with the question of where the capital is to be found, for all the balanced investment which it envisages. I have tried to make it clear in my discussion of it that the argument is primarily relevant to the problem of the demand for capital; it takes an increased supply of capital for granted. In my presentation balanced growth is an exercise in economic development with unlimited supplies of capital, analogous to Professor Lewis's celebrated exercise in development with unlimited labor supplies.

In reality, of course, capital supplies are not unlimited. It may be that the case for state investment stems chiefly from the fact that capital is scarce and that government efforts are necessary to mobilize all possible domestic sources of saving. Measures to check the expansion of consumer demand may be necessary to make resources available for investment but may at the same time weaken the private inducement to invest. This is a famous dilemma to which Malthus first called attention in his *Principles of Political Economy*. A case for state investment may clearly arise if and when the mobilization of capital supplies discourages private investment activity and so destroys the demand for capital. But this case is entirely separate from the principle of balanced growth as such. It might only be added that the capital supply problem alone creates a strong presumption against relying on the indiscriminate use of import restriction which may reduce a country's real income and therefore make it harder to increase the flow of saving.

Elsewhere I have tried to explain how the balanced growth idea is related to the classical law of markets. Supply creates its own demand, provided that supply is properly distributed among different commodities in accordance with consumers' wants. An increase in consumable output must provide a balanced diet. Each industry must advance along an expansion path determined by the income elasticity of consumer demand for its product. This simple idea must be the starting point in any expansion of production for domestic markets in the less developed countries, in so far as external demand conditions do not favor the traditional pattern of "growth through trade." Yet, as often happens in economic discussion, critics have tended to dismiss this idea either as a dangerous fallacy or as an obvious platitude. It is hardly necessary to add that the pattern of consumable output cannot be expected to remain the same in successive stages of development. The content of a balanced diet of a man with a thousand dollars a year will differ from that of a man with a hundred dollars.

The relation between agriculture and manufacturing industry offers the clearest and simplest case of balance needed for economic growth. In a country where the peasantry is incapable of producing a surplus of food above its own subsistence needs there is little or no incentive for industry to establish itself: there is not a sufficient market for manufactured goods. Conversely, agricultural improvements may be inhibited by lack of a market for farm products if the non-farm sector of the economy is backward or undeveloped. Each of the two sectors must try to move forward. If one remains passive the other is slowed down.

It is important in this connection to make a clear distinction between two concepts that are frequently confused: the marketable surplus and investible surplus of the farm sector. The farm sector's marketable surplus of farm products determines the volume of non-farm employment in manufacturing and other activities. It reflects simply the farm sector's demand for non-agricultural commodities. This is the concept that is relevant to the balanced growth principle.

An investible surplus of farm products represents an act of saving in the farm sector. It can conceivably result from a transfer of surplus labourers from the farms to capital construction projects: a food surplus may then arise through forced or voluntary saving in the farm sector for maintaining the workers engaged on capital projects. This is the concept relevant to the problem of capital supply. It is obvious that even a large marketable surplus of food need not involve any saving by the farmers. It presents a very helpful inducement, but does not in itself create the means, for capital investment outside the agricultural sector. A fuller discussion of the interrelationship between marketable and investable surpluses would take us too far from our present subject. It seemed desirable to mention the distinction here merely for the sake of conceptual clarity. So much for the relation between agriculture and industry.

Within the manufacturing field alone the case for balanced investment implies a horizontal diversification of industrial activities all pushing ahead, though naturally at varying rates. The objection can be made that such diffusion of effort and resources over many different lines of activity must mean a loss of dynamic momentum in the economy. This is possible. The dispersal of investment over a variety of consumer-goods industries can undoubtedly be carried to excess. The balanced growth principle can be and has been interpreted far too literally. Producing a little of everything is not the key to progress. The case for balanced growth is concerned with establishing a pattern of mutually supporting investments over a range of industries wide enough to overcome the frustration of isolated advance, in order precisely to create a forward momentum of growth. The particular factors that determine the optimum pattern of diversification have to do with technology, physical conditions and other circumstances that vary from country to country. There can be no standard prescription of universal applicability. We are concerned with a point of principle and cannot deal with the precise forms of its implementation in practice. Just as it is possible for manufacturing industry as a whole to languish if farmers produce too little and are too poor to buy anything from factories, so it is possible for a single line of manufacturing to fail for lack of support from other sectors in industry as well as agriculture; that is, for lack of markets.

2.2 BALANCED GROWTH: A CRITIQUE *

My principal point is that the theory [of balanced growth] fails as a theory of *development*. Development presumably means the process of *change* of one type of economy *into* some other more advanced type. But such a process is given up as hopeless by the balanced growth theory which finds it difficult to visualize how the "underdevelopment equilibrium" can be broken into at any one point. The argument is reminiscent of the paradox about the string that is equally strong everywhere

* From Albert O. Hirschman, *The Strategy of Economic Development*, Yale University Press, New Haven, 1958, pp. 51-5, 62-3, 65-70, 73. Reprinted by permission.

and that therefore when pulled cannot break anywhere first: it either will not break at all or must give everywhere at once. However, as Montaigne pointed out in considering this paradox, its premise "is contrary to nature" for "nothing is ever encountered by us that does not hold some difference however small it may be."

Oblivious of this "difference," the balanced growth theory reaches the conclusion that an entirely new, self-contained modern industrial economy must be superimposed on the stagnant and equally self-contained traditional sector. Say's Law is here made to reign *independently* in both economies. This is not growth, it is not even the grafting of somethin new *onto* something old; it is a perfectly dualistic pattern of development, akin to what is known to child phychologists as "parallel play." There are indeed instances of this kind of development, but they are usually considered conspicuous failures from both the social and economic points of view: the contrast between the Indian communities of the Peruvian altiplano and the Spanish mestizo economy along the coast comes to mind and so do the much decried enclave-type plantations and mining operations that have been set up in several underdeveloped countries by foreign concerns as perfectly self-contained units, far away from the danger of contamination by the local economy.

Naturally, this is not the picture that was in the minds of the authors of the theory. How can we then explain that they set up so unsatisfactory a model? I suspect the reason is that the very difficulty of the task of development has led them to an escapist solution. How many a Western traveler to an underdeveloped country has been bewildered and dismayed by the ubiquitous poverty and inefficiency, by the immensity of the task, and by the interlocking vicious circles! The temptation is strong then to leave all this backwardness alone and to dream of an entirely new type of economy where, in the words of the poet, "tout est ordre et beauté!"

One of the most curious aspects of the theory is the way in which it combines a defeatist attitude toward the capabilities of underdeveloped economies with completely unrealistic expectations about their creative abilities. On the one hand, the conception of the traditional economy as a closed circle dismisses the abundant historical evidence about the piecemeal penetration by industry that competes successfully with local handicraft and by new products which are first imported and then manufactured locally. It also disregards the evidence that, for better or for worse, some products of modern industrial civilization —flashlights, radios, bicycles, or beer—are always found sufficiently attractive to make people stop hoarding, restrict traditional consumption, work harder, or produce more for the market in order to acquire them. But, on the other hand, a people that is assumed to be unable to do any of these things and that is therefore entirely uninterested in change and satisfied with its lot is then expected to marshal sufficient entrepreneurial and managerial ability to set up at the same time a whole flock of industries that are going to take in each others' output! For this is of course the major bone that I have to pick with the balanced growth theory: its application requires huge amounts of precisely those abilities which we have identified as likely to be in very limited supply in underdeveloped countries. It is altogether inconceivable that a one-floor economy could set up such a "second floor" with its own forces or even with limited help from abroad; without thorough foreign colonization the task would seem to be hopeless. ...In other words, if a country were ready to apply the doctrine of balanced growth,

then it would not be underdeveloped in the first place.

...

According to the theory of balanced growth which we have discussed so far, the role of the state is to assure that simultaneity of investments in a large variety of enterprises which is believed to be needed to ensure the success of the individual ventures. A more sophisticated version of the doctrine and of the role it assigns to state action analyzes the anticipations rather than the possible actions of entrepreneurs. It states that, under a private enterprise system, entrepreneurs in underdeveloped countries will invest far less than is profitable from the point of view of society. The reason is that atomistic private producers cannot appropriate the external economies to which their activity gives rise, or that they cannot foresee the repercussions which will eventually make them into recipients of economies external to other firms but internal to their own. Private profit calculations fatally underestimate actual social benefits. In the opinion of Rosenstein-Rodan, the pessimistic anticipations of the entrepreneurs are correct as long as they remain atomistic producers; in that of Scitovsky, they are incorrect since they are eventually going to be recipients of pecuniary external economies. But the conclusions are similar in both cases. Production must be integrated and centrally planned as though it were taking place in a single "trust," for only in that case are the external economies going to be "internalized" with a consequent upward revision of profit estimates.

In one respect, the theory is no more than a variant of the balanced growth doctrine. It says: if ten projects could be undertaken jointly, lending each other mutual support in demand, any one of them would be more profitable than the same project undertaken in isolation. On the premises stated, this is undoubtedly correct. But it is also true that a country cannot undertake any number of projects just because they would turn out to be profitable *if* it undertook them. At any one time the available developmental skills of a country set some kind of a ceiling on the number of projects that can be undertaken simultaneously....

Having discarded [the] "pure" theory of balanced growth we must still consider a far less rigorous version, one that insists that if growth is not to be stunted the various sectors of an economy will have to grow jointly in some (not necessarily identical) proportion; no sector should get too far out of line, not because of demand but because of supply or "structural" considerations. For instance, if secondary industry grows, the food and raw material input needed by the workers and the machines will go up; if some of these requirements are imported, then an increase in exports is necessary, etc., etc.

In this form, the balanced growth theory is essentially an exercise in retrospective comparative statics. If we look at an economy that has experienced growth at two different points in time, we will of course find that a great many parts of it have pushed ahead: industry and agriculture, capital goods and consumer goods industries, cars on the road and highway mileage—each at its own average annual rate of increase. But surely the individual components of the economy will not actually have grown at these rates throughout the period under review. Just as on the demand side the market can absorb "unbalanced" advances in output because of cost-reducing innovations, new products, and import substitution, so we can have isolated forward thrusts on the supply side as inputs are redistributed among users through price changes, and at the cost of some temporary shortages and disequi-

libria in the balance of payments or elsewhere. In fact, development has of course proceeded in this way, with growth being communicated from the leading sectors of the economy to the followers, from one industry to another, from one firm to another. In other words, the balanced growth that is revealed by the two still photographs taken at two different points in time is the end result of a series of uneven advances of one sector followed by the catching-up of other sectors. If the catching-up overreaches its goal, as it often does, then the stage is set for further advances elsewhere. The advantage of this kind of seesaw advance over "balanced growth," where every activity expands perfectly in step with every other, is that it leaves considerable scope to *induced* investment decisions and therefore economizes our principal scarce resource, namely, genuine decision-making.

...

Development as a Chain of Disequilibria: As has been shown, the balanced growth theory results from comparing the initial point of underdevelopment equilibrium with another point at which development will practically have been accomplished. A certain impatience with the process that lies between these two points —i.e, for the process of development—is shown by the following quotation from a well-known article by Scitovsky:

Profits are a sign of disequilibrium; and the magnitude of profits under free competition may be regarded as a rough index of the degree of disequilibrium. Profits in a freely competitive industry lead to investment in that industry; and the investment in turn tends to eliminate the profits that have called it forth. Thus far, then, investment tends to bring equilibrium nearer. The same investment, however, may raise ... profits in other industries; and to this extent it leads away from equilibrium. . . . The profits of industry B created by the lower price for factor A, call for investment and expansion in industry B one result of which will be an increase in industry B's demand for industry A's product.

This in turn will give rise to profits and call for further investment and expansion in A; and equilibrium is reached only when successive doses of investment and expansion in the two industries have led to the simultaneous elimination of investment in both. It is only at this stage that ... the amount of investment profitable in industry A is also the socially desirable amount. The amount is clearly greater than that which is profitable at the first stage before industry B has made its adjustment. We can conclude, therefore, that when an investment gives rise to pecuniary external economies, its private profitability understates its social desirability.[1]

To my mind, the first part of this passage is a most pertinent portrayal of how development is set and kept in motion, but Scitovsky, considering the proceedings he describes unnecessarily laborious, proposes to short-circuit them and to reach in a single jump a new point of equilibrium where the "elimination of investment" has been accomplished. But, actually, development is a lengthy process during which interaction of the kind described by Scitovsky takes place not only between two industries, but up and down and across the whole of an economy's input-output matrix, and for many decades. What point in such a virtually infinite sequence of repercussions are we supposed to shoot at? Which intermediate expansion stages ought we to skip, and which ordinarily successive stages ought we to combine? Some skipping or combining may be possible, but with no more than the modest objective of speeding up development here and there. In general, development policy must concern itself with the judicious setting up of the kind of sequences and

1. Tibor Scitovsky, "Two Concepts of External Economies," *Journal of Political Economy,* April 1954, pp. 148-9.

repercussions so well described by Scitovsky, rather than with any attempt to suppress them. In other words, our aim must be to *keep alive* rather than to eliminate the disequilibria of which profits and losses are symptoms in a competitive economy. If the economy is to be kept moving ahead, the task of development policy is to maintain tensions, disproportions, and disequilibria. That nightmare of equilibrium economics, the endlessly spinning cobweb, is the *kind* of mechanism we must assiduously look for as an invaluable help in the development process.

Therefore, the sequence that "leads away from equilibrium" is precisely an ideal pattern of development from our point of view: for each move in the sequence is induced by a previous disequilibrium and in turn creates a new disequilibrium that requires a further move. This is achieved by the fact that the expansion of industry *A* leads to economies external to *A* but appropriable by *B*, while the consequent expansion of *B* brings with it economies external to *B* but subsequently internal to *A* (or *C* for that matter), and so on. At each step, an industry takes advantage of external economies created by previous expansion, and at the same time creates new external economies to be exploited by other operators.

. . .

Technical complementarity in the strict sense is usually defined as a situation where an increase in the output of commodity *A* lowers the marginal costs of producing commodity *B*. This will happen typically as a result of the following situations:

a. because *A* is an input of *B* and is produced under conditions of decreasing costs;

b. because *B* is an input of *A* and is itself produced under conditions of decreasing costs;

c. because *A* and *B* are joint products

(or because *B* is a by-product of *A*) and are produced under decreasing costs.

Because situations such as these have long been familiar to economists, complementarity is usually associated with economies of scale. But there is no need for so restrictive an interpretation. We can define complementarity as any situation where an increase in the demand for commodity *A* and the consequent increase in its output call forth an increased demand for commodity *B* at its existing price. This happens not only when the connection between the two commodities is via the production process. The connection between *A* and *B* may also arise because the increased *use* of *A* leads to greater demand for *B*. We are not thinking here of situations where *A* and *B* *must* be employed jointly in fixed proportions. In this case it would not make much sense to say that demand for *A* and the subsequent increase in its output provide an incentive for the production of *B*, as it is rather the demand for the good or service into which *A* and *B* enter jointly which explains the demand for both products. This is the familiar case of derived demand. But there are many situations in the course of economic development where the increased availability of one commodity does not *compel a simultaneous* increase in supply of another commodity, but *induces slowly*, through a loose kind of complementarity in use, an upward shift in its demand schedule. The phenomenon has been described under the apt heading "entrained want";[2] Veblen observed it long ago and effectively summed it up when he said that "invention is the mother of necessity" rather than vice versa.

An example of the rigid type of complementarity in use (best treated as derived demand) is cement and reinforcing steel rods in the construction, say, of downtown office buildings. Examples of the looser, "developmental" type of complementarity (entrained want) can be found in the way in which the existence of the new office buildings strengthens demand for a great variety of goods and services: from modern office furniture and equipment (still fairly rigid), to parking and restaurant facilities, stylish secretaries, and eventually perhaps to more office buildings as the demonstration effect goes to work on the tenants of the older buildings. Here again, failure to arrange for all of these complementary items from the start could be denounced as "poor planning" which ought to be avoided by centralized decision-making. But, just as in the case quoted by Scitovsky, an attempt to telescope the whole process would be futile because of the virtually infinite number of complementarity repercussions, and because of the uncertainty about a good many of them; moreover, such an attempt would miss the point that the profitable opportunities that arise as a result of the initial development move constitute powerful and valuable levers for subsequent development which are to be carefully nursed, maintained at some optimum level, and if necessary created consciously rather than eliminated.

The common feature of the various complementarity situations is that, as a result of the increase in the output of *A*, the profitability of the production of *B* is being increased because *B*'s marginal costs drop, or because its demand schedule shifts upward, or because both forces act jointly.

Put even more generally, complementarity means that increased production of *A* will lead to *pressure* for increasing the available supply of *B*. When *B* is a pri-

2. The term is used by H. G. Barnett in *Innovation: The Basis of Cultural Change* (New York, McGraw-Hill, 1953), pp. 148-51, with the exact meaning we have in mind here: "The fulfillment of one need establishes conditions out of which others emerge ... In most instances it is impossible for people to foresee [these emergent wants] even if they try ... Entrained wants are a consistent feature of motivational stresses for cultural change" (p. 148).

vately produced good or service, this pressure will lead to imports or larger domestic production of *B* because it will be in the *interest* of traders and producers of *B* to respond to the pressure. When *B* is not privately produced, the pressure does not transmute itself into pecuniary self-interest, and will take the form of political pressure for the provision of *B*. This is the case for such public services as law and order, education, satisfactory monetary and banking arrangements, highways, water, electric power, etc. Complementarity then manifests itself in the form of complaints about shortages, bottlenecks, and obstacles to development. Action in this case does not take place through the operation of the profit motive, but through group pressures on public authorities and agencies. . . .

The way in which investment leads to other investment through complementarities and external economies is an invaluable "aid" to development that must be consciously utilized in the course of the development process. It puts special pressure behind a whole group of investment decisions and augments thereby that scarce and non-economizable resource of underdeveloped countries, the ability to make new investment decisions.

The manner in which an investment project affects the availability of this resource is for us the principal measure of its contribution to further development. . . .

2.3 BALANCED VERSUS UNBALANCED GROWTH *

In this article we shall attempt to show that the questions posed by the controversy over balanced *versus* unbalanced growth have not been very fruitful, although each doctrine contains some valuable insights. Before we enter upon a discussion of the merits and faults of the doctrines of bal-

* From Paul Streeten, "Balanced *versus* Unbalanced Growth," *The Economic Weekly,* April 20, 1963, pp. 669-71. Reprinted by permission.

anced growth (BG) and of unbalanced growth (UG), it is necessary to clarify two questions to which the contributors to the debate have not given clear and satisfactory answers. The first question, most relevant in the present context of our discussion, concerns the role of planning; the second question the role of supply limitations and supply inelasticities.

In the controversy the role of government (or for that matter private) planning has not always been brought out clearly. In particular, it is not always clear whether the question under consideration relates to planning, or whether it relates to an attempt to explain development that takes place without planning, or with only an initial impulse of planning in the form of an investment project, while things are thereafter left to take their own course with market forces responding to demand and supply.

Nurkse thought that BG is relevant primarily to a private enterprise economy. It is (he argued) private investment that needs market inducements. In his doctrine, the choice between public and private investment and between direct controls and market incentives is mainly a matter of administrative expediency. But he seems to be wrong in this. The indivisibilities assumed in BG imply the need for coordination, i.e. planning, although it would, in principle, be possible to have either private or public coordination.

UG as propounded by Hirschman is consistent with, but does not require, initial *and* continued planning. His state administrators are—or should be—subject to the same kind of pressures as private entrepreneurs. The role of the state is both to induce and to repair disequilibria. Thus state action becomes a dependent, as well as an independent, variable. But again, on closer inspection it would seem that UG, to be most effective, does require planning and preferably state planning, because no private firm may want or be able to carry the surplus capacity and the losses, and because private horizons are too narrow.

It is not surprising that both BG and UG should, to be most effective, presuppose each (a different kind of) planning, for they are both concerned with lumpy investments and complementarities. Coordination is needed in order both to get things done that otherwise would not be done, and in order to reap the rewards of complementarities. Market forces look best after adjustments that can be made in infinitesimally small steps. This is why the concept "marginal" plays such an important part in neo-classical Western economic theory. It is also one of the important differences between developed and underdeveloped countries. In the former a new profitable investment project is normally small relative to the size of existing capital equipment (however measured), relatively to new investment, and relatively to the hinterland of facilities on which it can draw. In underdeveloped countries indivisibilities are more prominent and marginal adjustments rarer for at least four reasons.

First, both the existing stock of equipment and the additions to it are small compared with those in advanced countries with comparable populations. Since plant and equipment often have to be of a minimum size for technical reasons, the addition of a plant or of a piece of equipment makes a greater proportionate difference both to the stock of capital and to total investment.

Second, economic development is usually directed at moving people from agriculture to industrial enterprises. This normally implies an increase in the number of indivisible units.

Third, the necessary social overhead capital and the basic structure of industry (power, steel, transport, housing, government buildings) consist of large indivisible units.

Fourth, complementarities between enterprises and activities are likely to be more important in the meagre economies of underdeveloped countries, so that a given investment is more liable to require complementary and supplementary investments. Both BG and UG give rise to external economies. A cost incurred by A creates profit opportunities for B. If steps are taken to seize these opportunities at once and in one type of sequence (BG), the results will be different than if they are seized later and in a different type of sequence (UG). But there is no guarantee that A will be induced by market forces to incur these costs, indeed there is a presumption that he will not be so induced.

We next turn to the role of supply limitations and supply inelasticities in the controversy. Nurkse explicitly confined his discussion to the demand side. He assumed supplies to be available and asked what would investment have to be like to justify them? He wrote:

There is no suggestion here that, by taking care of the demand side alone, any country could, as it were, lift itself up by its boot-straps. We have been considering one particular facet of our subject. The more fundamental difficulties that lie on the supply side have so far been kept off-stage for the sake of orderly discussion.[1]

Nevertheless, the position of this chapter in his book and the emphasis laid on it have led to misinterpretations. If BG stresses *markets* as the main limitation on growth, UG in the Hirschman version stresses *decisions*. The implication of Hirschman's theory is that supplies will be forthcoming with relative ease if only the lack of decision-taking can be overcome. This shift of emphasis to an attitude, usually assumed either constant or automatically adjusted to precisely the required extent, should be welcomed. Hirschman

[1]. *Problems of Capital Formation in Underdeveloped Countries*, pp. 30-31.

has been charged with excessive preoccupation with *investment* decisions. Much of his book indeed focuses attention on them, but it is clear that he had a wider concept in mind, as is shown by his use of the terms "development decisions" and "developmental tasks."

Insofar as BG is concerned with the creation of markets through complementary investment projects and the inducement to invest by providing complementary markets for final goods, it stresses a problem which is rarely serious in the countries of the region. Final markets can often quite easily be created without recourse to BG, by import restrictions and, less easily, by export expansion.

On the other hand, although UG is correct in pointing to the scarcity of decision-taking in some countries, it should not be contrasted, but it should be combined with the provision of more supplies. The contrast drawn by UG between scarcity of physical resources and scarcity of decision-taking can be misleading. Those who stress resources say that decisions will be taken as soon as resources are available; those who stress decision-taking say that resources will flow freely as soon as adequate inducements to take decisions are provided. The former group of experts go out on missions and advocate high taxation in order to "set resources free," the latter recommend low taxation in order to "encourage enterprise."

Both views reflect misplaced aggregation and illegitimate isolation, two types of bias introduced by the careless use of Western concepts and models. No general formula will serve. The correct division often cuts across these categories. The question is what combination of resource policy, reform of attitudes (including "incentives") and of legal, social and cultural institutions, is necessary in a particular situation.

Moreover, the tendency of both BG and UG to underplay supply limitations diverts attention from the fact that planning must be directed as much at restricting supplies in certain directions as at *expanding* them in others. The policy package presupposes a choice of allocating limited supplies, i.e., supplies growing at a limited rate, and in response to certain stimuli, to the most important uses, combined with inducements to decisions of all kinds (not only investment decisions). These supply limitations are considerably less important in advanced industrial countries now and were less important in the early developing phase of many now advanced countries, like Sweden or the regions of recent settlement. These countries had almost unlimited access to capital at low interest rates, a reserve of skilled labour and plentiful natural resources. Again, certain underdeveloped regions in advanced countries (Southern Italy, the South of the USA) can draw on supplies but lack development decisions.

The models developed in the BG vs UG controversy seem to have drawn on this kind of experience from "ceilingless economies" which is relevant to South America but not to the entirely different problems of South Asia. The two important differences between, on the one hand, advanced countries now and in their development phase, and, on the other hand, the underdeveloped countries of South Asia are:

(1) that investments in advanced countries can more often be treated as marginal than in underdeveloped countries, and

(2) that advanced countries are and were high supply-elasticity economies with responses and institutions already adapted to economic growth.

Both doctrines have certain faults. The trouble with advocating UG is that, for countries embarking on development, unbalance is inevitable, whether they want it or not, and governments and planners do not need the admonitions of theoreticians. All investment creates unbalances because of rigidities, indivisibilities, sluggishness of response both of supply and of demand in these low-elasticity economies and because of miscalculations. There will be, in any case, plenty of difficulties in meeting many urgent requirements, whether of workers, technicians, managers, machines, semi-manufactured products, raw materials or power and transport facilities and in finding markets permitting full utilisation of equipment. Market forces will be too weak or powerless to bring about the required adjustments and unless coordinated planning of much more than investment is carried out, the investment projects will turn out to be wasteful and will be abandoned.

Insofar as unbalance does create desirable attitudes, the crucial question is not whether to create unbalance, but *what* is the *optimum* degree of unbalance, *where* to unbalance and *how much*, in order to accelerate growth; which are the "growing points," where should the spearheads be thrust, on which slope would snowballs grow into avalanches? Although nobody just said "create any old unbalance," insufficient attention has been paid to its precise composition, direction and timing.

The second weakness of UG is that the theory concentrates on stimuli to *expansion,* and tends to neglect or minimise *resistances* caused by UG. UG argues that the active sectors pull the others with them, BG that the passive sectors drag the active ones back. While the former is relevant to South America, the latter is relevant to South Asia. It would, of course, be better, as Nurkse would have liked it, if *all* sectors were active, and the wish may have been father of the thought behind these models. But the problem is how to activate them. Activation measures must take the form both of positive inducements and of resistances to resistances.

The UG model in the Hirschman version has the great merit, in comparision with many other models, of including attitudes and institutions, and in particular investment incentives, normally assumed fully adjusted to requirements, and of turning them from independent variables or constants into dependent variables. In particular Hirschman's discussion of forward and backward linkages is provocative and fruitful. It brings out the previously neglected effects of one investment on investment at earlier and later stages of production. But the doctrine underplays obstacles and resistances (also in attitudes) called into being by imbalance. Shortages create vested interests; they give rise to monopoly gains; people may get their fingers burnt by malinvestments and may get frightened by the growth of competition. The attitudes and institutions evolving through development will arouse opposition and hostility. Some of these resistances may be overcome only by state compulsion, but the governments of the "soft states" are reluctant to use force and the threat of force. Once again, the absence of this type of reaction from the models is both appropriate for Western countries and is opportune to the planners in South Asia, but it introduces a systematic bias and neglects some of the most important issues.

Turning now to BG, we have seen that its main weakness is that it is concerned with the creation of complementary domestic markets as an inducement to invest, whereas markets in the countries of the region can usually be created by import restrictions, and, where possible, export expansion. This relates to final goods and principally to consumers' goods. As far as intermediate markets are concerned, Nurkse came out in favour of UG (vertical imbalance) in his second Istanbul Lecture.[2] Social overhead investment provides

2. R. Nurkse, *Equilibrum and Growth in the World Economy,* pp. 259-78.

the conditions and inducements for con-sequential direct productive investment. As for horizontal balance, he believed that the case "rests on the need for a 'balanced diet'." [3] But he later drew a distinction between BG as a method and BG as an outcome or objective.[4] What remains of the doctrine is the emphasis on the comple-mentarity of markets for final goods as an ultimate objective for investment incen-tives. But not only is absence of markets not normally a serious obstacle to develop-ment; even where it is, it is by no means the main obstacle and, in any case, balanced growth cannot always remove it.

What is sound in BG is the stress on the investment package, on the need for coordination, on the structure of an invest-ment complex. But investment is not the only component in this package: and there is too much stress on the complementarity of final markets. What is needed is a package of policy measures containing

(a) complementary investments;

(b) actions to reform attitudes and insti-tutions, including the desire to invest, but also the ability and willingness to work, (which may involve raising *consumption*), to organise and manage and in particular to administer politically;

(c) a carefully thought-out timetable showing the sequence of the various meas-

3. "The difficulty caused by the small size of the market relates to individual investment in-centives in any single line of production taken by itself. At least in principle, the difficulty van-ishes in the case of a more or less synchronized application of capital to a wide range of different industries. Here is an escape from the deadlock; here the result is an over-all enlargement of the market. People working with more and better tools in a number of complementary projects be-come each others' customers. Most industries catering for mass consumption are complemen-tary in the sense that they provide a market for, and thus support, each other. This basic comple-mentarity stems, in the last analysis, from the diversity of human wants. The case for 'balanced growth' rests on the need for a 'balanced diet.'" *Problems of Capital Formation in Underdevel-oped Countries*, pp. 11f.

4. *Op., cit.*, p. 279.

ures which would be determined by tech-nological, political and sociological factors;

(d) controls checking undesirable or less desirable investments; and

(e) policies designed to weaken or elim-inate obstacles and inhibitions to develop-ment, including resistances induced by measures (a) to (d).

2.4 A BALANCED VIEW OF BALANCED GROWTH *

In the preceding section, the doctrine of balanced growth has been offered on the one hand as a possible solution and one with some educational merit for under-developed countries, but on the other hand as an incomplete, implausible, and even potentially dangerous solution. Perhaps it is well now to amplify this judgment by standing back and taking a broader view of the problems involved. For this purpose, the elementary sketch of an under-developed economy may be re-introduced. There are several distinct roads to eco-nomic growth.

1) In the first place and most obviously, there is the increase in productivity in agri-culture. It is not unnatural that foreign missions to underdeveloped countries should emphasize this road to economic growth: any visitor to an underdeveloped country will observe, first, that the bulk of the population—about 80 per cent in our sketch—is employed in agriculture; and, second, that agriculture is carried on at a particularly low level of productivity, not only in relation to agriculture in more advanced countries, but also in relation to other occupations in the same underde-veloped country. Higher productivity in agriculture must certainly be one of the main roads to economic growth. When it occurs it would normally solve the market-

* From Hans W. Singer, "Balanced Growth in Economic Development," *Economic Growth: Ra-tionale, Problems, Cases,* edited by Eastin Nelson, University of Texas Press, Austin, 1960, pp. 81-5. Reprinted by permission.

ing difficulty; the higher incomes of farmers will provide expanded markets for industries and, according to Engel's Law, part of the additional demand is likely to be for nonagricultural products. Note, however, that the solution of the marketing difficulty through higher agricultural productivity is by no means automatic: where the higher productivity results in a higher level of feeding for the extended family of the subsistance farmer, it is still clearly a good thing—but it does not remove the marketing difficulty from the path of structural change. Where improvements in agricultural productivity occur in relation to commercial crops, and even more so where they occur in relation to export crops, we can be reasonably certain that such improvements will create pre-conditions for growth, and enable us to dispense with the balanced-investment package as a specific remedy for marketing troubles. Where agriculture productivity rises within a system of subsistence farming, it should normally be possible for an enlightened government to link this rise in productivity with institutional changes that would utilize it as a foundation of growth. For example, where the higher agricultural productivity is accompanied by the offer of "incentive goods" to farmers which will induce them to develop a propensity to "truck, barter, and exchange" as their output increases, growth becomes possible as a result. Furthermore, an increase in agricultural productivity, in so far as it releases labor from the farms, creates part of that elasticity of factor supply which makes the balanced-investment package possible.

2) A second road to economic growth is improvement of productivity outside agriculture, specifically in industry. There is plenty of evidence to show enormous scope for such improvement. It would indeed be surprising if it were otherwise, considering the lack of experience in handling capital, the scarcity of managerial

skills, the absence of supporting managerial services and of external economies, and the absence of maintenance and repair facilities. We may perhaps add to this list the fact that the technology used is an alien growth imported from abroad, and was therefore not developed in line with the requirements and resource endowments of the under-developed countries. . . . Such nonagricultural improvements may be not so obvious, especially to the outside observer, as the need for higher productivity in agriculture. But even though agriculture may employ 70 per cent to 80 per cent of the total population, it does not normally account for more than half the national income. It follows that a given degree of improvement in the nonagricultural sectors will increase total real incomes by about as much as the same degree of agricultural improvement. Investments designed to raise nonagricultural productivity, by lowering real cost curves, will create "markets" where none existed before, and they do so without the need for a broadly based investment package.

3) The promotion of export trade is a third means of stimulating economic growth. The low-level equilibrium deadlock of real incomes and markets exists only in a closed economy, or for the world as a whole. In any individual underdeveloped country with significant foreign trade—and that means nearly all underdeveloped countries—some of the markets lie abroad in highly developed countries, and hence are not limited by the low domestic incomes. These markets are, of course, also limited: by real incomes abroad, by competition from possibly lower cost competitors, and by technological changes. Furthermore, the notorious instability of world commodity prices may make markets abroad particularly hazardous for the specialized exporter. All the same, export promotion offers a historically and analytically most important

method of by-passing the marketing dead-lock, offering opportunities for economic growth without the balanced-investment package.

4) A fourth means of improving the economic status of an underdeveloped country is import substitution. A country engaged in foreign trade has established domestic markets presently supplied by imports from abroad. Import substitution, like export promotion, thus offers an opportunity of growth in happy disregard of the need for an investment package. The protective tariff has historically been a major alternative to the balanced-investment package, in the early stages of development. Arthur Lewis' "Report on the Industrialization of the Gold Coast" provides the *locus classicus* for this unbalanced, yet effective, approach.

5) In relation to the improvement of productivity, there is a fifth approach to economic growth, via building up the economic infrastructure. Here, perhaps, investment in transport facilities is most obviously an alternative to the balanced-investment package as a method of creating new markets. The absence of markets in underdeveloped countries is not merely a question of the specific economic framework and institutions in which the incomes are earned. If the division of labor depends on the extent of the market, the market in turn depends on the extent to which certain facilities are available. Transport is the most obvious of these facilities. The doctrine of balanced economic growth is right in emphasizing the creation of markets as a key problem, but one can create markets by methods other than by inducing balanced demand.

6) Unbalanced investment, a sixth means of encouraging economic growth, and quite apart from foreign trade, appears at first paradoxical. It would be unrealistic to assume a state of perfect harmony— even the harmony of the deadlock—

between markets and supplies. The doctrine of balanced growth seems to assume that in making decisions on the allocation of resources in an underdeveloped country we start from scratch. That, of course, is not so. Rather, we start with a situation which incorporates the effects of previous investment and previous developments. This means that at any given point of time there are types of investment which are not in themselves balanced-investment packages, but which are complementary to existing investments, and which thus bring the total stock of capital nearer balance. We must thus distinguish between balance as the end result at which to aim, and balance as the method of approach. Where you start with imbalance, you need further imbalance in order to come closer to balance. It may be said that this still leaves the concept of the balanced-investment package valid, only stretching it over several investment periods. Thus, while we may be aiming at balance as an investment criterion, we achieve this objective by unbalanced investment.

We have now described six alternative approaches other than those singled out by the doctrine of "balanced growth." Each of these alternative approaches could conceivably, if successfully pursued, resolve the marketing deadlock which gave origin to the doctrine of balanced growth. Thus balanced growth should be judged not as a sole cure for the evil correctly diagnosed but as one of several possible cures. Which of the various cures will be the most appropriate will then depend on specific situations, and more particularly on the total volume of available resources. In this respect, the specific cure of the balanced-investment package does not compare well in the early stages of development because it requires large resources—in fact larger resources than most expositors of the doctrine seem to realize. The balanced-investment package cannot logically be confined to a group of projects which are self-sup-porting on the demand side; the package must include investment in agriculture and in the infrastructure. The cure is far from being the sole cure; in addition, it is an expensive cure and one which is most effective when taken as a mixture with other prescriptions.

But having thus defined the limitations of the doctrine, we are now perhaps in a better position also to appreciate its merits: the combination of self-supporting projects can serve to raise the productivity of invest-ment. In particular, it can prevent the creation of "white elephants"—projects without a market—which dot the landscape in so many underdeveloped countries. As between alternative appropriations of *given* resources, the balanced-investment package has an inherent superiority—wherever the available resources are sufficient for such a package.

There is another lesson which we can learn from the doctrine of balanced growth. The inducement to invest will be greatly increased by expectation of expanding markets and expanding incomes. Inflation-ary expectations are one way of increasing the inducement to invest; an expectation of real growth would be just as effective—perhaps more effective. It is not sufficient that complementary investment which will provide markets actually go forward; it is necessary also that it be seen or known, or at least assumed, to go forward. For this reason, in any development program of an underdeveloped country it is crucially important to create a general sense of moving forward. The very formulation of

development programs may be helpful in creating such a sense of moving forward—more specifically, I believe that this is also one of the most important effects of the community development movement in India. Balanced growth can play a part in improving what in trade cycle theory is perhaps rather vaguely called "the state of business confidence." A low-level deadlock of incomes and markets can be due to excessive self-justifying pessimism concern-ing future markets, particularly where there is a long history of stagnation or eco-nomic troubles. It is, however, not so easy for excessive optimism to be self-justifying —the inexorable limitation of resources stands in the way. Where the low-level equilibrium has been determined by exces-sive pessimism rather than by resource limi-tation, the doctrine of balanced growth acquires considerable theoretical as well as practical merit.

Finally, let us remember that the objec-tions to the doctrine of balanced growth will be greatly reduced and finally vanish as the available resources increase in the course of economic growth. Thus inter-preted, the doctrine should stimulate underdeveloped countries to undertake the necessary sacrifices in the early stages of development; it dangles before them a car-rot—the hope that one day when resources have become big enough, balanced-invest-ment packages will become possible. Hav-ing labored to the top, the balanced-investment package will help them to "slide down the other side of the roof," into the promised land of cumulative growth and compound interest.

3. MANPOWER AND EDUCATION

3.1 Investment in Human Capital—Note

Although the objective of adding to the stock of physical capital has dominated investment discussions, it has now become

evident that a high priority must also be assigned to investment in human capital. As part of the reaction to an excessive reli-ance on the accumulation of physical capital, it is increasingly recognized that the acceleration of development may be thwarted by a deficiency in the knowledge and skills embodied in human beings.

Many studies of economic growth in advanced countries confirm the importance of non-material investment. These statistical investigations indicate that output has increased at a higher rate than can be explained by an increase in only the inputs of labor and physical capital. The "residual" difference between the rate of increase in output and the rate of increase in physical capital and labor encompasses many "unidentified factors," but a prominent element is the improvement in the quality of inputs. Although some of this progress may be incorporated in physical capital, the improvements in intangible human qualities are more significant.[1]

Several studies of American growth, for example, indicate that the largest fraction of the rate of growth of income should be attributed to education and the growth of knowledge and know-how, as well as the increased efficiency of physical capital due to advances in technology and changes in economic organization.[2] One of the more extensive investigations attributes some 23 per cent of the growth in real national income in the United States between 1929

and 1957 to the increased education of the labor force and another contribution of approximately 20 per cent of total growth to the advance of "technological" knowledge and "managerial" knowledge which permitted more to be produced with a given quantity of resources.[3] The contributions of education and the increase in knowledge during this period were each larger than that due to the increase in inputs of physical capital, which contributed only 15 per cent of the total increase in real national income. Similarly, for the longer period 1889 to 1957 in the United States, another study concludes that among the more important causal forces at work in the process of productivity advance have been the growing relative outlays for education and health that have increased the average productive powers of the population, and the rising outlays for research and development that have improved the organization, processes, and instruments of production.[4]

These studies reveal that the usual concept of capital formation misses this important ingredient of economic development—the investment in human beings as productive agents. For purposes of measurement, capital formation is usually identified with the net increase of land, structures, durable equipment, commodity stocks, and foreign claims. But the capital stock should be interpreted more broadly to include the body of knowledge possessed by the population and the capacity and

1. Professor Schultz contends that the omission of economies of scale and the neglect of improvements in the quality of material capital are only minor sources of discrepancy between the rates of growth of inputs and outputs compared with the improvements in human capacity that have been omitted. T. W. Schultz, "Investment in Human Capital," *American Economic Review*, March 1961, p. 6.

2. Moses Abramovitz, *Resource and Output Trends in the United States since 1870*, National Bureau of Economic Research, Occasional Paper 52, New York, 1956, also in *American Economic Review, Papers and Proceedings*, May 1956, pp. 5-23; Robert M. Solow, "Technical Change and the Aggregate Production Function," *Review of Economics and Statistics*, August 1957, pp. 312-20; S. Fabricant, *Basic Facts on Productivity Change*, National Bureau of Economic Research, Occasional Paper 63, New York, 1959; John W. Kendrick, *Productivity Trends in the United States*, Princeton, 1961.

3. Edward F. Denison, *The Sources of Economic Growth in the United States*, Supplementary Paper No. 13, Committee for Economic Developement, New York, 1962; also, Denison, "Education, Economic Growth, and Gaps in Information," *Journal of Political Economy*, October 1962, pp. 124-9.

4. Kendrick, *op. cit.*, p. 14. According to Kendrick, over the period 1889 to 1957, the combined input index of physical capital and labor increased at an average rate of 1.9 per cent per annum, and the output index increased about 3.5 per cent per annum, leaving a "residual" increase of about 1.6 per cent per annum.

training of the population to use it effectively. Expenditures on education and training, improvement of health, and research contribute to productivity by raising the quality of human capital, and these outlays yield a continuing return in the future. If these expenditures are considered as capital expenditures, then the proportion of capital formation in national income in the rich countries would be much larger than is conventionally indicated in national accounts that treat these expenditures under the flow of goods to ultimate consumers rather than under capital. But since poor countries do not make many such investments in the formation of human capital, this broad interpretation of capital would not increase significantly the proportion of their national incomes devoted to capital formation. From this point of view, it may well be, as Professor Kuznets suggests, that instead of a difference in net capital formation proportions between 10 per cent in rich and, say, 3 per cent in poor countries, the true difference is closer to between 30 per cent or over and 3 per cent.[5]

While investment in human beings has been a major source of growth in advanced countries, the negligible amount of human investment in underdeveloped countries has done little to extend the capacity of the people to meet the challenge of accelerated development. The characteristic of "economic backwardness" is still manifest in several particular forms:[6] low labor efficiency, factor immobility, limited specialization in occupations and in trade, a deficient supply of entrepreneurship, and customary values and traditional social institutions that minimize the incentives

for economic change. The slow growth in knowledge is an especially severe restraint on progress. The economic quality of human capital remains low when there is little knowledge of what natural resources are available. the alternative production techniques that are possible, the necessary skills, the existing market conditions and opportunities, and the institutions that might be created to favor economizing effort and economic rationality. An improvement in the quality of the "human factor" is then as essential as investment in physical capital. An advance in knowledge and the diffusion of new ideas and objectives are necessary to remove economic backwardness and instill the human abilities and motivations that are more favorable to economic achievement.[7] Although investment in material capital may indirectly achieve some lessening of the economic backwardness of the human resources, the direct and more decisive means is through investment in human beings.

Emphasizing the weight that should be given to the growth in the quality of human resources, Professor Schultz illustrates the possible implications of the quality component as follows:

Suppose there were an economy with the land and the physical reproducible capital including the available techniques of production that we now possess in the United States, but which attempted to function under the following restraints: there would be no person available who had any on-the-job experience, none who had any schooling, no one who had any information about the economy except of his locality, each individual would be bound to his locality, and the average life span of

5. Simon Kuznets, "Toward a Theory of Economic Growth," *National Policy for Economic Welfare at Home and Abroad,* edited by R. Leckachman, New York, 1955, pp. 39-40.

6. Hla Myint, "An Interpretation of Economic Backwardness," *Oxford Economic Papers,* June 1954, pp. 132-63.

7. For psychological and sociological interpretations of the relationships between economic change and basic personality needs, motivations, and values, see D. C. McClelland, *The Achieving Society,* Princeton, 1961; George M. Foster, *Traditional Cultures and the Impact of Technological Change,* New York, 1962; E. E. Hagen, *On the Theory of Social Change,* Homewood, 1962.

people would be only forty years. Surely, production would fall catastrophically. It is certain that there would be both low output and extraordinary rigidity of economic organization until the capabilities of the people were raised markedly by investing in them. Let me now take a Bunyan-like step and suppose a set of human resources with as many but no more capabilities per man than existed as of 1900 or even as of 1929 in the United States. The adverse effects on production in either case would undoubtedly be large. To continue these speculations, suppose that by some miracle India, or some other low-income country like India, were to acquire as it were overnight a set of natural resources, equipment, and structures including techniques of production comparable per person to ours—what could they do with them, given the existing skills and knowledge of the people? Surely the imbalance between the stock of human and non-human capital would be tremendous.[8]

Recent experience with attempts to accumulate physical capital at a rapid rate in poor countries bears out the necessity of due attention to human capital. It has become evident that the effective use of physical capital itself is dependent upon human capital. If there is underinvestment in human capital, the rate at which additional physical capital can be productively utilized will be limited since technical, professional, and administrative people are needed to make effective use of material capital. In many newly developing countries the absorptive capacity for physical capital has proved to be low because the extension of human capabilities has failed to keep pace with the accumulation of physical capital.[9]

8. T. W. Schultz, "Reflections on Investment in Man," *Journal of Political Economy*, Supplement: October 1962, pp. 2-3.

9. For strong arguments that "the experience of planning seems to suggest that knowledge (and certainly not investment resources) is the most important scarce factor in underdeveloped countries with otherwise favorable social climate," see B. Horvat, "The Optimum Rate of Investment," *Economic Journal*, December 1958, pp. 751-3.

While the case for investment in human resources is gaining wider acceptance, the means of attaining an increase in this type of investment have still received only superficial consideration compared with the intensive investigations that have been made of the problems of investment in physical goods.

It is not difficult to identify the more important categories of activities that improve human capabilities. As Professor Schultz suggests, a typical list would be:

(1) health facilities and services, broadly conceived to include all expenditures that affect the life expectancy, strength and stamina, and the vigor and vitality of a people; (2) on-the-job training, including old-style apprenticeship organized by firms; (3) formally organized education at the elementary, secondary, and higher levels; (4) study programs for adults that are not organized by firms, including extension programs notably in agriculture; (5) migration of individuals and families to adjust to changing job opportunities.[10]

Underlying each of these activities, however, are a number of questions that should be studied more seriously.[11] At the outset, the problem of measurement presents several difficulties: is it possible to separate the consumption and investment part of expenditures on these activities? Can the particular resources entering into each of these components be identified and measured? Can the rates of returns from these activities be identified and measured? And can the rate of return on investment in education be compared with the rate of return on investment in some other alternative use? As yet, no completely satisfactory empirical procedure for answering these

10. Schultz, "Investment in Human Capital," *op. cit.*, p. 9.

11. The remainder of our discussion concentrates on education and training. For a consideration of human capital formation through health services, see Selma J. Mushkin, "Health as an Investment," *Journal of Political Economy*, Supplement: October 1962, pp. 129-57.

questions has been devised. Although a few studies have recently made noteworthy steps in the direction of measuring some consequences of an increase in tangible capital,[12] no empirical study of investment in human capital is yet free from some arbitrary elements, and more statistical evidence is needed.

Another problem of particular importance to a country engaged in development programming, is to determine at what phase of development the formation of intangible capital is most significant. It can be argued that a high rate of increase in the demand for improvements in the quality of inputs appears only at a fairly advanced phase of development. The early industrialization in Western Europe, for example, appears to have been accomplished without requiring as prerequisites marked improvements in skills and knowledge and health of workers.[13] And the contribution of education to American growth has been most pronounced in the more recent decades, while capital investment was more important in earlier decades.[14] Unlike the earlier historical situation, however, it may now be necessary to have a relatively high level of skill and much more knowledge to take advantage of the more complex equipment and techniques that may be obtained from advanced countries.

There are additional questions to be raised concerning what types of education should be emphasized, to what degree, and how soon. Some economists have such questions in mind when they criticize— from the viewpoint of the economic, though not social or moral, value—pro-posals for mass education or extensive systems of higher education in newly developing nations. They contend that these countries do not yet have an effective demand for large numbers of educated workers; it will take considerable time to raise the presently limited absorptive capacity of the economy for educated persons; and a poor country can not afford to pay for as much education as can rich countries.[15] Since educational outlays compete for resources that have an alternative use in directly productive investment, it is essential to determine what proportion of national income should be devoted to education. And within the educational system itself it is necessary to establish priorities for the various possible forms of education and training.

From the standpoint of accelerating development, the immediate requirements may call for emphasis on vocational and technical training and adult education rather than on a greatly expanded system of formal education. Considering its high cost and the problems of absorption that it raises, even the case for universal primary education is questionable. Professor Lewis expresses such skepticism in the following comments on African proposals:

The limited absorptive capacity of most West African economies today—especially owing to the backwardness of agriculture— makes frustration and dislocation inevitable if more than 50 per cent of children enter school. This, coupled with the high cost due to the high ratio of teachers' salaries to average national income, and with the time it takes to train large numbers of teachers properly, has taught some African countries to proceed with caution; to set the goal of universal schooling

12. For example, Mary Jean Bowman, "Human Capital: Concepts and Measures," in *Money, Growth, and Methodology,* Essays in Honor of Johan Akerman, Lund, 1961, pp. 147-68.

13. Cf. Schultz, "Investment in Human Capital in Poor Countries," in *Foreign Trade and Human Capital,* edited by P. D. Zook, Dallas, 1962, pp. 3-4, 11-12.

14. Denison, "Education, Economic Growth, and Gaps in Information," *op. cit.,* p. 127.

15. These arguments are cogently presented by W. Arthur Lewis, "Education and Economic Development," *International Social Science Journal,* Vol. XIV, No. 4, 1962, pp. 685-99; Thomas Balogh, "Misconceived Educational Programmes in Africa," *Universities Quarterly,* June 1962, pp. 243-9.

twenty years ahead or more, rather than the ten years ahead or less associated with the first flush of independence movements. Such a decision is regarded as highly controversial by those for whom literacy is a universal human right irrespective of cost.... On the other hand, considering that in most African territories less than 25 per cent of children aged six to fourteen are in school, a goal of 50 per cent within ten years may be held to constitute revolutionary progress.[16]

More immediately serious than the lack of universal primary education is the deficiency in secondary education. The most critical manpower requirement tends to be for people with a secondary education who can be managers, administrators, professional technicians (scientists, engineers, agronomists, doctors, economists, accountants, etc.), or sub-professional technical personnel (agricultural assistants, technical supervisors, nurses, engineering assistants, book-keepers, etc.). Lewis characterizes the products of secondary schools as "the officers and non-commissioned officers of an economic and social system. A small percentage goes on to university education, but the numbers required from the university are so small that the average country of up to five million inhabitants could manage tolerably well without a university of its own. Absence of secondary schools, however, is an enormous handicap.... The middle and upper ranks of business consist almost entirely of secondary school products, and these products are also the backbone of public administration."[17]

Also deserving of high priority is the infusion of new skills and knowledge into the agricultural sector. In order to achieve a system of modern agriculture, the quality of labor in agriculture needs to be improved as an input in its own right and also to allow the use of better forms of non-human capital (equipment, seeds, insecticides, etc.). In many countries that have experienced substantial increases in agricultural production, the key factor has not been new land or land that is superior for agriculture; nor has it been mainly the addition of reproducible capital. More importantly, the agricultural transformation has been based predominantly upon new skills and useful knowledge required to develop a modern agriculture.[18] Educational facilities for agriculture may also provide a way of encouraging rural school-leavers to take up work in the rural sector rather than migrating to the towns, and the special training of young school-leavers may allow them to act as the agents for introducing new and improved agricultural techniques.

For the broader problems of educational requirements, the making of "manpower surveys" (as discussed in the next selection) may furnish a useful basis for determining the principal skill shortages and what types of training activities should be emphasized. At least for the short term, the provision of agricultural extension services, training in mechanical and technical skills, and training in supervisory and administrative skills may contribute the most to fulfilling manpower requirements. After overcoming the immediate bottlenecks of scarce personnel in specific key occupations, the education system should then be devised to provide a balance between general education, pre-vocational preparation, and vocational education and training.

We may conclude that the recent attention to investment in human capital should prove salutary in cautioning against an overemphasis on non-human capital to the neglect of the more tangible factors. When considered for a poor country, however, investment in human capital calls for new approaches and special emphases that dif-

16. Lewis, *op. cit.*, p. 689.
17. *Ibid.*, pp. 688-90.

18. Cf. Schultz, "Investment in Human Capital in Poor Countries," *op. cit.*, p. 9.

fer from those in advanced economies. An extensive system of formal education is a commendable objective—but it must necessarily be a distant objective. Instead of attempting to imitate the educational system of an advanced country, newly developing countries may more suitably concentrate, at least in the early phases of their development programs, on methods of informal education and on the objectives of functional education. These efforts are less time-consuming, less costly, and more directly related to manpower requirements than is a formal educational system. As such, they are likely to prove most effective in improving the economic quality of human resources.

3.2 HUMAN RESOURCES DEVELOPMENT *

Most modernising economies are confronted simultaneously with two persistent, yet seemingly diverse, manpower problems: *the shortage of persons with critical skills* in the modernising sector and *surplus labour* in both the modernising and traditional sectors. Thus, the strategy of human resources development is concerned with the twofold objective of building skills and providing productive employment for unutilised or under-utilised manpower. The shortages and surplus of human resources, however, are not separate and distinct problems; they are very intimately related. Both have their roots in the changes which are inherent in the development process. Both are related in part to education. Both are aggravated as the tempo of modernisation is quickened. And, paradoxically, the shortage of persons with critical skills is one of the contributing causes of the surplus of people without jobs. Although the manpower problems of no two countries

* From Frederick H. Harbison, "Human Resources Development Planning in Modernising Economies," *International Labour Review*, Vol. LXXXV, No. 5, May 1962, pp. 2-5, 7-8, 20-24.

are exactly alike, there are some shortages and surpluses which appear to be universal in modernising societies.

The manpower shortages of modernising countries are quite easy to identify, and fall into several categories:

(1) In all modernising countries there is likely to be a shortage of highly educated professional manpower such as, for example, scientists, agronomists, veterinarians, engineers, and doctors. Such persons, however, usually prefer to live in the major cities rather than in the rural areas, where in many cases their services are most urgently needed. Thus, their shortage is magnified by their relative immobility. And, ironically, their skills are seldom used effectively. In West Africa and also in many Asian and Latin American countries, for example, graduate engineers may be found managing the routine operation of an electric power sub-station or doing the work of draughtsmen. Doctors may spend long hours making the most routine medical tests. The reason is obvious.

(2) The shortage of technicians, nurses, agricultural assistants, technical supervisors, and other sub-professional personnel is generally even more critical than the shortage of fully qualified professionals. For this there are several explanations. First, the modernising countries usually fail to recognise that the requirements for this category of manpower exceed by many times those for senior professional personnel. Second, the few persons who are qualified to enter a technical institute may also be qualified to enter a university, and they prefer the latter because of the higher status and pay which is accorded the holder of a university degree. Finally, there are often fewer places available in institutions providing intermediate training than in the universities.

(3) The shortage of top-level managerial and administrative personnel, in both the private and public sectors, is almost uni-

versal, as is the dearth of persons with entrepreneurial talents.

(4) Teachers are almost always in short supply, and their turnover is high because they tend to leave the teaching profession if and when more attractive jobs become available in government, politics, or private enterprise. The scarcity is generally most serious in secondary education, and particularly acute in the fields of science and mathematics. This shortage of competent teachers is a "master bottleneck" which retards the entire process of human resources development.

(5) In most modernising countries there are also shortages of craftsmen of all kinds as well as senior clerical personnel such as bookkeepers, secretaries, stenographers, and business machine operators.

(6) Finally, there are usually in addition several other miscellaneous categories of personnel in short supply, such as, for example, radio and television specialists, airplane pilots, accountants, economists, and statisticians.

I shall use the term "high-level manpower," or alternatively "human capital," as a convenient designation for the persons who fall into categories such as those mentioned above. The term "human capital formation," as used in this paper, is the process of acquiring and increasing the numbers of persons who have the skills, education, and experience which are critical for the economic and political development of a country. Human capital formation is thus associated with investment in man and his development as a creative and productive resource. It includes investment by society in education, investment by employers in training, as well as investment by individuals of time and money in their own development. Such investments have both qualitative and quantitative dimensions—i.e., human capital formation includes not only expenditure for education and training, but also the

development of attitudes toward productive activity.

As stressed earlier, a central problem of all modernising countries is to accelerate the process of human capital formation. Human capital, or high-level manpower, may be accumulated in several ways. It may be imported from abroad through a variety of means such as technical assistance, expatriate enterprises, hiring of consultants, or immigration. It may be developed in employment through on-the-job training, in-service programmes of formal training, management development seminars, part-time adult education classes, and many other means. It is also developed in employment through better organisation of work, creation of appropriate attitudes and incentives, and better management of people. It is accumulated through formal education in schools, technical training centres, colleges, universities and other institutions of higher learning. And finally, it may be developed as a by-product of modern military training.

The analysis of human capital formation is thus parallel and complementary to the study of the processes of savings and investment (in the material sense). In designing a strategy for development, one needs to consider the total stock of human capital required, its rates of accumulation, and its commitment to (or investment in) high-priority productive activities.

The rate of modernisation of a country is associated with both its stock and rate of accumulation of human capital. High-level manpower is needed to staff new and expanding government services, to introduce new systems of land use and new methods of agriculture, to develop new means of communication, to carry forward industrialisation, and to build the educational system. In other words, innovation, or the process of change from a static or traditional society, requires very large "doses" of strategic human capital.

The countries which are making the most rapid and spectacular innovations are invariably those which are under the greatest pressure to accumulate this kind of human capital at a fast rate. Here we may make two tentative generalisations:

First, the rate of accumulation of strategic human capital must always exceed the rate of increase in the labour force as a whole. In most countries, for example, the rate of increase in scientific and engineering personnel may need to be at least three times that of the labour force. Sub-professional personnel may have to increase even more rapidly. Clerical personnel and craftsmen may have to increase at least twice as fast as the labour force, and top managerial and administrative personnel should normally increase at a comparable rate.

Second, in most cases, the rate of increase in human capital will need to exceed the rate of economic growth. In newly developing countries which already are faced with critical shortages of highly skilled persons, the ratio of the annual increase in high-level manpower to the annual increase in national income may need to be as high as three to one, or even higher in those cases where expatriates are to be replaced by citizens of the developing countries.

The accumulation of high-level manpower to overcome skill bottlenecks is a never-ending process. Advanced industrial societies as well as underdeveloped countries are normally short of critical skills. Indeed, as long as the pace of innovation is rapid, the appetite of any growing country for high-level manpower is almost insatiable.

As indicated above, no two countries have exactly the same manpower problems. Some have unusually serious surpluses, and others have very specialised kinds of skill bottlenecks. Politicians and planners, therefore, need to make a systematic assessment of the human resources problems in their particular countries. Such assessment may be called "manpower analysis."

The objectives of manpower analysis are as follows: (1) the identification of the principal critical shortages of skilled manpower in each major sector of the economy, and an analysis of the reasons for such shortages; (2) the identification of surpluses, both of trained manpower as well as unskilled labour, and the reasons for such surpluses; and (3) the setting of forward targets for human resources development based upon reasonable expectations of growth. Such forward targets are best determined by a careful examination and comparison, sector by sector, of the utilisation of manpower in a number of countries which are somewhat more advanced politically, socially and economically.

Manpower analysis cannot always be based on an elaborate or exhaustive survey. It is seldom possible to calculate precisely the numbers of people needed in every occupation at some future time. But, whether statistics are available or not, the purpose of manpower analysis is to give a reasonably objective picture of a country's major human resources problems, the inter-relationships between these problems, and their causes, together with an informed guess as to probable future trends. Manpower analysis is both qualitative and quantitative, and it must be based upon wise judgment as well as upon available statistics. In countries where statistics are either unavailable or clearly unreliable, moreover, the initial manpower analysis may be frankly impressionistic. . . .

Once the manpower problems of a newly developing country are identified, a strategy must be developed to overcome them effectively. The essential components of such a strategy are the following: (1) the building of appropriate incentives; (2) the effective training of employed manpower, and (3) the rational development of formal education. These three elements are interdependent. Progress in one area is dependent upon progress in the other two. The country's leaders should not concentrate on only one or two of them at a time; they must plan an integrated attack on all three fronts at once.

The argument has been made that investments in formal education alone are not likely to solve either critical skill shortages or persistent labour surpluses in modernising societies. Investments in education are likely to contribute effectively to rapid growth only (1) if there are adequate incentives to encourage men and women to engage in the kinds of productive activity which are needed to accelerate the modernisation process; and (2) if appropriate measures are taken to shift a large part of the responsibility for training to the principal employing institutions. The building of incentives and the training of employed manpower, therefore, are necessary both as a means of economising on formal education and as a means of making the investment in it productive.

In the building of incentives, a cardinal principle is that the status and compensation attached to occupations should be related to their relative importance as measured by the high-priority needs of a developing society, and not to arbitrary levels of education, degrees, family status or political connections. This is essential for the accumulation of human capital and for its most effective utilisation. The surpluses of labour, particularly those connected with rural-urban migration and the unemployment of primary school leavers, may be reduced in part by a far-reaching programme of modernisation of agriculture and rural life as a counterpart to a programme of industrialisation. Because of rapidly increasing populations and the early emphasis on universal primary education, however, there will still be large numbers of unemployed or under-employed persons in most modernising societies.

The potentialities of fully utilising government agencies, private employers, expatriate firms and technical experts as trainers and developers of manpower, though very great indeed, are seldom exploited fully. Thus, a key element in the strategy of human resources development is to shift as much as possible the responsibility for training to the major employing institutions, and to provide the necessary technical guidance to enable these institutions to develop in-service training programmes along modern lines.

The third component of the strategy is wise judgment and prudent investment in building the system of formal education. This calls for giving priority to investment in and development of broad secondary education. It requires that the costs of universal primary education be kept as low as possible by applying new technologies which can make effective use of relatively untrained teachers and which can multiply the contribution of a very small but strategic group of highly trained professionals. Finally, in the area of higher education, the strategy stresses the need for giving priority to investment in intermediate-level training institutions and the scientific and engineering faculties of universities. But this does not mean that the production of liberally educated persons should be neglected.

The three essential components of the strategy are interdependent, and call for a well-designed and integrated attack on all three fronts at once. And it is imperative that the strategy of building and utilising human resources be an integral part of a country's national development programme. The strategy assumes that the politicians of the country are firmly committed to the goal of accelerated development, and that they have the will to do the things which are imperative for its attainment.

There are, however, obstacles which lie in the path of implementation of a consistent strategy of human resources development. The most formidable, perhaps, is traditional thinking. For example, those who have experience with traditional methods of elementary education are suspicious of new technologies which might reduce teaching costs. Most of the leaders of the underdeveloped countries are unaware of the great strides made recently in methodology of in-service training in the advanced countries. The thought of overhauling the wage and salary structure of government ministries is frightening. The idea of tampering with higher education to turn out larger proportions of sub-professional personnel is not consistent with the kind of indoctrination one may have had at Oxford, Cambridge or the Sorbonne. And the very thought that there is a strategic relationship between incentive, in-service training and formal education is strange and difficult to grasp. Yet those who preach the revolutionary doctrine of planned, accelerated growth—more rapid and more sweeping than anything before —must be prepared to reject outworn concepts and employ the most modern techniques available. In their approach to development, they must be more modern in many respects than the advanced nations from which they seek aid and advice.

The governmental structure of the developing countries is another obstacle. Thinking and planning tends to be in compartments. The ministries of education deal only with formal education, and some do not even have jurisdiction over technical education. Ministries of labour are concerned with employment standards and

some aspects of training skilled and semi-skilled labour. The ministries of industry, commerce, and agriculture are likely to be preoccupied with technical and financial questions. The economic development ministries or development boards, if they exist at all, are generally concerned with physical capital formation, the balance of payments, and other urgent economic questions. The traditional economic planners are likely to banish human resources development to that "no-man's-land" of social welfare. Thus, no ministry or board is in a position to see the problem as a whole. Each grasps rather blindly for some programme of manpower development, and in justification makes wild claims for its indispensable role in promoting rapid growth.

3.3 ROLE OF EDUCATION *

That education is one of the few sure roads to economic progress is a contemporary creed. But there are too few facts with which to support this faith, and stated in the usual way it is far too vague. We need to know *how* education enters into political or economic transformation, in what ways it interacts with other social processes, and in what sorts of time patterns. For which parts of the labor force is literacy essential? What, under various conditions, is the most fruitful allocation of resources between secondary and primary schooling, and with what distribution of responsibilities and costs? In what form and in which circumstances should technological training be given priority over academic? How do patterns of incentive and aspiration affect the outcome of this or that kind of schooling? How can incentives be modified to improve the con-

* From Mary Jean Bowman and C. Arnold Anderson, "The Role of Education in Development," *Development of Emerging Countries. An Agenda for Research,* The Brookings Institution, Washington, D.C., 1962, pp. 153, 155-60. Reprinted by permission.

tribution of education to diverse sorts of change? How different are the methods for transferring "know-how" from those that spread knowledge? When, where, and to what extent should resources be devoted to the formation of human capital rather than physical capital? Are there situations in which education may even obstruct economic advance? Though these questions are asked and even boldly answered by planners and economic advisers, the answers commonly are sophistic and wishful. Estimates of man-power needs and their educational implications facilitate planning, but they contribute little to identifying the ways in which this or that sort of education might impinge on the economy.

Five basic propositions underlie the approach to growth taken in this chapter and condition the kinds of hypotheses deemed important in identifying promising research.

1. Economic growth is a process of structural transformation. Because it involves basic changes in the structure of a society, it cannot be understood by empirical or theoretical approaches that assume too simple a continuity or that look primarily at aggregates and averages.

2. There are many alternative combinations of factors that can foster growth or prevent it. But there are limits to the substitutions consistent with given levels of development. This holds both within the educational sphere and as between education and other programs.

3. Attitudes and preferences within a population strongly condition the interplay between education and other aspects of development; they are also variables subject to change and influenced by the nature of perceived opportunities.

4. The "multiplier" and "external econ-

omies" concepts of the economists and the rates-of-diffusion analyses of geographers and sociologists constitute a promising framework for dealing with development. Sustained, relatively rapid growth depends on the strength of the multipliers.

5. The concept of "balanced growth" is either a contradiction in terms or highly ambiguous. Decidedly unbalanced growth may be the only potentially rapid growth for many underdeveloped countries. A breakthrough may call for planned imbalance. This does not, however, mean there is no need for coordination between educational and other developments nor does it reject the principle of complementarity in regard to the components of a concentrated push—perhaps best described as selectively focused "integrated sets".

Probably Johan Akerman has put more stress than any other economist on the significance of structural transformation in his theory of structural limits and transitions, which relates to political events as well as to endogenous economic change.[1] Though he has concentrated on the histories of today's industrialized nations, his work suggests questions about earlier stages of development and by implication about the role of education in different settings. Following his line of thinking, formal schooling and other types of education probably play different roles in some settings than in others. (This amounts to incorporating point 2 in point 1.)

Starting from a more orthodox orientation, Eric Lundberg reaches a similar position but within a single major structural frame. He cites Solow and Aukrust[2] who with other writers, especially at the National Bureau of Economic Research, dem-

1. Johan Akerman, *Theory of Industrialism* (Lund: Gleerup, 1960).
2. See R. M. Solow, "Technical Change and the Aggregate Production Function," *Review of Economics and Statistics* (August 1957); O. Aukrust and J. Bjerke, "Real Capital in Norway," *Income and Wealth Series VIII* (London: Bowes, 1959).

onstrate that increases in physical capital together with increases in the labor force explain only a part of the rise in national incomes since 1929. He then poses the question: Does this mean that allocation among investments is unimportant to economic growth? That is, if the total is relatively unimportant, can its parts be important? He concludes that they can be, and are. The averages are misleading, including declining as well as expanding industries; marginal rates of return on investments in the latter may be very high and play a major part in growth even though returns in the more stagnant sectors may be small or negative. This general proposition relates to early as well as later stages of development; applied to education, it requires consideration of marginal returns to different components in the education mix under varying conditions.

Though Akerman's and Lundberg's views differ in many ways, both challenge implicitly the meaning of "balanced" growth. Indeed that notion is questioned by conceiving of growth as structural change, especially when growth and structural change are rapid. Taken together with the more sociological studies of the influence of attitudes on societal processes and with the many studies of diffusion processes, such considerations lead to proposition (5).

Though most Western writers of late have argued for balanced development, there are important exceptions. Moreover, there is a respectable history behind some elements in the unbalanced growth approach. It is clearly involved in Joseph Schumpeter's cycle theory and in Edwin Gay's stress on "disruptive innovating energy." More recently related but different arguments have been presented by Hirschman and Streeten, among others, and even Nurkse admits a possible positive role for successive limited imbalances as a growth mechanism (distinguishing the mechanism

from the social end of "balanced development"). Soviet economists recently have been pursuing the idea of planned imbalance for growth, which is hardly surprising in the light of Soviet economic history. Amidst complex and mathematical models, one basic idea is essentially simple: rapid growth occurs, and must occur, unevenly, by concentrating effort now in one sphere and then (after a period of only partial digestion) in another. The arguments do not center on planning versus a "free" economy; in the Soviet as in the Schumpeter and Gay conceptions imbalances are important, though they differ with respect to how much imbalance occurs, in what forms, with what timing, and at what costs.

The position taken in this chapter shares the conception of successive imbalances as part of the growth mechanism, and it rests in part on some of the same economic arguments. However, it is in much greater degree a social-science as distinct from a strictly economic approach. It pays more attention to variations in socio-economic starting points, and there is a broader sort of multiplier and diffusion theory at its core.

This brings us back to propositions (3) and (4) concerning attitudes and diffusion. A few remarks here will anticipate later discussion. Because growth, especially in take-off and early stages, changes attitudes (by plan or incidentally), it necessarily entails conflict. Criticisms of aid programs commonly give too little recognition to this fact. Education that feeds into growth in such circumstances becomes entangled with complex processes of transforming attitudes; it is therefore inevitably a threat as well as a promise. Moreover, the less favorable the prevailing attitudes with respect to change, the more likely it is that a breakthrough will require concentrated efforts at particular points in the economy and in the educational system, with periods of highly visible and relatively extreme imbalance. Yet imbalance does not assure growth and may throttle it. Growth depends on unleashing multiplier and diffusion processes. These are not merely the multipliers of the economist's money-flow models or his external economies and inter-industry employment and investment multipliers; they are also attitude and education multipliers. They do not occur evenly through time and space. A more generalized multiplier and diffusion theory is needed, one that joins the approaches of the economist with those of other social sciences, and one that takes the time element more explicitly into account along with possible discontinuities and minimal reaction thresholds. Education falls into place in this sort of framework.

Finally, a sixth basic propostion should perhaps be added, though it is a derivative of what has been said. The fact that single factors in development cannot be isolated means that to understand the part education plays in any given situation (or the failure of educational advance to be followed by other sorts of development) requires viewing education in a broad context. Alternative sets of critical factors, each necessary for growth but alone insufficient, must be found. Both dissection of "education" into components and consideration of noneducational factors are involved. If this view is correct, attempts to assess the influence of education by studying aggregate inputs and outputs, while essential in plotting the scale of possible contribution from the human factor, must be inconclusive. Yet approaches from one or another special angle, a bit at a time, are the unavoidable steps in making a rounded picture. The crude data summarized below are such partial abstractions, used here mainly as bases for rapid incursions into vaguely known territory.

Briefly, comparisons made by the authors between educational indexes and per capita incomes around the world revealed the following:[3]

1. Correlations of literacy rates with income were very loose, and nonlinear. Only countries with 90 per cent literacy or better had 1955 per capita incomes of over $500, and, where literacy rates were under 30 per cent, incomes were under $200. However, countries with incomes under $100 had literacy rates ranging up to 60 per cent and those with incomes between $100 and $200 included countries with literacy as high as 70 to 80 per cent. Moreover, in the 30 to 70 per cent literacy range there was virtually no correlation between literacy and income.

2. Correlations between 1955 income and elementary school attendance in the 1930's were moderate ($r^2 = .59$) but lower than the reverse sequence relating 1938 income to 1950-1954 elementary school attendance ($r^2 = .71$). When countries with literacy rates of over 90 per cent in 1950-1954 were excluded, both correlations were lowered, but the difference between the two variances was sharpened, with r^2 values of .21 and .57 respectively.

3. Excluding countries with 90 per cent or more literate in 1950-1954, post-primary enrollment rates added virtually nothing to the correlation between 1950-1954 literacy and 1955 per capita incomes. The zero order correlation gave an r^2 of .43 and adding post-primary enrollment rates raised this only to .44.

4. Far Eastern countries had low incomes relative to their education indexes. However, for the world as a whole the amount of cultivated land per capita provided no explanation of the income variance unexplained by the various education

3. This analysis is to be published under the title "Concerning the Role of Education in Development" in a forthcoming symposium sponsored by the University of Chicago Committee for the Comparative Study of New Nations, Clifford Geertz, ed.

indexes. Neither did measures of energy potentials.

5. South American countries manifested diverse patterns, but predominantly they were characterized by stagnation in both educational and income development after reaching an intermediate educational position.

These findings point up the importance of examining the processes by which education may enter into and interact with other factors in economic development. Clearly, there are problems not only of take-off but also of sustaining educational diffusion as well as economic growth. Clearly, also, a relatively large elite is no guarantee of progress in the less developed areas. There can be wasteful investments in education as in any other sphere. And potentially fruitful investments in education can be wasted by failure of the society to make effective use of its educated people.

3.4 INVESTMENT IN THE SOCIAL INFRASTRUCTURE *

This idea [of investment in social and human capital] has proved attractive to many people, both economists and non-economists, and there have been attempts to consider how to strike a correct balance between investment in material capital and investment in human capital, between economic development and social development. Unfortunately, however, as currently stated, this idea remains rather vague, based upon an analogy which has not been systematically drawn. Thus, as a possible subject for discussion among social scientists of different disciplines, we may begin by drawing attention to some of the

conceptual problems as they appear to an economist.

To begin with, it should be noted that even with respect to material capital, there is no simple mechanical relationship between the amount of resources invested and the *value* of the capital formation which results from it. Although national income statistics automatically equate the two, it can readily be seen that say an amount of one million pounds of savings invested may result in capital goods which may be worth many times more or many times less than one million pounds, depending on how and where it is invested and how far the resultant capital goods serve the future productive requirements of the country and how far people value the products which these capital goods can help to produce. In the extreme case, it has not been unknown for large sums of money to be so wrongly invested as to serve no useful purpose so that the value of capital formation resulting from them is zero. The problems of trying to establish a causal quantitative relation between the expenditure on resources invested and the value of capital formation which results from it are multiplied manifold when we move from material capital to human capital. To start with the most general difficulty: in dealing with material capital the economists have a reasonably clear idea of what they mean by the productive structure and how an additional piece of material capital may contribute to it, either by changing and improving its efficiency or by fitting into an identifiable gap in it. But no such established conceptual framework exists when we move to human capital. By analogy, we must suppose that the value of a given investment in human capital will depend on its contribution to the "social infrastructure," either by improving and changing this infrastructure or by fitting into a gap in it. But what is this "social infrastructure" and in what

* From Hla Myint, "Social Flexibility, Social Discipline and Economic Growth," Paper presented to UNESCO Expert Working Group on Social Prerequisites to Economic Growth, Kyrenia, Cyprus, April 1963; mimeographed, UNESCO/SS/SP/13, Paris, December 1962, pp. 3-6.

direction do we wish to change and improve it?

At this point the economist will look askance at the social scientists from other disciplines, many of whom have been using the fashionable concept of "social and human capital" as much as some of the economists. If hard pressed to define the "social infrastructure" further, the economist can only carry the analogy one or two stages more. He would suppose that in the same way as there is an intimate connexion between the material production structure of a country and its natural resources, there would be a similar connexion between the social infrastructure and the social conditions and characteristics of a country. Material production structure represents the adaptation and improvement of natural resources through investment in material capital. Some investment would exploit the special advantages of these natural resources and other investment would make up for the deficiencies in these natural resources. He would then have to ask the other social scientists whether this analogy is meaningful when extended to cover the relationship between the social infrastructure and the social conditions of a country.

Carrying the analogy a stage further, the economist would point out that the consequences of a wrong choice of investment project may be very different between material capital and human capital. Frequently, a wrong investment in material capital and attempts to salvage it have a distorting effect on the whole production structure. For instance, a wrongly sited railway system or a "show piece" but uneconomic factory may be maintained by government subsidy, grants of exclusive monopolistic privileges or by protection against foreign competitors. But at the last resort a wrong investment in material capital can be scrapped when it proves too expensive to salvage. Wrong choice of investment in human capital will presumably have similar distorting effects on the social infrastructure, but wrong pieces of human capital cannot be scrapped; they tend to be self-perpetuating and have the habit not merely of distorting but actually of disrupting the social infrastructure. For instance, the growing problem of graduate unemployment in Asian countries, due to the production of too much of the wrong type of "human capital" is a very clear illustration of this danger.[1]

In this connexion, it may be noted that for the economist the material production structure of a country is a different thing from the economic institutions which mobilize resources and feed them into the production structure. But when we come to the concept of social infrastructure, the distinction between these two different functions is blurred. As currently used, the idea of social infrastructure seems to serve both as the social equivalent of the production structure which absorbs resources and also to have the more active function of the social and institutional framework which mobilizes and allocates resources. This makes assessment of the productivity in investment in human capital doubly difficult. For instance, increased educational opportunities, say through films, radio and other mass media, may widen the horizons of the people and stimulate the growth of new wants (through demonstration effects) and new ideas. This may possibly increase the long run productivity of the people and thus may be regarded as an improvement in the social infrastructure in the first sense. But on the other hand, the effect of these new educational opportunities may also weaken and disrupt the ability of existing social values and social hierarchies to mobilize resources and thus undermine the social infrastructure in the second sense.

1. See Hla Myint, "The Universities of South East Asia and Economic Development," *Pacific Affairs*, Summer 1962.

We started by saying that the conflicting requirements of social flexibility and social discipline in promoting economic development at the earlier pre-take-off stages of development can be illustrated by two approaches: the first in terms of the growth of the money economy and the second in terms of increasing investment in social and human capital. It now appears that this conflict is latent even if we concentrate on the second approach only although to some extent it is hidden by the vagueness in the concept of the "social infrastructure." Certain changes which might widen the educational horizon of a people and thus increase their longer run productivity might at the same time undermine the coherence of the social and institutional framework to mobilize resources to increase capital formation both in human and material capital.

This conflict may be further illustrated by human investment in higher education for economic development where the greatest long run increases in productivity have been frequently claimed. When people make this claim, they have two distinct ideas at the back of their minds. Firstly, they are thinking of the dynamic effects of higher education, in stimulating new discoveries and innovations and in adopting new methods of production. This implies a sort of intellectual yeast which will ferment and change the whole of the production structure and presumably the social infrastructure with it. Here the productivity of investment in human capital is conceived in terms of greater flexibility and adaptability of the social and institutional framework which will create favourable conditions both in stimulating changes and for receptiveness and adaptability to these changes. Secondly, they are also thinking of shortages of skilled people of particular types who are needed as "missing components" to be fitted into a desired pattern

of economic development. Of course some flexibility has to be allowed even in the most rigid and comprehensive type of planning. But it is fair to say that the *basic* reasons for claiming high productivity as a result of investment in education are different in these two types of argument. In popular terms, the first type of argument is thinking in terms of creating square pegs to fit into round holes with the hope that the pattern of holes will be stretched and changed into more productive directions. The second type of argument is thinking in terms of trying to create round pegs to fit into round holes, as though fitting the missing pieces into a jigsaw puzzle within the framework of a given and fixed pattern of production and planning requirements.

These conflicting considerations become bewildering when we look closely at the skilled manpower problems of any newly independent countries. Firstly, there is an obvious need to fill up the gaps left in the civil service, and those left in all sectors of the economy by departing foreign personnel. The missing components have to be produced to maintain the old economic and administrative structure. But at the same time there is a great desire to change very quickly "the old colonial structure," not only politically but also economically and socially. Logically, one might perhaps expect a great upsurge of a liberal educational policy encouraging individualism, enterprise and innovations to break down the rigidities both of the traditional and of the colonial systems. But given the prevailing intellectual atmosphere that such quick change can only be forced through by economic planning, the prevailing bias is against both economic liberalism and "liberal education" in favour of detailed skilled manpower planning integrated with programmes of technical education which ideally should specify the exact type of training and the exact number of trainees. Thus we get back to the problem of manufacturing the "missing components" for the jigsaw puzzle, the only trouble being that the old puzzle has been torn down and the new puzzle has not been constructed.

4. BIBLIOGRAPHICAL NOTE

1. The following references may be consulted for a more detailed analysis of various investment criteria: A. K. Bagchi, "The Choice of the Optimum Technique," *Economic Journal*, September 1962; K. A. Bohr, "Investment Criteria in Manufacturing Industries in Underdeveloped Countries," *Review of Economics and Statistics*, May 1954; M. D. Bryce, *Industrial Development*, New York, 1960; S. Chakravarty, *The Logic of Investment Planning*, Amsterdam, 1960; H. B. Chenery, "The Application of Investment Criteria," *Quarterly Journal of Economics*, February 1953; H. B. Chenery and K. S. Kretschmer, "Resources Allocation for Economic Development," *Econometrica*, October 1956; Joel Dean, "Measuring the Productivity of Capital," *Harvard Business Review*, January/February 1954; Maurice Dobb, *Economic Growth and Planning*, New York, 1960; Dobb, "Some Problems in the Theory of Growth and Planning Policy," *Kyklos*, Vol. XIV, No. 2, 1961; Otto Eckstein, "Investment Criteria for Economic Development and the Theory of Intertemporal Welfare Economics," *Quarterly Journal of Economics*, February 1957; W. Galenson and H. Leibenstein, "Investment Criteria, Productivity and Economic Development," *ibid.*, August 1955; Zvi Griliches, "Research Costs and Social Returns," *Journal of Political Economy*, October 1958; A. C. Harberger, "Cost-Benefit Analysis and Economic Growth," *The Economic Weekly*, February 1962; H. Leibenstein, "Why Do Economists Disagree on Investment Criteria? *Indian Economic Journal*, April 1958; Leibenstein, "Investment Criteria and Empirical Evidence—A Reply to Mr. Ranis," *Quarterly Journal of Economics*, February 1963; J. G. McLean, "How To Evaluate New Capital Investments," *Harvard Business Review*, November/December 1958; D. F. Ross, "The Costs and Benefits of Puerto Rico's Fomento Programmes," *Social and Economic Studies*, September 1957; A. K. Sen, *Choice of Techniques*, Oxford, 1960; A. Vaidyanathan, "A Survey of the Literature on 'Investment Criteria' for the Development of Underdeveloped Countries," *Indian Economic Journal*, October 1956. United Nations, ECLA, *Manual on Economic Development Projects*, New York, 1958.

2. In addition to the sources already cited in section 2, above, the balanced growth versus unbalanced growth controversy can be examined more intensively in the following references. The list includes readings on the various concepts of external economies which underlie advocacy of balanced growth. Some references also subject the balanced growth doctrine to historical analysis, and others relate the doctrine to foreign trade: H. W. Arndt, "External Economies in Economic Growth," *Economic Record*, November 1955; H. B. Chenery, "The Interdependence of Investment Decisions," in *The Allocation of Economic Resources*, edited by Moses Abramovitz and others, Stanford, 1959; M. Fleming, "External Economies and the Doctrine of Balanced Growth," *Economic Journal*, June 1955; J. R. T. Hughes, "Foreign Trade and Balanced Growth: The Historical Framework," *American Economic Review, Papers and Proceedings*, May 1959; M. Lipton, "Balanced and Unbalanced Growth in Under-

developed Countries," *Economic Journal,* September 1962; H. B. Malmgren, "Balance, Imbalance, and External Economies," *Oxford Economic Papers,* March 1963; J. M. Montias, "Balanced Growth and International Specialization: A Diagrammatic Analysis," *ibid.,* June 1961; H. Myint, "The Demand Approach to Economic Development," *Review of Economic Studies,* Vol. XXVII, No. 2; S. K. Nath, "The Theory of Balanced Growth," *Oxford Economic Papers,* June 1962; Goran Ohlin, "Balanced Economic Growth in History," *American Economic Review, Papers and Proceedings,* May 1959; Tibor Scitovsky, "Growth—Balanced or Unbalanced?" in *The Allocation of Economic Resources,* edited by Moses Abramovitz and others, Stanford, 1959; John Sheahan, "International Specialization and the Concept of Balanced Growth," *Quarterly Journal of Economics,* May 1958.

3. For supplementary readings on manpower and education, the following may be consulted: J. Bonner and D. S. Lees, "Consumption and Investment," *Journal of Political Economy,* February 1963; Adam Curle, *Educational Strategy for Developing Societies,* London, 1963; R. B. Goode, "Adding to the Stock of Physical and Human Capital," *American Economic Review, Papers and Proceedings,* May 1959; International Labour Office, "Youth Employment and Vocational Training Schemes in the Developing Countries," *International Labour Review,* September 1962; Nigerian

Federal Ministry of Education, *Investment in Education* (The Ashby Report), 1960; Organization for Economic Cooperation and Development, Policy Conference on Economic Growth and Investment in Education, *Challenge of Aid to Newly Developing Countries* (Vol. 3), *The Planning of Education in Relation to Economic Growth* (Vol. 4), Paris, 1962; UNESCO, Conference of African States on the Development of Education in Africa, *Final Report,* Paris, 1961; United States Papers Prepared for the United Nations Conference on the Application of Science and Technology for the Benefit of the Less Developed Areas, *Social Problems and Urbanization* (Vol. VII), *Human Resources* (Vol. XI), Washington, D.C., 1962. Several writings by T. W. Schultz are highly instructive on the role of education in development: "Capital Formation by Education," *Journal of Political Economy,* December 1960; "Investment in Human Capital," *American Economic Review,* March 1961; "Education and Economic Growth," in *Social Forces Influencing American Education,* edited by N. B. Henry, Chicago, 1961; "Investment in Human Capital in Poor Countries," in *Foreign Trade and Human Capital,* edited by P. D. Zook, Dallas, 1962. The special supplement of the *Journal of Political Economy,* October 1962, also contains a number of pertinent papers covering particular aspects of the problem of "Investment in Human Beings."

INDUSTRIALIZATION AND AGRICULTURE

THE ATTAINMENT of a proper balance between the establishment of industries and the expansion of agriculture is a persistently troublesome problem for developing nations. In earlier discussions of development priorities, deliberate and rapid industrialization was often advocated. Experience, however, has shown the limitations of an overemphasis on industrialization, and it is increasingly recognized that agricultural progress is a strategic element in the development process. Industrial development *versus* agriculture has become a false issue, and the concern now is rather with the interrelationships between industry and agriculture and the contribution that each can make to the other. It has also become apparent that the relative emphasis to be given to industry and agriculture must vary according to the country and its phase of development.

Most of this chapter is devoted to examining the specific problems of agricultural and industrial development as they have arisen in a number of countries. To furnish a background for the country applications, section one provides some general observations on the advantages of industrialization, while section two presents the case for concentrating on an increase in agricultural productivity and output. Section three then appraises the special arguments for industrialization through import-substitution.

It is clear that industrialization offers substantial benefits of a dynamic character that are important for changing the traditional structure of the economy, and the advocacy of industrialization may be particularly convincing for primary export countries that confront problems of a lagging export demand while having to provide employment for a rapidly increasing labor force (1.1). At the same time, however, it is essential to recognize that successful industrialization depends upon the attainment of an agricultural surplus, and that the pace of industrialization is confined by the rate of agricultural progress (2.1, 2.2). While sections 1 and 2 present arguments for emphasizing industry and agriculture, respectively, the dominant theme that emerges in this chapter is that industrial and agricultural development are not alternatives but are complementary and are mutually supporting with respect to both inputs and outputs.

The case of Japan (4.1) is especially instructive in demonstrating the contributions of the agricultural sector and the accomplishment of agricultural development alongside industrialization. The discussions of Latin American countries and Ceylon (4.2, 4.3, 4.6) illustrate some factors complicating a reliance on agricultural development. The case of Ceylon also indicates the relation of industrialization to an expansion of employment under conditions of population pressure. Professor Lewis's comments on industrialization in the Gold Coast (Ghana) and the West Indies (4.4, 4.5) provide a pertinent summary of the favorable and unfavorable conditions for industrialization. Finally, the discussion of the effects on the balance of payments of employment in non-agricultural sectors (4.7) stresses the need for easing the balance of payments by expanding agricultural output if an increase in industrial employment is to be feasible.

1. EMPHASIS ON INDUSTRY

1.1 INDUSTRIALIZATION OF PERIPHERAL COUNTRIES *

Historically, the spread of technical progress has been uneven, and this has contributed to the division of the world economy into industrial centers and peripheral countries engaged in primary production, with consequent differences in income growth. We are now at a transitional stage, in which this division is being gradually weakened, but it may take rather a long time to disappear. As the spread of technical progress into the periphery—limited originally to exports of primary commodities and related activities—is advancing more and more into other sectors, it brings with it the need for industrialization.

Indeed, industrialization is an inescapable part of the process of change accompanying a gradual improvement in per capita income. In response to differences in the income elasticities of demand and

in rates of increase in productivity, the active population is tending to shift—chiefly through the distribution of its increment—from occupations with a relatively low income elasticity of demand—principally primary production—to industry and other activities where this is relatively high.

This process has characterized the development of the industrial centers and is now advancing into the periphery. Industrialization of the centers is not a matter of dispute: it seems quite obvious that industrial countries should continue to industrialize. On the other hand, industrialization of the periphery has always been a controversial subject, not only in the centers, but also in the peripheral countries themselves. Although the opposition is receding, there are still some who consider industrialization to be a harmful diversion of productive resources from primary activities. Those who promote industrialization of the periphery are still credited with odd or ill-founded motives: the belief that industry makes nations wealthy while agriculture is a source of poverty; animosity towards

* From Raúl Prebisch, "Commercial Policy in the Underdeveloped Countries," *American Economic Review, Papers and Proceedings,* May 1959, pp. 251-5. Reprinted by permission.

the countryside, reasons of prestige, or the desire to achieve self-sufficiency or to imitate the centers.

Let the peripheral countries increase productivity in their primary activities through much-needed technical progress and thus expand their exports. Their rate of development will then be accelerated on a sound basis. So runs the argument.

Technical progress in export activities of these peripheral countries has undoubtedly been a great stimulus to their growth. But if this process is extended to other primary activities for internal consumption, where productivity is very low, and industry is not developed to absorb redundant manpower, then the inevitable outcome will be more disguised unemployment or downright unemployment.

Thus the plea for technical advance in primary production as an alternative to industrialization in order to improve standards of living defeats its own purpose, as some of the fruits of such technical advance will usually be transferred from the peripheral countries to the outer world, unless it is buttressed by a vigorous process of industrialization and increasing productivity in industry. The greater the inelasticity of demand for peripheral exports, the larger the proportion of the fruits that is so transferred.

Industry and technical advance in primary production are thus complementary aspects of the same process. And in this process industry plays a dynamic role, not only in inducing technical progress in primary and other activities, but in the new attitudes fostered by industrial development.

As in the centers, industrial development at the periphery responds to the same disparities in income elasticity as regards internal demand; and in addition to that, to the effects of similar disparities in foreign trade. It is a well-established fact that the income elasticity of demand for imports of Latin American primary commodities by the centers is generally lower than the income elasticity of demand for Latin-American imports of industrial products from these centers. This difference is frequently accentuated by measures to protect primary commodities in the centers, whereas, it is reduced by protection in peripheral countries, provided this is established between certain limits.

Let us take one instance: the case of Argentina. This country has followed the very mistaken policy of trying to stimulate industrialization to the detriment of agriculture, instead of promoting a balanced growth of both. In the recent ECLA study prepared at the request of the Argentine government, we examined a series of measures that might considerably increase exports through mechanization and other technical advances in agriculture. But even so, exports would only grow at the rate of 1.1 for every 1 per cent of growth of income, while the demand for imports was estimated with a coefficient of income-elasticity of 1.4 per cent, given the projected rate of income growth up to 1967 as compared with 1955. Similarly high elasticites for imports have been found in ECLA's studies for Brazil, Mexico, Colombia, and Peru.

In other words, in addition to the need for industrialization arising from the internal growth of Argentine income, there is the further need, because of the disparities between exports and imports just described, for substituting domestic production for imports of industrial goods.

The other aspect of this process is to be found in manpower figures. Indeed, the active population employed in agriculture in Argentina in 1955 represented 26 per cent of the total. Although this is rather a low figure for Latin America and exports are supposed to grow at a very high rate, we have estimated that, in the period considered, due to technical progress only about 10 per cent of the increment of active population will be absorbed in agriculture, whereas industry will have to absorb some 47 per cent of it.

Import substitution (defined here as an increase in the proportion of goods that is supplied from domestic sources and not necessarily as a reduction in the ratio of imports to total income) is the only way to correct the effects on peripheral growth of disparities in foreign trade elasticity. Let us take a numerical example to clarify this aspect of our problem. For the sake of simplicity, we shall assume that there is only one center and a periphery, having equal rates of population growth. Assuming that the center's rate of income growth is 3 per cent yearly and the income elasticity of demand for imports of primary commodities is 0.80 and that there is no import substitution, then the rate of growth of these imports will be 2.40 per cent (3 per cent $\times$ 0.80 per cent) per year.

Suppose now that at the periphery income elasticity of demand for industrial goods from the center is 1.30. If, in a balanced development process, the rate of growth of these imports is to be no higher than that of exports, then peripheral income cannot increase faster than 1.84 per cent per year. This is the rate which, combined with that coefficient of elasticity, gives the limit of import growth—that is to say a rate of 2.40 per cent, the same as that for exports.

Should peripheral income grow at a rate, say, similar to the 3 per cent of the center, its demands for imports of industrial products would grow at the rate of 3.90 per cent (3 per cent $\times$ 1.3 per cent) while exports of primary commodities would increase at the rate of only 2.40 per cent. To bridge the gap between these two rates, either the rate of increase of demand for imports would have to fall by 1.50 per cent, by means of import substitution, or industrial exports would have to be added

to the primary ones, or a combination of the two.

We have assumed the same rates of population growth at the center and periphery. If the rate is higher at the latter, as is the case in Latin America, industrialization has to be intensified in order to have the same per capita rate of income growth as the center. This is particularly necessary if the present differences in per capita income are to be gradually narrowed down.

We have seen that import substitution tends to correct the disparity in income elasticities of demand for imports and for exports. This does not mean that industrialization is not necessary in the exceptional cases—at least in Latin America— where there is no such disparity. It has been shown that industrialization also responds to internal disparities of demand. If exports of a particular country grow faster than its demand for imports, industry will still have to grow, but its contribution towards meeting total demand for industrial goods will decline while that of imports will increase. By contrast, when demand for imports tends to grow at a faster rate than exports, import substitution is necessary to correct this disparity, and then imports constitute a declining proportion of total demand for industrial goods.

On the other hand, a country whose exports grow at a very fast rate and constitute a relatively high component of its aggregate product is in a better position than others to accelerate its rate of economic growth; but this acceleration may induce a rate of increase in the demand for imports higher than the increase in exports, requiring import substitution to correct the disparity.

The acceleration of the rate of growth will be the more necessary if exports absorb only a small fraction of the increment of population. This is the peculiar case of Venezuela, where fast growing oil exports constitute 32 per cent of its total product, whereas they employ only 2.6 per cent of the total active population.

In the changing pattern of employment associated with the process of development, a declining proportion of the continuously increasing active population is needed for the growth of existing activities for the internal market, due to improvements in productivity. Therefore a part of the growing manpower is not required in these exisiting activities. Moreover, there is manpower that for the same reason is not needed to produce the present level of exports. All this redundant manpower has to be employed in the expansion of these exports and in new branches of industries for substitution purposes, as well as in other new activities. These new forms of employment are geared to internal and external demand elasticities and to different rates of increase in productivity.

In other words, in a dynamic economy redundant manpower is continually emerging as a result of technical progress, and it tends to be absorbed to meet the increasing demand generated by that very same technical progress.

In addition, there is a second form of manpower that has to be so absorbed. There are indeed vast numbers of marginal workers of low productivity rendering poorly paid personal services, as well as people engaged in other forms of precarious employment or disguised unemployment of a precapitalist character who should be moved to new jobs.

In the process of growth, at every level of per capita income, a certain proportion of this manpower is made available for transfer to other forms of employment, through shifts in demand as well as through technical changes in production.

For the sake of brevity, we will use the term "surplus manpower" to describe both these sources of labor and we will confine ourselves to that part of the surplus to be transferred to exports or new branches of industry for import substitution.

Redundant manpower as such does not produce any income and the real measure of the fruits of technical progress is the increment that accrues to the community when such manpower is transferred to new forms of employment. In addition to this increment, there is the net increase in income obtained by transferring available manpower from these precapitalist forms of employment of very low productivity to exports or industrial activities of much higher productivity.

2. EMPHASIS ON AGRICULTURE

2.1 ARGUMENTS FOR DEVELOPMENT OF AGRICULTURE *

The economic arguments for heavy emphasis on development of agriculture include the following:

(1) In some countries the modernization and mechanization of agriculture are necessary to free labor for industrial development.

* From Gustav F. Papanek, "Development Problems Relevant to Agriculture Tax Policy," *Papers and Proceedings of the Conference on Agricultural Taxation and Economic Development,* Harvard Law School, Cambridge, 1954, pp. 193-6. Reprinted by permission.

(2) The basic argument for agricultural priorities is the contention that agricultural and rural production can be raised rapidly and with little capital.[1] On the other hand,

1. Evidence cited includes the possibility of doubling crop production, or raising crops in previously uncultivated areas by irrigation with such low capital techniques as diversion dams, simple pumps and wells, and water spreading; the application of fertilizer which in the first year can provide a 200-400 per cent return; the use of improved seeds which can double or triple yields at an insignificant increase in costs; the local construction of improved fishing vessels, pottery and tools to save imports; the use of underemployed rural labor for the construction of schools, roads and housing.

the massive industrial development required to affect underemployment and to sustain a process of economic development, takes time and requires a massive infusion of capital from the developed area. Capital exports of the required magnitude are extremely unlikely in the forseeable future.

(3) Large-scale industrialization is precluded not only by the lack of capital, but also by lack of sufficiently widespread managerial and entrepreneurial ability, and institutional arrangements, and inadequate social overhead facilities such as transport, communications, and power networks. Considerable time would have to elapse before these basic facilities for large-scale expansion of industry become available.

On the other hand, rapid and large returns in the agricultural sector are possible with relatively minor changes in techniques, which the bulk of agriculture is able and willing to make, given suitable government policies.[2]

(4) Development of the rural sector is also capital-saving in requiring minimum expenditures for such overhead costs as housing, roads, social and health facilities, by obviating massive population movements. Industrializaton would require heavy expenditures to provide at least minimal facilities for the new city inhabitants.

(5) In addition to scarcity of domestic capital, many underdeveloped countries face a shortage of foreign resources. Development of agricultural production is often the fastest method for decreasing needed imports or increasing saleable exports.[3]

2. It is argued that improvements in techniques would not require mechanization of either agricultural or rural industry or the managing of much larger units, but only the substitution of steel for wood plows, of improved for traditional kilns.

3. E.g., India's balance of payments fluctuates largely with changes in its food import requirements; Burma's foreign exchange earnings are primarily dependent on rice exports, Pakistan's on cotton and jute, while Ceylon, Indonesia, Israel, Bolivia and others could take a substantial step

(6) Although it is acknowledged that technical improvements in agriculture sometimes require structural changes, many of these can be carried out without prior industrialization. For instance, although land reform would be greatly facilitated and be more acceptable politically without excessive population pressure, it can be carried out even where that pressure is greatest.

(7) Although it is acknowledged that variation in interest rates, tax concessions, and other fiscal measures will be less effective in the rural than in the urban sector, in encouraging reinvestment out of increased production, the use of more direct methods can be effective in this respect. This might, for instance, involve betterment assessments and development lotteries to channel resources through the government into investment, and the encouragement of direct reinvestment through subsidies, education, the creation of credit facilities, and land tenure improvement. Steps to increase savings or taxes are facilitated if a larger proportion of the population engaged in producing for investment remains in the rural area, where most of its requirements continue to be furnished by the family farm.

(8) In many underdeveloped countries the increased incomes resulting from development will express themselves mainly in an increased demand for food and clothing. Agriculture production, or imports, will therefore have to be increased in any case as part of the process of development, since it cannot be expected that all of the increased production will be reinvested.

This point is also important with respect to the popular support essential to any development program. Increased agricultural production satisfies the most urgently felt needs of the bulk of the population

towards the solution of their foreign exchange problem if they decrease their need for food imports.

and is the most rapid and dramatic demonstration of progress for the overwhelming majority of the population. Tangible evidence of progress, however small, is essential if democratic governments are to retain support during the initial development period when reinvestment requirements allow the population to benefit from only a fraction of the increased output. In this period, expectation can often be substituted for actual improvements in the level of living, if tangible evidence of progress is at hand....

The extent of government participation in rural development and its tax policies and methods depend not only on the relative role assigned to the rural sector, but also on the objectives established for the development and the methods used to reach these objectives.

Without attempting to be all-inclusive or mutually exclusive, the objectives which underlie agricultural programs in underdeveloped countries can generally be outlined under these headings:

1. An increase in production
2. Improvements in marketing
3. Changes in land tenure
4. A decrease in the disparities of income and wealth in the rural sector
5. The use of part, but not all, of any increase in production to raise the level of living of the rural population
6. Inducing population shifts from the agricultural sector to industry
7. The encouragement of investment and reinvestment.

2.2 AGRICULTURE'S CONTRIBUTION TO DEVELOPMENT *

The most important ways in which increased agricultural output and productivity contribute to over-all economic

growth can be summarized in five propositions: (1) Economic development is characterized by a substantial increase in the demand for agricultural products, and failure to expand food supplies in pace with the growth of demand can seriously impede economic growth. (2) Expansion of exports of agricultural products may be one of the most promising means of increasing income and foreign exchange earnings, particularly in the earlier stages of development. (3) The labor force for manufacturing and other expanding sectors of the economy must be drawn mainly from agriculture. (4) Agriculture, as the dominant sector of an underdeveloped economy, can and should make a net contribution to the capital required for overhead investment and expansion of secondary industry. (5) Rising net cash incomes of the farm population may be important as a stimulus to industrial expansion.

1. *Providing increased food supplies.* Apart from autonomous changes in demand, presumably of limited importance, the annual rate of increase in demand for food is given by $D = p + \eta g$, where p and g are the rate of growth of population and per capita income and η is the income elasticity of demand for agricultural products.[1]

Growth of demand for food is of major economic significance in an underdeveloped country for several reasons. First, high rates of population growth of $1\frac{1}{2}$ to 3 per cent now characterize most of the world's underdeveloped nations, so that growth of demand from this factor alone is substantial. As a result of international borrowing of knowledge and techniques in the public health field and the availability of such powerful weapons as DDT, the sulpha drugs, and penicillin, the decline in death rates is frequently sharp. This, in

* From Bruce F. Johnston and John W. Mellor, "The Role of Agriculture in Economic Development," *American Economic Review,* September 1961, pp. 571-81. Reprinted by permission.

1. K. Ohkawa, "Economic Growth and Agriculture," *Annals Hitotsubashi Academy,* October 1956, pp. 46-60.

combination with the slow decline in birth rates, has resulted in rates of natural increase substantially higher than those that characterized the presently developed countries during their "population explosion." Moreover, there is now only a weak relationship between the factors mainly responsible for the rise of natural increase and the factors determining the growth of a nation's income.

Secondly, the income elasticity of demand for food in underdeveloped countries is considerably higher than in high-income nations—probably on the order of .6 or higher in the low-income countries vs. .2 or .3 in Western Europe, the United States, and Canada. Hence, a given rate of increase in per capita income has a considerably stronger impact on the demand for agricultural products than in economically advanced countries.

The increase in farm output in Japan between the 1880's and 1911–20, which seems to have been of about the same magnitude as the growth of demand during that period, corresponded to an annual rate of increase in demand of approximately 2 per cent. With current rates of population growth and a modest rise in per capita incomes, the annual rate of increase of demand for food in a developing economy can easily exceed 3 per cent, a formidable challenge for the agriculture of an underdeveloped country. Moreover, as a result of the expansion of population in cities and in mining and industrial centers dependent upon purchased food, the growth of demand for marketed supplies is a good deal more rapid than the over-all rate of increase. Thus there are additional problems in developing transportation links and marketing facilities in order to satisfy the requirements of the nonagricultural population.

If food supplies fail to expand in pace with the growth of demand the result is likely to be a substantial rise in food prices leading to political discontent and pressure

on wage rates with consequent adverse effects on industrial profits, investment, and economic growth. There is scant evidence concerning the price elasticity of demand for food in underdeveloped countries. At least in the case of an increase in prices as a result of demand outstripping supply, there is a strong presumption that the price elasticity for "all food" is extremely low, probably lower than in economically advanced countries. Cheap starchy staple foods—cereals and root crops—provide something like 60 to 85 per cent of the total calorie intake in low-income countries, so there is relatively limited scope for offsetting a rise in food prices by shifting from expensive to less costly foods; and the pressure to resist a reduction in calorie intake is strong.

The inflationary impact of a given percentage increase in food prices is much more severe in an underdeveloped country than in a high-income economy. This is a simple consequence of the dominant position of food as a wage good in lower-income countries where 50 to 60 per cent of total consumption expenditure is devoted to food compared with 20 to 30 per cent in developed economies.

Owing to the severe economic and political repercussions of a substantial rise in food prices, domestic shortages are likely to be offset by expanded food imports, provided that foreign exchange or credits are available.[2] For some countries

2. Some underdeveloped countries have reacted to the social and economic problems resulting from food shortages and their inflationary consequences by instituting compulsory food collection, price controls, and rationing. It is easy to appreciate that considerations of social equity would lead to such measures in a low-income country; but from the standpoint of economic development the effects of an attempt to maintain such food distribution controls on a continuing basis are almost entirely unfavorable. Such programs tie up scarce administrative talent in a program of uncertain value that is usually ineffective as well; and they impede the growth of a market-oriented agriculture. Much higher returns are obtainable from a well-conceived program of agricultural development to expand total output rather than controlling its distribution. . . .

that are in a favorable position with respect to foreign exchange earnings this may be a satisfactory solution. But foreign exchange is usually in short supply and urgently required for imports of machinery and other requisites for industrial development that cannot be produced domestically. There is no simple or general answer to this question of import substitution that Chenery has described as "the most important and most difficult aspect of development programming ... "[3] In view of the potential that exists for increasing agricultural productivity it is likely to be advantageous to obtain the additional food supplies by increased domestic output rather than by relying on expansion of exports to finance enlarged food imports.[4] In any event, a static view of comparative costs may be misleading. The demand for imports of machinery and other items can be expected to increase as development proceeds, so the existing exchange rate is not likely to reflect the future demand for and supply of foreign exchange.[5]

The foregoing discussion has stressed the severe penalties attached to failure to achieve the "required" increase in output. This notion of a "required" increase in output should not be pushed too far; the price elasticity of demand for food is low but not zero and there is normally the possibility of adjusting supplies via imports.

3. H. B. Chenery, "Development Policies and Programmes," *Economic Bulletin for Latin America,* March 1958, p. 67.

4. This is, of course, merely a presumption, and it does not alter the fact that it is important to maintain price competition between domestic and imported foodstuffs, nor the fact that it is advantageous to import foodstuffs that cannot be produced efficiently at home, wheat imports in tropical regions being an important example. The availability of large quantities of U.S. agricultural surpluses on favorable terms has the effect of somewhat reducing the importance of measures to increase agricultural productivity and output in a developing country; but there remains the question whether such windfall supplies will be available on a continuing basis in quantities sufficient to satisfy a rapidly growing demand.

5. Chenery, *op. cit.,* p. 67.

Nevertheless, it is noteworthy that the demand for food is a derived demand determined essentially by the growth of population and of per capita incomes; and this characteristic of the demand for food cuts in both directions. Not only does it mean severe penalties for failure to expand food supplies in pace with the growth of demand, but is also implies that the returns on investment in expansion of food crops for domestic consumption fall off sharply if food supplies increase more rapidly than demand. There is thus a significant difference between the domestic demand for food products and the more expansible demand for agricultural exports (of a particular country) and for the miscellany of goods and services produced by "non-agriculture."

2. *Enlarged agricultural exports.* Expansion of agricultural exports is likely to be one of the most promising means of increasing incomes and augmenting foreign exchange earnings in a country stepping up its development efforts. A profitable export crop can frequently be added to an existing cropping system; the capital requirements for such innovations are often moderate and largely dependent on direct, non-monetary investment by farmers.

Development of production of export crops has a further advantage in catering to an existing market; and an individual country that accounts for only a small fraction of world exports faces a fairly elastic demand schedule. In view of the urgent need for enlarged foreign exchange earnings and the lack of alternative opportunities, substantial expansion of agricultural export production is frequently a rational policy even though the world supply-demand situation for a commodity is unfavorable.

There are, of course, disadvantages to heavy reliance on agricultural exports. And simultaneous efforts to expand exports of certain agricultural commodities in a number of underdeveloped countries involve the risk of substantial price declines, especially if the relevant price and income elasticities are low.

A longer-run goal is diversification which will lessen the vulnerability of an economy that depends heavily on export proceeds from one or a few crops. One of the rewards of the structural transformation associated with economic growth is the greater flexibility of a diversified economy. Of much greater immediate importance, however, is the fact that for most of the underdeveloped countries the introduction or expanded production of agricultural export crops can and should play a strategic role in providing enlarged supplies of foreign exchange.

3. *Transfer of manpower from agriculture to nonagricultural sectors*. To the extent that the Lewis two-sector model with its assumption of a perfectly elastic supply of labor is applicable, it follows that manpower for manufacturing and other rapidly expanding sectors can be drawn easily from agriculture. On the other hand, if the rural population is sparse and there is a good potential for expanding output of profitable cash crops, it may be difficult to obtain labor for a rapidly expanding capitalist sector. In any event, the bulk of the labor for the expanding sectors must be drawn from agriculture in the earlier stages of development simply because there is almost no other source. The experience of Japan where the conditions of the two-sector model were approximated, seems to indicate that the rate of investment was the limiting factor and that transfer of labor to industry was not a major problem.[6] In view of the potential that exists for increasing agricultural out-

put per man, it is to be expected that labor-supply problems in manufacturing and other growing industries will not be serious, provided that intelligent and vigorous efforts are made to enhance farm productivity.

4. *Agriculture's contributions to capital formation*. The secular decline of the agricultural sector and the structural transformation of an economy that characterize the dynamics of growth underscore the importance and difficulty of the problem of capital accumulation in an underdeveloped country. This is probably the most significant implication of Lewis' two-sector model in which the rate of capital formation determines the rate at which employment can be expanded in the capitalist, high-wage sector of the economy; and the rate of expansion of employment in the capitalist sector relative to the growth of the total labor force determines how soon the surplus of rural labor will be reduced to a point where wage levels are no longer depressed by the low level of productivity and earnings in the subsistence sector.

An underdeveloped country that is making determined efforts to achieve economic progress faces formidable requirements for capital to finance the creation and expansion of manufacturing and mining enterprises, for overhead investment in transportation and utilities, and in the revenue needed for recurrent expenditure for expansion of education and developmental services. These requirements are certain to outstrip the supply of funds available except in those countries which have large earnings from petroleum or mineral exports or particularly favorable access to foreign capital. The sheer size of the agricultural sector as the only major existing industry points to its importance as a source of capital for over-all economic growth. This presumption is particularly strong during the early stages of economic growth inasmuch as reinvestment of prof-

6. B. F. Johnston, "Agricultural Development and Economic Transformation: Japan, Taiwan, and Denmark," Paper prepared for an SSRC conference on relations between agriculture and economic growth, Stanford, November 1960, pp. 51-73.

its, historically the major source of capital accumulation, cannot be significant so long as the capitalist sector remains a small segment of the economy.

Since there is scope for raising productivity in agriculture by means that require only moderate capital outlays, it is possible for the agricultural sector to make a net contribution to the capital requirements for infrastructure and for industrial expansion without reducing the low levels of consumption characteristic of the farm population in an underdeveloped country. An increase in agricultural productivity implies some combination of reduced inputs, reduced agricultural prices, or increased farm receipts. Labor, being the abundant input in agriculture, is the principal input that will be reduced, and attention has already been given to agriculture's role as a source of manpower. Implicit in the earlier discussion of the need to expand agricultural production in pace with the growth of demand for food was the important proposition that stable or reduced agricultural prices can facilitate capital accumulation by preventing deterioration or even improving the terms of trade on which the industrial sector obtains food and other agricultural products.

Before considering the possibilities of securing a flow of capital out of agriculture, mention should be made of the ways in which the resource requirements of the agricultural sector can be minimized. The [most effective] approach to agricultural development...is one which minimizes requirements for scarce resources of high opportunity cost and which emphasizes the possibility of enhancing the productivity of the resources already committed to agriculture. It is also desirable for the capital requirements for agricultural expansion, including the increased outlays for fertilizers that are likely to be so important in this phase of agricultural development, to be financed as much as possible out of increased farm receipts that may accrue with the increase of productivity and output. Possibilities also exist for levying school fees, charges for land registration, and other fees that cover all or part of the cost of services provided for the farm population. But for many of the developmental services important to agriculture, it is *not* desirable to link services rendered with a charge to defray the cost. This is partly because individual farmers may not be able or willing to pay for such services, but more important is the fact that social returns to expenditures for research and extension to raise agricultural productivity may be much larger than the private benefits that can be appropriated by individual producers.

. . .

Political and institutional problems frequently make it difficult to translate the increased potential for saving and capital accumulation, made possible by increased agricultural productivity, into an actual increase in investment. Recent experience in India and Pakistan, for example, gives rise to doubts as to whether capital accumulation and economic growth will proceed at a "satisfactory" pace. Despite the stress that has been placed on promoting economic development, agriculture's contribution to investment and revenue requirements for government expenditure for current services seems to have declined; or at least there is evidence that agriculture's relative contribution to tax revenues has declined appreciably. Wald reports that whereas land revenues in India provided over 20 per cent of total tax revenue in 1939 they accounted for only 9 per cent of the tax receipts of India's central and state and provincial government in 1954 and only 5 per cent of total tax receipts in Pakistan in 1952.[7]

7. H. P. Wald, *Taxation of Agricultural Land in Underdeveloped Countries,* Cambridge, 1959, pp. 44n., 61-3.

The political difficulties in taxing the agricultural sector are often formidable, but it seems likely that insufficient recognition of the strategic role that agriculture can and should play in contributing to the capital requirements of economic development has been a factor in the failure to realize the potential for a higher rate of capital formation. Frequently, simple inertia and weaknesses in the tax system have been major factors; government revenues from land in the seven Part A states in India increased only 50 per cent between 1938–39 and 1951–52 whereas the index of wholesale prices of major agricultural commodities increased 550 per cent. On the other hand, inertia has contributed to high tax yields in instances in which tax revenues have been geared to rising world prices. The yield from the land tax in Burma declined from 40 per cent of total government revenue prewar to 5 per cent in 1952, but this was offset by the profits of the state agricultural marketing board which provided some 40 per cent of total government revenue.[8] The influence of the postwar rise in commodity prices was a particularly significant element in the large take of export taxes and marketing board surpluses in Ghana, Uganda, and other African countries.

The conclusion suggested so strongly by both theoretical considerations and historical experience is that in underdeveloped countries, where agriculture accounts for some 40 to 60 per cent of the total national income, the transition from a level of saving and investment that spells stagnation to one permitting a tolerable rate of economic growth cannot be achieved unless agriculture makes a significant net contribution to capital formation in the expanding sectors. If communist countries have an advantage in securing rapid economic growth, it would seem to lie chiefly in their ability to ride roughshod over polit-

8. *Ibid.*, pp. 54, 63.

ical opposition and divert a maximum amount of current output into capital accumulation. And agriculture has been a prime target in squeezing out a maximum amount of surplus for investment. In the Soviet Union compulsory collection of grain at artificially low prices was used to siphon off the increment in output originating in agriculture and to facilitate the forced-march development of industry. The rural communes in Communist China appear to be a device aimed not only at extracting the maximum possible surplus of capital from the countryside but a maximum labor effort as well.

Societies which value individual freedom and which limit the arbitrary power of government are unable and unwilling to apply the sort of coercion and drastic reorganization of rural communities involved in the collectivization drive in the Soviet Union and in the creation of the Chinese communes. But this should not blind us to the hard fact that an essential element of economic growth is, in Lewis' phrase, "the process by which a community is converted from being a 5 per cent to a 12 per cent saver ..."[9] In the earlier phases of development it is well-nigh certain that agriculture must play a major role in the process.

5. *Increased rural net cash income as a stimulus to industrialization.* One of the simplifying assumptions of the two-sector model is that expansion of the capitalist sector is limited only by shortage of capital. Given this assumption, an increase in rural net cash income is not a stimulus to industrialization but an obstacle to expansion of the capitalist sector.[10]

9. W. A. Lewis, *The Theory of Economic Growth,* Homewood, 1955, p. 226.

10. Lewis states that: "Anything which raises the productivity of the subsistence sector (average product per person) will raise real wages in the capitalist sector, and will therefore reduce the capitalist surplus and the rate of capital accumulation, unless it at the same time more than correspondingly moves the terms of trade against

It is true, of course, that investment decisions may in fact be influenced not only by the availability of capital but also by demand conditions and estimates of the future profitability of additions to capacity. Nurkse has been especially emphatic in stressing the importance of *opportunities* for profitable investment as a strategic factor influencing the rate of capital formation, and Lewis himself emphasized in his report on industrialization in the Gold Coast that increased rural purchasing power is a valuable stimulus to industrial development.[11] Nurkse has given this concise statement of the problem:

The trouble is this: there is not a sufficient market for manufactured goods in a country where peasants, farm laborers and their families, comprising typically two-thirds to four-fifths of the population, are too poor to buy any factory products, or anything in addition to the little they already buy. There is a lack of real purchasing power, reflecting the low productivity in agriculture.[12]

the subsistence sector." ("Economic Development with Unlimited Supplies of Labour," *Manchester School of Economic and Social Studies,* May 1954, p. 172.)

11. W. A. Lewis, *Report on Industrialization and the Gold Coast,* Gold Coast Government, Accra, 1953.

12. Ragnar Nurkse, *Patterns of Trade and Development,* Stockholm, 1959, pp. 41-2.

There is clearly a conflict between emphasis on agriculture's essential contribution to the capital requirements for over-all development and emphasis on increased farm purchasing power as a stimulus to industrialization. Nor is there any easy reconciliation of the conflict. The size of the market is particularly pertinent to investment decisions in industries characterized by economies of scale so that a fairly high volume of demand is needed to justify construction of a modern factory. But substitution of domestic output for imported manufactured goods often provides a significant addition to demand that does not depend upon an increase in consumer purchasing power. Furthermore, if capital requirements for developing infrastructure and capital-goods or export industries are large relative to the amount of capital that can be mobilized, insufficient consumer demand is unlikely to limit the rate of investment. Political considerations, of course, also play an important role in this determination. Although this is another of the policy issues for which no general answer is possible, it will normally be appropriate to emphasize the capital contribution from agriculture in early stages of the structural transformation.

3. IMPORT-SUBSTITUTION AND INDUSTRIAL PROTECTION—NOTE

It has become common to favor a policy of import-substitution through protective tariffs on industrial imports as a direct route to industrialization. Proponents of industrial protectionism adduce several special arguments—arguments that we should consider more seriously than the usual simple assertions about a "natural" inferiority of agriculture or the supposed necessity of industrialization to achieve a rising level of income.

Support for import replacement comes partly from an appeal to the experience of industrialized countries. Historical studies of some countries show not only that the share of industrial output rises with development, but also that the growth of industries based on import substitution accounts for a large proportion of the total rise in industry.[1] It is also true that "much of the

1. For evidence, see H. B. Chenery, "Patterns of Industrial Growth," *American Economic Review,* September 1960, pp. 639-41, 651.

recent economic history of some rapidly developing underdeveloped countries can be written in terms of industrialization working its way backward from the 'final touches' stage to domestic production of intermediate, and finally to that of basic, industrial materials."[2] At first, the country may import semifinished materials and perform domestically the "final touches" of converting or assembling the almost-finished industrial imports into final products. Later on, with the growth in demand for the final product, a point may be reached at which the import demand for intermediate components and basic goods is sufficiently high to warrant investment in their production at home; the market has become sufficiently large to reach a domestic production threshold.[3]

As with any interpretation of historical development, however, it is one thing to determine what has happened to make the course of development in one country a "success story" and quite another to infer from this experience that the same result could now be induced more rapidly in another country through deliberate policy measures. The historical evidence on the contribution of import-substitution to industrialization applies only to some countries; in other countries, the replacement of imports was not significant. Moreover, we should recognize that the rise of industry through import-replacement was in large part due to systematic changes in supply conditions, not simply to a change in the composition of demand with rising income.[4] The changes in factor supply—especially the growth in capital stock per worker and the increase in education and skills of all kinds—were instrumental in causing a systematic shift in comparative advantage as per capita income rose. But for

a presently underdeveloped country there is no reason to expect that a tariff on industrial imports would cause the supplies of capital, human skills, and natural resources to change in a way that would favor the substitution of domestic production for imports. The changes in supply conditions that occurred in other countries cannot now be duplicated simply by a policy of industrial protection.

Nor is industrial protection justified by reference to the historical pattern of industrialization working its way backward from the "final touches" stage to domestic production of formerly imported materials. On the contrary, this pattern demonstrates that it is the growth of imports which subsequently induces domestic production; in offering proof that a market exists, the imports can fulfill the important function of demand formation and demand reconnaissance for the country's enterpreneurs, and the imports can act as a catalytic agent that will bring some of the country's underemployed resources together in order to exploit the opportunities they have revealed.[5] For the objective of eventually replacing imports with domestic production, it would thus be self-defeating to restrict imports at too early a stage and thereby forgo the awakening and inducing effects which imports have on industrialization.[6] An increase in imports—not their restriction—is the effective way to prepare the ground for the eventual creation of an import-replacing industry. Only after the domestic industry has been established can the country afford to dispense with the "creative" role played by imports, and only then would there be a case for protection of the domestic industry. Although in promoting the demand for import substitutes, restrictions on imports allow the country to by-pass the difficulties of

2. A. O. Hirschman, *The Strategy of Economic Development*, New Haven, 1958, p. 112.
  3. *Ibid.*, p. 114.
  4. Chenery, *op. cit.*, pp. 624-5, 628-9, 644.

5. Hirschman, *op. cit.*, p. 123.
  6. *Ibid.*, p. 124.

having to build up internal demand simultaneously with supply,[7] nonetheless such a protective commercial policy is designed merely to replace imports; this in itself is no guarantee of cumulative growth. Even though industrialization may be initiated through import-substitution, there still remains the problem of sustaining the industrialization momentum beyond the point of import replacement.

.As already noted in Raúl Prebisch's statement (1.1), another special argument for industrialization via import-substitution rests on the contention that a peripheral country's demand for industrial imports increases much more rapidly than does the foreign demand for its exports, so that the country must supply all those industrial products which cannot be imported in view of the relatively slow growth of its exports. If we accept the contentions that there is disparity in the income elasticities of demand for imports and exports, that the industrial imports are essential and must be either imported or produced at home, and that the country has no other means of increasing its capacity to import, then there is *prima facie* a case for industrial protection to encourage import substitutes. What is relevant for individual primary exporting countries, however, is not the over-all income elasticity of demand for primary products but the prospects for their individual exports. It is unreasonable to believe that export prospects are equally unfavorable for foodstuffs, minerals, and raw materials, or for all commodities in each of these broad categories. Moreover, though the elasticity of demand for a commodity may be low on world markets, it may be high for the commodity from a particular source of supply. Nor can the future demand of industrial countries for imports be inferred simply from

their income elasticity of demand for imports. Their import requirements will also depend on their growth rates in income (a high growth rate may offset a low income elasticity of demand), on shifts of the long-term supply elasticities within the industrial countries (domestic output of certain minerals and fuels, for example, has not kept pace with demand, so that import requirements are rising relatively to income growth), and on the degree of liberalization in the importing countries' commercial policies. Without undertaking individual commodity and country studies, it is therefore difficult to gauge how applicable is the argument for industrialization because of a weak export position.

We should also allow for the fact that a developing country's capacity to import industrial products will depend not only on its export earnings, but also on the inflow of foreign capital, changes in the terms of trade, and the capacity to replace other imports (such as foodstuffs and raw materials) with domestic production. To the extent that these other factors may raise the capacity to import industrial products, there is less need for industrial protection.

The case is also weakened if in attempting to offset the limited demand for exports, the policy of import-substitution should in turn give rise to limitations on the supply side and deter exports. Such a worsening of the export situation may occur when the country's scarce financial and human resources are concentrated on industrialization, resources are diverted from the export sector, home consumption limits the available export supply, or the industrialization program is inflationary.

Another facet of the argument for replacing industrial imports with domestic production is related to the objective of expanding employment outside of agricul-

7. Cf. Gunnar Myrdal, *An International Economy*, New York, 1956, p. 276.

ture. It may be contended that industrialization is necessary to provide employment opportunities for the presently underemployed, to absorb manpower that would otherwise become redundant when agricultural productivity rises through the adoption of more advanced techniques, and to take up the increase in the size of the labor force as population grows.

The promotion of new employment opportunities is certainly a crucial component of development programming, and in this connection there is considerable point to the emphasis on industrialization. The relevant questions here, however, are whether investment should be directed toward import-replacing industries, and whether industrial protectionism is the most appropriate policy for facilitating the expansion of non-agricultural employment.

It is possible that the objectives of more employment and a more rapid rate of development are incompatible, and this conflict in social objectives must first be resolved. A policy of industrialization through import-substitution must also be compared with a policy of gradually inducing industrialization through agricultural improvement, or promoting industry through the production of manufactured exports (as discussed in Chapter VII, section 2). There is also a tendency to exaggerate the amount of employment that could be provided by substituting home manufacture for imports; as emphasized in the next section (selections 4.5, 4.6), the direct employment which can be provided by replacing imports with domestic manufacture is generally limited for a poor country.

Further, it can be questioned whether industrialization through protection is the best remedy for underemployment. The effect of surplus labor in agriculture is low productivity, but the remedy for this is capital formation, not industrialization as such. Although the surplus labor constitutes an "investible surplus," this surplus can be applied in various investment outlets, and we cannot simply conclude that the optimum resource use is in import-competing industries. We should also recognize that other policies might be more effective in stimulating labor mobility than would protection. When occupational mobility is restricted by institutional and cultural barriers, the supply responses to the price and income stimuli of protection are necessarily weak, and extra-economic measures are required in such forms as education and training, land tenure reforms, and policies that foster cultural change. Finally, we must distinguish between the mere availability of surplus laborers and their actual transference into productive employment as efficient and fully committed industrial workers. This raises all the complex problems of creating and disciplining an industrial labor force.[8]

A more sophisticated version of the employment argument is that industry should be protected by a tariff in order to offset the effects of an excessively high wage rate for labor in the importable manufacturing industries.[9] It is claimed that the wage differential between the agricultural and industrial sectors overvalues labor for the industrial sector in the sense that industrial wage rates exceed the social opportunity costs of employing more labor

8. Cf. W. Galenson (ed.), *Labor and Economic Development,* New York, 1959; W. E. Moore and A. S. Feldman (eds.), *Labor Commitment and Social Change in Developing Areas,* New York, 1960.

9. For a detailed analysis of this argument, see E. E. Hagen, "An Economic Justification for Protection," *Quarterly Journal of Economics,* November 1958; J. Bhagwati, "The Theory of Comparative Advantage in the Context of Underdevelopment and Growth," *Pakistan Development Review,* Autum 1962, pp. 342-5; J. Bhagwati and V. K. Ramaswami, "Domestic Distortions, Tariffs and the Theory of Optimum Subsidy," *Journal of Political Economy,* February 1963, pp. 44-50.

in industry. This may be due to the alleged fact that industrial wages are based on agricultural earnings, which are determined by the average product of labor in agriculture rather than by the marginal product of labor which is lower (compare the discussion of Lewis's model in Chapter II, section 5, above); or it may be due to market imperfections that make the gap between agricultural and industrial wages greater than can be accounted for by "net advantages" as between agricultural and industrial work. In either case, there is a distortion in the labor market which raises the private cost of labor in industry above its social opportunity cost (the marginal product of labor in agriculture). This results in an inefficient allocation of labor between agriculture and industry, and it also understates the profitability of transforming agriculture into manufactures.[10] It is therefore concluded that protection of manufacturing industry may increase real income above the free trade level by making the relative price of manufactures higher and facilitating the redistribution of labor from agriculture to import-competing industries.

This conclusion, however, can be criticized in several respects. In so far as it is concerned with absorbing underemployed agricultural labor into import-competing industries, this aspect of the argument is subject to the same qualifications raised previously for the general argument of expanding employment through industrial protection. More pointedly, with regard to the alleged distortion in the labor market, it can be questioned whether the mere existence of a differential between industrial and agricultural wages is proof of a distortion. To the extent that the wage differential might be explained entirely by rational considerations of differences in costs and preferences as between industrial and agricultural work, there is no genuine distortion.[11] Considering the other possible reason for a distortion in the labor market —that industrial wages are related to agricultural earnings, but these earnings exceed the marginal productivity of agricultural labor—we must recognize that this result is based on the assumption of surplus agricultural labor and the ability of the worker to receive the average product because the supply of labor is the family which works on its own account and not for wages. This consideration is not relevant, however, for thinly populated countries or for plantation labor. And, regarding the concept of surplus labor and any estimate of its extent, we should recall all the reservations discussed earlier in Chapter II, section 4.

Even if we assume, however, that the wage differential does represent a genuine distortion, we must still recognize that the effects of this distortion may be better offset by domestic policies rather than a tariff on industrial imports. The difficulty with protection by a tariff is that it seeks to remedy the distortion by affecting foreign trade whereas the distortion is in a domestic factor market.[12] In this case, a policy of subsidization of production of the import-competing commodity, or of taxation of agricultural production, would be superior

10. In technical terms, the wage differential against industry causes the feasible production possibility curve to be drawn inwards within the maximum attainable production possibility curve based on a uniform wage. It also makes the commodity price ratio diverge from the domestic rate of transformation, so that the optimum conditions characterized by the equality of the foreign rate of transformation, domestic rate of transformation in production, and domestic rate of substitution in consumption are violated in the free trade case. See, Bhagwati and Ramaswami, *op. cit.*, pp. 48-9.

11. For a list of conditions under which wage differentials do not represent a genuine distortion, see *ibid.*, pp. 47-8.

12. A tariff could make the foreign and domestic rates of transformation equal, but it destroys the equality between the domestic rate of substitution and the foreign rate of transformation.

to a tariff.[13] A policy of subsidization on the use of labor in the import-competing industry, or a tax on its use in agriculture, would be an even better solution; since it directly eliminates the wage differential, this policy yields a higher real income than would a tariff, and an even higher real income than can be attained by a tax-cum-subsidy on domestic production.[14] A tariff on industrial imports is thus the least effective way of offsetting a distortion in the labor market.

Although we have so far been skeptical about the validity of protectionist arguments for import substitution, there remain two arguments that have more merit—the infant industry case and the attraction of foreign investment argument.[15] Tempo-

rary tariff protection of an infant industry is generally accepted as a valid policy for establishing an industry that would eventually be able to produce at lower costs and compete favorably with foreign producers. Nonetheless, to justify government intervention, it is not sufficient to anticipate solely the realization of internal economies of scale. For if the future benefits were to accrue only to the firm, the investment might then still be made by a private firm without protection in so far as the firm can cover its earlier costs of growth out of its later profits. Protection should instead be based on the condition that the social rate of return exceeds the private rate of return on the investment. The social benefit is likely to exceed the private benefit in an infant industry for two special reasons that are particularly relevant for a newly developing country: the knowledge of new industrial production techniques acquired in the protected industry may also be shared with other producers, and the training of the labor force may also redound to the benefit of other employers. When external economies are present, social benefits will exceed private benefits, and market forces would not yield the social optimum output. To gain the additional benefits, government aid may then be advocated.

It should be realized, however, that protection causes society to bear not only the losses that would be incurred by the industry during its period of infancy, but also the cost to consumption in the form of higher-priced import substitutes during this period. The ultimate saving in costs, therefore, ought to be sufficient to compensate the community for the excess costs during the "growing up" period.

13. A policy of subsidization or taxation of domestic products could equate the domestic and foreign rates of transformation and the domestic rate of substitution. But since it does not eliminate the inefficiency of labor-use induced by the excessive wage differential, it achieves this equality along the production possibility curve that is within the maximum attainable production possibility curve.

14. A policy of tax-cum-subsidy on the use of labor could achieve the equality of the domestic rate of transformation, foreign rate of transformation, and the domestic rate of substitution, and it can do this along the maximum attainable production possibility curve. For in this case, the wage differential against the industrial sector is directly removed, and both the inefficiency in labor allocation and the divergence of commodity prices from opportunity costs are simultaneously eliminated.

15. We omit the external economies argument and the terms of trade case for protection. These arguments are analytically correct, but are not among the most relevant for import-substitution in a poor country. The external economies argument merges with the balanced growth doctrine (Chap. V, section 2). There is, moreover, no *a priori* reason why—among all possible alternative investment opportunities—we should expect the net external economies to be greatest in import-competing industries. And again, a policy of tax-cum-subsidy on domestic production may be shown to be superior to a tariff. Cf. Bhagwati and Ramaswami, *op. cit.,* pp. 45-7.

Although it is possible that a nation may succeed in improving its terms of trade by switching

production from exportables to import-substitutes, this policy has little practical relevance for poor countries that cannot exercise sufficient monopoly or monopsony power in foreign trade.

We should also be aware of how difficult it is in practice to select genuine infant industries, insofar as this entails forecasting changes in cost conditions and the magnitude of future external economies. Instead of attempting to impose selective tariffs of sufficient height to encourage particular industries, it may be more expeditious to place a uniform *ad valorem* tariff on a whole range of industrial products and then leave the selection to market forces.

Finally, when the social rate of return exceeds the private, the preferable policy, in a way analogous to the other cases of domestic distortions, would be a direct subsidy on facilities to further the "learning process" of new production methods, or provisions by the government for the training of labor. These subsidies are superior to a protective tariff, since they avoid the intermediate loss to consumption that occurs with protection.

Protection may, however, be an effective policy for fostering an import-replacing industry when its successful establishment depends on the acquisition of better technical knowledge and experience. For when the country imposes prohibitive tariffs, or other import restrictions, against foreign manufactures, the foreign manufacturer may be induced to escape the import controls against his product by establishing a branch plant or subsidiary behind the tariff wall. Although the protection would have little effect in attracting supply-oriented industries, the inducement may be significant for the creation of "tariff factories" in market-oriented industries. It may be particularly effective in encouraging the final stages of manufacture and assembly of parts within the tariff-imposing country when there is an import duty on finished goods while raw materials or intermediate goods remain untaxed. This assumes, of course, that a sufficiently high domestic demand exists for the product of the tariff factory. And in determining whether the attraction of additional private foreign capital provides a net gain, we must again recall the earlier discussion about the various costs and benefits of foreign capital (Chapter III, 5.1).

From the foregoing appraisal of the various protection arguments, we may conclude that they must be highly qualified, the costs of protection not underestimated, and superior alternative policies not overlooked. Beyond these analytical considerations, the actual experience of many developing countries with industrial protectionist policies also confirms the conclusion that developing countries are likely to overemphasize the scope for replacement of industrial imports. In many instances, the protectionist policies have resulted in higher prices, a domestic product of inferior quality, excess capacity in the import-competing industries, and a restraint on the expansion of exports—all without a net saving of imports since the replacement of finished import commodities has required heavy imports of fuels, raw materials, and capital goods, as well as foodstuffs in cases where agricultural development has lagged. Some indication of this overinvestment in import-replacing industry is provided in the country analyses of the next section.

Instead of following protectionist policies that cause an excessive emphasis on deliberate industrialization through import-substitution, more attention should be given to the possibilities of inducing a gradual process of industrialization through agricultural development, and to the potential of industrialization through the export of manufactured products. We shall consider the latter possibility in the next chapter.

4. COUNTRY APPLICATIONS

4.1 ROLE OF AGRICULTURE IN JAPAN'S DEVELOPMENT *

Perhaps the most outstanding feature of Japanese development is its rapidity, or what is even more important, the sustained character of the growth process.[1] What are the crucial factors which led to the economic breakthrough in the nineteenth century and made for sustained rapid growth in the ensuing period? The purpose of our paper is to supply a partial but relevant answer to this question: a study of the role of agriculture in modern Japanese economic development. This necessarily becomes a two-fold problem. Firstly, we outline the main features of Japanese agricultural development in its role as one of the major sectors of the economy. Secondly, we examine the relationships between agriculture and the other sectors during the growth process.

The discussion that follows attempts to accomplish these aims within certain clearly defined limits. Observations are generally macro-sectoral, and sub-sectoral material is introduced only for specific illustrations. Historically, we try to compare two rather long periods: period I, from the Meiji Restoration to World War I, and period II, from World War I to World War II. In spite of the sustained character of growth in Japan, the relative position of major sectors in the economy

changed considerably. As we will show, World War I marked a distinct structural change especially pronounced in the relations between agriculture and industry....

The analysis starts with a study of the period from 1878 to 1917. (Before 1878 statistical deficiencies are nearly insurmountable.) Out attention will primarily focus on two aspects of agricultural progress: output and productivity. Throughout these pages the term "productivity" is used in a conventional way, simply meaning product per worker or per unit area. These may be considered neutral measures and are of equal importance to all types of economic development. Within this framework we will deal with three principal questions:

1. What happened to output and productivity during the period?

2. What development took place in the structure of the producing unit?

3. How did the changing pattern of factor combinations affect output and productivity?

Although there exist statistical hurdles in analyzing changes in Japanese agricultural output, the overall picture is very clear. The expansion rate of food crops was high enough to outstrip the growth rate of population. Gross and net output of agriculture in real terms increased steadily throughout the period. The annual growth rate of net output from 1878 to 1917 averaged about 2.3 percent, while the growth rate of gross output was somewhat higher.[2] These observations can be verified with the data supplied in Table 1.

* From Kazushi Ohkawa and Henry Rosovsky, "The Role of Agriculture in Modern Japanese Economic Development," *Economic Development and Cultural Change,* October 1960, pp. 43-8, 50-51, 60-67. Reprinted by permission.

1. For general background, see Kazushi Ohkawa and Others, *The Growth Rate of the Japanese Economy since 1878,* (Tokyo: Kinokuniya Bookstore Ltd., 1957), especially part II; Bruce F. Johnston, "Agricultural Productivity and Economic Development in Japan," *Journal of Political Economy,* LIX, 6 (Dec. 1951); and Henry Rosovsky, "Japanese Capital Formation: The Role of the Public Sector," *Journal of Economic History,* XIX, 3 (Sept. 1959).

2. Our discussion is based on data fully presented in Ohkawa and Others, part II. By net output we mean gross output minus intermediate goods. Real term series result from dividing money values by an agricultural price index. It must be noted that the use of Japanese statistics before the 1920's inevitably involves errors and biases, and it is not an easy matter to ascertain the direction of these departures from reality.

TABLE I. AGRICULTURAL OUTPUT, 1878–1917 [a] (FIVE YEAR AVERAGES)

Year	Rice: Total output [b] (million bushels)		Rice: Yields (bushels/hectare)		General agricultural production index [c]
1878–82	147.53	(100)	59.72	(100)	100
1883–87	167.64	(113)	63.93	(107)	112
1888–92	192.87	(130)	70.38	(117)	123
1893–97	186.87	(126)	67.36	(112)	129
1898–02	210.70	(142)	74.30	(124)	147
1903–07	229.58	(155)	79.56	(133)	158
1908–12	250.91	(170)	84.87	(142)	176
1913–17	274.00	(185)	89.68	(150)	198

Year	Agricultural Gross Output (Million Y, 1928–32 prices)		Agricultural Net Output (Million Y, 1928–32 prices)	
1878–82	960	(100)	825	(100)
1883–87	1,088	(113)	934	(113)
1888–92	1,349	(140)	1,089	(131)
1893–97	1,420	(147)	1,196	(144)
1898–02	1,688	(175)	1,432	(173)
1903–07	1,842	(191)	1,517	(183)
1908–12	2,129	(221)	1,722	(208)
1913–17	2,306	(208)	1,829	(221)

Sources: Rice Output Yields—Japan, Norinsho, *Norin tokei,* 1868-1953 (Statistical Tables of Agriculture and Forestry) (1955), Table 9 and 18; Production Index—*Norin tokei geppo* (Monthly Review of Agriculture and Forestry Statistics) (May 1946); Gross and Net Output: Ohkawa and Others, pp. 58 and 72.

[a] Figures in parentheses show the series as relatives, 1878–82=100.

[b] Rice production figures are shown separately because it was the most important crop. Rice production statistics are generally conceded to be most reliable.

[c] The overall index of agricultural production, still classified as a tentative result by the Ministry of Agriculture, is included for general reference purposes. We are somewhat skeptical about its validity, because a higher overall rate than the rice expansion rate seems most unlikely. In fact, a comparison of the three main series—rice output, gross output, and net output—may raise some doubts about the statistical consistency of the materials. We share these doubts, and present all the available series to give an overall picture.

Turning next to productivity, let us first look at land productivity, obtained by dividing net output by arable land. If we assume yields per unit to have been 100 in 1878-82, they rose to 180 by 1913-17. (See Table II.) It must be remembered that during this period the area of arable land increased from 4,524 thousand hectares in 1884 to 6,084 thousand hectares in 1920. But this is an increase of only 35 percent, compared to an 80 percent increase in land productivity. This shows that gains in productivity were more important than new

land in achieving output increases, and suggests that land-saving technological innovations were of great importance. We will have to return to this matter below.

Estimating labor productivity is a very hazardous undertaking in the Japanese case mainly because the term "labor force" is conceptually and statistically treacherous. There are several estimates for the labor force and for the gainfully occupied population in agriculture, but it is still not possible to accept the figures with full confidence. Using the latest and best com-

putations, shown in Table II, the results are
as follows: labor productivity (net output/
labor force) increased annually by 2.6 percent. The trend was not entirely uniform;
towards the end of the period increases in
labor productivity tended to become
slower. Available sources indicate that
between 1898 and 1917 there took place a
small decline in the number of persons
gainfully occupied in agriculture. Thus,
increases in net output associated with a
reduction in the labor force suggest that
technological development took a mild
labor-saving form.

What are the implications of these output and productivity changes? They can
be understood only in conjunction with
other macro-economic data. In terms of
domestic events, the expansion of output
was almost large enough both to supply
the needed food for a rapidly growing
urban population, and to meet the increased food demand stemming from a rise
in real per capita income. As shown in
Table III, Japan was a net exporter of agricultural products until the 1890's; after that
she became a moderate importer of food.[8]

3. The figures of Table III tend to overstate the
imports of food crops. Japan became an especially
heavy importer of certain industrial crops in the
twentieth century; e.g. cotton.

During the period total population grew
at rates which varied from 0.8 to 1.3 percent
per year, while the income elasticity for
food has been estimated to have been about
0.6 to 0.7, a high figure as compared with
later periods.[4] Per capita real income
increased at about an annual rate of 2 percent.[5] Taken together, these data indicate
that the demand for food increased at an
annual rate of about 2 percent, and that
this increase was largely met by output
expansion, slight increases in arable land,
and a small reduction in the labor force.[6]
In this sense, excepting short-term fluctuations, the forces of demand and supply for
food were in near equilibrium during the
initial phases of Japanese industrialization.
The terms of trade between agriculture and
the other sectors lend support to this conclusion. From 1878 to 1917, they remain
extremely steady, as shown below, except
for cyclical fluctuations.

We have shown that Japanese agriculture grew in harmony with the other

4. Tobata and Ohkawa, chapter 4, section 1, pp.
166 ff. This calculation is based on aggregate time
series; family budget studies have shown slightly
different results.
5. Ohkawa and Others, p. 24.
6. Rate of population increase + rate of per capita income increase $\times$ income elasticity for food
= rate of increase of food demand.

TABLE II. INCREASES IN LAND AND LABOR PRODUCTIVITY, 1878-1917
(FIVE YEAR AVERAGES)

Year	Land productivity (net output/ arable land)		Labor productivity (net output/ labor force)		Labor force (thousands)	
1878–82	Y 17.3	(100)	Y 53.0	(100)	15,573	(100)
1883–87	20.5	(118)	60.2	(113)	15,511	(99)
1888–92	22.2	(128)	70.4	(132)	15,466	(99)
1893–97	23.8	(137)	77.7	(146)	15,397	(98)
1898–02	28.3	(163)	93.5	(176)	15,303	(98)
1903–07	28.5	(164)	99.9	(188)	15,184	(97)
1908–12	30.5	(176)	115.2	(217)	14,490	(95)
1913–17	31.2	(180)	125.2	(236)	14,613	(93)

Source: Computed from Table 1. Labor force estimates based on unpublished results of Ohkawa.

TABLE III. BALANCE SHEET OF AGRICULTURAL PRODUCTS
(FIVE YEAR AVERAGES)   Unit: Million Y

Year	Domestic supply	Domestic demand	Supply — Demand
1878–92	431	420	+ 11
1883–87	333	326	+ 7
1888–92	460	463	− 3
1893–07	632	663	− 31
1898–02	959	1,058	− 99
1903–07	1,230	1,425	−195
1908–12	1,501	1,754	−253
1913–17	1,787	2,186	−399

Source: Domestic supply—Ohkawa and Others, p. 58; Domestic demand—Tobata, Seiichi and Oh-kawa, Kazushi (eds.), *Nihon no keizai to nogyo* (The Japanese Economy and Agriculture) (Tokyo: Iwanami Shoten, 1956), ch. iv, sec. 1, Table 4.2.

sectors of the economy. In so doing, agriculture made a necessary contribution to rapid industrialization and urbanization. Inflationary pressures stemming from a shortage of food must have been minimal, and many underdeveloped areas today must envy this situation.

So far we have stressed the domestic role of Japanese agriculture, but, as is well known, its contribution was also notable in the expansion of international trade. Increases in output and quality improvement of such commercial products as silk cocoons and tea leaves were, in the early years, the primary basis for the rapid growth of semi-manufactured exports, such as raw silk and tea. Raw silk in particular remained an important export item even after World War I. The function of agriculture as an earner of foreign exchange was extremely important to the economic development of the country. In the absence of foreign loans, export surpluses were required to import foreign capital goods to be used in the modernization in industry. Before World War I these export surpluses largely originated in agriculture.

TABLE IV. TERMS OF TRADE BETWEEN URBAN AND RURAL SECTORS
(FIVE YEAR AVERAGES)   1928–32 = 100

Year	Price index of non-agricultural commodities (N)	Price index of agricultural commodities (A)	N/A
1878–82	44	44	100
1883–87	33	30	107
1888–92	34	34	100
1893–97	41	44	92
1898–02	53	56	94
1903–07	63	66	95
1908–12	68	70	97
1913–17	82	77	106

Sources: Computed from Ohkawa and Others, p. 130.

The industrial revolution in Japan was not preceded or accompanied by an agricultural revolution of the *Western type*.[7] There was, as we have seen, a rapid expansion of agricultural output combined with speedy industrialization, and "revolutionary changes" took place in a matter of decades. However, the increases in output and productivity were based on the traditional patterns of rural organization inherited, in the main, from the Tokugawa period. The small family farm, averaging about 1 hectare per household, the distribution between peasant proprietors and tenants, high rents in kind—all of these characteristics were maintained during the period. At the same time, there was no strong trend of land consolidation, and this preserved the scattered holdings of tiny plots of ground, nor was there evidence of a rural exodus to the urban areas by a *newly created* landless peasant class. During the early period of industrialization necessary increases in the labor force did indeed come from the rural areas. But laborers were usually young and left singly. There was only very little movement in terms of family units, and no formation of an agricultural proletariat.[8] Thus, a fairly typical Asian type of agriculture remained in existence and was utilized to promote impressive increases in productivity, while Western technology was making rapid progress in manufacturing...

The previous analysis implies that there

7. The term "agricultural revolution" is, at best, vague, and not all Western countries went through agricultural revolutions of the Western type. Here we only wish to underline the fact that no radical reorganization of the producing unit took place shortly before or after the Restoration. Earlier in the Tokugawa period, as Thomas C. Smith has clearly shown, a very peculiar type of agricultural revolution did take place. Cf. *The Agrarian Origins of Modern Japan* (Stanford: Stanford University Press, 1959).

8. See Tobata and Ohkawa, ch. iii, section 1, pp. 123 ff. and section 2, pp. 153–5.

must have been key improvements in Japanese agricultural practice in keeping with the small unit of production. Broadly speaking, two kinds of improvement took place in combination. The first kind took the form of land improvement, including better irrigation and drainage facilities and the reclamation of some arable land—mostly paddy rice fields. The second kind of improvement encompassed superior seeds, better methods of crop cultivation, and increased input of manures and fertilizers. The latter type of technological advance required increases in working capital rather than lumpy investment in fixed capital such as machinery or livestock. As such, these were methods of improvement within the reach of the small family unit. On the other hand, land improvement projects and reclamation required capital and labor beyond the reach of the individual farmer, and were carried out principally by landlords and the government.

. . .

Before World War I the incentives for investment in agriculture were not lacking. Landlords received a high rent in kind, and were interested in raising and stabilizing yields. Nominally rents were set on the basis of absolute amounts, rather than as a share of output, but the final rent paid tended to fluctuate in accordance with yield changes. These factors encourage entrepreneurship. Furthermore, during almost the entire period, the price of rice rose *pari passu* with the general price level, and this must have been an incentive to one and all to improve practices of cultivation. Also, the land tax burden was lessened with greater production. At this time, absentee owners were rare in Japan. Most landowners lived in the rural districts and frequently acted as leaders in introducing new methods suited to particular local conditions. The State also played an important role in developing locally suited technology. Local and Central Government established experimental stations and extension services, and provided technical and general education through organization and support of the school system.

. . .

In discussing the changing role of agriculture in Japanese economic development, especially when attempting to observe the economic facets of urban-rural relationships, we have so far ignored at least two important problems. The first has to do with the human factor—movement of the labor force to cities and sources of entrepreneurship—and this topic has been covered by others. The second problem deals with investment flows from the rural to the urban regions. Agriculture was a source of savings in the economy, and these savings were translated into investment, i.e. capital formation. At this juncture, it is almost impossible to provide a quantitative discussion of these investment flows. The data are not adequate, and we will therefore approach the issue indirectly.

We begin with the widely accepted assumption that large savings in agriculture could be and were in fact used for purposes of industrialization. The rationale of this assumption can be illustrated theoretically. Let us suppose that for the pre-World War I period the average growth rate of the economy was about 3.5 percent per year, and that the average capital coefficient was around 3 or 4. Then the average ratio of savings in the economy would be 10 to 14 percent—that is, simply the product of the growth rate and the capital coefficient. (We believe the figures to be close to reality.) The growth rate of net output in agriculture, as shown previously, was 2.3 percent per year during the relevant period, and it can be reasonably supposed

that the capital coefficient of this sector was lower than the national average.[9] This means that the required investments in agriculture were smaller than the savings generated by this sector—if the savings ratio was at least as large as the national level—and the resulting surplus could have been siphoned off to the non-agricultural sectors.[10]

Good evidence that the facts are in rough correspondence with the theory lies in the operation of the famous Meiji land tax. In an earlier section, we stressed the maintenance of high rents in kind in the face of steadily increasing agricultural productivity. A traditional landlord system and the device of the land tax allowed the government to exploit the existing situation by transferring income from one sector of the economy to the other.[11] It is not necessary to provide a detailed description of this tax, enacted in 1873. Let us only remind ourselves that, during a critical stage of Japanese economic development, the land tax was the main source of government revenue; its weight in the central govern-

9. We indicated previously that the key improvements in Japanese agriculture were not especially capital using. Certainly they were less capital using than Western industrial technology which was being adopted in the secondary sector.

10. In the initial stages of Japanese industrialization, foreign capital, on the whole, played a minor role. The Meiji Government borrowed considerable sums of money from great merchants, and in this way used some of the capital accumulation dating back to feudal times. The new government also established a modern banking and credit system in order to facilitate the creation of funds for industrialization. Also, the inflationary process, especially during the early period, by creating forced savings contributed to the intricate process of capital formation. All of these points, worthy of further study, are well beyond the limits of our paper. Here we only wish to stress that, in addition to the devices discussed above, the transfer of rural income and savings to the urban sector played a continuous and fundamental role in overall capital formation.

11. For an analysis dealing with almost the same problem and reaching similar conclusions, see Ranis, "Financing Japanese Development," *Economic History Review*, XI, 3.

TABLE V. COMPOSITION OF MAIN CENTRAL GOVERNMENT TAXATION REVENUE [a]
(FIVE YEAR AVERAGES)

Unit: Thousand Y

Year	Income tax	%	Land tax	%	Business tax	%	Customs duty	%	Total
1888–92	1,091	2.4	38,446	85.6	740	1.6	4,654	10.4	44,941
1893–97	1,599	3.3	38,679	80.4	1,335	2.8	6,483	13.5	78,096
1898–02	5,520	7.8	44,632	63.2	6,058	8.6	14,414	20.4	70,624
1903–07	19,907	15.5	71,579	55.8	15,710	12.3	33,835	26.4	141,031
1908–12	34,071	18.3	79,541	42.9	25,033	13.5	46,691	25.3	185,337
1913–17	51,249	26.0	73,983	37.6	25,334	12.9	46,245	23.5	196,811
1918–22	187,276	47.4	73,936	18.3	57,226	14.2	85,686	21.1	404,124
1923–27	206,692	45.0	71,204	15.5	58,835	12.8	122,264	26.7	459,218
1928–32	177,568	42.9	65,121	15.8	48,290	11.7	122,414	29.6	413,393
1933–37	267,695	49.4	58,175	10.7	62,132	11.5	153,751	28.4	541,753

Source: Tobata and Ohkawa, p. 375. Calculated from data provided by Tsunematsu.

[a] Revenue other than from the four main taxes—the so-called "miscellaneous revenue"—is excluded from the table. Before World War I it accounted for about 30 to 40 percent of total revenue; after the War its share rose to from 45 to 50 percent.

ment revenue structure is shown in Table V.

The changing role of agriculture comes out clearly in these data. Until 1913-17, the land tax—though steadily declining in significance—was absolutely the most important source of government revenue. The agricultural land tax formed 80 or 90 percent of the general land tax, and thus the main source of revenue had to be the net product of the farms. An income tax enacted into law in 1888 played only a minor role before World War I. It became important as agriculture faded out of the picture as the primary source of revenue, and as a dynamic force of further development.

The heavy burdens which the rural areas were required to shoulder during the course of development come out even more obviously in Table VI. Here we use Tsunematsu's estimates of the relative direct tax burden—central and local—on income produced, dividing the economy into two sectors: agriculture and non-agriculture. It may be surprising to note that the direct tax ratio remained consid-

erably higher in agriculture during the period. A very high tax rate was imposed on agriculture during the early years of development, while a very low rate prevailed outside; it is true, however, that the weight of the burden declined with time. The persistence of the agricultural tax load stems from heavy local tax rates, applied in rural prefectures, which were not reduced when productive capacity lagged.

By way of summary, let us take a brief look at the expenditure side of the government budget, concentrating on subsidies. Throughout the relatively long period of Japanese development, the government played a very important role, especially as an investor.[12] Subsidies were one method of government investment. While other methods (mainly direct investment) were quantitatively more important, subsidies do indicate to some extent the economic priorities of the regime. These changing priorities are apparent in Table VII, where we show the distribution of subsidies by industrial sectors.

12. See Rosovsky, "Japanese Capital Formation," *Journal of Economic History,* XIX, 3.

TABLE VI. DIRECT TAX RATIO TO INCOME PRODUCED
AGRICULTURE VERSUS NON-AGRICULTURE

Year	Agriculture		Non-Agriculture	
	Direct tax (thous. Y)	Ratio (%)	Direct tax (thous. Y)	Ratio (%)
1883–87	63,552	22.1	9,548	3.0
1888–92	58,479	15.5	9,779	2.3
1893–97	65,626	12.4	13,167	2.0
1898–02	99,050	12.1	35,378	3.2
1903–07	113,582	11.2	79,313	5.4
1908–12	153,441	12.5	132,196	6.4
1913–17	167,660	12.9	145,441	4.5
1918–22	295,672	9.2	431,081	5.4
1923–27	304,217	10.5	506,203	5.2
1928–32	205,450	9.7	421,311	4.3
1933–37	197,325	7.8	559,235	4.2

Source: Tobata and Ohkawa, p. 381. Computed from data supplied by Tsunematsu.

TABLE VII. SECTORAL COMPOSITION OF SUBSIDIES
(TOTAL = 100)

Year	Primary sector	Secondary sector	Tertiary sector	Miscellaneous
1891	–	58.8	2.3	37.9
1901	–	51.9	28.7	17.8
1911	0.8	38.0	30.9	30.3
1921	0.6	19.6	32.8	47.1
1931	10.8	40.2	10.9	38.1
1941	20.0	10.8	40.9	28.4

Source: Nakayama Ichiro (ed.), *Nihon keizai no kozo bunseki*, part ii, p. 159.

Throughout the entire period, the secondary and tertiary sectors were the main recipients of government subsidies. Manufacturing, shipping, armaments, and social overhead capital all received extensive support. More significant from our point of view is the varying picture in the primary sector. Until the 1920's practically no subsidies (although plenty of other help) were allotted to agriculture; after all, it was one of the major sources of surplus in the economy. But then the income flow seems to be reversed as agriculture begins to get some financial support from the government. We believe that the changing distribution of subsidies is symptomatic of a structural change in the traditional capital flow. In a sense the economy had turned a full circle. In the early period of development there was a net flow of capital from the rural to the urban areas. We think that this flow may have been reversed sometime after World War I. Admittedly this must remain a highly conjectural conclusion, and requires further detailed investigation before it can be accepted with the proper degree of confidence.

How does the Japanese experience fit the international pattern of development? In this section we will try to examine certain aspects of this question for the entire period of analysis: that is, from 1868 to the 1940's. International comparisons are technically and substantively intricate. Comparable and otherwise adequate series are in extremely short supply, and all too often a great deal of guesswork is involved. This is especially true for long-term comparisons. To minimize these problems our comparisons are restricted to a few basic and broad issues.

In common with all other developing countries, during Japanese industrialization there took place a decline in the relative share of income produced and labor employed in agriculture. The percentage of national income produced in the primary sector fell from 64 in 1878–82, to 36 in 1913–17, to 17 in 1938–42. The percentage of the labor force engaged in agriculture was 76, 59, and 44 during the same periods.[13] Both of these measures indicate a rather rapid transformation when compared to the data available for Europe.

Let us first consider the matter of income shares. European data are unfortunately unavailable for the period which would correspond to the initial phase of Japanese development. Beginning in the 1880's, when Kuznets' series start, we note that income produced in agriculture accounted generally for 40 to 50 percent of national income. By 1940, the European range lay between 27 per cent (Italy) and 13 per cent (Sweden)—excluding the United Kingdom.[14] Two conclusions follow: the income share of agriculture decreased at a much more rapid tempo in Japan than in Europe, and perhaps more important, the

relative position of Japanese agriculture in terms of income produced had reached the average European levels even before World War II.

The average European share of labor force in agriculture was much lower than in Japan. Around 1940 it ranged from 25 to 35 per cent (leaving out certain extreme cases.)[15] This naturally requires the conclusion that the relative level of *per capita* income in Japanese agriculture was much lower than the average level in Europe. And indeed this is hardly surprising in view of the structural difficulties of Japanese agriculture which were encountered in the period preceding World War II.[16]

15. *Ibid.*, Appendix Table 4. It might not be out of place to point out here that statistics dealing with the occupational breakdown of the labor force are frequently unreliable. For example, the Japanese figures classify as agricultural labor many persons who engage in so-called "by-employment" (usually small industry or services) and whose major source of income, especially on a household basis, may be from secondary or tertiary employment.

16. It may be of interest to make a few comparisons with the most recent and important case of agricultural take-off in Asia: the experience of Communist China. This has become possible with the recent authoritative study by Choh-Ming Li, *Economic Development of Communist China,* (Berkeley: University of California Press, 1958). He shows that in 1956, 40 percent of China's NNP was produced by agriculture (p. 110). Japan had reached nearly the same level by 1908–12 (Ohkawa and Others, p. 26), but China descended from 49.7 per cent to 40.0 per cent in four years, while this took Japan about fifteen years. The current cost ratio to net output in Chinese agriculture is around 74 per cent. This is roughly equivalent to the Japanese level in 1942. (Li, pp. 86-7, and Ohkawa and Others, p. 64). These differences seem largely due to the greater degree of mechanization in present Chinese practice. Li estimates the food grain output growth rate to be about the same as that of population, i.e. 2.5 per cent annually (p. 72). We have already shown that the pre-World War I rates in Japan were on the same level *with much lower population growth*. No simple analogy can be attempted between Meiji Japan and Communist China. It is, however, quite clear that the social costs of Japanese development were lower. Similar growth of output was achieved without collectivizations, communes, and other social strains.

13. Ohkawa and Others, pp. 26-27. The figure for 1878–82 has been tentatively revised to 76 per cent from the previous 82 per cent. See Ohkawa, Kazushi, "Yugyo jinko (1872–1920) no suikei—nogyo jinko" (Survey of the Gainfully Employed Population in Agriculture, 1872–1920), Hitotsubashi University Institute of Economic Research Working Papers, 1958.

14. Simon Kuznets, "Quantitative Aspects of the Economic Growth of Nations—II, Industrial Distribution of National Product and Labor Force," *Economic Development and Cultural Change,* supplement to Vol. V, No. 4 (July 1957), Appendix Table 2.

These brief comparisons suggest a number of questions which may serve to clarify the differences between the Japanese and the European patterns. First of all, what effect could have been expected from the economic level prevailing in Japan when she started to industrialize? The issue of "initial conditions" is frequently raised by economists when they consider the possibilities of economic development in currently backward areas. Often there is the feeling that the Western experience with industrialization is only of highly limited applicability because pre-industrial economic levels in Europe were much higher. These are complex problems, and the lack of data rarely allow quantitative analysis. In the case of Japanese agriculture, however, it may be possible to say something about the initial stages with the aid of productivity figures. At this time, of course, agriculture was the most important sector in the economy and therefore represents quite well the average economic level.

Let us look at levels of productivity prevailing in Asia today, and those which prevailed in Japan during the Meiji Era. The *Yearbook of Food and Agricultural Statistics* (1957) of the FAO cites the following national paddy yield averages for 1954-56 in bushels/hectare: China (Taiwan) 134.2, China (Mainland) 121.0, Malaya 98.5, Indonesia 84.8, Burma 74.5, Thailand 66.1, India 63.7, Philippines 58.8, and Japan 208.7. We know that Japanese paddy field yields were approximately 63 bushels/hectare in 1878-82, and it seems safe to assume that yields fluctuated between 60 and 70 bushels/hectare in the first decade of Meiji.[17] In other words, the level of rice farming land productivity at the beginning of Japanese economic development was similar to the current levels of Southeast Asia. It is reasonable to suppose that this was also true for labor productivity.

17. See relevant years of *Noshomusho tokeihyo*.

It is much more difficult to compare Japanese and Western productivity levels during the initial phases of development because the main crops were different. It is, however, plausible to suppose that average labor productivity was much higher in the West. Two main reasons may be given: the man-land ratio was much more favorable throughout Europe, and, for the most part, agricultural revolutions had preceded industrial revolutions.

We can now summarize the conditions of Japanese agriculture during the initial stages of industrialization by underlining two distinctive features: a very unfavorable man-land ratio and a relatively low level of labor productivity, implying a low level of general economic performance. Japan shared these features with most Asian countries, which as a group stood in contrast to average European conditions.

A second point which can explain the differences between the tempo of sectoral change in Japan and in the West involves the speedy progress of Japanese agriculture before World War I. This has already been described in some detail, but a few comparative points may be raised now. We hesitated to label these events as "agricultural revolution" because technical innovations did not bring about a change in the structure of the producing unit. On the other hand, it is worth noticing that changes in agriculture took place at a speedy rate, comparable perhaps to the most speedy rates of Europe. It is not possible to produce the statistics which would allow us to raise these statements from the level of assertion to the level of fact. Nevertheless, consulting such data as are available, we believe that the fastest growth rates of agricultural output and productivity in Europe hardly ever exceeded 2 and 1.5 per cent per year respectively.[18] If

18. We have made some rough calculations of the annual growth rates of real net product per man for several Western countries. Using data

so, one may call the Japanese case revolutionary progress.

Thirdly, it has already been observed that revolutionary progress in Japanese agriculture occurred not before but side by side with industrialization. This was not the typical European sequence. The concurrent and rapid changes in Japanese agriculture and industry suggest to us the possibilities of a peculiar and interesting model of economic growth. It would have to emphasize several key relations observed in Japan: an increasing trend in the subsistence level of the peasantry, increasing real wages in the industrial sector, almost balanced growth of output in agriculture and industry, high rates of saving and investment, and low capital coefficients. In the model, agriculture would perform the crucial functions of supplying output, net increments of the labor force, and a large share of savings, all in an institutional framework of enterpreneurial landlordism and a paternal government. A model of this type could, when compared to Western experience, clarify the *role* of Japanese agriculture in economic development seen in an international setting. . . .

The concurrence of rapid agricultural and economic development resulted in an unusual juxtaposition of sectoral growth rates. Just as industry was hitting its peak, agriculture went into a decline. In some sense the revolutionary developments in agriculture were short-lived, and this can be explained in terms of two major causes.

If we date the beginnings of Japanese economic growth in the 1870's—and for certain purposes this is perfectly legitimate —then the period of rapid agricultural

expansion lasted less than fifty years. This view, however, fails to consider the fact that the groundwork for progress in agriculture, as distinguished from the other sectors, started at a much earlier date. The achievements of agriculture before World War I are part of a long chain of events beginning in the eighteenth century. The unit of production, the system of tenure, and many other characteristics can all be traced back to the Tokugawa Era. A certain production potential existed at the time of the Restoration, and the introduction of some modern methods, the intensification of selected beneficial traditional methods, minimum fixed capital requirements, and a very dynamic economic climate, all help to account for the increases in output and productivity. But once this potential has been exploited within the inherited institutional framework and with almost unchanged factor proportions, further progress became much more difficult. By 1918, the traditional setting and rigid unit of production had become a limiting factor in further development.

Another reason for the rather short spurt of agricultural output and productivity is related to the general pattern of Japanese economic development. It must, however, be considered in conjunction with a few exogenous factors. The spurt of industrialization which started during World War I, efforts to cope with severe international competition abroad, enforced heavy industrialization in preparation for war in the 1930's—all these economic influences pressed the relative income share of agriculture into a less important place. These tendencies were reinforced by a factor which can only be called paradoxical. In spite of their very rapid expansion, the non-agricultural sectors grew barely sufficiently to absorb increases in the labor force produced by agriculture. This has meant that just before World War II an unfavorable man-land ratio of the Asian type, with

---

supplied by E. Ojala in *Agriculture and Economic Progress* (London: Oxford University Press, 1952), taking an average beginning and terminal period and assuming a compound growth between these two points, we get the following annual average growth rates: U.S.A. (1869–78–1909–18) 1.0; U.K. (1867–69–1904–10) 0.6; Sweden (1861–65–1906–10) 1.6. . . .

which Japan originally started, still existed, and that rapid industrialization and urbanization had not succeeded in significantly decreasing the absolute agricultural population. In turn, this limited the possibilities of technical progress in agriculture.

4.2 LATIN AMERICAN AGRICULTURAL POLICY *

Agriculture has developed slowly in most Latin American countries over the past few years. Where it has developed rapidly, the growth was caused by the incidental development of export products, particularly those for which there is a slowly but steadily increasing external demand.

The slow growth of agriculture has acted as a powerful deterrent to balanced general economic development. Moreover, the structural framework in which agricultural activities develop and the pattern of income distribution prevalent in that sector have also delayed the emergence of an adequate market for the absorption of the products of domestic industry.

Action to remedy the situation described above and to find ways and means of achieving the rapid development of agriculture and a more equitable distribution of agricultural income must therefore be taken without delay. This action might lead to the following:

(a) Use of idle or underemployed resources, particularly lobour;

(b) Expansion of demand for industrial goods and services as well as food and fibres produced by farmers;

(c) Import substitution in respect of foodstuffs and raw materials of agricultural origin—particularly those from outside the area—with a view to freeing foreign exchange which could be used to import

capital equipment both in order to achieve a more rapid process of industrialization and to provide agriculture with better equipment and a higher level of technique and production;

(d) Avoidance of an unduly rapid process of urbanization;[1]

(e) Improved living and nutritional conditions in rural areas.

A faster rate of agricultural development which would have far-reaching effects on the steady economic development of Latin America would call not only for full employment of the rural labour force throughout the year but also for the widespread adoption of improved agricultural techniques. In the first stage of an effort of this kind, production techniques should be adapted to the general conditions of abundant manpower and lack of capital, without forgetting that the degree of emphasis will vary depending on the area concerned. In other words, pilot stations should endeavour to introduce techniques calculated to produce the best combination of factors through full employment of the labour force and higher productivity by means of improved seeds, fertilizer, pesticides and hand-tools.[2] They should also seek to improve the quality of farm work and to undertake such projects as irrigation and drainage in order to lengthen the useful period of the farm year as much as possible. None of these improvements— nor the more equitable income distribution needed in order to expand the market—can be achieved without thorough institutional reforms designed to shake producers out of their present indifference to economic

* From Economic Commission for Latin America, "An Agricultural Policy to Expedite the Economic Development of Latin America," *Economic Bulletin for Latin America,* October 1961, pp. 1-3.

1. Recent experience in Latin America shows that, in countries with a high population growth rate, the manufacturing sector—even with a very high growth rate of the product of 8 to 10 per cent annually—cannot fully absorb the natural growth of the urban labour force and is even less able to absorb redundant rural workers.

2. Instead of adopting "imported" methods based chiefly on labour saving through mechanization.

incentives aimed at achieving the selective increases in agricultural production required by a growing country.

Full employment of the rural labour force may cause severe short-term disequilibria in the supply-demand balance and a surplus of food and other traditional products in Latin American countries suffering from heavy population pressure. In areas with a low percentage of rural population, a relatively high level of technique and a nearly optimum use of labour, much of the farm work will have to be mechanized in order to achieve an effective increase in production. In cases where production is uncertain because of a shortage or excess of water, full employment in agriculture cannot be attained without establishing a proper infrastructure. Moreover, improvement of means of communication to facilitate or permit agricultural development is essential throughout Latin America.

It is therefore felt that the accelerated development of agriculture in Latin America will require an intensive public works programme for the following purposes:

(a) to provide work for those who cannot immediately be employed in agricultural production proper because of the danger of surplus supply;

(b) to reduce seasonal unemployment as much as possible;

(c) to establish an adequate infrastructure as a basis for more efficient agriculture.

Inherent in the above programme is the construction, in due course and on a staggered basis, of irrigation and drainage works, roads, warehouses, schools and other public buildings, improvement of rural housing, etc. In order adequately to supplement this sort of escape valve for the rural labour force, processing industries suitably distributed in rural areas must also be established. Public investment in the rural sector will not only lead to the bene-

fits already mentioned but will also compensate for the sluggish rate of investment in the Latin American agricultural infrastructure. It should nevertheless be borne in mind that, while the coefficient of foreign exchange needed for this investment is very small, it does require domestic savings. It is therefore obvious that high priority must be given to these works until the bottleneck created by agriculture has been removed. Once this has been done, however, agricultural investment should be considered in the light of other investment possibilities within the broad framework of the economy as a whole, so that priority may be given to investments which would contribute to the best relative increase in the total product.

The interest shown by countries in this type of programme as a means of relieving social tensions through accelerated agricultural development, and the possibility that international assistance in this field may increase, point to the desirability of studying the general lines of an agricultural policy for Latin America, particularly with respect to the major institutional changes required for an adequate growth rate with which to achieve the desired objectives. This task requires governmental action in agriculture and other sectors of the economy. Until now this form of guidance—which has always existed to a certain extent—has at times been incomplete, sporadic and disjointed. Hence the importance of development programming, which is essentially nothing more than the orderly arrangement of governmental action in the economic field to promote the achievement of well-defined targets for the welfare of the community.

In spite of the efforts made and the favourable conditions which prevailed during the first ten post-war years, Latin America has not succeeded in achieving a position enabling its growth rate to exceed that of its exports. The growth rate of the product in Latin America is currently much lower than it was in the period 1945-55 and prospects for improvement seem to be somewhat limited unless the countries concerned adopt decisive measures to overcome certain obstacles, particularly of an institutional character. There are two major aspects to the problem. On the one hand, the external sector of the regional economy has weakened with the fall in prices, the deterioration in the terms of trade and the difficulty in securing outlets for agricultural (and other) products on the world market. On the other hand, the rate of expansion of the internal sector has been inadequate. The Latin American markets are growing too slowly, largely because of the unequal income distribution, aggravated in some countries during the past few years by monetary stabilization measures which were not accompanied by adequate investment programmes.

The situation created by the internal sector of the Latin American economies is largely attributable to the inadequate development of agriculture. A study of the growth rate and conditions obtaining in this sector point clearly to problems which would seem to require the urgent attention of Governments with a view to establishing a general process of expansion of the Latin American economy on a proper and durable basis.

The background to the problem of Latin American agriculture is the low average income level of the rural population. Taking Latin America as a whole, the contribution of a rural worker to the gross product is, on an average, less than one third of the contribution of a person engaged in activities other than agriculture. Moreover, available figures indicate that, in absolute terms, the differences are increasing instead of diminishing. Thus, between 1945-47 and 1955-57 the average income of a rural worker in Latin America, in terms of constant purchasing power, rose from 325 to 390 dollars, whereas that of an urban worker increased from 1120 to 1315 dollars.

The gap between rural and urban income is only part of the problem, because income distribution in agriculture itself is also very uneven. Although data on this point are lacking, it is perhaps in the rural sector that the sharpest contrasts may be found. In fact, while the vast majority of small landowners, landless peasants and rural wage-earners barely earn enough to live at a minimum subsistence level, a relatively small group of large entrepreneurs and property owners have huge incomes. The average income per major category—much of it being undisclosed, particularly at the upper end of the scale—shows that the *per capita* income of the entrepreneurial group is from 20 to 40 times larger than that of the vast majority of rural workers.

Although a situation similar to that prevailing in Latin America obtains in virtually every country in the world, there are factors which help to widen the gap in underdeveloped countries and, on the contrary, to narrow the breach in those industrial countries which, in addition to their high level of agricultural technology, have a better system of land distribution. Besides the vast differences in rural and non-rural income, there are also differences in the productivity of the persons employed in the various sectors of the economy. Agricultural productivity is usually low because of the uneven distribution of property, the inadequate systems of land tenure and use, and the archaic rural labour and recruitment systems which still obtain in many areas of Latin America. To all this must be added the shortage of capital and the lack of a proper infrastructure for the development of productive activities, widespread ignorance of—or failure to apply—agricultural techniques through which a better combination of factors under existing conditions can be secured and, very often, the absence of a policy of economic incentives and of structural changes directed towards the achievement of specific development targets.

Under the conditions described above, the growth of Latin American agriculture has been sluggish in most countries during the past few years. Taking Latin America as a whole, total agricultural production and the output of foodstuffs—expressed in *per capita* terms—are now less than they were before the last war. In the few cases in which agricultural output has grown rapidly, this was achieved primarily through the incidental development of export commodities—e.g. coffee, cotton and bananas—the foreign demand for which is slowly but steadily increasing....

The slow development of the agricultural sector in face of a rapid growth in population and in the total income generated by the economy has had important consequences for Latin America. On the one hand, the growing domestic demand for foodstuffs and agricultural raw materials has compelled some countries to withhold an increasing share of their staple export items, particularly meat, wheat, pulses, oilseeds and milk derivatives. On the other hand, many countries have found it necessary to expand their imports of foodstuffs to prevent a cut in supplies which might have increased existing inflationary pressures and depressed the nutritional level, already low and inadequate in large areas of Latin America.

In the circumstances, the gap between agricultural imports and exports narrowed considerably. Fortunately, the capacity to import did not suffer as much as might logically have been expected during the first ten post-war years. On the contrary, there was a marked improvement in the terms of trade as a result of which the purchasing power of net *per capita* exports declined by only 14 per cent at a time when the quantum dropped by over 40 per cent. However, the situation has changed sub-

stantially since 1957 because of the sharp drop in the price of a few agricultural commodities on the world market.

Notwithstanding the aforementioned structural defects and the relative stagnation of production, agriculture continues to be the chief economic activity for Latin America as a whole. Its contribution to the gross national product is close to 24 per cent.[3] Agricultural exports account for about two-thirds of the total value of Latin American exports. Lastly, over 50 per cent of the economically active population is engaged in farming.[4] That is why agricultural problems are so important and must be speedily solved in order to achieve a more rapid rate of general development and greater stability in the Latin American economies.

4.3 TRENDS IN AGRICULTURAL DEVELOPMENT OF COLOMBIA *

Agriculture is Colombia's major industry; it provides a way of life for two out of every three persons in Colombia. Domestic agricultural production makes the largest single contribution to the country's national income, supplies most of the country's food requirements and accounts for more than three quarters of Colombia's foreign exchange earnings.

Thus any sound and effective program for the further development of the economy of Colombia as a whole must include as an indispensable element measures that will achieve the fullest possible utilization of Colombia's many resources—human,

3. The industrial sector, next in importance, represents about 20 per cent.

4. The population classified as "rural" constitutes about 58 per cent of the total population of Latin America.

* From *The Agricultural Development of Colombia,* Report of a Mission organized by the International Bank for Reconstruction and Development at the request of the Government of the Republic of Colombia, Washington, D.C., May 1956, pp. 1-2, 32-7.

physical and financial—for agricultural development.

The mission of the International Bank which made a general economic survey of Colombia in 1949 included in its report an analysis of the agricultural situation and numerous recommendations for action. During the five and one half years since that report was submitted, substantial progress has been made in a number of directions in developing Colombia's agriculture.

Progress in agriculture has failed, however, to keep pace with the country's growing needs. While farm output has increased, the population and its requirements have likewise increased; agriculture has lagged behind various other sectors of the economy in providing higher standards of living for a constantly rising population.

Over the next decade agriculture would need to be expanded by 25% merely to keep pace with Colombia's increasing population, even without an improvement in the standard of living. If standards of living are to be raised, as they should be, the rate of growth must be even faster. The mission believes that a 40% increase in agricultural production by 1965 will be necessary to provide for the increase in population and a rise of 25% in consumption standards. Such a program would not achieve national self-sufficiency in agricultural products; it might be possible to eliminate imports except for wheat but this would require an increase of nearly 50% in production instead of 40%.

This is a challenging goal but it is one which the mission believes to be realistic and attainable. As the report demonstrates, however, there is no simple or easy path by which it can be reached. It will require an impressive mobilization of resources. It will require an approach from many directions at once. It will require dedication and wisdom—and it will require patience to forego spectacular early accomplishments in favor

of steady and soundly-based progress over a number of years.

A fundamental conclusion on which the mission's entire program is based is that Colombia's future agricultural needs cannot be met by the traditional system of extensive cultivation because sufficient new land of good quality is not available. While some increase in output can come from opening up new lands, the mission warns that this method will become progressively more difficult and may be reaching its end within a decade. The development program will have to be directed principally to measures that will bring about a steady and substantial increase of output on lands now in use and will lower the present high costs of production....

During the six years since the report of the International Bank's general survey mission to Colombia, substantial progress has been made in a number of directions in developing Colombia's agriculture; yet, when viewed as a whole in relation to Colombia's needs, progress has fallen far short of possibilities. Farm output has increased (although lack of reliable statistics makes it impossible to gauge the exact extent of the gains), partly through the assistance given by government but largely by private initiative. At the same time, the population and its needs have likewise increased. The overcrowded mountain sides under arable cultivation still look down on sparsely populated pasture valleys and, though some pasture land has been brought under the plow, the shift of land use from grazing to arable farming has been sporadic. Neither the opening of new lands for farmers from the overpopulated hilly areas nor the protection of the eroding slopes has become the subject of a planned and coordinated activity of the government.

While progress has been made in certain lines the situation has remained static in others, and in many important spheres the shortcomings noted half a dozen years ago go unremedied. The numerous unsolved problems of land tenure continue to lack attention, and to react harmfully on the productivity of the soil. Colombian agriculture continues in general to move in the same vicious circle of capital shortage, low productivity and high production costs.

In the meantime, the non-agricultural sector of the country's economy has been growing rapidly. Industrial development has drawn many people off the land. Thus, the percentage of the total labor force of Colombia engaged in agricultural production, 60.5 in 1945, fell to 54.3 in 1953, although the absolute numbers remained about the same.

The growth of industry in Colombia has led to an expansion of demand for agricultural products, notably fibers, but it has also resulted in many attractive alternative uses for capital; consequently, in the last five years the limited amount of capital in the country has been attracted to fields other than agriculture. The rate of capital formation in agriculture has lagged considerably behind that of industry; today, the total investment in machinery and equipment in the entire agriculture of Colombia is less than that of the Bavaria Brewery there.

Buoyant coffee prices and the rapid increase in industrial development have contributed to the inflationary process which has continued in Colombia during the past five years but is now levelling off. This has strengthened the tendency to hold large tracts of land as assets rather than as factors of production; the building up of cattle inventories has become a popular device for tax avoidance. The best land remains under-used and the areas where the potential for increased productivity is greatest (and so can contribute to checking inflation) are under-exploited.

Since 1949 there has been further road construction which is helping to break down regionalism, to create a national market for many products, and to reduce the locational protection of high-cost producers. Improvement in road construction has been notable though slow.

The government has been pursuing actively its policy of increasing national self-sufficiency in agriculture. To this end it has endeavored to promote domestic production by making farm machinery, seeds, fertilizers and credit more readily available, while discouraging low-cost imports of foodstuffs by high tariffs, quotas and the like.

To assist further in improving production and marketing, the government has embarked on a many-sided program, the execution of which has been entrusted to some dozen agencies, institutes and other bodies, official and semi-official. Some of these agencies are under the aegis of the Ministry of Agriculture; others are remote from it. Consequently, development has been sporadic, without adequate coordination and often on an individual commodity, rather than an over-all, basis. In this process the Ministry of Agriculture has divested itself of many of the functions normally performed by an executive branch of the government.

Remedial action is required in fields such as extension, education, research and statistics. The shortage of trained personnel for all these activities is acute. Gains have been made, however, in the field of research and a sound organization has been set up to handle certain aspects of it. The first government-sponsored major irrigation projects have been constructed and are in operation and the government has entered into the field of marketing through its marketing agency, the *Instituto Nacional de Abastecimiento* (INA). The *Caja de Credito Agrario Industrial y Minero* has expanded its activities; during the past five years its loans have risen six-fold.

Notable improvements have occurred in the private sector of the economy since 1950. Mechanization, particularly for preparatory tillage, has increased considerably, although its use is far from widespread, and far from what will be required to achieve necessary production targets in the future; large-scale production of cotton and rice has been undertaken and is being increased in several parts of the country. There has been a considerable expansion in the use of improved seed, fertilizers and pesticides.

But the underlying pattern has nevertheless remained largely unchanged. Progress has been uneven. There is little change in the general pattern of land use, technology and marketing. Such changes as have taken place have largely by-passed both the small-scale producer on the hillside lands sub-marginal to arable production and the large landowner engaged in livestock raising. Most progress has come about through the activities of a relatively new group on the scene—the tenant farmer with financial resources adequate to purchase machinery and to cultivate land on a considerable scale. Some landlords are doing likewise, particularly in or near the more densely populated urban areas where land values are very high. However, much greater development in this direction is needed.

Thus, although during the last six years there has been unquestionable progress in some aspects of Colombian agriculture, it has been uncoordinated and many aspects remain untouched. Now, as noted in the report of the earlier International Bank mission, the government has still to meet the challenge of developing a comprehensive and coordinated over-all farm policy, without which advances in scattered fields will be outweighed by the debilitating effect of stagnation and lack of organization elsewhere. If the national government is to assume the leadership which only it can give in framing and executing such a program, it is clear that considerably more resources must be made available than the meagre 1.76% shown for the Ministry of Agriculture in the national budget of Colombia for 1955, to carry through a program affecting a segment of the economy in which two out of three Colombians earn their living.

In the mission's view the overriding agricultural needs of present-day Colombia are:

1. To increase agricultural (including livestock) production so that a population which is increasing at the high average rate of 2.2% annually may be adequately supplied with food. The general level of nutrition appears already to be low. It is also necessary that production be expanded to provide the raw materials required for the rapidly developing industrial sector of the economy;

2. To reduce present high unit costs of production which are the reflection of inefficiencies and low productivity; and

3. To create the means by which the agricultural economy can be placed on a sound permanent basis.

In endeavoring to assess the degree required in the principal agricultural commodities the mission has had to use such data as are available, realizing fully their probable inaccuracy in many cases and respects.

In establishing an agricultural program it is convenient to formulate specific targets for the principal agricultural commodities. Such targets must be related to the expected growth in demand for agricultural products and must take into account realistically potentialities for increasing production in the agricultural sector itself. The mission feels that opportunities for expanding production on a reasonable cost basis will permit an over-all increase of 40% in agricultural production by 1965. With such an increase in production agricultural products would be available in sufficient quantity to permit the fulfillment of demands at income levels of 25% higher than now on a *per capita* basis, taking into account a 25% increase in population during the next decade. Imports of agricultural commodities would constitute the same percentage of total domestic consumption as they do today. It is possible that agricultural production might be increased at reasonable cost to an extent sufficient to eliminate imports of agricultural products other than wheat. This would require an increase of nearly 50% in agricultural production instead of 40%.

4.4 INDUSTRIALIZATION IN THE GOLD COAST (GHANA) *

Industrialization starts usually in one of three ways: (1) with the processing for export of primary products (agricultural or mineral) which were previously exported in a crude state; or (2) with manufacturing for an expanding home market; or (3) with the manufacture for export of light manufactures, often based on imported raw materials. . . .

The main difficulty in the way of capturing the processing of raw materials, and thus of getting the consuming countries to import a finished product instead of its raw material, lies in the superiority of the consuming countries as centres for manufacturing. This superiority is based both on long experience and also on the scale and variety of their manufacturing industries, which is the secret of efficient production. . . .

In this competition the underdeveloped country relies usually on two advantages: (a) low labour cost, based on low wages, and (b) an advantage in transport cost, if the material loses weight in the course of processing.

Low wages are not the same as low

* From W. A. Lewis, *Report on Industrialisation and the Gold Coast,* Government Printing Department, Accra, 1953, pp. 1-3.

labour cost. In comparison with the United Kingdom, labour cost is lower on the Gold Coast (Ghana) only if the difference in wages is great enough to offset the difference in productivity. The result varies very much from industry to industry. The difference in wages is fairly constant: money wages of unskilled labour are about four times as high in the United Kingdom as they are in the Gold Coast. So the wage cost of manufacturing is lower in the Gold Coast wherever it takes less than four men to do a job that one man would do in the United Kingdom. There are a great many occupations where the advantage in wage cost lies with the Gold Coast. This advantage then helps to offset the disadvantage in other costs—bigger fuel bills, greater cost of supervision, greater costs of maintaining equipment and so on—which every Gold Coast industry has to bear.

The likelihood of low labour cost offsetting the disadvantages of operating in a non-industrial environment is greatest where labour cost is a substantial element in total cost. This is partly a function of the ratio of labour to capital in the Industry. If an operation is performed mainly by machinery, with only a small element of labour, it is almost certain to cost more in the Gold Coast than in the United Kingdom because the cost of buying, erecting, and maintaining machinery is higher in the Gold Coast than it is in an industrial country. Low labour cost is most helpful in industries where the amount of capital used per head is small. Since the processing of heavy raw materials is usually very capital intensive, low labour cost is often not sufficient to offset the environmental disadvantages of local manufacturing.

It is more usually an advantage in transport costs which decisively favours the processing of raw materials on the spot. This advantage arises in the case of those raw materials which lose weight in the process of manufacture. For example, since it takes four tons of bauxite to make one ton of aluminum, transport charges are saved if bauxite is turned into aluminum on the spot, instead of being transported as bauxite to the country where the aluminum will be used. Similarly, it is cheaper to transport sawn timber than the equivalent logs, steel than the equivalent iron ore, sugar than the equivalent sugar cane, and so on. It is not, on the other hand, cheaper to transport cloth than the equivalent cotton, because very little fibre is lost in the process of manufacture. Neither is it cheaper to transport soap to the consuming market, rather than the equivalent oils, or rubber tyres rather than the equivalent latex.

One raw material which is always lost in the process of manufacture is fuel. If fuel is available side by side with the material which is to be processed, the producing country has thus a double advantage over all consuming countries which do not have their own fuel. A source of fuel is not always important, because some commodities supply their own fuel, in the form of waste. Thus, sugar factories, sawmills, and palm oil factories are usually self-sufficient in fuel....

The decisive factor locating the processing of raw materials is thus, to summarise, usually not low wage cost, but loss of weight in the process of manufacture. Thus it is not surprising that in the Gold Coast the chief cases in which processing before export occurs are the timber industry, where up to 40 or 50 per cent of the weight of the log is waste in sawmilling, the palm oil industry, where the waste, by weight, is even greater, and the removal of precious stones from the useless ores in which they are buried, where the waste is greater still....

Manufacture for the home market shares the problems of processing for export, and has also additional problems of its own.

There is the same disadvantage of manufacturing in a place where fuel is costly, engineering service expensive, public utilities inadequate and so on. And there is the same offsetting advantage, in some occupations at any rate, of having low wage costs. The transport factor, however, is different; the principles are the same, but the consuming market is now at home, instead of overseas. In the context of the Gold Coast, where fuel had to be imported, the transport factor may be summarised as follows:

Local manufacture is favoured in two cases:

(a) If the industry uses a heavy raw material which is available on the spot, local manufacture is protected against imports to the extent of the cost of transporting the raw material, e.g. cement, beer. Or,

(b) If the manufactured commodity is more bulky than the materials of which it is made, there is a similar protection, whether or not the materials themselves have to be imported, e.g., furniture, most assembly work, hollow-ware.

Local manufacture is at a disadvantage in two cases:

(a) If the raw material would have to be imported, *and* loses weight in the process of manufacture, the transport factor favours production in the country which has the raw material, e.g., steel. Or,

(b) If fuel requirements are large. In most industries fuel cost is less than 2 per cent of the value of the finished article, but in some industries it is as high as 15 per cent to 20 per cent. The cost of transporting fuel is eliminated when commodities are made where the fuel is to be found, e.g., steel, some chemicals.

Transport cost has little relevance:

(a) If the raw material has to be imported, but does not lose weight or acquire bulk in the process of manufacture. For transport cost is then more or less the same whether the country imports the raw material or the finished article, e.g., cotton weaving, cigarettes, soap. And,

(b) If fuel requirements are small—say only 2 per cent or so of the cost of the finished article.

Apart, however, from environment, wage cost, and transport cost, the prospect of manufacturing for the home market is dominated by one other consideration, namely the size of the local market in relation to the minimum size at which production can be done economically.

The size of the local market for manufactures depends, given the size of the population, upon how rich or poor the people are. In poor countries the local market for manufactures is very small because the people spend the largest part of their income upon food and housing, and have only a small surplus available for expenditure on manufactures. Most of this surplus has to be spent on clothes, and the clothing industries are almost the only ones which have any chance of success.

The development of manufacturing for the home market therefore essentially depends upon improving the productivity of other economic activities. As the incomes derived from agriculture, from mining and from other activities grow, the local market for manufactured commodities grows automatically, and this is what makes possible the creation of factory industries catering for a local demand.

From this point of view, the most usual path to progress is increasing efficiency in the production of food. In very poor countries nearly the whole of the population is required in agriculture just to produce enough food for the country. As efficiency in food production grows, the proportion needed to produce food diminishes. In fact the simplest index to productivity in a country is to ask what proportion of the population is needed in agriculture to produce enough food for the whole country. In the richest countries, such as

the United Kingdom, the United States of America and Australia, the answer is 12 per cent to 15 per cent, whereas in most underdeveloped countries 60 per cent or more of the people are required in agriculture to produce a standard of feeding only half as good as that which the more efficient countries produce with 12 per cent of their population.

Ever increasing productivity in agriculture affects manufacturing favourably in two ways. First, as the farmer's production grows, he has an ever-increasing surplus to offer in exchange for manufactures; ever-increasing productivity in agriculture means an ever-increasing market for manufactures. And secondly, as productivity grows, and the proportion of the population required in food production falls, labour becomes available for manufacturing industry.

In unenlightened circles agriculture and industry are often considered as alternatives to each other. The truth is that industrialisation for a home market can make little progress unless agriculture is progressing vigorously at the same time, to provide both the market for industry, and industry's labour supply. If agriculture is stagnant, industry cannot grow....

The most certain way to promote industrialisation in the Gold Coast is to lay the foundation it requires by taking vigorous measures to raise food production per person engaged in agriculture. This is the surest way of producing that large and ever-increasing demand for manufactures without which there can be little industrialisation.

There are two ways of increasing production per man in agriculture. One way is to increase the yield per acre; the other is to increase the number of acres worked per man.

To increase the yield per acre is usually the cheaper way. It requires first that there should be research, to breed the most productive seeds and livestock, to discover the best use of fertilisers, to determine appropriate crop rotations, and so on. The Gold Coast Department of Agriculture has done some work in these spheres, and has no doubt made the best use of the scanty resources at its disposal. But, in one sense, the surest way to industrialise the Gold Coast would be to multiply four or five times the resources available to the department for fundamental research into food production. And then, as the results become available, to multiply five-fold the funds available for extension work in the villages.

The number of acres that a man can work is a function of the amount of equipment he has. In the Northern Territories farmers are being taught to use the bullock and the plough, thereby multiplying by four the amount of land that a family can cultivate in one year. Elsewhere there are experiments in mechanical cultivation. Mechanisation is costly, especially as all its fuel has to be imported. But this is without doubt the line of progress. A high standard of living cannot be built upon an economy in which half the people are scratching the ground for food with a hoe.

One finds a certain complacency towards food production in the Gold Coast. There is, it is true, some alarm as to whether the demand for food may not outgrow the supply as further urbanisation takes place. This question is actively disputed in the highest government circles. Even this, however, is not the point which is being made here. For even if the supply of food were fully adequate to meet all likely demands upon it, it would still be true that the principal road to progress would be through intensified efforts to improve efficiency in production of food. Our concern is not with the amount of food available, but with food production per person engaged in agriculture. If the food supply were adequate, the Gold Coast would still be strain-

ing to have fewer farmers, each producing more, since this is the way to stimulate the other sectors of the economy. A vigorous agricultural programme is needed, not because food is scarce, but because this is the road to economic progress.

4.5 INDUSTRIALIZATION IN THE WEST INDIES *

The case for rapid industrialization in the West Indies rests chiefly on overpopulation. The islands already carry a larger population than agriculture can absorb, and populations are growing at rates of from 1.5 to 2.0 per cent per annum. It is, therefore, urgent to create new opportunities for employment off the land....

What is unproductive in the West Indies is not land but labour. In England one man year of labour will cope with 40 acres of wheat, but in the West Indies it can cope with only two acres of sugar. It is impossible for a man to get a decent standard of living from two acres of land in any staple crop in any part of the world (i.e. excluding truck crops). The only way that agriculture in the West Indies can be made to yield its workers the standard of living they require is by greatly reducing the number of persons employed per hundred acres and substituting mechanical power for human labour.

The same holds for peasant farming. The typical West Indian peasant is working on a holding of 2 or 3 acres. Near the towns money can be made in supplying fresh vegetables and flowers, which have a very high money yield per acre, even perhaps as much as 500 gross per acre per annum. But the market for such crops is very limited, and the bulk of the peasantry must depend on the staple crops. However

* From W. A. Lewis, "The Industrialisation of the British West Indies," *Caribbean Economic Review,* Vol. II, No. 1, May 1950, pp. 25, 28-31, 36-7. Reprinted by permission.

carefully the peasant may work his holding in such crops—and, of course, at present he is very backward—he cannot make 2 or 3 acres yield him a reasonable standard of living. He cannot get from 2 or 3 acres even the 6/- a day or more which he hopes to earn in the town, so that it is not at all surprising that there is a continual drift to the towns. If peasant agriculture is to be put on its feet, the number of peasants must be reduced drastically, in relation to the land that they now occupy, so that each family may be able to have a reasonable acreage (more equipment to work the land will also be needed).

In a word, if West Indian agriculture is to yield a decent standard of living, the number engaged in the present acreage must be drastically reduced—it must be something like halved, if current expectations of what is reasonable are to be fulfilled. But this is not practicable unless new employments can be found for those who would be displaced in the process. Until new employments can be created, mechanization and other increased use of capital quipment will be a doubtful boon, and major improvements in peasant agriculture will be impossible.

Now, agriculture could provide its own outlet if the islands had surplus lands lying idle on to which the surplus population could be moved.... Most of the islands have, indeed, lands now lying idle which were formerly cultivated, and especially lands which have never been cultivated, and which could be brought into use through drainage, irrigation or terracing. For more than a century, travellers through the West Indies have always been struck by the large amount of land lying idle, which they would expect in other countries to be cultivated. Partly this is an illusion, due to real difficulties of controlling the movement of water on the land. Nevertheless, there is no doubt that, if vigorous expenditure is devoted to water control

(drainage, irrigation, soil erosion), a fair amount of land now idle can be opened up for settlement.

Alas, the experts seem to agree—especially judging by their ten-year plans—that the area that can be opened up in these ways is not really very large. Pressure of population has already taken the people over most of the land that can be exploited without great expenditure, and, indeed, even on to much land from which they must withdraw in the future, in the interest of forest preservation and of soil conservation. There are some derelict estates, but these are either already being let in small parcels to tenants, or else rapidly being acquired by governments for land settlement. Swamps are being drained, and irrigation schemes are in hand, but much reading and enquiry leave the layman with the impression that the total amount of land which will be added to cultivation in the next twenty years is a relatively small fraction of the area already occupied.

If this impression is right, then agriculture in the islands will yield a decent standard of living only if the numbers engaged in it are drastically reduced, and this will be possible only if new employments can be created outside agriculture. The creation of new industries is an essential part of a programme for agricultural improvement.

This is not generally realised. There are still people who discuss industrialisation as if it were an *alternative* to agricultural improvement. In countries where agriculture is not carrying surplus population, industry and agriculture are alternatives. New Zealand, on the one hand, or England on the other, have to weigh carefully the respective merits of industry and of agriculture, and to decide on relative emphases. But this approach is without meaning in the West Indies islands. There is no choice to be made between industry and agriculture. The islands need as large an agriculture as possible, and, if they could even get more people into agriculture, without reducing output per head, then so much the better. But, even when they are employing in agriculture the maximum number that agriculture will absorb at a reasonable standard of living, there will still be a large surplus of labour, and even the greatest expansion of industry which is conceivable within the next twenty years will not create a labour shortage in agriculture. It is not the case that agriculture cannot continue to develop if industry is developed. Exactly the opposite is true: agriculture cannot be put on to a basis where it will yield a reasonable standard of living unless new jobs are created off the land. . . .

If the West Indian market is itself to support a large manufacturing industry, then the standard of living must first be greatly increased. The way to increase the standard of living, as we have already seen, is to make it possible for each worker to have at his disposal the produce of a larger acreage; i.e., greatly to reduce the number of persons in agriculture per 1,000 acres, without reducing the total output of agriculture. But this, as we have also seen means putting more persons into manufacturing industry. Thus the full complementarity of industry and agriculture stands revealed. If agriculture is to give a higher standard of living, then industry must be developed. But equally, if industry is to be developed, then agriculture must give a higher standard of living, in order to provide a demand for manufactures. The agricultural and the industrial revolutions thus reinforce each other, and neither can go very far unless the other is occurring at the same time. Those who speak as if the choice in the West Indies lay between agricultural development and industrial development have failed completely to understand the problem.

4.6 Providing Employment in Ceylon *

I assume in what follows that the basic need for development in Ceylon is the need for providing employment for the expanding population. If it were not for the population pressure the urge for development might not be so very great; for there is not at the moment a crushing problem of poverty and malnutrition such as there is in neighbouring countries. Development means change, and change involves disturbance of settled ways; how much disturbance people would stand, in order to secure a modest improvement in their standard of living in the future, is rather problematical. But in fact these issues do not come up, for the demands of the rising generation are peremptory. In an economy, organised as the Ceylon economy now is, there will not be places for the people who will be demanding places in a few years' time. Development is necessary in order that places should be found for them.

This is (of course) not to say that any development is possible which can itself *solve* the population problem. With birth and death rates as they are at present, the population will *go on* increasing rapidly, and there is no possible development which could enable an unlimited population to support itself on the island. It is inevitable that in the end the population pressure should be eased in other ways. But even if reproduction rates should fall at once to a level which is consonant with present mortality, the rise in population must continue for some considerable time. It is indeed sufficient, when approaching the question of development from this angle, to look on it as a matter of finding places for the rising generation that is already there.

* From J. R. Hicks, "Reflections on the Economic Problems of Ceylon," *National Planning Council Papers by Visiting Economists*, Colombo, 1959, pp. 9-11, 13-16.

There are countries in which development is mainly a matter of raising living standards; but in Ceylon one must regard that as secondary to the population question. I therefore propose to consider development in terms of what one might call a *horizontal* expansion—how to arrange things so that, after an appropriate time has elapsed, 125 people can earn as good a living (or as nearly as possible as good a living) as 100 do at present. Even horizontal expansion such as this, on the scale which appears to be necessary, is going to be a most difficult task; it will be well to avoid complicating our analysis (as the execution of any plan will doubtless be complicated in practice) with concern for other objectives.

It is clear, to begin with, that the required expansion cannot be achieved in the theoretically simplest way—by expanding all activities in the same proportion, using 25 per cent more labour in every industry and turning out 25 per cent more of all products. Basically this is not possible because there is not room for a simple uniform expansion of this sort in several of the agricultural industries; there is not 25 per cent more good tea land, 25 per cent more good coconut land, and so on. (This is more fundamental than the question of export demand; it is by no means unlikely that the demand for Ceylon's exports will be increasing, to more or less the required extent, in the time that is available.) It is the land shortage which makes it inevitable that the expansion should not be uniform—that the expanded economy should be something different from a mere replica of the present economy, reproduced on a larger scale.

Even uniform expansion (in a country where uniform expansion is possible) does of course absorb capital; if production is already much-capital-using, the absorption of capital may be very large. Ceylon is probably rather fortunate in this respect,

in that her methods of production (though quite productive) do not use a great deal of capital; thus if the land were available easily, horizontal expansion would be a simpler matter than it is in some other countries. But in fact more land (to be used in the same sort of way as the existing cultivated land is used) is not available except at very great cost in the investment of capital; capital is soaked up at Gal Oya to provide the same facilities as are provided in the Wet Zone by Nature herself. The natural obstacles to this method of expansion can thus be alternatively expressed by saying that the capital costs of uniform expansion are prohibitive.

Awareness of this obstacle suggests that at the next stage of our analysis we should allow it all possible strength. Let us now assume that there is to be no change in the agricultural sector, which is to continue to employ just about the same number of people and to produce just about the same output. The whole of the additional population has then got to be employed outside agriculture. This, of course, is only a provisional assumption; we want to see whether any solution at all is possible under this condition. Whether or not it is possible can best be tested in the following way.

We take it, for the moment, that the additional labour force is employed outside agriculture; and we consider the effect on the balance of payments. Exports and imports of the present size are already accounted for by the unaugmented population; but the additional workers, as they come to spend their wages, will increase the import bill by something like 25 per cent (if we assume that the additional population has the same propensity to import as the original population). Actually, the increase may be larger than this, since there is no increase in the supply of food, and the whole food supply of the additional population must therefore be imported. These additional imports have got to be paid for, and there are only two ways in which they can be paid for by the new activities. Either the new "industrial" population must export some of its own products; or it must sell its products to the rest of the population, in such a way as to displace goods formerly imported. The possibility of industrial exports, granted the present aptitudes of the Ceylon population, does not look very bright; it is therefore necessary to look closely to see whether the thing could be done in the other way. But I am afraid the answer is that that way also, if it is relied upon as the main solution to the dilemma, is not a way out.

One can check the thing up, in a rough sort of way, by the following calculation. The total value of the additional output of the new industries (if the Gross National Product is to be increased by 25 per cent) must be of the order of 1,200 million rupees (at 1956 prices). If one allows (i) for the import of raw materials (ii) for the imported goods which the newly employed buy out of their wages (iii) for the imported goods which the receivers of profit buy out of their profits—or, if foreign capital is employed, for the transfer of interest or dividends on that capital, which, so far as the balance of payments is concerned, acts like an additional import; taking all these things together, it seems hardly possible that the import drain, due to the additional employment, could be less than 50 per cent of the gross output. If this is to be covered by economising on other imports, there must be a diversion of purchasing power, by the rest of the community, from imports to the products of the new industries, of something like 600 million rupees. Since the total import bill, at present, is roundabout 1,600 million rupees, a diversion on this scale does not appear to be possible. It would certainly

not be possible by the simple competition of the new products with imports, on equal terms. Even if there were heavy government encouragement of the new industries, through taxation and prohibition of particular imports, and direct government purchase of the new products, it does not look as if so big a shift would be practicable. If one looks down the list of imports, as it is at present, it seems impossible to find 600 million rupees' worth of goods, at present imported, which could possibly be substituted by non-agricultural goods and services that could be produced in Ceylon.

The matter can indeed be checked up in another way. If the new industries are to produce a gross product of 1,200 million rupees, and are not to spend more than 600 millions of their gross earnings on imports, they must be able to spend the other 600 millions, directly or indirectly, on things produced at home. Some of this may be accounted for by what they buy from each other, but a good part will have to consist of things bought from the "old" sectors. It is very much a question whether, under the limitations under which we are at present proceeding, the "old" sectors could produce enough, in raw materials, or in finished goods or direct services, to meet the demands which we are postulating.

All these calculations are very rough. They could doubtless be improved very greatly by the use of more detailed statistical information than is available to me as I write; but it seems unlikely that refinement would make much alteration to the general impression. It can be concluded pretty safely that if there is no expansion in agricultural output, an expansion of the non-agricultural sectors, sufficient to absorb into employment the increase in population that is in prospect, is not practicable....

Any prolonged discussion of methods of raising agricultural output would clearly lie outside the scope of this paper. It is, in any case, a matter which lies outside my competence. There is only one point about it which may, indeed must, be made.

As we have seen, an expansion which is directed towards increasing agricultural employment is likely to be extremely expensive in terms of capital; but if, *in this sector*, output rather than employment is regarded as the main consideration, it is by no means clear that the capital cost need be high. What Ceylonese agriculture seems to require is better organisation, better methods of production, not a lot of capital investment. Improvement on these lines involves a good agricultural advisory service, and (no doubt) some credit facilities; it probably involves some rationalisation of holdings; and it no doubt requires a system of incentives, which will *impel* cultivators to a utilisation of the facilities offered. It is in this last direction that some new thinking seems to be most required.

The practice of food subsidies is already well established in Ceylon. The vital thing, from the point of view of the above policy, is not that subsidies should be reduced (as "uneconomic") but that they should be re-shaped so as to contribute as directly as possible to the improvement of efficiency. A flat subsidy on output is a very poor subsidy from this point of view. An attempt should be made to grade subsidies so that they encourage the use of superior methods; and, so far as the general subsidy is retained, to concentrate it at the margin, so that it gives the maximum stimulus to output at a given cost to the Treasury. This would be done if there were a subsidy on actual output, matched by a tax on 'normal' output; or, what comes to the same thing, a subsidy on output, which could be even more generous than at present, paid for by a tax (a universal tax, without exemptions) on land. The good farmer then finds that his receipts from the subsidy are a good deal higher than his payment of tax; the bad farmer is penalised by receipts from subsidy

that are less than tax. By such means the *incentive* can be made as large as one likes; but it is no use giving an incentive to the cultivator unless it is an incentive to do something which he is able to do. The provision of facilities for improvement should be the other side of the same policy.

A policy of this kind, aimed directly at the expansion of output, would not in itself at all necessarily expand agricultural employment. The rationalisation which it entailed might indeed tend, at least to some extent, in the opposite direction. The contention that such a policy is a coherent part, indeed an essential part, of a successful employment policy, needs therefore further justification.

All that is claimed here is that an increase in agricultural output makes it possible to expand employment (at reasonable real wages); not that the increase in output of agriculture expands employment at all automatically. Conditions are conceivable in which agricultural output might expand, and no favourable effects on employment would follow. This would happen ... if the whole of the earnings from increased agricultural exports were spent abroad; and there was a corresponding effect on the side of import-competing agricultural products (called for convenience "paddy"). Here, if the demand of the towns was shifted from imported rice to home-produced rice (at, we will suppose, much the same price), while the increased supply of home-produced rice came from improved efficiency, not increased employment, there would be no direct expansion of employment in agriculture; while, if the higher earnings of agriculturists were spent entirely upon imports, there would be no expansion in employment elsewhere. ...

What an increase in agricultural output does is to make a market for the products of potential new industries; it is impossible that new industries should arise unless there is a market for their products, but the existence of a potential market does not make the rise of such industries inevitable. There are further steps of great importance which have, at this point, to be considered.

It is possible, as we have seen before, for the government to channel the spending of the gains which follow from an expansion of agricultural output in such a way as to make a market for the products of new industries; but the industries which are brought into being in this way will not be efficient industries, they will not be such as to produce goods which are adequate substitutes for imported commodities, unless they can command an adequate capital supply. If the capital which would be needed for this purpose is not available, so that the labour which is newly employed (outside agriculture) has to be employed as "direct labour," without proper equipment, its productivity is bound to be low. What this sort of employment amounts to is familiar from the experience of many countries with "public works in relief of employment." Obviously this is not the sort of employment that is wanted. It is however an important consequence of our argument that even if nothing better than this is to be attained (with the extra mouths being fed on a tolerable standard) an expansion in agricultural output will still be needed. Otherwise the mere maintenance of the excess labour force, employed in doing nothing that is very useful, will impose a crushing burden on the economy.

If (as we must) we set our sights higher than this, the question of capital provision becomes urgent. It is (I insist) a prior problem to that of the form in which the new industries are to be organised, whether they are to be state enterprises or private undertakings; in either case much the same capital will be required. And in either case it is a point of prime importance that, in view of the limited resources of the Island for the manufacture of capital equipment, a large proportion of the capital equipment required will have to be imported. The question of capital provision is in consequence not merely a matter of saving (as it is in a closed economy); it is a balance of payments question once again.

It is not possible to suppose that the difficulty can be overcome, to more than a very limited extent, by the building up of capital goods manufacture within Ceylon. When one is dealing with a country the size of India, something useful in that direction can undoubtedly be done; but even India has involved herself in her present difficulties largely because of an excessive faith in this particular way out. It is only the simplest sorts of capital goods (building materials being the obviously important case) which can expect to command a market within Ceylon sufficient to enable their production to be carried on at an efficient size. One has only to consider that there are plenty of countries that can produce textiles efficiently; but there are very few countries which can keep a textile machinery industry going without considerable reliance on an export market. This is the kind of situation which repeats itself with one sort of specialised capital good after another.

The simplest way of avoiding this difficulty is to finance the new industries with external capital; if this can be done no more remains than the problems of financing interest or dividend payments...The possibility of this way out does however raise important questions of another character; it will be more convenient to come back to them after we have considered the possibilities of finance from internal sources, which one would accept to be a preferable form of finance, so far as it will go.

If one includes involuntary saving (through the budget, or even through credit creation) as part of the domestic saving which is in question, the extent to which domestic saving can be increased is in principle quite large. But it remains true, in view of the balance of payments consideration, that the amount of *useful* capital accumulation, which can be financed through domestic saving, is liable to be more circumscribed than would appear from a consideration of the saving potential alone. It may indeed seem at first sight that this is not so. Suppose that the proportion of investment expenditure, according to the best available plan, that must go on imports, is $x\%$; that the proportion of saving (private and governmental) which is at the expense of imports (the proportion, which would have been spent on imports, of the consumption which would have occured if the saving had not been made) is $y\%$; the balance of payments will then be deteriorated by the saving *and* investment if x is greater than y, improved if y is greater than x. It follows from our earlier discussions that there is a tendency in Ceylon for y to be quite large; it may therefore seem that it is possible for x to be quite large without resulting in any particular balance of payments trouble. But this does not allow for the point that we have already discovered—that it is necessary for the government to impose such checks as it can upon the propensity to import (y) in order to make a market for the new industries. If y is already written down for this reason, the danger of trouble in the balance of payments from a high import content of the investment that is undertaken becomes more serious. The size of x does indeed depend upon the character of the investment plan, and may differ very widely from one investment plan to another. There are some sorts of investment which can be undertaken quite easily, if the requisite saving is forthcoming; but there are others (as India is finding) which cannot be undertaken without a severe strain on the balance of payments.

The practical consequence to be drawn from this argument is however no more than an underlining of the moral we have drawn already. Once the balance of payments can be eased, not temporarily but as a long-run trend, by an expansion of agricultural output, the absorption into industrial employment of the expanding population becomes quite feasible; otherwise it will be very difficult indeed. One runs into the same conclusion by whatever way one approaches the problem....

4.7 Balance of Payments Implications: Asia and the Far East *

In the early postwar years, many countries of the region were faced with food shortage problems and a need for immediate rehabilitation of productive capacity, impaired by war damage and lack of replacement. The need for more food and foreign exchange to purchase new equipment from abroad led these countries first to rehabilitate and develop agricultural production, including cash crops, which offered greater possibilities for quick returns. On completion of the reconstruction programme, the inherent problem of vulnerability to external factors of primary exports, on which the economies of many countries rely heavily, re-emerged. The escape from this traditional weakness has invariably been sought in efforts to speed up the process of industrialization, particularly from the long-run point of view. These efforts are largely reflected in the patterns and changes that have been planned in the allocation of investment in the early plans following the reconstruction programmes. Thus, in these plans, Burma, Indonesia, and the Philippines, as well as mainland China, for different reasons, accorded priority to industry. Investment in this sector (manufacturing industry, mining and construction) was larger than that in agriculture (including forestry, fishery,

* From Economic Commission for Asia and the Far East, "Economic Development and Planning in Asia and the Far East," *Economic Bulletin for Asia and the Far East,* December 1961, pp. 11-12.

irrigation and community development). ... However, in most other countries, agriculture still claimed pride of place. The relatively smaller proportion of industrial investment in the public sector in the first plans of countries such as India, the Federation of Malaya and Thailand, is somewhat deceptive, for in India, at that time, industry in the private sector was proportionately quite substantial, and in the Federation of Malaya and Thailand industrial development has, according to announced government policy, been left largely to private investment.

The divergent trends indicated the renewed significance of the old argument of whether agriculture or industry should be given priority in planning for economic development, and this problem has grown increasingly acute in recent years. There were cases where countries, at first enthusiastic about establishing modern industries, discovered later that bottlenecks had been created because of the neglect of agricultural development. The reason for emphasizing industrialization is that industrial development would absorb rural underemployed persons into those fields of production where higher productivity is possible without reducing total agricultural output. This argument has to be scrutinized carefully, particularly with respect to whether there exists substantial *chronic* underemployment or just *seasonal* underemployment. But in either case (the latter would be worse), rapid industrial development without an improvement in agricultural productivity would create obstacles to further development, owing to shortage of food and agricultural raw materials. For if the supply of food and raw materials remained stable while demand for them rose on account of industrial development, either prices and wages would increase, or the balance of payments position would deteriorate. In the food-exporting countries of the region, the deterioration of the balance of payments situation would reflect the slow growth, if not the decline, of the exportable surplus. In the raw materials exporting countries, it would mean both an increase in food imports as well as a slow growth or decline of the exportable surplus, which, in many cases, tends to be aggravated by the trend of unfavourable terms of trade. In food-deficit but resource-diversified countries, such as China: mainland and India, it would mean a considerable expansion of food and/or raw material imports as well as a reduced or stagnant level of the exportable surplus of agricultural products. Table 1 shows that, in six countries of the region (Burma, Ceylon, India, Indonesia, south Korea and the Philippines), exports as a percentage of gross domestic product have decreased during the past decade, and only in three countries (China: Taiwan, Japan and Thailand) has it increased.

Such a situation can, of course, be remedied if the newly developing industries can earn or save foreign exchange. This is the main reason why, in the industrial development programmes of most countries of the region, the importance of foreign exchange earning and saving has been particularly stressed. However, as the import-replacing industries also tend to generate further demand for imports of capital goods, raw materials and fuels, and as the export markets for manufacturing goods are highly competitive, balance of payment difficulties, once they emerge, would tend to become so persistent that the countries concerned could hardly escape the trap, except for those few which had a slow rate of growth and/or particularly favourable markets for their major exports, *e.g.* the Federation of Malaya and Thailand. Again, Table 1 shows that, during the last decade, in spite of restrictions, imports as a percentage of gross domestic product have increased in six countries of the region (Burma, Ceylon, China: Taiwan, India, Japan, and Thailand), and decreased only in three (Indonesia, south Korea and the Philippines).

Over-investment in industry or neglect of agricultural development has actually caused such strain (especially through the shortage of foreign exchange), that in several countries of the region the existence of a sizeable idle capacity has become rather serious. In the Philippines, "it is estimated that the average level of operation of existing industrial plants is only about 50 per cent of rated capacity."[1] It was estimated in the current plan that raising the operating capacity from 52 per cent in 1957 to 70 per cent in 1960/61 would raise foreign exchange requirements for imports of raw materials from 55 to 73 per cent of merchandise imports in the corresponding years.[2] Again, in Pakistan, at the end of the fourth year of the first Five-Year Plan period, the rate of capacity utilization for some consumer goods industries, engineering and

electric industries making up about 25 per cent of the value added in large-scale industries, was on the average 50 per cent."[3] Idle industrial capacity in India and China: Taiwan also appears to be substantial. In such circumstances, the question is whether fuller utilization of existing plants should not be given priority over installation of new industrial undertakings, or whether agriculture should not be allowed to catch up with industry.

Recurrent deficiencies in the supply of agricultural products were not only due to limitations imposed on investment in agriculture, but also to the underestimation of possibilities in, and slow implementation of the task of increasing, the supply of agricultural commodities. The various cases of underfulfilment, either of the agricultural target as a whole or of specific commodities, may indicate inadequate appreciation of the importance of agricultural investment

1. National Economic Council, *Philippines Three-Year Programme of Economic and Social Development* (FY 1959/60–1961/62), p. 69.
2. *Ibid.,* p. 9.

3. Government of Pakistan, Planning Commission, *First Five-Year Plan: Preliminary Evaluation Report,* September 1959, p. 26.

TABLE I. EXPORTS AND IMPORTS AS PERCENTAGE OF GROSS
DOMESTIC PRODUCT, 1950 AND 1959

Country	Exports		Imports	
	1950	1959	1950	1959
Burma	21.1	19.4	13.8	19.3
Ceylon	38.1	29.1	28.5	33.2
China: Taiwan	10.0 [a]	11.7	15.6 [a]	17.3
India	5.7 [b]	4.8 [b]	5.8 [b]	6.9 [b]
Indonesia	7.7 [a]	4.9	5.2 [a]	2.6
Japan	7.5	9.9	8.8	10.3
Korea, South	1.0 [c]	0.8	5.8 [c]	3.5
Philippines	9.9	9.5	10.3	9.1
Thailand	10.0	15.4	11.3	18.3

Source: United Nations, *Yearbook of National Account Statistics,* and *Yearbook of International Trade Statistics.*

[a] 1951.   [b] As a percentage of net domestic product at factor cost.
[c] 1953.

in the plan and implementation. The agricultural sector, as at present organized in most countries of the region, offers great scope for the introduction of modern production techniques and organizational improvements, such as the consolidation of small holdings, pooling of agricultural equipment, or better use of existing resources. The slow response of the cultivator in the backward rural society to modern technological and institutional changes required for an increase in productivity emphasizes particularly the need for early attention to agricultural development. This is especially so in those countries where in recent years agricultural development has been rather neglected ... At present, several countries of the region are threatened by setbacks in the rate of economic growth, because of the lag in agricultural development, *e.g.* mainland China (although partly due to natural calamities), India and Pakistan (depending on foreign aid for financing food imports), Burma and the Philippines (through balance of payments difficulties), etc. These hard facts have forced many countries to raise the share of government investment in agriculture. Thus, in Burma, the share (including irrigation) was raised from 12 per cent in

the Eight-Year Plan to 27 per cent in the first and second Four-Year Plans. In India, while the second Plan increased considerably the share of investment in heavy industries, and thus aggravated the deficiencies in the supply of agricultural commodities during the second plan period, the share of government investment in community development as a means of increasing agricultural production was substantially raised in the third plan. In Pakistan, owing to the poor performance of agriculture under the first plan, government investment in agriculture (which is already high in the first plan) was slightly raised in the second plan. In the Philippines, the share of government investment in agriculture under total government investment in the economic sectors was increased from 22 per cent in the first Five-Year Plan to 31 per cent in the subsequent Three-Year Plan. The increase in the already relatively high share of agriculture in total investment under the second plans of China: Taiwan and the Federation of Malaya seems to indicate that, in the immediate future, sizeable investments in agriculture are still considered a favourable means of promoting economic growth.

5. BIBLIOGRAPHICAL NOTE

1. Some of the interrelationships between industry and agriculture that have been discussed in this chapter are established more rigorously in a number of models of a "two-sector" economy. Although the models tend to be highly formal, they provide considerable insight into why the lack of agricultural progress is one of the most serious obstacles to development; they provide criteria for allocating resources between the industrial and agricultural sectors; and they indicate conditions for an optimal growth path. Of special interest are

the following references: M. Dobb, *An Essay on Economic Growth and Planning*, London, 1960; R. Findlay, "Capital Theory and Development Planning," *Review of Economic Studies*, February 1962; R. M. Goodwin, "The Optimal Growth Path for an Underdeveloped Economy," *Economic Journal*, December 1961; G. O. Gutman, "A Note on Economic Development with Subsistence Agriculture," *Oxford Economic Papers*, October 1957; D. W. Jorgenson, "Development of a Dual Economy," *Economic Journal*, June 1961; Anne O.

Krueger, "Interrelationships Between Industry and Agriculture in a Dual Economy," *Indian Economic Journal*, July 1962; J. E. Meade, *A Neo-Classical Theory of Economic Growth*, New York, 1961; G. Ranis and J. C. H. Fei, "Unlimited Supply of Labour and the Concept of Balanced Growth," *Pakistan Development Review*, Winter 1961; Ranis and Fei, "A Theory of Economic Development," *American Economic Review*, September 1961; Ranis and Fei, "Capital Accumulation and Economic Development," *American Economic Review*, June 1963; A. K. Sen, *Choice of Techniques*, Oxford, 1960.

2. The following readings consider more specialized topics relating to agricultural development: J. C. Abbott, *Marketing Problems and Improvement Programs*, Rome, 1958; T. Balogh, "Agriculture and Economic Development," *Oxford Economic Papers*, February 1961; H. Barlowe, "Land Reform and Economic Development," *Journal of Farm Economics*, May 1953; H. Belshaw, *Agricultural Credit in Economies of Underdeveloped Countries*, Rome, 1959; B. O. Binns, *The Consolidation of Fragmented Agricultural Holdings*, Rome, 1950; P. K. Chang, *Agriculture and Industrialization*, Cambridge, 1959; D. Felix, "Agrarian Reform and Industrial Growth," *International Development Review*, October 1960; N. Georgescu-Roegen, "Economic Theory and Agrarian Economics," *Oxford Economic Papers*, February 1960; I. C. Greaves, *Modern Production Among Backward Peoples*, London, 1935; A. E. Kahn, "Agricultural Aid and Economic Development: The Case of Israel," *Quarterly Journal of Economics*, November 1962; Simon Kuznets, "Economic Growth and the Contribution of Agriculture: Notes on Measurement," *International Journal of Agrarian Affairs*, April 1961; W. A. Lewis, "Developing Colonial Agriculture," *Three Banks Review*, June 1949; J. W. Mellor, "The Process of Agri-cultural Development in Low-Income Countries," *Journal of Farm Economics*, August 1962; A. T. Mosher, "Research on Rural Problems," in R. E. Asher (ed.), *Development of the Emerging Countries*, Washington, D.C., 1962; W. H. Nicholls, "Investment in Agriculture in Underdeveloped Countries," *American Economic Review, Papers and Proceedings*, May 1955; Nicholls, "Industrialization, Factor Markets, and Agricultural Development," *Journal of Political Economy*, August 1961; Nicholls, "An 'Agricultural Surplus' as a Factor in Economic Development," *Journal of Political Economy*, February 1963; H. T. Oshima, "A Strategy for Asian Development," *Economic Development and Cultural Change*, April 1962; K. H. Parsons (ed.), *Land Tenure*, Madison, 1951; A. Pim, *Colonial Agricultural Production*, London, 1946; *Proceedings of the Eleventh International Conference of Agricultural Economists: The Role of Agriculture in Economic Development*, London, 1963; Y. A. Sayigh, "The Place of Agriculture in Economic Development," *Land Economics*, November 1959; T. W. Schultz, *The Economic Organization of Agriculture*, New York, 1953; United Nations, Department of Economic Affairs, *Land Reform*, New York, 1951, and *Progress in Land Reform*, New York, 1954; D. Warriner, *Land Reform and Economic Development*, Cairo, 1955; Warriner, *Land Reform and Development in the Middle East*, London, 1957; V. Wickizer, "Plantation System and Tropical Economies," *Journal of Farm Economics*, February, 1958.

3. Specialized aspects of the development of secondary industry are considered in the following: H. G. Aubrey, "Small Industry in Economic Development," *Social Research*, September 1951; G. B. Baldwin, *Industrial Growth in South India: Case Studies in Economic Development*, Glencoe, 1959; H. Belshaw, "Observations on Industrialization for Higher Income,"

Economic Journal, September 1947; M. D. Bryce, *Industrial Development,* New York, 1960; N. S. Buchanan, "Deliberate Industrialization for Higher Incomes," *Economic Journal,* December 1946; H. B. Chenery, "The Role of Industrialization in Development Programs," *American Economic Review,* May 1955; Ford Foundation, International Planning Team, *Report on Small Industries in India,* New Delhi, 1955; B. F. Hoselitz, "Small Industry in Underdeveloped Countries," *Journal of Economic History,* December 1959; E. A. J. Johnson, "Problems of 'Forced-Draft' Industrialization," *First International Conference of Economic History,* Stockholm, 1960; C. Leubuscher, *The Processing of Colonial Raw Materials,* London, 1951; W. A. Lewis, "Industrial Development in Puerto Rico," *Caribbean Economic Review,* December 1949; Lewis, "Industrialization of the British West Indies," *Caribbean Economic Review,* May 1950; Lewis, *Aspects of Industrialization,* Cairo, 1953; W. E. Moore, *Industrialization and Labor: Social Aspects of Economic Development,* Ithaca, 1951; C. A. Myers, *Labor Problems in the Industrialization of India,* Cambridge, 1958; H. W. Singer, "Problems of Industrialization of Underdeveloped Countries," in L. Dupriez (ed.), *Economic Progress,* Louvain, 1955; United Nations, Bureau of Economic Affairs, *Management of Industrial Enterprises in Underdeveloped Countries,* New York, 1958; United Nations, Statistical Office, *Patterns of Industrial Growth,* New York, 1960; United Nations, Department of Economic and Social Affairs, *Processes and Problems of Industrialization in Underdeveloped Countries,* New York, 1955.

VII

THE EXPORT SECTOR

A LONG WITH THE AGRICULTURAL AND INDUSTRIAL SECTORS, the export sector also plays a vital role in determining the rate and structural pattern of a country's development. Since most of the newly developing countries are strongly oriented toward foreign trade, it is important to consider the extent to which their development can be promoted through trade. Accordingly, this chapter concentrates on the problems connected with the transmission of development through trade. It is especially concerned with whether there is a conflict between market-determined comparative advantage and the acceleration of development—whether in pursuing the gains from trade, a country might limit its attainment of the gains from growth.

Materials in the first section present opposing views on this question. Raúl Prebisch and Gunnar Myrdal argue that the accrual of the gains from trade is biased in favor of the advanced industrial countries, that foreign trade has inhibited industrial development in the poorer nations, and that—contrary to what would be expected from classical trade doctrine—free trade has in reality accentuated international inequalities (1.1, 1.2). In contrast, Professor Haberler and A. K. Cairncross support the traditional position that foreign trade can contribute substantially to the development of primary exporting countries, and that the gains from international specialization merge with the gains from growth (1.4, 1.6). Adopting a more neutral position, Professors Hicks and Nurkse offer some special observations on the dynamic character of trade as a transmitter of growth (1.3, 1.5). An alternative explanation of why international trade has not induced more rapid development in the poorer countries is presented in the Note on the "carry-over problem," where emphasis is placed on characteristics of the export good as defined by the nature of its production function and the influence of domestic conditions within the primary exporting country (1.7).

In connection with the need for growth in export markets, section 2 explores the potential role for the export of manufactured goods. Following a general statement of the advantages to be derived from expanding manufactured exports (2.1), some special problems are noted in terms of the

338

possibilities for exporting light manufactures from the West Indies (2.2) and the measures for export promotion in Pakistan's Second Plan (2.3).

Besides being concerned about adequate growth in their export markets, newly developing countries are also anxious to remove the limitations on their development caused by instability in their export proceeds. In considering the exposed position of primary export countries, section 3 concentrates on the causes and effects of instability in export revenue (3.1, 3.2), and outlines various national and international measures for mitigating the instability. Special attention is given to the recent advocacy of some form of "development insurance fund" that would provide compensatory financing for the shortfalls in export earnings of developing nations (3.4, 3.5).

Proposals for regional integration, as a means of lessening the dependence on primary exports and accelerating development, have also gained increasing favor. The Note in section 4 appraises the contributions that a customs union or free trade area might make to the development of its member nations.

1. INTERNATIONAL TRADE AND INTERNATIONAL INEQUALITY

1.1 CENTER AND PERIPHERY *

In Latin America, reality is undermining the out-dated schema of the international division of labour, which achieved great importance in the nineteenth century and, as a theoretical concept, continued to exert considerable influence until very recently.

Under that schema, the specific task that fell to Latin America, as part of the periphery of the world economic system, was that of producing food and raw materials for the great industrial centres.

There was no place within it for the industrialization of the new countries. It is nevertheless being forced upon them by events. Two world wars in a single generation and a great economic crisis between them have shown the Latin-American

* From Raúl Prebisch, "The Economic Development of Latin America and Its Principal Problems," *Economic Bulletin for Latin America,* February 1962, pp. 1, 4-6.

countries their opportunities, clearly pointing the way to industrial activity.

The academic discussion, however, is far from ended. In economics, ideologies usually tend either to lag behind events or to outlive them. It is true that the reasoning on the economic advantages of the international division of labour is theoretically sound, but it is usually forgotten that it is based upon an assumption which has been conclusively proved false by facts. According to this assumption, the benefits of technical progress tend to be distributed alike over the whole community, either by the lowering of prices or the corresponding raising of incomes. The countries producing raw materials obtain their share of these benefits through international exchange, and therefore have no need to industrialize. If they were to do so, their lesser efficiency would result in their losing the conventional advantages of such exchange.

The flaw in this assumption is that of generalizing from the particular. If by "the community" only the great industrial countries are meant, it is indeed true that the benefits of technical progress are gradually distributed among all social groups and classes. If, however, the concept of the community is extended to include the periphery of the world economy, a serious error is implicit in the generalization. The enormous benefits that derive from increased productivity have not reached the periphery in a measure comparable to that obtained by the peoples of the great industrial countries. Hence, the outstanding differences between the standards of living of the masses of the former and the latter and the manifest discrepancies between their respective abilities to accumulate capital, since the margin of saving depends primarily on increased productivity.

Thus there exists an obvious disequilibrium, a fact which, whatever its explanation or justification, destroys the basic premise underlying the schema of the international division of labour.

Hence, the fundamental significance of the industrialization of the new countries. Industrialization is not an end in itself, but the principal means at the disposal of those countries of obtaining a share of the benefits of technical progress and of progressively raising the standard of living of the masses.

. . .

It was stated in the preceding section that the advantages of technical progress have been mainly concentrated in the industrial centres and have not directly extended to the countries making up the periphery of the world's economic system. The increased productivity of the industrial countries certainly stimulated the demand for primary products and thus constituted a dynamic factor of the utmost

importance in the development of Latin America. That, however, is distinct from the question discussed below.

Speaking generally, technical progress seems to have been greater in industry than in the primary production of peripheral countries, as was pointed out in a recent study on price relations.[1] Consequently, if prices had been reduced in proportion to increasing productivity, the reduction should have been less in the case of primary products than in that of manufactures, so that as the disparity between productivities increased, the price relationship between the two should have shown a steady improvement in favour of the countries of the periphery.

Had this happened, the phenomenon would have been of profound significance. The countries of the periphery would have benefited from the fall in price of finished industrial products to the same extent as the countries of the centre. The benefits of technical progress would thus have been distributed alike throughout the world, in accordance with the implicit premise of the schema of the international division of labour, and Latin America would have had no economic advantage in industrializing. On the contrary, the region would have suffered a definite loss, until it had achieved the same productive efficiency as the industrial countries.

The above supposition is not borne out by the facts. As can be seen in the indexes of Table 1, the price relation turned steadily against primary production from the 1870's until the Second World War. It is regrettable that the price indexes do not reflect the differences in quality of finished products. For this reason, it was not possible to take them into account in these considerations. With the same amount of primary products, only 63 per cent of the

1. "Post War Price Relations in Trade Between Under-developed and Industralized Countries," document E/CN.1/Sub.3/W.5.

finished manufactures which could be bought in the 1860's were to be had in the 1930's; in other words, an average of 58.6 per cent more primary products was needed to buy the same amount of finished manufactures.[2] The price relation, therefore, moved against the periphery, contrary to what should have happened had prices fallen as costs decreased as a result of higher productivity.

During the expansion of the last war, as in the case of all cyclical expansions, the relation moved in favour of primary products. Now, however, although there has not been a recession, a typical readjustment is taking place, with the result that prices of primary products are losing their former advantage.

The pointing out of this disparity between prices does not imply passing judgment regarding its significance from other points of view. It could be argued, on grounds of equity, that the countries which strove to achieve a high degree of technical efficiency were in no way obliged to share its fruits with the rest of the world. Had they done so, they would not have reached their enormous capacity to save, without which it might well be asked whether technical progress would have achieved the intense rhythm which characterizes capitalist development. In any case the productive technique exists and is at the disposal of those with the capacity and perseverance to assimilate it and increase their own productivity. All that, however, is outside the scope of this report. The purpose is to emphasize a fact which, despite its many implications, is not usually given the importance it deserves when the significance of the in-

2. According to the report already quoted. The figures for the thirties go only as far as 1938 inclusive. The data given are the Board of Trade's average price indexes for British imports and exports representative of world prices for raw materials and manufactured goods respectively.

TABLE I. RATIO OF PRICES OF PRIMARY COMMODITIES TO THOSE OF MANUFACTURED GOODS (AVERAGE IMPORT AND EXPORT PRICES, ACCORDING TO DATA OF THE BOARD OF TRADE) (1876–80 = 100)

Periods	Amount of finished products obtainable for a given quantity of primary commodities
1876–80	100
1881–85	102.4
1886–90	96.3
1891–95	90.1
1896–1900	87.1
1901–05	84.6
1906–10	85.8
1911–13	85.8
— —	—
1921–25	67.3
1926–30	73.3
1931–35	62.0
1936–38	64.1
— —	—
1946–47	68.7

Source: "Post War Price Relations in Trade Between Under-developed and Industrialized Countries," document E/CN.1/Sub.3/W.5, 23 February 1949.

dustrialization of the peripheral countries is discussed.

Simple reasoning on the phenomenon in question brings us to the following considerations:

First Prices have not fallen concomitantly with technical progress, since, while on the one hand, costs tended to decrease as a result of higher productivity, on the other, the income of entrepreneurs and productive factors increased. When income increased more than productivity, prices rose instead of falling.

Second Had the rise in income, in the industrial centres and the periphery, been proportionate to the increase in their respective productivity, the price relation between primary and manufactured products would have been the same as if prices had fallen in strict proportion to productivity. Given the higher productivity of industry, the price relation would have moved in favour of the primary products.

Third Since, as we have seen, the ratio actually moved against primary products in the period between the 1870's and the 1930's, it is evident that in the centre the income of entrepreneurs and of productive factors increased relatively more than productivity, whereas in the periphery the increase in income was less than that in productivity.

In other words, while the centres kept the whole benefit of the technical development of their industries, the peripheral countries transferred to them a share of the fruits of their own technical progress.[3]

...

3. "Post War Price Relations in Trade between Under-developed and Industrialized Countries," document E/CN.1/Sub.3/W.5, pp. 115-16:

"A long-term deterioration in terms of trade, such as has been found to obtain for primary producers over a long period, may be an effect of differences in the rate of increase in productivity in the production of primary commodities and manufactured articles, respectively. If we can assume that the deteriorating terms of trade for under-developed countries reflect a more rapid increase of productivity in primary commodities than of manufactured goods, the effect of worsened terms of trade would, of course, be less serious. It would merely mean that, to the extent that primary commodities are being exported, the effects of increased productivity are being passed on to the buyers of primary articles in the more industrialized countries. Although statistical data on differential rates of increase in productivity of primary production in under-developed countries, and production of manufactured articles in industrialized countries, are almost entirely lacking, this explanation of the long-term changes in terms of trade which were observed in this study may be dismissed. There is little doubt that productivity increased faster in the industrialized countries than primary production in under-developed countries. This is evidenced by the more rapid rise in standards of living in industrialized countries during the long period covered, from 1870 to the present day. Hence, the changes observed in terms of trade do not mean that increased productivity in primary production was passed on to industrialized countries; on the contrary, they mean that the under-developed coun-

In short, if, in spite of greater technical progress in industry than in primary production, the price relation has moved against the latter instead of in its favour, it would seem that the average income, *per capita*, has risen more in industrial centres than in the producer countries of the periphery.

The existence of this phenomenon cannot be understood, except in relation to trade cycles and the way in which they occur in the centres and at the periphery, since the cycle is the characteristic form of growth of capitalist economy, and increased productivity is one of the main factors of that growth.

In the cyclical process of the centres, there is a continuous inequality between the aggregate demand and supply of finished consumer goods. The former is greater than the latter in the upswing and lower in the downswing.

The magnitude of profits and their variations are closely bound up with this disparity. Profits rise during the upswing, thus tending to curtail excess demand by raising prices; they fall during the downswing, in that case, to counteract the effect of excess supply by lowering prices.

As prices rise, profits are transferred from the entrepreneurs at the centre to the primary producers of the periphery. The greater the competition and the longer the time required to increase primary production in relation to the time needed for the other stages of production, and the smaller the stocks, the greater the proportion of profits transferred to the periphery. Hence follows a typical

tries maintained, in the prices which they paid for their imported manufactures relative to those which they obtained for their own primary products, a rising standard of living in the industrialized countries, without receiving, in the price of their own products, a corresponding equivalent contribution towards their own standards of living."

characteristic of the cyclical upswing; prices of primary products tend to rise more sharply than those of finished goods, by reason of the high proportion of profits transferred to the periphery.

If this be so, what is the explanation of the fact that, with the passage of time and throughout the cycles, income has increased more at the centre than at the periphery?

There is no contradiction whatsoever between the two phenomena. The prices of primary products rise more rapidly than industrial prices in the upswing, but also they fall more in the downswing, so that in the course of the cycles the gap between prices of the two is progressively widened.

Let us now look at the explanations of this inequality in the cyclical movement of prices. It was seen that profits rise in the upswing and decrease in the downswing, thus tending to offset the disparity between demand and supply. If profits could fall in the same way in which they rose, there would be no reason whatsoever for this unequal movement. It occurs precisely because they cannot fall in that way.

The reason is very simple. During the upswing, part of the profits are absorbed by an increase in wages, occasioned by competition between entrepreneurs and by the pressure of trade unions. When profits have to be reduced during the downswing, the part that had been absorbed by wage increases loses its fluidity, at the centre, by reason of the well-known resistance to a lowering of wages. The pressure then moves toward the periphery, with greater force than would be the case, if by reason of the limitations of competition, wages and profits in the centre were not rigid. The less that income can contract at the centre, the more it must do so at the periphery.

The characteristic lack of organization among the workers employed in primary production prevents them from obtaining wage increases comparable to those of the industrial countries and from maintaining the increases to the same extent. The reduction of income—whether profits or wages—is therefore less difficult at the periphery.

Even if there existed as great a rigidity at the periphery as at the centre, it would merely increase the pressure of the latter on the former, since, when profits in the periphery did not decrease sufficiently to offset the inequality between supply and demand in the cyclical centres, stocks would accumulate in the latter, industrial production contract, and with it the demand for primary products. Demand would then fall to the extent required to achieve the necessary reduction in income in the primary producing sector. The forced readjustment of costs of primary production during the world crisis illustrates the intensity that this movement can attain.

The greater ability of the masses in the cyclical centres to obtain rises in wages during the upswing and to maintain the higher level during the downswing and the ability of these centres, by virtue of the role they play in production, to divert cyclical pressure to the periphery (causing a greater reduction of income of the latter than in that of the centres) explain why income at the centres persistently tends to rise more than in the countries of the periphery, as happened in the case of Latin America.

That is the clue to the phenomenon whereby the great industrial centres not only keep for themselves the benefit of the use of new techniques in their own economy, but are in a favourable position to obtain a share of that deriving from the technical progress of the periphery.

1.2 International Inequalities *

Our inherited economic theory would
...lead us to expect that international
inequalities should not be so large as they
are and not be growing. In any case this
theory does not furnish us with an explanation in causal terms of these inequalities
and their tendency to increase.

"The fact that many under-developed
countries do not derive the advantages
from modern transportation and commerce that theory seems to demand is one
of the most pertinent facts in the present
international situation and cannot be easily dismissed"—I am quoting from a recent
paper by a Swedish economist, Mr. Folke
Hilgert [1] ...

Hilgert points out that huge movements
of labour and capital from Europe have
transformed the plains in the temperate
belts into "white man's land" with high,
rapid and sustained economic development
and rising levels of living. "Yet the gradual filling of the 'empty spaces' has not
reduced the pressure of population in, for
instance, Asia's over-populated regions
where labour is most abundant."

Let us remember, however, that according to the classical doctrine movements
of labour and capital between countries
would not be necessary for bringing about
a development towards equalisation of
factor prices and, consequently, earnings
and incomes; in fact, the theory of international trade was largely developed on
the abstract assumption of international
immobility of all factors of production.
That trade itself initiated a tendency
towards a gradual equalisation of factor
prices was implicit already in the exposi-

tions by the classical authors, though their
method of stating the law of comparative
costs in terms of only a single factor,
labour—which, however, could have different "qualities" or degrees of "effectiveness"—turned the emphasis in other directions.

After Eli F. Heckscher's paper on the
equalising influence of trade on factor
prices and Bertil Ohlin's restatement of
the classical theory of international trade
in terms of a general equilibrium theory
of the Lausanne school type,[2] trade appeared more clearly as a substitute, or an
alternative, to factor movements in permitting an adjustment of industrial activity to adapt itself to the localisation of
natural and population resources with the
result that the relative scarcity of labour
and capital became less different. Upon
this foundation there has in recent years
been a lively discussion between the eco-
nometricians elaborating, under specific,
abstract and static, conditions, the relative
effectiveness of this tendency to equalisation of factor prices as a result of
international trade.[3]

The inadequacy of such theories for
explaining reality cannot be accounted for
by pointing to the relative breakdown of
the multilateral trading system as it func-
tioned prior to the First World War, a
change which is related as both effect and
cause to the increase of national trade
and payments restrictions. For, as Hilgert

* From Gunnar Myrdal, *Development and Underdevelopment*, National Bank of Egypt Fiftieth
Anniversary Commemoration Lectures, Cairo,
1956, pp. 9–10, 47–51. Reprinted by permission.

1. "Uses and Limitations of International Trade
in Overcoming Inequalities in World Distribution
of Population and Resources," *World Population
Conference*, Rome, 1954.

2. Eli F. Heckscher, "The Effect of Foreign
Trade on the Distribution of Income," *Readings
in the Theory of International Trade*, selected by
a committee of the American Economic Association, Allen & Unwin, London, 1950 (translation
from the Swedish original 1919); Bertil Ohlin,
Interregional and International Trade, Harvard
University Press, Cambridge, Mass., 1933.

3. The recent discussion of the problem of factor price equalisation as a result of international
trade was initiated by Professor Paul A. Samuelson in two articles in the *Economic Journal*, 1948
and 1949; for fuller reference see Svend Laursen,
"Production Functions and the Theory of International Trade," *The American Economic Review*, 1955, pp. 540 ff.

observes, a similar confrontation of the facts of international inequality with the theory of international trade for the period before 1914 reveals the same discord. And I would add that it is not self-evident but, indeed, very much up to doubt whether today a freer trade would necessarily lead to less of international inequality or whether in general trade between developed and (densely populated) under-developed countries has ever had that effect.

. . .

Contrary to what the equilibrium theory of international trade would seem to suggest, the play of the market forces does not work towards equality in the remunerations to factors of production and, consequently, in incomes. If left to take its own course, economic development is a process of circular and cumulative causation which tends to award its favours to those who are already well endowed and even to thwart the efforts of those who happen to live in regions that are lagging behind. The backsetting effects of economic expansion in other regions dominate the more powerfully, the poorer a country is.

Within the national boundaries of the richer countries an integration process has taken place: on a higher level of economic development expansionary momentum tends to spread more effectively to other localities and regions than those where starts happen to have been made and successfully sustained; and inequality has there also been mitigated through interferences in the play of the market forces by organised society. In a few highly advanced countries—comprising only about one-sixth of the population in the non-Soviet world—this national integration process is now being carried forward towards a very high level of equality of opportunity to all, wherever, and in

whatever circumstances they happen to be born. These countries are approaching a national harmony of interest which, because of the role played by state policies, has to be characterized as a "created harmony"; and this has increasingly sustained also their further economic development.

Outside this small group of highly developed and progressive countries, all other countries are in various degrees poorer and mostly also less progressive economically. In a rather close correlation to their poverty they are ridden by internal economic inequalities, which also tend to weaken the effectiveness of their democratic systems of government in the cases where they are not under one form or another of oligarchic or forthright dictatorial rule.

The relations between relative lack of national economic integration and relative economic backwardness run, according to my hypothesis of circular cumulative causation, both ways. With a low level of economic development follow low levels of social mobility, communications, popular education and national sharing in beliefs and valuations, which imply greater impediments to the spread effects of expansionary momentum; at the same time the poorer states have for much the same reasons and because of the very fact of existing internal inequalities often been less democratic and, in any case, they have, because they are poorer, been up against narrower financial and, at bottom, psychological limitations on policies seeking to equalise opportunities. Inequality of opportunities has, on the other hand, contributed to preserving a low "quality" of their factors of production and a low "effectiveness" in their production efforts, to use the classical terms, and this has hampered their economic development.

On the international as on the national level trade does not by itself necessarily work for equality. A widening of markets strengthens often on the first hand the progressive countries whose manufacturing industries have the lead and are already fortified in surroundings of external economies, while the under-developed countries are in continuous danger of seeing even what they have of industry and, in particular, their small scale industry and handicrafts outcompeted by cheap imports from the industrial countries, if they do not protect them.

It is easy to observe how in most under-developed countries the trading contacts with the outside world have actually impoverished them culturally. Skills in many crafts inherited from centuries back have been lost. A city like Baghdad, with whose name such glorious associations are connected, today does not harbour any of the old crafts, except some silver smithies, and they have adapted patterns from abroad requiring less craftsmanship; similarly it is only with the greatest difficulties that one can buy a book of Arabic literature, while cheap magazines in English or Arabic are in abundance.

If international trade did not stimulate manufacturing industry in the under-developed countries but instead robbed them of what they had of old-established crafts, it did promote the production of primary products, and such production, employing mostly unskilled labour, came to constitute the basis for the bulk of their exports. In these lines, however, they often meet inelastic demands in the export market, often also a demand trend which is not rising very rapidly, and excessive price fluctuations. When, furthermore, population is rapidly rising while the larger part of it lives at, or near, the subsistence level—which means that there is no scarcity of common labour—any technological improvement in their export production tends to confer the advantages from the cheapening of production to the importing countries. Because of inelastic demands the result will often not even be a very great enlargement of the markets and of production and employment. In any case the wages and the export returns per unit of product will tend to remain low as the supply of unskilled labour is almost unlimited.

The advice—and assistance—which the poor countries receive from the rich is even nowadays often directed towards increasing their production of primary goods for export. The advice is certainly given in good faith and it may even be rational from the short term point of view of each under-developed country seen in isolation. Under a broader perspective and from a long term point of view, what would be rational is above all to increase productivity, incomes and living standards in the larger agricultural subsistence sectors, so as to raise the supply price of labour, and in manufacturing industry. This would engender economic development and raise incomes *per capita*. But trade by itself does not lead to such a development; it rather tends to have backsetting effects and to strengthen the forces maintaining stagnation or regression. Economic development has to be brought about by policy interferences which, however, are not under our purview at this stage of the argument when we are analysing only the effects of the play of the market forces.

Neither can the capital movements be relied upon to counteract international inequalities between the countries which are here in question. Under the circumstances described, capital will, on the whole, shun the under-developed countries, particularly as the advanced countries themselves are rapidly developing further and can offer their owners of capital both good profits and security.

There has, in fact, never been much of a capital movement to the countries which today we call under-developed, even in earlier times—except tiny streams to the economic enclaves, mainly devoted to export production of primary products which, however, usually were so profitable to their owners that they rapidly became self-supporting so far as investment capital was concerned and, in addition, the considerably larger but still relatively small investments in railways and other public utilities which had their security in the political controls held by colonial governments. The bulk of European overseas capital exports went to the settlements in the free spaces in the temperate zones which were becoming populated by emigration from Europe. After the collapse of the international capital market in the early 'thirties, which has not been remedied, and later the breakdown of the colonial system, which had given security to the foreign investor, it would be almost against nature if capital in large quantities were voluntarily to seek its way to under-developed countries in order to play a role in their economic development.

True, capital in these countries is scarce. But the need for it does not represent an effective demand in the capital market. Rather, if there were no exchange controls and if, at the same time, there were no elements in their national development policies securing high profits for capital —i.e. if the forces in the capital market were given unhampered play—capitalists in under-developed countries would be exporting their capital. Even with such controls and policies in existence, there is actually a steady capital flight going on from under-developed countries, which in a realistic analysis should be counted against what there is of capital inflow to these countries.

Labour migration, finally, can safely be counted out as a factor of importance for international economic adjustment as between under-developed and developed countries. The population pressure in most under-developed countries implies, of course, that they do not need immigration and the consequent low wages that immigrants are not tempted to come. Emigration from these countries would instead be the natural thing. For various reasons emigration could, however, not be much of a real aid to economic development, even if it were possible.

And the whole world is since the First World War gradually settling down to a situation where immigrants are not welcomed almost anywhere from wherever they come; people have pretty well to stay in the country where they are born, except for touristing by those who can afford it. And so far as the larger part of the under-developed world is concerned, where people are "coloured" according to the definition in the advanced countries, emigration is usually stopped altogether by the colour bar as defined by the legislation, or in the administration, of the countries which are white-dominated and at the same time better off economically.

If left unregulated, international trade and capital movements would thus often be the media through which the economic progress in the advanced countries would have backsetting effects in the under-developed world, and their mode of operation would be very much the same as it is in the circular cumulation of causes in the development process within a single country ... Internationally, these effects will, however, dominate the outcome much more, as the countervailing spread effects of expansionary momentum are so very much weaker. Differences in legislation, administration and *mores* generally, in language, in basic valuations and beliefs, in levels of living, production capacities and facilities, etcetera make the national boundaries effective barriers to the spread to a degree which no demarcation lines within one country approach.

Even more important as impediments to the spread effects of expansionary momentum from abroad than the boundaries and everything they stand for is, however, the very fact of great poverty and weak spread effects within the under-developed countries themselves. Where, for instance, international trade and shipping actually does transform the immediate surroundings of a port to a centre of economic expansion, which happens almost everywhere in the world, the expansionary momentum usually does not spread out to other regions of the country, which tend to remain backward if the forces in the markets are left free to take their course. Basically, the weak spread effects as between countries are thus for the larger part only a reflection of the weak spread effects within the under-developed countries themselves.

Under these circumstances the forces in the markets will in a cumulative way tend to cause ever greater international inequalities between countries as to their level of economic development and average national income *per capita*.

1.3 DEVELOPMENT AND TRADE *

When capital is being accumulated in a closed economy, resources are being diverted from the making of goods for immediate consumption to the making of capital goods, which will increase capacity in the future. The extent of this increase in capacity (which is the productivity of the investment) depends, first, on the quantity of capital goods that can be made with the resources transferred (a matter of the present productivity of the capital goods producing industries); and secondly, on the extent to which future productivity will be assisted by the capital goods that are produced (that is to say, upon the productivity of the capital goods themselves). It will be useful, from now

* From J. R. Hicks, *Essays in World Economics,* Clarendon Press, Oxford, 1959, pp. 180–88. Reprinted by permission.

on, to look at these two components separately.

It is perfectly possible that there may be a closed economy in which the productivity of investment is high on both counts. The world itself is a closed economy, and about its performance in both directions there is not (perhaps) much to complain. There are instances (of which Russia, at some stages of her Communist experience, is no doubt the most striking) where a country has achieved great things in the way of economic progress, even though its economic intercourse with the outside world has been kept extremely small. But if we make the same distinction with reference to a more typically under-developed country, and suppose that it is endeavouring to develop as a closed economy, without foreign trade and without drawing capital from outside its frontiers, the picture which emerges does not look inviting. There will be few sorts of capital goods which it can produce from its limited resources; and these, it is only too likely, will be produced at high cost (so that few of them can be produced against a given volume of saving) or will be of unsatisfactory kinds. So that, on the other count, the contribution which such capital goods can make to capacity will itself be limited. An expansion, which operated under such restrictions as these, would not get easier as it went on; it is only too likely that it would grind to a stop.

The obstacles which I have in mind, in painting this picture, do not include the difficulty which must always arise in any development that starts from a condition of poverty: that capital goods producing industries must be built up from nothing (or almost nothing), and that the building-up, to a condition of full efficiency, is a process that must inevitably take time. That is a difficulty which everyone, at the corresponding stage, has had to meet; with determination and patience it can be overcome. What I do have in mind are the permanent reasons which make autarky inefficient; the basic diseconomies, which are familiar in the textbooks, of small *size*.

As the case has been traditionally set out, it runs in terms of the advantages of trading to a country with given supplies of the factors of production. It is not so often remarked that just the same principles are operative when it is a question of growth. The gain from trade is the difference between the value (to the country) of the things that are got, and the value (in the same sense) of the things that are given up. These values may be expressions of direct utility (to consumers); but they may also reflect indirect utilities, the utilities of capital goods as instruments of future production. By exchanging goods with less growth potential for goods with more growth potential (in the economy into which they are to be fitted), the progress which results from a given effort on the savings side can be quickened up.

The principal reasons why it is possible to make gains of this sort (why it is nearly always possible to make some gains) are two in number. The more obvious is concerned with natural resources. The ability to turn savings into capital goods, and to do so efficiently, depends upon the supply of other factors, of labour and *land*. From this particular point of view, it is not the quantity of land resources which is the most important; the variety is more important still. Modern technology has only succeeded in opening up such endless vistas of opportunities because of the variety of materials which it has found ways of combining; if a country's resources are very uniform, this is itself a thing which limits the development which it can achieve from its own resources alone. This is one of the reasons why a large country can afford a policy of self-containedness better than a small country; for a larger area will generally contain a wider variety of resources, if only because it extends over a wider variety of climates. It is nevertheless true that there are some small areas which are favoured with considerable variety; so that this disadvantage of self-containedness, though always present, is not always important to the same extent.

The less obvious reason, to which I now turn, is more strictly a matter of size. It is impossible to make sense of the phenomena of international trade unless one lays great stress upon *increasing returns* (the economies of large scale); and this is particularly important in the present connexion, because of the close connexion between increasing returns and the accumulation of capital.[1] It is a common situation in industry that there is a choice between a relatively 'primitive' and a relatively 'advanced' technique—the obvious difference between them being that the advanced technique requires more capital. So far as this is the only difference, we may expect that a country which is accumulating capital will naturally proceed from the more primitive to the more advanced method; but it may not be the only difference. For the profitability (or superior productivity) of the more advanced method is also, in many cases, a matter of the volume of output which is to be produced. The more advanced methods only become economic (in the sense of lowering costs, and hence of raising the national productivity) if they can be employed upon a sufficiently large scale. It follows that a small country, which had no trade, could not wisely adopt advanced methods in many of its industries. Its opportunities for the productive investment of capital would be restricted, simply because of its small size.

It is important to be clear just what we

1. The classical statement of the connexion is in Allyn Young, "Increasing Returns and Economic Progress" (*Econ. Jour.*, vol. xxxviii, 1928).

mean by size in this connexion. The size in question is the size of the market, the volume of output (of a particular commodity) that the market can absorb. This depends on population, but also on the wealth of the population. A very poor country, such as India or China, may have an enormous population; yet the real incomes of its people may be so low that the market which it offers for many sorts of manufactured goods may be quite moderate. (It should be emphasized that a market may be large enough to call forth all possible economies of scale in the production of final consumers' goods, but may not be large enough to do the same in the production of the capital goods which are to make those consumers' goods, or in many ancillary industries. All the stages of production must be taken into account.) A poor country is hampered, just as a small country is hampered, by diseconomies of small size. But it is of course true that when a country is large geographically, it can overcome this obstacle, provided that it can achieve some rate of progress; its economic expansion will enlarge the size of its markets, and will therefore enable it to overcome, at a later stage of its growth, the difficulties (of this sort) which hamper it at an earlier stage. When the country is small geographically, the obstacle is more permanent.

Even so, it is an obstacle that can be overcome—by trade, and consequent specialization. By concentrating its production on the things that it is best suited to make, it can achieve an output which is limited, not by its own size, but by the world market for such commodities. In spite of its small size, it can achieve, in its export industries, the full advantages of large scale which such industries are capable of attaining.

In principle, all this is well known; what I want to emphasize here is its bear-

ing on the productivity of investment. Suppose, for the moment, that savings are to be embodied in capital goods that are to be used in industries which produce for the home market. There is still a choice, whether to produce those capital goods at home, or to import them from abroad, paying for them by exports, or by the contraction of other imports. An increase in saving is a diminution of consumption; if the consumption reduction is a reduction of imports, funds are directly set free out of which capital goods can be imported; if it is a reduction in the consumption of home-produced goods, the labour which would have made those products can be transferred to production for export. Certainly, in this latter case, there is a problem of selling the additional exports; it may happen that this difficulty is such that it is, after all, more productive to produce the capital goods at home. But when we remember how difficult it will be for a small country to produce at home anything like the full range of capital goods that will be wanted, it becomes almost inevitable that there will be many capital goods which it is easier to acquire by the route of trade. It is especially important, in this connexion, that many of the most 'advanced' capital goods are among the things which are most affected by economies of large-scale production. The demand for them, from a country of moderate size, is bound to be rather small, and may be quite intermittent. The growth of its economy will proceed more rapidly if it imports them from abroad than if it insists upon producing them, somehow or other, at home.

The advantage which I have just been describing is indeed one that does seem to be generally appreciated. One does not observe that countries of moderate size are at all reluctant to import large quantities of capital equipment. It is only the greatest giants which attempt to manufacture for themselves anything like the whole range of capital goods which they need. Even those which are at the top of the second rank are willing, and often anxious, to import capital goods to a quite remarkable extent. Of course they export capital goods also; they have a lead in some lines and they are content to rely upon imports for others. There does indeed seem to be a tendency for international trade to be settling into a form in which it consists of an exchange of capital goods for materials, of capital goods for other capital goods, and materials for other materials; each country endeavouring to make its own consumption goods for itself, but relying on trade to provide it with the *variety* of materials that it needs, and with the capital goods which it could not make for itself in the quantities it requires except at prohibitive cost.

The structure of trade does seem to be tending in that direction; but before we accept the tendency as being satisfactory, we should see what it implies. We have so far been assuming that the capital goods which are imported are to be used in industries that produce for the home market; that is to say, although international trade is allowed to influence the terms on which savings are converted into capital goods, it does not influence the efficiency with which the capital goods are used—which was the further stage in the process by which accumulation becomes effective. There can be no doubt, at least in principle, that the same arguments which apply to the manufacture of capital goods apply also to their use. Here also it ought to be considered whether it is not possible that a larger quantity of products could be acquired through trade than can be acquired by direct production. If the trade alternative is selected, it implies that there will have to be an adjustment of a similar character to that which was discussed in the other case. What it means here is that

the new capital goods, instead of being wholly employed in direct production for the home market, will be partly such as will assist production for export. The additional supply of finished goods, which is the object of growth, and indeed in a sense *is* the growth, will then be acquired in exchange for additional exports, instead of being manufactured directly at home.

The advantages of this possibility ought always to be considered; and for almost any country there are likely to be some sorts of goods for which the case for such a procedure is extremely strong. One can nevertheless understand that it does often seem much less strong than the corresponding argument in the case of capital goods. The consumption goods can, very often, be produced at home after a fashion; if they are dear, or their quality is poor, that can be put down to "teething troubles"; given time, so it is said, we shall produce them just as well as anybody else. It is difficult to pay for imports by expanding exports; and the capital goods imports, which we cannot produce at home, must have priority. The easy way out is to have a heavily protected home market for consumption goods.

This, very broadly, is the way a great many "developing" countries are behaving; and from the point of view of each individual country, it is an intelligible, and may be a defensible, policy to adopt. It has, of course, its obvious dangers; inefficient industries, sheltered by the restriction of imports, have little incentive to improve their efficiency; they have a tendency to be centres of stagnation, not progress. There is, however, another less obvious consequence of the same policy which also requires to be noticed.

It is precisely this kind of policy, adopted by individual nations, which causes international trade (as a whole) to settle into the form of an exchange of capital goods against raw materials, the form which we previously noticed. The underdeveloped countries are themselves prone to this policy, but so are others also, for much the same reasons. Its general result is decidedly detrimental to the interests of the underdeveloped countries. For it perpetuates the distinction between the developed and the underdeveloped. It divides the countries of the world into two distinct types: one predominantly exporting capital goods (with a few materials and foodstuffs for which they have special advantages), and the other (the underdeveloped type) exporting materials and foodstuffs and nothing else. The only sort of development which is open to the latter countries, so long as this system continues, is the development of a limited range of protected industries, producing for the home market. The step from that kind of development to the further kind, which would genuinely put them on a par with the developed countries, of becoming exporters of manufactured goods, is made exceedingly difficult. For what that would mean, on this system, is that they would have to become exporters of capital goods —that is to say, they would have to develop a comparative advantage for goods of a type which is furthest away from the types which they are at present producing with the greatest success, for goods the production of which is highly capitalized and which are particularly subject to economies of large scale. The ladder by which they might climb up to, or towards, that point has been removed.

It has been removed, partly by the policies of others, but partly by their own. At least so far as the smaller underdeveloped countries are concerned, it is hardly possible that they can break right out of their economic confinement, unless they can become in some sense, however modest, exporters of manufactures. But the sorts of manufactured goods which it is least hopeless for them to export are those

which do not require too much capital, too much complicated organization, too many economies of large scale. And these are much more likely to belong to the consumption goods class than to the other.[2]

But what, it may be asked, is the moral? One cannot go to an underdeveloped country, which naturally feels that it owes a large part of such development as it has achieved very largely to its policy of protection, and advise it to take down its "defences," in the interests of wider gains, which can only accrue in the remote future, and which may well, even then, accrue to their neighbours rather than to themselves. One must content oneself with something more modest. One can suggest that the considerations, which have led (in Europe) to movements for Free Trade Areas and Common Markets, are not without relevance to the problems of the underdeveloped countries. If the day when they can hope to become exporters of manufactured goods to the "advanced" countries is in most cases very far off, it is by no means so hopeless (economically considered, though one sees the political obstacles) that they should get themselves, before very long, into a position where they can sell the easier sorts of manufactures to one another.

1.4 Dynamic Benefits of Trade *

I shall now positively and systematically state what I think the contribution of international trade to economic development was in the past and what it can be in the

2. It is no accident that the two small "underdeveloped countries" which have achieved a major economic expansion during the last ten years (Puerto Rico and Hong Kong) have done precisely this. But as the world is now tied up, there is no room for that "miracle" to be repeated, as it ought to be, many times over.

* From Gottfried Haberler, *International Trade and Economic Development*, National Bank of Egypt Fiftieth Anniversary Commemoration Lectures, Cairo, 1959, pp. 5-7, 9-14. Reprinted by permission.

future. My overall conclusion is that international trade has made a tremendous contribution to the development of less developed countries in the 19th and 20th centuries and can be expected to make an equally big contribution in the future, if it is allowed to proceed freely. It does not necessarily follow that a 100% free trade policy is always most conducive to most rapid development. Marginal interferences with the free flow of trade, if properly selected, may speed up development. But I do not want to leave any doubt that my conclusion is that substantially free trade with marginal, insubstantial corrections and deviations, is the best policy from the point of view of economic development. Drastic deviations from free trade can be justified, on development grounds,—and this is very nearly the same thing as to say on economic grounds—only if and when they are needed to compensate for the adverse influence of other policies inimical to economic development, for example, the consequences of persistent inflation or of certain tax and domestic price support policies. Let me guard against a possible misunderstanding. If I say that drastic interferences with the market mechanism are not needed for rapid development, I refer to trade policy and I do not deny that drastic measures in other areas, let me say, land reform, education, forced investment (if the projects are well chosen) etc. may not speed up growth. . . .

International division of labor and international trade, which enable every country to specialize and to export those things that it can produce cheaper in exchange for what others can provide at a lower cost, have been and still are one of the basic factors promoting economic well-being and increasing national income of every participating country. Moreover, what is good for the national income and the standard of living is, at least potentially, also good for economic development; for the greater the volume of output the greater can be the rate of growth— provided the people individually or collectively have the urge to save and to invest and economically to develop. The higher the level of output, the easier it is to escape the "vicious circle of poverty" and to "take off into self-sustained growth" to use the jargon of modern development theory. Hence, if trade raises the level of income, it also promotes economic development. . . .

In most underdeveloped countries international trade plays quantitatively an especially important role, that is, a larger percentage of their income is spent on imports, and a larger percentage of their output is being exported, than in the case of developed countries of comparable economic size. (Other things being equal, it is natural that the "larger," economically speaking, a country, the smaller its trade percentages.) Many underdeveloped countries are highly specialized also in the sense that a very large percentage of their exports consists of one or two staple commodities. . . .

This high concentration of exports is not without danger. One would normally not want to put so many of one's eggs into one basket. But the price of diversification is in most cases extremely high. I shall touch on that topic once more. At this point, let me simply say that a high level of concentrated trade will, in most cases, be much better than a low level of diversified trade. How much poorer would Brazil be without coffee, Venezuela, Iran and Iraq without oil, Bolivia without tin, Malaya without rubber and tin, Ghana without cocoa, and, I dare say, Egypt without cotton. The really great danger of concentration arises in case of deep and protracted slumps in the industrial countries—slumps of the order of magnitude of the Great Depression in the 1930's. In my opinion, and here I am sure the overwhelming majority of economists in the Western world agrees, the chance that this will happen again is practically nil.

The tremendous importance of trade for the underdeveloped countries (as well as for most developed ones, with the exception of the US and USSR, which could, if need be, give it up without suffering a catastrophic reduction in their living standard) follows from the classical theory of comparative cost in conjunction with the fact that the comparative differences in cost of production of industrial products and food and raw materials between developed countries and underdeveloped countries are obviously very great, in many cases, in fact, infinite in the sense that countries of either group just could not produce what they buy from the other.[1]

...

For our purposes I will distinguish among the changes which constitute economic development two types—those that take place independently of international trade and those that are induced by trade or trade policy.

As far as the first group—let me call them autonomous changes—is concerned, I can see no difficulty resulting from them for the applicability of the classical theory of comparative cost. Such changes are the gradual improvement in skill, education and training of workers, farmers, engineers, entrepreneurs; improvements resulting from inventions and discoveries and from the accumulation of capital—changes which in the Western world stem for the most part from the initiative of individuals and private associations, but possibly also from conscious government policies.[2]

These changes come gradually or in waves and result in gradually increasing output of commodities that had been produced before or in the setting up of the production of goods that had not been produced earlier. Analytically, such development has to be pictured as an outward movement of the production possibility curve (often called substitution or transformation curve). Depending on the concrete turn that autonomous development (including improvements in transportation technology) takes, the comparative cost situation and hence volume and composition of trade will be more or less profoundly affected. But since these changes only come slowly and gradually and usually cannot be foreseen (either by private business or government planners) in sufficient detail to make anticipatory action possible, there is no presumption that the allocative mechanism as described in the theory of comparative cost will not automatically and efficiently bring about the changes and adjustment in the volume and structure of trade called for by autonomous development.

I turn now to the second type of changes in the productive capabilities of a country which are more important for the purposes of my lectures, namely, those induced by trade and changes in trade including changes in trade brought about by trade policy. Favorable as well as unfavorable trade-induced changes are possible and have to be considered. Alleged unfavorable trade-induced changes have received so much attention from protectionist writers from List to Myrdal (which has induced free trade economists, too, to discuss them at great length), that there is danger that

1. In many cases very expensive and poor substitutes can be produced. There is not much sense in contemplating extreme situations. But if I were pressed to guess, I would say that the developed countries as a group, and a few of them individually, could get along without trade a little easier (although still at a terrific loss) than the underdeveloped countries.

2. I am not speaking here of policies concerning international trade such as the imposition of import restrictions. Changes resulting from trade policy measures are trade-induced and not autonomous changes.

the tremendously important favorable influences be unduly neglected. Let me, therefore, discuss the latter first.

If we were to estimate the contribution of international trade to economic development, especially of the underdeveloped countries, solely by the static gains from trade in any given year on the usual assumption of given [3] production capabilities (analytically under the assumption of given production functions or given or autonomously shifting production possibility curves) we would indeed grossly underrate the importance of trade. For over and above the direct static gains dwelt upon by the traditional theory of comparative cost, trade bestows very important indirect benefits, which also can be described as dynamic benefits, upon the participating countries. Let me emphasize once more that the older classical writers did stress these "indirect benefits" (Mill's own words).[4] Analytically we have to describe these "indirect," "dynamic" benefits from trade as an outward shift (in the northeast direction) of the production possibility curve brought about by a trade-induced movement along the curve.

First, trade provides material means (capital goods, machinery and raw and semifinished materials) indispensable for economic development. Secondly, even more important, trade is the means and vehicle for the dissemination of technological knowledge, the transmission of ideas, for the importation of know-how, skills, managerial talents and entrepreneurship. Thirdly, trade is also the vehicle for the international movement of capital especially from the developed to the underdeveloped countries. Fourthly, free international trade is the best antimonopoly policy and the best guarantee for the main-

3. This includes autonomously shifting.
4. In the neo-classical theory they have been somewhat neglected. The reason is perhaps that these factors do not lend themselves well to precise mathematical treatment.

tenance of a healthy degree of free competition.

Let me now make a few explanatory remarks on each of these four points before I try to show how they fit into, and complement, the static theory of comparative advantage.

The first point is so obvious that it does not require much elaboration. Let us recall and remember, however, the tremendous benefits which the underdeveloped countries draw from technological progress in the developed countries through the importation of machinery, transport equipment, vehicles, power generation equipment, road building machinery, medicines, chemicals, and so on. The advantage is, of course, not all on one side. I stress the advantage derived by underdeveloped countries (rather than the equally important benefits for the developed countries), because I am concerned in these lectures primarily with the development of the less developed countries.

The composition of the export trade of the developed industrial countries has been changing, as we all know, in the direction of the types of capital goods which I have mentioned away from textiles and other light consumer goods. This shift has been going on for a long time; it is not a recent phenomenon. But it has proceeded rapidly in recent years, and there is no reason to doubt that it will continue.

Secondly, probably even more important than the importation of material goods is the importation of technical know-how, skills, managerial talents, entrepreneurship. This is, of course, especially important for the underdeveloped countries. But the developed countries too benefit greatly from cross-fertilization aided by trade among themselves and the less advanced industrial countries can profit from the superior technical and managerial know-how, etc. of the more advanced ones.

The late-comers and successors in the

process of development and industrialization have always had the great advantage that they could learn from the experiences, from the successes as well as from the failures and mistakes of the pioneers and forerunners. In the 19th century the continental European countries and the U.S. profited greatly from the technological innovation and achievements of the industrial revolution in Great Britain. Later the Japanese proved to be very adept learners and Soviet Russia has shown herself capable of speeding up her own development by "borrowing" (interest free) immense amounts of technological know-how from the West, developing it further and adopting it for her own purposes. This "trade" has been entirely onesided. I know of not a single industrial idea or invention which the West has obtained from the East.[5] Today the underdeveloped countries have a tremendous, constantly growing, store of technological know-how to draw from. True, simple adoption of methods developed for the conditions of the developed countries is often not possible. But adaptation is surely much easier than first creation.

Trade is the most important vehicle for the transmission of technological know-how. True, it is not the only one. In fact this function of trade is probably somewhat less important now than it was a hundred years ago, because ideas, skills, know-how, travel easier and quicker and

cheaper today than in the 19th century. The market where engineering and management experts can be hired is much better-organized than formerly. There is much more competition in this field as well as in the area of material capital equipment. In the early 19th century Great Britain was the only center from which industrial equipment and know-how could be obtained, and there were all sorts of restrictions on the exportation of both. Today there are a dozen industrial centers in Europe, the US, Canada, and Japan, and even Russia and Czechoslovakia all ready to sell machinery as well as engineering advice and know-how.

However, trade is still the most important transmission belt. What J.S. Mill said 100 years ago is still substantially true: "It is hardly possible to overrate the value in the present low state of human improvement, of placing human beings in contact with persons dissimilar to themselves, and with modes of thought and action unlike those with which they are familiar.... Such communication has always been, peculiarly in the present age one of the primary sources of progress.[6]

The third indirect benefit of trade which I mentioned was that it also serves as a transmission belt for capital. It is true that the amount of capital that an underdeveloped country can obtain from abroad depends in the first place on the ability and willingness of developed countries to lend, which is of course decisively influenced by the internal policies in the borrowing countries. But it stands to reason—and this is the only point I wanted to make at this juncture—that, other things being equal, the larger the volume of trade, the greater will be the volume of foreign capital that can be expected to become available under realistic assumptions. The reason is that with a large volume of trade the transfer of interest and repayments on principal is

5. This statement is made on the authority of Prof. John Jewkes of Oxford who has made a close study of sixty major industrial innovations (in the Schumpeterian sense) and comes to the following conclusion: "The cases taken as a whole reveal that no country has a monopoly of inventive power. The outstanding names and groups are widely spread over many industrial countries. One significant exception is that in none of sixty cases studied had contributions been made by Russian workers subsequent to the Revolution. Before that date numerous names of distinguished Russian contributors crop up." J. Jewkes, "The Sources of Invention," *Lloyd's Bank Review*, Jan. 1958, p. 23....

6. *Principles of Political Economy.*

more easily effected than with a small volume of trade; and it would be clearly unrealistic to expect large capital movements if the chance for transfer of interest and repayments is not good. There is, furthermore, the related fact that it is much easier to get foreign capital for export industries with their built-in solution of the retransfer problem than for other types of investments which do not directly and automatically improve the balance of payments. This preference of foreign capital for export industries is regrettable because other types of investment (such as investment in public utilities, railroads, manufacturing industries) may often (not always) be more productive and may make a greater indirect contribution, dollar per dollar, to economic development by providing training to native personnel and in various other ways than export industries which sometimes (by no means always) constitute foreign enclaves in native soil. If the direct and indirect contribution of non-export industries to national income and economic development are in fact greater than those of the export industry, they should be preferred, because their indirect contribution to the balance of payments position will then also be such as to guarantee the possibility of smooth retransfer of principal and interest—*provided* inflationary monetary policies do not upset equilibrium entailing exchange control that then gets in the way of transfer. But with inflationary monetary policies and exchange control practices as they are in most underdeveloped countries, the preference of foreign capital for export industries is readily understandable and must be reckoned with and foreign capital in export is better than no foreign capital at all.

The fourth way in which trade benefits a country indirectly is by fostering healthy competition and keeping in check inefficient monopolies. The reason why the American economy is more competitive—and more efficient—than most others is probably to be sought more in the great internal free trade area which the US enjoys rather than in the antimonopoly policy which was always much more popular in the US than in Europe or anywhere else. The importance of this factor is confirmed by the fact that many experts believe that the main economic advantages of the European Common Market, towards the realization of which the first steps have just been taken, will flow from freer competition rather than merely from the larger size and larger scale production which it entails.

Increased competition is important also for underdeveloped countries, especially inasmuch as the size of their market is usually small (even if the geographic area is large). A reservation has nevertheless to be made. The first introduction of new industries on infant industry grounds may justify the creation of monopolistic positions, depending on the size of the country and the type of industry. But the problem will always remain how to prevent the permanent establishment of inefficient exploitative monopolies even after an industry has taken root and has become able to hold its ground without the crutches of imports restriction.

The general conclusion, then, is that international trade, in addition to the static gains resulting from the division of labor with given (or autonomously changing) production functions, powerfully contributes, in the four ways indicated, to the development of the productive capabilities of the less developed countries. Analytically we have to express that, in the framework of modern trade theory, by saying that trade gradually transforms existing production functions; in other words, that a movement along the production possibility curves in accordance with the pre-existing comparative cost situation, will tend to push up and out the production possibility curve.

1.5 PATTERNS OF TRADE AND DEVELOPMENT *

[It is] instructive to take a look at past experience and see how economic growth in certain areas was induced through international trade in the nineteenth century. The areas involved in this process of growth through trade were chiefly the so-called regions of recent settlement in the temperate latitudes outside Europe. These areas, in which the United States may be included, received a large inflow of labour as well as capital from Europe, but a basic inducement that caused them to develop was the tremendous expansion of Western Europe's, and especially Great Britain's, demand for the foodstuffs and raw materials which they were well suited to produce. Growth at the periphery was induced, through trade, by growth in the rising industrial centre.

Alfred Marshall referred to "the splendid markets which the old world has offered to the products of the new." [1] He forgot to mention the crucial point that these were growing markets, but this he probably assumed as a matter of course. The penultimate chapter of his *Principles* is entitled "General Influences of Economic Progress" and begins as follows: "The field of employment which any place offers for labour and capital depends, firstly, on its natural resources; secondly, on ... knowledge and ... organization; and thirdly, on ... markets in which it can sell those things of which it has a superfluity. The importance of this last condition is often underrated; but it stands out prominently when we look at the history of new countries." [2]

It was under the impression of this experience that Marshall made the following pronouncement: "The causes which determine the economic progress of nations belong to the study of international trade." [3] In the second half of the twentieth century this may seem to us a curious statement. It can be understood only in the light of certain historical conditions, and it embodies the particular experience of Britain's economic relations with the new countries overseas. Economic growth in these areas was due not to international specialization alone but more particularly to the fact that the character of trade was such that the rapid growth which was taking place in the centre was transmitted to the outlying new countries through a vigorous increase in the demand for primary products.

Trade in the nineteenth century was not simply a device for the optimum allocation of a given stock of resources. It was that too, but it was more than that. It was above all "an engine of growth." This profoundly important observation is one which we owe to Sir Dennis Robertson. [4]

It helps us to see things in perspective, but in doing so it serves also to limit the significance of classical trade theory to its proper sphere. The conventional tendency has been to credit international specialization as such with the spectacular growth of the new countries in the nineteenth century. In the light of Robertson's remark it may perhaps be suggested that classical specialization theory, which in the nature of the case is a static analysis, has derived more prestige from nineteenth-century experience than it has deserved. The dynamic nature of trade as a trans-

* From Ragnar Nurkse, "Trade Theory and Development Policy," in H. S. Ellis (ed.), *Economic Development for Latin America*, St. Martin's Press, New York, 1961, pp. 236-45. Reprinted by permission.

1. Alfred Marshall, *Principles of Economics*, 8th ed. (London, 1920), pp. 668-9.

2. *Ibid.*, p. 668.
3. *Ibid.*, p. 270.
4. D. H. Robertson, *Essays in Monetary Theory* (London, 1940), p. 214.

mitter of growth was overlooked during an era in which progress was taken for granted, like the air we breathe.

There is no doubt that international trade was peculiarly important in the conditions of the nineteenth century. In real volume it increased tenfold between 1850 and 1913, twice as fast as world production. Imperialism had very little to do with the expansion of trade. As was shown by J. A. Hobson himself,[5] the tropical colonies took a minor share in the growth of British trade. Continental Europe and the new countries outside as well as within the British Empire took the major share. The regions of recent settlement were high-income countries from the start, effective markets as well as efficient producers. Their development was part of the growth of international trade itself.

So much for the new countries. Elsewhere, in the truly backward areas, economic growth induced through international trade in some cases carried with it certain features that were, and still are, regarded as undesirable. It sometimes led to a lopsided pattern of growth in which production of primary products for export was carried on with the aid of substantial investment of foreign capital, while the domestic economy remained far less developed, if not altogether primitive. This picture applies especially to tropical areas. It is the familiar picture of the dual economy resulting from trade and from foreign business investment induced by trade. Areas of outpost investment producing for foreign markets often showed a lack of social as well as economic integration internally. Moreover, their export activities were subject to the familiar hazards of cyclical instability.

Nevertheless, even unsteady growth through foreign trade is surely better than no growth at all. Mr. Bauer has given impressive examples of progress resulting from peasant production for export in some parts of West Africa during the early half of the twentieth century.[6] Elsewhere foreign capital working for export has usually led to an additional demand for local labour, increased wage incomes, expenditures on local materials, new sources of taxation, and, in the case of mineral concessions, lucrative profit-sharing arrangements. All these benefits have helped to promote expansion in the domestic economy.

The traditional pattern of development through production for expanding export markets is not to be despised and ought not to be discouraged. Indeed, I should like to assume that all opportunities in this direction are fully exploited. The trouble is that in the mid-twentieth century, with a few notable exceptions, conditions for this type of growth do not, by and large, appear to be as promising as they were a hundred years ago.

Since 1913 the quantum of world trade has increased less than world production. To be sure, in the last five or six years we find the volume of trade in the non-communist world increasing at just about the same pace as production. But when we look at it more closely we find that it is chiefly among the advanced industrial countries that international trade has been expanding in the recent past. These countries, including above all the United States, are themselves efficient primary producers, especially of food. Their demand for exotic raw materials like crude rubber, silk, nitrates, jute, vegetable oils, hides, and skins has been, and will probably continue to be, affected by the growth of the chemical industry in the twentieth century.... Professor D. D. Humphrey in his voluminous study, *American Imports*,[7]

5. J. A. Hobson, *Imperialism,* 3rd ed. (London, 1938), ch. 2.

6. P. T. Bauer, *West African Trade* (Cambridge, 1955).

7. D. D. Humphrey, *American Imports* (New York, 1955).

attaches great importance to the technological factor. He esimates that, in its effect
on total United States imports, the displacement of imported raw materials by
synthetic products has more than offset
the 75 per cent reduction in the American
tariff which has taken place in the last
twenty years partly through duty reductions and partly through the effect of
price inflation on the burden of specific
duties. While tariff changes have mainly
affected imports of manufactured goods
from other industrial countries, technological displacement has particularly affected United States imports from the less
developed countries.

Only for minerals are conditions generally favourable, although even here it
should be noted that, first, the demand
for metals is affected by the increasing
efficiency of scrap collection and recovery
in the industrial countries. Second, mineral deposits are gifts of nature, and if
a country does not happen to have any,
it can do nothing in response to the rise
in world demand. Some countries that
have deposits fail to exploit them. Nevertheless, the point remains that while
Guatemala, for example, can at least try
to grow chicle, she cannot try to grow
nickel. Third, the export of minerals
involves in an obvious sense an element
of living on capital.

The growth of synthetic materials is
undoubtedly one explanation of the findings which Professor Kindleberger reaches
in his book on *The Terms of Trade: A
European Case Study*. This study lends
some support to the view that the poorer
countries' terms of trade have shown a
tendency to deteriorate. Kindleberger has
calculated industrial Europe's terms of
trade separately for various parts of the
world, including in particular two groups
of countries overseas, the areas of recent
settlement, not including the United
States, and the poorer countries (the rest

of the world in his grouping). Difficulties
due to quality changes and transport costs
apply to both groups. Both the new countries and the poor countries are exporters
of primary products and importers of
manufactured goods. From 1913 to 1952,
according to these estimates, Europe's
terms of trade with the areas of recent
settlement showed a 20 per cent improvement, while in trade with the poorer
countries Europe's terms seem to have
improved by as much as 55 per cent.[8]

Other recent studies have provided evidence that world demand for the poorer
countries' export products has tended to
rise much less than in proportion to the
production and incomes of the advanced
countries.[9] It is therefore not surprising
that, according to the report of the Contracting Parties to the General Agreement
on Tariffs and Trade, we find the following distribution of international trade in
the non-communist world in 1955. The
exports of twenty advanced industrial
countries (United States, Canada, Japan,
and Western Europe) to each other constitute as much as 40 per cent of total
exports. Exports from these twenty countries to all less developed countries outside the communist orbit amount to 25
per cent of the total. Exports from the
less developed to the advanced countries
represent another 25 per cent. Only 10

8. C. P. Kindleberger, *The Terms of Trade: A
European Case Study* (New York, 1956), p. 234.
9. For the post-war period this conclusion is
documented in United Nations, *World Economic
Survey, 1956,* and also in the annual report of the
Contracting Parties to the General Agreement on
Tariffs and Trade, *International Trade, 1955*
(Geneva, 1956).
For a longer period, Professor Cairncross has
made a careful statistical study of world exports
of manufactured goods since 1900 showing that
the manufactured goods which the industrial
countries export to each other have constituted a
steadily increasing proportion of their total exports of manufactured articles; A. K. Cairncross,
"World Trade in Manufactures since 1900," *Economia Internazionale,* November 1955.

per cent of the total are exports of the less developed countries to each other, even though the more than hundred countries in this group contain two-thirds of the total population of the non-communist world.[10] Why is it that so little of the coffee, tea, rubber, and tin produced in these countries goes to other countries in the same group? Obviously the main explanation is the low purchasing power of people in these countries, which in turn is a reflection of their low productivity.

The fact that the economically advanced countries are each others' best customers is now more than ever a central feature of world trade. It is chiefly within this small circle of countries that international trade is now expanding. With the leading exception of petroleum and a few other minerals, it can hardly be said that primary producing countries are enjoying a dynamic expansion in world demand for their exports....

In view of the tremendous growth of the American economy it is an extraordinary fact that, according to an official index, the real volume of American imports of agricultural products in 1955 was 15 per cent below the 1929 level. The 1955 quantum of United States imports of crude materials (excluding foodstuffs but including minerals) was only 23 per cent higher than in 1929, although the United States gross national product had increased by 116 per cent since 1929.

Professor T. W. Schultz in his paper on "Economic Prospect of Primary Products" shows that the demand for all raw materials, whether imported or domestically produced, has lagged far behind the increase in output in the United States. What we are considering therefore is merely the international aspect of a fairly general tendency. In a country amply supplied with capital and technical know-how, it seems a perfectly natural tendency for investment in research and development to displace crude materials with synthetic products made from a few basic elements of mostly local origin. These trends are not confined to the United States. They are affecting the trade of other advanced areas as well.[11]

If this is the situation of the mid-twentieth century, the mental habits which economists have inherited from the mid-nineteenth may no longer be altogether adequate. It will be recalled that Professor Hicks's analysis of the long-run dollar problem was based on what he described as "a change in economic atmosphere between the nineteenth and twentieth centuries." [12] His analysis in regard to the dollar problem was open to criticism, yet I believe that in emphasizing the varying incidence of productivity changes on international trade he made an important point, a point that had been noted some years earlier by Professor Haberler.[13] While Britain's ratio of imports to national income showed a rising tendency during most of the nineteenth century, the United States import ratio has been practically halved in the last five decades.[14] This has happened in spite of the fact that in short period comparisons the

11. A. K. Cairncross and J. Faaland, "Long-Term Trends in Europe's Trade," *Economic Journal,* March 1952, pp. 26-7.

12. J. R. Hicks, "An Inaugural Lecture," *Oxford Economic Papers,* June 1953, p. 130.

13. G. Haberler, "Dollar Shortage?," in S. E. Harris, ed., *Foreign Economic Policy for the United States* (Cambridge, Massachusetts, 1948), pp. 438-9.

14. United States exports as a percentage of gross national product fell from 5·7 per cent in the period 1896–1914 to 2·97 per cent in 1955. See W. Lederer, "Major Developments Affecting the United States Balance of International Payments," *Review of Economics and Statistics,* May 1956, p. 184.

10. *International Trade,* 1955. The figures given in this report exclude trade within the communist orbit. For the sake of comparability I have adjusted them so as to exclude trade between communist and non-communist countries as well.

United States typically shows a rather high income elasticity of imports. There seems to have been a long-run downward shift in the United States import function, resulting from changes in economic structure. It is not certain that tariff policy provides the major part of the explanation. It seems very likely that the incidence of technological advance has had a good deal to do with it.

The slight increase which has occurred in the last few years in the United States import ratio has been due to increased imports of finished and semi-finished manufactures. This has meant increased trade with other industrial countries, Canada, Western Europe, Japan. Imports of crude materials, largely from under-developed areas, have not regained their pre-war position in relation to United States gross national product. All this does not mean that the absolute volume of United States imports has failed to expand. It increased by 44 per cent from 1929 to 1955.[15] But notice two things. This increase is much less than proportional to the growth of United States output. Moreover, it is much less than the rate of growth of British imports in the nineteenth century, which during any comparable period showed a two to threefold increase in volume.

It is useful to keep in mind these elementary facts about American imports because the United States is now the dominant economy not only in world production but also in world trade. Some economists are more inclined to stress the future prospect of expansion in United States imports, but that is a debatable matter. It is never quite safe, and for present purposes really unnecessary, to engage in predictions. The facts for the recent past are sufficient to indicate a change in the economic atmosphere of international trade between the nineteenth and twentieth centuries.

It will be remembered that in Hicks's analysis of the dollar shortage, the balance of payments problem resolves itself into a terms of trade problem. This seems a plausible simplification. Any country in foreign exchange difficulties can normally restore its balance of payments by accepting a worsening in its terms of trade. In Hicks's model external balance is maintained by changes in terms of trade.

But can we not go a step further? There has been a tendency, in Britain and elsewhere, to exaggerate both the actual extent and the economic significance of changes in the terms of trade. We are sometimes apt to think of these changes as if the resources of each country were for ever committed to the existing export industries. This view may be all right for the short run, but in the longer run labour and capital within each country can usually move to other occupations, and do in fact move. If the relationship of export prices to import prices undergoes a marked increase or decline, it is entirely natural that factors of production should tend to move from export industries to import-competing industries or vice versa. This may involve simply changes in the allocation of *increases* in factor supplies rather than movements of existing factors. In any event, the point is that a change in the terms of trade tends to induce shifts in production and in the distribution of resources, which will tend to reverse or counteract the change in the terms of trade.

15. The quantum of crude material imports, as already stated, increased by only 23 per cent. The other commodity groups showed the following percentage increases from 1929 to 1955: crude foodstuffs, 33 per cent; manufactured foodstuffs, 55 per cent; semi-manufactures 76 per cent; finished manufactures, 52 per cent. Is it not possible, however, that the relatively small rise in imports of crude commodities may be due, not to a low rate of growth of United States demand, but rather to a deficiency on the supply side? The answer is in Professor Schultz's paper, where the strategic role of demand is clearly demonstrated.

What remains is growth and change in the volume of productive activity induced through international trade. On this view, changes in the terms as well as in the balance of trade are a transient and relatively insignificant element in the mechanism by which processes of economic growth (or decline) may be transmitted from one country to others.

This does not imply that shifts in external demand do not matter. Fortunate indeed is the country with an expanding export market for the commodity in whose production it has a comparative advantage; for it can then draw increasing supplies in limitless variety from the outside world. The suggestion is merely that, because of the possibility of internal factor shifts in response to varying price relationships, long-term trends in external demand conditions need not be reflected fully, if at all, in changes in the terms of trade.

In considering the international mechanism of development it is necessary at any rate to admit the possibility of variation in the conditions of growth transmission through trade. Just as the limited extent to which the United States economy transmits its own growth rate to primary producing countries is fully understandable in the light of its own abundant natural resources combined with its ample capital supplies and technical know-how, so the nineteenth century experience was conditioned by the fact that the industrial revolution happened to originate on a small island with a limited range of resources, at a time when the chemical industry was yet unborn.

As a result, the rate of growth in the import demand of the dominant economy of the twentieth century seems different from that of the nineteenth. If this is so, it is not certain that the less developed countries can rely on economic growth being induced from the outside through an expansion of world demand for their exports of crude materials.[16] In these circumstances reliance on induced expansion through international trade may not be able to provide the main solution to the problem of development. It is not surprising, therefore, that countries should be looking for other types of solution. It will be useful to keep these things in mind, because they form the background to the case for balanced growth which is now so greatly in vogue.

1.6 CONTRIBUTION OF TRADE TO DEVELOPMENT *

Let me begin ... by emphasizing the importance—indeed, the uniqueness—of the contribution that foreign trade can make to economic development. There is nothing necessarily regrettable about dependence on foreign trade. It is true that in engaging in trade a country puts itself at the mercy of external events: this is the price that any international division of labour exacts. But a country that seeks development must invite foreign influences if it is to succeed. It needs foreign equipment, foreign capital and foreign ideas. How can it pay for this equipment without earning foreign currency by exporting? Or arrange a transfer of capital, in or out, without those other transactions in goods

16. To ask the less developed countries to increase their export quantities of primary products in the face of a price inelastic and not an upward shifting demand schedule would be to ask, in effect, for an income transfer from poor to rich countries through a change in the terms of trade in favour of the latter. If one of several countries exporting the same primary commodity were to cut its export costs and prices, its export proceeds could indeed increase, but only at the expense of a fall in the other countries' export proceeds. The balance of payments adjustment process alone (whether through exchange rate variations or domestic price changes) would lead the latter to cut their export prices too, and all will be worse off at the end than they were at the start.

* From A. K. Cairncross, *Factors in Economic Development*, George Allen & Unwin, London, 1962, pp. 214-20, 223-8. Reprinted by permission.

and services that give effect to the transfer? Or allow the economy to be permeated with the ideas that are the seed of true development without the kind of contacts with foreigners that trade automatically produces? Trade is no mere exchange of goods, least of all when it takes place between economies at different stages of development. As often as not, it is trade that gives birth to the urge to develop, the knowledge and experience that make development possible, and the means to accomplish it.

The importance of foreign trade is particularly great in countries that lack an engineering industry and are obliged to import almost all their machinery. In such countries exports may easily become the limiting factor on productive investment and on the successful development of the economy. The common experience in under-developed countries is not that exports are already a dangerously large element but that they are not large enough to give adequate elbow room in the financing of new investment. A high level of exports enlarges the volume of imports of equipment that can be financed without endangering the balance of payments, and this greater degree of freedom makes it easier to take a long view and plan domestic investment without the constant interruption that destroys half its value.

There is nothing particularly surprising when external demand bears on a narrow sector of the economy. This presumably reflects the much higher productivity of resources, especially land, in some specialized use, such as the growing of coffee, than in any less specialized alternative use. Foreign trade opens up large possibilities of immediate gain by concentrating on a product that foreigners will buy and for which they will pay a relatively attractive price. It helps to transform subsistence into monetary economies by providing a market for cash crops, and raises the standard of living of monetary economies by bringing a higher return for the same effort. But it does not and cannot by itself do more than this. It does not, for example, result in an automatic modernization of agricultural methods; nor does it guarantee that the domestic market which it creates or widens will nurse local industry to factory-scale volume. The attitudes, practices and tenures of peasant cultivators may be little altered and they may buy their manufactures not from the towns but from abroad. Development may be blocked by a social structure that keeps the response to economic forces within narrow channels and itself withstands transformation by those forces. An expanding foreign demand will not be translated into a self-sustaining process of development in every sector of the economy unless many other conditions are fulfilled simultaneously. But the chances are that if these conditions are not fulfilled the same obstacles will stultify development so long as the forces of change are purely economic.

I confess to some scepticism about the supposed ineffectiveness of foreign trade in producing innovation and development. It does not strike me as entirely plausible to speak as if foreign trade could be contained within an enclave without transmitting its dynamic influences to the rest of the economy. How can one contain the so-called demonstration effects? By what magic is a steel mill supposed to revolutionize an economy while a railway or a copper smelter leaves it essentially unchanged? Every new departure is initially an enclave and it takes time for all innovations to work through and be absorbed. The influence of foreign trade may also make itself felt slowly. Sometimes the influence is bound to be indirect; there is not much in an oil refinery that will transform the agriculture of an Arab country. But indirect influences are not to be discounted: they may embrace half the profits of the oil companies and a good deal of free technical education for the local staff. As Professor Swerling has pointed out, "the tax machinery can remove much economic remoteness even from mineral enclaves."

Most of the countries that we now think of as advanced have been at one time or another dependent on just as narrow a range of exports. Japan in the early stages of industrialization was heavily dependent on exports of silk, the United States and Canada on exports of grain, Britain on exports of wool, or, at a later stage, on textile manufactures which once supplied over 70 per cent of her export earnings. If you want to make a start you must use what you have, not lament that the other fellow who is ahead of you is less highly specialized. The more foreign exchange is felt to be a bottleneck, the more important it is to foster in every possible way the limited range of activities from which foreign exchange can be derived.

Yet the risks of specializing on a narrow front are very real. In the long run there is the danger of a substitute produced at lower cost by factory methods; in the short run there is the danger of wide fluctuations in price. Of these two the long-run danger is the more alarming even if, so far, it has been rare for a natural product to be superseded by a synthetic one. The world's consumption of cotton, rubber, jute, butter and other products threatened by substitutes is higher than ever before in spite of the rise of synthetics. The function of the synthetic product has generally been to supplement an inelastic natural supply and meet rapidly expanding industrial requirements rather than to displace the natural products altogether.

Far too much emphasis is put in current literature on the forces operating to limit or diminish the demand for primary produce and far too little on the constant opening up of new requirements through-

out the world as the standard of living rises. It is a useful exercise to list the major raw materials in use today and consider how many of them were available, even a hundred years ago. Steel and petroleum are barely a hundred years old. In 1860 aluminum was a precious metal used like platinum in royal gifts. Rubber, newsprint, synthetic fibres are for all practical purposes twentieth century creations. Nor is it only the advanced countries that benefit when new materials emerge. The less advanced countries, with luck, can shift from one crop to another or find within their borders the mineral products that technological change brings to the front. If there are losers through the obsolescence of materials, there are gainers as well.

There are, it is true, limitations on the range of produce that the under-developed countries can supply. It is perhaps significant that most of them—particularly those in Asia and Africa—lie in the tropical latitudes and are highly dependent on the world market for tropical produce. This means that they are partly screened from competition with the advanced countries except when science produces a substitute or when high prices make the development of substitutes commercially attractive. They are not screened, however, from competition with one another. They have between them an enormous population—Asia alone has half the world's population—and the competition is correspondingly intense. Any one country may have advantages of climate or soil that give it some shelter in its chosen field; but among all the tropical countries there are sure to be some that are almost equally well placed. Thus, so long as they keep within the usual round, they are not likely to do much better than their neighbours. They may, for a time, enjoy a run of luck as producers of bananas or coffee or rubber; but if they do, other tropical countries will soon join in and put an end to any exceptional gains. Indeed, if they export tree crops (which form about one-quarter of total exports from this group of countries) the gains are only too likely to be followed by exceptional losses once new plantings have had time to come into production either at home or in competing countries. In minerals, on the other hand, the competition of other tropical countries is without special significance, the success of individual countries being governed largely by geological factors peculiar to each.

The situation confronting agriculture in an under-developed tropical country is thus essentially different from the situation faced in the countries settled from Europe during the nineteenth century. The latter were all or nearly all in temperate latitudes and could supply the industrial centres of Europe with foodstuffs in *replacement* of the higher-cost foodstuffs produced there. The specialization between the old world and the new was on a basis that brought low-cost farmers overseas into competition with high-cost farmers in Europe and gave to the development of the newer countries all the leverage of a large cost-differential. The new countries were in a very real sense the frontiers of an older economy. But the under-developed countries of today are selling in a more inelastic market.

This is so for two reasons. In the first place such elasticity as there is derives from competition with other products, not from substitution for a similar, home-produced commodity. The Canadian wheat-farmer found it easier to sell his wheat in the British market because British farmers were able to switch from grain to grass, but the only kind of substitution that Brazilian coffee-producers can profit from is substitution on the part of consumers. Secondly, exports of tropical produce bear a much higher relation to world

output than exports of primary produce from temperate latitudes. The principal consumers of coffee, rubber, sugar, and so on, lie outside the producing countries so that domestic demand is largely unaffected by changes in output and price. Canadian wheat is a very small fraction of the world crop but Brazil produces nearly half the world's coffee. A given increase in the Canadian wheat crop or in Canada's exports of wheat involves, therefore, far less disruption in the world market than an equal proportionate increase in the cultivation or exportation of Brazilian coffee.

This brings me to what seems to be the central issue. Is the market for the exports of the under-developed countries so inelastic that it no longer provides a satisfactory engine of growth? Is their development being cramped by stagnation of world demand for their traditional exports?

That the nineteenth century process of growth-transmission works rather differently nowadays is not in dispute. The under-developed countries are no longer the frontiers of an expanding world economy and the division of labour between them and the individual countries of North America and Western Europe does not involve those vast territorial shifts in primary production that lie behind the rapid growth of world trade in the nineteenth century. In the middle of the nineteenth century that growth averaged about 13 per cent annually, the total volume trebling within thirty years largely as a result of the inflow into Europe of primary produce from countries overseas.[1] Since the scope for similar displacements is now far more limited and the industrial countries are less willing to see their agriculture contract further, it is unlikely that trade will ever grow so fast again over so long a period. To the extent that the

1. A. H. Imlah, *Economic Elements in the Pax Britannica*, pp. 96-7, 190.

under-developed countries have to rely on exports of tropical produce, there can be very little displacement of production and the rate of expansion is bound to be limited by the growth of world demand. For other products, however, notably base metals and petroleum, this limitation does not apply.

It is an illusion to suppose that, even in the nineteenth century, mere pressure of demand was sufficient to transmit development from one country to another. It certainly did not by itself ensure the *industrial* development of primary-producing regions. The fact that the United States ultimately became the leading industrial nation should not blind us to the failure of the Southern States, from which came a high proportion of American exports of primary produce, to undergo industrialization or to enjoy the rapid growth experienced in the north. Latin America remained comparatively under-developed. Australia and New Zealand, although enjoying a high standard of living and far from negligible as producers of manufactured goods remain, as exporters, almost exclusively dependent on primary produce.

Again, the countries to which European growth was most successfully transmitted were already comparatively rich countries. Although their development was geared to the supply of export markets, they already had a sufficiently high standard of living to provide an opening for domestic manufacturers. The countries that remain under-developed started from a much lower level so that their domestic market is narrower and far less favourable to the building up of local industries. The example of Japan, however, shows that there is no insuperable difficulty in starting from a low level provided the industries that take root are not confined within the limits of the domestic market.

It was possible in nineteenth century development for a growing foreign trade to accompany a still more rapidly growing domestic market. This was certainly true, for example, of the United States after the Civil War. There was nothing inconsistent between reliance on exports of primary produce to open up new investment opportunities and a shift in the sources of consumer goods in favour of indigenous producers. This shift might come about through the unassisted operation of market forces or it might be induced or accelerated by protective policies. The important point is that foreign trade could remain the driving force behind an economy even when exports were a diminishing fraction of total production. A demonstration that exports are being outpaced by production does not prove that the motor force which exports provide is running down. On the contrary, it is more likely to mean that the process of growth transmission is really working, that the domestic market is being transformed, and that an industrial structure is taking shape within a hitherto non-industrial economy.

...

...if we take a longer view and, rather than accept the past decade as the touchstone of future prospects, look back as far as 1913, we do not find any conspicuous lag in exports from the under-developed countries. Each of the poorest continents in the world—Africa, Asia and Latin America—had a larger share of world exports in 1953 than in 1913. In both years they had a quite negligible share of world exports of manufactures, but their exports of primary produce had by 1953 overhauled those from the three richest continents—North America, Europe and Australasia. Forty years earlier they had differed in the ratio of 1:2, by 1953 the difference had almost disappeared.

Whether one takes a long view or a

short, these aggregates are of limited value in interpreting what is going on in the under-developed countries. Every under-developed country is unique and is affected by the market conditions and prices for its own products and not by the movement of index numbers. To aggregate or average the experience of the group of countries that we think of as under-developed is to presume common elements that may have no real existence.

Nevertheless, it may help to give some concreteness to my argument if I turn at this point to consider just what the under-developed countries as a group do export and what part trade plays in their economy. For simplicity I shall divide the world into the three poorest and the three richest continents, the first group being made up of Africa, Asia and Latin America and the second of Europe, North America and Oceania. This means that one or two advanced countries such as South Africa and Japan will be included in the group of poor countries but their exclusion would make little difference to the results. At times I have been obliged to use a grouping prepared by GATT which adds Australasia to the three poorer continents and labels the mixture "non-industrial areas." The Communist bloc of countries is excluded throughout, unless otherwise indicated.

The so-called non-industrial areas, on examination, turn out to be very far from non-industrial. According to GATT they import only about one-third of their consumption of manufactures, and this proportion is falling.[2] The remaining two-thirds of their consumption of manufactures is produced at home. Many of them already have a flourishing textile industry and some of them are net exporters of textiles. Of the manufactured goods which they import, a high proportion consists of capital goods, base metals, and so on, while manufactured consumption goods are relatively small, constituting not much more than 10 per cent of total imports. Nor are they by any means entirely dependent on foreign markets for the sale of their primary produce. This is particularly true of food and feeding stuffs; nine-tenths of the output is consumed at home while only the remaining tenth is exported. Many of the foodstuffs that form their staple diet are quite unimportant in foreign trade. Exports of fuel and raw materials (including materials of agricultural origin) take a higher proportion of total production—on the average, about two-fifths,[3] and sometimes, as in the oil countries, nearly 100 per cent.

Just as it is a mistake to think that under-developed countries have no industries, so it is a mistake to think of them as the major sources of primary produce. Every country is a primary producer, and the more advanced it is, the larger, broadly speaking, is its output of primary produce. There can be few countries that fail to grow at least half their food supply or to produce a wide range of raw materials. It is true that some advanced countries employ very little of their manpower in agriculture and that their raw materials are often manufactured rather than mined or grown. But the fact remains that the advanced countries produce more food and more raw materials than the less advanced countries. What they import from the less advanced countries meets only one-tenth of their requirements of food and one-quarter of their requirements of raw materials.[4] Nor are they all net importers. Some of them are large exporters, and the three richer continents account for roughly half of world exports of primary produce. They are in fact larger exporters, just as they are larger produc-

3. *Ibid.*, p. 13.
2. *International Trade 1959*, GATT, 1960, p. 14.   4. *Ibid.*, p. 14.

ers, of primary products than the so-called primary-producing countries.[5]

The less advanced countries, in the same way, are importers as well as exporters of primary produce: indeed, their imports are half as large as their exports. Thus it is quite wrong to think of the world as if it could be divided into two sets of countries, the advanced and the less advanced, with primary produce flowing exclusively in one direction. On the contrary, international trade brings the primary producers of every country into competition with one another, and the margin of advantage does not necessarily shift steadily in one direction.

Seven items or groups make up nearly three-quarters of the total exports of primary produce from the under-developed countries. Listed in order of size they are: petroleum, beverages, textile, fibres, base metals, sugar, oilseeds and fats, and rubber. The same group of items make up less than 40 per cent of the exports of primary produce from the developed countries. But what is perhaps of more significance is the change that has taken place over the past century. For the seven items selected the share of the under-developed countries in world trade has risen from 43 per cent to 64 per cent. For all other items, representing nearly half the total volume of world trade in primary products, the share of the under-developed countries has remained a little below 30 per cent. It has been where their share was already high that it expanded most.

On the other hand there has been an unmistakable tendency towards a contraction in their exports of cereals and livestock produce. Exports from the developed countries, especially those in North

5. This is true only if we exclude Australasia from the primary-producing countries. See my "International Trade and Economic Development," *Kyklos*, Vol. XIII (1960), p. 549.

America and Australasia, have shown a corresponding expansion. The three under-developed continents supplied 31 per cent of world exports in 1913 and only 21 per cent in 1953. No doubt this trend is partly associated with American aid. But by itself this is far from adequate to account for it, and it seems to have a deeper origin in the pressure on available land in some under-developed countries and the efforts at industrialization in others.

Exports of cereals and livestock products are a comparatively small proportion (about 7 per cent) of total exports from the under-developed countries. Exports of other foodstuffs are much larger—over one-third of the total. Of these exports, tea, cocoa and coffee, in which they come near to having a monopoly of foreign trade, form nearly half, and other tropical produce, such as sugar, oilseeds and fats and tobacco make up most of the other half. Thus within the food group there is a large tract over which competition is limited. In food that can be grown in temperate latitudes the under-developed countries have either contracted or show little expansion. But in tropical foodstuffs they have enjoyed a rapid growth. For example, they were supplying 73 per cent of world exports of sugar in 1953 compared with 64 per cent in 1913. For the group of foodstuffs other than cereals and livestock products (in which their share contracted) and beverages (in which their share was virtually 100 per cent) they improved their share of the world market quite perceptibly.

Foodstuffs, however, account for less than half the total exports of primary produce from the three poorer continents. Petroleum, crude and refined, accounts for about one-quarter (depending upon how the exports are valued) and raw materials, including those of agricultural as well as of mineral origin, unwrought metals and crude fertilizers, for nearly one-third. For materials as for foodstuffs there is some tendency for the exports of the developed and under-developed continents to be in non-competing groups. Nearly all the world's output of rubber and jute, over 40 per cent of its petroleum and a high proportion of its hides and skins, mineral ores and crude fertilizers, come from the under-developed areas. But in other textile fibres and in base metals they are in direct competition over a wide area.

From this analysis of the trade of the under-developed countries I draw four conclusions.

First of all they are highly dependent on a very narrow range of exports. A large proportion of these exports consists of gifts of nature: petroleum, mineral ores, crude fertilizers. How much a country can earn from exports of this kind is largely a matter of luck and of willingness to make use of foreign capital. Other exports suffer from great variability in supply and low elasticity of supply. The source of these exports tends to be either foreign-owned plantations or peasants who may lack the means, the knowledge or the incentives to adopt modern methods of production. On top of all this nearly all capital equipment has to be imported, and a shortage of foreign exchange frequently sets a sharp limit to the scale and firmness of any forward planning of investment. These facts point strongly to the desirability of widening the range of exports wherever possible and developing domestic sources of the simpler types of imported manufactures.

Secondly, it would seem that exports from the under-developed countries are governed less closely by the level of world demand than is usually supposed. Where they are in direct competition with the more advanced countries, their share of the market depends also on the terms on which they are able to compete: on the

movement of their costs and in the alternatives which they can choose. If their exports have lagged behind the exports of the more advanced countries, this is partly because they have been running a large external deficit (now of the order of $5000—$6000 m. a year) and this necessarily implies some downward drag on their exports compared with the exports of the countries from which they buy. Other, but not unrelated, factors tending to hold back their exports have been inflation, relatively high prices, and the encouragement of other sectors of their economies.

Thirdly, since agriculture is by far the most important activity and is usually directed more towards domestic than export markets, there is everything to be gained by trying to expand agricultural production. Without a general improvement in agricultural production and incomes, the mass of the population will remain hungry and poor and domestic industry will be stifled for lack of markets. Such an improvement is not dependent on some precise rate of growth of exports. An expanding foreign market can, however, contribute, both by putting more cash in the hands of the cultivators and by introducing a competitive element that may make technical change in agriculture more acceptable.

But what, fourthly, if agriculture proves unresponsive and the government has to think of industrialization without any expansion in foodstuffs? The fact that under-developed countries produce about two thirds of the manufactured goods which they consume shows that some progress towards industrialization has already been made. Industrial development *is* occurring, assisted by higher export earnings and foreign investment and loans. But the industries that have grown up are not, as a rule, very efficient. It is curious, for example, that Latin American countries meet nearly all their own textile requirements but have a negligible share in each other's markets or, indeed, in any foreign market.

One of the principal obstacles to more rapid industrialization is the limited scale of operations in a manufacturing plant supplying only the domestic market of an under-developed country. It is precisely this limitation which international trade can remove. If, therefore, we are anxious to encourage development in the poorer countries and doubt whether agricultural expansion will clear the way for industry, might we not turn to a new model of the traditional engine of development and see what could be done through freer trade in manufactured goods?

1.7 THE "CARRY-OVER" PROBLEM—NOTE

The foregoing materials raise a central question: why has not a process of export-induced development followed upon an expansion of the export sector? Notwithstanding the possibility of lagging exports in more recent decades, most of the under-developed countries have experienced long periods of export growth. In most cases, after a country was exposed to the world economy, its exports grew markedly in volume and in variety. Yet, despite their secular rise, exports have not acted as a key propulsive sector, propelling the rest of the economy forward. Although the classical belief that development can be transmitted through trade has been confirmed by the experience of many countries that are now among the richest in the world, trade has not had a similar stimulating effect for countries that have remained underdeveloped. Why has not the growth in exports in these countries carried over to other sectors and led to more widespread development in the domestic economy? What has limited the "carry-over" from the export sector?

As noted above (1.1, 1.2), some critics of the classical position contend that the very forces of international trade have been responsible for inhibiting development. They argue that the development of the export sector by foreign capital has created a "dual economy" in which production has been export-biased, and the resultant pattern of resource utilization has deterred development. This argument, however, tends to contrast the pattern of resource utilization that actually occurred with some other ideal pattern. More relevant is a comparison between the actual pattern and the allocation that would have occurred in the absence of the capital inflow. There is little foundation to the assertion that if there had been no foreign investment, a poor country would have generated more domestic investment; or that, in the absence of foreign entrepreneurs, the supply of domestic entrepreneurs would have been larger. Contrary to what is often implied by the critics of foreign investment, the real choice was not between employing the resources in the export sector or in domestic production, but rather between giving employment to the surplus resources in export production or leaving them idle.[1] It is difficult to substantiate the argument that foreign investment was competitive with home investment, or that the utilization of resources in the export sector was at the expense of home production.

Another contention is that trade has impeded development by the "demonstration effect": the international demonstration of higher consumption standards in more developed countries has allegedly raised the propensity to consume in the less developed countries and reduced attainable saving rates. By stimulating the

1. Cf. Hla Myint, "The Gains from International Trade and the Backward Countries," *Review of Economic Studies*, Vol. XXII (2), No. 58, (1954–55); "The 'Classical Theory' of International Trade and the Underdeveloped Countries," *Economic Journal*, June 1958, pp. 317-37.

desire to consume, however, the international demonstration effect may also have operated on incentives and been instrumental in increasing the supply of effort and productive services—especially as between the subsistence sector and the exchange economy. This positive effect on the side of factor supply may have more than offset any negative effect on saving.

More serious is the argument that international market forces have transferred income from the poor to rich nations through a deterioration in the terms of trade of the less developed countries. The main elements of this argument have been summarized by Raúl Prebisch in selection 1.1, above. The significance of this argument is also overdrawn, and it can be questioned on both theoretical and empirical grounds. The alleged trend is based not on the measurement of prices within the poor countries, but rather on inferences from the United Kingdom's commodity terms of trade or the terms of trade between primary products and manufactured products.[2] This does not provide a sufficiently strong statistical foundation for any adequate generalization about the terms of trade of poor countries.[3] The

import-price index conceals the heterogeneous price movements within and among the broad categories of foodstuffs, raw materials, and minerals; no allowance is made for changes in the quality of exports and imports; there is inadequate consideration of new commodities; and the recorded terms of trade are not corrected for the substantial decline in transportation costs. The introduction of new products and qualitative improvements have been greater in manufactured than in primary products, and a large proportion of the fall in British prices of primary products can be attributed to the great decline in inward freight rates. The simple use of the "inverse" of the United Kingdom's terms of trade to indicate the terms of trade of primary producing countries involves therefore a systematic bias which makes changes appear more unfavorable to the primary exporting countries than they actually were.

Even if it were true that the less developed countries experienced a secular deterioration in their commodity terms of trade, the question would still remain whether this constituted a significant obstacle to their development. The answer depends on what caused the deterioration and whether the country's factoral terms of trade and income terms also deteriorated. If the deterioration in the commodity terms is due to increased productivity in the export sector, the single-factoral terms of trade (commodity terms corrected for changes in productivity in producing exports) can improve at the same time. As long as productivity in its export industries is increasing more rapidly than export prices are falling, the country's real income can rise despite the deterioration in the commodity terms of trade: when its factoral terms improve, the country benefits from

2. United Nations, Department of Economic Affairs, *Relative Prices of Exports and Imports of Under-Developed Countries,* New York, 1949, pp. 7, 13-24; W. A. Lewis, "World Production, Prices and Trade, 1870–1960, *"Manchester School,* May 1952, p. 118.

3. For detailed criticisms, see R. E. Baldwin, "Secular Movements in the Terms of Trade," *American Economic Review, Papers and Proceedings,* May 1955, pp. 267ff., P. T. Ellsworth, "The Terms of Trade Between Primary Producing and Industrial Countries," *Inter-American Economic Affairs,* Summer 1956, pp. 47-65; T. Morgan, "The Long-Run Terms of Trade Between Agriculture and Manufacturing," *Economic Development and Cultural Change,* October 1959, pp. 6-17; Gottfried Haberler, "Terms of Trade and Economic Development," in H. S. Ellis (ed.), *Economic Development for Latin America,* New York, 1961, pp. 275-97; Jagdish Bhagwati, "A Skeptical Note on the Adverse Secular Trend in the Terms of Trade of Underdeveloped Coun-

tries," *Pakistan Economic Journal,* December 1960; G. M. Meier, *International Trade and Development,* New York, 1963, pp. 58-63.

the ability to obtain a greater quantity of imports per unit of factors embodied in its exports. Also possible is an improvement in the country's income terms of trade (commodity terms multiplied by quantity of exports) at the same time as its commodity terms deteriorate. The country's capacity to import is then greater, and this will ease development efforts. When due weight is given to the increase in productivity in export production and the rise in export volume, it would appear that the single-factoral terms and income terms of trade actually improved for many poor countries, notwithstanding any possible deterioration in their commodity terms of trade.

Having rejected the view that international trade operated as a mechanism of international inequality, we must look to other factors for an understanding of why trade has not had a more stimulating effect in underdeveloped countries. A more convincing explanation focuses on the differential effects of the various export goods, according to characteristics of their production functions, and on market imperfections and sociocultural impediments within a poor country.

The nature of the export good's production function has a close bearing on the extent of secondary changes elsewhere in the economy beyond the primary increase in export production.[4] With the use of

4. Although more empirical research is needed, some illustrative cases are suggested by D. C. North, "Location Theory and Regional Economic Growth," *Journal of Political Economy,* June 1955, pp. 249-51; Dudley Seers, "An Approach to the Short-Period Analysis of Primary-Producing Economies," *Oxford Economic Papers,* February 1959, pp. 6-9; R. E. Caves and R. H. Holton, *The Canadian Economy,* Cambridge, 1959, pp. 41-7; J. V. Levin, *The Export Economies,* Cambridge, 1960; B. C. Swerling, "Some Interrelationships Between Agricultural Trade and Economic Development," *Kyklos,* Vol. XIV, No. 3 (1961), pp. 377-9; R. E. Baldwin, "Export Technology and Development from a Subsistence Level," *Economic Journal,* March 1963, pp. 80-92; M. H.

different input coefficients to produce different types of export commodities, there will be diverse "backward linkage" effects: when some exports grow, they provide a strong stimulus for expansion in input-supplying industries elsewhere in the economy, while for other exports the input coefficients may be such as to provide little opportunity for the emergence or growth of other sectors in the economy. The use of different factor combinations will also affect the distribution of income: in broad terms, the relative shares of profits, wages, interest, and rent will vary according to whether the export sector is dominated by mining, plantation agriculture, or peasant farming. Along with the variation in the internal distribution of the export income, the structure of demand and saving propensities are also likely to differ. By favoring groups with a higher propensity to consume domestic goods than to import, the resultant distribution of income from some export commodities is more effective in raising home demand. If income increments go to those who are likely to save large portions, then the export sector may also make a greater contribution to the financing of growth in other sectors. An additional important "factor contribution" from the export sector to other sectors may be the provision of skilled labor, or the diffusion of organizational and administrative skills.

Whether export production leads on to the development of modern processing techniques is also of considerable importance in determining the extent of the "carry-over" from exports. For the machine processing of raw materials or foodstuffs raises supply requirements and increases employment and income in other activities supporting the export sector. In so far as output of the export industry

Watkins, "A Staple Theory of Economic Growth," *Canadian Journal of Economics and Political Science,* May 1963, pp. 141-58.

becomes an input for other industries, processing activities provide "forward linkages." The degree to which the various exports are processed is also highly significant in determining external economies: the processing of primary product exports by modern methods is likely to benefit other activities through the spread of technical knowledge, training of labor, demonstration of new production techniques that might be adapted elsewhere, and the acquisition of organizational and supervisory skills. In contrast, growth of the export sector will have a negligible carry-over if its techniques of production are the same as those already in use in other sectors, or if its expansion occurs by a simple widening of production without any change in production functions. If the introduction or expansion of export crops involves simple methods of production that do not differ markedly from the traditional techniques already used in subsistence agriculture, the stimulus to development is clearly less than if the growth in exports entailed the introduction of new skills and more productive recombinations of factors.

As will be discussed more fully in section 3 below, fluctuations in export proceeds also affect the development process: the larger is the amplitude of fluctuation, the more disrupting is the effect on employment, real income, capital formation, resource allocation, and the capacity to import. Since exports differ in their degree of fluctuation, and in revenue earned and retained at home, their repercussions on the domestic economy will also vary.

In short, the stimulus from exports will differ among countries according to the nature of their export-base. The stimulus can be expected to be stronger under the following conditions: the higher is the growth rate of demand for the export good, the greater is the direct effect in the export sector on employment and personal income, the more export expansion involves a change in production functions rather than a simple widening process, the more the distribution of export income favors those with a higher marginal propensity to save, the more the export sector makes a "factor contribution" to other sectors, the more productive is the investment resulting from any saving of export income, the more investment in exports creates opportunities for investment elsewhere, the more it makes a "market contribution" by drawing inputs from other domestic sectors, and the more stable are the export receipts retained at home. Some exports fulfill these conditions more readily than others, and countries specializing on these exports will enjoy greater opportunties for development.

Even with a strong stimulus from exports, however, the transmission of growth from the export-base to the rest of the economy will still be contingent upon other conditions in the economy. The weak penetrative power of exports in underdeveloped countries is to be explained not only by a possibly weak stimulus from a particular type of export, but also by the host of domestic impediments that limit the transmission of the gains from exports to other sectors even when the stimulus may be strong. The carry-over from exports has been restrained by all the market imperfections noted in previous discussions—the factor immobility, price rigidity, isolated markets, ignorance of technological possibilities, and other characteristics of economic backwardness. As long as the domestic economy remains fragmented and compartmentalized, the transfer of resources to more productive employment is restricted, and the linkage of markets and their subsequent extension are limited.

Moreover, many inhibiting factors are associated with the lack of political development and with sociocultural customs and institutions that perpetuate the traditional society. In the absence of prior political development and changes in the social structure and the values of a traditional society,[5] the secondary round of activities induced by an expansion in any sector is cut short, and it is difficult to produce further transformative effects elsewhere in the economy. In view of these persistent domestic obstacles, we should not be surprised that the stimulus from trade has not drawn a greater response.

It follows that if a more extensive carry-over from exports is to be achieved, domestic obstacles must be removed. Many of the policy implications in the preceding chapters have already referred to the need for reducing the fragmentation and compartmentalization of the economy. To accomplish this, alternative forms of economic and social organization are required, and policy measures must aim at diminishing the prevalence of semi-monopolistic and monopolistic practices, removing restraints on land tenure and land use, widening the capital market, promoting credit and marketing facilities, and increasing investment in transportation, communication, education, and manpower training.

It also follows that the stimulus from the export-base should be as strong as possible. While domestic obstacles may have accounted for the weak carry-over of exports in the past when export markets were expanding, it may be contended (as Nurkse does, 1.5) that exports no longer enjoy a strongly rising world demand and do not now provide a sufficient stimulus for development in the first instance. If exports are confined to a slow rate of growth, then there can be little scope for development through trade even

5. In this connection, we may recall Rostow's emphasis on the preconditions necessary for a take-off (Chap. I, 1.3, above).

if the domestic obstacles are removed. To counter this "export pessimism," it is all the more necessary for underdeveloped countries to raise productivity in agriculture in order to ensure that their primary exports are competitive on world markets, and to prevent home consumption from causing a limitation of their export supplies. Further, it is important that the less developed countries pursue policies that will ensure that they specialize as much as they can in exports with the highest growth prospects. To do this, a country must have the capacity to reallocate resources—to shift, for instance, from exporting a foodstuff which may have only a slowly growing demand, to the export of an industrial raw material or a mineral for which the demand may be rising more rapidly. Of special significance is the country's potential for taking advantage of new export opportunities in manufactured goods. The exportation of manufactured commodities may play a strategic role in transmitting development to some poor countries that have a favorable factor endowment and can gain a comparative advantage by utilizing labor-intensive methods. In the next section, we shall consider more fully the issue of export stimulation, giving particular attention to the opportunity for exporting manufactures. Efforts at regional integration may also promote trade in manufactures among the developing nations themselves, as will be discussed in section 4, below.

Export prospects may also be improved by a more liberal importation policy on the part of advanced countries. A removal of trade restrictions is beneficial not only for the more traditional primary exports, but also for encouraging new manufactured exports. The export market for primary products might also be expanded if industrialized nations avoided artificial supports for the substitution of primary products by synthetic materials. And along with the liberalization of trade, it is vitally important that the less developed countries should be able to look forward to the maintenance of high rates of growth in the advanced countries to which they export.

Finally advanced countries can contribute by supporting policies to stabilize export proceeds. High and stable levels of employment in industrial nations will help reduce the short-term fluctuations in export proceeds, but, in addition, national and international measures might be advocated to achieve greater short-run stability in international commodity markets. Various possible remedies for the short-term fall in export earnings are examined in section 3, below.

2. EXPORT STIMULATION

2.1 ADJUSTMENTS IN FOREIGN TRADE *

Three main lines readily suggest themselves along which under-developed countries may direct their efforts to strengthen their external position:

(a) Expansion of traditional exports of primary products (in raw or processed form).

(b) Development of home production to replace imports of manufactured goods.

(c) Development of home production to generate new exports of manufactured goods.

These three avenues do not, of course, exhaust the possibilities. In some cases home production of foodstuffs can be and should be increased to replace imports. Moreover, imports of some goods—luxuries—may be altogether eliminated without any intention of replacing them, though in this case positive steps need to be taken to prevent the diversion of domestic resources into production of the undesired goods. Let me, however, concentrate on the three main lines of approach which I have described.

A country is bound to do what it reasonably can to maintain and expand the

market for its traditional exports, but there are nevertheless several negative considerations to be borne in mind. One of these is the familiar complaint that the demand for primary products is relatively inelastic with respect to price; this need not deter any one country from seeking to increase its share of the market but may be a more serious difficulty if a number of countries are simultaneously trying to do so. Another equally well-known objection is that the typical under-developed country is already uncomfortably dependent on one, or at best very few, export commodities and should seek to spread its risks. A third consideration, particularly relevant to problems of economic growth, is that the further development of a country's traditional exports of primary goods makes little contribution towards the creation of "external economies" for industry and thus does not help very much even indirectly to initiate a more balanced economic growth.

The second approach—the development of home production to replace imports of manufactures—is free from the particular objections just mentioned and is bound to be followed both as a means of strengthening the external balance and as a way of getting started on the road to industrialization. The main effort to industrialize is likely, in the first instance, to take the form of substitution for the customary

* From Hal B. Lary, "Economic Development and the Capacity To Import—National Policies," *Lectures on Economic Development,* Faculty of Economics (Istanbul University) and Faculty of Political Sciences (Ankara University), Istanbul, 1958, pp. 135-8. Reprinted by permission.

imports of manufactures while the demand for other types of imports grows. Even so, there are several conditions to be kept in mind. An under-developed country can well afford to replace those imports the production of which requires relatively large amounts of labour, but it will need to proceed cautiously in trying to replace those which are costly in terms of their capital requirements. A second consideration is that the replacement of imports can, at best, operate within definite limits: there comes a time when the possibilities of economizing on foreign exchange in this way are exhausted while foreign exchange needs are likely to continue to grow. Finally, import substitution does nothing to strengthen the composition of exports by increasing their variety.

These are arguments not for opposing the expansion of traditional exports or the replacement of imports by home production but for considering carefully also the possible return from the third line of attack: the production of manufactured goods not only to meet home demand but also for export. In addition to the advantages already suggested, it is only through the development of production for export that poor countries with limited home markets can hope to become efficient in industries where economies of scale are important. Moreover, since export industries have to compete in a wider market, they are likely to be more progressive than those catering exclusively to home demands, and this is likely to have an all-round favourable effect.

The difficulty of competing with the already established exports of the more developed economies is, of course, very great. It is a matter both of the initially higher costs at which the new industries of the less developed countries would have to operate and of institutional factors, such as existing trade ties. In time, the cost disadvantages could be overcome. In-stitutional barriers to the development of exports may prove to be more difficult. The very attempt of an under-developed country to make use of its most abundant resource, manpower, is likely to give rise to charges of social dumping by its competitors.

I confess to some difficulty in finding historical examples to support this argument in favour of trying to establish export industries at an early stage of economic development, but that is perhaps because of the still greater difficulty of finding any under-developed countries (as I have defined them) that so far could be said to have got well started on the road to economic development. The example of Japan is almost unique. India has also become a major textile exporter, however, and now proposes to develop the production of such items as sewing machines and bicycles for sale abroad. Among the smaller countries, the case of Yugoslavia is perhaps even more to the point: it exports 50 per cent of its production of electric motors, 40 per cent of its production of railway rolling stock, and 30 per cent of the output of its shipyards, and it proposes to expand tremendously its production of aluminum, chiefly for export. These Yugoslav industries are all instances where economies of scale are likely to be significant.

The sort of bold export endeavour I have in mind is also illustrated by a recent press announcement of a new $20 million rayon plant to be put up in Israel, half of whose output will be exported in competition with the big established firms in the United Kingdom, Germany, the Netherlands and Japan. The Israeli Government is apparently underwriting about one-third of the cost while the remainder is, so it seems, being subscribed from abroad. It also appears that experienced American management will take an active part in the enterprise.

This Israeli project, even though perhaps not motivated exclusively by business considerations, suggests ways in which under-developed countries might seek to combine local financing with both investment funds and management experience from abroad. It should be possible to work out management contracts over a sufficient period of years to provide for the repayment of external obligations (facilitated by the fact that much of the production would be for export) and to train local management to take over at the end of the period.

2.2 EXPORTING MANUFACTURES *

We must...conclude that the West Indies...is an overpopulated area where shortage of natural resources is an obstacle to economic development.

Now the classical economists, in particular Ricardo, made much of this fact that the shortage of natural resources is an obstacle to economic development, when they were writing about the development of a closed economic system. They foresaw economic stagnation for the world as a whole arising out of this obstacle. But when they were writing about an open economy they came to quite a different conclusion. Taking not the world as a whole but any particular part of it, they rescued it by bringing in the law of comparative costs. Even if a country is short of natural resources it can nevertheless make a good living by importing the products of natural resources and exporting the products of labour and capital. This is whence we derive the proposition that any overpopulated country in which development is taking place—we notice the qualification, in which development is taking place—will have to import more

* From W. A. Lewis, "Employment Policy in an Underdeveloped Area," *Social and Economic Studies,* September 1958, pp. 46-8, 71-3. Reprinted by permission.

and more food and raw materials and to export manufactures in exchange. This proposition is well exemplified by history, ancient and modern. In ancient history by the development of ancient Greece; in modern history by the development of Britain, Germany, Japan and India, (whose exports are already more than half manufactures). If our analysis of the West Indian territories is correct the same must happen in due course in the West Indies.

Now this proposition, although it has the full backing not only of economic theory and of economic history, ancient and modern, is for some reason always resisted in the West Indies. We have had a series of official reports which have denied it. They have said in effect: "The West Indies is obviously agricultural. Land is obviously its main resource; obviously the most important thing to do is to develop the land, and any talk about industrial development for export market is silly." This is complete nonsense. This kind of statement can be made of any country at the appropriate stage of its development. You could have said of England in 1800: "England is obviously agricultural, most of its people are engaged in agriculture. Land is its main resource. Obviously England should concentrate on agriculture and any talk of industrial development for export markets is silly." One could have said that of Germany in 1850, or of the United States as late as 1900. It is obviously nonsensical. What is important in this context is not where the country now is, but what its future must be, having regard to the limits of its natural resources and to the principle of comparative cost.

The persistence of this attitude is hard to understand. In 1949 I was asked by the Caribbean Commission to write a report on this subject. In the light of this analysis I turned to consider what possible markets there might be for light manufactures exported from the West Indies. I said that the countries in a similar position to the West Indies, especially Latin America, were likely to develop the same kind of manufactures as the West Indies, so that it was useless to look for major markets there. One should look for markets rather to the countries which were well endowed with industrial resources, particularly with heavy industry; these would find it profitable to concentrate on manufacturing heavy industries, and would be able to import light manufactures. I gave Britain as an example. At once several people said that I was talking through my hat, as Britain being a highly developed industrial country, would not import manufactures. Well within the next three or four years Britain developed an enormous importation of textiles from India and Hong Kong, revealing a market which if the West Indies had gone into it would have provided a very substantial level of employment here for us. What was the difference between India and Hong Kong on the one hand, and the West Indies on the other? ... I suggest to you among other phenomena a lack of initiative, a lack of imagination, a lack of willingness to take the risks of developing an export trade in manufactures. This willingness to take risks is not evenly spread throughout the world, but we shall have to develop it here if we are to make a living from our meagre resources.

Now I hope you will not misunderstand me. I have never anywhere suggested that industrialization is the one and only solution for West Indian problems. The West Indies, or any other country, has to make the best use of every resource that it has; of land, of water, of mountain scenery, of climate, and of skill; every conceivable resource that we have must be exploited to the full. All I have said on this subject is that when we have exploited everything

that we can exploit to the full we will find ... that the net result will be that we have developed ourselves as importers of food and raw materials and as exporters of manufactures. ...

The question has been raised: Where is the market for these exports? As I said before, $30 billion worth of manufactures is being imported in the world today and this is increasing at the rate of 4 per cent per annum. We must disabuse ourselves of the idea that there is no market for our manufactures, or that protective tariffs are such that no one is likely to buy our manufactures. The fact is that manufactures are being bought. One per cent of the world trade in manufactures equals the whole national income of Jamaica. If Jamaica were to capture a fraction of 1 per cent of something which is growing by 4 per cent per annum its whole problem would be solved.

We must get the problem in perspective. As someone said when talking of migration—there is an enormous difference between the small country and the large country. You cannot solve the overpopulation problem in India, where there are 400 million people, by exporting them to the U.K., but when you are talking about the B.W.I., with its 3½ million people, it is a different problem. The same is true for manufactures. The problem for India is entirely different from the problem for the B.W.I. What we are talking about is capturing a tiny fraction of something which already exists and which is already growing at an enormous rate. Let us rid our minds of the idea that this cannot be done.

This is not to say that it is easy to capture part of this trade. It will be difficult to accomplish. There will be many problems in trying to capture a share of the world trade in manufactures. Let me dispute the proposition that the problem is primarily one of distance. The importance of distance is two-fold: (1) transportation costs, (2) maintaining contact with the market. Transportation cost is for a wide range of manufactures a negligible phenomenon—e.g., it is not true that England exports more to Europe than to the rest of the world because it is next-door. Distance is highly important for some items but for a wide range of manufactures the cost of transporting goods is not terribly important. Let us not be frightened by the fact that we are 3,000 miles away from England. We are 3,000 miles away from England yet England can export to us, so why can't we export to them?

Much more important is the question of the type of manufacture. In a study I did for the Caribbean Commission I went into this in great detail and tried to pick out the most suitable types of manufactures. There are types of manufactures that are not dependent on having cheap fuel and cheap ores. We must depend on light manufactures where fuel costs are not more than 1 per cent or 2 per cent of total cost. We must choose what we manufacture. We can have heavy industry for the local market. We can have our own building industry, make our own cement, import iron and steel already smelted and make things for the local market but for the export market we have to concentrate on light goods. We must concentrate on these because it is not so profitable for the big countries to manufacture these for themselves.

On the question of maintaining contact with the market there are two crucial problems in selling: (1) price, (2) salesmanship. Those who have studied this problem agree that salesmanship is more important than price. You can sell things that are more expensive if you know how. What handicaps the British in selling manufactures is not the price—over a wide range of commodities British prices are highly competitive—but the British do not know how to sell, how to maintain a sales organization and how to give the market what it wants.

For the B.W.I. the problem is not that there is no world market, nor that we are far away from the market, but can we develop people with the right kind of initiative and attitudes and the capacity to build up and create the right kind of organization for selling manufactures. Looked at from the angle that you wish to capture only 1 per cent of the world trade it does not seem a difficult problem, but looked at from the angle of initiative and organization it is a difficult problem. Few countries in the world are successful at this.

There is not much use in saying: let us find a Jamaican or a Trinidadian with initiative; we have got some particular kind of material, we have skill and capital, let us build up an industry and then let us look for the market. It is much better if you say: there in Britain or in the U.S. is a man who has got the contacts, the market and the organization, let us get him to come and establish an industry here. This is the real secret of the Puerto Rican success.

Exporting enough manufactures is a difficult problem even for Britain with 200 years experience. But the point is not whether it is a difficult or an easy problem. The point is that there is a problem which must be solved. The fact that it is a difficult problem only means that we have to go at it all the harder.

2.3 Export Promotion in Pakistan's Second Plan *

The Plan was originally published in 1960 and is to run from 1 July 1960 to 30

* From GATT Programme for Expansion of International Trade, Trade of Less Developed Countries, Development Plans: Study of the Second Five Year Plan of Pakistan, Geneva, 1962, pp. 8-9, 15-21.

June 1965. . . . The aim of the Second Plan is to increase the gross national product by 24 per cent. In view of the anticipated increase in population of about 11 per cent, this would mean an increase per capita of about 2.5 per cent per annum if all the programmes are effectively implemented. In 1960/1961 this target was met, real national income increasing by 4.2 per cent.

The highest priority is attached to increasing agricultural production and an over-all increase of 14 per cent is projected. In this sector the primary aim is to attain national self-sufficiency in foodgrains within the five-year period, and allocations have been made with this aim in mind. The development of export crops is also planned.

A substantial increase is proposed in industrial production: the value added in production is projected to rise by somewhat over 60 per cent in large and medium-scale industry, and by 25 per cent in cottage and small-scale industry. Industrial development is to be aided by the encouragement of private enterprise and the removal of superfluous restraints on the economy. Basic industries are to be encouraged where economically feasible. Special emphasis is to be placed on the development of small-scale industries, both because of their intrinsic merits and because of their employment potential. Industries are also to be encouraged when they stimulate agricultural development or which support small-scale industries. It is inevitable that in the industrial sector the Plan should stress both import substitution and export development.

Export promotion and export-oriented investment are to form an important part of economic policy in Pakistan during the Second Plan Period. Investment under the Plan is to be made wherever possible in sectors producing for export. Domestic consumption is to be curtailed so that an exportable surplus will exist. It is hoped to achieve this by the levying of excise taxes. The possibility of using compulsory export quotas has also been discussed. The Plan faces uncompromisingly the need for austerity and for the diversion of goods in growing demand at home to the export market.

In common with other less-developed countries Pakistan has traditionally relied on the export of a narrow range of basic commodities for which demand is inelastic and whose prices fluctuate unpredictably. In the case of Pakistan, partition cut across traditional patterns of production. The desirability of a more diversified export structure is clear, but despite lack of financial resources it has been found essential to give assistance to infant industries attempting to break into the export market. The Export Bonus Scheme came into effect in January 1959. Under the Scheme all exports, except raw jute, raw cotton, hides and skins, wool, rice, tea and (later) cotton yarn which were traditional export items, earn negotiable bonus vouchers for a percentage of their f.o.b. value which allow the import of a wide range of commodities. The Scheme has effectively stimulated the export of new products and has been an important factor towards a more liberal import policy. Exports covered by the Scheme were valued at Rs.456 million in 1959, Rs.672 million in 1960 and Rs.695 million in 1961, and vouchers issued amounted to Rs.6 million, Rs.138 million and Rs.159 million respectively. Some goods not previously traded in significant quantities are now being exported in increasing amounts. These include fuller's earth, dry dates, medicinal herbs, crude glycerine, cement, files, gold thread, household utensils, reedboard, maize starch, marble blocks, molasses, tents, oxygen gas, brushes and cotton canvas. It has been recognized that the operation of an incentive for a very short period, or the existence of uncertainty on its operation would considerably reduce its effectiveness in stimulating the establishment of new export industries. It has therefore been decided to continue the export bonus scheme at least for the duration of the Second Plan period.

In connexion with the stimulation of exports of traditional products careful consideration has been given to the reduction of export duties, notably those on cotton and jute. The Plan, referring to this, felt the case for a reduction to be stronger in the case of cotton, where the tax was felt to act as a disincentive to the production of cotton for export in raw form, than in the case of jute. It was however pointed out that raising the price of jute would discourage consumption and promote the use of substitutes in the consuming countries.

The Plan considers the direction of Pakistan's export trade as well as its commodity composition. There is a need to develop new markets as well as new export products. Traditionally intra-Commonwealth trade has been of primary importance to Pakistan. The main importers of Pakistani goods among Commonwealth countries are the United Kingdom and India. It should, however, be noted that during the fifties the countries now forming the European Economic Community have absorbed a larger share of Pakistan's exports than has the United Kingdom. In general the developed countries have imported the bulk of Pakistan's exports and the Plan recognizes that it will be an important part of Pakistan's export policy to promote trade with the developing countries in Asia and Africa.

Table 1 sets out projected foreign exchange earnings during the Second Plan period by main export groups. These export items face uncertain markets but the projections are inevitably based on the assumption that world market conditions will not be subject to violent fluctuations.

The projections are also based on the assumption that the production targets of the Plan will be achieved. It is estimated that total foreign exchange earnings will rise from an annual level of Rs.1,970 million in 1959/60 to about Rs.2,450 million in 1964/65, an over-all increase of nearly 15 per cent. Of the increase, about three quarters is likely to be accounted for by manufactured goods and one quarter by exports of raw materials. Despite this it can be seen that for some time to come the Pakistan export trade will be heavily reliant on a few basic crops.

The Plan anticipates that the world market for jute goods will expand by at least 1.2 per cent per annum during the Second Plan period. Rapid expansion seems unlikely as jute is meeting stiff competition from paper and to a lesser extent from other fibres as a packaging material, while bulk handling tends to impede expansion of the packaging material market as a whole. About 15 to 20 per cent of world jute production is, however, used for non-packing purposes of which the manufacture of floor coverings is the most important. This is a growing market and the danger of the substitution of other materials is less. It is considered possible that the consumption of jute for non-packaging purposes may increase by 4 per cent per annum or even more.

The entire increase in exports is expected to take place in the form of manufactured goods. In 1964/65 the production target for raw jute has been fixed at 7.3 million bales, of which 4.4 million would be exported unprocessed. The target for jute looms has been set at 12,000 by 1964/65 so that at least 380,000 tons of jute goods could be produced. If markets are favourable, this should leave at least 290,000 tons for export in that year. On these assumptions, raw jute would earn Rs.800 million of foreign exchange in 1964/65 and jute goods Rs.340 million.

TABLE I. PROJECTED FOREIGN EXCHANGE EARNINGS DURING SECOND
PLAN 1960–65
(Million rupees and per cent)

	1960/61 actual		1964/65 projection		Total Second Plan
	Mil. Rs.	*%*	*Mil. Rs.*	*%*	*Mil. Rs.*
Raw jute	870	39	800	33	4,100
Jute manufactures	320	14	340	14	1,600
Raw cotton	200	9	260	11	1,100
Cotton manufactures	120	3	220	9	800
Hides and skins	70	3	70	3	350
Wool	80	4	80	3	400
Miscellaneous exports	270	12	400	16	1,500
Invisible receipts	280	13	280	11	1,400
Total	2,210	100	2,450	100	11,250

An increase of some 10 to 15 per cent in world consumption of cotton appears to be a likely estimate in the Second Plan period. As Pakistan provides only about 5 per cent of world cotton exports there seems to be scope for increased sales if supplies can be made available at competitive prices. A production target of 2.3 million bales has been set for 1964/65, compared with the estimated production of about 1.7 million bales in 1959/60. The adoption of the target contained in the Plan was conditioned by two factors, i.e. that cotton faces severe competition on the world market from over-production and from artificial fibres, while at home it shares claims on acreage with essential foodgrain crops. While the acreage which can be devoted to cotton growing is limited, the Plan does foresee an increase in the production of high quality cotton. Comilla cotton grown in East Pakistan is a very high quality harsh short-staple cotton and commands a premium price over all other comparable varieties. During the past five years, production of Comilla cotton has varied between 14,000 to 19,000 bales. The demand for this cotton could reach 50,000 bales and more if supplies could be assured. At present production fluctuates widely between 10,000 and 55,000 bales as it depends on shifting cultivation by nomads. It is assumed that by 1964/65 it will be possible to export 650,000 bales of raw cotton. The export price of raw cotton has been assumed to be only 400 rupees per bale, at which price Pakistan would be fully competitive in world markets.

The cotton processing industry has been developed almost entirely by private enterprise and is the premier manufacturing industry of the country. Its importance from the point of view of the country's foreign exchange position is very great. In 1950/51 the country imported cotton manufactures worth Rs.625 million. These imports, which it is estimated would have cost about Rs.900 million in 1960, have been eliminated and cotton yarn and cloth worth about Rs.200 million were sold abroad in 1959/60. Between 1954–59 yarn production was doubled. By 1959 production of yarn and cloth was valued at about Rs.1,000 million and the industry employed about 150,000 persons providing more than one third of all employment in large scale industry. Capacity was sufficient to meet domestic requirements of cotton textiles in the coarse and medium varieties and to provide a margin for export until 1959 when shortages began to develop due to the unimplementation of First Plan targets. The average consumption of domestically produced cloth during the First Plan period was 12 yards per caput. Domestic demand is expected to rise to 14.5 yards by 1965. To maintain domestic supplies and textile exports the Plan proposes a target of 2.5 million spindles by 1965. While the Plan acknowledges that forecasting in this field is particularly difficult, it expects exports of cotton manufactures to fall off and not to return to the 1960 level until 1964/65. By this time it is assumed that 50 million pounds of cotton yarn and 225 million yards of cotton cloth will be exported.

Existing woollen spindlage can meet internal requirements by establishing operations on a multi-shift basis. Capacity in the worsted textile industry is now 3.5 million pounds while demand is estimated at 4 million pounds. No increase in capacity is proposed during the Plan period because of the foreign exchange burden of imported raw materials including wool tops, dyes and chemicals. Exports of wool and wool products are expected to remain stable during the Second Plan period at roughly Rs.80 million per annum. Most of the wool which is suitable for manufacturing carpets is now being exported raw. It is proposed to convert a part of this into yarn for use in the domestic manufacture of carpets. The Plan, therefore, proposes to set up a carpet-wool spinning unit based on indigenous wool. It is further proposed to establish a wool bureau on the lines of the International Wool Secretariat which is, among other matters, to be responsible for trade promotion.

The present annual production of hides and skins is estimated at 16 million pieces,

valued at Rs.135 million. Of these only about 6 million pieces are tanned in Pakistan, the balance being exported in the raw state. During the First Plan period an average of Rs.50 million in foreign exchange was earned per annum from the sale of hides and skins. It is hoped to raise this average to Rs.70 million per annum during the Second Plan period.

Better handling of raw hides and skins, notably through more careful flaying, can substantially increase foreign exchange earnings. Foreign exchange earnings can also be increased considerably by exporting processed goods rather than raw hides and skins. An expert report puts the net foreign exchange earnings which could result from the expansion and improvement of tanning and leather fabrication at more than Rs.90 million per year. It is estimated that an additional Rs.20 million could be earned by improving the quality of raw hides and skins. It will be important to secure adequate quality control for products destined for the export market.

The export of leather in the form of finished leather goods is also a promising possibility. With technical advice on design and quality, small units can manufacture excellent leather goods such as bags, footwear, wallets, belts and finished leather goods for which there is a large export market. The Small Industries Corporation will devote attention to strengthening small industries.

At the outset of the Second Plan period about 54 million pounds of tea were produced per annum after processing. In the calendar year 1960, however, exports of tea were valued at only Rs.10 million compared with an average of Rs.29 million in the three previous years since the rise in domestic consumption had reduced the surplus available for export. In September 1960 the Government called a Convention of Exporters at which representatives of trade and industry met to recommend methods of reaching the objectives for exports laid down in the Second Plan. It is hoped that at the end of the Second Plan period 22 million pounds of tea, valued at Rs.49 million, will be exported per annum.

Exports of *fish* are expected to earn at least 50 million rupees per annum during the Plan period.

It is hoped that it will be possible to export about 70,000 to 95,000 tons of superior *rice* per annum during the Second Plan period.

It is proposed to increase production capacity for *mechanical paper* and *newsprint* by 15,000 tons during the Second Plan period. While demand for paper products, notably for packing purposes, is bound to increase, it is thought that about 11,000 to 12,000 tons of newsprint and about 8,000 to 9,000 tons of mechanical paper should be exported annually by the end of the planning period.

An *oil* refinery is being established in Karachi and its by-products, notably gases, will be available for a wide range of important synthetic fibres and other products. This, together with other chemical plants, based on natural gas of which there are large deposits in West Pakistan, is expected to provide a surplus of Rs.90 million for export in 1963/64 and subsequent years.

Production of *sports goods* gives employment to thousands of workers in West Pakistan. Most of the production is exported and enjoys a high reputation although there has been some fall in exports. The Small Industries Corporation will undertake the modernization of this industry in order that it may maintain and strengthen its position on the world market. It is expected that present exports, valued at about Rs.10 million per annum, could thereby be increased.

Miscellaneous exports such as those discussed above and others based on small scale craft production, are expected to rise in value from the Rs.190 million annual average during the First Plan period to a level of Rs.400 million in 1964/65. A small increase in invisible receipts is also assumed in the Plan coming mainly from increased earnings of shipping, air and insurance services, as well as from tourism.

Total foreign exchange earnings during the Second Plan period are expected to be about Rs.11,250 million or an annual average of 2,250 million. In 1960/61 foreign exchange earnings had already reached a level of Rs.2,210 million compared with the annual average during the First Plan period of 1,912 million.

3. STABILIZATION OF EXPORT PROCEEDS

3.1 Special Problems of Primary-Exporting Countries *

Heavy dependence on staple exports has not been a highly popular national policy in the postwar period. The severe depression of agricultural prices in the Great Depression, identification of primary production with colonial political status, dis-

* From Boris C. Swerling, "Some Interrelationships Between Agricultural Trade and Economic Development," *Kyklos,* Vol. XIV, No. 3, 1961, pp. 379-86. Reprinted by permission.

advantageous bargaining position vis-à-vis the Western nations who controlled wartime shipping, and vulnerability to technological developments of external origin, all have played a part in creating that attitude. There are, besides, certain real disabilities associated with extreme specialization, disabilities that public policy has failed adequately to relieve.

Difficulties arise, *first*, from the contrast between the product mix of world trade and that of domestic agricultural systems

TABLE I. AGRICULTURAL COMMODITIES: EXPORTS
% WORLD PRODUCTION 1956/1957

Percentages	Commodities
0-10	Rice, maize, meat, olive oil
10-30	Barley, wheat, cottonseed [1], tobacco, cheese, butter, jute
30-50	Soybeans [1], peanuts [1], sugar (centrifugal), cotton, wool, linseed [1], palm oil
50-90	Copra [1], coffee, tea, cocoa
90-100	Rubber, abaca, palm kernels [1]

Source: United Nations, *Commodity Survey 1959*. New York, 1960, p. 14.
1. Oil equivalent.

(see Table 1). Although trade in wheat and rice ranks high in value terms, staple carbohydrates of widespread dietary use lean heavily on domestic supplies. World commerce gives a relatively larger role to tree crops than to field crops of sustained demand or the diversified feed-live-stock economy. Tree crops, which are especially characteristic of tropical exports, are subject to economic instability in an exaggerated form, arising out of long gestation periods, prolonged periods of excessive prices while tree plantings adjust, difficulties of anticipating future output from widespread plantings not well reported in official statistics, problems of anticipating market requirements at the late future date when new supplies will be forthcoming, low variable costs when plantings come into commercial bearing, and corresponding susceptibility to protracted periods of low prices.[1] Instabilities peculiarly the result of agricultural supply structures are accentuated by the long time lags of ocean shipment,[2] by the role of the world market as residual supplier when domestic crops fall short or domestic requirements

are suddenly enlarged, and by cyclical fluctuations in the demand for raw-material imports.

To be sure, the factors affecting commodity instability themselves change in the course of time.[3] Successive phases of US strategic stockpiling have had their destabilizing effects on world markets, but current holdings together with accumulated surpluses of American agricultural produce do provide some unilateral assurance against major commodity inflation. While the moderate severity of postwar industrial recessions to date has tempered one of the major sources of international instability, commodity stocks and consequently international commodity shipments are prone to behave in volatile fashion so long as inventory fluctuations remain an important element of cyclical disturbance. Nor have changes worked necessarily to reduce commodity instability. The inclination of the USSR to enter or withdraw from particular commodity markets on short notice and often for political reasons introduces a factor not easily amenable to anticipation or control. Primary producing countries enjoying new political status have by their own acts set in motion serious commodity disturbances, if one recalls only Iranian oil, Cuban sugar, or Congo copper. Emergence of the US as a major exporter of fats and oils creates some additional variability for that commodity group, inasmuch as important elements in world supplies are merely by-products from the American point of view. That is notably true of lard and tallow, related to their respective livestock cycles, and to cottonseed, but even soybeans have some of this characteristic when grown in rotation with corn. US disposal policies, on the other hand, have operated for the most part so as not to disrupt world prices,

1. E. W. Zimmermann, *World Resources and Industries*. Rev. ed., New York, 1951, Chap. 22.
2. Cf. M. Abramovitz, *Inventories and Business Cycles*. New York, 1950, pp. 182-184, and 207-217.

3. Cf. K. E. Knorr, "The Quest for a Stabilization Policy in Primary Producing Countries," *Kyklos*, Vol. XI, 1958, Fasc. 2, pp. 224-230.

and fluctuations in international cotton shipments have been met by wide swings in American exports while competing sources of supply have enjoyed a less exposed position.

Secondly, and beyond the patterns imposed by individual commodities, the primary exporting country tends to register distinctive structural features, to which Seers directs appropriate attention. It is not merely that market behavior of a limited range of export commodities dominates the level of economic activity, the volume of government revenues, and the capacity to finance development programs. In addition, specialized resources defy classical assumptions on the greater domestic than international mobility of factors, and restrict that ability to adjust quickly to new opportunities upon which important trading gains often depend.[4] It is broadly correct to say that national income of this type of country tends to be limited by the ability to finance essential imports rather than by available manpower or productive capacity; investment, by the ability to import capital goods, rather than by the rate of savings; and consumption, by the capacity to import consumer goods, rather than by the level of national income.[5] Inventory fluctuations become a particularly important economic variable, and the cyclical pattern of expenditures depends a good deal on the capital-labor proportions and social organization in the particular export commodity enjoying market strength or weakness at a given moment. Wide variability in foreign exchange earnings is not matched by any comparable capacity to finance the higher level of reserves needed to cope with export contingencies.

Thirdly, decided inequalities in the bargaining status of primary-exporting countries reinforce their exposed position. A country exporting coffee, bananas, or sugar may produce a trivial portion of world supply yet rely overwhelmingly on proceeds from this single crop. Though crop variability in a single country or region may occasionally be sufficiently important to affect the world price, the prices alike of exports and of imports are more customarily determined by factors operating in the advanced countries. It is not uncommon for a foreign business enterprise and its investment decisions to outrank the scale of indigenous governmental operations. The need to maintain exports to finance essential imports, and the desire to avoid the burdens of carrying stocks, are further factors weakening bargaining position on the export side.

A *fourth* matter of concern is the alleged long-run tendency for the commodity terms of trade to run against primary commodities and in favor of manufactured goods. It should be recalled that the Korean commodity boom gave rise to professional views of the opposite sort. Jewkes, for example, argued that each advance of industry throughout the world, by turning the terms of trade in agriculture's favor, will tend to make industrialization less easy,[6] and it was also contended that a serious lag in agricultural production will tend to retard the growth of world demand for manufactured imports.[7]

Morgan, after subjecting the statistical evidence and much of the literature to

4. G. Myrdal, *An International Economy, Problems and Prospects.* New York, 1956, p. 255.

5. *World Economic Survey,* p. 12.

6. J. Jewkes, "The Growth of World Industry," *Oxford Economic Papers,* February 1951, p. 14.

7. W. Y. Elliott, *et. al., The Political Economy of American Foreign Policy.* New York, 1955, p. 79. Even during the early 1950's E. S. Mason's view was that any substantial movement of price relationships in favor of primary commodities would be the result of national policies of self-sufficiency rather than physical limitations of supply, "An American View of Raw Materials Problems," *Journal of Industrial Economics,* November 1952, p. 5.

critical review,[8] finds no general worsening of the price position of primary producers, quite aside from the relevance of the barter terms-of-trade concept or corrections to adjust for changes in commodity quality or composition.

Fifthly, primary-producing countries are particularly vulnerable to adverse policy decisions in the advanced countries. Tariff and quota systems that favor imports in less processed form deny to the region of export fabricating operations entirely appropriate to their natural economic endowment, and this is reinforced when production has been explicitly developed to service manufacturing enterprises in developed countries. European excise levies on coffee, tea, tobacco and the like tend to reduce the volume of trade and hence the foreign exchange earnings of tropical exporters, quite apart from certain regressive aspects so far as the distribution of fiscal burdens are concerned.[9] Directly and indirectly, agricultural research has been fostered to an uneconomic degree on temperate crops, with the advanced industrial countries employing their scientific endowment to the competitive disadvantage of more promising regions in the tropics. Primary-production, which is likely to be relatively efficient in less developed countries, is the very sector that receives tender governmental treatment in many advanced nations.[10] Important income transfers occur when an International Materials Conference or wartime shipping control limits upward movement in commodity prices, and the real purchasing power of accumulated foreign exchange balances responds to monetary,

fiscal and exchange-rate policy of the industrial countries.

Such considerations lead on by easy degrees to arguments that specialization on primary export has been positively harmful to the country of origin. Milder versions of this approach stress structural maladjustment: that overseas primary production was pushed beyond the limits of comparative advantage by the metropolitan countries;[11] that an unbalanced infrastructure was developed, with transportation in all colonial areas leading to the sea;[12] that the 19th century division of labor between industrial and agrarian nations tended to perpetuate the contrast in their economic structure;[13] or that private foreign investment retarded economic development in the capital-importing country by diverting local savings and enterpreneurship from domestic to export activities.[14] One may point to the effect of plantation crops upon Java's population size, rather than upon its well-being, or emphasize the disadvantages that a persistent trade surplus imposes upon a primary-exporting country. In its extreme form, the argument is developed in frankly Marxist terms.[15] Even a superficial look at the debates of the United Nations General Assembly will verify the extent to which the exploitation theme is skillfully employed for ideological ends. Whether rooted in truth or falsehood, attitudes growing out of earlier trade patterns now inhibit the functioning of private instrumentalities that were important carriers

8. T. Morgan, "The Long-Run Terms of Trade between Agriculture and Manufacturing," *Economic Development and Cultural Change,* October 1959, pp. 1-23. See also J. Viner, *International Trade and Economic Development,* Glencoe, Illinois, 1952, pp. 141-7.

9. GATT, *Trends in International Trade,* pp. 103-10.

10. *World Economic Survey,* p. 66.

11. W. Y. Elliott *et al., op. cit.,* p. 185.

12. J. B. Condliffe, *The Commerce of Nations.* New York, 1950, p. 318.

13. W. S. and E. S. Woytinsky, *World Commerce and Governments: Trends and Outlook.* New York, 1955, p. 11.

14. H. W. Singer, "The Distribution of Gains between Investing and Borrowing Countries," *American Economic Review, Papers and Proceedings,* May 1950, p. 476.

15. P. A. Baran, "On the Political Economy of Backwardness," *Manchester School,* January 1952.

of economic development in the past, and the same attitudes affect the position that non-industrial nations take on current issues of international politics.

Trade has been affected in various ways by the shift in social priorities associated with political developments of the post-war period. An independent India has not been prepared to let high export prices outbid its domestic consumers for essential foodstuffs, such as oilseeds. One attribute of Dominion status within the British Commonwealth is the inclination and the ability to bargain more effectively for the use of the Sterling Area's dollar pool.[16] As the Gold Coast became Ghana, the application of Marketing Board reserves to purposes of stabilization declined relative to those of general public expenditure. American foreign aid tends to be more acceptable to independent African countries than to the administrators of dependent overseas territories.[17] Xenophobia has been aroused against the resident aliens who are frequently in charge of actual trading operations; the cosmopolitan outlook even of the native trader becomes suspect; and nationalization of import-export instrumentalities has been pursued as an independent objective, distinct from broader issues of government ownership or public investment.

In the process, sight has often been lost of the special advantages that a high level of trade can bring to less developed countries. Foreign exchange is a most flexible form of resource; governments inclined to a liberal economic system can effect desirable resource allocation with minimum *dirigism* by instituting appropriate commercial policies; and import duties and export taxes are effective fiscal devices for

economic systems in which scarce administrative skills must be carefully husbanded. The tax machinery can remove much economic remoteness even from mineral enclaves. The long list that includes nations like Ceylon, Cuba, Uruguay and Ghana surely do well to model their commitment to trade after New Zealand and Denmark, the Netherlands and Japan. Only countries of broad expanse and diversified resources can hope to match the low trade-output ratios experienced by the USA and the USSR. The contrasting post-war experiences of Argentina and Canada provide an interesting commentary on the results of, respectively, starving and stimulating the primary sectors of an economy.

If specialization on staple exports is to have its due, public policies concerning primary products will require far more imaginative treatment than they have hitherto received. Myrdal rightly stresses that advance in social welfare within the advanced industrial countries has not been matched by a parallel concern for vulnerable groups who reside beyond the national border. The United States has maintained an ambivalent attitude towards international commodity agreements, participating for those commodities (such as wheat and sugar) for which a supported price has served American interests while remaining, at least until very recently, a non-intervention purist towards South American staples[18] and disowning the parity principle at the water's edge. Not that the stabilization of individual commodity prices is necessarily the appropriate approach. The argument is made elsewhere for protecting the income of domestic farmers by a social-insurance measure,[19] and a comparable approach to

16. Cf. J. Polk, *Sterling, Its Meaning in World Finance.* New York, 1956, pp. 137, 165.

17. On the other hand, colonial producers in recent decades have typically enjoyed more assured market outlets than have been available to the export staples of independent nations.

18. M. S. Eisenhower, *Report to the President: United States-Latin America Relations,* December 27, 1958, pp. 10-12.

19. B. C. Swerling, "Income Protection for Farmers: A Possible Approach," *Journal of Political Economy,* April 1959, pp. 173-86.

international stabilization problems has also had some attention.[20] The social costs involved in shifting resources are recognized and to a limited extent met by the European Social Fund provided for in the Rome treaty, and this approach also has wider potential use. If unorthodox approaches are countenanced, certain petroleum exporters might seek means of advancing their people's welfare by investing capital abroad rather than at home, just as the American farmer might increase his returns by investing less in agriculture and more in other sectors. Primary-exporting countries do have special trading problems that need to be better understood and more satisfactorily dealt with.

3.2 FLUCTUATIONS IN EXPORT EARNINGS *

As is well known, the prices of most primary products in international trade vary more sharply from year to year than those of most industrial products. While foodstuffs are less affected by cyclical variations in demand than all industrial materials or manufactured products, most materials of agricultural origin are subject to irregularities in export supply and import demand arising from crop fluctuations, and most primary product markets are much affected by oscillations in demand arising out of changing expectations as to the future course of prices. However, the reason for the differences in price behavior between primary and manufactured products lies not so much in any special instability of import demand or export supply for the former as in the fact that in the case of primary products both demand and supply are as a rule less responsive to changes in price than in the case of manufactures. With the exception

of a few commodities, whose prices are stabilized by understandings between producing firms or by governmental action, primary products are supplied to world markets under much more competitive conditions than are industrial products. Thus, whereas manufacturers, as a rule, seek to maintain fairly steady prices in the face of variations in demand, allowing the quantities they supply to vary, primary producers are more likely to maintain the quantities supplied, leaving prices to vary.

According to UN studies,[1] the mean year-to-year variation in the prices of individual primary commodities averaged some 13 per cent over the period 1900 to 1958.[2] Instability was particularly severe in the period between the two World Wars, when year-to-year changes amounted to 15-16 per cent; before World War I and again in the years 1948–1958, the average change appears to have been close to 11 per cent[3]....

The volume of exports from the average primary producing country varies from year to year as much as, if not more than, the price. This is true of individual primary products exported from individual countries in the interwar period and also for the over-all exports of individual countries in the postwar period.

For most of these countries, taken individually, the elasticity of world demand for their exports is high, the elasticity of home supply low. Export prices vary in the main with market conditions abroad, and only in a few cases do home supplies have

20. *World Economic Survey*, p. 128.

* From "Fund Policies and Procedures in Relation to the Compensatory Financing of Commodity Fluctuations," *International Monetary Fund Staff Papers*, November 1960, pp. 4-7, 12-18.

1. *Instability in Export Markets of Underdeveloped Countries* (New York, 1952) and *World Economic Survey, 1958* (New York, 1959).

2. The result appears to be roughly the same whether or not the war and immediate postwar years are included.

3. These figures are unweighted arithmetic means of year-to-year changes, disregarding signs, in the U.S. dollar prices or unit values of some 25-32 individual commodities. The changes are expressed as percentages of the higher of the two annual figures.

a significant influence on price. Export quantities, however, vary mainly with supply conditions at home and are only slightly responsive to price changes.

The proceeds accruing to individual countries from exports of primary commodities have on the average varied more, but not very much more, from year to year than have either export price or export volume. This is true both for exports of individual primary products from individual countries in the interwar period and for over-all exports of individual primary producing countries in the postwar period.

In the absence of counteracting policies, including the use of compensatory financing, a high degree of instability in a country's export proceeds will give rise to four other kinds of burdensome instability: instability in the incomes earned in export industries, relative to those earned in other sectors of the economy; instability in general money incomes and prices; instability in external purchasing power; and, as a consequence of these, instability in real expenditure, particularly real investment.

Fluctuations in the money value of exports tend directly to induce similar fluctuations in the incomes of those who produce for export; and indirectly, through their repercussions on private consumption, private investment, and public expenditures, they tend to generate income fluctuations in other industries.

To some extent, fluctuations thus generated in domestic incomes can be alleviated by governmental action involving contractionary policies in periods of high export proceeds and expansionary policies in periods of low proceeds. The arrangements, which are very widely used, for stabilizing the prices and incomes of agricultural producers, including those producing for export, constitute perhaps the most powerful of these stabilizing devices, but something can also be done by more general budgetary and monetary policies.... Indeed, a certain amount of budgetary offsetting will take place automatically if tax rates are kept unchanged. In some countries, however, stabilization operates more effectively against deflationary than against inflationary impulses. It is often more difficult for governments to run a budget surplus or contract credit when exports boom than to run a deficit and expand credit when exports slump. Even when price stabilization schemes for export commodities exist, their profits in good times may be used to finance developmental and other public expenditure while their losses in bad times give rise to budget deficits financed by the banking system. The appearance of one-sided stabilization may sometimes be due mainly to the persistence of an underlying inflationary trend, now stimulated, and now retarded, according as the influences from the export sector are inflationary or deflationary. In most cases, however, it is probable that, over the longer run, export instability as such has a net inflationary effect.

Fluctuations in the importing power of exports or of external receipts, unless offset, tend to give rise to fluctuations in imports.... The imports of primary producing countries in the postwar period, though moving more closely with external receipts than with exports alone, have in some cases moved rather differently even from the former, because of the leeway provided by reserves. However, in the average primary producing country, the magnitude of year-to-year variations in imports (12.2 per cent) has been practically the same as that of variations in the importing power of exports. Fluctuations in imports as severe as those which have occurred in some countries are likely to be associated with sizable variations in real consumption or investment. To the extent that the instability in exports or other foreign exchange receipts reacts through its monetary repercussions on the level of domestic production for the home market, the variations of real expenditure will be even greater, in absolute magnitude, than those of imports. In particular, the flow of real expenditure on investment is likely to suffer interruption, both because of the sensitivity of investment to general prosperity and because of its high import component. Such instability in investment and consumption clearly has undesirable implications from both social and economic standpoints.

To some extent, the adjustment of imports to fluctuations in exports tends to arise more or less automatically as a result of the variations in money prices and incomes to which these export fluctuations give rise. Such influences on income, however, operate with a certain time lag, so that incomes and import demand go on rising for some time after export proceeds have turned down. Moreover, when, as is frequently the case, export fluctuations are superimposed on a domestic situation characterized by persistent inflationary pressure, it is not surprising that any incipient decline or even leveling off in export proceeds should suffice to provoke a payments crisis. At this point, countries often have recourse, first, to an intensification of restrictions on imports and payments and, later, in order to escape from the resulting complications and the serious contraction of their foreign trade, to an adjustment of the exchange rate.

Many of the adverse consequences of export instability that have been discussed above are experienced in some degree by industrial as well as by primary producing countries. For many primary producers, however, the effects of export fluctuations are more severe and difficult to cope with, partly because the level of per capita income is low, but mainly because the fluctuations are superimposed on a static, or at least insufficiently progressive, long-term trend in importing power....

Two broad lines of policy have been applied or suggested to alleviate the problems arising from short-term fluctuations in the value of exports of primary products. One approach aims at stabilizing the proceeds that countries derive from the export of particular primary products, mainly through stabilizing the prices at which the products are traded internationally. The intention of this approach is to curtail at the source all the various forms of instability, internal as well as external, that have been described above as consequential on fluctuations in export proceeds. The other approach is to offset the fluctuations in the external purchasing power of exports, or of foreign exchange receipts in general, by various forms of compensatory financing. The two approaches are not mutually exclusive but can be applied in conjunction. Unlike arrangements that seek to stabilize export prices, compensatory financing will do nothing directly to iron out the income fluctuations in primary producing countries that result from export fluctuations; any stabilization of domestic incomes, whether in the export sector or in the economy generally, will require separate measures of monetary and budgetary policy.

Compensatory financing is usually considered by those discussing commodity problems to involve international transfers, on a grant or loan basis. The concept, however, should logically be broadened to include variations in the accumulation and decumulation of national reserves of gold and foreign exchange. This is the general use of the term "compensatory financing" in the context of balance of payments analysis. Reserve movements, loans and repayments, and unilateral transfers of various sorts can all, in principle, be used to offset fluctuations in a country's external receipts from exports and other items, and thus to permit some stabilization of imports. Thus conceived, compensatory financing offers a comprehensive way of mitigating fluctuations in a country's external purchasing power; and the fact that in some forms it can be carried out by purely national action and in others by bipartite arrangements with international organizations or individual foreign countries frees it from some of the difficulties of international negotiation that beset most attempts at the stabilization of export prices.

3.3 TECHNIQUES OF STABILIZATION *

Instability of export proceeds is the joint result of fluctuations in prices and quantities. Prices can be stabilized, but the more obvious remedy for quantity fluctuations is some form of countercyclical lending or reserve accumulation. It seems hardly worth while, therefore, to spend much time on price stabilization, unless prices can be shown to represent the major part of the problem.

The impression that countercyclical lending holds out more promise than price stabilization will indeed obtrude itself with increasing force in the course of this paper....

To prove that price fluctuations are important does not imply that they are necessarily bad. Discussions of stabilization occasionally, and no doubt inadvertently, convey the impression that price fluctuations are bad *per se*. Of course they are not; they are the essential mechanism for the allocation of resources. Price movements are the signal to increase or reduce production of a commodity. The question is whether the signal is reliable, and how strong it has to be to produce a given effect.

Doubts as to the reliability of price signals arise when we remember the short-

* From Henry C. Wallich, "Stabilization of Proceeds from Raw Material Exports," in Howard S. Ellis (ed.) *Economic Development for Latin America,* St. Martin's Press, New York, 1961, pp. 344-9, 353-9. Reprinted by permission.

run speculative as well as the cyclical nature of many price movements. Presumably we do not want to see sugar mills dismantled, coffee trees uprooted or neglected, or copper mines abandoned in response to a price drop that fails to reflect the long-run trend of demand.

Doubts as to the effectiveness of a given signal originate precisely from the opposite and more realistic concern. Because price movements in the short run are often misleading, producers may be hesitant to react too quickly or too intensively, although the signal may later prove correct. For some products, this fact may mean extreme price movements for prolonged periods. A lesser signal might suffice, if the producers were given time to react to it. On the side of contraction, inelasticity of supply usually is even more pronounced. Hence the familiar spectacle of surpluses overhanging the market and depressing prices for many years. And, finally, there is the possibility of a cobweb situation—high prices cause over-production, which depresses prices and production, which leads to high prices and renewed over-production, which in turn leads ... and so *ad infinitum.*

It is generally agreed that the signals given in raw material markets are frequently so misleading or extreme that it seems entirely legitimate to counteract them, even in a free market system. What is not compatible with a free market is a modification of the long-run trend of prices—the true signal that prices are designed to give.

The merits of stabilization, however, have been questioned from still another point of view. It has been argued that the fluctuations experienced by raw material producing countries may be beneficial rather than harmful to their economic development. The reason suggested is that more capital may be formed when incomes are high only periodically, with large profits going to export producers, than when they are more stable and more evenly distributed.[1]

How strong is this argument? There is considerable doubt about the implied analysis of the savings process itself. It may be that the establishment of a higher living standard, based on a temporarily high income, would cut into saving when income falls again and so lead to lower total saving over the cycle. But there are still other reasons for questioning the boom and depression pattern as a promoter of economic development in raw materials producing countries. One is that during the boom, when savings from export profits are at their peak, the country's resources are already fully employed, in the sense in which this can be said of under-developed countries. There are no idle resources then to be mobilized so as to employ the boom-time saving. As a corollary, the savings themselves are in effect invested in the foreign exchange reserves generated by the export surplus. The liquid resources which the exporters hold are just their counterpart, which can be used without inflationary consequences only by liquidating the foreign exchange holdings.

A second reason for questioning the boom and depression pattern is the fascination that it seems to exert on business men in the countries so afflicted. The big killings under such conditions are always to be made in the country's principal commodities, be they sugar, coffee, wool, or cotton. Other profit possibilities seem to pale into insignificance. This engenders a kind of raw material mentality that leans towards speculation rather than towards some more stable but less dramatic activity. It is not an attitude helpful to the development of new industry.

1. Sir Sydney Caine, "Instability of Primary Product Prices—a Protest and a Proposal," *Economic Journal*, September 1954.

The same is to be said of the general sense of instability that permeates an economy dominated by raw material fluctuations. It moulds the economic climate, infuses uncertainty into all plans, and narrows the investment horizon. Economic development is the victim.

Attempts have been made to salvage the instability doctrine on the grounds that depressions themselves have often been a cause of development. Whereas moderate prosperity allows everybody to carry on in his accustomed way, sudden adversity becomes the mother of initiative. This, however, is a picture appropriate to the 1930s. Today, few countries have need of adversity to stimulate their developmental imagination. Stability—at a high level—seems to be what is most needed.

In the end, the success of the development drive will itself do much to overcome the problem of instability. Through diversification of raw materials output, the impact of fluctuations, whether mitigated by stabilization schemes or not, will be lessened. Through the reduction of raw material exports to a small fraction of the national income, the weight of their instability will be reduced. But many years may go by before this solution is attained. Meanwhile we have to continue to search for a solution to the commodity problems of the present and of the immediate future.

We have established so far that price fluctuations do play a major role in the instability of export proceeds. Also, we have noted that these price fluctuations are often larger than necessary to perform their allocative function....

Buffer pools, quotas, and purchase contracts appear to be the basic generic types of stabilization tools. Their subvariants are endless—domestic and international, private and governmental versions of buffer pools; quotas on production, exports, imports, or consumption; purchase contracts for long or short periods, conditional or unconditional, for small or large parts of total output, with prices fixed or flexible, and so forth.

While there is nothing basically new in this field which seems to call for attention at this time, recent experience has thrown some light upon the respective merits and demerits of the various tools.

Buffer Pools From a purely abstract point of view, buffer pools are probably the ideal stabilization device. They resemble the open market operations of a central bank in that they do not interfere with the working of the market. They merely change the balance of supply and demand. In the abstract, a buffer pool could be operated without danger of running out of money or out of stocks—if men of good judgment, who could adjust their price policy flexibly in the light of events and who were independent of politics, could be found to administer it.

This ideal situation, however, conspicuously fails to prevail. In practice, therefore, buffer pools are probably the least promising of all devices. One important difficulty is the question "Where is the money coming from?" The producer countries are those most interested in stabilization but usually also those least able to afford it. The consumer countries often have the resources but lack an immediate vital interest. In fact they must fear that they would be putting prices up against themselves. The United States and Canada, being producers as well as consumers, do not fit into this pattern, but so far this has not necessitated any change in the conclusion that buffer pools are hard to finance.

Next, there is the difficulty of agreeing on policy—on the price range, volume of operations, and the like. Agreement might impose itself during the down phase under the imperative need to make stabilizing purchases. During the upswing, producers would scarcely welcome efforts to hold down prices. Buying is easy, selling is hard.

Then, in the absence of production and export quotas to protect the buffer pool, there is always the prospect that some countries might use it to create easy foreign exchange for themselves. Export subsidies and special exchange rates might provide the means to that end. Finally, the present division of the world into different currency areas would hamper the functioning of buffer pools.

Quotas In the case of quotas of all kinds, the situation is the reverse. Quotas are bad theoretically because they imply misallocation of resources. They protect inefficient producers, freeze markets, and probably keep supply below the optimum. Quotas have the advantage, however, of being manageable. They avoid accumulation of stocks, require no financing, and do not call for continuous operating decisions. Some past base year, however arbitrary, can usually be made to serve as a standard to facilitate delicate decisions. In practice, quotas would probably have to be combined with buffer pools, in order to provide the necessary short-run flexibility of supply.

Purchase Contracts Last, there is the long-term contract typified by the International Wheat Agreement. Such an agreement has the advantage of preserving the free market as an allocator of resources and an indicator of trends, provided not all supplies are covered by it. The technical problems of a purchase contract are quite manageable, although difficulties grow as the agreement is drawn tighter to make it more effective. The purchase contract has the grave disadvantage, however, of creating a two-price system. It requires domestic controls of some sort and buffer stocks to implement it, and it is quite apt to put the participating governments into the commodities business. In an extreme case, it may become nothing but a payment by the government of one country to that of another, without ever touching the producer or consumer. I shall argue below that this may be the best way of compensating for commodity fluctuations. There is no reason, however, to conduct such an operation under the guise and with all the paraphernalia of an elaborate commodity stabilization agreement.

Different commodities are likely to react differently to each of these devices and to various combinations of devices. Solutions are complicated by the existence of different commodity grades with corresponding price differentials, by seasonalities, by the currency problems both of producer and consumer countries, by differences of production costs and marketing power among producer countries and the ensuing difference in their respective willingness to participate in restrictive schemes, and a host of other factors. We have too little experience to be able to generalize with any confidence. This brief enumeration of problems seems appropriate, however. It should leave no doubt as to immense practical difficulties to be overcome. If any further evidence were needed it is supplied by the paucity of agreements that have come into existence and by the rather indifferent success of a good part of this small number.

The discussion so far has been in good part an account of difficulties, problems, and obstacles. Does any of it point towards some particular form of action? What are the prospects that such action may materialize?

Action is possible on two planes—the national and the international. It is generally thought that, to be effective, action in the commodity field must be international. This is the explanation often given for the experience of countries that have tried to go it alone, like Brazil, or that have banded together in insufficiently comprehensive groups, like the sugar producers under the Chadbourne Plan. This explanation, however, is only partly correct. It

applies where the goal is to improve the long-term trend of prices. It does not apply where the desire is only to eliminate the effects of short-run fluctuations. The benefits inherent in the elimination of short-run fluctuations, which underlie the United Nations' experts' recommendations, can be achieved by purely national action. An international agreement is not absolutely necessary.

The national stabilization that I am referring to has nothing to do with price support schemes of the familiar kind. In fact, it does not attempt to influence the price of commodities. All that a country has to do if it wants to neutralize the effect of price fluctuations is to adopt the technique of the West African Marketing Boards, or some refinement of it.[2]

By means of a flexible tax and subsidy, a country could insulate domestic producers against world market fluctuations. It would sell its commodities for whatever they would bring, paying or taxing its producers in accordance with the difference between the stabilized and the world market price. It would accumulate exchange-reserves in good times and draw them down in bad times. The stabilized prices would have to be adjusted from time to time, of course, to keep them in line with evolving trends in the world market. A country following this policy would not stabilize the world price, but its domestic economy and its imports would behave as if the price had been stabilized.

The national approach has certain obvious difficulties, otherwise we should see it in action more frequently. It is lacking in the discipline that international action might provide. It runs into the fact that politically it is not easy to tax away producers' gains from rising prices, nor to sterilize the domestic and foreign exchange

2. P. T. Bauer and F. W. Paish, "The Reduction of Fluctuations in the Incomes of Primary Producers," *Economic Journal,* December 1952.

resources accruing from this tax. Further-more, national action would allow differ-ent countries to make different assump-tions as to future price trends. This might lead to a breakdown of some of the national plans, and also to changes in rela-tive market shares. Shifts in market shares might result also if some producer coun-tries stabilized in this form while others did not, because of the impact of domestic stabilization upon supply.

These are potent objections to the national approach, and I am not suggest-ing seriously that it is to be widely recom-mended. The reason why I have empha-sized it is rather because the widespread lack of interest in it points to an important conclusion. I shall set it forth briefly.

The national approach, despite its weak-nesses, is, after all, a possibility, and one which could be seized by any country with-out waiting for international agreements which are known to be unlikely. Many countries are practising a rudimentary form of it when they support domestic farm prices, or when they try to conduct a counter-cyclical policy in their foreign exchange reserves. With few exceptions, however, these practices are very far from constituting a clearly conceived and firmly adhered-to system.

The conclusion to which this failure to embrace the national approach points is clear: producer countries are not willing, on the whole, to make major efforts or sacrifices for the sake of the kind of sta-bility that the national approach can pro-vide. This kind of stabilization, as I pointed out earlier, is one that does not seek to modify the terms of trade—it is *pure* stabilization. Pure stabilization evi-dently is not a goal to inspire great effort and enthusiasm. What underlies the wide-spread urge to do something for commodi-ties must, therefore, be a desire, not for stable prices, but for higher prices.

This interpretation poses a dilemma for contemporary expert opinion. As I men-tioned earlier, the present climate of non-partisan opinion, for which there is a good deal to be said, inclines to the belief that commodity agreements should not be allowed to alter long-run price trends. The unwillingness of policy-makers to make more effective use of the national approach seems to indicate that they do not fully share the views of the technicians.

In this final section of my paper, which deals with action, we must face these politi-cal realities. All technical difficulties aside, commodity agreements aiming at pure stabilization are not likely to be adopted because they do not offer enough to the producer countries. Commodity agree-ments promising better terms of trade may be worth the sacrifices, in terms of political discipline, that are required. The question is whether the consumer countries are prepared to co-operate.

At first sight it would not appear in their interest to do so, and that has been the predominant attitude up till now. However, the consumer countries, and particularly the United States, recognize that the economic development of other countries is in their own interest. Favour-able terms of trade are an important resource for development. The consumer countries cannot, therefore, take it for granted that a commodity agreement that worsens their own terms of trade must necessarily be hostile to their long-range interests.

In addition, the consumer countries are interested in establishing reliable sources of supply of raw materials. This is a second reason why, prejudices apart, they should not necessarily look with disfavour upon commodity schemes that do not redound to their immediate price advantage.

An action programme in the field of raw materials stabilization should there-fore take account of these two thoughts: first, to be successful, an agreement should hold out to the producer countries some prospect of better terms of trade, and second, the agreement should justify this feature by stressing the developmental aspect for the producer countries and the raw materials supply aspect for the consumer countries. To these principles I would add the proviso that our concept of what constitutes a commodity agreement should not be drawn too narrowly. Countercyclical lending geared in some way to fluctuations in raw materials proceeds would, by this test, fall under the general heading of commodity agreements.

A stabilization agreement between a group of producer and a group of consumer countries that shifts the terms of trade against the consumer countries is, in effect, a transfer of income from one group to the other. The real income of the consumers is reduced, that of the producers is increased. In the abstract, the governments of the consumer countries might as well impose a tax and pay the proceeds to the governments of the producer countries. The effect upon their respective real national incomes would be identical, except for tax friction and the like. But once we begin to think in terms of transfers of income, we are bound to notice that to effect the transfer by paying higher prices for commodities is not a very efficient way.

In the first place, to transfer or redistribute income internationally through higher commodity prices means to give most of the benefits to a particular producer group in the exporting countries. Whether the benefit goes only to the wealthy owner or trickles down to his labour is not the main issue here. In either case, the larger part of the population, which is only indirectly connected with the export industry, benefits only indirectly.

In the second place, the higher prices will tend to intensify the raw material character of the exporting economies. An outright shift of resources to the raw

material sector may be impeded by the quantitative restrictions that will probably be required to implement the scheme. But the implications for economic development in general would perhaps not be wholesome.

In the third place, the income transfer reaches the recipient countries in the form of income, not of investible capital. Probably only a small fraction of the additional income will be saved and invested. The bulk will go into consumption. If the same amount were transferred as an investment grant, or even as a loan, it would do much more for economic development.

Finally, an income transfer via high raw material prices depends for its size not only on the price but also on the volume of exports. Quantity fluctuations make up an important part of total fluctuations in export proceeds. An income transfer by loan or grant could be tailored so as to compensate for proceeds fluctuations resulting from both price and quantity fluctuations.

Contrary considerations may no doubt present themselves. The raw material countries may specifically want to increase the income of their export industries, if these have been suffering. Usually these industries are the backbone of the economy, and often it is difficult to shift resources away from them as a part of a countercyclical policy. Alternatively, the raw material countries may siphon off the benefits through taxes or multiple exchange rates. The consumer countries on their side may want to strengthen their sources of supply and may therefore prefer the price stabilization technique to a generalized income transfer.

In the case of the United States, it is even conceivable that commodity agreements may some day be favoured as a means of giving foreign aid if political objections to overt aid continue to build up. Admittedly, the prospect seems remote, in view of the well-known attitude of the American Government toward commodity agreements.

The conclusions that I would derive from this discussion are as follows. The prospect for pure stabilization agreements is poor, because they do not offer enough. Stabilization agreements that aim at changing the terms of trade are not in principle undesirable because they can be made a vehicle of developmental financing. They are merely inefficient because ordinarily developmental financing can be carried out more effectively by overt income transfers than in the concealed form of better terms of trade. I would suggest, however, that the concept of a commodity agreement be broadened so as to include countercyclical loans and grants designed to compensate for raw materials fluctuations. If that be conceded, a good case can be made for commodity agreements.

3.4 CONCLUSIONS ON INTERNATIONAL COMPENSATORY MEASURES *

We began our work by examining the question: "Is there a situation calling for action?" We are satisfied that there is. Instability in commodity markets has been serious in recent years, and there are no good reasons, short of international action in one form or another, for expecting the situation to change greatly in character for a number of years ahead.

The amplitude of fluctuations in the value of trade in individual primary commodities has not been so wide as during the inter-war period, but the improvement seems hardly commensurate with the advance in the internal stability of the industrial countries. If the variations in primary commodity trade were oscillations about a strongly rising trend, the problem would

* From United Nations, Department of Economic and Social Affairs, *International Compensation for Fluctuations in Commodity Trade*, Report by a Committee of Experts, E/CN.13/40, New York, 1961, pp. 66-73.

be less acute. In fact the total value of this trade in recent years has grown but slowly in absolute terms; thus, as trade in manufactures has expanded, the share of primary commodities in total world trade has declined.

The adverse effects of instability in commodity trade, particularly in the less developed of the primary producing countries, are numerous. Fluctuations in export proceeds add greatly to the difficulties of maintaining stable internal economies. Instability handicaps the planning and realization of economic development expenditure, both public and private, and of social programmes as well.

While noting that the direct impact of fluctuations in commodity trade is worse for the under-developed countries than for advanced economies, we are also impressed by the strong mutual interest in lessening and off-setting this impact. International effort of a many-sided character is called for. The fact that our report concentrates on measures of compensatory finance is not intended to exclude concurrent effort to promote stability by other means.

Having satisfied ourselves that a situation exists which calls for compensatory measures in one form or another, we next turned to a discussion of what these measures might be. It was natural that the Committee should first examine the relevance to the situation of existing sources of international liquidity—namely, countries' reserves of foreign exchange together with their access to the resources of the International Monetary Fund. In any case it was clear that those responsible for our terms of reference intended this.

Bearing in mind the vulnerability of primary producing countries to instability in export proceeds, there can be little doubt that their need for foreign exchange reserves is generally more intense than that of industrial countries. Yet, for various reasons the reserves held by primary producing countries generally do not reflect this; they have in fact become less adequate in recent years. Furthermore, their capability of pursuing compensatory policies with their own resources is limited. For such countries the question of access to the resources of the Fund therefore assumes special weight.

It is clear that the Fund is already engaged in compensatory financing of importance to some of its members. With its recently enlarged resources and increasing experience in dealing with the problems of primary producing countries, the Fund is capable of considerably augmenting this activity. Our discussion of the Fund's role as a compensatory instrument revolved around two points: the degree of certainty with which members can count on drawing upon the Fund in time of need, and the adequacy now or potentially of Fund resources and policies in relation to the dimensions of the problem.

Our conclusions on the role of the Fund have emerged reasonably clearly … and [are] repeated here:

(a) In so far as drawings on the Fund are automatic, a country whose export proceeds fall has reliable access to a source of compensatory financing. At present only 25 per cent of a member country's quota comes close to being automatically available. Any significant increase in this percentage which the Fund could institute would be a valuable step towards providing compensatory financing to meet the needs of primary producing countries when threatened with the adverse impact of a decline in export proceeds.

(b) A large-scale increase in the degree of automatic drawing rights on the Fund would, however, be inconsistent with the necessity of ensuring reasonably prompt repayment of drawings. Unless the basic nature of the Fund is altered, therefore, we do not believe that it is practicable to offset the major part of a decline through enlarging the degree to which the Fund's transactions are automatic. Given this view, the main prospect of advance towards greater certainty of drawings for members must lie in closer relations between the members and the Fund. Through the increased use of stand-by arrangements or consultative procedures, the Fund should aim to clarify with interested members the conditions which would assure that the full use of quota without waiver (Fund holding of 200 per cent of a member's currency) or even more will be readily granted, if it appears justifiable according to forecasts of commodity markets and other relevant considerations.

(c) We are impressed, furthermore, by the severity of the problem created by fluctuations in export proceeds of the magnitude likely to be experienced by many countries. Bearing this in mind, we feel that even if a reasonable degree of progress is made by the Fund in the direction indicated, in many cases the uncertainty attached to drawings on Fund quotas of the dimensions required—or the limitations on national policies that must be accepted to reduce this uncertainty—will offer a serious handicap to the important object of continuity in developmental expenditure. At the same time, we feel that it may not be feasible for the Fund to adjust its policies even further than is suggested above.

These are important conclusions, for they reveal our considered doubt whether the Fund's activities, present or likely, offer a complete answer to the need for measures to affect instability in the export trade of primary producing countries. This applies particularly to the under-developed countries in view of the special importance of maintaining continuity in their developmental expenditure. It is right, nevertheless, to stress our view that the Fund can and should play an increasing role in this form of compensatory financing.

Long-term capital transfers also lend themselves to certain possibilities of compensatory financing. We have taken note of several developments in this regard which appear to offer some promise of contributing to a greater continuity of development expenditure in the face of commodity fluctuations.

If long-term capital is to be employed effectively in a compensatory manner, it is important that the agencies concerned adopt policies which will permit a measure of variation in the rate of its utilization. For this purpose it is desirable that such capital be available to finance the broad range of imports required for developmental expenditure, whether in the public or private sector, and not be unduly limited to specific projects. There is room for the further development of long-term loans and grants which are compensatory in effect as a useful supplement to more general compensatory measures.

Having concluded that the existing instruments of compensatory finance are not likely to offer an adequate solution to the problem with which we were asked to deal, we devoted a substantial part of our deliberations to proposals which call for new and different approaches. These are grouped together ... as insurance proposals...

The basic risk to be insured is a decline in export proceeds, however defined, which is due to instability in commodity trade. A degree of insurance would perhaps be possible by a pooling of the risks among the vulnerable countries; but to insure the solvency of a pool including only such countries would require extremely large contributions. In view of the fact that the risk to be insured is generally greatest for those countries least able to compensate for it from their own resources, such premiums would be inordinate. We do not consider this a practical approach; and in any case, because of the mutual interest involved, we favour an arrangement which embraces both developed and underdeveloped countries even if on unequal terms with respect to the distribution of cost and benefits.

This approach was not adopted without first examining proposals which might be mutually balanced in the sense that countries sustaining a loss during a specified period from a change in prices would be compensated by transfers from countries enjoying a gain from the same price movements. We do not, however, consider this a fruitful line of inquiry: the technical difficulties of negotiating and operating such schemes are formidable, and, what is more, it would be hard to justify arrangements under which substantial transfers from under-developed to advanced countries might be required.

Of the proposals to give financial compensation for declines in export proceeds, those we regard as most feasible partake of the nature of social insurance and presuppose a willingness of advanced countries to contribute on the understanding that their direct benefits will not equal their contributions. We envisage a central fund ("development insurance fund") into which all member countries would pay contributions and against which members would make financial claims which would be paid automatically in stated circumstances. Since the claims would reflect the relative degree of instability in the export proceeds of the participants, there would be a net transfer of payments predominantly or exclusively to the participating under-developed countries.

As indicated by its name, the object of a "development insurance fund" would be to provide a form of compensatory finance which would ensure a greater continuity in foreign exchange income (taking actual export proceeds together with compensation) and thus to protect under-developed countries against setbacks in their development caused by instability in world commodity markets. In devising machinery to this end, several problems must be faced which we have not been able to sift fully in the time at our disposal. We are clear that something less than full compensation for declines in export proceeds is desirable. This would greatly lessen the danger that difficulties which are chronic rather than short-term may be ignored by the recipient countries and also offers safe-guards against possible abuse.

For the same reasons, it is important that benefits should be adjusted for losses resulting from longer-term trends in export proceeds. Also, the variety of situations of different countries would have to be taken into account in adopting particular principles of operation. We reject any idea that all declines in the export proceeds of participants should be covered regardless of origin or persistence.

As regards the terms on which compensation might be paid, we have considered two main types of arrangement and certain variants of each. In one type (referred to as type I) a claim would be met by a final cash settlement. In the other (type II), settlement would take the form of a contingent loan repayable under certain circumstances. We can see certain possible advantages in a combination of the two types of settlement.

We have thought it useful to estimate the possible orders of magnitude of the gross claims that might be made on a fund set up along the lines indicated, assuming in this instance that all participants are eligible to present claims. Under conditions like those of recent years (1953–1959) and assuming compensation equal to 50 per cent of the short-fall in export proceeds adjusted by a minimum deduction ranging between 2.5 per cent and 10 per cent of the base value of proceeds, it appears that the under-developed countries would have had claims ranging on the average between the

equivalent of $466 million and $246 million yearly, and industrial and high-income producing countries between $142 million and $12 million.

With the time at our disposal we were unable to consider many important aspects of financing a "development insurance fund." In principle, it would appear desirable to constitute the fund by the payment of fixed annual contributions plus an initial capital subscription sufficient to enable the fund to meet possible claims arising from an initial period of unusually large shortfalls in export proceeds. Contributions might be assessed on the basis of a stipulated percentage of exports for the underdeveloped primary producing countries and on the basis of national income for other countries, with the possibility of taking account of differences in the average *per capita* income of such countries.

If a "development insurance fund" is established, we see the possibility of its being used to carry out certain additional but related functions under appropriate safeguards. Thus, it might finance a supplementary system of crop insurance to mitigate the effect on a country's balance of payments of additional imports required because of fluctuations in domestic agricultural output. Also, in the event of a serious recession in the industrial countries, the "insurance fund" might liberalize temporarily the rules governing compensation payments.

The establishment of compensatory machinery on the principles sketched above necessarily implies, in our view, the condition that the benefits will be effectively utilized, especially to promote the development of the countries likely to be the principal recipients. We do not, however, regard it as practicable to trace whether compensation has been used specifically for particular purposes or desirable otherwise to impose detailed conditions on the use to be made of compensatory payments.

What is important is that a receiving country adopt the necessary policies to make effective use of benefits and to facilitate the working of the scheme, and that the net contributors be assured that these objects will be pursued.

We would emphasize that these insurance proposals should be regarded as being complementary, not alternative to the development of the existing instruments of compensatory action. For one thing, the coverage of risk proposed is only partial. Furthermore, other agencies, notably the International Monetary Fund, are equipped to deal with balance-of-payments contingencies other than a decline in export proceeds.

Our final view is that, given the necessary political acceptance, the insurance proposals set forth in this report appear to be workable. Many technical problems have become apparent even in the brief time at our disposal, and we cannot give unqualified assurance that further study can be overcome. We are entirely clear that the possibilities for additional fruitful action are enough to warrant the Commission on International Commodity Trade and other interested international bodies in setting such work on foot.

For reasons related both to our terms of reference and the time available, we did not attempt a systematic review of direct measures of commodity stabilization....

No attempt was made to judge whether existing international commodity agreements are effective in stabilizing fluctuations in export proceeds. We have noted, however, that buffer stocks are likely to be more effective if held and financed as an integral part of international commodity arrangements.

Perhaps our most interesting and important conclusion in relation to direct commodity stabilization is the importance of identifying difficulties which, if neglected, are likely to lead to persistent trends adverse to the interests of under-developed countries. This observation applies to the effective operation of compensatory arrangements no less than to direct stabilization measures. We strongly endorse the growing practice of holding meetings of importing and exporting countries within the framework of the United Nations, meetings which frequently become formalized in continuing study groups.

Arising from the importance for stabilization efforts of coping with structural problems is another point, the significance that must be attributed to providing expanding markets for the exports of under-developed countries. If the necessary growth of such exports is to be fostered, there is scope for constructive and sympathetic commercial and fiscal policies on the part of advanced countries. As a rule of economic strategy in the general interest, we consider that the advanced countries should recognize a certain priority in primary production for the under-developed countries.

In reviewing the implication of our conclusions, we have operated with a strong presumption against the setting up of additional international administrative agencies. This may be required to give effect to any insurance proposals, but it is premature to be specific on this point. One approach would be to provide the necessary finance for a "development insurance fund" as a trust fund to be administered by the most suitable existing organization.

As regards the approach to stabilization through direct commodity arrangements, we have stressed the importance of consultation through study groups within the framework of the United Nations. Any formal international commodity agreements or understandings include the requisite administrative provisions, and this calls for no further comment. We do consider it desirable, however, that acute commodity problems—particularly those which appear intractable when considered narrowly—be singled out for attention in an appropriate United Nations forum. This procedure may provide a useful political impetus to their solution.

3.5 COMPENSATORY FINANCING OF EXPORT FLUCTUATIONS *

In 1960, in response to an earlier request by the Commission on International Commodity Trade, the Fund prepared a study explaining its policies and procedures bearing on the compensatory financing of fluctuations in foreign exchange receipts from the export of primary commodities.[1] The main points in this study may be briefly summarized as follows:

(1) The provision of foreign exchange to Fund members to assist in the compensation of short-term fluctuations in the balance of payments constitute a legitimate use of Fund resources.[2] Among such fluctuations are some that arise primarily from variations in export prices and proceeds. However, in order that balance of payments deficits from this cause should be suitable for financing by the Fund, the member's policies must be such as to enable it, with the financial assistance it obtains from the Fund, to overcome its difficulties within a reasonably short period of time.

(2) It would be neither practicable nor desirable to make the amount of such assistance dependent on any automatic formula, or to provide any separate form of Fund assistance to deal with export fluctuations alone. The reasons for this are (a) that judgment is required to determine

the extent to which export fluctuations require, and are suitable for, compensatory financing in the light of the balance of payments as a whole, and the extent to which any compensation required should be provided by international transfers rather than by national reserve movements, and (b) that, if the Fund should give too much of its assistance automatically, its ability to influence countries toward the adoption of appropriate policies would be seriously impaired. Requests for drawings for all purposes in accordance with the Articles of Agreement are, however, treated liberally if they are within the gold tranche or the first credit tranche.

(3) Fund quotas (at the end of 1959) were considered adequate to provide for its primary exporting members a supplement to liquidity which, in the majority of cases, should be sufficient, in conjunction with their own resources, to enable them to deal with payments problems created by short-term fluctuations in exports or in receipts from abroad of the order experienced since World War II, provided they did their best to keep their income and costs adjusted to the longer-run changes in their external purchasing power.

(4) There appeared (as of the same date) to be no reason why a shortage of Fund resources should be a factor limiting the amount of assistance that the Fund would otherwise consider it desirable to extend to its members.

(5) Consequently, it was concluded that "members of the Fund that are taking appropriate steps to preserve internal financial stability and to maintain their balance of payments in equilibrium, taking good years with bad, and that are otherwise making satisfactory progress toward the fulfillment of the Fund's purposes can anticipate with confidence that financing will be available from the Fund which, in conjunction with a reasonable use of their own reserves, should be sufficient to enable

---

* From International Monetary Fund, *Compensatory Financing of Export Fluctuations,* Washington, D.C., February 1963, pp. 3-6, 9-14.

1. "Fund Policies and Procedures in Relation to the Compensatory Financing of Commodity Fluctuations," *Staff Papers,* Vol. VIII (1960-61), pp. 1-76.

2. Since the presentation of this study in April 1960, Fund transactions with primary exporting countries have greatly increased. Outstanding drawings by low-income primary exporters have nearly doubled over the last 3 years.

them to overcome temporary pay-ments difficulties arising from export fluctuations." [3]

Since the study summarized above was submitted to the United Nations in April 1960, the subject of compensatory financ-ing has been actively considered within the framework of the United Nations (UN) and of the Organization of American States (OAS), in particular by the UN Committee of Experts which reported in January 1961, [4] and by the OAS Group of Experts which reported in April 1962. [5]

In general, the international bodies in which the matter has been discussed have displayed understanding toward the Fund's policies on compensatory financing, as outlined above (including the restricted scope given to automatism in Fund trans-actions), and appreciation for the assist-ance which the Fund has been able to give under its present rules to primary exporting countries having export difficulties. How-ever, certain suggestions have been made for changes in policy that would permit an enhancement of the Fund's role in com-pensatory financing. Moreover, it has been argued that, even if the Fund should make a reasonable degree of progress in the direc-tion indicated, enough uncertainty would remain in the minds of governments as to their ability to draw on the Fund to justify the consideration of other possible international measures of compensatory financing. The suggestion has therefore been made that some new financial insti-tution separate from, though possibly affil-iated with, the Fund is needed to provide compensatory financing for export fluctua-tions, in amounts or of a kind or with a

3. *Ibid.*, p. 4.
4. United Nations, *International Compensation for Fluctuations in Commodity Trade* (Report by a Committee of Experts, E/CN.13/40, New York, 1961).
5. Organization of American States, *Final Re-port of the Group of Experts on the Stabilization of Export Receipts* (Washington, D.C., 1962)

degree of automatism that is either not praticable or not desirable for the Fund. In pursuance of this line of thought, the above mentioned UN Committee of Experts worked out schemes for a devel-opment Insurance Fund, which have sub-sequently been elaborated by the UN Secretariat, whereas the scheme of the OAS Expert Group is on a loan basis. . . .

The type of automatism envisaged in the various proposals that have been put forward—automatism of the "export com-pensatory" rather than of the "all purpose" type—has two principal features:

(1) A mathematical formula would be used to determine whether, and to what extent, exports in a particular year are to be considered so abnormally low as to require compensation, or so abnormally high as to permit the repayment of com-pensation received previously. No judg-ment would be made by the lending agency, in the light of any other informa-tion that might be available, as to whether, in a particular situation, the formula yields a reasonable estimate of normal exports.

(2) The lending agency, whether the Fund or a new agency, would make credit available to a country without question whenever the formula pointed to a statisti-cal justification on export grounds alone. No regard would be paid to the over-all balance of payments need for such credit, to the likelihood that the country would be able, in the light of the policies it was pur-suing, to repay the credits that were being granted or, in some proposals, to the amount that the country has already bor-rowed. The country itself could, of course, refuse to take up credits to which it was entitled or could repay credits before maturity.

With regard to the first point, the proposals now under consideration have assumed, virtually without question, that when exports are below the average for, say, the three preceding years they can safely be assumed to be abnormally low so that compensation would be appropriate. Statistical experiments, covering the post-war period, recently made for a large number of primary exporting countries, suggest, however, that this is by no means generally the case. The fact that exports in any given year have been lower (or higher) than they were in preceding years is very often an indication of a downward (or upward) trend which may well persist for some years to come. Export proceeds that seem low in relation to those of preceding years may well appear in retrospect as rather favorable. It follows from this that automatic formulae based on past and current export data can, at best, yield only rather unsatisfactory estimates of the true trend of exports. In the absence of foreknowledge of future exports, the least inaccurate estimate of the normal level in any given year is likely to be one that attributes a great weight to the exports of the year itself. Even when this is done, however, the extent to which it is possible to adjust export proceeds by adding or subtracting compensatory receipts or repayments so as to bring them closer to their true norm or to reduce their instability is limited.[6]

While great uncertainty must always attach to any attempt to estimate the medium-term trend or norm of exports, it is reasonable to assume that a better estimate could be made by the exercise of judgment based on an analysis of the causal factors at work than by any mathematical formula, however skillfully contrived, which is based on the mere statistical magnitude of current and previous exports.

In regard to the second aspect of automatism—the granting of credit irrespective of the general balance of payments

situation or of the policies of the country receiving assistance—it may be useful to set out existing Fund policies and their rationale.

Under present Fund policies "members are given the overwhelming benefit of the doubt in relation to requests for transactions within the "gold tranche," that is, for drawings which do not increase the Fund's holdings of the currency beyond an amount equal to the member's quota. The Fund's attitude to requests for transactions within the 'first credit tranche'—that is, transactions which bring the Fund's holdings of a member's currency above 100 per cent but not above 125 per cent of its quota—is a liberal one, provided that the member itself is making reasonable efforts to solve its problems. Requests for transactions beyond these limits require substantial justification. They are likely to be favorably received when the drawings or stand-by arrangements are intended to support a sound program aimed at establishing or maintaining the enduring stability of the member's currency at a realistic rate of exchange."[7]

In the higher tranches, the Fund has therefore wished to be satisfied that a sound set of policies is being followed. The Fund may have reached this conclusion before the question of a drawing arose—e.g., if it has a stand-by arrangement with the country in question. If such policies are being followed, no change in them would be needed to meet payments difficulties that are due solely to temporary situations in foreign markets, or to such factors as a temporary fluctuation in crops. The mere fact of a falling off in exports would not be taken as an indication that a corrective program was necessary or that the corrective program already envisaged should be intensified. On the other hand, a need for corrective policies might arise

6. See J. Marcus Fleming, Rudolf Rhomberg, and Lorette Boissonneault, "Export Norms and Their Role in Compensatory Financing," Part I, *Staff Papers*, Vol. X (1963), pp. 98–124.

7. International Monetary Fund, *Annual Report*, 1962, p. 31.

either because the decline in exports appeared to foreshadow a lasting weakening of the country's balance of payments or because (though the export decline itself might be purely temporary and self correcting) the country's monetary and financial policies were such as to provoke, sooner or later, balance of payments difficulties even under satisfactory export conditions. Recognition by the Fund of the need for corrective policies in either of the two circumstances outlined above does not mean that the Fund has seized the occasion of a member country's financial plight to press for immediate adoption of the full range of what might be construed as "ideal" policies; for example, the elimination of all payments restrictions, the adoption of full currency convertibility at an effective par value, the abolition of all multiple rates, etc. Reference to the policies followed in regard to these matters by the many countries that are using the Fund in the second or higher credit tranches or that have stand-by arrangements permitting such use would dispel at once the notion of such an approach by the Fund. In accordance, however, with the purposes set out in Article I of the Fund's Articles of Agreement, Fund assistance, at least beyond the gold tranche, is not made available to any country that makes no effort to move toward the elimination of those aspects of its exchange and monetary policies that are detrimental to the interests of the member itself or those of other members.

The general case against providing compensatory credit without inquiry into general balance of payments need or into the policies of the country concerned has been argued at length in "Fund Policies and Procedures in Relation to the Compensatory Financing of Commodity Fluctuations,"[8] and these arguments have not, in

general, been challenged. As suggested by the UN Committee of Experts, a country exposed to export fluctuations might feel more secure if it had access to resources on which it could draw without having to satisfy any international organization or lending government as to the type of domestic or international economic policy it was pursuing. Moreover, it is possible that the availability of international credit on an automatic basis at times when exports are low, and the necessity of repaying such credit at times when exports are high, would have some effect in inducing countries to attempt to keep their domestic expenditures and imports on an even keel, on the basis of reasonable expectations as to the medium-term trend of their exports and other receipts. These potential advantages, however, have to be weighed against the disadvantages of automatic credit geared to a single element in the balance of payments. In this connection it may be appropriate to mention two considerations in particular:

(1) Even a statistically accurate determination that exports in a particular year are below normal implies nothing at all as to the cause of the shortfall. The cause may be a decline in world demand or a crop failure brought about by a natural calamity. But the reason may also lie in domestic inflation, leading to increasingly overvalued exchange rates, government purchases for stockpile at prices above those prevailing in world markets, or other national policies. When declines in exports occur, a most careful consideration of their possible causes is needed in order to determine whether some of them may not be open to remedial action by the country itself, so as to prevent export declines in the future if similar circumstances recur.

Thus, while it is desirable that countries have access to financial means to compensate for fluctuations in exports, it is not particularly desirable, and may be against

8. *Staff Papers,* Vol. VIII (1960-61), pp. 1–76.

the genuine interest of the country concerned, that this finance should be provided automatically and without an exploration of the causes of the decline in exports and the measures that might be taken to improve exports in the future.

In this connection, it should be pointed out that the benefits which a country derives from reaching an understanding with the Fund as to the policies appropriate to its situation may extend beyond the financial assistance obtained from the Fund itself. In such circumstances, agreement with the Fund is likely to strengthen opinion abroad and at home regarding the country's creditworthiness, and thus to facilitate the attraction of capital from other sources, official as well as private.

(2) The total amount of short-term credit made available to a country by one agency or under one arrangement cannot be totally divorced from the amount made available on similar terms by another agency or under another arrangement by the same agency. It would be shortsighted to think that a country would be fully justified in borrowing a relatively large amount on short term to compensate for an export shortfall while totally disregarding the amount that it had already borrowed on short term for other purposes. Prudent countries would themselves see to it that their total indebtedness did not exceed what they could reasonably expect to repay, and this would take into account all indebtedness of a similar character. It would seem to be dubious wisdom to set up the terms of lending of an international agency in such a manner as to put governments under internal pressure to borrow sums that they themselves might consider beyond the bounds of prudence. If there are sensible limitations on total short-term borrowing, these limitations should be taken into account not only by the borrowing country itself but also in the policies of the international agency extending the credit.

4. REGIONAL INTEGRATION AND DEVELOPMENT—NOTE

Some of the questions raised above— how to increase the gains from trade, stimulate exports, stabilize export proceeds —are now receiving increasing attention in the context of regional economic integration. Various degrees of integration are possible,[1] but most interest centers on the potential role of customs unions and free trade areas.[2] Even though practical results are as yet only modest, there have been several proposals for economic union among underdeveloped countries, and more active efforts toward their establishment might be expected. As a basis for appraising specific proposals, we consider in this Note the benefits that might be derived from a customs union or free trade area and the difficulties that are likely to be encountered in their formation.

Advocates of an economic union believe that its formation will accelerate the devel-

1. At a level less general than a customs union or free trade association, regional integration might be directed simply toward "sectoral integration"—that is, the removal of trade restrictions on only a selected list of commodities, or the treatment of the problems of some one industry as a whole on a regional basis.

Beyond free trade in goods, a more comprehensive economic union might allow for the free movement of factors of production, a common monetary system, and the co-ordination of economic policies among the member countries. We are concerned here with only the implications of free trade in goods.

2. While both a customs union and free trade area provide for free trade among the member countries, a customs union also adopts a common external tariff.

opment of the member countries by (a) stimulating the establishment and expansion of manufacturing industries on a more rational basis, (b) increasing the gains from trade, and (c) providing benefits from intensified competiton.

In many developing countries import requirements are now growing rapidly, but the export-based capacity to import is insufficient to allow an unrestricted demand for imports. To meet the need for imports of essential materials and capital goods in face of a deficiency in foreign exchange, many countries have adopted a policy of deliberate import-substitution in consumer goods. When each country restricts its imports, however, and attempts to substitute home production, industrialization is unduly compartmentalized, and the uneconomic multiplication of import-competing industries is wasteful. In contrast, if manufacturing industry can be encouraged in the context of a customs union or free trade area, it may attain a higher level of productivity than now results from industrial protection in each country.

To reach an efficient scale of output, a modern manufacturing plant may have to produce a larger output than the low level of home demand in a single underdeveloped country can absorb. By pooling markets through the removal of internal trade barriers, a free-trade union might thus provide a sufficiently wide export market to make economies of scale realizable. Within a union, secondary industry can become more efficient as specialization occurs in the member country that acquires a comparative advantage. At the same time, the other constituent countries may now replace their imported manufactures from outside the union and thereby be able to spend a higher proportion of their foreign exchange on outside imports that are essential but cannot be produced efficiently within the union. A more rational pattern of production and trade within the region may therefore be an important result of integration.

The extension of the market, together with the inducement to get behind the external tariff wall, may also be particularly effective in attracting direct private foreign investment in manufacturing. And over time, there is the further possibility that new industries can become increasingly competitive on world markets and eventually be able to export manufactured goods to non-member countries. But this depends first on establishing a sufficiently wide market within the union to allow operation of a manufacturing industry on a large enough scale.

An expansion of trade among the member countries is also expected to result from the removal of trade barriers. If this takes the form of replacing high-cost producers within the region by lower-cost producers, the effect is one of "trade creation."[3] The gains from trade are then increased since the international division of labor is improved as resources shift into more efficient production. On the other hand, some of the intra-union trade may merely replace trade that formerly occurred between members and nonmembers. When the formation of an economic union has this "trade-diverting" effect, the international division of labor will be worsened if the outside source of supply is actually a low-cost source, and its product now becomes higher priced within the union because of the external tariff. In this case, there is an uneconomic diversion of output from the low-cost outside source to the high-cost supplier within the union, and the gains from trade are diminished.

In considering whether trade creation or trade diversion is likely to dominate in a particular union, we have to take into

3. Jacob Viner, *The Customs Union Issue*, New York, 1950, pp. 48-52.

account the pre-union level of tariff rates among the members, the level of the post-union external tariff compared with the pre-union tariff levels of each member country, the elasticities of demand for the imports on which duties are reduced, and the elasticities of supply of exports from the members and foreign sources. Conditions are more propitious for trade creation when each member's pre-union duties are high on the others' products, the members are initially similar in the products they produce but different in the pattern of relative prices at which they produce them, the external tariff of the union is low compared with the pre-union tariff levels of the members, and the production within the union of commodities that are substitutes for outside imports can be undertaken at a lower cost.

The formation of a free-trade union might also result in an improvement—or at least the forestalling of a deterioration in—the region's commodity terms of trade. This is possible if there is a reduction in the supply of exports from the union, or the demand by members of the union is reduced for imports from outside, or the bargaining power of the members in trade negotiations is strengthened. But unless the members of the union are the chief suppliers on the world market or constitute a large part of the world market for their imports, they are unlikely to be able to exercise sufficient monopolistic or monopsonistic power to influence their terms of trade by raising duties on their trade with the outside world or by inducing outsiders to supply their goods more cheaply. Moreover, when free trade is confined only to the region, there is the risk of retaliation through the formation of other economic blocs. A union may thereby inhibit the realization of the more extensive gains from the "universal" approach to free trade.

Finally, regional integration might be beneficial in encouraging competition among the member countries. Technical efficiency in existing industries might then be improved as marginal firms are forced to reduce their costs, resources are reallocated from less efficient to more efficient firms, and monopolies that had previously been established behind tariff walls are no longer in a sheltered position. Further, the stimulation of competition within each country may yield not only a better utilisation of given resources, but may also raise the rate of growth of productive resources. This may result from stronger incentives to adopt new methods of production, to replace obsolete equipment more rapidly, and to innovate more rapidly with more and better investment.[4]

In practice, however, a number of objections have been raised against proposals for regional integration, and actual negotiations have encountered serious difficulties. As is true for a union among even advanced countries, political problems take precedence, nations will guard against a sacrifice of their sovereignty, and the administration of the union may be extremely complex. For underdeveloped countries, these problems tend to be especially acute since many have only recently gained political independence, newly established national governments may be excessively concerned with their own national interests and needs, and the administrative requirements may be beyond their present capacity. Aside from the political and administrative difficulties, there are also several economic objections to a union.

To begin with, it may be argued that the case for an economic union is in reality weak when the constituent countries have not yet established many industries. Limitations on the supply side may be more of a deterrent to the creation of an

4. See Paul Streeten, *Economic Integration*, Leyden, 1961, pp. 26–7.

industry than is the narrow market on the side of demand. If production conditions do not also improve, the mere extension of the consumer market will not be sufficient to create industries. Moreover, when manufacturing industry is only at a rudimentary stage in the member countries, there is not much scope for eliminating high-cost manufacturers within the region. Nor is there much scope for realizing the benefits of increased competition when there are not yet similar ranges of rival products, produced under different cost conditions, in the several member nations. A union will not cause substantial improvement in the utilization of resources unless industries have already been established but need wider markets than the national economy can provide for the realization of economies of scale, and the member countries have been protecting the same kinds of industry, but have markedly different ratios of factor-efficiency in these industries to factor-efficiency in non-protected branches of production.

It has been pointed out that the case for a union is strongest among countries that have little foreign trade in proportion to their domestic production, but do a high proportion of their foreign trade with one another.[5] When these conditions prevail, there is less possibility for introducing, within each member country, a distortion of the price relation between goods from other member countries and goods from outside the union, and more of a possibility for eliminating any distortion by tariffs of the price-relations between domestic goods and imports from other member countries. There is therefore greater likelihood that the union will improve the use of resources and raise real income.

5. R. G. Lipsey, "The Theory of Customs Unions: A General Survey," *Economic Journal,* September 1960, pp. 507–9. This conclusion rests, however, on the assumption that there are no productive economies of large scale.

A union among underdeveloped countries, however, is unlikely to conform to these conditions. The ratio of foreign trade to domestic production is generally high for these countries, and the actual volume of intra-regional trade is normally only a small proportion of the region's total foreign trade. The gain from regional integration would therefore be small. The basic difficulty is that, with existing trade-patterns, the formation of a union is likely to cause a considerable amount of wasteful "trade diversion." Over the longer run, comparative costs and trade-patterns may change, and economies of scale may give rise to competitive advantages as development proceeds, so that the scope for "trade creation" will become greater within the union. But the immediate gain is small, and the longer run prospects for the creation of new trade are not likely to influence current decisions to join a union.

Besides the possibility of "trade diversion," other undesirable consequences may result from a union. The member countries are unlikely to benefit equally, and some members may feel that others are gaining at their expense. A country may have a strong comparative advantage in only primary products and will sell to other members only goods that it could as readily export to outside countries. At the same time, manufacturing industry may become highly localized within one country in the union, and the other members may then contend that if they too had been able to adopt tariff protection against their partners, they would have also been able to attract industry. A non-industrialized member country may further complain that in buying from an industrialized partner, instead of importing from the outside, it is losing revenue equal to the duty on outside manufactures. And, with a common external tariff, member countries no longer have the discretionary power to use variations in the tariff for the purpose of adjusting their national revenues to their own requirements. The internal strains that arise from uneven development among the member countries may thus make it extremely difficult to preserve a free-trade area. It may be possible for the union to correct some of the inequalities through a system of public finance transfers among members, a regional development bank, encouragement of free factor movements, regional policies for the location of industry, the pooling of overhead costs of public services, or co-ordination of development policies. But unless the union is strong enough to adopt these other measures and distribute the gains more evenly, its stability may be threatened.

We may conclude that while there are potential benefits to be derived from an economic union, especially over the longer run, the immediate gains should not be over-estimated, and due attention must be given to the possible undesirable consequences. If a union is to be effective, it must be a strong one—and most proposals for regional integration do not yet show the promise of sufficient cohesion. Although a comprehensive form of union may not now be practicable for most underdeveloped regions, there are still substantial advantages that can be derived from a more *ad hoc* functional type of regional co-operation that operates within a framework broader than that of simply sectoral integration but narrower than a free trade area or full customs union. Until the risks of joining a free-trade union are diminished, the intermediate approach may therefore be the most feasible alternative, even though a customs union may be the ultimate objective.

5. BIBLIOGRAPHICAL NOTE

1. The following readings offer various interpretations of the problem of development-through-trade: R. E. Baldwin, "Patterns of Development in Newly Settled Regions," *Manchester School of Economic and Social Studies*, May 1956; Baldwin, "Export Technology and Development from a Subsistence Level," *Economic Journal*, March 1963; P. A. Baran, "On the Political Economy of Backwardness," *Manchester School of Economic and Social Studies*, January 1952; K. Berrill, "International Trade and the Rate of Economic Growth," *Economic History Review*, April 1960; J. Bhagwati, "Immiserizing Growth: A Geometrical Note," *Review of Economic Studies*, June 1958; Bhagwati, "Growth, Terms of Trade and Comparative Advantage," *Economia Internazionale*, August 1959; Bhagwati, "Economic Development and International Trade," *Pakistan Economic Journal*, December 1959; A. K. Cairncross, "International Trade and Economic Development," *Kyklos*, Vol. XIII, No. 4, 1960; Bhagwati, "International Trade and Economic Development," *Economica*, August 1961; H. B. Chenery, "Comparative Advantage and Development Policy," *American Economic Review*, March 1961; G. Haberler, *International Trade and Economic Development*, Cairo, 1959; J. R. Hicks, *Essays in World Economics*, Oxford, 1959, chap. 8; H. G. Johnson, *International Trade and Economic Growth*, Cambridge, 1958, chap. III; Johnson, "Economic Development and International Trade," *Pakistan Economic Journal*, December 1959; C. P. Kindleberger, "Foreign Trade and Economic Growth: Lessons from Britain and France, 1850 to 1931," *Economic History Review*, December 1961; J. V. Levin, *The Export*

Economies, Cambridge, 1960; A. N. McLeod, "Trade and Investment in Underdeveloped Areas: A Comment," *American Economic Review,* June 1951; G. M. Meier, *International Trade and Development,* New York, 1963; Hla Myint, "The Gains from International Trade and the Backward Countries," *Review of Economic Studies,* Vol. XXII (2), No. 58, 1954–55; Myint, "The 'Classical Theory' of International Trade and the Underdeveloped Countries," *Economic Journal,* June 1958; G. Myrdal, *Rich Lands and Poor,* New York, 1957; D. C. North, "Location Theory and Regional Economic Growth," *Journal of Political Economy,* June 1955; R. Nurkse, "Some International Aspects of the Problem of Economic Development," *American Economic Review, Papers and Proceedings,* May 1952; Nurkse, *Patterns of Trade and Development,* Stockholm, 1956; Nurkse, "International Trade Theory and Development Policy," in *Economic Development for Latin America* (H. S. Ellis, ed.), New York, 1961; R. Prebisch, "Commericial Policy in the Underdeveloped Countries," *American Economic Review, Papers and Proceedings,* May 1959; K. N. Raj and A. K. Sen, "Alternative Patterns of Growth Under Conditions of Stagnant Export Earnings," *Oxford Economic Papers,* February 1961; D. Seers, "An Approach to the Short-Period Analysis of Primary Producing Economies," *Oxford Economic Papers,* February 1959; Seers, "A Model of Comparative Rates of Growth in the World Economy," *Economic Journal,* March 1962; J. Sheahan, "International Specialization and the Concept of Balanced Growth," *Quarterly Journal of Economics,* May 1958; H. W. Singer, "The Distribution of Gains Between Investing and Borrowing Countries," *American Economic Review, Papers and Proceedings,* May 1950; United Nations, Economic Commission for Asia and the Far East, "Trade Policy as a Means of Implementing or Promoting Economic Development," *Economic Bulletin for Asia and the Far East,* May 1957; J. Viner, *International Trade and Economic Development,* Glencoe, 1952.

2. Problems of export stabilization for primary exporting countries are considered in the following: P. T. Bauer and F. W. Paish, "The Reduction of Fluctuations in the Incomes of Primary Producers," *Economic Journal,* December 1952; S. Caine, "Instability of Primary Commodity Prices: A Protest and a Proposal," *Economic Journal,* September 1954; J. S. Davis, "Experience Under Intergovernmental Commodity Agreements," *Journal of Political Economy,* June 1946; M. Fleming et al., "Export Norms and Their Role in Compensatory Financing," *International Monetary Fund Staff Papers,* March 1963; Food and Agriculture Organization of the United Nations, *Report of the FAO/ECAFE Centre on Policies to Support and Stabilize Agricultural Prices and Incomes in Asia and the Far East,* Rome, 1959; M. Friedman, "The Reduction of Fluctuations in the Incomes of Primary Producers," *Economic Journal,* December 1954; R. Frei (ed.), "Stabilization and Development of Primary Producing Countries: Symposium II," *Kyklos,* Vol. 12, No. 3, 1959; General Agreement on Tariffs and Trade, *Trends in International Trade; A Report by a Panel of Experts,* Geneva, 1958; A. I. MacBean, "Problems of Stabilization Policy in Underdeveloped Countries," *Oxford Economic Papers,* October 1962; R. F. Mikesell, "Commodity Agreements and Aid to Developing Countries," *Law and Contemporary Problems,* Spring 1963; R. M. Stern, "International Compensation for Fluctuations in Commodity Trade," *Quarterly Journal of Economics,* May 1963; B. C. Swerling, *Current Issues in Commodity Policy,* Princeton, June 1962; United Nations, Department of Economic Affairs, *Instability in Export Mar-*

kets of *Under-Developed Countries*, New York, 1952, and *Commodity Trade and Economic Development*, New York, 1953; P. L. Yates, *Commodity Controls: A Study of Primary Products*, London, 1943.

3. The following may be consulted for a more intensive consideration of regional economic integration as a means of accelerating development: R. L. Allen, "Integration in Less Developed Areas," *Kyklos*, Vol. XIV, No. 3, 1961; B. Balassa, *The Theory of Economic Integration*, Homewood, 1961; R. S. Bhambri, "Customs Unions and Underdeveloped Countries," *Economia Internazionale*, March 1962; S. Dell, "Economic Integration and the American Example," *Economic Journal*, March 1959; R. F. Harrod, "Economic Development and Asian Regional Cooperation," *Pakistan Development Review*, Spring 1962; H. G. Johnson, "The Economic Theory of Customs Union," *Pakistan Economic Journal*, March 1960; H. Kitamura et al., "Special Issue on Asian Trade," *Pakistan Development Review*, Winter 1962; R. G. Lipsey, "The Theory of Customs Union: Trade Diversion and Welfare," *Economica*, February 1957; Lipsey, "The Theory of Customs Unions: A General Survey," *Economic Journal*, September 1960; J. E. Meade, *Problems of Economic Union*, London, 1953; Meade, *The Theory of Customs Unions*, Amsterdam, 1955; R. F. Mikesell, *Intra-Regional Trade and Economic Development*, Washington, D.C., 1958; R. L. Sammons, "Proposals for a Common Market in Latin America," *Public Policy*, Cambridge, 1960; T. Scitovsky, "International Trade and Economic Integration as a Means of Overcoming the Disadvantages of a Small Nation," *Economic Consequences of the Size of Nations* (E. A. G. Robinson, ed.), New York, 1960; United Nations, Economic Commission for Latin America, *The Latin American Common Market*, New York, 1959; J. Viner, *The Customs Union Issue*, New York, 1961.

VIII

SCOPE OF DEVELOPMENT PLANNING

WHILE ALL THE FOREGOING CHAPTERS have had some policy implications, we now want to bring the leading policy issues together in a more systematic fashion. This chapter and the next focus directly on the choices that confront governments undertaking development planning. Before concentrating on specific techniques of development planning, we first consider in this chapter the general case for planning and the question of its scope.

Some of the materials in section 1 argue against the effectiveness of the price system for attaining the objectives of development (1.1, 1.2, 1.3). The market mechanism is criticized as being either ineffective, unreliable, or irrelevant for the problems now encountered by developing nations. It is contended that the price system exists in only a rudimentary form in many underdeveloped countries and that market forces are too weak to accomplish the changes needed for accelerated development. Even a fairly well-defined price system may be considered unreliable, it is claimed, when market prices of goods and factors are not a true reflection of the opportunity costs of these goods and factors to society. Above all, it is believed that the price system must be superseded when the determination of the amount and composition of investment is too important to be left to a multitude of individual investment decisions, and when the tasks of the economy entail large structural changes over a long period ahead instead of simply marginal adjustments in the present period.

On the other hand, it may be argued that the objections to the market system are relatively unimportant compared with the essential functions of the market, and that the disadvantages of detailed planning by a central authority are far more serious than the deficiencies of the market system. As Professor Johnson stresses, the market is extremely valuable in the context of development as an administrative instrument that is relatively cheap to operate (1.4). Development policy might therefore be better devoted to improving and strengthening the market system than to supplanting the market with detailed controls.

In section 2, we consider the argument that a "big push" in the form of a high minimum amount of investment is necessary to overcome the obstacles to development (2.1). As between the relative roles of the public and private sectors, advocates of a "big push" assign a decisive position to the public sector in determining directly the amount and composition of investment. Criticizing the "big push" argument, Professor Ellis emphasizes the limits of possible gain, the risks and costs of an accelerated rate of investment through state intervention, and the merits of alternative policies (2.2). Although it is instructive to review the "balanced growth" doctrine (Chapter V, section 2) for its relation to the "big push" theory, it should be noted that the principle of balanced growth is not a necessary component of the big push theory, and balanced growth need not be dependent upon a large amount of public investment or dominance of the public sector.

To indicate the extent to which the public sector is being emphasized in development programming, section 3 examines in more detail the public expenditure programs of several developing countries. Summary data are provided on the share of the public sector in the spending of the national income for several countries in Asia and the Far East (3.1); the allocation of public investment by economic sectors is also indicated (3.2). The next selection offers, on the basis of African experience, some cautionary comments that deserve attention when interpreting the role of public investment and considering the management of public enterprises that are established as part of the development program. The last three selections concentrate on the developmental role of investment in the public and private sectors of Nigeria, India, and Ceylon (3.4, 3.5, 3.6).

1. DEVELOPMENT PLANNING AND THE PRICE SYSTEM

1.1 THE FLAW IN THE MECHANISM OF MARKET FORCES *

The free and unimpeded mechanism of market forces would lead to a maximum national income according to the liberal classical doctrine. Disregarding an ethical value-judgment about personal income distribution and special cases of increasing

* From Paul N. Rosenstein-Rodan, "Programming in Theory and in Italian Practice," in Massachusetts Institute of Technology, Center for International Studies, *Investment Criteria and Economic Growth*, Cambridge, 1955; Asia Publishing House, Bombay, 1961, pp. 19-22. Reprinted by permission.

returns to scale the maximum would also be an optimum national income. Any conscious deliberate active economic policy designed to influence the amount and the composition of investment could not, according to this school, raise national income in the long run. It is the contention of this paper that the opposite is true, that an economic policy designed to influence the amount and composition of investment can raise the rate of economic growth and increase national income.

Maximization of national income would be reached, according to the "liberal" school, by the working of the mechanism of supply and demand on assumption of competitive conditions and of small changes per unit of time, in four stages or "equilibria": (1) allocation of given stock of consumers' goods, (2) allocation of production on assumption of given stock of *equipment*, land, and labor, (3) allocation of investment on assumption of given stock of labor, land, and capital. A fourth equilibrium condition is provided by Say's law.

It is true that the price mechanism works perfectly under those assumptions in the first stage, i.e., in allocation of given stocks of consumers' goods. It works less perfectly, but tolerably well, in the second stage, when we replace the assumption of given stocks of consumers' goods by flows of supply of these goods from given stocks of equipment, raw materials, and labor.

The price mechanism does not work in this sense, however, in the third equilibrium when we drop the assumption of given fixed capital and assume that the amount and composition of investment is to be determined by a multitude of individual investment decisions.

The individual investment decision may lead to nonoptimum allocation of resources for the following reasons:

a. The investor maximizes the private, not the social net marginal product. External economies are not sufficiently exploited. Complementarity of industries is so great that simultaneous inducement rather than hope for autonomous coincidence of investment is called for.

b. The lifetime of equipment is long (say ten years) so that the investor's foresight is likely to be more imperfect than that of the buyer and seller or of the producer. The individual investor's risk may be higher than that confronting an over-all investment program. The costs of an erroneous investment decision are high; punishment in the form of loss of capital afflicts not only the investor but also the national economy.

c. Because of the indivisibility (lumpiness) of capital, large rather than small changes are involved. Yet the price-mechanism works perfectly only under the assumption of small changes.

d. Capital markets though often well organized are notoriously imperfect markets, governed not only by prices but also by institutional or traditional rationing quotas.

The investment theory is indeed the weakest link in the "liberal" theory.

It is finally recognized even by the strongest advocates of a free economy that an equilibrium between aggregate demand and aggregate supply (i.e., the dynamic monetary equilibrium) cannot itself be ensured by trusting to the automatic responses of a free economy. This task can only be discharged by a deliberate policy. Without an equilibrium of aggregate demand and aggregate supply, however, prices cease to be reliable parameters of choice and the price mechanism breaks down.

The automatic responses of the market economy do not ensure an optimum allocation in two out of four markets. They allocate efficiently stocks of consumers' goods, and supplies of these goods flowing from stocks of equipment, but they do not function efficiently in the fields of investment and monetary equilibrium.

Programming is just another word for rational, deliberate, consistent, and coordinated economic policy. It is only spelling out explicitly what was always attempted implicitly in any monetary (fiscal and commercial) policy. Like Mr. Jourdain who talked prose all his life, programming at least in the field of monetary policy was always practiced, though it used shorthand rules of thumb or the "practical man's flairs, hunches, instincts and insights" rather than fully spelled out "White Papers" on output and employment. Neutral Government is as unrealistic an assumption as Neutral Money.

Monetary (fiscal and commercial) policy is a form of programming using indirect means for the achievement of its aims and targets. In its first pre-Wicksellian stage its only aim was equilibrium between aggregate demand and aggregate supply without distinguishing too clearly between investment and consumption. It became more purposeful in its second post-Wicksellian stage differentiating between and choosing its impact effects on various sectors of national income. In its third post-Keynesian stage it aims not only at *a* monetary equilibrium but at one which assures full employment and more and more also one (not necessarily the same) which assures the optimum rate of growth. In this third stage programming concerns not only the amount but also the composition of investment.

The *aim* of programming is to assure the maximum national income through time. For this purpose it tries to maximize the amount and to optimize the composition of investment. The *means* employed may be either indirect (monetary, fiscal and commercial policy as well as providing information on economic trends besides other incentives and disincentives) or direct (public investment). Even if no direct means were to be employed programming would be necessary in order to inform investors of short- and long-run trends, notably of intersectoral demands resulting from complementarity of industries (revealed by a periodically revised input-output table) and of indirect effects of investment on future demand of domestic, imported, or so far exported goods. Such information might guide and favorably influence the composition of investment.

The need for an active economic policy,

even if it were to employ only indirect means, can hardly be denied. Agreement on this point may conceal, however, two different conceptions. The "liberal" considers State intervention as an occasionally necessary medicine. "Nobody denies that clean living is the best way to good health, but this is really not a sufficient reason to deny that it is sometimes necessary to take medicine." This view is based on the assumption that private investment decisions normally lead to an optimum position. The other view considers that a continuous active economic policy, beyond measures to assure an equilibrium between aggregate demand and aggregate supply, is necessary, since the multitude of dispersed individual uninfluenced decisions will not lead to the maximization of national income. The real question is how far programming should extend, what it should cover, what degrees of "freedom" it should leave between and within the various economic sectors....

1.2 ON PLANNING IN BACKWARD COUNTRIES *

Planning is at the same time much more necessary and much more difficult to execute in backward than in advanced countries.

In the first place, planning requires a strong, competent and incorrupt administration. It must be strong enough to be able to enforce its measures, such as to collect taxes from the peasantry, or to enforce a rationing system without black markets, measures which even so ancient a government as that of France has not found itself fully able to enforce. It must have a competent administrative service, with trained personnel, able to understand the large issues that are at stake, and to act reasona-

---

* From W. Arthur Lewis, *The Principles of Economic Planning,* George Allen & Unwin Ltd., London, 1952, pp. 121-8. Reprinted by permission.

bly and rapidly. And it must be free of all charge of corruption, since, whereas men will bear many restrictions from a government which they believe to be acting fairly and solely in the public interest (however mistakenly) without respect of persons, they will sooner or later resist violently measures which are corruptly administered, however acceptable the measures themselves may be.

Now a strong, competent and incorrupt administration is just what no backward country possesses, and in the absence of such an administration it is often much better that governments should be *laisser-faire* than that they should pretend to plan. This was indeed the essence of the case for *laisser-faire* made by eighteenth century writers, who saw the mess that was made by weak, incompetent and corrupt governments, and sought therefore to confine the activities of government within the narrowest practicable limits, so as to minimise the damage that they might do. The alternative approach was that of Lenin, who fully realised the impossibility of using a backward administrative service for planning, and who sought therefore to create, in his Communist Party, a highly trained and disciplined priestly order, on which he could rely to carry out his instructions. At least we may say this: the first objective of planners must be to create an administrative machine that can do the work of planning; to train young men academically and in the tasks of administration, and to weed out mercilessly the incompetent and the corrupt. And, secondly, in the meantime no administration should be loaded with tasks more numerous or more delicate than it can handle; the quantity and forms of planning should be limited strictly within the capacity of the machine.

In backward countries governments have usually much leeway to make up in fulfilling the normally accepted functions of governments long before they get on to more controversial matters. The usual public works are usually in a deplorable state. Roads and communications have to be planned; rivers to be brought under control, to put an end to flooding, and utilised for irrigation and electric power; water supplies must be conserved, and pipes laid to bring water to reasonably accessible places; elementary public health measures are wanting, the draining of swamps, the control of infectious disease, the regulation of sanitation, the establishment of a public health service. Forests, schools, geological research, hospitals, courts, police—one could continue this list at length. City dwellers in Western Europe or the U.S.A. take for granted a vast network of government services which are absent or grossly inadequate in backward countries, and which it is the recognised first duty of governments to provide.

But the difficulty which faces these governments is that they cannot expand their own services unless they can raise money to pay for them, and they cannot raise all the money they need because their peoples are too poor. They are therefore driven to concern themselves with measures to increase the national income. This is the sense in which planning is more necessary in backward countries. In advanced countries the national income increases steadily from decade to decade even if the government does not "interfere" in economic life. But in many backward countries there is either stagnation or retrogression, and a progressive government is naturally driven to enquire what plans it may make to bring about economic progress.

The crux of the problem is usually a backward system of agriculture—lack of scientific knowledge, poor equipment, inefficient marketing, insecure tenure, an uneconomically small scale of operation, and, frequently also, rural overpopulation. There are recognised remedies—an agricultural extension service, cooperative and other provision of credit, cooperative and other reorganisation of marketing, legislation to protect the security of tenants—but they make little headway unless the interest and enthusiasm of the farmers is awakened and held. Once the farmers begin to desire progress almost all difficulties can be overcome, but so long as they are apathetic and uninterested very little can be done. The first task of progressive governments in the sphere of agriculture is to arouse the enthusiasm of their people for new knowledge and new ways of life. How to awake and capture enthusiasm is the first problem in mass education. It is also politically the first task of new popular governments, and it is because only new popular governments can capture such enthusiasm that it is only in the countries which have had such governments that there has been substantial progress in agriculture among backward peoples in the last thirty years.

The most difficult of all the agricultural problems is the small size of holdings in peasant countries, frequently of five acres or less. All such countries have to go through an agrarian revolution at the end of which is some form of large scale agriculture, whether it be the capitalist farm, or the collective farm, or the state farm, or merely the family farm, working large areas with machinery but without hired labour. In the past an agrarian revolution has always been violent, even where, as in England, the violence may have been cloaked in Parliamentary forms. It remains to be seen whether popular governments can awaken sufficient enthusiasm for their mass education programmes to carry through such revolutions in future by consent. So far the omens are unfavourable. Popular revolutions have just the opposite result. Large estates are broken up into small uneconomic holdings sometimes not exceeding five acres, with disastrous effects on productivity. Techniques for combin-

ing democracy with large scale agriculture have still to be worked out.

Large scale agriculture usually requires fewer people per acre than small holdings, and therefore where the countryside is overpopulated and there are not enough new lands reclaimable by drainage or irrigation, it is not desirable to make an agrarian revolution without providing new employment opportunities outside agriculture. An agricultural and an industrial revolution always go together, the first releasing the labour which the second draws off the land. Governments of backward countries have therefore to put into their agricultural programmes projects for industrialisation.

Since this problem is one of disguised unemployment it is sometimes suggested (for example by implication in the Bombay plan for India) that it can be solved, as is unemployment in industrial countries, simply by increasing the quantity of money. But this is not so. Suppose that the government starts to build roads, and creates the money to pay wages and salaries. In the first place, the propensity to import is very high; much of this money goes abroad to import food, clothes, bicycles and so on. There is then a strain on the balance of payments unless exports can be increased correspondingly, but this is not easy, and cannot be achieved even by devaluation. If it were achieved, the quantity of goods on the home market would be correspondingly reduced—the extra imports go to receivers of the new incomes, but receivers of old incomes have now to yield up part of the old produce to these same people and part for export, and so there is inflation created at home. The situation is then the same as if the government controlled imports and did not allow the new money to be spent abroad. This, in practice, is what it has to do; control of the exchanges is one of the first things planners have to do in backward countries because they are not able to expand exports adequately in view of their high propensity to import.

Control of the exchanges does not, however, solve the problem; the new money then circulates at home and forces prices up. In an industrial country this would cause entrepreneurs to take on labour, and output would expand rapidly. But in an agricultural country as likely as not when prices rise the farmers begin by consuming more of their own produce, thus reducing the amount available to the towns and raising prices still further. They next go to the towns with their extra money to buy imported goods, and on finding that these are now in short supply (because the circulation of new money has increased the demand but not the supply) they may return home and reduce their sowings. This, for example, is what happened in Russia until agriculture was collectivised, and was one of the chief reasons why the Government was so anxious to bring the farms under its control. In an industrial country an increase in the quantity of money increases employment and output, but in an agricultural country, even when there is unemployment, open or disguised, an increase in the quantity of money frequently reduces output.

It follows that if governments of backward countries try to finance their investments by creating money they will cause inflation. Investment must be financed either by taxation, or by borrowing. In very backward countries the propensity to import is almost unity; that is, almost all extra income is spent on imports, and even local borrowing cannot finance investment unless the lenders either lend out of foreign reserves, or reduce their own demands on imports to the full extent of the propensity to import.

It also follows that more positive steps are needed than the mere creation of money if the unemployed are to be absorbed in productive enterprise. In an industrial country there are entrepreneurs eager to respond to the prospects of increased profits by installing new industrial enterprises and engaging workers. But in an agricultural country the enterprise and experience are confined to agriculture and to commerce. Moreover, because the "external economies" are large in industrial production, small isolated factories seldom pay, and entrepreneurs will not easily establish in new areas when they have a choice of old areas already well supplied with cheap power laid on, with trained industrial labour, with information services, and with all the other accessories of a developed industrial centre. In these days if one wishes to develop secondary industries, one must do it on a large scale, and deliberately set out to create the facilities which factories use in common, and which cannot be provided cheaply on a small scale. That is why the trading estate, financed by government, is now the established technique for developing depressed areas. And it is also why, once an area has started to decline, it tends to decline cumulatively; and once it has started to expand, it tends also to expand cumulatively. Any backward country which wishes to encourage industrialisation—and they nearly all must if only as a part of their agricultural programme—must, as a minimum, set about building a trading estate, and offering inducements to industrial entrepreneurs to set up in its territory.

Foreign capital cannot be avoided, even if the government decides to build and operate all the plants itself. The machinery must come from abroad, and the workers who build the factories, the roads, the factory workers' houses and so on will want to spend a large part of their wages on imported goods. Some foreign exchange can be found by using a strict exchange control to cut out all luxury imports, and to pare down even necessaries; and by using what is thus saved to buy machinery. (There must be corresponding taxation or borrowing to mop up the incomes thus diverted to the home market, in order to prevent inflation.) But backward countries are too poor to be able to provide much capital simply by cutting down luxuries. If they are to industrialise substantially they have either to cut severely into the consumption of necessaries, or else to borrow abroad. A ruthless dictatorship can cut consumption to the desired extent, but a democracy will always have to rely largely on foreign capital in its early stages of development.

The quickest way to ease the strain on the foreign exchanges, and to reduce the dependence on foreign borrowing, is to plan the new investment in such a way that its produce becomes rapidly available, and adds to exports or can be substituted for imports. Export industries have first priority. Next comes food. In most backward countries output is low partly because people are undernourished or malnourished. Investments which increase the output of food, such as by irrigation, or reclaiming lands, or increasing manuring or livestock, are of the greatest urgency, especially if they are such as to yield their results rapidly. There is also a high propensity to import food, so such investments quickly reduce the strain on foreign reserves. Then there are the clothing industries and building materials, which also have a high import propensity. Weaving, knitting and the making of clothes and of boots and shoes are simple industrial processes, and are always among the first to be developed. Building materials depend on the existence of suitable local earths and forests; where these are available they should be rapidly exploited.

Now industry cannot flourish if there are no industrial resources whatever in the territory—especially if there is no source whatever of power—and however overcrowded an area may be, if it has no industrial resources it must seek other sources of employment—a tourist industry, a film industry, or failing all else employment in other lands that permit migration. Industry depends also on a sizeable home market. There are many areas that are very overcowded, but which nevertheless have too small a total population to be able to support industry. The world will get into a mess if each small backward political unit embarks upon industrialisation. The remedy for most of these units is political and economic federation, which, by widening the market, increases specialisation, and makes it possible to develop economically.

There are also backward countries whose problem is not overpopulation but under-population, perhaps the classical example being the colony of Northern Rhodesia whose population of one and a half million is dispersed over an area three times the size of Great Britain. In such countries the problem is rather that of husbanding one's resources. To build roads, schools, waterworks and other capital goods all over the country would be much too costly. One must start in small areas, encourage the population to concentrate there, and move outward only as numbers increase. How to plan new settlements systematically is a subject as old as Gibbon Wakefield, and one in which new techniques have been developed in recent years, especially by the Dutch in the out islands of the former Netherlands East Indies. The problems here are quite different from those of the overpopulated backward areas.

It can thus be seen that planning in backward countries imposes much bigger tasks on governments than does planning in advanced countries. The government has to do many things which can in advanced countries be left to entrepreneurs.

It has to create industrial centres, to put through an agricultural revolution, to control the foreign exchanges most strictly, and in addition to make up a great leeway of public services and of ordinary economic legislation. And all this has to be done through a civil service that is usually much inferior to that of an advanced country. Why then do backward countries take more readily to planning? Because their need is also so obviously much greater. And it is also this that enables them to carry it through in spite of error and incompetence. For, if the people are on their side, nationalistic, conscious of their backwardness, and anxious to progress, they willingly bear great hardships and tolerate many mistakes, and they throw themselves with enthusiasm into the job of regenerating their country. Popular enthusiasm is both the lubricating oil of planning, and the petrol of economic development—a dynamic force that almost makes all things possible. We in the United Kingdom felt this during the war, and can understand the claims of Russia in the 1930s or of Jugoslavia today to have awakened this dynamic enthusiasm and to be conquering all things with it. Even the most backward country will progress rapidly if its government knows how to tap this dynamic force.

1.3 THE CENTRAL ROLE OF PLANNING *

Planning appears to have been widely accepted as an essential and pivotal means of guiding and accelerating economic development in under-developed countries. That the functioning of the traditional economies left alone may perpetuate stagnation and wide fluctuations, that private initiative unaided may not easily gather

* From United Nations, Economic Commission for Asia and the Far East, "A Decade of Development Planning and Implementation in the ECAFE Region," *Economic Bulletin for Asia and the Far East*, Vol. XII, No. 3, December 1961, pp. 1–2.

sufficient momentum to generate economic growth, that the market mechanism with all its imperfections cannot be solely relied on for mobilizing and utilizing effectively the available resources to achieve a maximum possible rate of growth—these are the basic reasons for planned economic development. Broadly speaking, planning inevitably involves at least some centralized decision-making and some government action in effecting such decisions in a co-ordinated way.

There are in the real world no completely planned and completely unplanned economies; planning is obviously a matter of degree. In the countries of the region, the degree of planning varies widely. Thus, there is on the one hand the centrally planned economy in mainland China (and also north Korea and north Viet-Nam) where most labour, material and equipment resources are allocated by the Government to the majority of the production units, which dispose of the major part of their products according to central direction. On the other hand, there is the predominantly private enterprise economy of Japan, in which planning means chiefly projection by the Government, of the economic activity (including that of the Government) and the influence of the Government on the rate of growth through fiscal and monetary policies. In between these two extremes, come the other countries of the region with different shades of "mixed economy," in which planning contains two important elements, namely (i) the government's direct utilization of saving to carry out investment and management of resources for production, particularly in providing economic and social infrastructure, and (ii) the government's measures to facilitate, stimulate, guide and even control private economic activity. It goes without saying that in all these countries, regardless whether their economy is centrally planned, predominantly private enterprise, or "mixed," the government plays the common role of creating the general conditions for development, e.g. political and monetary stability, and of making known the available resources and development potentialities. Depending on the degrees of planning, countries of the region encounter different problems. Since information on the centrally planned economies of the region is not readily available, and Japan's problem of planning is of quite a different dimension, this paper will deal largely with the other countries of the region which are under a system of "mixed economy" embarking upon a planned economic development from the present low income level.

Practically all countries of the region are now receiving guidance from a plan of some sort of further economic development. India has embarked upon its third plan, other countries are completing their second plans, and still others are implementing their first plan. The immediate driving force for the preparation of a first plan to symbolize entrance into the planning field varies among countries of the region. In some countries, such as India, it sprang from the conviction that "planning is essentially an attempt at working out a rational solution of problems," and that economic planning means "utlitizing more effectively the potential resources available to the community."[1] ... In other countries, such as Indonesia, it came from the idea that a development plan would give more substance to political independence. In still others such as the Republic of China and the Republic of Korea, it arose chiefly from the need to secure foreign aid.

Whatever its motivation and scope, the first plan usually represented national aspirations, and brought to focus the national objectives of development; in this

[1]. Planning Commission, Government of India, *The First Five-Year Plan*, p. 7.

way it tended to arouse the enthusiasm of the people and enlist their support towards the common goal. Implicit in the resort to planning is the recognition of the importance and the vast increase (both in strength and in variety) of government functions.

In subsequent plans, the investment programmes are generally more comprehensively formulated, their segments more interrelated, and development policies and measures more co-ordinated, although much still remains to be desired. ...

The scope and comprehensiveness of development plans vary widely among countries of the region. The first plans were almost invariably a summation of a number of individual projects in the public sector, many of which were already being implemented. Some of the plans contain certain aggregate targets, such as the rate of increase of national income in India's First Five-Year Plan and the extent of absorption of the unemployed in Ceylon's Six-Year Investment Programme. Others, such as the Afghanistan First Five-Year Plan, do not provide aggregate targets, for lack of statistics on national income and employment. Even in those first plans where income and employment targets were given, the functional relationship between the investment programme as a whole and the expected increase in national income and employment was hardly more than a guess, because of lack of accurate information on the capital/output ratio and capital/labour ratio.

The comprehensiveness of a plan depends chiefly on the stage of development of the economy, the availability of statistical data and the supply of qualified planners. In the period of early postwar rehabilitation or under conditions of political instability or inflation, it has not been advisable to introduce a comprehensive plan. In such circumstances, efforts were naturally concentrated on sound reconstruction projects or stabilization programmes. This was the case of the first plans in China: Taiwan and south Korea. When severe inflation prevails a comprehensive plan may become unrealistic and impracticable, for it is difficult to evaluate development projects correctly under a distorted cost price structure, and the introduction of a relatively ambitious investment programme may aggravate economic instability. Lack of stability was perhaps the main reason which made Indonesia's and south Viet-Nam's first five-year plans practically inoperative.

Shortage of statistical data and qualified planners are the main reasons why several comparatively less developed countries of the region cannot produce a comprehensive plan. Judging from their stages of development, it may be practicable for them to begin with a plan containing mainly a number of technically feasible and economically justifiable individual projects, without too much emphasis on aggregate income, employment targets and inter-industry co-ordination. Of course, in the evaluation of individual projects for inclusion in the plan, external economies and other indirect benefits should, as far as possible, be taken into consideration. In any case, in the foreign-trade-oriented economies, inter-industry imbalance can be corrected and adjusted largely through imports, particularly when a large amount of foreign aid is available. The important thing for these countries is a start in the right direction. However, development policies suitable to their economic system and needs should be designed and included in their first plans to guide, foster and stimulate economic activity in the private sector. The absence of income (and employment) targets would mean that the nation would be unable to grasp in a nutshell what the plan was meant to achieve; yet it would not necessarily deprive the

plan of its operational value if the projects included are well conceived and development policies well designed.

Gains in experience and improvement in the availability of statistical data have tended to make the subsequent plans more comprehensive.

Generally speaking, a comprehensive plan should consist at least of the following parts:

(1) Objectives and aggregate targets, primarily in terms of national income and employment;

(2) A public investment programme with distribution of development expenditures among major sectors, chiefly for building up the economic and social infrastructure;

(3) A projection of private investment among various major sectors;

(4) Policy measures (especially in the fiscal, financial, foreign trade, foreign exchange and foreign investment fields) to stimulate, direct and influence private investment;

(5) A programme, co-ordinated with (4), for financing public and private investment from domestic and foreign sources, including particularly the government budget and foreign exchange budget;

(6) Sectoral programmes containing individual projects; and

(7) Policies aiming at basic institutional changes, including land reform, labour policy, etc.

1.4 THE MARKET MECHANISM AS AN INSTRUMENT OF DEVELOPMENT *

In recent times, there has been a retreat both in economic theory and in economic policy from the nineteenth-century ideal of the unfettered market as a principle of economic organization. But the economic

* From Harry G. Johnson, *Money, Trade and Economic Growth*, George Allen & Unwin Ltd., London, 1962, pp. 152–3, 156–9, 160–63. Reprinted by permission.

pros and cons of this retreat have been fully debated, and the economist consequently has a great deal to say about the relative merits of the market as contrasted with other methods of economic organization, and the circumstances appropriate to each.

The subject of planning and the market in economic development is, therefore, one which falls definitely within the field of the economist. Before I go on to discuss it, I must define more precisely what I mean by it. "Planning and the market" may be interpreted in two different ways. First, it may refer to the contrast between direction of the economy by Government and the policy of *laissez-faire*. This is not my subject, though in a wider philosophical and historical context it offers much to discuss. For example, though *laissez-faire* and direction are often regarded as opposites, if one looks to the history of economic development one finds (as Professor Easterbrook has shown[1]) that economic development is almost invariably a process in which planning and direction on the one hand and freedom of enterprise on the other play their part, and are mixed. There is almost no case in which economic development has been entirely planned or entirely unplanned. The usual pattern is one of some framework of control by Government, within which the entrepreneur provides his services—a mixture of bureaucracy and enterprise, in which bureaucracy takes care of the major risks of development and enterprise faces and overcomes the minor ones. Another relevant point that Easterbrook makes is that an economy which succeeds in finding

a formula for growth tends to repeat that pattern after it has become inappropriate. For example, Britain has gone on trying to work the internationally-oriented pattern of her nineteenth-century development; Russia has been very successful in developing heavy industry but has not yet solved the problem of agriculture.

The alternative interpretation takes planning, in the sense of a general direction of the economy, as an established principle, and considers the market as an alternative to other and more direct means of detailed control. Given the general framework of economic planning, there is still a choice between two alternative methods of looking after the details. One is by direct detailed planning by a central authority, the other is by leaving the working out of details as far as possible to the operation of the market. (There is a third alternative, in which the Government is itself the entrepreneur and investor, which I shall consider later.)

This alternative interpretation is the one I shall be using: I shall discuss the question of the market mechanism as against detailed planning as an instrument of economic development. I should like to make it clear from the start that I am going to make a strong case for the market, as the preferable instrument of economic development, on two main grounds. The first is that the achievement of the desired results by control methods is likely to be especially difficult and inefficient in an underdeveloped economy; at this point I should like to remind you that a large part of Adam Smith's argument for *laissez-faire* was the inefficiency and corruption he saw in the Governments of his time. The second is that the remedies for the main fault which can be found with the use of the market mechanism, its undesirable social effects, are luxuries which underdeveloped countries cannot afford to indulge in if they are really serious about

1. Professor Easterbrook's analysis was presented in the Marshall Lectures at Cambridge University in the spring of 1956. Unfortunately these lectures have not been published, but some of the ideas are available in W. T. Easterbrook, "Long Period Comparative Study: Some Historical Cases," *Journal of Economic History*, XVII, No. 4, December 1957, 571–95.

attaining a high rate of development. In particular, there is likely to be a conflict between rapid growth and an equitable distribution of income; and a poor country anxious to develop would probably be well advised not to worry too much about the distribution of income.

I am going to make a fairly strong case for the market, because the market figures relatively little in the literature of economic development, and the theoretical analysis which economics has developed in relation to markets is often overlooked or disregarded. . . .

I now want to recapitulate briefly the various economic functions of the market and the price system as a method of economic organization. I shall be brief, as the argument is a familiar one.

In the first place, the market rations supplies of consumer goods among consumers; this rationing is governed by the willingness of consumers to pay, and provided the distribution of income is acceptable it is a socially efficient process. Secondly, the market directs the allocation of production between commodities, according to the criterion of maximum profit, which, on the same assumption, corresponds to social usefulness. Thirdly, the market allocates the different factors of production among their various uses, according to the criterion of maximizing their incomes. Fourthly, it governs the relative quantities of specific types of labour and capital equipment made available. Fifthly, it distributes income between the factors of production and therefore between individuals. Thus it solves all the economic problems of allocation of scarce means between alternative ends.

These are static functions; but the market also serves in various ways to provide incentives to economic growth. Thus the availability of goods through the market stimulates the consumer to seek to increase his income; and access to the market pro-

vides an opportunity for inventors of new goods and technical improvements to profit from their exploitation. Moreover, the market serves particularly to provide an incentive to the accumulation of capital of all kinds: first to the accumulation of personal capital in the form of trained skill, since such skill earns a higher reward; and second to the accumulation of material capital, since such capital earns an income.

The argument, then, is that a properly functioning market system would tend to stimulate both economic efficiency and economic growth. And it is important to note that the market does this automatically, while it requires no big administrative apparatus, no central decision-making, and very little policing other than the provision of a legal system for the enforcement of contracts.

All this sounds very impressive; but it is clearly not the whole of the story. What, then, are the objections to the market, how serious are they, and what should be done about them in the context of economic development? I shall discuss these questions in some detail. But first I shall state briefly the central theme of my discussion. It is that in many cases the objections to the market can be overcome by reforming specific markets, so as to bring them closer to the ideal type of market; and that to overcome other objections to the market may be very expensive and may not prove to be worthwhile—in other words, the defects of the market mechanism may on balance be more tolerable than they look at first sight.

Now, what are the objections to the market? They can, I think, be classified into two main types. One type of objection is that the market does not perform its functions properly. The other type of objection is that the results produced by the functioning of the market are undesirable in themselves.

I begin with the first type of objection, that the market does not perform its function properly. Here it is useful to draw a distinction between two quite different sorts of cases—those in which the market operates imperfectly, and those in which a perfectly functioning market would not produce the best results.

Imperfect operation of the market in an underdeveloped country may be attributable to ignorance, in the sense of lack of familiarity with market mechanisms and of awareness of relevant information, or to the prevalence of other modes of behaviour than the rational maximization of returns from effort. In the first case, the appropriate Governmental policy would seem to me to be, not to assume from the market the responsibility for allocative decisions, but to disseminate the knowledge and information required to make the market work efficiently and provide the education required to use it. The second case implies a more fundamental obstacle, not only to the use of the market but also to economic development itself, and suggests that successful economic development requires a basic change in social psychology. To my mind, it raises a serious question of fact. Is it really true that people in underdeveloped countries are strangers to the idea of maximizing gains? The idea that they are is very common in the literature and policy-making of economic development; one of its manifestations is the implicit assumption that both supplies and demands are completely price-inelastic. I am very sceptical about this, partly because of Bauer's work and partly because at least some of the actions of Governments in underdeveloped areas presuppose that even the poorest producers are susceptible to price incentives. I personally do not think one is justified in assuming as a general proposition that ignorance and illiteracy necessarily imply that men are not interested in making

money. If it is true, there will be serious difficulties in the way of economic development; but again, the appropriate Governmental policy would seem to be to educate the people in the practice of rational economic behavior.

Even if the market functions perfectly, it will not produce the best possible results by its own criteria if there is a difference between social and private benefit or cost. This type of case may be particularly relevant to economic development; it includes the case of increasing returns to scale, and can be extended to include the possibility that technical progress or capital accumulation tend to proceed more rapidly in industry than in agriculture. But it raises an immediate question of fact—whether divergences between social and private benefit or cost are numerous and important or not. This is an important question, but one on which we do not know very much for certain. The theory of increasing returns is logically intriguing, but the influence of increasing returns still has to be disentangled from that of technical progress in historical growth. Again, it is a fact that few advanced countries are not industrial; but this by itself does not establish the wisdom of a policy of forced industrialization in an underdeveloped country. Aside from the question of fact, the existence of divergences between social and private returns does not necessarily indicate a need for the government to replace the market mechanism; instead, the operation of the market can be perfected by the use of appropriate taxes and subsidies to offset any divergences between social and private returns.

I now turn to the second type of objection to the market, the point of which is not that the market does not work in the way it should, but that the results produced are undesirable in themselves. Here, I think, there are two major objections to the market. The first is that the income distribution produced by the market is unjust and socially undesirable. The distribution of income through the market depends on the wealth and talents of different individuals, and on their individual skill in seeing a profitable opportunity of employing their money or labour. If they make a wise or lucky choice, they may obtain a much higher income. The objection is that this method of determining the distribution of income is not just. But if you attempt to intervene in the distribution of income, you immediately encounter the problem that such intervention interferes with the efficiency of the market system. If people are not allowed to enjoy the income they could obtain by their decisions, their decisions in turn will be affected, and the efficiency of the system will be impaired. There is, therefore, a conflict between economic efficiency and social justice. The extent and importance of this conflict is likely to vary according to the state of economic development. The more advanced a country is, the more likely are its citizens to have consciences about the distribution of income, and to accept the high taxation necessary to correct it without disastrously altering their behaviour; and on the other hand, the higher the level of income reached, the less serious will be any slowing down of the rate of growth brought about by redistribution policies. An advanced country can afford to sacrifice some growth for the sake of social justice. But the cost of greater equality may be great to any economy at a low level of economic development that wishes to grow rapidly, particularly as it is evident that historically the great bursts of economic growth have been associated with the prospect and the result of big windfall gains; it would therefore seem unwise for a country anxious to enjoy rapid growth to insist too strongly on policies aimed at ensuring economic equality and a just income distribution. I

should add that the problem may not be in fact as serious as I have made it out to be, since in the course of time rapid growth tends in various ways to promote a more equal distribution of wealth.

. . .

I have been discussing the objection to the results of the market system on the grounds that it produces an undesirable distribution of income. A second objection of the same sort is that the free market will not produce as high a rate of growth as is desirable. I think there is a strong case for this objection, because people's actions in regard to saving and investment depend very much on their guesses about the future. Now people are likely to know their own current requirements better than the Government. But the requirements of the future have to be looked at not from the individual or family point of view or that of the nation as a collection of individuals, but from the point of view of the ongoing society. The needs of society in the future, many economists agree, tend to be underprovided for by the free market.

Even if the conclusion that state action is desirable to raise the rate of growth is accepted, this conclusion nevertheless does not carry with it a number of corollaries which are often attached to it. In particular, it does not necessarily imply that the state ought to undertake development saving and investment itself. Private enterprise may be more efficient than the Government in constructing and operating enterprises, so that the best policy may be to stimulate private enterprise by tax concessions, subsidies, and the provision of cheap credit. Similarly, it may be preferable to stimulate private saving by offering high interest rates, rather than by forcing savings into the hands of the state by taxation or inflation. One argument against a policy of low interest rates and forced saving is that it may in the long run contribute to the inequality of income distribution. The reason is that the poor or small savers are mainly confined to low-yielding fixed-interest investments, directly or indirectly in Government debt, because these are safe and easily available, whereas the larger savers can invest their money in higher-yielding stocks and shares or directly in profitable enterprises. There is, therefore, an opportunity here for Government both to stimulate saving for development and to improve the distribution of income.

There is another reason for being wary of the proposition that the state should undertake development investment itself —the danger that if the Government undertakes investment itself, especially if its administrators are not too clear on their objectives, the result will be the creation of vested industrial interests inimical to further development, and resistant to technical change.

To summarize the foregoing argument from the point of view of development policy, it seems to me that much of development planning could usefully be devoted to the improvement and strengthening of the market system. This does not imply the acceptance of all the results of *laissez-faire*, especially with respect to the rate of growth; but there are reasons for thinking that too much emphasis on a fair or ethical distribution of income can be an obstacle to rapid growth.

The argument I have presented has been concerned mainly with one side of the case for the market. The other side concerns the costs and difficulties of controls, in terms of the manpower costs of the administration they require, and their effects in creating profit opportunities which bring windfall gains to some members of the community and create incentives to evasion which in turn require policing of the controls. I have touched on that side of the argument sufficiently frequently to make it unnecessary to elaborate on it further.

Instead, I shall comment briefly on international markets in relation to economic development, since so far I have been implicitly concerned with internal markets. Economic development planning inevitably has a strong autarkic bias, by reason both of its motivation and of the limitation of the scope of control to the national economy. Nevertheless, international trade can play an important part in stimulating and facilitating the development process. Access to foreign markets for exports can permit an economy with a limited domestic market to exploit economies of scale, and the potentiality of such exports can serve as a powerful attraction for foreign capital and enterprise. Similarly, the capacity to import provided by exports can give a developing economy immediate access to the products of advanced technology, without obliging it to go through the long and perhaps costly process of developing domestic production facilities. Economic nationalism and excessive fear of the risks of international trade, by fostering aversion to exploiting the advantages of the international market, can therefore retard economic development unnecessarily.

One further comment on the international aspects of the market and economic development seems to me worth making. Discussion of the international side of development has been mostly concerned with commodity trade and commerical policy. But in fact one of the most important ways in which the world market system is imperfect is with respect to the international mobility of capital and labour. The problem of international capital movements has received a fair amount of attention, labour mobility and immobility much less. Now, the process of economic development in the past, especially in the nineteenth century, was characterized by vast movements, not only of capital, but also of labour, about the world. The mass movement of labour between countries has now been more or less shut off by the growth of nationalism. I believe it is important to recognize this restriction on international competition, and its implications for programmes of economic development. It means—looking at the world economy as a whole—that the solution to the problem of maximizing world output cannot be approached directly, by bringing labour, capital technology, and natural resources together at the most efficient location; instead, the other productive factors have to be brought to the labour. To a large extent, "the economic development of underdeveloped countries" is a second-best policy,[2] in which gifts of capital and technical training by advanced to underdeveloped countries are a com-

2. See J. E. Meade, *The Theory of International Economic Policy, Volume II: Trade and Welfare* (London: Oxford University Press, 1955), and R. G. Lipsey and Kelvin Lancaster, "The General Theory of Second Best," *Review of Economic Studies*, XXIV(1), No. 63, 1956–57, 11–33.

pensation for the unwillingness of the former to consider the alternative way of improving the labour to resources ratio, movement of the labour to the resources. The fact that development is a second-best policy in this respect may impose severe limitations on its efficiency and rapidity.

To conclude, I have been concerned with the role of the market in economic development; and I have aimed at stressing the economic functions of the market, in automatically taking decisions about various kinds of allocations of economic resources, and the place in economic development programmes of improvements in market organization and methods. I have been advocating, not a policy of *laissez-faire,* but recognition of the market as an administrative instrument that is relatively cheap to operate and may therefore be efficient in spite of objectionable features of its operations. The general assumption on which I have been arguing is that economic development is a process of co-operation between the state and private enterprise, and that the problem is to devise the best possible mixture.

2. THE "BIG-PUSH" ARGUMENT

2.1 THE THEORY OF THE "BIG PUSH" *

An institutional framework different from the present one is clearly necessary for the successful carrying out of industrialisation in international depressed areas. In what follows arguments are submitted tending to show why the whole of the

* From Paul N. Rosenstein-Rodan, "Problems of Industrialization of Eastern and South-Eastern Europe," *Economic Journal,* June-September 1943, pp. 204–7; "Notes on the Theory of the 'Big Push,'" in Howard S. Ellis (ed.), *Economic Development for Latin America,* St. Martin's Press, New York, 1961, pp. 57–8, 60–62, 65–6. Reprinted by permission.

industry to be created is to be treated and planned like one huge firm or trust.

The first task of industrialisation is to provide for training and "skilling" of labour which is to transform Eastern European peasants into full-time or part-time industrial workers. The automatism of *laissez-faire* never worked properly in that field. It broke down because it is not profitable for a private entrepreneur to invest in training labour. There are no mortgages on workers—an entrepreneur who invests in training workers may lose capital if these workers contract with another firm. Although not a good investment for a private firm, it is the best investment for the State. It is also a good investment for the bulk of industries to be created when taken as a whole, although it may represent irrecoverable costs for a smaller unit. It constitutes an important instance of the Pigovian divergence between "private and social marginal net product" where the latter is greater than the former. Training facilities (including transport and housing) of one million workers per annum would involve costs of certainly more than £100 million per annum—a sum which may be too great to be borne by the State (or the Eastern European national economy) if taken *apart* from the costs of the 50% participation in its own "Eastern European Industrial Trust" that we shall propose. It should be counted as capital investment in the Eastern European Industrial Trust (E.E.I.T.).

That is not, however, the most important reason in favour of such a large investment unit.

Complementarity of different industries provides the most important set of arguments in favour of a large-scale planned industrialisation. In order to illustrate the issues involved, let us adopt the somewhat roundabout method of analysing two examples. Let us assume that 20,000 unemployed workers in Eastern and South-Eastern Europe are taken from the land and put into a large shoe factory. They receive wages substantially higher than their previous meagre income *in natura*. It would be impossible to put them into industry at their previous income standard, because they need more foodstuffs than they had in their agrarian semi-unemployed existence, because these foodstuffs have to be transported to towns, and because the workers have to pay for housing accommodation. If these workers spent all their wages on shoes, a market for the

products of their enterprise would arise representing an expansion which does not disturb the pre-existing market, and 90% of the problem (assuming 10% profit) would be solved. The trouble is that the workers will not spend all their wages on shoes. If, instead, one million unemployed workers were taken from the land and put, not into one industry, but into a whole series of industries which produce the bulk of the goods on which the workers would spend their wages, what was not true in the case of one shoe factory would become true in the case of a whole system of industries: it would create its own additional market, thus realising an expansion of world output with the minimum disturbance of the world markets. The industries producing the bulk of the wage goods can therefore be said to be complementary. The planned creation of such a complementary system reduces the risk of not being able to sell, and, since risk can be considered as cost, it reduces costs. It is in this sense a special case of "external economies."

It may be added that, while in the highly developed and rich countries with their more variegated needs it is difficult to assess the prospective demand of the population, it is not as difficult to foresee on what the formerly unemployed workers would spend their wages in regions where a low standard of living obtains.

Two other types of "external economies" will arise when a system of different industries is created. First, the strictly Marshallian economies external to a firm within a growing industry. The same applies, however (secondly), to economies external to one industry due to the growth of other industries. It is usually tacitly assumed that the divergence between the "private and social marginal net product" is not very considerable. This assumption may be too optimistic even in the case of a crystallised mature competitive economy. It is certainly not true in the case of fundamental structural changes in the international depressed areas. External economies may there be of the same order of magnitude as profits which appear on the profit and loss account of the enterprise.

The existing institutions of international and national investment do not take advantage of external economies. There is no incentive within their framework for many investments which are profitable in terms of "social marginal net product," but do not appear profitable in terms of "private marginal net product." The main driving-force of investment is the profit expectation of an individual entrepreneur which is based on experience of the past. Experience of the past is partly irrelevant, however, where the whole economic structure of a region is to be changed. An individual entrepreneur's knowledge of the market is bound to be insufficient in this case because he cannot have all the data that would be available to the planning board of an E.E.I.T. His subjective risk estimate is bound to be considerably higher than the objective risk. If the industrialisation of international depressed areas were to rely entirely on the normal incentive of private entrepreneurs, the process would not only be very much slower, the rate of investment smaller and (consequently) the national income lower, but the whole economic structure of the region would be different. Investment would be distributed in different proportions between different industries, the final equilibrium would be below the optimum which a large E.E.I.T. could achieve. In the international capital market the existing institutions are mostly used to invest in, or to grant credit to, single enterprises. It might easily happen that any one enterprise would not be profitable enough to guarantee payment of sufficient interest or dividend out of its own profits. But the creation of such an enterprise, e.g., production of electric power, may create new investment opportunities and profits elsewhere, e.g., in an electrical equipment industry. If we create a sufficiently large investment unit by including all the new industries of the region, external economies will become internal profits out of which dividends may be paid easily.

Professor Allyn Young's celebrated example elucidates our problem. He assumed that a Tube line was to be built in a district and that an accurate estimate was made of costs and receipts. It was found that the rate of profit would be below the usual rate of yield on investments obtainable elsewhere. The project was found not profitable and was abandoned. Another enterprising company bought up the land and houses along the proposed Tube line and was then able to build the line. Although the receipts from the passenger traffic would not pay a sufficient rate of profit, the capital appreciation on the houses and land more than made up the deficiency. Thus the project was realised, the Tube line was built. The problem is: Is it desirable—i.e., does it lend to an optimum allocation of resources and maximisation of national income—that this form of capital gain (external economy) be included as an item in the calculus of profitability, or is it not? Allyn Young hints that it is not desirable because the capital appreciation of houses and land along the Tube line due to an influx of people from other districts has an uncompensated counterpart in a capital depreciation of houses and land in districts out of which people moved into the Tube-line district. Agricultural land in Eastern and South-Eastern Europe will, however, not depreciate when the agrarian excess of population moves out. In this case external economies should be included in the calculus of profitability.

. . .

"There is a minimum level of resources that must be devoted to . . . a development program if it is to have any chance of success. Launching a country into self-sustaining growth is a little like getting an airplane off the ground. There is a critical ground speed which must be passed before the craft can become airborne. . . ."[1] Proceeding "bit by bit" will not add up in its effects to the sum total of the single bits. A minimum quantum of investment is a necessary, though not sufficient, condition of success. This, in a nutshell, is the contention of the theory of the big push.

This theory seems to contradict the conclusions of the traditional static equilibrium theory and to reverse its famous motto, *natura non facit saltum*. It does so for three reasons. First, it is based on a set of more realistic assumptions of certain indivisibilities and "nonappropriabilities" in the production functions even on the level of static equilibrium theory. These indivisibilities give rise to increasing returns and to technological external economies. Second, in dealing with problems of growth this theory examines the path towards equilibrium, not the conditions at a point of equilibrium only. At a point of static equilibrium net investment is zero. The theory of growth is very largely a theory of investment. Moreover, the allocation of investment—unlike the allocation of given stocks of consumer goods (equilibrium of consumption), or of producers' goods (equilibrium of production)—necessarily occurs in an imperfect market, that is, a market on which prices do not signal all the information required for an optimum solution.[2] Given an imperfect investment market, pecuniary external economies

have the same effect in the theory of growth as technological external economies. They are a cause of a possible divergence between the private and the social marginal net product. Since pecuniary, unlike technological, external economies are all-pervading and frequent, the price mechanism does not necessarily put the economy on an optimum path. Therefore, additional signalling devices apart from market prices are required. Many economists, including the author, believe that these additional signals can be provided by programming. Third, in addition to the risk phenomena and imperfections characterizing the investment equilibrium, markets in under-developed countries are even more imperfect than in developed countries. The price mechanism in such imperfect markets does not provide the signals which guide a perfectly competitive economy towards an optimum position.

Indivisibilities of inputs, processes, or outputs give rise to increasing returns, that is, economies of scale, and may require a high optimum size of a firm. This is not a very important obstacle to development since with some exceptions (for instance in Central America) there is usually sufficient demand, even in small, poor countries, for at least one optimum scale firm in many industries. There may be room, however, only for one or a few firms with the obvious danger of monopolistic markets.

As Allyn Young pointed out, increasing returns accrue to a firm not only with the growth of its size but also with the growth of the industry and with the growth of the industrial system as a whole. Greater specialization and better use of resources become possible when growth helps to overcome indivisibilities generating pecuniary external economies. The range

1. Massachusetts Institute of Technology, Center for International Studies, *The Objectives of United States Economic Assistance Programs* (Washington, 1957), p. 70.

2. See P. N. Rosenstein-Rodan, "Programming in Theory and in Italian Practice," in Massachusetts Institute of Technology, Center for International Studies, *Investment Criteria and Economic Growth* (Cambridge, Massachusetts, 1955).

of increasing returns seems to be very wide indeed.[3]

Social overhead capital is the most important instance of indivisibility and hence of external economies on the supply side. Its services are indirectly productive and become available only after long gestation periods. Its most important products are investment opportunities created in other industries. Social overhead capital comprises all those basic industries like power, transport, or communications which must precede the more quickly yielding, directly productive investments and which constitute the framework or infrastructure and the overhead costs of the economy as a whole. Its installations are characterized by a sizeable initial lump and low variable costs. Since the minimum size in these basic industries is large, excess capacity will be unavoidable over the initial period in under-developed countries.[4] In addition, there is also an irreducible minimum industry mix of different public utilities, so that an under-developed country will have to invest between 30–40 per cent of its total investment in these channels. Since over-all vision is required as well as a correct appraisal of future development, programming is undoubtedly required in

3. The capital-output ratio in the United States has fallen over the last eighty years from around 4 : 1 to around 3 : 1, while income per head, wage-rates, and the relative importance of heavy industry were rising. This is due to technical progress (change in production functions), increasing returns on balance (increasing returns prevailing over decreasing returns), and to the rising demand for labour-intensive services characteristic of high-income economies. It is my conviction that increasing returns played a considerable part in it.

4. We may distinguish in fact between the developmental social overhead capital which provides for a hoped for but uncertain future demand and the rehabilitation social overhead capital which caters to an unsatisfied demand of the past. The first with its excess capacity will necessarily have a big sectoral capital-output ratio (10–15 : 1); the second, through breaking bottlenecks, has a certain high indirect productivity and a much lower capital-output ratio.

this lumpy field. Normal market mechanisms will not provide an optimum supply.

Social overhead capital is characterized by four indivisibilities. First, it is indivisible (irreversible) in time. It must precede other directly productive investments. Second, its equipment has high minimum durability. Lesser durability is either technically impossible or much less efficient. For this and other reasons it is very lumpy. Third, it has long gestation periods. Fourth, an irreducible minimum social overhead capital industry mix is a condition for getting off the dead-end.

Because of these indivisibilities and because services of social overhead capital cannot be imported, a high initial investment in social overhead capital must either precede or be known to be certainly available in order to pave the way for additional more quickly yielding directly productive investments. This indivisibility of social overhead capital constitutes one of the main obstacles to development of under-developed countries.

Relatively few investments are made in the small market of an under-developed country. If all investment projects were independent (which they are not) and if their number grew, the risk of each investment project would decline by simple actuarial rules. The lower marginal risk of each investment dose (or project) would lead to either higher or cheaper credit facilities and these would thus constitute internal economies. In reality, however, various investment decisions are not independent. Investment projects have high risks because of uncertainty as to whether their products will find a market.

Let us restate our old example, at first for a closed economy. If a hundred workers who were previously in disguised unemployment (so that the marginal productivity of their labour was equal to zero) in an under-developed country are put into a shoe factory, their wages will constitute additional income. If the newly employed workers spend all of their additional income on the shoes they produce, the shoe factory will find a market and will succeed. In fact, however, they will not spend all of their additional income on shoes. There is no easy solution of creating an additional market in this way. The risk of not finding a market reduces the incentive to invest, and the shoe factory investment project will probably be abandoned. Let us vary the example. Instead of putting a hundred previously unemployed workers in one shoe factory, let us put ten thousand workers in one hundred factories and farms which between them will produce the bulk of the wage-goods on which the newly employed workers will spend their wages. What was not true in the case of one single shoe factory will become true for the complementary system of one hundred factories and farms. The new producers will be each other's customers and will verify Say's Law by creating an additional market. The complementarity of demand will reduce the risk of not finding a market. Reducing such interdependent risks naturally increases the incentive to invest.

A high minimum quantum of investment requires a high volume of savings, which is difficult to achieve in low income, under-developed countries. There is a way out of this vicious circle. In the first stage when income is increased due to an increase in investment which mobilizes additional latent resources, mechanisms must be provided which assure that in the second stage the marginal rate of saving is very much higher than the average rate of saving. Adam Smith's dictum that frugality is a virtue and prodigality a vice has to be adapted to a situation of growing income. Economic history does not show

that the proportion saved from the increase in income was higher than the previous average rate of saving.

A zero (or very low) price elasticity of the supply of saving and a high income elasticity of saving thus constitute the third indivisibility.

These three indivisibilities and the external economies to which they give rise, plus the external economies of training labour, form the characteristic pattern of models of growth of under-developed countries.

The economic factors discussed so far give only the necessary, but not the sufficient, conditions of growth. A big push seems to be required to jump over the economic obstacles to development. There may be finally a phenomenon of indivisibility in the vigour and drive required for a successful development policy. Isolated and small efforts may not add up to a sufficient impact on growth. An atmosphere of development may only arise with a minimum speed or size of investment. Our knowledge of psychology is far too deficient to theorize about this phenomenon. This does not make it a less important factor. It may well constitute the difference between necessary and sufficient conditions for success.

2.2 A Critique *

...the theories I am considering have several characteristics which warrant their being grouped together. For one thing, these theories are generally strongly interventionist, at least so far as concerns the assumption of responsibility by the state for a greatly increased rate of saving, and—extending out from this basis according to the predilections of the individual writer—to more or less, and generally more, control (and sometimes operation)

* From Howard S. Ellis, "Accelerated Investment as a Force in Economic Development," *Quarterly Journal of Economics*, November 1958, pp. 486, 491–5. Reprinted by permission.

of the specific lines of investment and production. Secondly, these "big push" theorists usually consider manufacture as inherently superior to primary production as a vehicle of development. These two characteristics are so general that I shall terminate the list with these alone for greater emphasis; but it would be tempting to point to the frequency also of an inflationary bias in writings of this sort, to autarkical leanings and to a fondness for general equilibrium planning as implied by linear or nonlinear programming. But the interventionist and other features of these theories, upon which I shall want to comment later, are their overtones rather than their substance.

The substantive bases for an accelerated rate of investment through state intervention are principally three: a demographic argument, a line of reasoning involving the propensity to consume (or to save), and thirdly, conclusions reached from the technical discontinuities or "lumpiness" of investment. Let me say clearly in advance that in no case do I reject the reasoning completely; but that in all cases I attach much greater weight than do the proponents of these theories to the limits of possible gain, to the risks and costs of the proposed line of action, and to the merits of alternative policies.

...

The chief basis upon which the "big push" of investment has been justified, since its original enunciation by Paul Rosenstein-Rodan a decade and a half ago, has been the possibility of realizing extensive external economies, and this ground is still a favorite with nearly all writers of this persuasion. But the great offset to the possibility that domestic development programs should give rise to further external economies has been definitively set forth by Professor Viner: foreign trade makes available to the developing country the much more substantial economies realized upon world markets, independently of home investment.[1] This fact is now recognized by Professor Rosenstein. But he fails to give overt recognition to the further fact adduced by Viner that the newly developing countries nowadays are chiefly primary producers, and, as such, investment for exports and for marginal import substitutes, where external economies are presumably negligible, occupies a very large part of total investment. For this entire sector, the "big push" loses its specific justification from external economies.

We are left then with that portion of production for the domestic market which does not substitute for imports. Still, this can be a very substantial field, embracing purely local consumer goods production and most public utilities—transportation, communication, power, water and sewerage facilities, and the like. Even here, however, there are limits to potential external economies. Viner points out that certain investments—presumably in the case of fairly inelastic demand—are cost-reducing rather than output-expanding. Since external economies depend upon expansion of output in the initial industry, they become negligible for this category of investment. I should like to call attention to two further limitations of considerable significance. In the field of purely domestic goods, a large fraction will be personal services and very light industry (a good deal of food and raiment production) in which the "chunkiness" of fixed investment is unimportant because fixed investment is itself a small fraction of costs. Since external economies are simply internal economies in adjacent industries, their

1. Jacob Viner, "Stability and Progress: the Poorer Countries' Problem," First Congress of the International Economic Association, Rome, September 6–11, 1956; mimeographed paper, pp. 27–31. [Reprinted in Douglas Hague (ed.), *Stability and Progress in the World Economy*, New York, 1958.]

significance is correspondingly small in these cases. It is furthermore worth remembering that, in the case of public utilities, potential external economies do not pertain to the cost of the *equipment* of these industries if it can be more cheaply imported.

Taken together, all of these limitations need not entirely remove the possibility of external economies. But they are neither as universal as often supposed nor, when they actually exist, as substantial. Furthermore and finally, though their existence does increase the productivity of the economy for given magnitudes of investment, they do not constitute a reason for a *concentration of investment in point of time* if—as would appear probable in any but the smallest countries—the "chunkiness" of individual investments levels out to a fairly full utilization of capacities in the aggregate for all capital facilities together. This is a decidedly relevant consideration if "accelerated investment" is taken, not as simply synonymous with more investment continuously, but as a "big push" followed by a lower rate.

Beyond its substantive theoretical basis in the population, savings, and external economies arguments, the doctrine of accelerated rates of investment has overtones for policy which its proponents, I am sure, would not be content to have ignored. One of these is the predilection for manufacturing over agricultural and other primary industries. In part this predilection may simply reflect a sentimental desire to see the country "independent" of its neighbors, particularly the richer ones; but in part it may rest on rational arguments, such as the improvement in labor morale which is supposed to attend factory production, the cultural and demographic effects of large cities, which are supposed to be favorable to economic progress, and the risks of primary production from the fluctuations of world markets.

On the other hand, agricultural and primary types of production have in their favor that they utilize the relatively abundant factors of land and labor and economize capital; that characteristically in the less developed countries they provide two-thirds or more of the national income; and that, by the same token, they supply the chief wherewithal for industrial imports and investment in general.

It would scarcely seem necessary at the present stage of the debate concerning economic development to say that the merits of investment in agriculture versus industry have to be settled according to the peculiarities of each country. By consequence, whatever merits may inhere in crash programs of investment may just as well be associated with agriculture—irrigation, drainage, transportation facilities, reform of fragmented land-holdings, etc.,—as with building industrial plants; in particular cases, indeed, more so.

Somewhat similar reflections would be germane to the penchant of the "big push" economists for planning, state direction of investment, and extensive controls. Linear programming, for example, is essentially an information service, and the benefits of its information may just as well be made available to private as to public entrepreneurs. In and of itself, linear programming does not supply any rationale for accelerated investment. If it should appear desirable to supplement private voluntary savings by the fiscal arm of the state, the funds can be lent to private firms. The theoretical underpinning of accelerated investment program pertains to a *rate* of investment, and not necessarily to government controlled investment. Ordinary economic motivations of the individual and the firm are a powerful engine of economic progress. It would be regrettable if the economists of the free world created an impression to the contrary.

What, in conclusion, may be said of the

general merits of the "big push" philosophy of economic development? As a starting point for development some kind of impulse is, of course, necessary; a change from stagnation is not likely to come by almost imperceptible degrees. Economic historians and cultural anthropologists have pointed to various prime movers in economic change: to the roles of the foreign trader and foreign capital, to immigration and the transfer of techniques, to the process of technical innovation itself, to cultural change, and to political revolution. Among these, intensive programs of state investment, as in the Japanese and Russian cases, should certainly take their place. But they are by no means the only or even the chief channel through which development can be achieved; and the demographic advantages, the capital accumulation, and the external economies to be expected from crash programs of government investment can easily be overrated.

A statistical summary of recent economic development throughout the world by John H. Adler reaches the important conclusion, among others, that "a relatively low level of investment 'pays off' well in the form of additional output."[2] The author emphasizes this conclusion most sharply in connection with India and Pakistan; but the chief reason for this conclusion, the prevailingly low capital-output ratio, is also characteristic of many other of the less developed countries of Asia and Latin America as his statistics reveal. Thus it appears that it is far from generally true that a massive injection of capital is a precondition of growth.

A general weakness of the "big push" doctrine is that it frequently ignores the conditions for *evoking* the investment to which it ascribes such potency in the general picture of development, as well as neglecting the conditions under which investments, once made, can be fruitful. It is through the assumption of a *deus ex machina*, the state, which does all or most of the investing, that this theory is able to avoid the problems of securing not only the saving, but also the willingness to undergo risk, which is implied in investment. And it is only through a singular narrowness that the theory often implies that it tells the whole story of the successful operation of the economy, once the investment is made.

In point of fact, the conditions for the evoking of private investment and the conditions for the profitable use of capital are largely the same. I should place high upon this list the existence of stable and honest government, the absence of inflation, and the accessibility of the economy to the gains of foreign trade and commerce. But other factors, such as the improvement of general and technical education, the amelioration of agriculture (which bulks large in nearly all low-income countries), and progress along the family-limitation front would seem to be equally critical. Taken together, or in some cases even singly, we would seem to have identified a number of factors in economic progress which could outweigh a burst of state-engineered investment.

Some food for thought concerning programs of intensive investment would seem to be offered by certain points made recently by Simon Kuznets. His statistical and historical studies lead to the conclusion that "current international differences in *per capita* income are congealed effects of past differences in the rate of growth of *per capita* income." How far would it be necessary to go back into the history of the more advanced countries to reach levels comparable to the *per capita* incomes of the currently less developed countries? The answer is that we should have to go back

2. John H. Adler, "World Economic Growth—Retrospect and Prospects," *Review of Economics and Statistics,* XXXVIII (Aug. 1956), 279; cf. also, 283.

about ten decades to reach the current income level of Latin America and about fifteen decades for that of Africa and Asia.[3] Thus, even at a very early stage in

3. Simon Kuznets, "Quantitative Aspects of the Economic Growth of Nations," in *Economic Development and Cultural Change,* Vol. 5 (Oct. 1956); see especially pp. 23–5.

the industrialization of Western Europe, per capita incomes were probably as high as in Latin America today and certainly higher than in Asia and Africa. The economic development of the most advanced countries, at least, scarcely seems to be the result of crash programs.

3. PUBLIC SECTOR AND PRIVATE SECTOR

3.1 Increasing Role of the Public Sector *

It is common knowledge that governments of today have grown more intimately involved in the social and economic life of nations practically all over the world. This study of the postwar trends in public finance, therefore, begins with a review of the forces which have shaped the growth in the functions assigned to the public sector in the countries of the ECAFE region. In the process a distinction is made between planning and state control, and between the size of the public sector and the area of its influence.

The postwar period in Asia witnessed a complete transformation in the political status of a number of countries and territories. Twelve of these gained their freedom, thus increasing the number of independent nations in the ECAFE region from six before the war to eighteen by 1959.

The metropolitan countries in their stewardship had largely concerned themselves with the maintenance of law and order and the provision of basic welfare services. In the economic field, in accordance with the laissez-faire traditions of the late nineteenth century liberalism, the activities of the state had primarily been

* From United Nations, Economic Commission for Asia and the Far East, "The Increasing Role of the Public Sector," *Economic Survey of Asia and the Far East 1960,* Bangkok, 1961, pp. 53–6.

concentrated on the construction (and maintenance) of roads, railways, irrigation and other utilities. Direct participation in agricultural, industrial or commercial pursuits was rarely undertaken; the state restricted itself to the provision of basic facilities, including information, education and research.

Of course, laissez-faire did not altogether reign supreme. The national interests of the metropolitan powers demanded that the state encourage economic pursuits aimed at procuring raw materials for their industries, and markets for their industrial products. The development of commercial crops—tea, rubber, jute—and the extraction of minerals—petroleum, iron ore, tin, antimony, tungsten, manganese—bear testimony to their efforts in this direction. Even so, the development of the export and import sector was to a large extent left to private enterprise; the state confined itself to the provision of transport and other facilities for the movement of the goods between hinterland and port.

The dynamic export production and foreign trade sectors were dominated by the nationals of the metropolitan countries and certain immigrant minorities. The mass of the indigenous population was engaged in subsistence agriculture and handicrafts. In agriculture, techniques remained antiquated, yields remained stagnant, and the producers remained on the verge of subsistence. Handicrafts were adversely affected by cheaper factory-made goods imported from abroad. The establishment of peace and tranquility and the provision of welfare facilities led to an upsurge in population. Although malnutrition generally, and famines and epidemics periodically, acted as a brake, the population kept on increasing, and, for lack of any other alternative, kept pressing on the meagre resources of the soil.

The independent nations also fared no better. Foreign impact had created a few industries and laid down a few railway lines in mainland China. However, the country remained subject to periodic civil wars and encroachments on its sovereignty by major western powers and Japan. Other independent countries remained more or less in the simple agrarian stage, except for isolated enterprises dominated by private foreign capital, of which an outstanding example was the exploitation of petroleum in Iran by the Anglo-Iranian Oil Company.

Japan alone constitutes an exception. From 1868 onwards, the twin objectives of building up a militarily strong and economically prosperous nation led the state to participate in practically all phases of economic activity and community life. Before the turn of the century, primary education was made compulsory, a network of railroads was built and a system of development banks was established. Financed in the early years by land taxes and in the later years by other direct taxes, the Government remained closely associated with industrial activity; it built pilot units for coal, steel and textile production. The ties between the Government and the large business houses—the *zaibatsu*—which were established in the Meiji era (1868–1912) grew steadily stronger until, in the nineteen-twenties, major political parties were closely associated with big business firms.

In the period after the war, the government ments of the under-developed countries of the region could not but assume a direct responsibility for pulling their economies out from a long-drawn stagnation. The vicious circle of low productivity, low incomes and low savings could not be broken by private enterprise alone; the population-resource ratio turned adverse in many countries. The predominant dependence of the working force on agriculture and the low rate of national saving required to be altered. More productive capital per head had to be provided if low productivity were to be raised. However, efforts in this direction had serious economic and social ramifications. The task entailed raising the productivity in agriculture and providing of social overhead capital. The former objective called for institutional changes in land ownership and in the division of produce from land. As regards the second objective, the major characteristics of social overhead capital—long periods of gestation, the "lumpiness" of investment, and the indirect routes of pay-off—made them unsuitable for initiative by private enterprise. Both the economic characteristics of investment, and the societal changes called for, made it inevitable that the role for the public sector would be predominant.

With the objective of economic and social development firmly in mind, the countries of the ECAFE region, in the postwar period, have stressed the need to make the most efficient use of national resources. The actual extent of planning has varied from country to country. Mainland China and other centrally planned economies of the region have attempted to implement plans affecting their entire economies. In other countries the plans deal only or mainly with the major programmes to be implemented in the public sector and, in several of them, lay down production and investment targets for the private sector. The plan in Japan, on the other hand, started out as a set of economic projections over the plan period.

The concept of planning in the countries of the region has developed from separate sources. Mainland China (and northern Korea and northern Viet-Nam) have drawn on the Marxist philosophy according to which the state is to be the only entrepreneur during the stage of transformation of the capitalist society into the socialist one. It is in pursuance of this politico-economic philosophy that the state assumes control over the entire economic apparatus. Planning is a corollary, in the sense that, if the state is to be responsible for the physical allocation of the entire productive resources, there has to be a central plan of such allocation. In that sense, planning in the centrally planned economies in Asia, as in eastern Europe, has become a consequence of the "all-inclusive" role designed for the public sector.

The fountainheads of planning in other ECAFE countries spring from the post-Depression evolution of economic thinking and the practical experience in managing the wartime economies. Keynesian economics, as it has developed, assigns a central role to the public sector in the industrialized countries in levelling out the zigzags of private investment in order to avoid the trade cycles and in filling the gaps left by the secular deficiency in demand in order to avoid a high level of chronic unemployment. Private or personal consumption is assumed to be a stable function of incomes; the unstable element is private investment; the state has to adjust its outlays both on consumption and on investment if it wishes to achieve both a stable and high rate of employment.

The postwar policies of the industrially developed economies in North America and western Europe, and of Japan in Asia, have on the whole followed the stabilization directives for the public sector. Contrary to the prewar period, the postwar experience of these countries has, on the whole, been one of a relative excess of demand. The state has therefore not generally been called upon to make good a long-term deficiency in demand by a high rate of outlays designed to maintain full employment. The newly developing countries, on the other hand, picked upon this aspect to frame their economic policies; these came to be based on the critical relationship between investment and the growth of national income. And, if the private sector was not forthcoming in the drive to secure the rate of investment which was deemed desirable, the state had to step in.

The experiences of the war had posed the problem in a practical way, both for the industrial economies and the under-developed ones. Governments of the countries engaged in war were called upon to assume responsibility for the national allocation of resources in an attempt to squeeze out the optimum amount that could be diverted to the war effort. Thinking developed in this direction and the experience gained had a tremendous impact on the postwar policies of the under-developed countries. If, on a relatively sudden call, the economies could manage to divert 15-20 per cent of their output to purposes of destruction, why, in times of peace, could they not divert a higher figure than the traditional 5-7 per cent of their output in order to secure economic development? Could not the governments, as in wartime, *plan* the national allocation of resources in order to wage the infinitely more satisfying war against hunger, disease and poverty in general? It was symptomatic of this type of thinking that even before the war had ended, the pre-Independence Government of India and the then Government of China had set up machinery to evolve plans of national development when peace was restored.

Peace and independence only strengthened the two legacies of the war—the centralized allocation of resources and state control. The two are not inseparable except in mainland China. The former involves national planning, which may or may not imply a large share for the public sector in the actual control over resources. As to the latter, the countries have been more or less pragmatic in their approach. Except, again, in the centrally planned economies, where state control of almost the entire productive apparatus has been adopted on ideological grounds, the countries of the region have left both agriculture (constituting the bulk of their productive economy) and handicrafts and small-scale industry in private hands. Even in large-scale industry, the state has stepped in less on grounds of doctrine than of necessity, since private enterprise was either unwilling or unable to start off. As a result, the extension of the public sector has varied from country to country, though practically all have subscribed to the need for planning. The real reasons for the extension in the size of the public sector have lain in the very character of the social and economic investments called for in the process of economic growth. This, however, is not to deny that socialist thinking has played a part in strengthening the role of the state. Because of its political and moral appeal to the poor masses, several governments have declared that their economic objectives are directed towards attaining a socialist society; no country, other than mainland China, however, has gone in wholeheartedly for the elimination of private enterprise, for the sake of a socialist economy *per se*. If the state's tentacles have spread, this has been the necessary consequence of the desire to telescope a hundred years' progress into ten—or, in economic terms, quickly to increase—even double or treble—the traditional rate of national investment in a decade or less.

There is no clear-cut measure of the absolute size of the public sector which would enable us to make inter-country comparisons or to show the trends over a time period. The present methods of national or social accounting permit four possibilities of measuring it. The first is to measure the claim of the public sector on the national wealth or resources such as manpower and the stock of real capital. A second would involve assessing the share of the public sector in the spending of the national income on goods and services for consumption and investment. A third measure would involve a computation of the contribution made by the public sector, in terms of wages of all public sector employees and profits of public corporations, to the national total of factor incomes. Finally, it may be possible to indicate the degree of income redistribution occasioned by the public sector, as measured by the magnitude of taxation and other transfer payments (net of receipts) from the private sector.

In any such measurement, however, there is the major difficulty of defining what constitutes the public sector. The countries of the region differ considerably in the scope of their budgets or in the manner in which they classify them. The coverage of the public sector in terms of administrative authorities—the central, the state and local governments—or in terms of the inclusion or exclusion of public enterprises falling within the scope of each of these authorities, varies from country to country. Even the "publicness" of public enterprises shades off all the way from the wholly state-owned and state-operated enterprises to the substantially privately owned and privately operated activities. These difficulties are compounded by the absence of uniformity either in the defini-

TABLE I. ECAFE COUNTRIES: SHARE OF PUBLIC SECTOR IN GROSS NATIONAL EXPENDITURE
(Per cent of gross national expenditure)

Country and year	Total government expenditure	Current and capital transfer payments to private sector	Net claim of the public sector
Burma			
1951	14.4	2.1	13.4 [a]
1958	27.9	1.6	26.7 [a]
Ceylon			
1950	19.4	3.3	16.1
1958	25.6	6.1	19.5
China: mainland [b]			
1950	16.0	...	16.2 [c]
1958	32.7	...	32.7 [c]
Taiwan			
1951	25.4	0.4 [d]	25.0
1958	33.1	2.5	30.6
India [e]			
1950	9.3	1.0	8.3
1958	16.5	2.5	14.0
Indonesia			
1951	16.2	...	16.2 [c]
1958	19.7	...	19.7 [c]
Japan			
1950	23.8	7.9	15.8
1958	26.3	6.9	19.3
Korea, southern			
1953	13.2	2.8	10.4
1958	24.3	6.1	18.2
Pakistan [e, f]			
1950	9.7	0.4	9.3
1958	15.3	1.5	13.8
Philippines			
1950	11.2	1.1	10.0
1958	11.4	0.9	10.5
Thailand			
1950	10.8	...	10.8 [c]
1958	14.2	2.1	12.1

[a] Including inventory changes: +1.2 per cent of gross national expenditure in 1951 and +0.4 per cent in 1958.

[b] The concept of national income differs in mainland China from the one commonly used in private enterprise economies. It refers to material production only, and excludes economic activities not contributing directly to material production such as public administration and defense and personal and professional services. The estimates refer to net national income or product. ...

[c] Including transfer payments.

[d] Excluding capital transfers, figures for which are not available.

[e] Net national expenditure.

[f] Expenditure includes net payments of state trading schemes; net receipts are included under revenue

tions or in the methods of computation of the national accounts and by the varying degree of reliability of the basic data from which these accounts are prepared. In view of these difficulties, there is need for caution in interpreting the public finance data presented in this study for inter-country comparisons.

The first of the four measures, namely, the public sector's claim on real national wealth, could not be obtained. We have no clear measure of the nation's capital resources—land, equipment, buildings, etc.—and cannot therefore ascertain the draft made on them by the public sector. The measurement of the growth of the working force employed in the public sector is also subject to statistical difficulties. Except, in the case of Japan, an annual breakdown of manpower and employment is not available. The occupational distribution of population is available from the population censuses for a few countries only on a decennial basis....

Table 1 presents the available data relating the second of the four measures described, namely the share of the public sector in the national allocation of the total supply of final (as distinguished from intermediate) goods and services, including those received in foreign aid. The data presented are more truly indicative of the countries between two time periods; they are less truly representative of inter-country differences owing to the incompleteness of statistics of public enterprises. For mainland China the statistics exclude "co-operative" and "joint state-private" sectors which were substantially under government control. If these were included, the share of public sector would amount to 97 per cent in 1957. For the other ten territories for which it was possible to make an assessment, the public sector's claim on goods and services, net of transfer payments to the private sector, amounted to between 10 and 30 per cent

of the national total in 1957 or 1958. This provides a slightly wider range than that of the gross national product absorbed by the public sector in western Europe in 1957—between 15 and 25 per cent.

3.2 PHYSICAL INFRASTRUCTURE VS. DIRECTLY PRODUCTIVE ACTIVITIES *

Among investments in the field of economic development, a major division exists between investment in "physical infrastructure" or "overhead capital for the economy as a whole," such as transport, power, etc., and investment in directly productive activities, such as agriculture, manufacturing industry, etc. The proportion of investment as between these two broad fields in the public investment programme of any given country, should be appraised in the light of the corresponding proportion in the private sector. In a country where the private sector is relatively large, government investment in "directly productive activities" is bound to be proportionally less than in a country where the private sector is relatively small. Government investment in physical infrastructure, especially transport and power, is, however, not so flexible. In developing countries, such investment is not attractive to private entrepreneurs, because returns are small and the amount of capital required is generally beyond their capacity. Yet basic economic facilities are needed in almost every type of production, and their benefits to other sectors of the economy are immense. As the marginal social benefits are so much in excess of marginal private benefits, government investment in these fields has, therefore, invariably ranked high in all development plans of countries of the region.

The high share of investment in trans-

* From United Nations, Economic Commission for Asia and the Far East, "A Decade of Development Planning and Implementation," *Economic Bulletin for Asia and the Far East*, December 1961, pp. 8–10.

port and communications among all economic sectors is a common feature of
almost all current plans. Even in the group
of countries (Ceylon, India, Pakistan and
the Philippines) with the lowest proportions, it accounted for about one-fourth of
the total public invesment. In these countries, existing transport facilities meeting
present needs appear to be relatively more
adequate than in other countries where the
existing transport means are either insufficient to meet present needs or future
demand as a result of economic expansion,
or require substantial rehabilitation. In six
countries of the region (Burma, Cambodia,
Iran, Nepal, Thailand and south Viet-
Nam), the share of investment in transport
and communications is 40-50 per cent (see
Table I). To some extent, the relatively
high figures reflect the much larger share
of public than private investment in this
particular branch of physical infrastructure.

The share of power development in total
physical investment outlays of the government sector is relatively low in current
plans. The Federation of Malaya ranks the
highest, with 27 percent, followed by Pakistan, the Philippines, south Viet-Nam and
India with 16-20 per cent, and Burma,
Cambodia, Ceylon and Nepal, with 10-15
per cent.

The external economies argument behind the strategy of heavy investment in
basic economic facilities presupposes that
development in directly productive activities, especially in manufacturing industry, has been hampered by the lack of
transport facilities or power supply. While
this appears to be true in some countries
or some areas in a particular country, with
private enterprise, an adequate market
organization and sufficient final demand,
the strategy may not work in areas where
these elements of ability to invest are lacking. Under the latter conditions, excess
investment in physical infrastructure may
result in extensive idle capacity for at least

some time before "the ability to invest"
grows sufficiently. It may happen, for
instance, that a highway is built before it
is justified by the volume of traffic, so that
it is little used and therefore left without
adequate maintenance. Such idle capacity
is clearly a waste of resources which could
be devoted more productively to agriculture or industry.

Thus in the Eight-Year Development
Plan of Burma, heavy investment in electric power and transport and communications, amounting to 77 per cent of the total
public investment in economic sectors,
appeared to be excessive. It is reflected in
the comparatively low rate of growth with
a high rate of investment (high capital/
output ratio), and the intensification of the
foreign exchange scarcity.

It is therefore not without reason that
questions of the following kind were
raised: "if we endow an under-developed
country with a first-class highway network,
with extensive hydroelectric and perhaps
irrigation facilities, can we be certain that
industrial and agricultural activity will
expand in the wake of these improvements? Would it not be less risky and more
economical first to make sure of such
activity, even though it may have to be
subsidized in view of the absence of adequate transportation and power, and then
let the ensuing pressures determine the
appropriate outlays for SOC (social overhead capital) and its location?"[1]

However, this "pressures" approach also
has its disadvantages. Physical infrastructure projects, such as roads, railways and
hydroelectric power stations are generally
large projects characterized by bulkiness.
Their construction requires a rather long
time. If it has to wait until demand for
their services has accumulated to the extent
of exercising pressure, time may be lost and
the time required to extend other needed

1. A. O. Hirschman, *The Strategy of Economic
Development,* (Yale University Press, 1959), p. 93.

TABLE I. ALLOCATION OF PUBLIC INVESTMENT BY ECONOMIC SECTORS
(*in percentage*)

Country	Plan period	Planned(P) or actual(A)	Agriculture[a]	Industry and mining[b]	Electric power	Transport and communications	Others	Total
Burma	1952/53–1959/60	P	12	12	26	50	—	100
		A	16	31	19	34	—	100
	1952/53–1955/56	A	14	39	15	31	—	100
	1956/57–1959/60	P	27	28	17	28	—	100
		A	18	22	23	37	—	100
	1961/62–1964/65	P	27	12	10	49	2[c]	100
Cambodia	1960 –1964	P	27	14	10[d]	43	6[e]	100
Ceylon	1960 –1968	P	30	32	13	26	—	100
China: Taiwan	1957 –1960	P	23[f]		57[f]	20	—	100
Fed. of Malaya	1956 –1960	P	33	2	27[d]	38	—	100
	1956 –1960	A	30	2	31[d]	37	—	100
	1961 –1965	P	37	2	27[d]	34	—	100
India	1951/52–1955/56	P	42[g]	11	15[g]	32	—	100
		A	41[g]	7	17[g]	35	—	100
	1956/57–1960/61	P	28[g]	24	11[g]	37	—	100
		A	21	29	12	39	—	100
	1961/62–1965/66	P	24	30	18	27	—	100
Indonesia	1956 –1960	P	32	26	16	26	—	100
	1956 –1958	A	27	22	10	41	—	100
Nepal	1956/57–1960/61	P	33	9	11	41	6[h]	100
Pakistan	1955/56–1959/60	P	41[i]	17	17[i]	25	—	100
		P	39[i]	22	17[i]	22	—	100
	1960/61–1964/65	P	43[i]	17	16[i]	24	—	100
Philippines FY	1957 –1961	P	22	28	20[d]	30	—	100
FY	1960 –1962	P	31	24	17	28	—	100
Singapore	1961 –1964	P	10	38	29[d]	23	—	100
Thailand	1961 –1966	P	42	8	3	47	—	100
Viet-Nam, south	1957 –1961	P	43[j]	13	—	44[k]	—	100

Sources: National Development Plans. . . . As far as possible investment figures are used; in case where they are not referable, figures refer to development outlays.

Notes: Figures do not always add up to 100 because of rounding off.

[a] Generally agriculture includes agriculture, irrigation, forestry and fishery; in Cambodia, India, Indonesia, Nepal and Pakistan, it also includes community development.

[b] Industry and mining include mining, manufacturing industry, and construction whenever it is separately given in the plans.

[c] Trade only.

[d] Including small amount of water supply for industrial and other purposes.

[e] Expenditures on public enterprises.

[f] 40 per cent of investment on Shihman reservoir multi-purpose project is allocated to irrigation and 80 per cent to power; the estimate is based on the proportion of estimated future income which will be derived from irrigation and power respectively.

[g] Outlays on multi-purpose projects have been arbitrarily divided and added respectively to irrigation and power according to the proportion of investment allocation (excluding multi-purpose projects) to both sectors. The proportions are 57:43 and 56:44 respectively for the planned and actual figures in the First Five-Year Plan and 53:47 for the planned figures in the second Five-Year Plan.

[h] Mainly Rapti valley project.

[i] Investment in multi-purpose project is arbitrarily divided and added to irrigation and power

assistance to directly productive fields prolonged. Such assistance, regardless of its form (subsidies, protection, etc.) also amounts to a waste. Moreover, the response to public pressure of the authorities responsible for providing physical infrastructure tends to be weak and slow in under-developed countries. There are many examples of power plants, even of moderate capacity, which took a rather long time to complete, although the authorities concerned seemed not to mind much about the complaints of the public.

Balanced development between physical infrastructure and directly productive fields appears to be an inevitable conclusion. The actual implementation of this general principle depends, to a large extent, on a continuous and accurate assessment of the growth in both sectors, and on timely adjustments in the planning and implementation of the individual projects concerned. In this connexion, it is important that a projection of the future demand for transport services, power and other basic economic facilities should first be made on the basis of the projected or planned growth of the directly productive activities.

3.3 PUBLIC TARGETS AND PUBLIC INVESTMENT *

It is important to remember the difference between targets in the public sector and targets in the private sector. The former are the direct responsibility of the

* From United Nations, Economic Commission for Africa, *Problems Concerning Techniques of Development Programming in African Countries,* E/CN.14/42/Add. 1, December 18, 1959, pp. 45–7, 85–8, 108–11.

government and they should, therefore, be in the nature of firm undertakings, subject only to the normal revisions of the development programme. Targets in the private sector are no more than what the government expects to happen; or would like to happen or will try to make happen by its economic policies. Private targets state the assumptions on which the government proceeds in framing its public expenditure programme and the other measures and policies contained in the development programme. But they cannot be put forward with the same firmness as public targets, since government measures to influence private actions—encouragement or discouragement—are never quite certain in effect, and the achievement of these private targets will depend on the responses of individuals and business units. Moreover, insofar as the individuals or business units concerned may be foreign investors, their responses are not easily influenced by the government. For all these reasons, targets in the private sector cannot be held with the same firmness as public targets.

Among the public sectors, the more social sectors, such as health and education, are in a special class. A number of recent investigations in more advanced countries have pointed, with great unanimity, to the conclusion that of the total increase in productivity per man hour only a minor part has been due to the increased input of capital and natural resources per worker; the major part has been due to an increase in output per unit of capital and natural resources used as well as per unit of labour. This strongly points to the importance of "human investment" as factors in

---

respectively according to the proportion of investment (other than multi-purpose projects) in irrigation and power. In the second Five-Year Plan, it was stated that, within the total allocation of the water and power development programme, about 35 per cent is exclusively for water development, 30 per cent for investigation surveys and miscellaneous schemes. The last two segments have been divided and added to irrigation and power respectively according to the ratio of 35:30. The same proportion has been applied to the corresponding First Five-Year plan figures.

ʲ Including power.   ᵏ Public works.

increasing output. However, the relationship between expenditure on health and education on the one hand and the resulting output on the other hand is rather different from that, say, between bricks and buildings. In the first place, better health and better education are by themselves desirable development objectives, even if they do not contribute to output; this is not the case with bricks. Secondly, the relationship between health and education and output is usually more remote and unpredictable than the relationship between bricks and buildings. Thirdly, the relationship is not technological but a matter of general economic and social analysis; no input-output tables exist to describe this relationship, and experience elsewhere is not much help. In the fourth place, there usually is no market demand as a guide to the volume of education and health services required, as there is with buildings. For all these reasons, targets for health and education expenditure are normally treated as "autonomous targets," i.e. they are fixed without much reference to either aggregative target or to sectoral targets, but more in accordance with what a country "can afford"; or what it "needs." The possible guidelines are the percentages either of total national income or of total public expenditure directed into various types of health and education programmes.

...

Historically, development programming has started from the need to formulate multi-annual public investment programmes. While development programming has become much more than a public investment programme this remains an important part of it.

The first problem arising is one of definition. The development programme should set out the government's intended developmental expenditure, together with other measures and policies and its picture of the economy as a whole. But what is "development expenditure"? The easy answer—and the traditional answer—is to identify "development expenditure" with capital expenditure. This, however, is not only wrong, but it is also misleading. It is wrong because not all capital expenditure is developmental, nor is all developmental expenditure capital. Expenditure on splendid public buildings is capital expenditure but not necessarily developmental, even though it may be included in the development programme. The salaries of agricultural extension workers are developmental, but they are recurrent expenditure, not capital expenditure. The identification of developmental expenditure with capital expenditure is misleading because it draws developmental expenditure into the identification (in itself misleading) of recurrent expenditure with ordinary revenue, and of capital expenditure with borrowing.

The question of definition and classification of expenditure is important as a first step in drawing up a public expenditure programme, as an integral part of an economic development programme. The United Nations has organized regional "workshops" on the problem of economic and functional classifications of government transactions. Such schemes of classification cover the expenditure in the entire public sector and set it within the context of the economy as a whole. It helps to bring out more clearly the interrelationships between the public and the private sector and, thus, develops information essential for development programming. At the same time, the economic and functional classifications provide a convenient basis for distinguishing development expenditure from other public expenditure.

Economic development programming sets the public expenditures programme within the context of the economy as a whole. In the first place, the proper way of financing the public expenditure depends on the financing of private investment which in African countries is always an important and frequently the major part of total developmental investment. If private savings plus inflow of private foreign capital are insufficient to finance private developmental investment without undue recourse to inflation, the public expenditure programme (even that part of it which is capital expenditure "below the line") may have to be financed out of ordinary revenue, and the government may have to make public revenue available to private investors. On the other hand, if private savings plus inflow of foreign capital should be amply sufficient to cover private developmental investment needs— not a very likely case—the public expenditure programme, even part of the current expenditure, can be safely covered through various forms of borrowing or even creation of money. Development programming leads necessarily away from a purely "fiscal" view. But this does not mean that the old fiscal canons of finance have become useless and should be thrown on the scrap heap.

Secondly, development programming indicates that the benefits of public investment are not measured by the production directly arising in the public sector, and even less by the public revenue to which they give rise. Rather, they are measured by the total increase of production made possible as a result of public investment whether this increase in production accrues in the private sector or the public sector. But again, this does not mean that the revenue producing character or otherwise of different public expenditures projects should be entirely disregarded. Far from it: the degree in which subsequent increases in output can be "ploughed back" into new investment is of great importance

to the development programming approach, as we have already seen.

Thirdly, the financing of public and private investment must be seen as a whole. Private savings are considered to be available to finance public investment, if in the context of the development programme public investment deserves higher priority than the private investment which would otherwise be financed. Whether the private savings are transferred to the public sector by taxation, or by borrowing, or by credit rationing to the private sector or by other means is a question of technique, not of principle. But the opposite is also true. If private developmental investment is deemed to have priority over public investment, the public savings (surplus of revenue over expenditure as well as the government's access to external resources of public finance) should be made available to finance private developmental investment. This can be done by subsidizing private investment, or by setting up public credit institutions for private investors, or by reducing taxation; again, this is a matter of technique....

It will be noted that development programming is neutral as to what are proper spheres of public and private investment. That is a matter to be decided on other grounds. The technique of development programming is applicable whether the realm of public investment is widened, as a matter of philosophy or efficiency, or whether it is narrowed. Although it is commonly believed that development programming implies a bias in favour of public investment, this is not the case provided that those formulating the programmes beware of an elementary fallacy. It is a fact that public investment programmes can be drawn up with much more assurance, certainty and detail than private investment programmes which are at best a guess of what large numbers of private persons are likely to do under such stimuli as the government provides. In any case, those formulating the development programme are officials more closely in touch with government departments than with private investors. But it is a fallacy to conclude, because public investment is more easily predictable and more easily controlled by those formulating development programmes, that public investment for that reason is more important to development than private investment. Thus put, the fallacy involved is evident, and development programming can be seen to be a neutral technique. . . .

It may be worth repeating that a development programme is more than a public investment programme. But a public investment programme is an essential part of a development programme. The efficient implementation of a development programme depends vitally upon the efficient running of those public services and those public enterprises which are established or extended as part of the development programme.

Efficient management of enterprises is a problem in African countries in the private as well as the public sector. Shortage of skilled management is, in fact, one of the prime symptoms, as well as one of the prime causes, of under-development. The over-all shortage of managerial skill leads to two conclusions:

(a) That it is not easy for public services and public enterprise to secure the services of skilled management from the national private sector. In many cases, that would be robbing Peter to pay Paul.

(b) The management standards of public services and public enterprise must be judged in the context of the general shortage of managerial skill in the country. One cannot expect the impossible.

The shortage of managerial skill is largely due to a lack of experience. The best way of learning to manage is to manage. This creates a dilemma. The obvious solution would be to engage the services of expatriate managers, both for public and for private enterprises. This, however, is expensive, and in the public sector especially there may be political objections. Moreover, if the expatriate managers, however skilled, fail to train local managers to a higher standard of skill, the vicious circle of lack of experience and lack of managerial skill is perpetuated. Often, the solution will be to recruit expatriate managers but at the same time assure the training of local personnel.

The management of public services and enterprises requires different qualities and different traditions from normal administrative public service. Where the public enterprise is more of a routine nature, e.g. post office functions, the difference may not be sufficient to create special problems. In the case of more directly developmental services and enterprises, however, the good civil servant is not necessarily a good manager—and even the good civil servant may be rare. In many countries, an attempt is made to solve this dilemma by placing public services and enterprises outside the normal machinery of civil service administration; e.g. special public or semi-public corporations with varying degrees of autonomy. This may well be a suitable arrangement for most or all African countries . . . but it carries also a danger. In development programming, it is very important that such autonomous or semi-autonomous services or enterprises be brought fully into the scope of the development programme. The coordination of the policies of such public agencies and public enterprises with normal civil service departments is an essential part of programming, whatever the legal form of the various enterprises may be. How to reconcile autonomy for the sake of managerial efficiency, with coordination of policies for the sake of efficient programming is a big problem.

Public enterprises of a more specialized character are nearly always conducted outside the civil service routine. This applies, for instance, to development banks and other public financial institutions.

Public enterprise and investment usually lack the normal test of efficiency, namely profits or losses. In development programming, this test is in any case not necessarily accepted, since development programmes are derived from the idea that the working of the market mechanism alone is not necessarily sufficient to produce the maximum rate of development, or to produce the most desirable type of development. While some departure from the profit-loss test is inherent in development programming, yet it remains true that the profit-loss test remains at least a valuable point of departure in private enterprise. Unless specific reasons to assume the contrary are presented, a profitable enterprise benefits the economy, and an unprofitable enterprise hurts it. This cannot be assumed with public enterprise where the purpose frequently is to enable other sectors to make profits, rather than to make profits itself. Various theoretical devices have been suggested to introduce a modified profit-loss guide line even in public services and public enterprise, but they are too far-fetched to be of practical application in African countries at the moment.

In practice, other tests and standards of efficiency must be devised. An example would be frequent comparative cost analysis, careful market research and efficiency auditing. All these matters are of concern to development programmers since the implementation of the programme strongly depends on the efficiency of public enterprise. The measures necessary to increase the efficiency of public enterprise are not, however, directly under their own control, and they are often a matter for specialized inquiries.

It has been authoritatively pointed out [1]

that lack of managerial experts and scarcity of managerial skill applies more strongly to large-scale than to small-scale enterprise. This is in itself an argument for watching closely whether the development programme does not give too much emphasis to large projects as compared with small projects. It is also an argument for watching carefully whether a given project is suitable for public administration—which must almost by definition be limited to large-scale enterprise. While not normally suited for the direct administration of small-scale enterprise, public action is, however, well suited to the aid of small-scale enterprise by providing common services, credit facilities, technological research institutes, technical advice and other valuable aids. Such possibilities should always be carefully looked into in any development programme. Managerial failures can be particularly fateful in the case of large-scale enterprise. In the case of public services, it should also be remembered that whereas good public services have a high "multiplier" or stimulating effect on the economy as a whole, so badly run public services can have a "multiplier" effect in reverse, a widely discouraging effect. A development programme cannot be efficient if it assumes standards of managerial perfection in the public sector which cannot be satisfied.

3.4 INVESTMENT IN THE FEDERAL DEVELOPMENT PROGRAM OF NIGERIA *

The principal feature of Nigeria's First National Development Plan, 1962—68, is its gearing for growth—growth, that is, not in the sense of achieving spectacular immediate or even short-term results, but rather

[1] See W. Arthur Lewis, *Theory of Economic Growth*, pp. 81–3.

* From Federal Government of Nigeria, *Federal Government Development Programme 1962-68*, Federation of Nigeria, Sessional Paper No. 1 of 1962, pp. 1–5.

in the sense of laying a solid and enduring foundation for future expansion—an essential prerequisite in Nigeria's evolution towards a self-sustaining economy.

In considering the Federal Government's Development Programme two factors must be borne in mind. Firstly, the conception and execution of a National Plan is such that the Programme of any one Government cannot be judged in isolation or be regarded as complete in itself. In other words, the Development Programme of each of the four Governments forms but one essential part of a composite and coherent whole. Thus, the Federal Government's Programme must be viewed against the background of the general objective of the National Plan and the prospects for the Nigerian economy in the coming years.

Secondly, the Federal Government has an exclusive constitutional responsibility for certain major fields of governmental activity. These include:

(i) the defence of the nation and internal security;

(ii) the development of communications of nationwide significance; telecommunications, major trunk roads, railways, sea and airports, etc.;

(iii) the expansion of electric power;

(iv) certain major aspects of higher education, including medical education;

(v) pure research in the fields of primary production and mineralogy;

(vi) provision for services within the Federal territory of Lagos;

(vii) the creation of financial institutions appropriate to a sovereign state and the maintenance of confidence in these institutions.

It follows, therefore, that the role of the Federal Government within the over-all National Plan must necessarily differ considerably from those played by Regional Governments. Nevertheless, the Federal Government recognises clearly that it also must be responsible for providing a bold lead to Regional Governments in the achievement of the major objectives of the Plan. It is for this reason, for example, that it has accepted to provide by way of loans and grants, a total sum of up to £25,000,-000 towards the expansion of activities in the field of primary production.

At its Tenth Meeting held in 1959, the National Economic Council laid down that a National Development Plan should be prepared for Nigeria with the objective of the "achievement and maintenance of the highest possible rate of increase in the standard of living and the creation of the necessary conditions to this end, including public support and awareness of both the potential that exists and the sacrifices that will be required."

The major objective of the First National Plan is to maintain and, if possible, surpass, the average rate of 4 per cent per year in the growth of Gross Domestic Product. To realize this aim, it will be necessary to invest approximately 15 per cent of the Gross National Product each year and to ensure that, as much as possible, of this gross investment, whether undertaken by the Government or by private business, is channelled into the directly productive sectors of the economy. The Governments of the Federation fully realise that this high rate of investment will, of necessity, require a substantial amount of foreign assistance and of capital imports. It must be expected, therefore, that the import surpluses will increase but this trend is important to enable the economy to absorb external finance and to permit some increases in the level of living. In order to avoid hardships on the population, and distortion in the priorities of the Plan, every effort will be made to prevent inflationary price rises through monetary and fiscal policies and to avoid, as far as possible, the control of imports through quantitative restrictions and exchange controls.

The Governments of Nigeria realise that

only the achievement of a substantial rate of growth of the economy will make it possible to raise the average level of living and to provide the Nigerian people with the means for increased employment, and improved education and health. In order to achieve this rate of growth, the Governments have recognized that as large a volume of resources as possible must be allocated into the directly productive sectors of the economy. For this reason, the National Plan accords the highest priority to agriculture, industry and technical education.

The total capital expenditure programme of the National Plan amounts to £676.5 million over the six-year period. Of this sum, approximately 14 per cent has been allocated to Primary Production and 13 per cent to Trade and Industry. Thus, the two sectors which have been accorded top priority in the Plan will account for more than one quarter of the total capital expenditure over the period. Equally notable is the fact that more than 70 per cent of the total capital expenditure is to be devoted to those sectors which contribute directly

to economic growth—primary production; trade and industry; electricity; the transport system; communications; and irrigation and industrial water supplies. As Table I shows, there has been a substantial shift in the composition of capital expenditure, from administrative to developmental expenditure, compared with the 1955-61 Economic Programme.

Of particular interest is the major shift in emphasis which is to occur in those sectors which have been accorded highest priority in the Plan. The following illustrates the change in emphasis that has occurred:

The expected financing for the Programmes of the four Governments may be summarised as follows:

Within the total National figure of £676.5 million, the capital expenditure programme for the Federal Government amounts to £412.5 million. This includes the expenditure by Federal Statutory Corporations and by the wholly-owned Nigerian National Line and Nigeria Airways. The expenditure to be incurred directly by the Federal Government is expected

TABLE I. DISTRIBUTION OF CAPITAL PROGRAMMES AMONG MAJOR EXPENDITURE
CATEGORIES (ALL GOVERNMENTS) 1955-61 AND 1962-68

	1955-61 Plan	1962-68 Plan
Development expenditure	50.8%	71.7%
Social overhead expenditure	19.9%	20.9%
Administrative expenditure	29.3%	7.0%

TABLE II. DISTRIBUTION OF CAPITAL EXPENDITURE ON AREAS OF MAJOR
EMPHASIS (ALL GOVERNMENTS) 1955-61 AND 1962-68

	1955-61 Plan		1962-68 Plan	
	Expenditure (£ million)	Percentage of plan expenditure	Expenditure (£ million)	Percentage of plan expenditure
Primary production	8.7	3.7%	90.7	13.4%
Trade and industry	6.9	2.9%	89.6	13.3%
Education	18.8	8.0%	69.8	10.3%

TABLE III. SOURCE AND USE OF FUNDS FOR ALL GOVERNMENT CAPITAL PROGRAMMES,
1962/63-1967/68

	£
Resources from all sources	1,212.6 million
Less Recurrent expenditures	953.6 million
Available for capital programme	259.0 million
Planned capital expenditure	676.5 million
Less Underspending	25.0 million
Requirements for capital programme	651.5 million
Less Domestic resources available for capital programme	259.0 million
Gap to be financed	392.5 million
Less Assumed foreign aid*	338.8 million
Uncovered gap	53.7 million

* Assumed at 50 per cent of Planned capital expenditure.

TABLE IV. SOURCES OF FUNDS FOR FEDERAL CAPITAL PROGRAMME

	£
Total Recurrent revenues, 1962-68	487 million
Less Recurrent expenditure	460 million
Available for capital development from recurrent surpluses	27 million
Internal resources of statutory corporations	80 million
Domestic borrowing and central bank	63 million
Mobilisation of Nigerian external resources	10 million
Other accumulated federal government funds	20 million
TOTAL	200 million

to amount to £238 million, or 58 per cent of the total Federal Development Programme.

As has been indicated above, the Governments of the Federation expect to receive approximately one half of the total cost of the capital programmes by way of foreign loans and grants. The Federal Government intends, therefore, to mobilise from its own resources some £200 million towards the financing required for its Programme. This may be summarised as follows:

The major step forward in the economic development of Nigeria which is the aim of the National Plan is fully reflected in the Federal Government Development Program. In particular, investment will not, as hitherto, be largely limited to projects which are of exclusively Federal concern, but will be broadened to embrace new activities, particularly in the fields of agriculture and education. The allocation of investment in the Federal Government's Programme is directed towards:

(i) The production of adequate, cheap and reliable supplies of electric power to meet the rapidly increasing demand and without which the industrial and economic development of the Nation would be seriously delayed. In this connection, special mention must be made of the Niger Dams project, to which the National Economic Council has accorded the highest priority and which, it is anticipated will also provide important agricultural, fisheries and navigation benefits.

(ii) A major increase in investment by

the Federal Government in the field of Agriculture, coupled with more intensive research into natural resources and mineral wealth.

(iii) A positive approach to industrial development, both by promoting the establishment of a Development Bank and by direct Government participation in industry on a massive scale, particularly to support high priority programmes and to induce growth in the economy. Attention is drawn to the proposed Iron and Steel Industry which is expected to stimulate the establishment of a number of other related industries.

(iv) The maximum possible investment in the development of technical, secondary and higher education so that the future manpower requirements of the nation may be met by Nigerians in the shortest practicable time.

(v) The development of communications and a co-ordinated transport system, making the fullest use of the particular advantages of the various forms of transport available.

TABLE V. FEDERAL CAPITAL EXPENDITURE PROGRAMME 1962-68
DISTRIBUTION BY SECTOR

£ million

	1955-61 *Programme*		1962-68 *Programme*	
	Actual expenditure 1955-61	%	*Planned expenditure* 1962-68	%
I. ECONOMIC				
1. Primary production	1.2	0.8	20.5	5.0
2. Trade and industry	3.8	2.6	44.0	10.7
3. Electricity	7.0	4.8	98.1	23.8
4. Transport	49.9	34.0	104.0	25.1
5. Communications	12.1	8.3	30.0	7.3
6. Water excl. irrigation	2.0	1.4	1.8	0.4
II. SOCIAL OVERHEAD				
7. Education	6.8	4.6	29.2	7.1
8. Health	2.9	2.0	10.3	2.5
9. Town and country planning	17.4	11.9	23.2	5.6
10. Social welfare	0.4	0.3	2.7	0.7
11. Information	1.0	0.7	2.3	0.6
III. GENERAL ADMINISTRATION				
12. Judicial	0.1	0.1	0.3	0.1
13. General	35.7	24.4	43.9	10.6
IV. FINANCIAL OBLIGATIONS				
14. Financial obligations	6.1	4.1	2.2	0.5
Total	146.3	100.0	412.5	100.0
I Development	76.0	51.9	298.4	72.3
II Social overhead	28.4	19.5	67.7	16.5
III General administration	35.7	24.4	44.2	10.7
IV Financial obligations	6.1	4.1	2.2	0.5
Total	146.3	100.0	412.5	100.0

(vi) A limited expansion of services in the Federal Territory of Lagos commensurate with the increasing ability of the population of Lagos to sustain such services.

(vii) The strengthening of the defence and internal security forces.

(viii) Restraining investment in all other fields to the minimum levels required to accelerate growth in these sectors of higher priority.

. . .

In accordance with the classification of the capital budgets to be used for the National Plan, 1962-68, programmes are grouped according to the major economic sector in which they lie, regardless of where administrative responsibility may be. This is illustrated by Table V (p. 456).

3.5 INVESTMENT IN THE PUBLIC AND PRIVATE SECTORS OF INDIA *

The Plan includes outlays both in the public and the private sectors. In the public sector, a distinction is made between investment expenditure and current outlays, the latter representing expenditure of the

* From Government of India Planning Commission, *Third Five Yar Plan, A Draft Outline*, June 1960, pp. 25-7, 51-2.

nature of staff, subsidies, etc. The Third Plan envisages a total investment of Rs. 10,200 crores, of which Rs. 6,200 crores will be in the public sector and Rs. 4,000 crores in the private sector. Including the current outlay estimated as Rs. 1,050 crores, the total outlay in the public sector will be Rs. 7,250 crores. Investment in the public sector also includes a sum of Rs. 200 crores corresponding to transfers from the public sector for capital formation in the private sector. In Table 1 below, outlay and investment in the Third Plan are compared with those in the Second.

It will be seen that the Third Plan provides for an increase of about 51 per cent in the total investment, of about 70 per cent and about 58 per cent respectively in the investment and outlay undertaken in the public sector, and about 29 per cent in the private sector investment.

The following Table shows the distribution of outlay and investment in the Third Plan (Table II).

The investment in the economy increased over the First Plan from Rs. 500 crores to nearly Rs. 850 crores per annum. By the end of the Second Plan it is expected to reach an annual level of Rs. 1,450 crores to Rs. 1,500 crores. By the end of the Third

TABLE I. OUTLAY AND INVESTMENT IN THE SECOND AND THIRD PLANS *

| | Public Sector | | | (Rs. crores) | |
	Plan outlay	Current outlay	Investment	Private sector **	Total investment
Second Plan	4600	950	3650	3100	675
Third Plan	7250	1050	6200	4000	1020

* Two expressions in common use may be briefly explained:

(1) *Investment* is expenditure on the creation of physical assets (*e.g.,* buildings and plant and equipment), including expenditure on personnel required for putting up these assets. The expression corresponds broadly to expenditure on capital account.

(2) *Current outlay* corresponds broadly to expenditure on revenue account on plan schemes, it is expenditure other than that classified as 'investment'.

** These figures do not include investments financed out of resources transferred from the public sector.

TABLE II. OUTLAY AND INVESTMENT IN THE THIRD PLAN

| | Group | Public sector | | | Private sector investment | (Rs. crores) Total investment |
		Plan outlay	Current outlay	Investment		
1	agriculture, minor irrigation and community development	1025	350	675	800	1475
2	major and medium irrigation	650	10	640	—	640
3	power	925	—	925	50	975
4	village and small industries	250	90	160	275	435
5	industry and minerals	1500	—	1500	1000	2500
6	transport and communications	1450	—	1450	200	1650
7	social services	1250	600	650	1075	1725
8	inventories	200	—	200	600	800
9	total	7250	1050	6200	4000	10200

Plan the annual investment is likely to be in the range of Rs. 2,500 crores. Investment by public authorities rose from about Rs. 200 crores per annum to about Rs. 450 crores by the end of the First Plan and is likely to rise to about Rs. 800 crores by the end of the Second Plan, the corresponding level expected to be reached at the end of the Third Plan being about Rs. 1,500 crores.

The general pattern of investment in the Second Plan is being continued in the Third, but in the public sector there is greater emphasis on agriculture, industry and power and on certain aspects of social services. The distribution of plan outlays in different sectors according to the Second and the Third Plan is given in the Table below (Table III).

Investment in the private sector falls broadly into two parts, namely, (a) investment relating to the organised sector of industry, mining, electricity and transport, and (b) investment which is dispersed extensively over fields like agriculture, vil-

TABLE III. DISTRIBUTION OF PLAN OUTLAY IN THE PUBLIC SECTOR

| | | Outlay | | (Rs. crores) Percentage | |
		Second plan	Third plan	Second plan	Third plan
1	agriculture and minor irrigation	320	625	6.9	8.6
2	community development & Co-operation	210	400	4.6	5.5
3	major and medium irrigation	450	650	9.8	9.0
4	total 1, 2 & 3	980	1675	21.3	23.1
5	power	410	925	8.9	12.8
6	village & small industries	180	250	3.9	3.4
7	industry & minerals	880	1500	19.1	20.7
8	transport & communications	1290	1450	28.1	20.0
9	total 5, 6, 7 & 8	2760	4125	60.0	56.9
10	social services	860	1250	18.7	17.2
11	inventories	—	200	—	2.8
12	grand total	4600	7250	100	100

TABLE IV. INVESTMENT IN THE PRIVATE SECTOR

	Second Plan		(Rs. crores) Third Plan estimates *
	Original estimates	Estimated investment on the revised basis *	
1 agriculture (including irrigation)	275	675	850
2 power	40	40	50
3 transport	85	135	200
4 village and small industries	100	225	325 *
5 large and medium industry and minerals	575	700 **	1050 *
6 housing and other construction	925	1000	1125
7 inventories	400	525	600
8 total	2400	3300	4200

* These figures represent aggregate investment in the private sector, including that financed out of resources transferred from the public sector.
** These figures do not include investment by way of modernisation and replacement.

lage and small industries, rural and urban housing etc. Data regarding the second category are necessarily very rough, but in recent years more precise information has become available in respect of the organised private sector.

. . .

Investment in the private sector covers not only organised industry, mining, electricity and transport, but also large and dispersed fields like agriculture, village and small industries, rural and urban housing, etc. It is not possible with the data available to present a meaningful scheme of financing the investments in this entire sector. A broad view as to the feasibility of the proposed scale of investment has to be taken on a comparison with past trends. [Table IV above] sets out the likely levels of investment under major heads in the private sector in the Third Plan period as compared to the initial estimates of the Second Plan and the estimates of investment as now revised in the light of the studies made in the Reserve Bank.

It will be seen that as compared to the levels of private investment in the Second Plan as now estimated, the Third Plan proposes a substantial step-up mainly in the field of large and medium industries—from Rs. 700 crores to Rs. 1,050 crores. The increases envisaged in the other sectors are relatively small and it is assumed that they will be financed from their normal sources which include savings by agriculturists, by those engaged in arts and crafts and in trade and small industries, borrowings from unorganised or semi-organised lending agencies and also to an extent, from governmental and Reserve Bank assistance. Self-financing or financing from these diverse sources represents such a large proportion of the total resources that go into investment in these fields that it is difficult to attempt anything like a precise picture of the scope and possibilities in regard to each of these sources.

The problem, then, is regarding the finances required for the investment programmes for large and medium industries. Here again considerable guess-work is involved, but some broad estimates have been given in the chapter on Industries and Minerals. Of the total investment of Rs. 4,200 crores in the private sector Rs. 200 crores will, as mentioned earlier, be provided by way of transfer of resources from the public sector. Considerable assistance by the Reserve Bank to agriculture, small-scale industries and some select financial corporations dealing with the private sector is also envisaged. Moreover, external assistance to the private sector may be of the order of Rs. 300 crores. The trends of investment in the private sector during the Second Plan and the growing readiness of private enterprise to avail itself of the new opportunities being created by the development process warrant the hope that the financing of the order of investment proposed in the private sector will not present insuperable difficulties.

Ultimately, of course, the question is one of the adequacy of total resources available in the community for investment. The needs of finance both for the public and for the private sector have to be met from the common pool of domestic savings together with the quantum of external assistance forthcoming. Every effort has to be made to secure adequate availability in regard to both these.

3.6 Investment in Ceylon's Ten-Year Plan *

The main operative part of the Plan is the investment programme. The investment programme reflects the priorities of relevance to a development strategy for Ceylon. Broadly it provides for a rapid spurt towards industrialisation; for the expansion of export earnings through raising the output of plantation crops; for import saving and the provision of domestic requirements in respect of a variety of products in agriculture, animal husbandry and fisheries, for meeting national needs in the field of social services, particularly education, health and housing; and for achieving levels of activity and expansion

* From National Planning Council of Ceylon, *The Ten-Year Plan, Colombo*, 1959, pp. 68-9, 76-8.

over different fields sufficient for the fullest absorption of the country's growing manpower resources.

The total cost of the programme, in other words the total investment cost of the Plan, covering both the public and the private sectors, over the entire 10-year period 1959–1968 is Rs. 13,600,000,000. These investments are distributed over the major fields of activity as follows (Table I).

. . .

The magnitudes discussed so far are national aggregates covering the economy as a whole. They relate to combined totals of investment to be made by both the public and private sectors of the economy. As mentioned in a previous section, however, there is an essential difference in the nature of an over-all plan as it relates to the public and private sectors respectively. The investment programmes for the public sector are the direct responsibility of the government which is the operational agency for implementing them. These programmes could thus reflect actual investment decisions that have or would be taken by government. It is true that within the public sectors there are differences in the degree of firmness behind the several individual programmes presented here. Despite these differences, however, the public sector programmes fall into a distinct category from the point of view of planning. The programmes for the private sector are of a different nature. They are essentially in the nature of estimates of the performance which can be expected from this sector given the conditions and opportunities that would prevail over the 10-year period. Since the performance of the private sector can be closely influenced by governmental policies and measures it is implicit that government policy would be directed towards bringing forth this performance.

It is likely that the big increase in devel-

TABLE I. TOTAL GROSS INVESTMENT (1959—1968 INCLUSIVE)

(At market prices of 1957)

Sector	Amount Rs. million		Percentage of total	
Agriculture		3,110		22.9
Main Export Crops				
Tea	507		3.7	
Rubber	411		3.0	
Coconut	315		2.3	
Other Agriculture and Animal Husbandry				
Irrigation and land development	1,092		8.0	
Specific agriculture crops and animal husbandry	785		5.8	
Fisheries				
(Excluding fisheries harbours)		218		1.0
Industry		2,714		20.6
Large and medium	2314		17.0	
Small-scale and cottage	400		2.9	
Electricity		826		6.1
Transport and communications		1,946		14.3
Roads	516		3.8	
Railways	301		2.2	
Ports	372		2.7	
Aviation	48		.4	
Posts and telecommunications	153		1.1	
Vehicles and miscellaneous	556		4.1	
Construction		325		2.4
Social investments		3,571		26.3
Housing	2,725		20.0	
Health	446		3.3	
Education	400		2.9	
Public Administration		180		1.3
Other Services		711		5.2
GRAND TOTAL		13,600		1.000

* The small discrepancy between the total and the constituent items is due to rounding.

opment activity within the government sector as envisaged in the Plan would be accompanied by a parallel stepping up of activity in the private sector. It is not planned that government activity would provide all the requirements of the economy. Even the implementation of governmental programmes and projects involves the use of several services and products supplied by the private sector. An expansion in investment activity in this sector is therefore provided for in the Plan.

It should, of course, be clear that the role of the public sector in the effective realisation of the Plan is dominant. It is necessary for the State to ensure that the several measures vital for the transformation of the economy are in fact undertaken. Crucial investments have to be made in several fields—particularly new ones—which are strategic to economic growth. The government must ensure that these are made on a scale and at a pace which measure up to national needs. All this would involve the creation of several new enterprises in the public sector and the expansion of existing ones. It would involve in fact a substantial growth in this sector as a whole not only in absolute but in relative terms as well. Moreover the influence of government policy would obviously not be confined to the public sector. It would embrace the magnitude and direction of investment in the private sector as well. This is indeed implicit in the very concept of planning.

A distribution of the investment totals of the Plan between the government and the private sectors is shown below. The distribution is not inflexible. A division can be made fairly clearly when the investments fall into categories which belong exclusively to one or the other of the sectors. It can also be made where the investments are based on firm and detailed programmes which indicate separately public and private outlays. When these requirements are not satisfied however—and as indicated there are parts of the plan for which this holds—only a rough division is possible. This division could vary as detailed programmes and policies come to be formulated.

The figures presented below are based on a division between investments to be made by or financed by government and investments made or financed by the private sector. This does not, of course, necessarily correspond to a division based on public or private ownership. Government loans and investment subsidies to the private sector are generally included in the investment outlays of government except where they could be attributed to specialised governmental lending agencies. However, the distribution cannot be made with absolute accuracy. In the division which follows the category government embraces both central and local government and also public enterprises. "Non-monetised" investments representing the value of self-help contributions are shown separately.

TABLE II. GOVERNMENT AND PRIVATE INVESTMENT BY SECTORS, 1959–68 (INCLUSIVE)

Sector	(Rs. million) Non-monetized	Government	Private	Total
Tea	—	156	351	507
Rubber	—	194	217	411
Coconut	—	41	274	315
Specific agricultural crops & animal husbandry	—	321	464	785
Irrigation	110	982	—	1,092
Fisheries	—	208	10	218
Large scale industry	—	1,613	701	2,314
Small scale industry	40	360	—	400
Electricity	—	826	—	826
Transport	100	1,652	194	1,946
Construction	—	90	235	325
Housing	435	908	1,382	2,725
Public administration	100	926	—	1,026
Other services	70	100	541	711
	855	8,377	4,369	13,600

4. BIBLIOGRAPHICAL NOTE

1. The literature on the general topic of planning and the price system is extensive, but the following references may be cited for the particular problem of assessing the relative merits of the market mechanism and planning in the context of development: Hugh G. J. Aitken (ed.), *The State and Economic Growth*, New York, 1959; H. H. Aubrey, "The Role of the State in Economic Development, *"American Economic Review, Papers and Proceedings,* May 1951; T. Balogh, "Economic Policy and the Price System," *Economic Bulletin for Latin America*, March 1961; P. T. Bauer, *Economic Analysis and Policy in Underdeveloped Countries*, Durham, 1957, chap. 3; A. K. Cairncross, *Factors in Economic Development*, London, 1962, chap. 19; Amlan Datta, *Socialism, Democracy and Industrialization*, London, 1962; Maurice Dobb, *An Essay on Economic Growth and Planning*, London, 1960, chap. I; Dobb, "Some Problems in the Theory of Growth and Planning Policy," *Kyklos*, Vol. XIV, 1961; H. S. Frankel, "United Nations Primer for Development, *"Quarterly Journal of Economics,* August 1952; A. H. Hanson, *Public Enterprise and Economic Development*, London, 1959; R. F. Harrod, "Dynamic Theory and Planning," *Kyklos,* Vol. XV, No. 1, 1962; A. O. Hirsch-man, "Economic Policy in Underdeveloped Countries," *Economic Development and Cultural Change*, July 1957; K. William Kapp, "Economic Development, National Planning and Public Administration," *Kyklos,* Vol. XIII, No. 2, 1960; E. S. Mason, *Economic Planning in Underdeveloped Areas*, New York, 1958; G. Myrdal, *Rich Lands and Poor,* New York, 1957, chap. VII; R. M. Solow, "Some Problems of the Theory and Practice of Economic Planning, *"Economic Development and Cultural Change,* January 1962; J. J. Spengler, "Public Bureaucracy, Resource Structure, and Economic Development, *"Kyklos,* Vol. XI, 1958.

A number of relevant papers are also contained in the volume *Organization, Planning, and Programming for Economic Development,* United Nations Conference on the Application of Science and Technology for the Benefit of the Less Developed Areas, Vol. VIII, Washington, 1962.

2. The "big push" argument is elaborated more fully in the following: H. S. Ellis, "'Big Push' Theories of Economic Development," *L'Industria,* No. 2, 1957; H. Leibenstein, *Economic Backwardness and Economic Growth*, New York, 1957, chap. 8; T. W. Swan, "Circular Causation." *Economic Record*, December 1962.

IX

TECHNIQUES OF DEVELOPMENT PLANNING

HAVING INTRODUCED in the preceding chapter the case for a large measure of government direction over the rate and pattern of development we should now turn to an appraisal of the techniques and applicability of development planning. Taken together, the materials in this chapter indicate the nature of the available programming techniques, some problems connected with their operational use, and the significance of their effects in practice. Proceeding beyond the theory of development planning to a review of planning practice, we want especially to distinguish between the techniques discussed in development literature and those that have actually been used in various countries.

The materials in section one relate to the formulation of a development plan. This entails an explicit and systematic designation of objectives, the estimation and mobilization of necessary resources, and the allocation of resources. Particular attention is given to a survey of representative types of models that may be used for determining consistent sets of alternative policies (1.1, 1.2, 1.3). Primarily aggregate models are examined, supplemented by sector and inter-industry analysis, in order to ensure consistency in the development program. While such models have been useful in improving the formulation of development plans, their application is still beset with practical difficulties, and it is essential to recognize their possible abuse in development planning (1.5, 1.6).

In so far as planning efforts have concentrated on the role of investment and the allocation of new investment, the materials in the second section relate to the objectives and choice of implementation policies for sectors and projects. For the public sector, special attention is given to budgetary reforms to improve the formulation of public expenditure policy (2.1). Broad features of a programming approach to resource allocation are examined (2.2, 2.3, 2.6), as well as some of the experience with the more special problems of project evaluation (2.4, 2.5).

On the basis of country experience, section three offers an appraisal of the methods and impact of development planning in practice. To provide a

464

framework for judging case studies, Professor Lewis's comments point up a number of elements that should be considered in assessing a development plan (3.1). Some of these factors are examined in a summary review of planning experience in Africa (3.2) and Asia and the Far East (3.3). More detailed attention is then given to the experience of India as an especially illuminating case for the study of the actual performance of the economic planning mechanism (3.4, 3.5, 3.6).

Finally, the Note in section four submits some general conclusions on the present state of development planning. While this Note and other selections in this chapter may appear critical of specific plans, it should be realized that there can be considerable value to the planning process itself. The active process of development planning may indeed be of even more benefit than the actual plan—for it may demonstrate the need for the collection and use of more empirical information, may promote the dissemination of knowledge, clarify objectives and choices, and indicate the political and administrative preconditions necessary for the implementation of a plan.

1. FORMULATING A DEVELOPMENT PLAN

1.1 USE OF MODELS IN PROGRAMMING *

The elaboration of development programmes relies on the existence of a certain number of interrelationships in the economy. Whether a system of such relationships, which constitutes an "economic model," is explicitly formulated or implicitly assumed is not important. The soundness of a programme will depend largely on whether and to what extent the relevant relationships have been taken into account in formulating it. The purpose of this article is to examine representative types of models that are now being used in some countries for national economic and industrial planning purposes, and to attempt a preliminary evaluation in the light of the available experience under the United Nations technical assistance programme and elsewhere. Emphasis must be

* From United Nations, Department of Economic and Social Affairs, "Use of Models in Programming," *Industrialization and Productivity*, Bulletin 4, April 1961, pp. 7-15.

laid on the preliminary character of any findings or judgments expressed in this study....

An economic model is an organized set of relationships that describes the functioning of an economic entity, whether it be a household, a single industry or a national economy, under a set of simplifying assumptions. As mentioned above, all economic reasoning is based implicitly or explicitly on models, but this study is concerned only with those models, or explicit relationships within a model, that can be expressed in quantitative terms and for which data can be assembled. The data and relationships required for constructing a model are usually either based on the *past* experience of the economy concerned or "borrowed" from economies considered to be sufficiently similar. Before using such models for planning purposes it is necessary either to adopt certain specific assumptions with respect to the country's future or to adjust the historical relationships to allow for prospective changes. The extent to which the quantitative value and the direction of the changes in the relationships are correctly anticipated determines the reliability of the model for planning purposes.

Models can be applied to the determination of economic policies in two different ways. In the first and simpler case, it may be desired to determine the effects of a particular set of economic measures, for example, of investment in certain sectors. The measures and other data are taken as given, and the model is used to trace their effects throughout the economy.[1] In the second case, a certain set of objectives is specified, such as a given rise in income or employment or a given reduction of a balance of payments deficit, and the model is used to determine the most appropriate policy measures to achieve these objectives. Although both types of analysis are valuable for programming purposes, the second will be given particular attention. In the first place, underdeveloped economies are more likely to think of programming in terms of choice of policy measures; in the second place, the use of models has its greatest advantage over more intuitive methods precisely for this type of analysis.

A policy model of the second type consists of the following elements:

(1) A specified set of *objectives*—such as maximum income, full employment, reduced balance of payments deficit—which defines the objectives of the development programme;

(2) A set of *instrument variables* related to the policy measures that a government intends to use to achieve its objectives. Examples of instrument variables are levels of savings, production and investment by sector, exports, or other magnitudes that it is intended to influence in some way. The instrument variables are

affected by measures such as subsidies, taxes, or direct public investment to achieve a given level of output;[2]

(3) *Other variables,* not directly affected by government action, but which are necessary for an adequate analysis of the economy, such as consumption of individual commodities, and prices of commodities and of productive factors;

(4) *Economic relationships* in the form of equations containing the variables mentioned above. Such equations may *(a)* describe the behaviour of an economic entity in terms of a response of one economic variable to a change in another variable (for example, a consumption function); *(b)* express a technological relationship (for example, a production function), or *(c)* take the form of accounting identities that must hold true in any economy, such as the equality of total supply and demand. These last equations impose constraints upon the values of the component variables that must be simultaneously satisfied in order to obtain a programme that is at all feasible.

A solution of a model consists of a set of values for the instrument variables that satisfies all the equations in the model. As a rule, values of some of the variables are fixed by prior analysis and the model itself determines the values for only as many variables as there are equations. The same basic model may be solved for different variables. For example, the Harrod-Domar model in its simplest form states that the

---

1. These models are sometimes called "projection" models, in contrast to the second type of "decision" models.

2. In some cases, the model is devised to determine the measures directly—the percentage increase in direct taxes, tariffs, or the amount of government investment and so forth—that will be necessary and sufficient to achieve the objectives. This type of "decision model" in the strict sense necessitates that the economic parameters of the model be known with a degree of accuracy which is generally achieved only in highly developed economies. For this reason such models are not discussed in the present study. For a detailed discussion of these, *see* J. Tinbergen, *On the Theory of Economic Policy* (North-Holland Publishing Company, Amsterdam, 1952).

rate of growth of income depends on the proportion of income saved and the capital-output ratio. According to the circumstances, different combinations of two variables will be taken as given and the equation solved for the third. The model may thus serve to determine either the rate of growth that can be achieved with a given economic structure, the savings rate required to attain a given rate of growth, or the upper limit of the capital-output ratio if both growth and savings rates are fixed.

All of the models used in development programming are basically similar because they describe the same set of economic phenomena, except that in the various models some relationships are selected as being of greater relative importance for a given situation. The choice among the various relationships will be determined by the economist according to the terms of reference of his task, including the general political and economic goals which have been set up by the authorities. It is true that the terms of reference may be very general and vague; or the goals which are pre-set by the authorities—such as "raising *per capita* income," "providing full employment," and "reducing the gap in the balance of payments"— may be competing ones or mutually inconsistent. In such cases, the economist will have to decide for himself which key variables are to be considered for the construction of his first preliminary model. Whether the initial choice of the relationships is based on economic intuition or is given beforehand, this first model could be checked subsequently by constructing a more complex model through the addition of other elements. The ultimate test of a model is that it should make the best use of the available information and analytical resources within the time available for its construction.

A few general observations may be added on the relationship between models, programming and the type of economy of a country. A model provides a systematic framework for economic programming; the purpose of programming, in turn, is to provide for an effective government economic policy which is consistent with the goals pursued. The nature of the development programme, and consequently the type of model, will differ in accordance with the nature and extent of government intervention and the type of instruments used. In principle, the effectiveness of economic programming based on the use of models is not necessarily related to any particular type of economic structure. Thus, programming can be usefully applied in economies ranging from those based predominantly on private enterprise to centrally planned economies where the government is fully in control of directing national economic activities. This study is primarily concerned with use of models in economies of the former type; among countries of this group, government intervention in the economy varies within a fairly wide range (for example, as in the Netherlands, Puerto Rico, India and Israel), yet programming and planning techniques have been applied with considerable success in some of them.

There are three types of models used in development programming:

(1) *Aggregate models*, which apply to the entire economy and deal with production, consumption, investment and the like as single aggregates;

(2) *Sector models,* which apply to individual sectors;

(3) *Inter-industry models,* which are concerned with the relationships of the productive sectors of an economy with each other, and of each of these sectors with other entities of the economy.

It may be helpful to indicate some of the uses of each of these types. *Aggregate models* are used to determine possible growth rates in national income; the division of the national product among consumption (public and private), investment and exports; the required volume of domestic savings, imports and foreign financial assistance to carry out a given programme. *Sector models* are used to determine levels of production and consumption by economic sectors and to explore alternative production possibilities within individual productive branches. *Inter-industry models* serve to determine the demand for intermediate products and capital goods (including imports), and their solution provides for a mutually consistent set of production levels by economic sectors, and imports for the whole economy. It will be clear, however, from the following discussion that this subdivision is to some extent arbitrary, since, in practice, the dividing lines are not always so clear-cut.

Aggregate models: The relations most commonly included in an aggregate model are the following:

(1) A consumption-income (or savings-income) relation;

(2) A production function, relating national product to the input of capital and labour;

(3) An import function, relating import requirements to the level of national income or its components;

(4) The definition of domestic product on the expenditure side as the sum of consumption plus investment plus government expenditure on goods and services plus net exports of goods and services or—on the income disposal side—as the sum of consumption outlay plus net taxes plus savings;

(5) A certain number of "constraints" or limitations on resource use, such as: (*a*) the demand for labour cannot exceed the supply; (*b*) investment cannot exceed domestic savings plus net import of capital; (*c*) imports cannot exceed foreign exchange earnings plus net receipts from foreign loans and grants.

In most cases, not all these relations are used in the construction of the initial model. It is customary to focus on one or two of the resources considered to be of strategic importance in a given situation and on the relevant behaviour equations.

When capital is felt to be the main bottleneck in economic growth, as in the case in many of the underdeveloped countries, the typical equations of the aggregate model can be consolidated into the Harrod-Domar equation. This simplification ignores or treats as given data—at least initially—the labour factor and the import requirements and determines the maximum growth achievable from the rate of investment and its "productivity" as measured by a capital-output ratio. Further refinements may be introduced into this simplified model to allow for other variables or objectives other than income growth.

In the case of Morocco and in the Greek five-year plan, the Harrod-Domar model was applied on an aggregate basis with no distinction among sectors. A capital-output ratio was applied to the over-all income target to estimate an aggregate investment figure. In the Algerian ten-year plan, and the plan frame for the Indian second five-year plan, capital requirements were calculated on a sectoral basis. In both plans the income targets and investment requirements were set initially on an aggregate basis; the over-all projections were then broken down by sectors. In the case of India, four main sectors were singled out: investment goods; factory-produced consumer goods; small-scale industry and agriculture, and services. The total investment figure was allocated among these sectors on the basis of priorities and the resulting rise in sectoral income and employment was projected consistently with the assumed priorities and over-all targets. In the case of Algeria, the economy was divided into nine sectors. Sectoral capital-output ratios were then applied, and the resulting rates of growth and investment requirements by sectors were reconciled with the first aggregate estimates by a process of successive approximations. A twenty-seven-sector input-output table was used for that purpose. The capital requirements were then compared with the available supply of capital, the internal capital formation being estimated on the basis of the marginal propensity to save. The difference between investment requirements and internal savings (both public and private) provides a measure of the required foreign financial aid, unless the investment programme is scaled down. The process of adjusting investment requirements to capital availabilities in a capital-short economy is a process of successive approximations; it involves repeated evaluation and reevaluation of the projects making up the investment plan by a process of successive eliminations and substitutions so as to achieve a balance between the demand for, and supply of, capital.[3]

Although a Harrod-Domar model is principally centred on the capital factor, it can also be used to indicate the extent to which it would be possible to achieve full employment of labour. The increase in employment which may be expected to result from the investment programme can be estimated by using either a labour-capital or a labour-output ratio. The former method was used in India; the latter in Algeria. It may then be found that significant gaps exist between the resulting direct increase in employment and the desired employment targets. In such a case, unless the employment target is abandoned as unachievable, certain other labour-using

activities, which are unrelated to the planned investment, may be suggested by the planner to fill the gap.

If labour is taken as a starting point in planning, national product will be projected, as a first approximation, on the basis of the available labour supply and the labour-output ratio. The implications of the resulting growth in output can then be ascertained from the remaining conditions. Compliance with constraints 5 (b) and 5 (c) mentioned above will determine the amount, if any, of requirements in foreign capital. If the latter is not available, a different pattern of national growth based on lower investment requirements and lower imports will have to be devised, unless the initially stated employment targets are reduced.

In Ceylon, a model was used in which the prime objective was to provide employment for the unemployed and underemployed labour force, taking into account the anticipated natural increase in the labour force by the end of the ten-year plan period. On the basis of the projected labour force and an assumed level of labour productivity, an estimate was made of the national product at the end of the period and during the intervening years. The distribution of this aggregate product among the various sectors was made as follows. In the case of consumption, it was done by introducing an assumption of a slight rise in *per capita* consumption, in conjunction with appropriate income-demand elasticities. Production for export demand was projected as an exogenous variable, and an aggregate gross investment figure was estimated. The estimates of domestic consumption, exports and investment provided the basis for a projection of import requirements and of the balance of payments. This first round of estimates showed a significant balance of payments gap which led to the next step, namely, an estimate of the required expansion of exports and

3. Various methods of project evaluation are described in part II of United Nations, *Manual on Economic Development Projects* (Sales No.: 58.II.G.5), prepared by the Economic Commission for Latin America.

development of import-substitute industries. Employment in the various sectors was then projected on the basis of the production levels thus obtained, and the aggregate labour requirements compared with the estimated labour supply. In this case, there appeared a wide gap between the two. Only a limited amount of additional direct employment could be accounted for by the proposed investment. The residual unemployment was assumed to be taken care of by increases in employment in small-scale industry and services on which, however, no quantitative conclusions could be reached because of lack of data.

In the projections made by the Economic Commission for Latin America, the balance of payments deficit is considered to be a major limitation to growth, at least in the short run. Foreign exchange availabilities determine the possible imports of raw materials and investment goods, and the achievable increase in national product. An aggregate model is constructed which projects national product on the basis of the supply of foreign exchange. The latter is, in turn, determined by estimates of prospective exports, terms of trade and capital inflow. In a formal sense, this model is analogous to the previous two, and is usually combined with one or the other of them.

The model approach is most valuable when several constraints have to be taken into account simultaneously. Instead of starting with one of the simplified versions indicated above, all the limitations to growth are specified from the start, and a solution of the set of simultaneous equations is arrived at which determines the rate of growth compatible with all of them....

The solution of the models described in the preceding sections is reached by a process of successive approximations. Attention is centred first on one restriction—

that of the assumed key factor; the other restrictions are then brought into the picture, by a trial-and-error procedure, in a second or subsequent round of calculations.

The technique of successive approximations, which has been used in a great many countries, is well brought out in the planning for Tunisia, which was carried out with United Nations technical assistance. The planning began by constructing a series of aggregate investment-income projections for the period from 1957 to 1971, which were based on a set of alternative assumptions of capital-output ratios and the share of capital formation in gross domestic product. In the computation of these parameters, the past performance of the economy, among other things, was taken into account. A parallel projection was made of aggregate consumption—both public and private—which assumed different rates of increase by major groups of consumers, including government. This projection was based on the expected changes in the demographic structure of the economy and in the structure of employment. These two sets of projections provided the basis for calculations of the required import surpluses. Among the series of alternative projections thus obtained, one plan frame was selected as most realistic in the light of the restrictions on investment and foreign exchange resources. The plan outline for the final year of the planning period was then elaborated in more detail by estimating the availability of and uses for a certain number of major products (approximately 160) in the consumer goods, investment goods and intermediate goods categories. The demand for consumer and investment goods was calculated by an appropriate breakdown of the projected aggregate figures of consumption and investment. Domestic output was then estimated on the basis of the present production plus the prospective output from new investments, taking into account domestic demand and the potential export possibilities. These estimates were, in turn, used to determine the demand for intermediate products. By equating the domestic supply of these major products with the demand, it was possible to project import requirements and export availabilities.

These data for the major products were then used as the basis for a twenty-two-sector input-output matrix, in order to arrive at a more complete projection for the entire economy. The gaps in the outputs and inputs, as well as the projections of the distributive shares of the domestic product, by sectors, were filled by using coefficients from the input-output table of 1957. This process was carried out through successive approximations until a balanced matrix was reached. Finally, estimates were made for employment on the basis of the projected growth in output in major sectors of the economy, partly by calculating demand for labour force to achieve the required growth, and partly by assuming certain changes in labour productivity.

Sectoral Models: The first attempts to establish a development programme usually start from an assessment of the prospects in individual sectors of the economy. Such a procedure is followed when data for an over-all model are lacking although information may exist with respect to individual projects. The drawback of this approach is that the development programme tends to become a collection of assorted projects which are not part of an integrated total. It is not possible either to evaluate these projects on a consistent basis or to check the total inputs against the over-all availability of resources. This section will assess the experience of various countries in formulating national programmes in this way, which may be designated as a "from the bottom up" approach.

Although the project approach apparently dispenses with the use of methods, some implicit, if not explicit, general economic relationships are inherent in the criteria used to evaluate the projects. It is common, for example, to give priority to those that earn or save foreign exchange and also to favour those that employ local labour. The weights to be given to these and other criteria can only be adequately determined from some sort of over-all analysis. If no such over-all analytical framework exists, there is a danger that individual projects will be evaluated under different assumptions and different criteria.

The project approach to planning has been particularly used in countries where the industrial sector is relatively little developed, such as Ghana (five-year plan, July 1959-June 1964), Cambodia (five-year plan, 1960-1964), Jamaica (ten-year plan, 1957/58-1966/67) and, to some extent, in the first five-year plans of India (1951/52-1955/56) and Pakistan (1955/56-1959/60).

The procedure followed in Pakistan provides a good illustration of the way in which a set of projects is made consistent with an over-all analytical framework covering the availability of resources and an assumed rate of income growth. Lists of projects were first drawn up, by sector, on the basis of technical feasibility and market demand. Since the total of the resulting claims on government financial resources and foreign exchange supplies greatly exceeded their availability, priorities were allocated to the various sectors and to individual projects within each sector, in order to arrive at a feasible over-all programme. The criteria used in allocating such priorities were the contribution of the project to the national income and its impact on the balance of payments. Further adjustments were required to make the planning of different sectors consistent with one another, and to avoid bottlenecks in the production of power, and of cement or other critical materials. This called essentially for projections of the demand for and supply of these key commodities, and the establishment of physical balance-sheets.

The Ceylon ten-year plan also proceeded initially from programmes for selected key sectors, based on certain assumptions concerning the contribution of these sectors to the economy as a whole, and, to the extent possible, upon analyses of the demand and supply factors for each of these sectors. The resulting sectoral data were then aggregated by successive approximations, taking into account the over-all plan targets and the specific assumptions which were made concerning the movement of the main aggregates of the economy, such as investment and consumption. In this way a consistent set of macro-economic and micro-economic projections was achieved.

The problem of integrating sector projections into a consistent plan is discussed in the reports of several United Nations experts. An expert advising Israel noted that planning had previously been done on a sector basis, and that no need had been felt for an organized and integrated plan. The effect of this piecemeal approach was that the price structure had become distorted on account of numerous taxes and subsidies which, however, did not achieve the desired reduction in the country's balance of payments deficit. Since a significant reduction of this deficit was considered to be imperative, the adviser's task consisted in preparing an aggregate plan which would provide a general framework for an effective co-ordination of sectoral plans and policies.

In Viet-Nam, an adviser discussing the consistency of the national plan and the sectoral plans made by individual ministries noted that, in that country, the cumulative effect of sectoral plans led to over-ambitious and unrealistic targets. In such a case, there may be a lack of balance between resource requirements and availabilities which may lead to a failure to complete the projects.

Planning techniques involve estimates of the demand for particular commodities. Such demand projections can be carried out by various methods: extrapolation of past trends; experience of other countries in similar fields, and an analysis and projection of the economic variable determining the demand. In the case of intermediate demand, a detailed analysis involves the use of an input-output model, to be discussed below, but in many cases simpler models may serve the purpose.

The simplest model for the analysis of consumer demand relates the consumption of each commodity to the total consumer demand—or the total disposable income—in the economy. This relationship can be estimated either from cross-section studies of consumer budgets at a particular time or from an analysis of changes in consumption over time as income has varied. The two methods were combined in the ECLA studies of Colombia and Argentina, in which consumption was first projected on the basis of demand elasticities from household budget studies. The results were then adjusted in the light of recent trends to take account of price changes, population shifts and other factors.

As was pointed out previously, sector projections were used in all countries before the input-output techniques came into existence; they are also used widely even where the latter do exist. They have the advantage of economy in time and effort since they can be made without constructing elaborate input-output matrices. Where the data for an input-output table are of poor quality, or there is little interdependence between the economic sectors, such partial projection techniques may yield results as accurate as those provided by input-out models. However, they do have the weakness that indirect and secondary consequences may be frequently forgotten or ignored. Care should be taken when using these projections to make their limitations explicit, and to make some allowance also for indirect and secondary effects if these are considered to be of significant magnitude....

Inter-industry models: Inter-industry models range from simple input-output matrices to more complicated linear programming models. This article is mainly concerned with the simpler types, which are widely used in programming; a brief discussion will be presented of the applications of linear programming techniques.

Input-output models analyse explicitly the relationships among different sectors of the economy. In the applications for development programming, the economy is generally subdivided into from fifteen to thirty or more production sectors and from three to five or six sectors of final use. The variables in the model are the levels of final use, production, and imports of each group of commodities. The levels of final use are usually determined outside the model and the demands for intermediate products and imports are determined from the solution of the model.

The input-output model may be considered as a breakdown of the aggregate models considered above. Instead of a single equation for total supply of goods and services and their use, there is an equation for each sector of production. Similarly, the use of capital, labour and imported materials is estimated separately for each using sector instead of on an aggregate basis. Input-output models therefore take into account the effects of changes in the composition of demand and output in estimating the requirements of such entities as capital, foreign currency and skilled labour, in contrast to aggregate models, which assume—for instance, in the projection of capital requirements—a single over-all capital-output ratio.

In its usual form the input-output model assumes a linear relationship between the output of a sector and its input requirement. From this assumption it is possible to estimate the effect on other sectors of an increase in output in one industry. When technological changes or economies or diseconomies of scale are anticipated, an allowance can be made for changes in input-output coefficients.

Inter-industry models are primarily applicable in economies that have achieved a certain degree of industrial development and hence have a substantial volume of inter-industry transactions. As a rule of thumb, it may be suggested that this is the case in countries having at least 15 per cent of the gross national product originating in industry or having a *per capita* national income of $150 or more.

Input-output models have several uses in development programming.

(1) They provide for individual branches of the economy estimates of production and import levels that are consistent with each other and with the estimates of final demand.

(2) The solution to the model aids in the allocation of the investment required to achieve the production levels in the programme and it provides a more accurate test of the adequacy of available investment resources.

(3) The requirements for skilled labour can be evaluated in the same way.

(4) The analysis of import requirements and substitution possibilities is facilitated by the knowledge of the use of domestic and imported materials in different branches of the economy.

(5) In addition to direct requirements of capital, labour and imports, the indirect requirements in other sectors of the economy can be estimated.

(6) Regional input-output models can also be constructed for planning purposes to explore the implications of development programmes for the particular region concerned, as well as for the economy as a whole. Such regional tables have been con-

structed and used for planning purposes in Italy, where there is a clear regional distinction between the North and the South, and where a large programme for the development of the South has been under way for some time....

Some early uses of input-output models to analyse long-term development prospects were made in projections for Italy (1951-1956) and the Netherlands (1950-1970). The method has since been applied in development studies of Colombia, Argentina and Peru by the Economic Commission for Latin America, and in five-year to ten-year projections for Mexico, Tunisia, Algeria and other countries or areas. In most cases, models containing twenty to thirty sectors are used for analytical convenience.

The main problem in applying input-output analysis to developing countries is to allow for structural changes that may be taking place. These consist of substitutions of domestic productions for imports, of changes in technology and other shifts in the structure of intermediate demand. The following examples illustrate the methods of handling these problems.

The Italian input-output projections dealt with both technological changes and import substitutes. An important change in technology was expected to result from the increasingly widespread replacement of imported coal by domestic natural gas and certain other potential energy sources. These potential fuel replacements were estimated in a fuel balance-sheet; the input-output calculations were then adjusted to the new fuel pattern by a method of successive approximations. The fuel balance-sheet, which estimated the total demands for fuel in standard units of heat, was based on the expansion of fuel-consuming industries, on the economic and technological feasibility of meeting the demands of these industries with alterna-

tive fuels and on the special conditions affecting fuel supplies. The results of these estimates were then fed back into the input and output projections in order to trace their repercussions throughout the economy.

With regard to import substitutes, a set of marginal import figures was estimated for each of the two hundred product classes, namely, the fraction of additional requirements expected to be covered by imports rather than by domestic production. These import coefficients, each of which was an independent estimate of import substitution possibilities, were based partly on the average import proportions of the base year, partly on those of more recent years, and the rest on marginal trends in imports from one year to the next.

The ECLA input-output studies for Colombia, Argentina and Peru also focus upon the problem of import substitution. Projections were first made with existing ratios of imports to domestic production in order to determine the required amount of import substitution. In each sector, an assessment of production possibilities on technological and economic grounds was then undertaken. The study of Peru, in particular, illustrates the usefulness of the input-output technique in bringing together in a consistent way engineering and economic estimates in a country where statistical data are not entirely adequate.

The Mexican input-output projections, in which a United Nations adviser participated, provide another example of a procedure sufficiently flexible to allow for structural changes. A projection was first made for the period from 1955 to 1965, using the input coefficients of 1950 corrected for intervening price changes. The direct effects of changes, such as import substitution, increased consumption of electric power and other structural changes in consumption patterns, were then studied in independent projections and the indirect effects of these changes throughout the economy were estimated by feeding them into the model.

An important use of the input-output studies made so far is in checking the over-all requirements of a development pro-gramme or of an important specific project against the availabilities of such factors as capital, foreign currency and manpower. The indirect repercussions of the contem-plated developments throughout the econ-omy are often of equal or greater importance than the direct effects, and it may be difficult to evaluate them ade-quately if the traditional instruments of analysis are used. Thus, for instance, the checking of a preliminary investment pro-gramme in detail through the input-output method has made it possible in several cases, for example, in Argentina and Israel, to detect inconsistencies in the original formulation, and has led to adjustments of investment allocations in certain sectors.

Experiments with input-output analysis in some countries where industry plays a relatively minor role have not yet led to practical applications, presumably because of lack of data. Even where this is the case, however, the preparation of a rough input-output table is often a useful way to organ-ize the data that do exist and to indicate areas where inconsistencies and other deficiencies obtain and further investiga-tion is needed. A number of unpublished tables are known to have been prepared for this purpose for various countries. A related use of the input-output table is to serve as an intermediate step in the con-struction of a system of national accounts.

In order to overcome some of the techni-cal limitations arising from the assump-tions of the input-output models indicated above, inter-industry relations may be formulated in the more general framework of linear programming. This technique takes into account imports and alternative techniques of production as separate vari-ables, or "activities." It can also take account more effectively of such factors as shortages of capital, foreign exchange limi-tations and availabilities of specific natural resources.

A linear programming model describes economic functions, such as production, consumption, transportation, exporting and importing, as "activities." The levels at which these activities are carried on are the variables in the model. Several alterna-tive techniques of producing the same commodity can be included, as can alterna-tive uses of the same resources. In this way the model constitutes a formalized descrip-tion of the alternative ways of using exist-ing resources to satisfy specified needs. The input-output model can be thought of as a simplified linear programming model in which the choice of production activities and of imports and exports is specified in advance, thereby reducing the number of variables in the model.

The solution to a linear programming model consists in finding the most eco-nomical way of achieving a given set of objectives. In one formulation, targets for the expansion of national income and limitations on its composition are specified; the minimum amount of foreign borrow-ing consistent with these objectives is then taken as the test of efficiency. In another case, resources (including foreign invest-ment) are given and the national income is to be maximized. The solutions also provide sets of equilibrium prices that help to determine the efficiency of alternative programmes.

Two applications of linear programming to India illustrate its potential usefulness for development analysis. A United Na-tions planning expert constructed a four-teen-sector model designed to determine the optimum allocation of investment for a hypothetical ten-year programme. He was able, for example, to show the interrelationships among investments in such sectors as steel, coal and machinery and to compare costs and results of alternative investment expenditure in various industries.[4] Although his results were intended —because of the limitations in the data— to be merely illustrative, they suggest a number of possible applications in other under-developed countries. The main value of this study seems to be in making apparent the interrelationships among policies adopted in different sectors of the economy.

Another study of Indian planning used a linear programming formulation to check the efficiency of investment and prices implicit in the plan frame four-sector model.[5] The analysis did not support the conclusions that had been reached in the Indian plan frame as to the relative efficiency of investment in different sectors of the economy. It pointed out inconsistencies between the implicit factor prices assumed in the model and the actual factor price relationships in India. Thus, it indicated the need for revisions in the model or in its interpretation, which had not been apparent when the plan was originally formulated.

The main practical obstacle to the use of linear programming models lies in their greater demand for statistical information. The technology of industries that do not yet exist may be described on the basis of engineering projects or of coefficients "imported" from other countries, but care must be taken to use comparable classifications of products and to correct for price differences.[6] Furthermore, a comparison of the efficiency of alternative techniques is feasible only when production is broken down into smaller, more homogeneous classifications than have so far been used for input-output analysis, since the latter assumes parallel variations among the activities that are aggregated in a given sector.

For these and other reasons, it is likely that the use of linear programming models for formulating development programmes will not be of wide-spread use in the near future. These models do, however, have a considerable value in exploring the consistency of development alternatives, even when some of the parameters used in the analysis are no better than reasonable approximations.

1.2 AIMS AND MEANS OF PROGRAMMING *

It is useful to distinguish between two broad classes of problems, sometimes called analytical and policy problems. Analytical problems, in this context, are the usual problems of economic analysis, whose objective is to explain the course of economic variables when a number of *data* are given. These data are, on the one hand, phenomena of an extraeconomic character, that is, natural, psychological, technical, or institutional phenomena. On the other hand, they may be economic phenomena or variables outside the geographical area considered—usually a country. The data can be such things as crop yields, tastes of the population, technological coefficients, or tax rates. An important subdivision of the category of data in the context of our problem is that which can be influenced

4. J. Sandee, "A Long-term Planning Model for India," 1959 (United Nations mimeographed document TAO/IND/22/Rev.1).

5. R. Komiya, "A Note on Professor Mahalanobis' Model of Indian Economic Planning", *Review of Economics and Statistics,* February 1959, pp. 29-35.

6. Although input coefficients are interpreted in input-output and linear programming as being ratios in physical terms, they are normally measured in value terms.

* From Jan Tinbergen and Hendricus C. Bos, *Mathematical Models of Economic Growth,* McGraw-Hill Book Company, Inc., New York, 1962, pp. 1-10, 116-17. Reprinted by permission.

by government policy, to be called *means* or *instruments of economic policy,* and data which cannot be influenced. Policy problems, in our context, are problems in which the logic of analytical problems is partly inverted. Those data which are means or instruments of economic policy are no longer considered as given, but rather as unknowns. Inversely, some things are supposed known about the economic variables which are the unknowns in analytical problems. Assumed known are the *aims* of the policy considered; that is, either the precise values of some variables, to be called *target variables,* must be given or some function of them, to be called *social welfare function* or *social utility function,* must be a maximum. Thus, in development policy it may be that some fixed targets are set—a 20 per cent rise in national income and a 10 per cent rise in employment, say—or that the government aims at an optimum combination of national income, employment, and regional income distribution. The former type of problem, characterized by a set of fixed targets, requires that the number of instruments used be at least equal to the number of targets. There is less of such a condition in the case of the latter type of problem, but there must be at least 1 *degree of freedom,* that is, something to choose; otherwise nothing can be made a maximum....

The most general way of putting the problem of long-term development policy is to say that total welfare or social utility over a long period should be maximized, in principle even an infinitely long period. This welfare is dependent on a number of economic variables for all time units in the period. Among these variables, consumption stands out, but distribution of consumption over regions or groups, and variables like employment, as well as others, will also influence welfare. The problem therefore necessarily is a very complicated one, and the planner may have considerable need for simplification.

One important method of simplifying the solution of the problem is to break it down into steps or *stages,* which can be tackled in succession. More specifically, for development planning it seems appropriate first to deal with the problem of distributing consumption over time without entering into the composition with regard to individual commodities, and next to deal with the composition. This means that first a macroproblem is set in which the intricacies of distribution over time are given full attention, and that as a second stage a microproblem is solved. More precisely, the microproblem itself may be considered in a succession of stages, each referring to the proper allocation of investment between industries in a single year.

To be sure, the procedure may well be incorrect, and it has to be proved that, as a first approximation, it can be accepted. The authors believe that this proof is possible.

Other methods of simplification are to be found in the *choice of the variables.* Thus, consumption only, as the main variable, may be assumed to determine welfare. As a second approximation, one of the other variables only may be added, for example, employment. Instead of maximizing consumption over a long period, in certain circumstances, income may be maximized, where the amount spent on investment stands for additional consumption later.

The means of development policy applied in different countries depend very much on the preferences of their governments with regard to the *economic order.* In communist countries, where a much larger portion of the means of production is publicly owned, a much larger number of means of policy are available than in noncommunist countries. It would be inexact to say that all acts of the managers of publicly owned production units are themselves means of economic policy, since not all these acts can be controlled by the government. But clearly the grip of the government on such decisions is much tighter than in the case of privately owned production units. As a first approximation it may be said that investments in all industries in the public sectors are instruments of policy, and these are less numerous, although by no means unimportant, in noncommunist countries. Further important instruments are the other well-known instruments of public finance, that is, public expenditure for other than investment purposes, taxes, and subsidies.

In most, though not all, communist and in some other countries, prices are an instrument of policy, including the "prices" of labor, wage rates, and the "prices" of capital, interest rates.

In smaller countries the instruments of trade policy (duties and quantitative restrictions) have a considerable impact on the economy.

Planning, or programming, of development is an activity which to a considerable extent is independent of the precise development policy pursued by a government, that is, independent of the means applied in such policy. Even a policy that relies only on indirect ways to influence production may be well served by advance planning that charts the most desirable course of production and its components. This is true wherever complicated and time-consuming processes are involved: inconsistencies can be at least partly avoided by advance planning.

Planning differs from pure forecasting in that it is based on the assumption that the future course of production and other economic variables can be influenced, and it aims at indicating the most desirable course. What constitutes the most desirable course depends very much, however, on the aims set and the means to be admitted.

Historically the desirability of planning has become clear because of the inconsistencies that may exist among measures designed by various ministries or departments and divisions if those measures are based on a partial analysis only. The assumptions made by an electricity board may be incompatible with those made by a department of agriculture or a board of trade.

Planning is an almost continuous process. At regular, fairly short intervals, plans have to be revised in the light of new information. This new information may consist of figures about external data of a random character such as crops or about systematic changes in the other data; it may consist also of figures about the economic variables which have materialized meanwhile and which may deviate from those expected, first, because the data deviated from expectations and, second, because the relationships assumed are different from the real relationships.

Programming of development requires a number of different abilities and types of knowledge. As a rule the process consists in estimating such a large number of figures that first of all considerable organizing abilities are needed. The way in which the large number of people necessarily involved in the process cooperate and the way their various acts succeed each other and fit into the general pattern are by no means arbitrary or unimportant. It is a common misunderstanding that activities can simply start at the bottom of the pyramid of agencies and that the coordinating role of the center comes in later. There is a certain optimum degree of centralized directives to be emitted first, so as to avoid the most primitive inconsistencies in the work done by the base. This example may illustrate the role of organization. Its role is also very important because an essential feature of efficient planning consists in planning in as short a time as possible.

But the work proper of calculating the figures also requires a number of different abilities, mostly not present in one single man. It requires, in other words, the cooperation of a large number of specialists, first of all, specialists in various technological fields. This is particularly true for the appraisal of investment projects in many different sectors. It is true also, but to a lower degree, for the estimation of future demand, if this is to a high degree dependent on technical development. Then, specialists in the economic field are needed, vested with knowledge of the prospects and peculiarities of a number of markets. They have to take care of the estimation of exports in the first place, but also of home sales. They often need the help of statisticians and econometrists. In the third place, specialists in the broader field of sociology and psychology have to play their part, more particularly if industrialization is extended to new areas, and if the way of life of formerly rural people is involved. Social and political experts may also be useful to judge the priorities in these fields when it comes to changing social insurance, wage systems, industrial democracy, and tax systems.

Finally there is a special role for those economists whom we nowadays call macroeconomists.

The task of macroeconomists is the one of coordinating much of the work done by the other experts, but not coordinating it in the sense of organizing it. The coordination meant here is of a more abstract nature. The macroeconomists have to see to it that no inconsistencies creep into the system of figures which ultimately constitute the plan.

In principle there is only one way to take care of this task; in practice there are more, since we have to work with approximations and trial-and-error procedures. In order, however, to give at least a sharp theoretical description of the task, let us take the ideal method for a while. It is essentially of a mathematical or, if that term is preferred, of a logical character. The complete operation, in all its details, of an economy and the human beings populating it can be described by a mathematical model of a much more complicated and sophisticated nature than anything we know in reality. To deny this is equivalent to denying the possibility of the scientific treatment of the operation of society. It does not imply the assumption of determinacy in the old sense, since we have the tool of stochastic variables, representing—in physics as well as economics, to cite only two examples—those elements of "freedom" sometimes invoked against the assumption of determinacy. The essence of a model is precisely that of an orderly and, in a sense, complete administration of knowledge. It is for this reason that the model supplies us with the tools of coordination.

A model consists of a number of elements, now to be considered from the formal side only.... A model consists of (1) a list of variables, to be subdivided into known and unknown or exogenous and endogenous variables in the analytical sense used above; and (2) a list of relationships or equations specifying the links of any type that exist between the variables, to be subdivided into definitions, balance equations, technological and institutional equations, and behavior equations. Each equation represents a set of *links* or *reactions* with a causal direction, sometimes symbolized by arrows directed toward the variable affected. The links represented in one equation are those meeting in one variable at one point of time and together responsible for the size that variable will take at that time. In each equation, therefore, those variables occur which influence the variable in which the links meet. There are other elements too in the equations, representing a third element of the model:

(3) coefficients. They describe the intensity with which one variable affects, through one particular link, another variable. (Additive constants will be considered coefficients too.) They are typical of what is sometimes called the structure of the mechanism or organism.

The elements of a hypothetical ideal model of society can be used to analyze the process of planning and the coordinating task of the macroeconomist in it.

The figures which ultimately are to form the plan are the values of a number of the variables, more particularly the endogenous variables of the model. These variables are the outcome or, mathematically speaking, the solutions of the system of equations, given the exogenous variables, some of the endogenous variables at earlier time periods, and the coefficients. Since, in principle, they are interdependent, it cannot be that the variables referring to the agricultural sector are calculated by the agricultural experts, those of the textile sector by the textile experts, and so on. They can be calculated only by one man who solves the system of equations, perhaps helped by a machine.

This does not mean, fortunately, that this man has to unite in himself all the knowledge incorporated in the whole model. Both other elements, the equations and the coefficients, can be established one by one, and open up the possibility of decentralization and specialization of jobs. Also, the choice of variables that should be included in the list is a matter that can be decided upon in a joint discussion. The establishment of an equation describing the supply of agricultural products—or of one of them—not only can be left to the agricultural specialist, but definitely should be undertaken by him. Similarly, the establishment of other relations must be the task of other specialists. In the light of modern statistical methods, our statement has to be qualified: the choice of the variables and the mathematical shape of each equation are typically the tasks of the specialist in the field concerned. The actual determination of the coefficients may sometimes be a problem requiring centralized work. Yet the so-called a priori estimation of coefficients as well as the judgment of coefficients obtained by a centralized simultaneous-equations approach is profitably left to the specialist.

This, then, would constitute a reasonable division of labor between the coordinating macroeconomist and the specialist: the list of variables to be included should be based on suggestions from all specialists, discussed together; nature of equations and variables to be included, a priori estimation of coefficients, and a posteriori judgment of coefficients determined by simultaneous-equations method are tasks of the specialists, each in his own field; simultaneous determination of coefficients, as far as necessary, and the solution of the system of equations are typically the tasks of the macroeconomist. The latter is a specialist not in any material field but in interdependency problems.

It is the contention of the authors that this task, in fact, and not only in theory, can best be accomplished with the aid of a mathematical model. It does not follow from this statement that it could not be done otherwise. In fact, most development plans have been made without such a model, by methods of trial and error at different levels. Nor is it the opinion of the authors that the coordinating macroeconomist should aim at establishing this ideal model, which was the basis of their reconnaissance-in-principle, at least not in the short run.... The authors are in favor of approximative methods to be called *planning in stages*.

Yet the authors feel that the core of a development plan should be formed by some type of mathematical model. Such a model, or a combination of them for various stages, has clear advantages typical of systematic treatment. Outstanding general advantages are clarity and consistency, that is, the avoidance of inner contradictions. But there are more. As already set out in the previous subsection, a mathematical treatment yields a natural subdivision of the work into well-defined separate tasks that can be tackled in succession. In addition, a mathematical treatment offers some of the advantages of roundabout production: at relatively little extra cost, alternative calculations can be made which enable us to judge at least some of the *confidence intervals* or *limits of reliability* and to judge the effects of alternative policies.

The mathematical models to be used in development programming...have to satisfy a number of conditions which distinguish them from the vaster category of all conceivable models and which limit the degree of their complexity. They must be applied practically, "here and now," above all in underdeveloped countries. It is perhaps not each of the conditions separately but the combination of them that sometimes causes much trouble or limits their scope. Therefore, it goes without saying that the models to be used must be *complete* in the sense that they cover the whole economy and do not overlook phenomena of vital importance. They must be *correct* also in that they use coefficients which are in reasonable agreement with reality. By themselves these conditions are self-evident and common to all serious models. It is the combination with other conditions which we must now discuss.

The coefficients we are using must be more or less known, that is, no extensive or novel research, not yet generally recognized as pertinent, must be needed to determine the coefficients. Some of the more theoretical models presented in recent theoretical literature contain a host of relations of which we have not the slightest knowledge. Such models must be excluded from a practical program...Of course, work on them must go on in the universities and research institutes. These models may bring out features of vital importance which we are not yet aware of. It may well be that some of our policies of today will have no success because we did not know enough about these features. But we cannot base calculations on unknown relations.

Another condition our models must satisfy is that they must be manageable, and, more particularly, manageable by those who have to handle them. In part this is a question of the quality of the staff available to planning agencies. The models should not be too difficult and too elaborate. Both terms are very vague, to be sure, and leave much to the question of taste. We do not believe in models with hundreds of variables, at least for the time being....

To a certain extent the models must also be understandable to those who have to use the results of planning. This is even more vague an idea than the one of manageability. Almost none of the models here presented will appeal as such to the politicians whom they have to serve. They will have to be explained to them by the planners. Much will depend then on the didactic abilities of the latter. The general tendency of this part of the argument imposes a further restriction on the use of complicated concepts. What matters more perhaps is that no model should be made unnecessarily complicated. Often there are elegant ways of representing the main features of a mechanism or organism in a relatively simple way. In modern economic language our recommendations are: never use unnecessary boundary conditions or unnecessary input-output relations....

As has been said in the preceding sections, we are in favor of a method of development programming to be called *planning in stages,* which stands at variance with the more ambitious method of establishing one very complicated model for a simultaneous solution of all problems. In a general way, planning in stages is an attempt first to determine a few of the most important ("strategic") variables and later to determine others, thus coming to greater detail and gradually covering a longer period. Before going into some of the concrete features of the method, we may present a general argument in favor of it. The method is a special case of the well-known and old mathematical—and general scientific—method of successive approximations (or "decreasing abstraction"). This latter constitutes not only a semiscientific procedure for purely applied calculations but also, in many cases for lack of better, the only way out for scientific research. This is true in such cases where a more direct or precise method does not or does not yet exist. Since in many cases the accuracy of the approximative method can be increased at will, it can be used in general proofs of scientific statements. Its scientific "rank" should not therefore be misunderstood.

What matters more for the practice of planning, however, is that in order to reach a certain numerical result the method of successive approximations often requires less effort than the exact method, where it exists. In practice, numerical results need not be absolutely exact, but have to have only a margin of error below a certain prescribed limit. Thus, if we have to calculate the figure 1.003^4 up to three decimal places, there is no need of the complete "correct" calculation; the approximative answer $1 + 4 \times 0.003 = 1.012$ suffices. The gain of time and effort is considerable. As is well known, development in power series is a general and frequently used device to which the preceding remarks apply.

A few remarks may be added already on the concrete *stages of development planning* which we recommend....

As a rule the first stage may consist of a macroeconomic study of the general process of production and investment, along the lines suggested by Harrod-Domar models or by similar, somewhat more complicated models. The aim of this first stage should be to determine, in a provisional way, the rate of savings and the general index of production. A second stage may consist then in specifying production targets for a number of sectors over a fairly long period. A third stage, if needed, may go into more detail for a shorter period, giving figures for a larger number of smaller sectors. A fourth stage may consist in "filling the plan out" with individual projects. Intermixed with this succession there may be stages of revision of the previous stages. Thus, the figures of the second stage may already enable the planner to revise some of the coefficients used in the first stage and to re-do, therefore, the first stage. After a fixed interval of time, new data will be available and this may lead to another revision, combined or not with shifting the period of the plan.

This was an example only. Other stages may be called for by the situation. There is no need for fixed rules; adaptability is one of the virtues of the planner. In a slightly different sense, "stages" come in also by what could be called "partial" models, designed to highlight a detail. Market analyses for separate export products, especially the smaller ones, are good examples. So are models about locations conditions in some big individual project.

. . .

In conclusion, some practical suggestions may be made regarding the computation of a development program for a national economy over a given planning period. The following stages in such a computation seem to make sense.

1. The most desirable general rate of development, that is, the rate of increase in national income at constant internal prices,

is estimated with the aid of a simple macromodel, using provisional data on the capital coefficient for the nation as a whole and on foreign investment to be expected. The estimate must be based on an intuitive comparison between future advantages and present disadvantages of an increase in saving.

2. A choice is made on the number and exact definition of sectors to be considered.

3. Home demand for finished products is estimated for all years of the planning periods on the basis of the projection of income and investment, assuming no structural changes.

4. Demand for existing export products is estimated for all years of the planning period, assuming no price changes.

5. Current demand for intermediate products—as far as represented in the choice of sectors—is estimated on the basis of final demands computed under stages 3 and 4. Among these are imports.

6. Contributions to the national product to be obtained from a unit of new investment in each of the sectors and of possible new sectors are estimated, partly on the basis of data on individual projects, partly on the basis of general knowledge on learning curves and on the influence of the size of an enterprise on its costs.

7. If exports found under stage 4 fall short of imports found under stage 5 by an amount surpassing expected capital imports, new exports or import-replacing production volumes are estimated in the sectors contributing most (per unit of new investment) to national product so as to equilibrate the balance of payments. Sectors with high comparative advantages may even be expanded to such an extent that the corresponding prices fall, the consequences of which must then be estimated.

8. Similar variations in the production program may be envisaged in order to fulfill other aims of development policy, such as employment or distribution objectives.

9. With the aid of sector capital coefficients, or an "investment input matrix," the investment needs may now be specified in a more precise way, according to the supplying sectors and on the basis of gestation lags.

10. If total investments needed each year, calculated under stage 9, are deviating too much from the investment volumes assumed under stage 1, this latter calculation can now be corrected and all the subsequent estimates revised.

11. The investment program may now be "filled" with individual projects, taken in the order of attractiveness as found under stage 6.

1.3 THE FRAMEWORK OF A DEVELOPMENT PLAN *

This paper has the needs of the largest British territories of the Caribbean mainly in mind (Jamaica, Trinidad, British Guiana and Barbados), and takes account of their level of social, economic and political development. But its conclusions may be more widely applicable. The paper deals mostly with technical needs, particularly how a plan should be drawn up. What should be in the plan is of course something about which it is not possible to generalize very much. It largely depends on local circumstances....

The fundamental problem, which is becoming more and more obvious, is how to achieve an increase in national production fast enough to enable the labour force to be kept in employment, and also to enable *per capita* income to rise. There are two reasons why government will increasingly consider economic policy as a *national* problem, taking into account the private sector as well as economic decisions under the government control: the pres-

* From Dudley Seers, "Economic Programming in a Country Newly Independent," *Social and Economic Studies,* Vol. XI, No. 1, March 1962, pp. 34-41. Reprinted by permission.

sure of population increase and the growing unwillingness of people to tolerate
unemployment and destitution. . . .

The expression of political objectives
within a quantitative framework, showing
a possible future economic situation, provides a way of judging whether a total
political programme is both adequate and
feasible. It helps to bring out the fact that
choices have to be made (e.g. between
higher tax rates, population control and
import licensing), and indicates broadly
what sets of policies would be (taken
together) "responsible," in the sense of
being consistent with each other and with
likely trends of variables outside the government's control. Above all, it gives the
government some chance of anticipating
roadblocks in the growth process, and of
taking action to remove or circumvent
them.

The key forecasts: The programme is
therefore built around a set of projections
for some future year, at least four years
hence (the plan year). The initial steps
are two-fold: to forecast what the population will be, and how large will be the
labour force in the plan year. These are
not easy matters. The former involves
deriving trends from censuses and from
registrations, which may be of doubtful
(and changing) reliability. The latter
means estimating first what is the existing
labour force, on the basis of a guess at the
existing scale of unemployment, allowing
for those who would be applicants for
work, if it were available; then this estimate is carried forward to the plan year
by forecasting the population of working
age and likely changes in the fraction of
this group that will be seeking work.

One has to make some assumption about
changes in *per capita* income. On the one
hand, this is a statement about desired rates
of economic growth; on the other it is a
forecast about productivity trends. A provisional figure is used here, and (like several

other key assumptions) this can be varied
later if the programme does not fit.
Together with the population projection,
it provides one with a target rate of growth,
and thus a target domestic product in the
plan year.

The central aim of economic policy can
be described as achieving the desired rate
of growth, without a foreign payments
crisis and without inflation. Quantitatively,
these require three types of *ex ante* balance:

(i) In foreign payments, to avoid loss
of revenues;

(ii) In savings and investment, to avoid
global inflationary pressures;

(iii) In supply and demand for individual commodities, to avoid sectoral inflationary pressures. . . .

Balance in foreign payments: Let us take
these three balances one by one. The starting point is an estimate of the likely level
of foreign exchange receipts, commodity
by commodity. Taken in conjunction with
some anticipated level of capital inflow, a
level which may later be revised (see
below), this forecast of exports implies how
much imports the country will be able to
afford. As will emerge below, this is of
great significance, since the more pessimistic one is about exports, the more rapid a
rate of internal change in the economic
structure is implied. A provisional allocation of imports can be made between different types of product.

*Matching the structures of demand and
supply:* After this, some attempt must be
made to forecast the level of the main categories of demand. The balance between
consumption and investment is something
for which one makes a working hypothesis,
to be checked later against estimates for
the needs of capital formation (see below).
Within total consumption (public and private) some breakdown should be made,
e.g. between food, clothing, other goods
and services. This involves using any clues
available on income-elasticities of demand,

e.g. those derived from local household budgets by cross-section analysis; those obtained from time series; and those to be found in the experience of other countries. The need for intermediate products can also be estimated. Historical analysis may show that these are functions of the domestic product, and cross-section analysis for other countries may also be helpful. On the supply side, some attempt must be made to draw up estimates of output which add up to the target national product. But this is not the only requirement. For each category of commodity, if there is to be equilibrium, local industries must bridge the gap between demand and imports.

I am assuming that the pace of growth, and the anticipated rise in imports, permit this sort of balance to be maintained. It might easily turn out that the first draft of the plan showed imbalances in various sectors. It might prove impossible to allocate imports in any way that would provide sectoral balances. Assuming that we cannot increase the rate of overseas borrowing, this would indicate the need, either to aim at a slower rate of growth for the economy as a whole than was originally envisaged, or to attempt a faster rate of growth in certain key sectors. In the case of certain luxuries, such as consumer durables, some shortages may be acceptable—the price rises engendered need not spread to other areas of the economy, since the real incomes of only a small percentage of the public will be affected. It may even be that this would lead to some rise in savings, since money intended for these goods may not be fully diverted to other objects. Moreover, the shortages will stimulate local manufacturers to accelerate their plans to produce substitutes for unobtainable imports.

On the other hand, the political programme may not envisage a programme of "controlled inflation" of this type, and there may not be sufficient administrative capacity to keep it under control if many commodities are affected. Local substitutes for imports are likely to be expensive, and their production may increase strains on other sectors such as transport and power, leading to inflationary pressures throughout the economy. It is up to the politician to say whether he is prepared to go along this road, or whether it would be preferable to choose a less ambitious programme, with all the risks of another sort implied by (perhaps) growing unemployment. The relation between anticipated trends in exports and in population will determine how acute this dilemma will be.

Projections of demand and output can be put in as much detail as statistics permit and as circumstances require. If an input-output matrix exists, so much the better. If it is available for two separate years in the past, better still, because it will then be possible to get some clue on the variability of coefficients, and to derive demand-elasticities that are consistent with productive coefficients. But in a very small country, such as Barbados, detailed commodity breakdown may not be very necessary: as a first stage, details of different types of consumption could be omitted, so as to enable a planning office to rough out the complete picture. All sorts of intermediate statistical patterns may be used, depending on the nature of the economy, and the statistics available....

Balancing savings and investment: The next balance, of savings and investment, will show how the level of investment could be financed out of foreign borrowing, out of a surplus in the government budget and out of private savings. The government budget forecast will take account of anticipated revenue (perhaps assuming, in the first place, unchanged tax rates); and of plans for the public services, especially education. The figure for foreign borrowing (if any) will come out of the balance-of-payments account. One's view on how savings may be expected to grow in the future, depends on recent trends in levels of savings. This account will, of course, balance in the event, because it is an identity, but if the forecast implies an *ex ante* shortage of savings, the balance will be achieved by price inflation.

Let us go back to the question of forecasting the level of investment. One starts by asking how much investment will be needed, taking account of the capacity required to obtain the planned output levels in each sector, and of the needed basic social capital. This capital cannot, of course, be provided in the plan year itself. What one wants is a schedule of investment in each year up to and including the plan year. One cannot avoid making some sort of explicit or implicit use of capital-output ratios here (preferably by sector), unsatisfactory though these are. Past and overseas experience may be some guide. Fortunately, one can generally get, as a starting point, the investment and output plans of the main firms, especially in export industries, and one has the forecast level of public investment.

In this table too, it is almost certain that an imbalance will appear at the first attempt. The account may imply an unreasonably high demand for private savings. One therefore makes adjustments to achieve consistency. Most probably one first investigates the possibilities of higher taxes, then reconsiders the possibilities of foreign borrowing, and finally looks harder at one's programme of investment.

One should, during this whole process, make as explicit as possible what types of projections are being made, whether the variable concerned is something over which the government has little control, e.g. exports, or whether it represents a major political objective, such as the level of employment, or whether it is a reasonable guess of the value of a variable which depends on others (for example, the de-

mand for food, which can be related to the anticipated level of income).

But even when one has a consistent set of projections clearly defined in this way, this is really only the beginning. For there should be some attempt to see, by drawing up alternative sets of estimates, what might happen if some of the key "autonomous" variables (e.g. population or exports) turned out to be different from what has been anticipated, and also to show the implications of different possible targets for *per capita* income, and of unexpected levels of the dependent variables, due to changes in propensities or co-efficients (especially the capital-output ratios). These alternatives are particularly necessary for export-orientated economies, since the course of future exports is always rather uncertain, and the pace of industrialization necessary for a given rate of economic growth will depend very much on the forecasts used for leading exports.

In some respects the implications of the programme should be worked out in greater detail. In the first place, an attempt should be made to assess, very roughly, the consequences for income distribution. Secondly, the manpower requirements of each sector should be forecast (using productivity trends), in order to see whether the composition of the programme is compatible with a high level of employment, and in order to give some clue on the needs for training labour and professional people.

Lastly, an attempt should be made to show the main magnitudes, particularly in the savings-investment table, to be expected during the intervening years before the year for which the main sets of projections are made. For this purpose, one should make use of what government expenditure is really needed each year to maintain growth. It is a well-known weakness of most colonial development "plans" that they show what are really sums of departmental projections, which tail off alarmingly after two or three years, because departments do not anticipate what new projects they will be starting then; if some attempt were made to relate these estimates to projections for the economy as a whole, more reasonable figures would have to be used. Here one comes into the field of short-term projections. A simplified version of the three tables described above, perhaps without commodity detail (except in exports) would provide the general framework for each year's budget.

One might ask what guidance one could get from a study of comparative costs to see whether the projected line of development is really economic. A method has in fact been devised by Professor Chenery (see *American Economic Review,* March 1961) for using "shadow" prices to indicate the economic line of development, these "shadow" prices taking account of external factors, such as the advantages of reducing dependence on foreign trade or the existence of unemployed labour. In practice, one feels that this is more complicated than can feasibly be attempted by planning offices in the immediate future. The problem will present itself rather as one of how technically plausible estimates can be made which will be consistent with something like full employment. What one might, however, ask oneself is whether it is really worthwhile to expand some existing high-cost industries, if there is no reasonable expectation that with larger scale of output these costs might be reduced. One can in fact probably only apply the comparative cost test in specific cases, and even then one may find one has to ignore the implications of a comparison of this kind, at least when existing prices are used for the calculations.

The projections should be adjusted in the light of experience. The extent to which this can be done depends on how much resources the economic planning office has available, and what are the other claims on these resources. For example, tourist re-

ceipts may rise more rapidly than had been expected. This will change one's outlook on how much imports can be afforded and therefore how much one has to change the structure of output. Ideally the whole set of estimates should be revised from time to time, so as to make it possible for the general strategy of economic policy to be modified. It will be easier to do this, if various sets of estimates have been already worked out, on different assumptions. Revision would help achieve what will occur in any case, a steady improvement in the technique of making projections.

This whole discussion pre-supposes, of course, that statistics are available to enable one to draw up projections and revise them.

1.4 PLANNING ECONOMIC DEVELOPMENT *

In the socialist countries and in the countries following a national revolutionary pattern we plan economic development, because economic development would not, under historic conditions existent, take place by itself automatically. Consequently it must be planned.

What is the essential of planning economic development? I would say that the essential consists in assuring an amount of productive investment which is sufficient to provide for a rise of national income substantially in excess of the rise in population, so that *per capita* national income increases. The strategic factor is investment, or more precisely productive investment. Consequently the problem of development planning is one of assuring that there be sufficient productive investment, and then of directing that productive investment into such channels as will provide for the most rapid growth of the productive power of national economy.

These are the essential tasks of develop-

* From Oskar Lange, *Economic Development, Planning and International Cooperation,* Central Bank of Egypt, Cairo, 1961, pp. 10-13, 15-17. Reprinted by permission.

ment planning. The problems which planning faces can be divided into two categories. One is the mobilisation of resources for purposes of productive investment, the other is the direction of the investment into proper channels. These are the essential problems implied in planning.

The first problem is that of mobilising resources for investment. Taking the experience of the socialist countries and of the countries following a national revolutionary pattern, a certain picture of methods employed for that mobilisation of resources can be drawn. These methods consist in the following: one is, and that is the method which was paramountly applied in the socialist countries, nationalisation of industries, finance, trade and the use of the profits thus derived for purposes of investment. The other method, which particularly plays a role in the countries following the national revolutionary pattern, is nationalisation of foreign owned natural resources and the use of the profits from these resources for investment purposes.

A further method is the contribution of the peasants in countries where agrarian reforms are carried out. The peasants are required, in turn, to make some contribution to the state finances, which are used for purposes of investment. This frequently does not suffice and an appeal is made to resources derived from general taxation, public loans and, in certain cases, also to deficit financing.

These methods of raising resources for investment are applied both in socialist and national revolutionary countries in various proportions. There is, also, a method which plays a particularly important role in the national revolutionary countries, and which in certain socialist countries during a transition period play a role too. This is the inducement of private savers to undertake productive investment. This implies inducing private industrialists, traders, landowners, and financial groups, to invest

a considerable part of their income in the direction which is conducive to assuring the country's rapid economic development, that means essentially investment in production. This can be achieved by various ways such as, for instance, taxation of unproductive uses of wealth, compulsory saving, restrictions of distributions of profits and of such uses of profits as do not consist of productive investment, compulsory loans and all kinds of other measures. Finally, import of foreign capital may be also a source of financing productive investments. . . .

Thus there is a whole catalogue of means applied in various proportions in different countries which provide the resources necessary for substantial productive investment. By substantial productive investment I mean investment which is large enough to achieve a break-through, or as some economists call it—to produce the "take-off," the passage from stagnation to intensive development. This obviously cannot be done by small amounts of investment which are likely to peter out in a great number of minor projects. Sufficient investment is required to produce a real, a qualitative change in the structure of national economy. This is one problem of developmental planning, namely to secure these resources for productive investment.

The second problem is the direction of investment and here I shall distinguish three sub-problems. The first is how to allocate investment so as to assure the most rapid growth of production; the second is how to secure balanced development of the economy, balance between the different branches of national economy; the third is how to assure efficiency of the use of resources in economic development, how to avoid waste and resources. These are three sub-problems of the general problem of directing investment so as to assure economic development.

The first sub-problem is the most important one. It is concerned with choosing such types of investment as will most rapidly increase the productive power of the economy. This implies a concentration of investment in fields which increase the capacity of further production; that means building up the industries which produce means of production. It is only through development of the industries which produce means of production that the production capacity of the economy can be raised.

This can be done, however, either directly or indirectly. It is done directly through investing in the construction of, say, power plants, steel plants, machine industries, raw material production and so on. It is done indirectly through foreign trade: instead of investing directly in the production, say, of certain machines it may be possible to get these machines from abroad by investing in the production of such commodities which can be sold abroad in order to import the machines required. Thus the productive power of the economy can be increased either directly through investing in the production of means of production, or indirectly through developing export industries which make it possible to import in the future the needed means of production. Which of these two methods is used depends on all kinds of circumstances, of existing facilities for developing either directly the output of means of production, or for producing commodities for export. However, if investment in exportable commodities is undertaken then obviously it must be associated with importation in exchange for these exports of machinery, steel and other means of production to increase the country's productive power.

However, investment in the production of means of production is not the only type of investment needed. There are two complementary types of investment which are necessary. One is investment in agriculture to increase food production. The experi-

ence of economic planning, particularly in the socialist countries, has shown that with the growth of industrialisation, with an increasing part of the population being employed in industries or transport services and so on, a considerable surplus of agricultural products is needed to feed the non-agricultural population. Consequently complementary to the investment in the development of the output of means of production must be investment in agriculture to increase agricultural output. Also a certain amount of investment in industries producing consumers' goods for the population is required, for the standard of living rises with the expansion of industrial employment and output. These are then the chief directions of developmental investments. The first one is the stategic one, the one which brings about economic development, and the other two are of a complementary nature necessary in order that economic development can proceed smoothly.

Finally, there is one important field of developmental investment, namely investment in the general economic infra-structure of the country, such as transport facilities, roads and also social services. These, too, are complementary investments needed to assure smooth economic development. However, they by themselves are not a factor bringing about development. One of the problems in many, if not most, underdeveloped countries was—and this was a part of the colonial or imperialist system—that there took place a large construction of this economic infra-structure purely for the needs of colonial exploitation, and not for development of the productive power of the country.…

There are two kinds of balances which must be secured: one is the physical balance and the other is financial or monetary balance. The physical balance consists in a proper evaluation of the relations between investment and output. In the countries which have already experience in economic planning investment coefficients are computed. These coefficients indicate the amount of investment and also the composition of that investment in terms of various kinds of goods needed in order to obtain an increase of output of a product by a given amount. For example, how much iron, how much coal, how much electric power is needed in order to produce an additional ton of steel. On this basis the planned increase in output of various products is balanced with the amounts and types of investment. It is also necessary to balance the outputs of the various sections of the economy because, as we know, the output of one branch of the economy serves as input for producing the output of another branch. For instance, the output of iron ore serves as an input in the steel industry. In the last mentioned field a special technique, that of input-output analysis has been developed.

The physical balancing mentioned is necessary in order that the output of the different branches of the economy proceed smoothly. This is a condition of the internal consistency of the plan. If this condition is not observed bottlenecks appear. The plan cannot be carried out because of physical obstacles, such as lack of raw materials, of manpower etc.

The second kind of balancing is monetary balancing, assuring monetary equilibrium in the economy. This consists in establishing an equilibrium between the incomes of the population—wages, incomes of peasants and others—and the amount of consumers' goods which will be available to the population. If the amount of incomes, or more precisely that part of the incomes which is spent for purposes of consumption, should turn out greater than the amount of available consumers' goods, inflationary processes develop. Thus the financial or monetary balance must establish an equilibrium between the part of incomes devoted to consumption and the output of consumers' goods. Further it must establish equilibrium between the part of incomes of the population which will be used for private investment and the amount of investment goods made available to private investors. Finally, in the public sector a balance must be established between the financial funds made available for investment purposes and the amount of investment goods which will be produced or imported. In addition to these balances it is necessary to establish the balance of foreign payments and receipts. The financial balances are an important part of planning. Just like the lack of physical balance leads to physical obstacles to the smooth process of production, so the lack of financial balance leads to disturbances in the supply and demand for physical commodities, and finally also to physical disturbances in the process of production.

Looking backwards upon the experience of the countries which applied planning as a tool of economic development, I must say that it usually turned out to be difficult to maintain the proper financial balance. Few of these countries escaped inflationary processes during certain periods. These processes were due to the wage bill rising more rapidly than the output of consumers' goods. However, in theory and with the experience which has been gained in earlier years it is today quite possible to plan the financial equilibrium of economic development in a way which avoids inflationary processes.

A last point—to be only mentioned briefly—is that of securing efficiency in the use of resources in the process of economic development. This is connected with the use of the price system. The function of the price system in economic planning is twofold. Prices serve as means of accounting, namely as a means of evaluating cost of production, value of output, and comparing the two. For this purpose it is necessary to have a proper price system which reflects the social cost (and in the short run—the scarcity) of the various means of production and the social importance of the various products. Without such a price system, cost accounting would not have any objective economic significance. This is one role of the price system; the other role is that of an incentive.

The plan of economic development has two aspects: in the public sector it is a directive to various public agencies and enterprises to do certain things, e.g. to invest that much in such a way, to produce in such a way at such a cost. With regard to the private sector, the plan has not the power of a directive, but is a desire expressed which must be followed by creating such incentives as will induce private producers to do exactly the things which are required from them in the plan. It is quite clear and does not require further explanation that with regard to the private sector the price system, including interest rates, is an important incentive serving to induce the private sector to do things required from it in the plan. But also in the public sector the need for incentive exists. It is not sufficient just to address administrative directives to public agencies and public enterprises. In addition to that it is necessary to create such economic incentives that the public agencies, enterprises etc. find it in the interest of their management and their employees to do the things which are required from them in the plan. This again requires a proper price system.

Thus the price system plays in planning a role both as a basis of accounting and as an incentive inducing the people to do the things required from them in the plan. A certain general observation may be made here. It seems rather general historical experience that in the first phase of economic development, particularly industrialisation, the problem of a proper price system is not the most important one. In both the socialist and the national revolutionary type of economic development we find that in the first period the main problem is not that of the details of accounting or incentives. The main problem is assuring rapid growth of productive capacity. The question of rapidity of growth overshadows the more subtle questions of high grade efficiency. It is more important, for instance, to develop at all the machine industry than to do it in the most efficient manner. Too much preoccupation with the subtleties of economic accounting may hold up action and slow down progress. It is only on a higher stage of economic development, when the national economy has become more complex and diversified, that the problem of efficiency and incentives become increasingly important. It is then that the subtleties of assuring the highest efficiency of economy through proper cost accounting, through properly established incentives, etc. come into play.

Thus—not wanting to minimise the importance of the problem—I do believe that it is not the most important problem in the first stage of economic development. In this first stage, the take-off stage, the real issue is to mobilise the necessary resources for productive investment, to allocate them to the branches of the economy which most rapidly increase the productive potential of the country, and to do so by the most productive technological methods. At a later stage more subtle aspects of planning come into play. Thus a certain crudeness of planning in the early stages of economic development is, I believe, quite justified.

1.5 PROBLEMS OF DEVELOPMENT PLANNING *

The basic problem of development planning is the organization of resources for growth. In this, the problem does not dif-

* From Wolfgang F. Stolper, "Comprehensive Development Planning," Paper prepared for the Economic Commission for Africa Working Party in Addis Ababa, January 1962, mimeographed, pp. 1, 3-6, 8-13. Reprinted by permission.

fer essentially from what it is in the so-called developed countries, except that in developed economies there exists a market and numerous institutions which can be used for the carrying out of planning ideas. The problem which development planners face in under-developed countries is four-fold. Firstly, they frequently lack the signalling system which a well-functioning market provides; secondly, they also lack the institutions by means of which ideas which might crystallize can be put into practice; thirdly, in under-developed countries there does not exist a sufficient number of people who can take the place even of a crudely working price system; and fourthly, basic information of a technical sort, particularly with respect to agriculture, is frequently enough not there, or is available only in a form in which it is not usable. Experience in many countries indicates that it would be fatal to ignore the price mechanism; this is true even in such centrally planned economies as the Soviet Union or East Germany. And it is not a realistic alternative to say that a government can take the place of a supposedly non-existent entrepreneur class.

Any comprehensive development planning must, in my opinion, make use of all the resources which the country has: there should be no ideological blocks to the employment of both as much state activity and as much private activity as can be possibly executed....

The lack of data and the shortage of trained personnel dictate, in my opinion, the following approach to comprehensive planning.

First, no man can know the future. This is especially true in open economies dependent to an unusual degree on the prices for their export products....

It follows that any long-range plan must be flexible. The view is all too common that a Five-Year Programme—or whatever happens to be the mystic number chosen—

is a blueprint for the future which should be altered as little as possible. It is, in fact, the view of the plan as a five-year capital and recurrent budget. On the other extreme is the cynical view of the Plan as a series of telephone numbers that can be changed at will. But any realistic plan should provide primarily a sense of direction and consistency. It must, as far as Government expenditure is concerned, still be translated every year into the details of a budget. It must, therefore, be specified every year in the light of the then available information and the then available resources. Now, obviously, some projects have larger horizons than others: tree crops take longer planning than field crops. Oil drilling or a steelmill more than textile mills, bottling plants or even cement plants. But the tempo of road building, of electricity expansion, of sewerage and water expansion and in fact of most programmes can be adjusted quite easily. Hence, while the long-run plan should give direction and over-all priorities, the details remain to be ironed out annually or even more frequently. It is realized that this will lay planning open to continuous political interference which in dictatorships is even more frequent and irrational than in countries that have the check of open debate. But the alternative is the carrying out of programmes even after changing events have shown them to be undesirable....

The central direction, and the sense of where the economy is going must come from an over-all view of the economy. But because any knowledge of local conditions, if it exists at all, can be found only on the spot the execution of the plan and the detailed planning itself must be decentralized. Moreover, any plan which does not envisage a vigorous growth of a private sector both in agriculture and in industry is doomed to have slower growth rates than could be otherwise achieved....

I envisage a comprehensive plan to consist essentially of three parts: a capital budget for government; recurrent expenditure budgets for government; and policies towards the private sector. In addition, both recurrent expenditure and the policies require frequently the building of institutions, and everything requires the best possible use of the market mechanism, even if it exists in only an imperfect form.

The basic task of comprehensive planning is to ensure consistency and feasibility and to permit a rational determination of priorities. Any generally trained economist who is familiar with general equilibrium theory, particularly in its modern form of inter-industry economics, knows that the characteristic of an economy is the high degree of inter-relationships among its various parts. To some extent, it is a characteristic of an underdeveloped economy that its major links are through exports and imports with the outside world while the internal flows are relatively small. I have frequently wondered to what extent this is due to our ignorance of the true facts, and to what extent it truly reflects reality that there are relatively minor internal flows. We take it, for example, much too much for granted that food crops are primarily grown for subsistence when in fact a casual visit to any market indicates that almost any produce—millet, guinea corn, maize, kila nuts, rice, pepper, groundnuts, and what have you—is domestically traded. ...

No individual project can be evaluated in isolation. Whether it should or should not be executed will depend on the alternative uses which can be made of the capital requested and the manpower available. To ensure consistency, some over-all view has to be gained. The easiest and best developed method of doing so is through the development of national income statistics. ...

The uses to which such a national income account ... can be put [are] as follows. First, the politically determined targets in growth terms can be worked out. The projections of gross product at, say, x per cent, can be shown to be feasible by showing the implications which this growth would have. Thus, if in the past y per cent of income had to be invested to achieve x per cent of growth and if the composition of past investment among major sectors is known, it is a fair assumption that the same investment will carry the same rate of growth, unless its composition is drastically changed.

The aggregate model can, secondly, be used to determine—in admittedly rough terms—the order of magnitude of the foreign exchange gap that will develop. This permits the planner some view of whether his investment targets are realistic. It also gives him some clue how he may have to change the composition of investments to reduce the foreign exchange gap. Moreover, it is quite easy to vary such growth models and to build into them various price changes. It may be found that any inflationary trend very quickly tends to spill over into imports and tends to make it increasingly difficult to meet the required import finance.

The same model can also be used to determine the real limits of the investment programme in yet another manner. It is my firm conviction that the real limits to any governmental development programme is the ability to carry recurrent cost. It is virtually impossible to get foreign aid for recurrent cost, with the major exceptions of education and possibly health. Any development programme will raise recurrent costs. These recurrent costs can be translated with relatively minor effort into government absorption of goods and services in the national income sense. If the recurrent costs involved in the programme together with the normal administrative cost become too big and too large a percentage of GDP [Gross Domestic

Product] is to be allocated, therefore, to government consumption, this will reduce the available resources in other directions and require either a further lowering of consumption or an increase in the imports to be financed. If it is politically decided that no further sacrifices can be put upon consumers and if it is not feasible to finance a larger import gap, the over-all programme must be reduced.

Finally, the aggregative model is necessary to catch all the indirect repercussions which the investment programmes, whether by government or private persons, will have; particularly on import goods. No amount of adding of individual projects will give the total effect on imports because of these indirect repercussions. The development planner in particular who is aware of the foreign exchange content of many projects should be aware of the probability that he may run into balance of payments trouble even if he got foreign aid for all the foreign exchange content of each project. The aggregative model allows some assumption of the additional gap created by indirect repercussions and therefore of the additional percentage required either through the country's own resources or through general balance of payments support.

Any aggregative model can therefore be used to provide a planning framework into which projects and programmes are integrated. . . .

The heart of any development programme is an action programme consisting of well thought through projects. What distinguishes the comprehensive approach from a mere list of projects is, first, that an attempt is made to relate the various projects towards each other; secondly, that an attempt is made to take indirect effects into account; thirdly, that an attempt is made to relate policies for both the public and the private sector to the projects; and

finally that an attempt is made to make the various projects feed into each other in timing, manpower planning, size and so forth.

It should be repeatedly stressed that many basic facts of the African economies are not known and that, therefore, it will not always be possible to get the necessary facts. Nevertheless, it is surprising how much can be learned if the right sort of questions are asked. It should also repeatedly be stressed that projects must be profitable within a reasonable time. It is not an argument that can be defended economically or politically to say that a loss industry is justifiable because it gives employment; alternative better uses of the capital would have given more employment, as profits can be reinvested while losses require constant subsidies, prevent investment elsewhere, and therefore hamper development.

The intellectual framework of detailed planning is inter-industry economics. The techniques developed by Tinbergen, Chenery, Chakravarty and others must, of course, be imaginatively adopted to circumstances. No one in his right mind proposes to set up a system of equations, calculate the matrix and solve it to get the answers. It is questionable whether this would be worthwhile even if the data were available. In any case, we would not have sufficient facts to feed a high-powered modern calculating brain.

The basic problem of development is the allocation of resources in such a manner as to increase the availability of resources. Once the problem of how much consumption increase is to be permitted politically is settled, the major problem becomes one of resource allocation. The major scarcities in most African economies are skilled manpower and capital. Skilled manpower must, therefore, be allocated to raise production and not only capital. With African economies being open, foreign exchange allocation and earnings as well as saving become of paramount importance....

The indirect cost and benefits must be as far as possible evaluated. This, it seems to me, is the heart of comprehensive development planning: that one keeps constantly the interrelation with other parts of the economy in mind. The factual questions must be asked in such a manner that the answers when they are received can be fed into other programmes, into budgets, manpower estimates, foreign exchange budgets, and even that they can be used by an existing development corporation anxious to invest capital or attract a foreigner with lures of a prospective profitable market and capital participation. I am not preaching perfection but only the beginning of an attempt to look at a plan *in toto* and to evaluate projects within a context. The reason is, to state the point *ad nauseum,* that all our decisions in economics are of a "more-or-less" nature and not of an "either-or" nature; that we rarely will condemn a project outright but will mainly question its size and timing and that we will make the manner of its execution and indeed whether and when it is to be executed dependent upon other decisions taken simultaneously. There is, to repeat another point already made, some notion around that if only enough unprofitable enterprises are started somehow the economy will grow. Some vague and misunderstood concept of external economies and balanced growth will usually be mentioned.... Moreover, there is never any virtue in investing money at a loss, even if the money is available and not at the time usable for other projects. Opportunity cost for funds is measured in interest rates which are quite high throughout the world. And losses mean that you come out with less resources than you started with, which is not development....

It is, of course, impossible to do more than one thing at a time. What distinguishes comprehensive planning from a mere list of projects is not that there is no such list of projects but that the final list has been arrived at in the process of making the various individual programmes consistent with each other. They all must be added up, must be matched against each other and against the available resources. Only in this manner can some less profitable projects be shown to be undesirable. Because only then can it be conclusively shown that the execution of a less desirable project will interfere with a more desirable one. Only then can it be shown that the true choices are between a programme with a "more" and a programme with a "less" growth inducing distribution of investments. It goes without saying that the final decision must be made by the Ministers on a political level, and that is as it should be because a rapid economic development is only one of several possible and possibly conflicting political aims. I should not worry widely about the possible conflict. It is the characteristic of an optimal situation that no further improvement in one direction can be made without a deterioration in another. After all, how do you know that you are on top of a mountain and not in a saddle? All you have to do is to take steps in different directions. If the only way is down, you know you are as high as you can go. The technician must, however, have made a clear case in which the choices to be made are plain to the politician:

more projects mean more taxes and/or internal borrowing and/or foreign aid;

expansion in one direction must be balanced by contraction in another if tax increases, etc., are to be avoided;

execution of lower payoff projects will stimulate growth less than that of higher payoff projects; it will therefore reduce potential government revenues and potential domestic savings; it will therefore lead to a less fast growth in consumption, investment, employment and growth than possible in the circumstances.

All this can never be shown by treating individual projects in isolation. Nor can a sensible answer to what is a desirable project be found without tracing through as many of the repercussions as it is feasible to do in the admittedly rough circumstances with which the planner is faced.

1.6 DESIGNING A PRACTICAL PLAN *

Economic planning performs four functions: the first task is that of evaluating potentials; the second of translating objectives into programs and actions; the third is forming the basis for choosing among alternative programs in light of limited resources; and the fourth is that of co-ordination.

I would like to utilize these four functions as the framework for my discussion. However, since my topic deals with the problem of planning in practice, namely, the designing and administering of a regional development plan, I would like first to discuss briefly the problems of practical planning.

I think that this is a very important subject because, too often, the discussions concerning development planning make it appear as though we are dealing with an exact science and that each step follows logically from an almost superhuman concept of what ought to be done in the development of a particular region. For example, I have read of plans to develop particular areas which propose to utilize advanced techniques such as inter-industry schemes, linear programming methods, operations research and advanced econometric methods. These descriptions tend to leave the reader with the feeling that development planning has left the field of polit-

* From Alvin Mayne, "Designing and Administering a Regional Economic Development Plan with Special Reference to Puerto Rico," *Regional Economic Planning* (Walter Isard & John H. Cumberland, eds.), Organisation for Economic Co-operation and Development, Paris, 1961, pp. 142, 144-7, 151-3, 155-6.

ical pressures, hunches and guesswork, to take its place among the exact sciences. Too often, upon investigation, one discovers that these plans, which are nicely printed and bound, are placed upon shelves where they gather dust when they are not being used for a conference.

It would be useless to design a development plan which requires operational authority to articulate it if powers necessary are not available for use by the administration. Thus, in a democracy, a plan which calls for dictatorial powers for accomplishment is of no value. On the other hand, in sectors of the economy where social injustices may develop, plans which call for a completely *laisssez-faire* operation will be unacceptable in a society truly dedicated to social betterment of its population.

It is necessary to create a plan which can operate within the range of the legal latitude available to the administrators. This does not mean that the laws on the books must be regarded as frozen, but rather that there is no use in generating plans and programmes which would be operative only with legal changes which are unlikely to occur.

The financial feasibility of any plan is important. A plan which calls for expenditures of funds in excess of the potential financial resources is, of course, doomed. Again, this does not mean that the methods of generating financial resources must be taken as unalterable, but before recommending plans calling for increased financial resources the planner should take a hard look at the possibility of raising taxes, increasing borrowing of funds and deficit financing.

The practical planner must realize that decision-making with respect to the allocation of resources, by both government and private enterprise, is a continuing process. While the planner may feel that the current method of decision-making is not adequate, he must recognize that there is already a decision-making apparatus in being. Part of the task of the practical planner is to develop the strategic and tactical measures whereby the decision-making techniques called for by the development plan can gradually replace existing decision-making operation. A head-on collision between the existing and proposed decision-making apparatus will generally spell failure for the newer technique. The strategy of the take-over must be subtle and virtually unnoticed.

In creating a development plan for a region the practical planner will soon find that there are quite a number of conflicting objectives. The first source of conflict will be the objectives which are pressed upon him by the immediate conditions under which he finds himself. There will be strong pressures for development plans to contain programmes which will show immediate results and will raise the level of living of the present generation. On the other hand, the practical planner will soon recognize that due to limited financial administrative and human resources, it takes time to achieve desired objectives and a plan which concentrates on short-range objectives will not only fail in achieving longer-range goals but will also fail in satisfying the shorter-range measures.

The second source of conflict with respect to the objectives will result from the opposition of regional to national objectives. It may be in the interest of the national objectives to try to concentrate on particular areas which can most fruitfully be developed. However, if one is charged with planning the development of a particular region it may be difficult to obtain special assistance from the national government required by the area. For example, in Puerto Rico, in attempting to create a Public Housing Program which is realistic for Puerto Rico, it has been necessary to deal with the national standards which

were developed for the mainland and do not fit either the economic or physical conditions of Puerto Rico. The same situation exists with respect to monetary controls. The control mechanism set up the Federal Reserve System (the central bank) for controlling the flow of funds, proves to be a hardship to Puerto Rico, which is undergoing an entirely different type of development than that of the general economy.

The third major conflict in objectives, with which the practical planner must contend, is the conflict between the economic, social and physical planning objectives....

Closely allied to the conflict of economic and social objectives is the fourth problem faced by the practical planner, namely, the objectives for the individual are frequently in conflict with the objectives for the economy or society as a whole. The desire to give maximum individual liberty would frustrate all types of economic and social planning and the probable long-run development of the economy. The ability of the individual to dispose of his property, real or otherwise, in any manner which he wishes, may frequently clash with the development of the plan. The practical planner, in developing his plans, must consider the degree of freedom which this society is going to allow individuals and the degree to which the government is willing to take over decision-making with respect to the disposal of most of the resources. For example, an agricultural master plan was developed for Puerto Rico without seriously considering the role that the private individual as a decision-maker is entitled to play. Since the mechanism to translate the plan into action required considerably less private decision-making than would be conceded in the Puerto Rican society for some time to come, the plan had to be discarded and considered useless except as an interesting research project.

Finally, there is the conflict which is

constantly present in the democratic nations, namely, the relative roles of the public and private sectors. Too often the decision is made on the basis of previous ideological notions without considering the particular problems in developing a region. One of the greatest accomplishments of Puerto Rican planning has been the taking of a pragmatic view of the relative roles which the public and private sectors should play. Wherever possible, there has been an attempt to mix them and to find that combination which results in the maximum efficiency.

The first step that a practical planner must take is to make a quick survey of the characteristics of the society and the economy with which he is to deal. The inventories that concern him are the natural, human and financial resources, and the market and service industry potentials. Each regional economy and each society is endowed with a varying amount of these resources with respect to quality and quantity. . . .

The inventory of various resources serves two purposes for development and planning. First, the inventory represents a preliminary diagnosis of the situation and enables the advisors to indicate to the decision-makers which sectors, functional and geographic, have the greatest potential for growth. It is possible also to indicate the types of administrative organizations and legislation needed to provide the incentives and climate necessary to induce the feasible development. Thus, action of an enabling character can frequently be initiated without waiting for a final and complete plan for development. The second value of the inventory is that it enables the quantitative forecasting of growth potentials in such a way that the other three functions of planning may be implemented with continuous guidance given to the decision-makers in an integrated planning process.

It is important that, as soon as possible, the decision is made as to the type of profile which will be projected. There are two basic approaches to the building of economic and social models and projections. One method is to draw a picture of what is desired for future time without paying too much attention to the feasibility of achieving such an economic and social model. This approach is based on the belief that with economic and other forms of planning it is possible to accomplish most of the desired objectives. This procedure involves, and attempts to find, a series of incentives and programs which will accomplish the goals.

The second method is not to start from an *a priori* picture of the end result but to analyze the developments which have been occurring and to estimate the potentials of growth which are likely to exist. The incentive programmes are then tailored to fit the present and foreseeable circumstances. They are used to foster the probable developments which are considered more desirable. If the economic and social projections reveal developments likely to occur, but which are not considered desirable, then an analysis of forces which are required to alter the course of development must be developed. Once this is known, the programmes and incentives to accomplish this alteration can be brought to bear on the future progress of the economy.

The weakness of the first method is that it requires, for purposes of implementation, more authority than is generally possessed by a government. It tends to generate claims on scarce resources far in excess of the available supplies. The result may be a misallocation of scarce resources to the point where inefficiency and loss of output may occur. In addition, confusion tends to prevail if the desired goals become accepted as a forecast and if hopes fail to materialize. Decisions are then made on the basis of fictitious possibilities.

The second method has a greater chance of success because it is built on forces and potentialities which are already under way or whose development can be foreseen. It is the responsibility of the government therefore, to provide the setting which will enable the desired growth to take place. Feasible rates of growth have already been built into the model to the extent that it is possible to understand the nature of the forces which are operating. The danger of this method is, of course, that it will be too conservative.

It is my belief that the planning of government programs is best served if the profile of the future is based on the second method, namely, a forecast of the nature of the changes which are most likely to occur. . . .

A picture of how to prepare a model might be obtained by looking very briefly at the methods utilized in forecasting the growth of the Puerto Rican economy until 1975. The projections were expressed in terms of the national income accounts. The economic model was constructed by assuming that the basic generating forces in the Puerto Rican economy resulted from:

    i. expenditures for the purchase of goods and services in Puerto Rico by outside forces such as the United States economy and the Federal government, and

    ii. the investment of capital goods which are paid for by outside capital and/or savings of the Puerto Rican economy.

To facilitate analysis, the sectors of the economy were classified into two groups: those which might be considered generating and those which tend to be secondary, largely taking their growth pattern from the developments which occurred in the generating sectors. The generating sectors were as follows:

    i. manufacturing for export;

    ii. agriculture for export;

    iii. contract construction;

    iv. Federal government expenditures, and

    v. Commonwealth government expenditures.

The funds for the net income generated in producing agricultural and manufactured products for export come from outside of Puerto Rico and, therefore, represent a net injection of funds into the Commonwealth economy. Net income arising in contract construction was also included because activity in that sector is attributable to the investment of funds derived principally from external sources rather than from local savings. Net income arising from Federal government expenditures is comprised mainly of salaries and wages paid to civilian employees and members of the Armed Forces physically located in Puerto Rico. Since these payments are financed by taxes paid by the mainland economy, they also represent a net injection of funds into the Commonwealth economy.

The derived portion of the economy included the remaining activities such as manufacture and agriculture for local consumption, trade, services, etc., in which the activity is dependent generally upon the level of income for the economy as a whole. The level of the derived portion of the economy tends to vary with the changes in the determining sectors. Because of the great leakage of income due to the inability to import, the multiplier for the derived industries tends to be relatively low.

When these projections were put together they provided an estimate of the rate at which production and national income would grow. A series of checks was made as to the internal consistency of these estimates:

    i. determination was made of the rate at which production had been expanding during the last years to see whether the new projections were out of line, and

ii. studies were made of the capital ratios so as to determine whether there would be sufficient investment funds forthcoming to sustain the projected level of the output.

Once the rate of investment was determined the past history was reviewed both from the standpoint of feasibility of achievement, in terms of the task of constructing the facilities involving the capital investment, and the availability of funds. The availability of funds depends, in Puerto Rico, on external as well as internal investment. In recent years the rate of external investment has been about 50 per

cent of the total. Under the assumption that the industrial climate vis-a-vis the United States would remain roughly the same, it was possible to estimate the nature and extent of capital funds which would flow into the Puerto Rican economy from the United States. Next, the local sources of saving for investment were analyzed in light of their potential growth by studying the various accounts which were likely to generate savings. In light of the increasing level of income and the generation of business savings and depreciation funds, it appeared that the contribution of local savings would rise sufficiently to meet the demand. Thus, a cross-check was made through the use of two different methods of analysis.

2. ALLOCATING DEVELOPMENT RESOURCES

2.1 THE BUDGET AND PUBLIC EXPENDITURE POLICY *

Public expenditure policy, in its quantitative and qualitative aspects, is reflected and recorded in the government's budget. Therefore, any systematic discussion of public expenditures must start with an account of the process of budget preparation. When speaking about "the budget," most people, including politicians, mean the administrative or "conventional" budget. In this budget expenditures are classified according to the administrative units, such as departments responsible for the implementation of the activities for which public funds are appropriated. In countries with a democratic form of government, the administrative budget is an

* From John H. Adler, "Public Expenditures and Economic Development," Paper presented to Conference on Fiscal Policy, Santiago, Chile, December 1962, pp. 5-11. To be published by the Organization of American States. Reprinted by permission.

essential instrument to delineate the spheres of influence of the executive and legislative branches of government. The appropriation process enables the legislature to set the level and determine the composition of governmental outlays. The appropriation procedure, together with the activities of special control organs, such as the Court of Accounts, provides the framework within which the legislature assures that the appropriated sums are expended "legally," i.e. within the limits and for the objectives prescribed in the budget.

The administrative budget, geared primarily to this particular political and legal control function, performs a useful role and indeed an indispensable one. It is not sufficient, however, to assure the coordination of public sector operations with the development efforts of the economy as a whole, whether these efforts take place within the framework of a development plan or program or not. Its limitations have become more obvious in recent times as government budgets have grown in size and complexity and attempts have been made to remedy these deficiencies.

Traditional budget procedures suffer from two major difficulties. First their coverage is usually incomplete. The normal budget does not cover all public sector operations, not even those carried out by the central government. The operations of autonomous and semi-autonomous agencies are almost inevitably—as it were, by definition—excluded. To be sure, in virtually all countries there exist autonomous or semi-autonomous agencies whose operations are not recorded in the budget, although they fall clearly within the perimeter of the public sector. In developing countries, however, the number of public entities outside the public budget is usually large and their activities are of major importance in determining the direction and pace of the development process. In Latin America in particular autonomous agencies are numerous and their role in the development process is great. In some countries the tendency to create autonomous agencies has obviously gone too far. . . .

Decentralization of public sector activities has merit and is justifiable in some cases. But the proliferation of autonomous agencies is objectionable, the more so when the increase in their numbers indicates merely the failure of the regular departmental machinery to cope with the problem of public administration in a developing economy. . . .

Where responsibility for public sector activities is spread over many centers of decision, it becomes very difficult, not to say impossible, to frame a consistent policy for the public sector as a whole. This is especially true with regard to capital investment. Unless steps are taken to coordinate public investment activities

with each other and with those of the private sector one cannot expect public investment resources to be properly allocated.[1]

Therefore measures must be taken to provide decision makers with a comprehensive picture of public sector operations. This does not imply that all details of all autonomous agencies should be included in the budget. But it should be possible to learn from the budget what funds are used to subsidize the operations of the autonomous agencies and to finance their investments, and what use is being made of these agencies' own resources (i.e. depreciation funds and net earnings).

Another drawback of conventional budgeting is its emphasis on the cost aspect of government expenditures. The administrative budget shows the cost to government of acquiring goods and services. It does not relate this cost to the results achieved, i.e. to the benefits which the economy derives from public expenditures.

In recent years new methods of budget classification which are particularly useful for developing countries have been devised. They can be of great help in developing countries in the formulation of public expenditure policy.

They may also serve to show the way for the modernization and rationalization of public administration. A number of Latin American countries have already changed the presentation of their budgets, and others have started with reform plans. . . .

The budget reforms follow various lines and have various primary objectives. The functional budget and the performance budget are devices of particular usefulness for the improvement of public expenditure policies and for the preparation of public

[1] It may be noted in this connection that the widespread practice of earmarking taxes for the use of particular agencies or for special purposes increases the danger of misallocation.

expenditure plans as part of a development program.[2]

The functional budget provides a basis for a rational choice among competing objectives of public expenditure. It classifies public expenditure by specific governmental function, such as defense, health, education, promotion of agriculture, etc.[3] This procedure is clearly superior to the classification of expenditure by different administrative units....

Performance budgeting is more than a classification device. It constitutes a new approach to budget formulation and budget execution. Its main objective is to provide a mechanism for measuring the benefit of the various items of public expenditures, and to relate benefits to costs incurred. It also can be used to set targets for the various functions to be performed by the same administrative unit in a budget period.

The functional budget indicates the maximum cost than can be incurred in financing the activities pertaining to a particular function of government. When allocating money between, say, primary education and vocational training, policy makers already have some ideas about the comparative benefit to be derived for society as a whole from these outlays. They may be based to some extent on an objective analysis of such variables as the projected population growth, regional imbalances in the provision of educational facilities, and other factors.

All allocational decisions imply some sort of a cost-benefit notion, although the assessment of prospective benefits may have been arrived at in an intuitive way and purely political considerations may also have influenced the decisions. But the functional budget can do no more than indicate *ex post* whether the maximum amount of the projected costs has been exceeded. It does not provide any means to detect whether the projected benefits have in fact materialized, assuming that they have been expressed in terms of an objective unit of measurement, such as the additional number of children that would go to school as a result of the training of teachers.

In the preparation of the performance budget, however, the relation of benefits to cost can be carried considerably further. Performance budgeting presupposes an explicit determination of the objective to be attained by an outlay and thereby involves almost inevitably some cost-benefit calculations, based either on past performance, or some other relevant information.

Performance budgeting becomes of course virtually indispensable if the budget, or a part of the budget, forms a part of a development program. In a mixed economy, the hard core of a development program is a program of public expenditures, chiefly to finance capital projects but also to pay for "supporting" activities (e.g., research, training, education). The program objectives are stated in terms of specific targets and projects and thus becomes the goal of the budget, or of a series of budgets, to provide funds to reach these targets and to carry out these projects.[4]

[2]The "economic" budget classification is only indirectly relevant in this context. Its chief objective of classifying all public receipts and expenditures as current, capital or transfer operations is necessary for the preparation of national accounts. Only insofar as national accounts serve as a basis for decisions regarding public sector operations, is the economic budget a tool of expenditure policy.

[3]Cf. the scheme, suggested in the United Nations *Manual for Economic and Functional Classification of Government Transactions* (New York, Sales No. 58.XVI.2), Table 25.

[4]Performance budgeting, particularly within the framework of a development program, may also have important side effects. It may permit an evaluation of administrative arrangements and improvements in the allocation of functions to be performed by various departments of governments and at various levels of government.

2.2 Choice of Policy Instruments *

There has been little systematic analysis of the relative merits and defects of the policy instruments available to under-developed countries. Since control of international trade is administratively simpler than many other types of policy, there has been a tendency to rely heavily on it as a way of influencing the pattern of domestic production, without recognizing the drawbacks to exclusive reliance on this set of instruments. Colonial areas have been forced to devise other measures, since protection was denied to them, but they have rarely pursued over-all development policies. The need for a greater variety of measures to promote development has now been widely recognized, but there is still inadequate consideration of the range of alternatives available.

In its need to change the pattern of resource use over a relatively short period of time, the promotion of development resembles (in lesser degree) the problem of mobilization for war. The suitability of various instruments for the latter purpose has been widely discussed, and the experience of the United States and other countries has been analysed in some detail. A similar study of the actual effects of development policies is needed before very firm recommendations can be made to the under-developed countries, but some general comments may be in order.

Characteristics of instruments: Policy instruments may be classified in various ways: by the sectors of the economy on which they operate, by their use of prices or quantities as variables to be manipulated; by the extent to which they can be effectively controlled by the government, by the effect that they have on private incentives and freedom of choice, etc. In

* From Hollis B. Chenery, "Development Policies and Programmes," *Economic Bulletin for Latin America*, Vol. III, No. 1, March 1958, pp. 55-60.

Table I representative instruments are classified according to the extent of their application (general versus specific) and their mode of operation (through prices or quantities). The general instruments act on broad aspects of the economy—the money supply, the government budget, investment, consumption—and are widely used in developed and under-developed countries alike. The specific instruments are applied differentially to individual sectors of the economy, as illustrated by subsidies, tariffs, or Government investment.

To achieve a given effect on production, or use of any commodity, there is a choice between controlling a price and controlling a quantity. In this respect, tariffs are an alternative to quotas, differential interest rates are an alternative to capital rationing, and subsidies to private producers are an alternative to production by the government. These measures differ in their effects on prices and consumer choices, in administrative convenience, in the predictability of their results, and in other respects. A choice between quantity and price variables as instruments must therefore be made by balancing the advantages and disadvantages in each case.

Some of the main issues of economic policy are concerned with the choice between general and specific instruments and between using prices and quantities as control variables. There is a strong case to be made for using general instruments rather than specific ones. The rates of interest, taxation, and exchange are the orthodox means of exerting Government influence in a *laissez-faire* economy. Their immediate objectives are stability in prices and the balance of payments and the prevention of unemployment. Growth is left to free market forces. The manipulation of interest rates and exchange rates allows market forces in each sector to determine where expansion or contraction of production and consumption will take place. These

TABLE I. CLASSIFICATION OF POLICY INSTRUMENTS

	Area of policy	Price Variables — Instrument	Price Variables — Variables affected *	Quantity Variables — Instrument	Quantity Variables — Variables affected
General	Monetary	interest rate	(1) level of investment (2) cost of production	open market operations	(1) money supply (2) prices
General	Fiscal	personal income tax / corporate income tax	(1) consumption and saving / (1) profits (2) investment	Government expenditure	(1) national income (2) price level
General	Foreign Trade	exchange rate / general tariff level	(1) cost of imports (2) price of exports (3) balance of payments	exchange auctions	exchange rates
General	Foreign Investment	taxes on foreign profits	level of foreign investment	foreign loans and grants	(1) investment resources (2) exchange supply
General	Consumption	general sales tax	consumption	social insurance, relief, other transfers	(1) consumption (2) income distribution
General	Labour	wage rates	(1) labour cost (2) profits and investment (3) labour income	emigration and immigration	labour supply
Specific	Production	taxes and subsidies / price control	(1) profits and production (2) investment	Government production / Government research and technical assistance	level of production / cost of production
Specific	Investment	interest rates / tax exemptions	(1) profits (2) investment by sector	Government investment capital rationing / restrictions on entry	level of investment / (1) prices and profits (2) level of investment
Specific	Consumption	specific sales taxes	consumption by commodity	Government services (health, education)	(1) consumption (2) income distribution
Specific	Trade	export subsidies / tariffs	(1) price to consumer (2) profits on domestic production / (1) profits and investment	import quotas and prohibitions / exchange controls	(1) level of imports (2) domestic prices
Specific	Labour	wage subsidy	(1) labour cost and use (2) profits and investment	labour training	supply of skilled labour
Specific	Natural Resources	taxes and subsidies	(1) cost of production (2) rate of exploitation	surveys, auxiliary investment, etc.	rate of development

* All taxes affect Government revenue and saving in addition to the variables cited.

instruments therefore interfere less with the choices of producers and consumers than do measures which discriminate by sector. They also require a less detailed analysis for their use and do not substitute Government judgment of what is desirable for the action of market forces.

The need for specific instruments to supplement general measures derives from the deficiencies in the price mechanism which apply primarily to specific sectors of the economy. When these factors prevent the achievement of a satisfactory rate of growth, the problem is to devise policy measures which will improve on the working of the competitive economy without losing the advantages of private initiative and the automatic adjustment of the price system.

In designing policies for specific sectors, there is an argument for using price rather than quantity instruments which is based on reasoning similar to the case for general over specific instruments. Taxes and subsidies distort the choices open to producers and users of a commodity less than do allocation systems or other quantitative restrictions and hence are conducive to greater flexibility and over-all economic effciency. Furthermore, the administrative requirements for price intervention of this type are generally less than for quantitative controls.

Despite the general case in favour of using the price system, there are several situations in which quantitative measures may be needed:

(i) When it is necessary to limit consumption of an essential commodity in short supply (e.g., imported goods), the tax needed to bring about a given reduction in use might result in such high prices that the burden of the reduction would fall on lower income groups. In this case, price controls and rationing may be preferable on welfare grounds.

(ii) Where a minimum increase in production is essential to production in other sectors—as in the case of power, transport and various auxiliary facilities—the price needed to ensure adequate private investment may be too high or the response of private investors too uncertain. In this case, quantitative measures, such as Government investment, may be more efficient because the cost to the society is less or the outcome more predictable.

(iii) In general, where controls are needed for only a short period, as in the case of temporary shortages, it may be desirable to allocate supplies to more essential uses rather than upset the general price structure and distort investment decisions by allowing prices to rise. Quantitative measures are also likely to have more predictable effects in this case.

In these examples, it is the dynamic elements in the situation and the deviation from a desirable income distribution which provide the principal arguments for using quantitative measures of control.

Specific measures for investment allocation: Although the specific measures listed in Table I affect both current production and the allocation of investment resources, it is the latter aspect that is crucial for the future course of development. The various instruments affect investment decisions through the availability and cost of primary inputs (labour, natural resources, imported commodities); through the supply of inputs from other sectors (raw materials, overhead facilities); through the demand for output (sales taxes, export subsidies); through profits (taxes, subsidies); and through measures directly related to the process of investment (interest rates, capital rationing, restrictions on entry, direct Government investment). There is therefore a considerable variety of choice between quantity and price instruments and among measures more or less directly related to a particular investment.

The *a priori* arguments concerning some of the principal measures for influencing investment decisions run somewhat as follows:

(i) *Measures of protection*. As indicated earlier, protective devices are perhaps the most common instruments for influencing the pattern of investment. For this purpose, tariffs are generally preferable to quantitative restrictions—quotas, prohibitions, exchange controls, etc.—for reasons already indicated. Quantitative restrictions prevent competition with domestic producers regardless of price, raise prices to users and limit demand, and require an elaborate administrative mechanism and detailed economic analysis to be effective. Quotas also involve a loss of revenue to the Government, as compared with the use of tariffs, unless the profits of importers can be recovered through taxes.

The cases where quantitative measures may nevertheless be needed derive from the principles given in the previous section. In cases of extreme shortage of foreign exchange, tariffs (or devaluation) may be too uncertain in their results and quotas or exchange restrictions may be adopted as emergency measures.

The effect of quantitative restrictions on investment in domestic substitutes for imports or in sectors using imported commodities is generally less certain than that of tariffs. Allocations are subject to variation according to the amount of exchange available, and the profitability of domestic production is harder to determine than in the case of a tariff.

As instruments for inducing investment in new types of production, subsidies may be preferable to either quantitative restrictions or tariffs because the price is not raised above the level of world prices. Total demand is therefore greater and using sectors are not penalized in export markets. The cost of this technique in Government expenditure must be weighed against its benefits, however.

Protection from foreign competitors is only one factor in the expansion of domestic production. Also required are entrepreneurs, capital, skilled labour, raw materials, etc. When some of these are lacking, the restriction only serves to reduce imports and raise prices to consumers. Trade restrictions are therefore a rather uncertain method of directing investment unless combined with other measures affecting factor supply, and they frequently have undesirable secondary effects.

(ii) *Government investment versus incentives to private investment*. Although the arguments concerning trade restrictions are based mainly on economic considerations, the choice between Government investment and incentives to private investors involves social and political factors to a large extent. In countries that do not have strong ideological preferences for either private or Government enterprise, the usual approach is to rely on private investment except in cases where it cannot be expected to work in the public interest (e.g., monopoly) or in which its performance has been demonstrably deficient. Since the reaction of investors to various incentives (tax reduction, guaranteed markets, low interest rates, etc.) is subject to considerable uncertainty, such incentives are more likely to be adequate when a general objective is to be achieved—e.g., import substitution, increase of industrial employment—than when increases in output in specific sectors are required. Because of this uncertainty, the extent to which reliance on private investment is desirable can be determined only by an actual trial of specific measures.

Another alternative for securing investment in given sectors when tax incentives are thought to be inadequate or too costly to the treasury is the intervention of a Government agency as entrepreneur but not as a long-term producer. This may be done through development corporations, which sell their investments to private enterprises as they become profitable, or through mixed corporations, in which the role of the Government declines as the enterprise becomes established.

The assumption underlying all these measures is that it is bad for the Government to continue permanently as a producer in most fields. There is a widespread view (shared by the present writer) that the lack of incentives to efficiency in Government operations makes private operation preferable even where conditions are not favourable to the initial undertaking of the investment by private enterprise. In the absence of more objective evaluations of the experience with Government and private enterprise in various countries, it is impossible to support this conclusion empirically, and it is by no means universally held among democratic Governments. In countries such as India, for example, an attempt is made to ascertain the relative merits of public and private investment in specific fields rather than starting from this premise. Even in these cases, however, the sectors that are chosen for Government investment are limited in number and characterized by specific structural features (economies of large scale production, importance of the product, tendency to monopoly, etc.).

The possibility of attracting foreign investment adds a further element to the problem. To the argument against Government investment must be added the loss of additional investment resources, while the argument against private foreign investment must include the removal of profits from the economy and the future burden on the balance of payments. A purely economic evaluation would probably weigh the value of the additional investment resources and managerial tal-

ents more heavily than the cost of obtaining them (particularly where there are unemployed labour and natural resources because of lack of these factors), but the decision is infrequently made on purely economic grounds.

Quantitative analysis and choice of instruments: The preceding discussion has been entirely in qualitative terms, which at best leads to the establishment of certain cases to which particular policies apply. The identification of an actual situation with the relevant case often depends on the results of quantitative analysis. Such factors as the extent of the excess demand for imports, the future amount of unemployed labour, the magnitude of the shift in resources needed in particular sectors, and the importance to the rest of the economy of a given investment, can only be determined from such an analysis. The initial study of development possibilities should be designed to permit a choice of policy instruments in different fields. Once this has been done, the long-term programme can be formulated in more specific terms which take account of the instruments chosen.

The importance of a quantitative analysis for the choice of policy instruments will be determined in part by the presence or absence of the following factors:

(i) Economies of scale in production;

(ii) The possibility of imports and exports;

(iii) The use of the product in other sectors of production;

(iv) The predictability of demand.

In the production of consumer goods, the main objective of the development programme is likely to be a certain degree of substitution of domestic production for imports, but the choice of sector can be left to market forces. Quantitative analysis may be needed to determine the amount of employment and exchange saving which should be aimed at in the consumer goods industries, but not to determine the choice of sector.[1]

At the other extreme, the amount and distribution of investment in overhead facilities must be determined entirely from a quantitative analysis of future production because the alternative of imports is not available and output is needed to permit investment and production in other sectors. In some cases the choice between public and private investment will also depend on the amount of output required.

Choices among policy measures in the intermediate goods sectors are more affected by the outcome of the quantitative analysis than are those in consumer goods because demands derive from the planned outputs of the using sectors. Economies of scale are also more prevalent, and there is thus more interdependence among investment plans in earlier and later stages. While imports provide alternative sources of supply for many intermediate goods, some investments will not be undertaken unless there is a domestic supply of materials available. To ensure the carrying out of several interconnected projects, Government intervention in some form is likely to be necessary because the risk to private investors would be too great. Investments centring on steel production—ore, transport, power, iron and steel, fabricating—provide a good example. Once the initial investments have been made, however, most of them will prove suitable for private ownership and operation.

The advantage to the economy—in terms of the social productivity of the total investment—of inter-related projects of this type cannot be accurately determined from a partial analysis of each

1. This statement is not true where economies of scale are important as in the case of automobile production, because then the profitability of investment depends on an estimate of the quantity that would be demanded at the expected level of income.

investment taken separately because the profitability of one may understate its contribution to the total. This dynamic type of external economy (as opposed to the technological external economies of static analysis) can only be taken account of adequately in the framework of an over-all analysis.

Types of development programme: A development programme is an analysis which provides a basis for designing and carrying out development policy. There is, however, no sharp distinction between programming and policy making, since each influences the other. The main function of a programme is to make different policies consistent with each other. Ideally, it should go further and help to select the best policies and the best means of carrying them out. The decision to make a development programme does not constitute an endorsement of increased Government intervention, or of any other particular set of policy instruments, therefore.

The nature of the analysis contained in a development programme is determined in part by the information available and in part by the instruments which are being considered. For simplicity, three general types can be distinguished, which I will call aggregate programmes, sector programmes, and over-all programmes.

Aggregate programmes consist mainly of national accounts analyses and projections of other magnitudes such as industrial production, labour force, average productivity, etc. These projections are often combined with a more detailed analysis of certain aspects of the economy, such as the balance of payments, the sources of Government revenue, etc.

Programmes of this kind were used by most Western European countries during their period of post-war recovery as a guide to the use of general policy instruments affecting investment, employment, and the balance of payments. The technique of making such programmes has reached a high degree of perfection in the work of the Netherlands Planning Bureau. In the Western Hemisphere, Puerto Rico has prepared a long-term programme of this kind each year since the war to guide its development policy.

Aggregate programmes provide a fairly adequate basis for the use of general policy instruments, but they do not furnish a check on the consistency of the results in specific sectors nor on the balance of payments. They are more likely to be adequate when the composition of production and consumption does not change too much as income increases, and when the market mechanism works well in directing investment and production decisions. From this point of view, the reconstruction of the European economies was easier to analyse than the pattern of growth of the under-developed countries of Asia and Latin America.

Sector programmes are analyses of the demands and investment prospects in individual branches of production. Their main function is to determine the relative priority of investments within the sector. Investment programmes for the whole economy (or for all resources controlled by the Government) are sometimes constructed by merely adding up the high priority projects in each sector.

The sector approach is generally recognized to be inadequate as a basis for development policy because it does not provide a test of the consistency of the decisions made in each sector, nor a way of comparing high priority projects in one sector with those in another. It has nevertheless been the principal basis for development policy in Latin America and in most under-developed countries until quite recently. The defects in the sector approach are less serious in primary-producing economies than in those which have reached a high degree of industrialization and hence have a greater amount of inter-dependence among the various sectors.

Over-all programmes combine the elements of aggregate programmes and sector programmes in varying degrees. The analysis may start from over-all projections or from sector analyses, but in the final result they must be reconciled. It is only by some check of this kind that the consistency of the simpler models used in the two partial approaches can be tested.

Over-all programmes combining aggregate and sector analyses have been prepared in several countries of Europe (e.g., Norway, Netherlands, Italy) and South-East Asia (e.g., India, Pakistan, Philippines). In Europe, the main purpose of the sector analysis is to check the consistency of the over-all analysis, since Government intervention on a sector basis is limited, but in South-East Asia the programmes are intended to co-ordinate specific investment policies affecting a number of sectors. In Latin America, the ECLA studies of Colombia and Argentina have a similar purpose although they are more illustrative in nature.

The need for over-all development programmes is most acute when large structural changes are required to establish or restore a process of balanced growth. Large balance of payments deficits, unemployment, bottlenecks in over-all facilities, and lack of growth may each be evidence of such conditions. These conditions may of course be merely symptoms of an excess or deficiency of total demand, and the diagnosis of structural disequilibrium must try to identify the problems which would exist if inflationary (or, less often, deflationary) forces were offset. The design of policy in such circumstances is likely to call for an over-all analysis, however, whether the policy measures selected are general or specific in nature.

Development policy should include measures to increase the volume of specific resources available, especially the level of saving, as well as their allocation among alternative uses. The first type of policy relies more on general than on specific instruments and thus depends less on the establishment of a programme, and to a large extent the two aspects of policy are separable.

2.3 SECTOR EVALUATION USING ACCOUNTING PRICES *

Accounting prices are a convenient tool for evaluating investment projects in different sectors of the economy. The accounting price of an input, such as capital, labour, or foreign exchange, represents its "opportunity cost" or the loss to the economy that would result from a reduction in its supply by one unit. A factor that is expected to be in short supply should have an accounting price higher than its market price, while one that is surplus should have a valuation that is lower than its market price.

In order to formulate consistent sector plans, analysts in different sectors should make the same assumptions about the accounting prices (scarcity values) of the principal industrial inputs. These normally include capital, foreign exchange, different qualities of labour, and a few commodities. These initial estimates will have to be derived from the over-all analysis and, like other planning data, revised at a later stage.

The most important accounting price for industrial planning is probably the valuation given to foreign exchange, since almost any industrial project to reduce imports will appear profitable if this value is set high enough. In an optimum development plan, the accounting price of foreign exchange would be equal both to the incremental cost of earning foreign exchange

---

* From United Nations, ECAFE, *Formulating Industrial Development Programmes, Development Programming Techniques Series No. 2,* Bangkok, 1961, pp. 17-19, 20-23.

through exports and to the incremental cost of saving foreign exchange through import substitution. The former may be easier to estimate in many cases because there are relatively few potential exports, at least in the near future. In Pakistan, for example, an initial estimate of the value of foreign exchange in the first five-year plan was based mainly on an analysis of the supply and demand conditions for jute and jute products, which are the largest element in Pakistan exports.

An initial estimate of the accounting price of capital can be based on the interest rates paid by private investors, with allowance made for differences in risk among different types of loan. Where there are promising development possibilities, subsequent calculation may show that this rate understates the value of capital to the economy, since an integrated development programme may well raise the return on capital above its present levels.

A tentative estimate of the accounting prices of different types of skilled labour can be based on the cost of moving workers from villages to industrial areas, providing them with housing and other facilities, and training them. This procedure assumes that there is no surplus of skilled labour but ample supplies of agricultural and unskilled labour.

Although all of these estimates should be revised to reflect the supply and demand conditions revealed in the plan itself, initial estimates of some sort are very useful to ensure a consistent basis of evaluation for different sectors....

Once the range of possible sectors for investment has been narrowed down by using general economic and technical considerations, it is desirable to make a more precise evaluation of representative types of production in each sector. The data required for this evaluation are the inputs of labour, capital goods, and principal materials, expressed in value terms. The analysis of individual commodities and projects, which requires more detailed information on inputs in physical terms, is deferred in this procedure until a set of sector projections has been worked out.

The main choice to be made for most of the industrial sectors is whether a given group of commodities is to be imported or produced domestically, but the further possibility of exports must be considered for some industrial commodities. The choice among foreign exchange earning and saving sectors should be based primarily on the total resources required per unit of foreign exchange earned or saved.

The comparison of value of output to cost of input may be stated in any one of the following forms:

(i) Social return on total resources used throughout the economy:

$$\frac{\text{Total value of output}}{\begin{array}{c}\text{Cost of total labour, capital,}\\\text{and natural resources}\end{array}}$$

(ii) Social return to resources used in a given sector:

$$\frac{\begin{array}{c}\text{Value of output minus cost of}\\\text{purchased materials and}\\\text{depreciation}\end{array}}{\begin{array}{c}\text{Cost of direct labour}\\\text{and capital}\end{array}}$$

(iii) Social return to capital used in the sector:

$$\frac{\begin{array}{c}\text{Value of output minus cost of materials,}\\\text{depreciation and labour}\end{array}}{\text{Investment}}$$

For import substitutes and exports, output should be valued at the foreign price multiplied by the accounting price of foreign exchange.

Of these alternative measures, the second and third make use of accounting prices to add up the cost of inputs; the first requires an estimate of the total capital and labour used throughout the economy, and uses only the accounting prices of labour and natural resources. Since it is easier to calculate accounting prices for inputs than to try to trace the total capital, labour and natural resources required, one of the last two formulations is recommended. The remainder of the discussion is based on the use of the third formula, the return on capital.[1]

In the preliminary evaluation of sectors, it is sufficient to calculate the social return on capital used in each sector on the basis of the estimated accounting prices of labour, foreign exchange, and perhaps a very few commodities such as power and transportation that are undervalued at market prices. For other inputs, market prices can be used, with allowance for taxes and other differences between production cost and market prices. The calculation of the social return on capital can then be based on the rate of private profit in the sector adjusted for the differences between accounting prices and market costs of the indicated inputs. In symbols this calculation may be given as:

$$\frac{\text{Social return}}{\text{on Capital}} = \frac{(XP_x - LP_l - MP_m) + (X\Delta P_x - L\Delta P_l - M\Delta P_m)}{I}$$

1. The only difference between formula (ii) and (iii) is that labour cost is subtracted from the value of output in (iii) to give the return to investment alone. A number of examples of calculations using these two formulae are given in the United Nations, *Manual of Economic Development Projects* (Sales No.:58.II.G.5), 1958, Part II.

Where X is output, L is labour, M is purchased materials plus maintenance and depreciation and P_x, P_l, and P_m are their market prices. The terms ΔP_x, ΔP_l, and ΔP_m are the differences between acounting and market prices. The first expression in parentheses is equal to private profit and the second expression is the sum of the corrections made to private profit....

This first evaluation of production costs and social profits in different sectors serves two purposes. First, it forms the basis for setting up a sector programme.... Second, it provides a better estimate of the accounting prices, which will be used in the evaluation of individual projects. For the initial programme, sectors are selected in which the return to capital is highest, making some allowance for the diversity of projects within each sector. The acounting price of foreign exchange can then be calculated as the cost of earning or saving foreign exchange in the marginal sector, namely, the sector in which there is the lowest return to capital.

Planning authorities that do not explicitly estimate accounting prices can follow this general approach in an approximate way by giving different weights to balance of payments effects, employment effects, etc. It can readily be shown that the proper weights to be used in this case can be determined from the accounting prices, and that in principle the two approaches are equivalent.[2] For example, if the accounting price of foreign exchange is 50 per cent higher than its market value, the net effect of a project on the balance of payments should be given a weight of .5 in addition to the effect on the national income. This is equivalent to valuing all foreign exchange costs and earnings at a price of 1.5.

The weight for labour use is determined in the same way.

The great advantage of the use of the single test of social profitability based on acounting prices instead of a series of criteria for project evaluation is that accounting prices reduce the difficulty of weighting the separate criteria. Labour and foreign exchange are assigned their opportunity costs rather than some arbitrary value, and these estimates are revised in the course of establishing the programme. The same procedure can be applied to the evaluation of projects in all sectors of the economy and to the choice of techniques for producing a given output.

Not all the factors affecting the choice of projects can be included in the calculation of the social return on investment. Although some indirect benefits—such as labour training,—can be given a social value others cannot. For example, allowance should be made for the expected increase in labour productivity over time and for any benefits to other industries that may result from domestic production of a given commodity. Regional diversification may also have to be introduced as a modification to the estimate of social value.

2.4 PROJECT EVALUATION *

Project analysis is the third and most specialized of the three levels into which the planning process has been divided. Its relation to sector analysis corresponds to the relation between sector and aggregate analysis. In both cases, one proceeds from the more general to the more specific, and the analysis becomes narrower in scope and more specialized in content. The majority of decisions taken by governments to implement development programmes apply to individual commodities and projects,

2. See H. B. Chenery, "Comparative Advantage and Development Policy," *American Economic Review*, March, 1961 and United Nations, *Manual on Economic Development Projects, loc. cit.*, p. 206.

* From United Nations, ECAFE, *Formulating Industrial Development Programmes, Development Programming Techniques Series No. 2,* Bangkok, 1961, pp. 31, 38-40, 57-9.

and an over-all development plan is of only limited value unless it can be translated into these more specific terms.

The relationships between sector and project analysis are schematically indicated in the following chart . . .

trial sectors, but it requires a more extensive study of individual elements. Whereas sector analysis is applied only to the typical cost and demand conditions in the industry, project analysis takes into account a variety of supply and demand factors that are

SUGGESTED PROCEDURE FOR INDUSTRIAL PROGRAMMING

SECTOR ANALYSIS	PROJECT ANALYSIS
First phase: *The Initial Sector Programme*	*Second phase:* *Initial Project Evaluation*
1. Estimation of sector demand 2. Preliminary estimate of output 3. Initial allocation of capital and foreign exchange 4. Initial selection of sectors 5. Calculation of initial accounting prices 6. Initial sector programme	1. Screening of candidates for investment 2. Selection of best projects for each sector 3. Adjustment for technical interrelations 4. Comparison among sectors
Third phase: *Revised Sector Programme*	*Fourth phase:* *Revised Project Evaluation*
1. Revision of production and import proportions 2. Revised sector projections 3. Revised accounting prices	

Once the likely sectors for expansion of domestic production have been identified, alternative ways of increasing domestic production must be considered. The main choices are: (*i*) more efficient use of existing plant, (*ii*) expansion of existing plants and (*iii*) construction of new plants. In most cases, these choices will require the design of several alternative projects, so that all of the implications of a given decision can be studied.

In designing a project to produce a given commodity or set of commodities, a further range of choices must be considered. What range of commodities is to be produced? What technique of production is to be used? Should the plant be built to satisfy only the present level of demand, or should it have a larger scale in order to allow for increased demand in the future? These choices are to a large extent interdependent. . . .

Project evaluation utilizes principles similar to those . . . for the evaluation of indus-

peculiar to the commodities and production technique under consideration.

The choices among industrial projects can be divided into two types: (*i*) choice among projects in the same industrial sector, and (*ii*) comparison involving different sectors. Although the same general principles apply to both, it is convenient to concentrate on the choices within a single sector of industry as a first step. Revisions in the allocation of investment among sectors can then be made on the basis of the marginal or borderline projects in each sector. It is not assumed that projects in the same sector produce identical outputs, however, because the decision as to the range of products to be manufactured is part of the general problem of investment choice.

As in the choice among sectors, the basic criterion that is recommended for comparing projects is the social return on the capital invested in each alternative use. In the simplest case, in which a single homogenous commodity is produced by each alternative with no economies of scale, no differences in quality, and no differences in regional effects, the calculation of the social return on each project is a simple matter. The starting point is an enumeration of the inputs of materials, labour, and capital required by each plant. Labour, imported materials, and exports or import substitutes are valued at accounting prices. The remaining inputs are valued at market prices except for a few important elements, such as electric power and transport, for which the market price may seriously understate the amount of resources used in the production. In these cases accounting prices should be calculated also....[1]

Since actual projects depart to some extent from these assumptions, an allowance for these differences must be incorporated into the evaluation procedure. The main factors, most of which are taken up in more detail in succeeding sections, are as follows:

(*i*) *Variation in output over time.* This factor is particularly important in projects with a long interval between the initiation of construction and the attainment of full scale operation, as in hydroelectric power projects. To make projects comparable when the time pattern of outputs or inputs varies, a discounting of future costs and values is necessary. The result can be expressed either as the sum of all the discounted values (the present value) or as the value of the equivalent constant output.[2]

(*ii*) *Variation in the range of commodities produced.* Different production techniques usually produce different qualities of product and have varying degrees of flexibility in their adaptability to a change

in product. These considerations often offset the advantages of automatic machinery and large-scale production in less developed countries, because the smaller scale techniques are generally more flexible....

(*iii*) *Scale and location effects.* The existence of economies of large-scale production requires an estimate to be made of the increase in demand over time in order to select the optimum scale of production.... Offsetting these potential economies are the disadvantages of overconcentration of industry in a few centres, the increase in transport costs, and the complexity of operation of large-scale plants. Only some of these effects can be evaluated by quantitative methods; the others require a balancing of unquantifiable elements, such as the desirability of decentralization of industry.

(*iv*) *Non-market effects of production* may differ for different plants in the same industry, and even more for plants in different industries. The use of a more advanced technique provides training to labour and management that is of value for long-term industrial development although it is not reflected in the accounting price calculation. Other social benefits and costs, such as the reduction of undesirable waste, must also be considered.

The effects of these complicating factors may be minimized by first comparing projects within a given sector and only later reexamining the choice of sectors. Focussing on the choice of ways of producing a given set of commodities makes it possible to introduce qualitative elements which are harder to apply when different sectors are being compared....

The second phase of the planning procedure, leading to the initial selection of industrial projects, may be summarized as follows:

(1) *Selection of promising commodities for domestic production...*

(2) *Selection of the best projects in each sector.* Once the productivity of investment

---

1. An alternative procedure is to calculate the additional investment required in supplying these inputs and add it to the direct investment.

2. The details of these calculations are explained in the United Nations, *Manual on Economic Development Projects,* pp. 198-202.

in each project has been estimated by means of accounting prices, the projects should be compared to others in the same sector of industry, many of which produce similiar products or close substitutes. For homogeneous commodities having uniform supply and demand conditions for all plants, such as cotton textiles, there will be a single best type of design for new plants. In this case, the programme for cotton textiles can be stated as expansion of plants A, B, C ...plus construction of a certain number of new plants of a given type. However, in an industry in which supply conditions vary from plant to plant, such as food processing, cement, steel, and most of the earlier stages of manufacturing, it is usually necessary to specify individual locations and plant sizes for new plants instead of just the total capacity. Furthermore, when transport costs are a significant fraction of the delivery cost of the commodity, the location of demand must be allowed for in deciding on the sector programme.

The initial formulation of a sector programme can be done by choosing the projects with the highest productivity of investment (or lowest social cost) to satisfy the calculated demands for each commodity in the sector. In sectors where economies of scale are important, plants of different size should be considered as alternatives, ... and the calculation should include the variation in demand over time rather than just the demand within the plan period.

In case of substitutes for imports, the demand estimate provides an upper limit to the total increase in output, but within this limit decisions should be based on a comparison between the productivity of investment and the accounting price of capital. For this purpose, the output is valued at the cost of imports, using the accounting price for foreign exchange. If the productivity of investment computed on this basis is higher than the accounting

cost of capital, the project should be included in the programme....[3]

When the sector programme has been formulated on a trial basis, the productivity of investment in the least profitable (marginal) projects should be determined for use in the subsequent revision of the programme and the calculation of accounting prices. The best projects that may have been excluded because of lack of demand or because their profitability was less than the cost of capital should be noted in case a later revision of the sector analysis shows a greater demand or a change in the accounting price of foreign exchange or capital. These sub-marginal projects will then be reconsidered in the light of the changed demand and price data.

(3) *Adjustment for technical interrelations.* Before making a general revision in the sector analysis, the production levels in plants that are closely interrelated should be adjusted to make them consistent.... This type of adjustment allows for non-market as well as market interrelations and is limited to sectors such as chemicals and metal-working in which the profitability of a given plant may depend to a large extent on the existence of others as suppliers or users.

(4) *Comparison of productivity among sectors.* A comparison of the productivity of investment in differert sectors is needed as a basis for revising the sector estimates. Since the initial screening was carried out on a rather intuitive basis, the more detailed calculations are likely to reveal investment opportunities that had been overlooked and to show sub-normal returns in some of the candidate sectors.

The comparison among sectors should be based on an estimation of the productivity of investment in the least profitable

3. Alternatively, the cost of saving foreign exchange can be computed and compared to the accounting price of foreign exchange. The results will be the same by both methods.

projects included in each sector programme and the most profitable projects excluded. These give a rough estimate of the marginal productivity of investment in each sector. In making this calculation, allowance should be made for changes in the price of the output wherever this is possible, since in some cases a substantial increase in production will imply a lowering in price. Initial market prices may therefore exaggerate the value of the commodity to the economy. For all importable commodities, the cost of imports at the accounting value of foreign exchange provides an upper limit to the price, and in practice this is the only element in prices that can be determined with any accuracy. Fortunately, the great majority of industrial commodities are importable and the limit to their value can be assessed in this way.

2.5 Capital Intensity in Industry *

The determination of the appropriate capital intensity—that is, the right combination of factors of production—in the industry of an under-developed country is one of the key issues involved in formulating a programme of industrialization. It arises in respect of both the "macro-economic" aspect of planning for the industrial sector as a whole and the "micro-economic" aspect of designing a given plant or project. At the general planning level, it may involve a choice between over-all objectives—such as maximizing employment or maximizing income—in assigning priorities as between individual industries. It may involve decisions on the relative importance to be given to long-run and short-run considerations in setting up industrialization targets, the emphasis to be given to "heavy" or "light" industry, and the tempo of industrialization itself. At the level of actual design of plants, it

* From United Nations, Bureau of Economic Affairs, "Capital Intensity in Industry in Under-developed Countries," *Industrialization and Productivity,* Bulletin 1, April 1958, pp. 5-6, 19-21, 23.

may involve a choice—if a choice is technologically possible—between alternative techniques allowing different combinations of machinery and manpower. At both levels, decisions may be influenced by non-economic as well as economic considerations.

A number of experts have been sent out under the United Nations technical assistance programmes to advise governments of under-developed countries on various industrial problems ranging from over-all industrial planning and programming to organizational and production problems of individual plants. In the course of their work, the experts have faced either directly or implicitly some of the above-mentioned problems. It is the purpose [here] to analyse the relevant material in the reports of some of these experts and to appraise both their approach to the problem and their recommendations on the subject. . . .

Before evaluating the recommendations of the experts, it may be useful to discuss briefly the meaning they attach to the concept of capital intensity.

In a number of reports, this concept is used in an ambiguous way. Most experts mean by it the amount of capital per worker—presumably, fixed capital per man employed. Others refer to capital-output ratios, while still others refer to input of labour (or equipment) per unit of output, Some experts use alternatively several of these relationships.

Many experts refer not only to capital-intensive or labour-intensive *processes* but also to capital-intensive or labour-intensive *industries*. They apparently consider that there is an implicit correlation between capital per worker (or capital per unit of output) and type of industrial output. Thus, industries producing "light" consumer goods are generally identified with labour-intensive production and those producing "heavy" producer or capital goods with capital-intensive production.

In addition, capital intensity is also related by some experts to the scale of operation, "labour-intensive" production being largely identified with small-scale or medium-scale industries and "capital-intensive" production with large-scale industries.

It must be pointed out, as regards the concept of capital intensity, that various statistical measurements of it have been suggested in the economic literature, none of which is generally accepted.... It may be observed here that not only is the economic significance of the indicators still uncertain and their mutual relationship imprecise, but that actual statistical data are relatively scarce. Further research on the conceptual and statistical aspects of the problem is desirable if the usefulness of these tools in economic analysis and in economic planning is to be enhanced....

Both the recommendations of the experts for over-all policy and those for individual projects reflect a wide variety of views on the appropriate capital intensity of investment in industry. Some arguments seem to proceed from somewhat dogmatic attitudes. Some positions are, in fact, clearly conflicting, when for instance an appraisal of conditions in the same country leads to quite opposite conclusions.

While all policy recommendations are based on economic considerations—discussed below—those for a general policy along labour-intensive lines lay considerable emphasis on the social aspects of the problem. The proposals for a capital-intensive policy pay less attention to these aspects. The recommendations of engineers proceed essentially from technological considerations. They evidence in many cases a ready and sometimes indiscriminate resort to mechanization. The potential labour-displacing effect of the latter is seldom paid attention to, and techniques are rarely chosen with the specific aim of creating employment. Among the proposals by engineers, there are few, if any, which entail alternative factor combinations.

In many cases, no over-all policy directives have been formulated by the governments. In other cases, government policies exist, expressing the desirability of preventing the labour-displacing effect of mechanization, but these do not appear to have percolated to the technical level. Even when government policies have been formalized in an economic plan, they may not be explicit enough to guide technicians in the field. There is thus often little, if any, link between the "macro-economic" policy directives and the action of technicians in charge of carrying out individual projects. This aspect is important—particularly in planning—since general policy decisions can be meaningful and effective only if correctly implemented on the project level.

As pointed out by one expert, the adoption of objectives or planning targets, which precedes and determines the choice of means to achieve them, is to a large extent a political problem. National authorities have to decide whether to strive for self-sufficiency or rely on international interchange; what weights to attach to the social, economic, technical or even strategic considerations involved in setting up certain types of industry; the extent to which the government finds it desirable or feasible to intervene in the process of development; in particular, what controls it is prepared to impose; whether it should emphasize long-run or, alternatively, short-run measures of development and a faster or slower tempo of industrialization. While the present conditions and foreseeable developments in resources, prices of raw materials and factors of production, and in domestic and foreign markets affecting the country concerned may limit the scope of possible alternative policies, a measure of choice between basic objectives, which may be expressed by different systems of priorities in allocating resources, exists in most cases.

Such a choice depends not only upon an evaluation of economic and technical conditions and potentialities, but on the political and social order that a country may wish to achieve in the course of its development.

It will be noted that both labour-intensive and capital-intensive industrialization policies advocated by experts have certain common economic objectives. Both aim at raising the level of output and income through developing the industrial sector. Both recognize the importance of solving the problem of chronic under-employment which exists in most under-developed countries. Both agree that industrialization requires an increase in labour productivity. A major divergence between the two views arises through the fact that proponents of labour-intensive industrialization would achieve these results through obtaining the largest amount of employment per unit of invested capital, while the others would, from the outset, concentrate the investment resources of the country in industrial branches yielding a high productivity regardless of the labour-absorptive capacity of such investment. Proponents of the latter view readily recognize that labour-intensive development would, in the short run, bring about larger employment for the same invested capital, but point out that little, if any, cumulative increases in income and employment would be attained in the long run. In their view, absorption of the unemployed is a second priority goal, to be achieved only after an adequate rate of investment in basic productive capacity has been reached; from then on, both income and employment will rise more, and faster. It is the higher productivity and correspondingly higher surpluses available for capital formation generated by capital-intensive investment that proponents of such indutrialization emphasize.

There is no doubt that most experts advocating labour-intensive industrializa-

tion policies lay emphasis on short-run rather than long-run aspects. They stress primarily the employment-creating effect and, while recommending that labour productivity should also be increased, do not make clear how an adequate rate of capital formation—which should solve the problem of full utilization of the country's manpower in the long run—is to be achieved.

In the absence of external sources of financing, the accumulation of an adequate amount of such surpluses for capital formation is unquestionably a basic requisite to a rapid and cumulative process of growth of production and employment over the years. Some supporters of labour-intensive policies recognize that surpluses can be generated in adequate amounts only through raising productivity of labour sufficiently in excess of its real wages; that capital-intensive techniques do yield higher productivity and, in the long run, result in a faster tempo of industrialization. They point out, however, that labour productivity is affected not only by the quantity of physical capital per worker, but also by the nature and quality of the equipment and its appropriateness to conditions in under-developed countries, and by such factors as a better rate of utilization of plant capacity, proficiency of management and worker efficiency in terms of skill and effort. They are confident that an appreciable rise in productivity may be achieved in labour-intensive industries, which, together with the increase in employment, will, slowly but gradually, enlarge incomes and investment resources. This will make possible, later on, the establishment of more capital-intensive industries, if necessary.

Under either policy, it is thus implicitly assumed, first, that a surplus will be generated and, second, that savings out of this surplus will somehow be consistently channelled into further investment. With regard to the first point, it will be noted that the magnitude of the surplus depends on the number of workers employed, the productivity of labour, which is in turn a function of capital per worker employed, and the level of real wages. All these magnitudes are interrelated. All other things being equal, a rise in wages would clearly reduce the surplus. Pressure on wages will increase with the rise in productivity and will be likely to be stronger under conditions of industrialization along capital-intensive lines. Controls to restrict consumption and encourage capital formation may have to be used, whatever the form of the industrialization process; to be effective, such controls might need to be particularly severe under a capital-intensive type of industrial development, the more so as the requirements of an accelerated rate of capital formation are bound to give rise to heavier inflationary pressures. This is often one of the reasons for which, in spite of the slower tempo of industrialization of the labour-intensive type, preference is given to the latter by some experts.

As regards the second point, many experts consider that the fact that redundant labour and scarce capital entail low wages and high interest rates constitutes not only a basic argument in favour of government policies of labour-intensive industrialization, but also a strong incentive for private investment in industries allowing the use of labour-intensive techniques. It must be borne in mind, however, that while a price relationship favouring labour- intensive industrialization may often exist, the market prices of the factors may not always reflect their endowment, and the relationship may be adversely affected. ...

The problem of alternative techniques for a given industrial process remains to be considered. In many cases, the choice may in fact be non-existent or at least severely limited. As is well known, certain industrial operations can be carried out only by standard processes of relatively high capital intensity, so that more labour-intensive techniques are inapplicable. This accounts for the fact that in many industrial sectors in under-developed countries highly capitalized techniques are used in spite of the existence of abundant manpower available at low wages. Still, in such industries, certain ancillary operations—for instance, materials handling, packaging and the like —may lend themselves to alternative techniques. Aside from industries where basic processes are technologically inflexible, there are a large number of industries where alternative factor combinations are applicable in major processing operations.

To reveal such technological alternatives, and make possible the determination of a proper "factor-mix" in specific industrial operations, a great deal of research is required in a new and relatively little explored field. The macro-economic tools of the economist who measures capital intensity in terms of statistical aggregates are inadequate for that purpose. ...

The information which would be gradually evolved through such research would facilitate the task of planning authorities and help in the preparation of programmes of industrial development; in particular, it might be combined with and enhance the value of the planning techniques based on linear programming. ... It would help to establish a more direct link between general policy directives at the planning level, and their implementation in individual projects; thus, the target of maximizing employment of labour to the extent consistent with achievement of an acceptable level of productivity could, in many cases, be translated in practical terms on the actual project level. As mentioned earlier, such a link is at the present time rarely in evidence. Conversely, such information should make it possible for planning authorities better to appraise proposals by engineers for the establishment of new industries or the expansion of existing ones, from the point of view of the general objectives of the plan.

2.6 PROGRAMMING APPROACH TO RESOURCE ALLOCATION *

Although it may in many instances be necessary to rely primarily on . . . marginal criteria for lack of data on the rest of the economy, it is important to have some way of testing larger changes and of evaluating the errors that are introduced by the marginal procedure. Furthermore, without a more comprehensive analysis it is impossible to reconcile fully the conflicting policy implications of comparative advantage and growth theory.

The difficulties of partial analysis increase with the number of modifications that have to be applied to market prices in order to arrive at social value. Both the factor-intensity ratios and the partial productivity measures assume that there is one principal restriction on the system, the scarcity of capital. They do not allow for the fact that in allocating capital according to any one of these rules some other restriction on the system, such as the supply of foreign exchange, of skilled labor, or of a particular commodity, may be exceeded.

The programming approach to resource allocation begins with the problem of balancing supply and demand for different commodities and factors of production. Until quite recently, practical programming methods have been more concerned with ensuring the consistency of a given allocation of resources with certain targets than with testing the efficiency with which resources are used. Historically speaking, the programming approach is thus the operational counterpart of the theory of balanced growth, from which much of its conceptual framework is derived.

* From Hollis B. Chenery, "Comparative Advantage and Development Policy," *American Economic Review,* Vol. LI, No. 1, March 1961, pp. 31-3, 38-41. Reprinted by permission.

One of the earliest attempts at formulating a comprehensive development program for an underdeveloped area was Mandelbaum's illustrative model for Southeastern Europe. . . . He starts, as many subsequent programs have done, from an estimate of the increase in national income required to absorb a prospective increment in the labor force. The allocation of capital and labor is made initially from demand estimates and by analogy to the structure of more advanced countries. The principle of comparative advantage is only introduced intuitively in modifying the initial projection. The main test of resource allocation is the balance of demand and supply for each sector and factor of production.

The development of mathematical programming methods makes it possible to carry out this type of analysis in a much more precise way. In several countries, consistent development programs have been formulated by using input-output analysis, as in the studies of the Economic Commission for Latin America. It is only with the development of linear programming, however, that it is possible to reconcile the consistency criteria and the productivity criteria in a systematic way.

A link between the test of consistency (feasibility) in resource allocation and the test of productivity (efficiency) is provided by a consideration of the price implications of a given allocation. Assume that a set of production levels has been worked out so as to be consistent with the available supplies of labor, capital and natural resources, given the structure of consumer demand and the country's trading possibilities. These sector product and trade levels constitute a "feasible program." Any such program implies a unique set of commodity and factor prices if the economy is in equilibrium. If production activities are assumed to operate at constant costs, linear programming provides a method of calculating the "shadow prices" corresponding to the equilibrium conditions, in which the price of each commodity is equal to its cost of production. Prices are determined by the solution to the following set of simultaneous equations, one for each production activity included in the program:

$$a_{1j}P_1 + a_{2j}P_2 + \cdots + a_{nj}P_n = 0 \quad (j = 1 \cdots n)$$

where a_{ij} is the input or output of commodity or factor i by activity j, and P_i is the shadow price of commodity or factor i. The input coefficients may be measured at existing prices or in other convenient units. In an open economy, activities of importing and exporting are also included in the system, and the price solution contains the equilibrium price of foreign exchange....

The use of shadow or "accounting" prices in evaluating investment propects has been suggested by Tinbergen, Frisch, and Chenery. Although Tinbergen does not use a linear programming framework, his accounting prices for factors have the same meaning as shadow prices: the opportunity cost implied by a given resource allocation.[1] He suggests computing the costs associated with a project by using accounting prices; any project that shows a positive net return over cost (including capital cost) should be approved. This test is equivalent to the SMP [social marginal productivity] criterion, as shown below.

The general linear programming problem is to maximize the value of a linear objective function subject to linear constraints. In development programs, the principal constraints are that the demands for commodities and factors should not exceed their supplies; the function to be maximized is usually taken as the national income. Alternatively, the objective may be the achievement of a given increase in

output at minimum cost in investment (including foreign investment). Other social objectives, such as a minimum employment level or a specified degree of regional balance, can be included as additional restrictions on the program. The instrument variables can also be constrained to fall within specified limits, as in the models of Frisch....[2]

Although the example given here contained only one technique of production for each commodity, linear programming methods readily encompass alternative techniques. In a trial application of linear programming to Indian planning, Sandee includes three alternative ways of increasing agricultural output—increased use of fertilizer, irrigation, and extension services —which are substitutes over a limited range. The four alternative techniques for producing textiles cited by Galenson and Leibenstein could also be more properly evaluated in a programming model in which the cost variation associated with their different requirements for materials, maintenance, and skilled labor could be included. However, it is only necessary to include alternative techniques in a programming model when the choice between them depends on the outcome of the solution. Probably in most cases the range of shadow prices can be foreseen accurately enough to determine in advance which technique is more efficient for a given country. The initial assumption can always

1. Tinbergen defines accounting prices as those "that would prevail if (i) the investment pattern under discussion were actually carried out, and (ii) equilibrium existed on the markets just mentioned" [i.e., labor, capital, foreign exchange markets].

2. Frisch is one of the strongest advocates of the use of linear programming for development planning, as indicated in the preface to a recent methodological study: "In the beginning of 1959, during my work as a United Nations expert in Cairo, I was confronted with the problem of working out a methodology for *optimal investment programming* in a rapidly expanding underdeveloped country. I have always believed— and my Cairo experiences have confirmed it—that such a method must be formulated in terms which ultimately make the problem amenable to linear programming. Otherwise one is practically certain to be taken by surprise afterwards in unexpected balance of payments difficulties and other troubles."

be verified after the analysis has been completed by using the resulting prices.

Linear programming can be extended to include many of the indirect effects of investment that are suggested by growth theory. The production of trained labor, the effect on savings, or other indirect benefits can be considered as joint outputs whose value can be specified in the objective function. Similarly, indirect costs of production, such as the provision of housing to urban workers, can be included as additional inputs. The shadow prices computed from such an expanded system will therefore reflect nonmarket as well as market interdependence to the extent that it can be specified in quantitative form.

In formal terms, it is also quite easy to extend the programming model in time and to compute future prices for commodities and factors. The measurement of social profitability could then be made against a pattern of changing future prices. Given the degree of uncertainty attached to all future economic magnitudes, however, this is not likely to be a very useful procedure beyond the customary five-year planning period except in the most general terms. It would, however, be desirable to estimate the change in the equilibrium prices of foreign exchange and labor over a longer period of time, since these are the most important variables in choosing among investment projects.

Investment criteria and comparative advantage: The linear programming approach provides a convenient link to the principle of comparative advantage because the optimal pattern of trade is determined simultaneously with the optimum allocation of investment. The model is considerably more general that that of market equilibrium because it allows for different social objectives and takes account of costs and benefits other than those entering the market. The limitations to the programming model are of two sorts: the form of the restrictions that are specified, and the omission of relationships that cannot be expressed in quantitative form.

The introduction of inelastic demands or increasing costs does not create any more theoretical difficulty in a programming model than in the corresponding general equilibrium system, although the computational aspects of such models have not been widely explored. The accounting prices perform the same function as guides to proper allocation, but the test of social profitability must be applied in marginal rather than average terms. In development programs, this modification is particularly important in the case of exports, where the price elasticity of demand is often rather low. As Nurkse points out, marginal comparative advantage for the underdeveloped countries may for this reason be quite different from that inferred from the average costs and prices of primary exports.

The existence of increasing returns creates the same problem for the programming model as it does for equilibrium theory. Marginal-cost pricing is not sufficient to determine whether an investment should be undertaken, and the total cost of alternative solutions must also be considered. Although practical methods of solving programming models containing decreasing costs are now being developed, they do not give allocation criteria that rely only on accounting prices. It is approximately correct to say that beyond a certain output level country A has a comparative advantage in the production of steel, but the precise determination of the break-even point depends on the level of output in other sectors also.

The most serious theoretical qualification to the principle of comparative advantage comes from the type of nonquantitative interdependence among sectors that is assumed by Hirschman. If, as he supposes, one growth sequence is more effective than another because it economizes on decision-making ability or provides a greater incentive to political action, a set of criteria having little or nothing to do with comparative advantage is implied. The empirical significance of these psychological and sociological factors remains to be established, but they lead to a conflict that cannot be resolved in economic terms.

When the practical limitations on information and analysis are recognized, the possibilities of conflict between comparative advantage and growth theory are greatly increased. . . . An aversion to risk-taking may be a valid reason for limiting the extent of specialization in the export of primary products beyond the amount that would be optimum in the light of more accurate information. An inability to measure the extent of economies of scale, labor training, and other sources of external economies also makes possible a continuing disagreement as to their magnitude.

3. DEVELOPMENT PLANNING IN PRACTICE

3.1 ON ASSESSING A DEVELOPMENT PLAN *

In assessing a development plan we have to consider three matters: first, its contribution to policy-making, secondly its size, and thirdly its priorities.

Policy-Making: I put policy-making first because I am convinced that sound economic policies are more important to economic development than mere expenditure of money by the Government. In private enterprise systems the amount the Government has to invest is always less than half of the total capital formation required in the country. It is therefore important to adopt policies which encourage private investment to come forward in the right magnitude in the right places. Resistance to this has been strongest among those who do not know how large are the total sums required if an even moderate rate of development is to be achieved. In my experience, resistance crumbles as soon as the figures are demonstrated.

Resistance has crumbled remarkably in all under-developed countries in the past ten years in relation to investment in manufacturing industry and in mining. Everywhere these countries are now competing

in trying to create a framework which will encourage private investment. They do industrial research, set up propaganda bureaus, offer tax concessions, pass legislation to secure titles to land and to minerals, and spend lavishly on entertaining, persuading and helping business men. That this pays off is amply illustrated by the parts of the world where it is done on a substantial scale.

Attitudes have not been changed so radically in relation to agriculture. There is greater reluctance to grant concessions for agricultural enterprises than for mining or for manufacturing. More important, little progress is being made anywhere in Africa or in Asia (other than in India) in creating an appropriate framework for small farming—in tackling the fragmentation of farms, in providing adequate agricultural credit, in organising adequate agricultural extension services, in building subsidiary roads, dams and irrigation facilities, or in controlling agricultural debt. Agriculture is still the Cinderella of development programmes.

In the field of housing there is even less understanding of the need to create an encouraging framework for private investment, in view of how little money the Government has, in relation to housing needs. Nearly always one finds that the

---

* From W. Arthur Lewis, "On Assessing a Development Plan," *Economic Bulletin of the Economic Society of Ghana,* May-June 1959, pp. 2-16. Reprinted by permission.

planners of housing policy are discussing mainly how many houses the Government is going to build. A little arithmetic shows that the number of houses the Government can afford to build is, even at the most generous estimate, only a small fraction of the houses needed. The major problem is to encourage private building, and in countries where only a few people live in rented accommodation, the main problem is to help people build better houses for themselves. Self-help building schemes are now making their appearance. It is also coming to be understood that the Government must not fix rents at un-economic levels unless it has the money and can afford to build all the houses which private building is thereby discouraged from providing. In effect, the main objective of housing policy, in poor countries, should be to use such money as is available to stimulate building by others, rather than for the Government to build houses itself.

I think that Ghana's experience under the First Development Plan proves my proposition that policy is more important than expenditure. Very large sums of money were spent by the Government, but since the industrial, agricultural, mining, and housing policies were inappropriate, very little increased productive capacity resulted from these large expenditures. There was a remarkable increase in public facilities, such as roads, schools, electric power, water supplies, and so on, but remarkably little increase in the output of commodities. Considering also how much was wasted by overloading the building industry, one can say without hesitation that the country would have made more progress if it had spent less and had had better economic policies. So I deduce that the most important question to ask, when assessing a development plan, is whether the policies are adequate to stimulate private investment in the production of commodities. I do not think that this is fully realised in Ghana,

where some people seem to be hypnotised by the magic of large numbers. However, the Second Development Plan, as drafted, laid great emphasis on creating an appropriate framework, through reasonable policies and institutions.

Size: This brings me to expenditure. What is the right size for a development programme? There is no scientific answer to this question. One must use one's judgment.

The normal way of making a development programme is to begin with an assessment of what the country needs. Every Minister or Department is asked to list projects and expenditures which it would consider to be beneficial. This approach provides no answer to the question how large a development programme should be. The needs of under-developed countries are virtually unlimited. Anybody could make a development plan for Ghana, for instance, which provided for spending £G1,000 million over the next five years, and which was thought reasonable in relation to the country's need for water supplies, better roads, hospitals, schools, factories, agricultural equipment, irrigation works, and so on. Yet, any individual who based his personal expenditure programme upon his needs, without regard to his resources, would soon be written off by his fellow men as irresponsible. In determining size, the basis of a development plan is not needs, but resources.

For most countries, the principal limitation on the size of the programme is now money. There are some fortunate countries where the limitation is not money, but physical resources. This was the case with Ghana under the First Development Plan. The Government tried hard to complete the Plan in five years, and at all times had more than enough money to do so, but was unable to do so. At the beginning the physical limitation was the capacity of the building industry. Construction is normally about two-thirds of capital formation, and so a sudden attempt to increase capital formation is always frustrated by lack of trained construction workers, insufficiency of building firms, and difficulties of supervision. The result, as in Ghana, is that projects cost twice as much as they should, contractors make enormous profits, works are badly designed or badly built, and everything takes much longer to achieve than was expected. This limitation is temporary, since the construction industry can expand and in time does expand to whatever extent is required. Thus, whereas the capacity of the construction industry was a bottleneck in most countries in the early nineteen-fifties, this is no longer the case. Ghana could probably increase its 1958 expenditure on capital formation by 50 per cent without running into any major construction bottlenecks.

A more serious limitation in underdeveloped countries now is political and administrative capacity. To carry out a programme, decisions must be made at the right time, preliminary researches must be made, blueprints ordered at the right time, contracts placed at the right time, and so on. Not enough importance is attached to the absence of preliminary researches, which are a bottleneck to absorptive capacity. You cannot decide suddenly to invest in mines, without first having the geological surveys made, and this takes time. You cannot build hundreds of factories in five years, if each factory is to be properly studied, carefully designed and located, and fitted into appropriate commercial arrangements for its materials, labour, management, and the marketing of its products. The political aspect of administrative competence is also important. If reasonable decisions are to be made, the people who have to make decisions must be appointed on merit, and not merely for political or racial reasons. Contracts must be awarded to people who are capable of carrying them

out, and not merely to political friends. We hear much about corruption in underdeveloped countries, but the harm done by bribery or by theft seldom exceeds hundreds of thousands of pounds a year, and though morally deplorable, is quite small when compared with the harm which is done by appointing people to big jobs which they are not competent to do properly. Most under-developed countries are in this sense incapable of executing large development programmes. The larger the programme, the less preparation is given to each project, and the greater is the number of incompetent people appointed to public service. Programmes fall into arrears, are over-costly, and are badly executed. Ghana is much better off than most other countries in this respect, because it has inherited traditions of public probity which put its administrative performance well beyond that of more than half the members of the United Nations.

In most of the under-developed countries today the main limitation on the size of the programme is lack of money. Leaving aside the possibilities of credit creation, which are not relevant in West Africa, most countries either do not raise enough in taxes, or cannot borrow enough money to carry out the programmes which they could conveniently administer.

. . .

One important element in deciding how large a development programme should be is to look at the effects of the programme on the ordinary budget. Capital expenditure carries with it recurring commitments, so one way of discovering how much capital to spend (assuming that you can raise the capital) is to assess how much recurrent expenditure the country can afford to bear. There is no point in building schools or hospitals, if you cannot find the money to pay teachers or nurses. And there is no sense in borrowing, if you will not be able to meet the debt charges.

It follows that one of the ways of assessing a plan is to look carefully at what that plan says about the future of the recurrent budget. If it says nothing, or very little, one can deduce either that the planners have forgotten that capital expenditure carries recurrent commitments, or else that the recurrent commitments are so large that they prefer to hide the fact that they are biting off more than they can chew.

Priorities: Under this heading I deal with a number of topics which do not normally receive sufficient consideration.

First, basic surveys are usually starved of funds. I refer here to geological surveys, soil surveys, mapping, marine biology, the measurement of river flows, and fundamental agricultural research. Moreover, the officials responsible for these surveys have become so used to not having the money they need, that they no longer even ask for it. The economist planner has to knock at their doors and plead with them to ask for more money. Frequently they reply that they could not get the bodies even if the money were available, because salaries are inadequate.

Next, one should look at basic training. In these days, the favourite sons in West Africa are elementary education and University education. Elementary education is being pushed so rapidly that nobody knows what to do with the half illiterates who are now forsaking the countryside and crowding the towns. At the other end money is being poured out on University education to produce, at £2,000 to £3,000 per pupil per year (because there are not enough students) what the students could get elsewhere at a cost to the Government of only £600 per pupil per year. Meanwhile, the real bottleneck in Africa, which is secondary education, is hopelessly neglected. I am very glad to know that Ghana intends to give a lead in this matter to

the rest of Africa. Everywhere people are concerned about technical training, for nurses, secretaries, foremen, agricultural assistants, medical assistants, and other intermediate grades. The basis for this is secondary education, and one can judge any African plan by the extent to which this is realized. I say African plan, because this is an African problem. In most of Asia, 10 per cent of the children receive secondary education, whereas in most of Africa the figure is less than 1 per cent.

The third element to look for, in a development plan, is the basis on which the demand for the services of public utilities has been estimated. This is usually quite haphazard. Perhaps somebody is bitten with the bug of electricity, and puts in twice as much as is needed; or as in Ghana, in the first Five-Year Plan, the estimator is conservative and puts in only half as much as is needed. Similarly with roads, water supplies, port services, railroads and telephones. This is the point where economists pride themselves that their techniques have something to offer. They make mathematical exercises, estimating the growth of demand. They speak of the need for consistency between public and private intentions, and they even use input-output tables to demonstrate appropriate relationships. Actually, this is the area where precise estimation matters least, because mistakes find themselves out rapidly. If the planner neglects to provide adequate services, a bottleneck develops, people fuss, and the mistake can be corrected quickly. Fortunately too, if the planner provides too much service, he is not in error for long, since rapidly growing populations and productivities soon produce enough extra demand to catch up with over-capacity. The difficulty arises not in matching public supply to the needs of private commerce, but in deciding how much service to provide for domestic consumers. How high a priority should one accord to water supplies in the village, to rural electrification, to providing good road surfaces even where road traffic is small, to hospital and medical services, to broadcast rediffusion, to decent prisons, and to such other consumer facilities? These are matters for political decision. I can only answer for myself that I put these high above the prestige expenditures which clutter up so many programmes.

The next thing to look for in a development plan is the balance between what is being done for the countryside, and what is being done for the towns. It is easy to test a development programme for this by splitting up its proposed expenditures on an area basis, and calculating how much will be spent in the capital, and how much in the rest of the country. There is always a curious disparity between what the Ministers want, and what back-benchers in Parliament want. The back-benchers mostly come from the countryside, and they press the demands for water supplies, roads, hospitals, and the like. The Ministers, however, live in the capital. I have never known a Cabinet which was not persuaded that the most important thing to do with public money was to beautify the capital, leaving only scraps for rural development. Thus the capital becomes an imposing facade which impresses the tourists until they go into the countryside and see how little has been done for the great majority of the people living in the villages. The capital does not stay beautiful for long. The concentration of development there attracts people to flood into it from the countryside, and the slums multiply even faster than the magnificent structures.

The remedy for this lies in the machinery for making the development plan. One can take it as axiomatic that any programme which is made by a planning office in the capital, using data from the central ministries, will be a bad plan from this point of view. A plan should be prepared at the grassroots, by a large number of provincial committees. One cannot escape the fact that it will fall to the centre to determine the distribution of funds between the provinces, but if the provinces are well organised, and have made good plans for themselves, their needs cannot be disregarded as easily as happens when there are no provincial committees.

One should look next at the flow from the countryside to the towns, i.e., at the rate of urbanization. In most underdeveloped countries urbanization is occurring too rapidly. People are coming into the towns faster than the towns can provide jobs, houses, busses, water, electricity, and other amenities. Measures are required at both ends, to diminish the flow from the countryside, and also to improve the facilities in towns.

It is not easy to diminish the flow from the countryside. The impact of primary education is only one reason for this flow, which would occur even if the school curricula were better designed to fit rural children for rural life. Towns have substantial advantages over the countryside in terms of amenities, and will always attract people....

Lastly, I come to the question of prestige expenditures. In every country of the world, rich or poor, politicians believe that the greatness of their country is demonstrated by one or another kind of large useless expenditure. The United States strains to put more and more planets into orbit around the sun. The United Kingdom was unhappy without hydrogen bombs. France has an irrepressible taste for colonial wars. In the more ridiculous of the underdeveloped countries the leaders go in for flashy uniforms, palaces, toy armies, television, innumerable embassies, military parades, and other symbols of splendour. In the more sensible of the under-developed countries the weakness for prestige shows itself not so much in the objects of expenditure which are desirable in themselves, but in doing on a lavish and magnificent scale what could be done much more cheaply, and especially in lavish expenditure on airports, model towns, and imposing public buildings. Since these manifestations are universal and inevitable, there is not much point in grumbling about them. There may even be something to be said for some expenditure of this kind. Most of us derive some satisfaction from wasting our own money on prestige objects and the nation as a whole is the same. Everybody takes some pride in seeing fine structures going up in one's country, and only a few realise that the cost is less money spent on giving the villages water, schools, or sanitation. Those of us who know the cost can only hope that prestige expenditure will be kept to reasonable proportions. I would give high marks to a development programme in which only 10 per cent of the expenditures was in nonsense of this kind, whereas a programme in which the figure reached 30 per cent would seem to be well below par.

One way of keeping down such expenditures, is to have a development programme made openly. The programme should be made not by the Cabinet, but by a Committee of public persons especially charged to make it, such as the Planning Commission in India, or the Planning Commission in Senegal, or Tunisia, and elsewhere. The procedure is to appoint a representative Committee consisting of some officials and some private persons, including business men, trade unionists, and members of Parliament. They consider material submitted by the Regional Committees and the proposals made by ministries and government departments, and publish what in their opinion would be the best plan.

In this way one keeps to a minimum prestige objects, expenditures on political roads, excessive glorification of the capital, and similar defects. The Government is not, of course, obliged to accept what such a Committee recommends any more than it is obliged to accept the report of any other commission of inquiry. But if it wishes to add or exclude projects, it must give its reasons; and so it is less likely to make indefensible decisions than is the case where the whole plan is made in secret under the control of the Cabinet, without the public having the benefit of an impartial nonpolitical report with which to compare what the Government proposes.

Of course, all the foregoing presupposes that the published Plan is a serious document, in the sense that the Government means to do what it contains, and means not to do what is excluded. This is not always the case. A development programme can be used as a means of window-dressing, and is often so used. The Government omits from the plan things which it intends to do but prefers not to talk about, such as some prestige expenditures; and it puts into the plan things which will impress some readers, but which it does not intend to do. When the programme is obviously grossly excessive, because the Government has not had the courage to eliminate the lesser priorities, one cannot take it seriously at all, since it is clear that the Government cannot fulfill its promises, and it is also more than likely that what gets done will be determined rather by political pressures than by objective urgency. For this there is no remedy other than a strong public opinion, which does not exist in most under-developed countries. But this means that what must be assessed eventually is not what the Government says it will do, but what it actually does.

3.2 PLANNING IN AFRICAN COUNTRIES *

In treatises on development programming a distinction is often made between two techniques in establishing a development plan: a programming approach and a project approach. The programming approach starts from overall targets of national income, and estimates subsequently the concomitant levels of consumption, capital formation, imports, exports and other relevant aggregates of the economy. In a further analysis these totals may be broken down by certain sectors, exchanges and relationships between which may be calculated and fitted into a consistent framework. Thus one can arrive at a more or less detailed description of the economy during a certain period, or at some future date, on certain assumptions regarding external factors as well as the coefficients of the system. This picture of the future economy yields indications of the policies to be followed if the economy is to reach the targets fixed and maintain the desired equilibrium. A further analysis of the sectors leads to a detailed formulation of the projects to be carried out in the context of the plan.

The other possible approach, the project approach, is to start at the other end, from individual projects proposed which could be worked into a comprehensive plan. Cost-benefit calculations regarding the direct and indirect impact of such projects on the economy can be added to give, together with certain general extrapolations, e.g. of population increase, an overall picture of the changes to be expected in the economy. The aspects of projects to be taken into account are, on the one hand, increases in production, income, employment, exchange earnings, tax receipts and the like, and, on the

* From United Nations, ECA, "Survey of Development Programmes and Policies in Selected African Countries and Territories," *Economic Bulletin for Africa,* Vol. I, No. 1, January 1961, pp. 74-7.

other, requirements of capital, materials, labour of varying types of skill, foreign exchange, and extra demands put on public facilities etc. This approach, which should in theory result in the same kind of plan as the programming approach is, however, rare in practice.

Some countries in Africa, including most of those on the shores of the Mediterranean, have adopted the programming approach in their planning. However, development plans in Africa are usually not comprehensive: they are mainly public capital expenditure programmes containing no projections, objectives or targets for the private sector. Even though they contain lists of projects, these plans should not be confused with the project approach to development programming described in the previous paragraph; for these plans take no, or very limited, account of the impact of the projects on the economy. As far as demands on resources are concerned, the only aspect usually assessed has been capital costs, although in recent years, in an increasing number of cases, the effect on current budgets has been estimated and taken into consideration. The only benefits normally estimated have been direct benefits, i.e., no explicit account has been taken of the wider repercussions on the economy. As a consequence, it has always been difficult in these plans to establish proper priorities and make rational comparisons between projects. The plans concerned are therefore more truly government capital expenditure programmes than development programmes proper, even though certain expenditure items are sometimes included that are not, in a narrow sense, capital expenditure. The most noteworthy of such items are certain agricultural development expenditures which, although of a non-recurring nature, cannot properly be defined as outlay on the construction of capital works. In contrast, the

TABLE I. PUBLIC CAPITAL EXPENDITURE IN DEVELOPMENT PROGRAMMES

	Govt. Capital expenditure in US $ per head per annum	Percentage Distribution						
		Agricultural	Industry	Electricity	Transport and communications	Education	Health	Other
Nigeria (Fed. of)	55/60	2	3	2	8	61	4	3	19
(rev. 58)	55/60	2	2	1	8	59	5	1	24
(rev. 59)	55/62	1	1	1	7	56	6	2	27
Togo	49/54	2	8	—	—	58	5	17	12
Rhodesia & Nyasaland	57/61	12	3	—	45	41	4	4	3
(Fed. of)	59/63	7	2	—	44	35	8	6	5
Uganda (rev. 57 [a])	55/60	4	4	3	26	15	7	5	40
Southern Rhodesia	57/61	9	13	—	28	19	2	38	
Kenya	54/57	5	26	1	—	13 [k]	10	4	46
	57/60	3	38	—	1	14 [k]	9	4	34
Nyasaland	57/60	4	22 [e]	—	— [e]	10	8	—	60
Ivory Coast	47/56	7	16	—	3	64	17		
	58/62	10	33	3 [h]	2	30	12	4	16
Malagasy Republic	59/62 [b]	8	38	1	1	36	7	8	9
Togo	54/59	3	33	—	—	43	4	6	14
	59/60 [c]	2	22	—	—	43	7	14	14
Sudan	59/61 [d]	8	39	2	2	36 [n]	13		8
Portuguese Overseas Provinces [1]	59/64	4	40 [f]	—	—	45	7		8
Ghana	59/64 [m]	40	7	8	31	15	9	13	17
Western Nigeria	55/60	3	3	20	3	12	22	6	34
(Rev. 58)	55/60	3	3	17	2	17	17	8	36
	60/65	5	23	14	2	15	8	2	36
Eastern Nigeria	58/62	1	5	8	—	23	25	5	34
(Rev. 60)	58/62	2	4	8	—	25	21	5	37
Ethiopia	57/61	2	7	10	11	54	5	3	10
Morocco	58/59	10	35	4	2	15	10	3	31
United Arab Republic (Egypt)	59/61 [d]	33	24 [g]	29	3 [g]	23	21		
Algeria	59/63	44	23	7	7	22	12	3	26

[1] All overseas provinces including those outside Africa.
[a] Including expenditure by the Uganda Electricity Board.
[b] Excluding European Development Fund Expenditure.
[c] Fund for Assistance and Cooperation and European Development Fund Programme.
[d] Capital development budgets for the years 59/60 and 60/61.
[e] The Shire river valley project included in agriculture.
[f] Natural resources development; presumably agriculture and mineral prospecting.
[g] The high dam included in agriculture.
[h] Expenditure for mineral prospecting.
[j] 3% to be spent on investments in publicly owned mines.
[k] Excluding railways.
[m] Including expenditure on the Volta river project.
[n] Including expenditure by the Sudan Railways.

N.B. Figures for expenditure in US$ are not strictly comparable: they have been converted at prevailing exchange rates, which do not necessarily,—and do not in fact in this case—reflect the relative price levels in the different countries and territories.

plans referred to often contain genuine capital items which would appear in any normal government capital budget and which do not constitute a special effort to stimulate the economic development of a country, the most striking example being the capital expenditure on the maintenance of local security and public order and the construction of government administrative buildings which is included in many of the recent development plans in Africa....

Certain countries have decided to embark on the elaboration of a comprehensive plan; some have taken only the first preparatory steps, while others have determined an analytical framework and decided on general directives to be pursued. These plans form a special group in so far as they cannot be called fully articulated comprehensive plans; but as they contain projections of certain aggregates of the economy, they incline towards overall programmes.

The percentage distribution of public capital expenditure is shown in Table 1 in order to illustrate policies pursued by the various governments. In the cases of Ethiopia, UAR (Egypt) and Algeria only, the patterns of expenditure have been determined within the context of overall plans; all the other countries and territories listed have "plans" which may be more appropriately referred to as "public capital expenditure programmes."

The development programmes encountered in Africa can best be classified, first according to the techniques applied and, secondly, according to the lines of economic policy followed. In the case of comprehensive plans, these lines are, in principle, unambigously determined by the system, although in practice there still remains much room for manoeuver, particularly in the selection of the policy instruments. Where capital expenditure programmes are concerned, however, the lines of economic development are more or less freely chosen by the government and therefore offer a useful criterion for classifying these programmes. In the following pages attention will be focussed mainly on economic investments, social and particularly administrative investments being treated only by implication.

Classification:

1. Capital expenditure programmes with emphasis on infrastructure development:

(a) Programmes related to evacuation of primary products, concentrating mainly on transport, and possibly education and health. Examples are: Federation of Nigeria, Northern Nigeria, and many other countries and territories in Africa in their earlier plans.

(b) Programmes indirectly related to industrialization, adopted by countries which do not or need not take direct action to encourage industrial development but which concentrate on electricity production, in addition to transport and possibly other infrastructure expenditure. Examples: the Federation of Rhodesia and Nyasaland, and Uganda.

2. Capital expenditure programmes with emphasis on directly productive investments:

(a) Programmes which stress agricultural development to the point of a genuine agrarian and land reform with a view of reorganizing the productive structure and to developing domestic markets. Examples of this category are: Southern Rhodesia and Kenya.

(b) Programmes stressing the expansion of existing agricultural patterns and designed to increase quantities available for export and to improve the quality of the products. Many countries fall within this group. Examples...are: the Ivory Coast, Togoland, the Malagasy Republic, Nyasaland and the Sudan.

(c) Programmes emphasizing industrialization, e.g.: Ghana, Western Nigeria, and to some extent Eastern Nigeria, and the 1958/59 plan for Morocco which, however, contains a rather far-reaching agricultural programme as well.

3. Overall programmes:

Programmes of countries which have started on comprehensive planning and which have made projections of an overall framework of the economy but have not arrived at a fully articulated comprehensive plan. Examples... are the work done in: Mali (former French Sudan), and largely also the plan for: Ethiopia, and the FAO studies of Morocco and Tunisia.

4. Comprehensive programmes comprising detailed and articulated sector programmes, such as the plans (so far as they are known) for: Morocco, Tunisia, UAR (Egypt), and Algeria.

The dividing lines between the groups are not as sharp as may appear from this classification, which is introduced merely for convenience and should not be taken too literally.

3.3 INDUSTRIAL PLANNING IN ASIA
AND THE FAR EAST *

Formulation of development programmes inevitably requires the establishment of some planning agencies. Their methods of work will naturally differ with the scope of their functions and the extent of their plan coverage. In addition to the formulation of a plan or programme, planning agencies in some countries may be concerned with the policies and procedures for its implementation and with periodic assessment of plan achievements.

In most ECAFE countries, industrial planning is not a single-agency function; it is the product of a decentralized process

* From United Nations, ECAFE, *Formulating Industrial Development Programmes, Development Programming Techniques Series No. 2*, Bangkok, 1961, pp. 102, 104-18, 125-32.

in which several institutions and organizations, both governmental and non-governmental, take part. Planning units located in the government not only consolidate the projects proposed by the public corporation and private enterprises but also initiate proposals on the basis of resource surveys and technical studies made available to them. The central planning agency evaluates such programmes, fills in the gaps, where necessary, and integrates them into an industrial development programme consistent with the country's overall resources and objectives....

The plans differ in their coverage according to whether a partial or sectoral plan or a well-integrated multi-sectoral plan is contemplated. In this respect, the ECAFE countries can be divided into three groups:

(1) those which have integrated multi-sectoral plans embodying plan objectives and policy instruments;

(2) those which have well formulated plans mainly for public investment, mostly in social overheads; and

(3) those which have a string of isolated projects....

There is a considerable variation in the role of planning agencies in different countries of the ECAFE region. Planning machinery in countries falling under group (1) e.g. Ceylon, mainland China, India, Japan, Pakistan and the Philippines, consists of well-formed bodies concerned in varying degrees with the formulation, co-ordination and implementation of plans. In most of the countries, the plans are implemented through various Ministries and special agencies. The main function of the central planning authorities is to prepare plans and co-ordinate plan activities. In mainland China, planning until 1957 was highly centralized and practically all the targets were set by the central authorities in Peking. In 1956, the short-term planning functions of the State Planning Commission, *i.e.*, the formulation and supervision of annual plans and the day-to-day adjustments were taken over by a new body, the National Economic Commission, so that the State Planning Commission could concentrate on long-term economic development. Furthermore in 1957, the control of many industries was removed from the Ministries in Peking. It was recognized that there were a number of industrial units which would not necessarily benefit from centralized control and should better be placed under the control of dispersed management. These decisions, coupled with the decision to restore a limited free market in the field of agriculture and an increased freedom of choice within the state trading mechanism, reflect a trend towards an increasing degree of decentralization within in an essentially central planning framework. . . .

In countries falling under groups (2) and (3), the planning agencies appear to have a rather limited scope with respect to the formulation, co-ordination and execution of plans. For instance, in Burma the National Planning Commission is concerned with the implementation of programmes through the annual budgeting process rather than with the formulation of plans. In Cambodia, the Ministry of Planning is in charge of preparing plans but, due to lack of proper co-ordination, there is a great deal of divergence between the Ministry's targets and those put forward by government departments which are supposed to carry them out. The plan of Iran is a financial framework of development expenditure and the Plan Organization is primarily an executive agency responsible for the development and implementation of projects on its own authority within the financial limits determined by the Parliament. It has no responsibility to co-ordinate and advise on any activities not financed from its own funds. . . .

Industrial planning objectives The objectives of industrial planning in the countries of the region seem to have been derived from the overall objectives set forth in their economic development plans. Improvement in the level of living, expansion of employment opportunities and attainment of a balance in international payments are the three objectives most commonly found in the plans of the ECAFE countries. Usually they are all mentioned together in a brief statement of objectives, and it is difficult to distinguish which of them receives greater emphasis or priority; nor is it clear how the different objectives are reconciled. Furthermore a critical examination of the plan documents reveals the inclusion under objectives of what are basically means or instruments.

Broadly speaking, an emphasis on increasing national income together with some concrete estimates of the proposed increase are to be found in the plans of Burma, China: mainland and Taiwan, ceylon, India, Japan, Pakistan and the Philippines. Many of these plans also indicate saving (investment) at the base period, over-all increase needed in investment to attain the target increase in income and the required increase in the rate of saving. . . .

Expansion of employment opportunities is almost an equally important objective of many plans, notably of Ceylon, the Federation of Malaya, India, Japan and Pakistan. Almost all these plans give population projections and estimates of anticipated addition to the labour force and the employment opportunities to be created. Ceylon is an instance of a well-articulated plan in terms of employment; quantitative estimates of the increase in labour force to be absorbed in various sectors appear to be one of the guiding considerations in arriving at the planned investment outlay and its distribution. In other countries with expansion of employment as one of the plan objectives, decisions on the magnitude of investment do not seem to follow directly from considerations of employment targets; on the other hand, figures of increment in labour force to be absorbed are estimated from investment in different sectors of the economy. In most of the plans an appreciation of the need for increase in employment has led to an emphasis on the expansion of labour-intensive small-scale industries.

The objective of achieving balance in international payments in some of the plans is indicated by the emphasis laid on import-replacement and export industries. Usually, both methods are stressed, and it is difficult to discern which receives greater emphasis. The balance of payments objective is closely linked with the emphasis on diversification of production in the export-oriented economies vulnerable to external fluctuations. In the Ceylonese plan, high priority is attached to the need for import-saving production and for expansion of exports, particularly in agriculture. China: Taiwan stresses increase in exports in order to meet the import requirements of development programmes. In the Third Five-Year Plan of India, top priority has been given to the achievement of self-sufficiency in foodgrains and to an increase in agricultural production to meet the requirements of industry and exports; past experience indicates that this is essential to enable the economy to save scarce foreign exchange resources for importing the increasing volume of necessary producer goods. In Pakistan, improvement in the balance of payments has been the principal consideration in determining various production targets and the highest priority has been attached to increasing agricultural production. The Pakistan plan stresses the establishment of new capacity in those industries which earn or save foreign exchange or use mainly domestic raw materials. In the Philippine plan, increased efforts to develop dollar-saving industries, such as steel, basic chemicals, fertilizer, pulp and paper, textile, etc., and an intensive programme to increase the production of dollar-earning exports, such as copra, abaca and tobacco, are advocated to insure the economy against an unfavourable balance of payments position.

In achieving plan objectives, industrial development in the public sector has claimed particular attention in Ceylon, China (mainland and Taiwan), India and Japan.

In Burma, the lowest priority is given to industry in the government's spending programme, and the initiative for the development of industries is left to the private sector.

It is one of the major objectives of the Ceylonese Plan to take a decisive step forward over the next ten years towards industrialization; domestic industrial production is estimated to increase from 21 per cent of total supplies in 1957 to 40 per cent by 1968.

In the First and Second Five-Year Plans of mainland China, industry, particularly capital goods, is given the highest priority. While the First Five-Year Plan was heavily biased in favour of modern large-scale industries, increased attention was paid in the Second Plan to the development of small-scale industries often using traditional labour-intensive methods.

The Federation of Malaya places greater emphasis on agriculture and social services in its development plans. Industrial development is left to the initiative of the private sector and is limited by the small size of the home market and poor export prospects for manufactures.

In the Second and Third Five-Year Plans of India, rapid industrialization with particular emphasis on the development of basic and heavy industries is one of the plan objectives. It is recognized that such industries will significantly increase national income and employment only in the long run. Also it is expected that with the acquisition of capital, skills and technical know-how, the growth of the economy will become self-sustaining and increasingly independent of foreign assistance....

Although the Pakistan plan seeks to encourage the expansion of industries, the emphasis is on agriculture and social overheads, and one of the chief objectives in the industrial development programme is to earn or to save foreign exchange. The plan also seeks to prepare the base for industrialization and for self-generating growth, but the importance of these objectives as operational goals does not seem to be an overriding one.

The Philippine plan recognizes industrialization as one of the important objectives to meet the requirements of the domestic economy, particularly in consumer goods....

Figures of the percentage of industrial investment in total planned outlay for some countries of the ECAFE region are presented in Table 1 to show the quantitative importance of industrial investment in total plan outlay.

Industrial planning in public and private sectors: In most of the ECAFE countries, the private sector is responsible for a large share of investment outlay for industrial development. As mentioned... many of the countries in the region plan for public investment or for isolated projects, and do not attempt to present any development programme for the private sector. A well-integrated multi-sectoral plan, on the other hand, requires an assessment of investible resources available to the private sector, particularly when the state undertakes an important role in planning. In most of the ECAFE countries, demarcation of the spheres of activity between the private and public sectors is guided by pragmatic rather than doctrinaire considerations.

In the Ten-Year Plan of Ceylon, though there is no general restriction as to industries in which the private sector is not allowed to operate, a rather comprehensive list of industries has been reserved for the public sector in the process of actual implementation.

In mainland China, apart from state enterprises, there are large joint state-private undertakings whose production and management have already been brought under state planning step by step, with consequent changes in operation and management. The second plan points out the need for a reorganization of the large number of scattered small and medium joint state-private enterprises which are gradually to adapt themselves to the planned management of the state. The plan also observes that some handicrafts may be allowed to carry on production individually under the leadership of the handicraft co-operative organizations and to produce and market all their products by themselves.

It was observed in India's First Five-Year Plan that the private and public sectors could not be regarded as two separate entities but as parts of a single organism. Fulfilment of social needs and objectives of planning, as against motivation of profits alone, were held to be the guiding principle for the private sector....

The cardinal principle in the Second Five-Year Plan of Pakistan is that there should be no complete reservation of industries for the public sector except defence industries. However, the government should participate directly only in those enterprises which are essential for over-all development and where private capital is not forthcoming. Thus the implementation of the industrial development programme rests largely with private enterprise for which incentives are to be

TABLE I. SHARE OF INDUSTRIAL INVESTMENT IN TOTAL INVESTMENT
IN SELECTED ECAFE COUNTRIES

Country	Plan	Investment allocation in industries as a percentage of		
		Total invest. in public sector	Total invest. in priv. sect.	Total invest. in both sectors
Ceylon	Ten-Year Plan	23	16	21
China (Mainland)	First Five-Year Plan			58
	Second Five-Year Plan			60
China (Taiwan)	Second Four-Year Plan	49	58	51
Fed. of Malaya	Second Five-Year Plan	13		
India	Second Five-Year Plan	19	24	24
	Third Five-Year Plan	27	32	29
Iran	Second Seven-Year Plan	10		
Nepal	Five-Year Plan	6		
Pakistan	Second Five-Year Plan	10	38	21
Philippines	Three-Year Programme	18	27	24

maintained. The Plan further classifies the agencies responsible for investment into public, private and semi-public sectors. The semi-public sector is financed partly by the government and partly by the private sector and also enjoys more administrative autonomy than the agencies in the public sector.

In the Philippine Three-Year Programme, the basic policy provides that efforts to bring about economic development be undertaken primarily by the private sector, with the government limiting itself to (a) projects which the private sector is unwilling or unable to undertake because of huge initial capital outlays, (b) social overheads including public works and utilities, (c) education, research and surveys, industrial assistance, extension and public health, and (d) all other services necessary for the development of the private sector. Under the current programme, the state is also required to encourage private investment in what are considered to be strategic areas of industrial development, particularly the textile, pulp and paper, cement, glass and ceramics, agricultural tools and implements, and food-processing industries.

The relative importance of the public and private sectors in some of the ECAFE countries is indicated by the proportion in which total and industrial investment are distributed between the two sectors. In Table II the relevant figures are presented. It will be noted that the role of the private sector in industrial development is dominant in Pakistan and the Philippines, whereas the public sector is more important in Ceylon, China (Taiwan) and India.

Period of plan: Some of the development plans stress the desirability of having an overall view of the growth of the economy over a period of say, fifteen to twenty years. The perspective plan provides the framework for the formulation of medium-term and short-term plans. The medium-term plans may be for a period of four, five, seven or even ten years, and specify the principal objectives and measures to be adopted. Planners in the region also appreciate the need for annual plans within the framework of medium-term plans to enable revisions in the light of results achieved each year and of developments in the domestic and international economic situation. The main distinction between the medium-term and short-term plans on the one hand, and perspective plans on the other, lies in the assumption that, while the former are basically operational plans, the latter provide them with broad directions to which they should conform. Despite a general awareness of the need for perspective plans, detailed investment programmes for sectors over a long period, incorporating as integral parts the specific short-term plans, have not been worked out....

In the Second Five-Year Plans of India and Pakistan, it is observed that five-year plans must also be viewed in the perspective of developments to be undertaken over a longer period. A degree of temporary imbalance has been regarded as necessary in order to facilitate more rapid and better-balanced developments over a longer period. This is considered to be particularly true with respect to education, manpower and basic industries, power and transport, where the investments are of a lumpy nature and are better assessed in the light of developments over periods longer than five years.

Both India and Pakistan make long-term projections of national income. In the second Indian plan, certain assumptions have been made about the rate of growth of population, the proportion of increase in national income which could be ploughed back into investment and incremental capital-output ratio; it is suggested that, compared to 1950–1951, national income could be doubled by 1967–1968 and *per capita* income, by 1973–1974. Another important objective to be achieved by the end of the fifth plan (1975) is the reduction of the proportion of population dependent on agriculture, from the present level of about 70 per cent to about 60 per cent through industrialization.

In Pakistan's Second Five-Year Plan, it is proposed to double the existing level of national income in the fourth plan period (ending 1975) and to quadruple it in the sixth (ending 1985). This growth pattern, it is felt, requires a rate of growth of 20 per cent during the second plan period, rising to 25 per cent during the third and 30 per cent during the fourth and fifth plan periods. These aggregative

TABLE II. SHARE OF PRIVATE SECTOR IN PLANNED INVESTMENT
IN SELECTED ECAFE COUNTRIES

Country	Plan	Percentage share of private sector in	
		Industrial investment	Total investment
Ceylon	Ten-Year Plan	27	34
China (Taiwan)	Second Four-Year Plan	43	38
Fed. of Malaya	Second Five-Year Plan	n.a.	57
India [a]	Second Five-Year Plan	42	39 [b]
	Third Five-Year Plan	43	39
Pakistan [c]	First Five-Year Plan	n.a.	36
	Second Five-Year Plan	71	39
Philippines	Three-Year Programme	77	69

Note: n.a. = not available.

[a] The percentage share of private sector in industrial investment in the Indian plans includes mineral, whereas for other countries, it relates to industries only. Nor does it include investments financed out of resources from the public sector.

[b] While the plan provision was 39 per cent, the actual figure works out at 46 per cent.

[c] Includes investment of the semi-public sector financed by funds from the private sector.

projections in the Indian and Pakistan plans are obtained by applying the simple Harrod-Domar model and the rationale underlying the basic quantitative assumptions does not appear to have been worked out in detail. Moreover, the plan documents of these countries do not provide long-term sectoral projections in the light of which the aggregate projections relating to national income could be assessed....

Methods of allocation: The determination of the amount of investment in the industrial sector is one of the essential tasks of industrial planning. A tentative draft programme is worked out for the industrial sector, usually by aggregating schemes and projects submitted by various governmental and non-governmental agencies. The investment requirement of the industrial sector obtained in this way is assessed in the light of available resources including estimated foreign aid likely to be forthcoming during the plan period....

In fixing production targets and allocating investment outlays, various *ad hoc* procedures based on considerations of demand and supply have been used by the countries of the region. The Ceylonese plan relies heavily on an assessment of the potential markets for different industrial products on the basis of estimates of import requirements, increase in national income and population growth. Two sets of projections of import demand for the plan period were made by the Planning Secretariat; the low projections do not allow for any rise in the levels of living or increase in the rate of investment, whereas the high ones take into account not only the expected increase in population but also allow for some increase in levels of living and substantial increase in the rate of investment. The import projections thus obtained provide an idea of the size of the expected market for industrial products. Assuming

that it is potentially possible to replace two-thirds of these imports by domestic output, the scope of industrialization via import replacement has been assessed. In industries, domestic production as a percentage of total supplies is estimated to increase from 21 in 1957 to 40 in 1968. The emphasis is on the production of consumer goods whose imports are estimated to fall from 58 per cent of total imports in 1957 to 40 per cent in 1968 as a result of the programme of industrialization.

Mainland China emphasizes the development of capital goods and heavy industries as an important plan objective. One of the governing principles in the first and second plans is that capital goods industries must grow faster than consumer goods. Allowance is made for the development of the consumer goods industry to keep pace with the rise in the purchasing power of the people. As regards the method of allocation of resources, and the fixing of production targets, mainland China follows the well developed principles of centralized planning. Basic decisions relate to a conscious moulding of the pattern of economic development by regulating the proportions in which goods are produced and accordingly, the proportions in which economic resources are distributed among the various branches of production. The performance and fulfilment of this task depend on the preparation of estimates of balance relating to the economy's material, financial, and labour resources. These balance sheets comprise two parts, namely, utilization of resources needed and consumption of the products among the various economic branches. These balance estimates are first formulated for basic products and then combined by branches and sectors. Furthermore, projections are obtained on the basis of techno-productivity indices. The material balances are particularly designed to ensure the consistency of the needs of one industry with the production goals of the industries that supply it and the consistency of the various goals with the overall availability of resources. Important in this connexion are the balance estimates of iron and steel, building materials, fuel and power, grain and industrial crops, textiles and other products of light industries. Material balances must be consistent with the labour plan and financial plan. The labour plan contains, in addition to wages and productivity, estimates of skilled and unskilled labour, by sectors, by regions and for the economy as a whole. The financial plan mainly consists of the balanced estimates of the money income and expenditure of the population and the budget. In the planning of manufactured consumer goods, estimation of the wages bill, taxes, retail prices, and money income is an important factor. In view of the poor quality of economic data in mainland China, the balance estimates suffer from various inaccuracies, necessitating frequent changes and adjustments in the plans....

In the second and third plans of India, sectoral allocation of resources within industry has been governed by the emphasis placed on steel and machine building and the manufacture of producer goods. The Indian plans indicate a gradual shift towards import replacement in case of basic capital goods, reinforced by a favourable resource base. With respect to consumption goods, the aim is to meet all essential needs, but some restraint in consumption is regarded as unavoidable in the case of goods of a luxury or semi-luxury character. In the Second Five-Year Plan, the investment allocation for producer and capital goods amounted to 84 per cent of total investment in large-scale industries, leaving only 16 per cent for consumer goods. In the Third Five-Year Plan, this trend in favour of producer goods industries is to be given a further impetus, with the main emphasis on machine-building

industries. The rationale of detailed allocation between sectors seems to derive from various *ad hoc* considerations....

Pakistan has stressed balance of payments considerations in allocating resources and fixing industrial targets in the second plan. More or less complete replacement of imports has been shown to be practicable in the case of jute goods, cotton and woollen textiles, sugar, pulp and paper, newsprint, cardboard, cigarettes, bicycles, sewing machines, cycle tyres and tubes and a large number of light engineering and electrical products.

The Philippine Three-Year Programme also stresses the factor of import replacement in the allocation of resources within industry. Availability of local resources is taken into explicit consideration in the production of import substitutes. In the absence of domestic raw materials, the policy of importing and processing them at home, as illustrated by the textile industry, is advocated. The industrial programme of the Philippines, besides aiming at the production of import substitutes, also emphasizes the domestic production of basic raw materials to feed existing industries such as metallic products and chemicals; and the development of textile, wheat flour, pulp and paper, cement, ceramics, plate glass, petroleum refining, leather tanning, food manufacturing, and cottage industries....

Sector priority considerations: The investment costs of the industrial sector, obtained on the basis of considerations mentioned above, were usually added to the investment programmes of the other sectors to yield the first over-all tentative investment cost of the plan. A series of revisions then follow in which the sectoral allocations are readjusted in line with the total estimated resources, particularly foreign exchange. In such a process of adjustments, certain core projects (*e.g.* iron and steel in mainland China and India and fertilizers in Pakistan) are retained irrespective of foreign exchange costs. Trimmings called for by these readjustments are usually carried out on the basis of priority considerations.

Priority criteria borne in mind in the selection of industries are:

(1) industries having a large foreign exchange benefit coefficient;

(2) producer goods industries having the effect of reducing the import component of future development expenditure;

(3) industries using indigenous raw materials;

(4) consumer goods industries meeting essential needs;

(5) industries making the largest net contribution to national income per unit of investment.

The above merely represents the multiplicity of factors that are taken into consideration in fixing of priorities. Determination of the order of priority requires the weighing of these various factors, and this has not generally been done quantitatively except in the Philippines.

In China (Taiwan), decisions as to the establishment or priority of an industrial project are largely influenced by the extent of the market. A project is established where its product is urgently needed in sufficiently large quantities or can be manufactured with indigenous materials or by-products of existing industries, provided, however, that no technical difficulties arise and that a part of the capital and foreign exchange requirements can be met by United States aid. The project would not be given up unless the cost of production is considered to be excessively high. Because of the availability of aid such criteria as capital-output ratio and employment-investment ratio are relegated to a place of secondary importance.

In line with the basic objective of laying the foundation for accelerated economic growth, the Second Five-Year Plan of India prescribed the following industrial priorities:

(1) increased production of iron, steel and heavy chemicals and development of heavy engineering and machine-building industries;

(2) expansion of capacity of other developmental commodities and producer goods such as aluminum, cement, chemical, pulp, dyestuffs, phosphatic fertilizers, and essential drugs;

(3) modernization and re-equipment of important national industries such as jute, cotton textiles and sugar.

As a continuation of this policy, the Third Five-Year Plan envisages expansion and diversification of capacity of the heavy engineering and machine-building industries, including alloy tools and special steel, iron and steel and ferro-alloys, and increase in the output of fertilizers. There is also to be increased production of major producer goods like aluminum, mineral oils, basic organic and inorganic chemicals. In view of the high foreign exchange cost of such a development programme, the expansion of consumer goods industries having a substantial import component has perforce a low priority....

In Pakistan, the Planning Commission carried out a number of studies on comparative foreign exchange benefits and social profitability of various industries. Having thus established the comparative eligibility of industries, the emphasis given to various projects was determined by a number of factors, the main one being the importance of the product to the national economy, the potential demand for it and the export possibilities. A noteworthy feature of the foreign exchange benefit calculation has been the subtraction of the potential foreign exchange lost due to non-export of the domestic raw materials from the total foreign exchange earned or saved in each case.

The industrial priorities formula [1] used in the Philippine Plan is based on four factors, namely, the proportion of net value added by the industry concerned to its total investment (inclusive of circulating capital), the balance of payments ratio expressed as the proportion of net foreign exchange earned or saved by the industry to investment, utilization of domestic material ratio, and the ratio of wage bill to investment. These four rating factors are given certain weights and are then aggregated to arrive at the over-all priority rating. The industrial priorities formula of the Philippines is based on partial analysis and consists basically in selecting and encouraging types of productive activities which would use relatively little of the scarce factors (capital and foreign exchange). While such an approach offers immediate and objective criteria for planning, the planning authorities feel that the growing complexity of the Philippine economy may eventually render the industrial priorities formula difficult to apply in practice.

The above study of various priority considerations indicates the use of qualitative weights rather than accounting prices. However, such use of qualitative weights can be taken to be an implicit application of the accounting price concept. Pakistan has had the unique experience in the use of accounting prices for assessing the priority of industrial sectors and projects in the First Five-Year Plan. Since Pakistan had not yet followed India, the United Kingdom, and other countries in devaluing its currency, it was thought desirable to use an accounting exchange rate to allow for the distortion in the value of imports and exports. The rate applied was largely a matter of judgement; however it was based on a calculation of the rate that

1. For details, see *The Five Year Economic and Social Development Programme,* National Economic Council, Philippines, pp. 253-78.

would be necessary to make the most promising export and import substitutes yield a competitive return on the resources used ... The accounting price of foreign exchange was used to calculate the social profitability of the main projects being proposed for public investments by the Pakistan Industrial Development Corporation ... Although the data on which it was based were rather rough in some cases, this calculation of social profitability was of considerable value in determining priorities among the industrial sectors.

Project priority considerations: Once the eligibility of industries is determined on the basis of sectoral priorities, the next step is project selection and combination on the basis of feasibility with respect to resources, particularly foreign exchange and technical manpower. The problem of priorities in project selection, besides being subject to general industrial priorities, requires supplementary criteria with respect to scale and choice of technology drawn up in the light of employment targets and resource availability.

In China (Taiwan) owing to limitations of the domestic market the production capacity of a new project is usually kept relatively small at the beginning. However, provision is made for future expansion in order to develop the project into an economical unit as the demand for its product rises. The development of the polyvinyl-chloride (PVC) industry is typical of this approach; starting with an initial capacity of 4 metric tons per day in 1953, the capacity was expanded to 40 metric tons per day by 1960 through the addition of units at various periods in response to increase in domestic and export demand.

In India, plans for the lay-out of the three steel plants have taken into account the possibility of their further expansion in later years. Further, the Indian plans have recommended as a first priority the expansion of units which are regarded as operating below the optimum scale to attain the optimum scale of production. . . .

In the Pakistan Second Plan, no attempt has been made to specify the size of individual units as the bulk of the industrial investment is to take place in the private sector. However, studies have been made as regards the minimum economical scale of operations in industries. In Pakistan, the plan allocations were deemed to be large enough to permit each industry to set up at least one unit of medium size. While selecting the optimum size of plants, the technological possibility of increasing their scale by the addition of new units has been kept in mind.

The choice of technology posed to the countries the conflict between the objectives of maximum output and saving on the one hand and of providing maximum employment on the other. Attempts were made to achieve a balance between them. Labour intensive methods were favoured in the production of consumer goods by assigning an important role to the development of small-scale and cottage industries, since the choice of production methods in the case of producer goods is largely limited by technological considerations and quality requirements.

In the Second Five-Year Plan of India, it was estimated on the basis of studies relating to employment and investment coefficients of various small-scale industries, that 38 per cent of the additional employment in the industrial sector was likely to be generated in cottage and small-scale industries; the corresponding proportion of investment outlay (public and private) on cottage and small-scale industries to total planned investment outlay was of the order of 25 per cent. In the Draft Third Five-Year Plan of India, investment allocation for cottage and small-scale industries has been reduced to about 15 per cent of total investment in the industrial sector.

While the Pakistan Second Plan recognizes the role of small-scale industries in creating additional employment opportunities, it discourages any perpetuation of an uneconomic structure. The programme, therefore, is oriented towards adapting small industries to changing technological, economic and social conditions.

In most of the countries having a large sector of small-scale industries, need for increased efficiency in small-scale manufacture is emphasized. The plans advocate the development of small-scale industries as ancillary to large industries by linking them, as regards their requirement of raw materials, to large industrial concerns and by providing power and other facilities to the rural areas.

3.4 Lessons from India's Industrial Growth *

There can be no doubt . . . that our industrial revolution has started in right earnest; and the Planning Commission is justified in their statement that "The past decade has witnessed the beginning of an industrial revolution in India. . . ."

Reviewing the position as a whole, there is no doubt that with the exception of agriculture, the other growth factors in the economy have all recorded significant increases, in many cases well over the general industrial index, thus testifying to the validity of the contention that India has now started on her industrial revolution.

When we look at the way in which this growth in industrial output, and especially its growth factors, has been brought about, we find that it is largely due to the initiative taken by the State under the stimulus of newly acquired independence and the logic of planned development aimed at accelerated economic growth.

* From V. K. R. V. Rao, *Some Reflections on the Industrial Revolution Now in Progress in India,* Walchand Memorial Lecture Series, Bombay, 1962, pp. 2, 4-10. Reprinted by permission.

This is clear from the pattern of public investment and outlay during the period. The State has gone in for large programmes of investment in transport and communication facilities, generation of electric power, expansion of minerals including oil, irrigation and agricultural extension, production of steel, fertilisers and some other basic and intermediate goods, establishment of machine tool and machine fabricating industries, and technical education. It is this heavy investment in economic and social overheads that has created the necessary background for the stimulation of industrial production in the private sector. The private sector has also been stimulated by the closed economy that has accompanied planning with its severe restrictions on imports of consumption goods and the greater availability of foreign exchange for capital goods and maintenance imports. The more or less guaranteed domestic market that this has created has acted as a tonic to private industry and led to its growth and expansion on a larger scale and in a more diversified manner than was actually contemplated in the Plan targets. The private sector has also been assisted in securing foreign exchange for its capital requirements by government sponsorship before foreign financial organisations like the International Bank, the International Finance Corporation, the Export-Import Bank and some other banking institutions. Government help to the private industrial sector in securing domestic finance has also been considerable directly through the different financial institutions like the Industrial Finance Corporation, the Industrial Credit and Investment Corporation, the National Industrial Development Corporation and the Refinance Corporation of India. According to Shri K. P. Mathrani of the Industrial Finance Corporation, such direct financial assistance by way of loans and credits given to the private

sector in industry has totalled Rs.224 crores during this period or about 24% of the total estimated investment of Rs.945 crores made in the organized industries in the private sector during the two Plan periods. In addition, the International Finance Corporation and certain other institutions have been given guarantees for deferred payments and under-written capital issues, aggregating to Rs.40 crores during this period. If this amount is added to the assistance given to the private sector in organised industry in actual cash, the contribution of the State to private industrial finance during the period comes to nearly 28% of the total investment. In addition to this there has been substantial indirect financial assistance given by Government to private industry by way of tax concessions aimed at promoting investment such as double depreciation allowances, development rebates, and tax holidays. While it is not possible to give a quantitative estimate of this assistance, there can be no doubt about its substantial character as is seen by the comparatively low elasticity of tax contribution of the gross profits earned in the private industrial sector during the last ten years. It is surprising therefore to hear from time to time about the controversy on the public *versus* the private sector, with its implicit assumption that the public sector has been developing at the expense of the private sector. On the contrary, the bulk of the investment and current outlay incurred by Government during this period has been for the purpose of facilitating development in the private sector; and that this policy has also succeeded is amply borne out by the phenomenal increases in output and diversification that have taken place in the private sector in organised industry during this period....

The public sector itself has been active in the industrial field, besides creating economic and social overheads that benefit the development of both public and private industries. As I have said earlier, the public sector has, in recent years, especially during the Second Plan period, gone in for the direct development of some of the intermediate and basic industries necessary for the acceleration of industrial growth. Thus total public sector outlay on industries and minerals amounted to Rs.974 crores during this period; Rs.870 crores out of this was spent during the Second Plan period and amounted to 56% of the total investment in organised industry both public and private, during the period. Steel has been the major item in this activity; and also other heavy industries like heavy machine building plant, foundry-forge plant, heavy electrical project, coal mining machine plant, and machine tools; and basic industries like fertilisers, organic chemicals, aircraft, electronics, transport equipment, coal, lignite, oil and atomic energy. The share of the public sector in organised manufacturing industries is expected to increase from 2% on the eve of the First Plan to nearly 25% at the end of the Third Plan and in mineral production from 10% to about 34%....

This industrial development in the public and private sector has had perforce to lean heavily on imported supplies of machinery and equipment, and of basic and intermediate goods. Thus imports of capital goods increased in value from Rs.132 crores in 1950–51 to Rs.327 crores in 1960–61 or by 148%. Imports of intermediate goods increased from Rs.333 crores to Rs.503 crores or by 51% during the period. Imports of consumption goods increased from Rs.153 crores to Rs.200 crores or only 31%. The extent of foreign aid by way of both loans and grants used for the financing of development amounted to Rs.1631 crores during this period, in addition to withdrawal from our sterling balances of Rs.647 crores. In other words, to finance the essential imports required

for our economic development during the first ten years of planning our export earnings had to be supplemented by foreign funds to the tune of Rs.2278 crores. During the Third Plan period, it is expected that in addition to our export earnings, we will need at least Rs.3200 crores, which will still leave the economy with some underutilised capacity for want of maintenance imports and some shortfalls in investment for want of sufficient foreign exchange to get all the equipment needed for implementing the Plan targets. It may be interesting to note that the foreign exchange component of the investment contemplated in industry alone in both the public and private sectors during the Third Plan period amounts to Rs.1185 crores or 42% of the total outlay; and this is so in spite of the industrial development that has taken place during the Second Plan period in the field of basic and intermediate goods and of machinery and equipment. It is clear, therefore, that our industrial revolution has only commenced; and this impression is strengthened by the increasing dependence on maintenance imports during the Third Plan period for the full utilization of industrial capacity already created in the country. We have still a long way to go before we can call ourselves an industrialized country.

We may now pass on to the question of how far the industrial development that has taken place during the last ten years has resulted in the implementation of the social and economic objectives set out by the Planning Commission and in various statements of government policy that have been made during this period. There can be no doubt that the employment objectives set out in the Plan have not been fulfilled and to the extent that industrial development has formed the sheet anchor of this policy, our industrial revolution has not succeeded in its objective. As regards the overall position, the Planning

Commission have conceded that the employment targets of neither the First nor the Second Plan have been fulfilled and that the back-log of unemployed will stand at 9 million persons on the eve of the Third Plan, with unemployment having increased by 3.7 million during the Second Plan period....

The second objective laid down is a sufficient increase in the volume of basic consumption goods, to enable a rise in the common man's level of living during the Plan period. Here again, results achieved are disappointing from the point of view of the objective set out for achievement. We have already seen that the largest rises that have taken place are in the field of capital goods and intermediary goods and though this is a desirable feature from the growth standpoint, it does not fulfil the consumption objective in the short period. The grand strategy of the Second Plan which left the fulfilment of the consumption targets largely to small-scale and cottage industries has not succeeded; and among the consumption goods in the organised sector the output of which has recorded a significant rise during the period, basic necessities find but a small place. In fact, it is in the field of upper and middle class consumption goods and durable consumption goods which are largely beyond the reach of the masses that we find the most significant increases in industrial output. It appears that to the extent that organised industry in consumption goods—and this is almost wholly within the private sector—has recorded significant increases in output, it is the requirements of the U-sector and of the middle classes that are being met and not those of the masses. Whether this requires a reorientation of planned development in the consumption goods sector of organised industry is a question that has to occupy the attention of the planner, if he wants the industrial revolution now in progress in India to fulfil the objective of improving mass consumption levels within the Plan period.

A third objective set out in the Plan is reduction in inequality of incomes and in concentration of economic power.... From material already published and available to the public . . . it appears that there has been some increase in the concentration of economic power alongside India's industrial growth during this period. Growth appears to have been more in terms of both expansion and diversification in the case of the larger rather than the smaller units. Though this may not be uniformly true all along the industrial line, it appears to be true of the more significant sectors in industrial development. If this appearance is found to coincide with reality, it means that this is one more field in which India's industrial revolution has failed to keep pace with the social and economic objectives set out in the Plans. As regards inequality of income, material available is really inadequate for giving even a tentative answer; but if one can speak on an impressionistic basis, it appears that India's industrial growth during the last ten years is being accompanied by the emergence of a managerial and an entreprenurial class that is comparatively well off and is beginning to swell what may be called the U-sector among the Indian people. Whether this is desirable or not depends upon the view one takes of how far the monetary incentives at present employed in the acceleration of India's industrial growth are functionally necessary and constitute an inescapable economic price for eliciting the supplies needed of such managerial and entreprenurial personnel. The answer also depends upon the alternatives available, that will be both realistic of achievement and consistent with the fundamental ideals underlying our Constitution, our social philosophy and our spiritual values. I do not feel confident enough at this stage to venture an answer to these questions.

What is clear, however, from what I have said so far, is that it is not easy to go in for an industrial revolution and at the same time seek fulfilment of the social and economic objectives set out before the country, at any rate within the short period. Whether there is any fundamental conflict between the two which imposes the necessity of choice or whether there is a way of reconciling them and if so what sociological, psychological, institutional and other measures are necessary for this purpose are all questions I shall only raise without attempting to answer them at this stage.

Let me now pass on to a review of the industrial development of this decade from the point of view of the mistakes that have been made and the lessons they contain for the future. To begin with, there have been serious shortfalls in the industrial targets that were set out in the Second Plan. Thus the three new steel plants constructed during the Second Plan period still have their teething troubles and have contributed an additional output of only 0.6 million tons as against the targeted figure of 2 million tons. The other fertiliser plants in the public sector at Nangal, Neiveli, and Rourkela have all been delayed by one or two years, as has also the Heavy Electrical Project at Bhopal. The Heavy Machinery, the Mining Machinery and Foundry/Forge Project, which should by now have been quite advanced in their construction, are still in their initial stages; and instead of making a valuable contribution to the Third Plan will only begin to yield output at the end of it. Even the Tata Iron and Steel Company have failed to reach the output of saleable steel that was forecast for them in 1955 by the Tariff Commission. Shortfalls have occurred in the very industries which are of crucial importance from the point of view of

growth and thus deprived the economy of the benefits reckoned for the start of the Third Plan. Examples are paper and cement plant machinery, heavy castings and forgings, aluminum, newsprint, raw films, chemical pulp, soda ash, caustic soda, dyestuffs, and cement. Moreover, the actual cost of many of the projects has been much more than was originally estimated, the three steel plants alone having moved upward in their cost from an estimated Rs.425 crore to an actual Rs.620 crores. The overall investment in industry during the Second Plan period has gone up from Rs.1244 crores to Rs.1620 crores, in spite of which 30% increase, the physical targets achieved are only to the extent of 85 to 90%. Industry in the private sector has expanded no doubt; but in spite of licensing and controls, a part of this increase has been outside the Plan, a great deal of unutilised capacity has been created and maintenance imports have to be brought in increasing amounts for getting dividends from the investments made in this manner. Technical personnel of adequate quality are not available in sufficient number in spite of the vast increase in the facilities of technical education that have been created; and managerial talent of high calibre have begun indulging in the highly profitable game of merry-go-round, with the same persons rotating round an increasing number of increasingly profitable positions. The public sector has still to find its feet in the difficult art of economic administration under governmental constraints and audit restraints. Industrial planning in the public sector has still a long way to go in co-ordination, advance dove-tailing of supplies and requirements, technical competence, and timely production; while industry in the private sector has still to learn to act in a nationally planned framework and go in for maximum production, minimum cost and increasing reliance on domestic supplies. There is no doubt that

advance is taking place in the industrial field, but it cannot be described as a planned advance in the technical sense either in the public or in the private sector; and the problems that this creates do no credit to the philosophy of planned development.

It is a pity that we have not yet learnt the lesson that our industrial experience of the last ten years contains in such rich abundance. Thus the Third Plan talks of several projects which it has included in its overall estimates of cost as "being in very preliminary stages of formulation in respect of scope, processes, location, and other relevant particulars." Allocations fall far short of preliminary estimates in both the public and private sectors in industry and elicit the open admission that the physical targets postulated in the Third Plan are not likely to be achieved at the end of the Plan period. The Planning Commission go on to add that "it is difficult to forecast with any degree of accuracy which projects will get delayed and spill-over into the Fourth Plan and which of the physical targets will not be achieved." And this is in the context of a planned economy and in the eleventh year of planned development. Even the overall determinants of growth, which are so crucial for the implementation of individual industry targets, do not seem to be planned sufficiently either in terms of adequacy or timeliness or location, so that in the very first year of the Third Plan the air is heavy with the cry of shortages of power, fuel and transport. Resources raised are not adequate; and even the resources which are actually raised do not seem to be suffering from optimal utilisation. And then there is the dreaded problem of unemployment and with it the question of choice of techniques, the release of productive energy in a nationally dispersed manner, and balanced regional development. There is also the allied problem of the economics and

ethics as also the sociology of a dual society. The price to be paid for industrialisation is very high indeed, and we have not yet learnt either to assess its extent or find remedies for reconciling it with our established social and value objectives.

3.5 INDIAN PROGRAMMING TECHNIQUES *

To begin with, it will be useful to straighten out three questions of terminology. Each involves a pair of concepts that can helpfully be distinguished in one's analysis of the Indian—or of any other—central economic planning process. But in each case analysts often talk as though the contrast between the two concepts were greater than it really is.

First, there is the difference between *plans* and *planning*. Nearly everyone would agree that Indian planning is most significantly viewed as a continuing decision-making process, not just as an intermittent production of certain blueprints or documents. Yet the "plans" per se are, after all, nothing but the decisions that the process yields. The issue that those who emphasize this distinction actually are trying to get at is that of the rhythm of the process. In order to allow for the long lead times on many items, to keep planning problems manageably simple, and to economize a country's limited skills and energies for planning itself, it has become customary to program national development efforts in three-, five-, seven-, or other multi-year chunks. However, this sensible procedure can backfire if, by attaching an artificial importance to the economy's five-year (or three- or seven-year) accomplishment, it causes planners to ignore intra-period changes or the need for smooth transitions from the late Second-Plan years to the first Third-Plan years, and so on.

* From John P. Lewis, *Quiet Crisis in India*, Brookings Institution, 1962, pp. 116-29, 135-6. Reprinted by permission.

Indian planning never has been totally at the mercy of this kind of astigmatism. In principle the once-every-five-years exercises have never been regarded as more than major stock-takings and reformulations of a longer-term program that is subject meanwhile to constant review and frequent (usually year-by-year) revision and reauthentication. Nevertheless, as we shall see, Indian planning has displayed some unnecessary jerkiness in its inter-Plan and intra-Plan phasing of expansion projects.

Second, in trying to make sense of a planning process, it often is helpful to distinguish between issues of *technique* and those of *administration*. In what follows I shall frequently have occasion to point, on the one hand, to technical considerations that arise out of the planners' underlying economic models or out of the types of analysis they use for particularizing the strategies emerging from such models, or that concern the statistical limitations under which they work. On the other hand, we shall encounter problems that seem to be essentially matters of bureaucratic, political, and/or constitutional structure and relationship. Yet what is striking in the Indian case, I think, is the extent to which we shall find these two procedural strands of the planning process intertwined. Virtually all of the difficulties are ones to which *both* technical and administrative factors contribute. When we talk about problems of planning "technique," we are talking usually about the way issues tend to shape themselves for economist-type planners, whereas the administrative and organizational specialists view the same issues in terms of their own training and experience. Both types of specialists are needed in an effective planning organization, but their concerns are very much of a piece.

Finally, there is the alleged contrast between *planning* and *implementation*. It is convenient to draw a distinction, as I have a number of times in these pages, between development planning and development administration, and it may even have a certain impressionistic validity to say, as I have, that the "Indians are better planners than doers." But, it must be emphasized, no conclusive evaluation of a government's planning can be made in isolation from the quality of its administration. Moreover, this is not just because the pragmatic test of any plan is the action to which it gives rise. The fact is that "planning" and "implementation" are parts of the very same continuum. They are loosely assigned labels for different ranges of the same decision-making process. Seen in one of its dimensions, that process can be graded from general to specific. Typically, we call decision making at one end of this spectrum "planning" and at the other end, "implementation," but in many ways it is the intermediate range of the spectrum that is the most interesting. It makes not the slightest difference whether these intermediate decisions are called "detailed planning" or "(broad) plan implementation," but it means everything to the planning-*cum*-implementation process that they be made in timely and cogent fashion.

This last point is as apposite as any for indicating what this chapter undertakes to add to the present critique of the Indian economic development effort. To appraise the serviceability of the Indian planning process it is not sufficient to conclude, as I have, that the general development strategy emerging from it, while inviting amendment, is on balance eminently worthy of support. For if the strategy is to be made good, it must be connected to specific operational decisions by more detailed kinds of planning. And in the Indian case it is precisely in the realm of such implementational planning that there is the greatest room for improvement.

The issue of comprehensiveness and internal consistency In a sense the government of India made its choice once and for all between "piecemeal," or project-by-project, economic planning and "comprehensive" planning back at the beginning of the fifties, when it committed itself to the pursuit of a series of over-all development plans and set up a permanent Planning Commission to provide the central staffing for the effort. However, government's commitment to comprehensive planning meant little as long as such planning consisted simply of assembling a collection of state and ministerial projects that had few requirements for internal consistency other than that the sum of the outlays on particular projects should add up to the total stipulated cost of the program. The First Five Year Plan followed traditional government budgeting practice in this sense; it was a collection of discrete projects with very little interdependence. The major ministries of the government instinctively favored such a planning approach; they were jealous of the new Planning Commission's potential encroachment on their decision-making prerogatives; and, thanks partly to the fact that the Commission's only members of political stature other than its chairman (the Prime Minister) were the ministers of these same line ministries, the latter were able to hold the Commission to a fairly modest role during the early fifties — even though it had accumulated a substantial full-time staff.

The great procedural achievement of Indian planning during the period when the Second Five Year Plan was being formulated was, I think, establishment of the principle of the central importance of internal consistency in development design. Under the aggressive intellectual leadership of a few key planning technicians (notably Professor P. C. Mahalanobis) and with the active personal support of the Prime Minister, it came to be accepted that traditional budgeting practice was an extremely bad procedural model for those major portions of the planning problem that required the balancing of goals and particular expansion programs, of outputs and inputs, of the output of one industry with those of others, and of many variables through time. Here internal consistency was of the essence, and here, it was therefore recognized in principle, the traditional budgetary practice of leaving the initiation of program design entirely to the operating agencies would not work. Instead, if planning were to be coherent, yet not infernally tedious, the initial design would have to be formulated by a central group that viewed the economy as a whole — and then, of course, tested, modified, and recast its scheme in consultation with the operating agencies before submitting the whole program for political approval.

In principle, India has not wavered from this essential planning postulate since 1955. But for reasons that we shall next examine, it achieved only highly imperfect application during the Second-Plan period, and there is still reason to doubt the effectiveness with which it is being and will be implemented during the Third Plan.

Second-plan and Third-plan programming techniques In formulating the Second Five Year Plan and during most of the period of that Plan India's central development designers fell far short of fully carrying out the mandate for internally consistent programming. The Second-Plan exercise did start with the development of a so-called "plan-frame" that, for a preliminary document of that period, was a cogent piece of central design work. Nevertheless, the plan-frame itself was sketchy. For example, it and the early chapters of the Second-Plan document that were fashioned after it still, like the First-Plan window dressings before them, placed major reliance upon operationally meaningless and purely notional projections of the economy's over-all capital-output ratio. In many instances the connections between the general Plan framework set forth at the beginning of the Second-Plan document and the more specific industry and sector chapters that filled up the bulk of the book were tenuous; a number of the latter still had the look of piecemeal agency programs.

Worst of all, the phasing of the expansion programs during the latter half of the fifties was highly unsatisfactory. Planners tried to do their decision-making too much in a single five-year lump. Perhaps the worst aberration was in the area of private investment, where the entire five-year allocation of foreign exchange for this sector was made available at once. When, to everyone's dismay, private investors proceeded to use up the bulk of this ration in the first two years of the Plan period, the result was the well-known foreign-exchange crisis of 1957–58 and a consequent foreign-exchange stringency that continued to impede, not only further expansion, but current production in many industries during the balance of the Plan period.

Phasing was highly imperfect also in the public sector, where very little provision was made for those projects that would need to be started in the late Second-Plan years and completed early in the Third Plan if a steady thrust of expansion from Plan to Plan was to be maintained. Moreover, as the Second Plan unfolded, many temporary interindustry inconsistencies developed. Cement capacity was installed considerably before there was a need for it. Steel lagged badly and coal and coal washeries, even worse. There were other similar difficulties. Some of these, of course, were the result of engineering problems and other physical difficulties

that could not have been foreseen. But much of the trouble was chargeable to bad detailed planning.

The spotty procedural record of the Second Plan reflected a weakness of programming technique. We have already noted that the excessive deference shown by the Indian planners to orthodox Western saving-centered development theory has tended to curb the boldness of their efforts to activate idle resources. I have argued, however, that India's main production strategy has in fact, despite its saving-centered pretenses, fortunately been foreign-exchange-centered. But now we come to another charge that must be chalked up against the Second Plan's saving-centered orthodoxy. For, while the latter did not particularly impair the production strategy, it did impair the planners' technical implementation of that strategy in two ways.

In the first place, orthodox theory lured the planners into what was, for the time being at least, a technical blind alley. It suggested that the proper analytical sequence for particularizing the production program was first to determine the volume of total (unspecified) investment to be undertaken in the Plan period and only thereafter to go on to the question of investment allocation. And when the working programmer did move on to this "subsidiary" (but, as a practical matter, all-important) question of program composition, orthodox development economics of the time had only an exceptionally arid, abstract literature on "investment-choice criteria" to offer him. Since 1955 that literature has been considerably enriched. We now have had sophisticated endorsements of "social marginal product" as the best ground for investment choice, alternative advocacy of attention to the varying "re-investment quotients" of different projects, fresh emphasis on the applicability of refined benefit-cost calculations, and, from the burgeoning field of mathematical economics, some promising speculations about the possibilities of applying linear programming and other relatively sophisticated quantitative techniques to the investment-choice problem.

Nevertheless, I would make the considered (although herein unsupported) assertion that, even today, none of the standard theory on the criteria for investment choice offers a serviceable *primary* technique, given the present and near-term availabilities of economic data in India, for determining the commodity and industry composition of the Indian expansion program. The best of the orthodox theorizing offers the Indian planner some helpful hints, but still no directive guidance. In 1955–56 the hints were even less helpful, and the designers of the Second Plan, after fumbling a bit, simply stopped short of attempting to make explicit linkages between their aggregative plan and the specific investment (or project) choices along the route that conventional development theory seemed to indicate.

In the second place, the homage that the designers of the Second Plan paid to inappropriate theories was partly to blame, I think, for their failure fully to exploit the availability of an alternative, less elegant, but far more workable, technique for linking up specific projects with general expansion goals. This was implicit in the foreign-exchange-pivoting production strategy that, theory aside, they were in fact evolving. It was the technique of "planning backward" from final demand targets, which becomes usable *if* it can be assumed that, by a target year, the economy's production mix should match its consumption or end-use mix quite closely.

The "planning-backward" procedure consists first in establishing a set of broad final-demand goals indicating the magnitudes of general government services, of public-sector and private-sector current capital formation, and of personal consumption (in the light of the predicted volume of disposable personal income) that can be expected to fit within the economy's expanded real income that is being projected for the target year. Second, these broad demand goals can be broken down into sufficient commodity or commodity-group detail (for example, through the use of studies of income-elasticities of consumers' demand for food-grains, cotton cloth, and various categories of consumer hardware, and other studies of the typical construction-versus-equipment breakdown of different categories of investment) to establish a serviceable array of final-product output targets for the Plan period. Third, calculations can be made of the outputs of primary and intermediate products that should be available for supplying the requirements of final-goods production. Fourth, once the whole array of output targets is compared with existing capacities, planners can identify those expansion projects (and their several inputs, including particular-investment requirements) that are needed to bring particular industrial capacities up to the targets. And then finally planning backward, the planners can work out the specific phasings required to keep the whole process in concert and on schedule.

Now the foregoing, of course, is a dangerously oversimplified statement of procedure, even for our purposes; no satisfactory programming analysis can be quite as streamlined or one-directional as the one just described. At each of the analytical steps indicated the tentative results must be cross-checked for their physical and financial feasibility, and when this is done, modifications at other, logically prior steps in the analysis frequently will be indicated. Thus, even if it is exclusively of the type I have suggested, programming analysis is more likely to follow a round of successive approximations than a straight line from firm goals to firm particular-industry requirements. Furthermore, practical planning inevitably requires a combination of analytical approaches. At the time of any given planning exercise, for example, there always are some unfinished expansion projects to which heavy commitments of resources have already been made, and almost invariably, whatever the new final-demand projections of the planners are, the opportunity costs of not finishing these projects as quickly as possible will exceed the costs of so doing. Moreover, there are always a certain number of multi-purpose infrastructure and basic industry installations that so plainly will be needed by just about any conceivable pattern of expanded production that they can sensibly be pushed before many of the details of a comprehensive production program have been worked out. Thus there must in practice be certain kinds of specific *ad hoc* planning and some "planning forward" from existing capacities and existing uncompleted projects as well as the planning backward from final-demand targets.

Granting all of this, it nevertheless seems to me that, when it came to choosing the general technique for Indian programming, the planning-backward approach was the one really practical one that the Indian planners had available for achieving an effective marriage between aggregative and detailed planning. As we have seen, the technique's basic objective (to minimize imports) was highly appropriate in the Indian case. It would not be sensible or desirable, of course, to seek absolute self-sufficiency. But the Indian economy's need and potentialities for import substitution were great enough that it was possible to expand the outlined programming analysis to allow on the one hand, for the omission from the production program of imports for which there are no substitutes and, on the other hand, for the addition to it of projectible exports without seriously undermining the production guidance that the final-demand projections could afford. Moreover, the series of quantitative estimates required by this approach — of final-demand goals, of the latter's commodity composition coarsely broken down, of the requirements for primary and intermediate products by major commodity groups, and of the investment and other major inputs required for different industrial categories—were within potential reach of Indian technical skills and Indian statistics. While none of these needed estimates could be formulated with sufficient refinement to suit the taste of an economist who chose the role of a skeptic, it was possible for the Indians to generate serviceable data at each of these programming steps.

But now we come to the rub as far as Second-Plan design was concerned. It was *possible,* I say, to do a reasonably good job of planning backward from final-demand targets. But it was not easy; many of the data required were not ready-made. In particular, two kinds of data gaps needed filling: First, quite obviously, the approach did call for explicit formulation of final-demand targets, and this could not readily be done in the absence of a historical series of final-demand estimates to serve as a base for the projections. Curiously enough, official Indian national income statistics included no such series. There was a related need, moreover, for income-elasticity and other studies to be used in developing a commodity breakdown of final demand, and these too India in the mid-fifties largely lacked. Second, and basically more formidable, there was an urgent need for a great mass of technical-coefficient data showing what kinds of inputs were required for producing what outputs—how much steel and cement per average unit of industrial construction, how much machinery and electricity per ton of cement, and so on. Such data were essential for translating requirements for finished goods into requirements for unfinished goods and for converting all output requirements into investment and other input requirements.

The basic technical shortcoming of Indian planners at the time the Second Plan was formulated was their failure to bestir themselves very actively to fill these data gaps that inhibited the spelling out of a final-demand-oriented production program. It may be argued, of course, that the planners at this juncture simply did not have enough time to get much accomplished in this respect. However, I suspect that the fact that the planning-backward approach had little respectability in the eyes of orthodox development theorists accounts to a considerable degree for the data gaps.

The Second Plan's lack of explicit final-demand estimates and of a comprehensive array of technical coefficient data did not, as we have seen, prevent the mounting of a production program that was more faithful than not to the import-substitution strategy. Demand projections were used in setting a number of particular-commodity output targets, and, on the whole, the planners showed a pretty good intuitive sense of what the shape of target-year final demand should be. But by failing to project and publicize a set of final demand goals the planners robbed themselves of the most cogent justification that could be offered for the mixed bag of primary-, intermediate-, and final-goods targets they postulated; by failing to assemble an adequate array of data on inter-industry requirements, they stumbled into some of the bottleneck problems already noted; and by failing fully to exploit the planning-backward approach, they passed up the best available defense against the phas-

ing errors by which they were subsequently haunted.

By the time the Third Five Year Plan was formulated Indian planning had undergone an inconspicuous but important transition in these respects. Throughout the formulation period and in the final Third-Plan document itself...the Planning Commission persisted in its curious, passively stubborn refusal to present any formal statement of even moderately detailed final-demand goals. Yet I can attest that this time most of the "mixed bag" of commodity output targets were related to final-demand models, not just intuitively, but by explicit calculations contained in some of the Planning Commission's unpublished working papers. Moreover, during the interim there had been a significant accumulation of income-elasticity and other studies that could facilitate the projection of particular final-product categories. Most important of all, the government had acquired a formidable collection of technical coefficient data, thanks mainly to the initiative taken by Pitambar Pant, Chief of the Planning Commission's Perspective Planning Division. These data, as I have noted in another connection already, were, and had to be, assembled catch-as-catch-can. They are of an uneven quality, and there was no assurance that the various technologies they reflected were the appropriate ones for India to pursue. Nevertheless, Pant's tireless effort to assemble these nuts and bolts data and his incitement of the government's operating wings to check and refine them created the opportunity, more than did any other one thing, for Third-Plan programming to be an internally consistent exercise.

These are encouraging developments, and, on the whole, Indian planning seems to be on the way to making good their promise. However, there is still cause for concern about technical problems, particularly over the crucial matter of phasing.[1] This is a particularly slippery subject to judge from afar or through the reading of official documents. However, the last time I saw Indian planning first-hand, in the early summer of 1960, the Third-Plan projections of specific industry growth still, in many cases, were not based on realistic estimates of what the actual (as opposed to targeted) Second-Plan accomplishment would be; the Third-Plan goals had not been broken down into any series of closely calculated *annual* national income, industrial output, and foreign-exchange balances; the majority of the major industrial projects proposed generally for the early years of the Third Plan, had not had their design, contracting, manpower, investment, and import-requirement phasing worked out; and there was serious question still whether the Plan made sufficient provision in its later years for enough Fourth-Plan starts to maintain a steady thrust of expansion into the succeeding period.

While the final Third-Plan document includes some emphatic language, as well as some evidence, indicating a determination to eradicate this sort of programming fuzziness, I think it is fair to conclude that the radical improvement in Indian programming techniques that had been under way for the previous five years had not yet been fully consolidated at the time of the Third Plan's adoption. There was still room for a more explicit recognition of the merits of the planning-backward approach, and there was still need, as a means of implementing that approach, for an explicit formulation of final-demand targets.[2]

1. See W. B. Reddaway, "Importance of Time Lags for Economic Planning," *Economic Weekly* (Bombay), Annual Number (January 1960), and "Phasing a Development Plan," Special Number (June 1960).

2. In the course of drafting this section I have

Administrative impediments to the marshaling of facts Indian economic statistics are better than those of many economically underdeveloped countries, and there are instances—notably that of the technical coefficient data already cited—where

felt a growing desire to address a conciliatory (if not self-protective) aside to those fellow economists who may have been irritated by my failure, in explaining and advocating the planning-backward approach, to re-emphasize certain programming complications that already have been recognized in earlier chapters. These include the facts (1) that relative commodity and factor prices are sure to change during the course of the development effort, (2) that even within the restraints imposed by a foreign-exchange-economizing strategy, there is room for choosing between readily substitutable products with different input requirements, and (3) that there is also room, in the case of some particular products, for choosing among alternative technologies. It may be asked, how does the planning-backward approach take care of these issues? The answer is that, while it has no special magic for resolving them, as a general programming technique, it can readily incorporate into its analytical pattern any particular solutions to these problems that may be devised. For example, as fast as the opportunities for technological choice and for limited product choice are recognized, the planning-backward approach can adopt the same procedure that already has been suggested in the case of produce-or-import decisions: In spelling out the output-target and input-requirement implications of the final demand goals, it can make its process choices and its product choices on a comparative-cost basis. Throughout its analysis it can make more general use of "shadow prices"—for example, in the case of domestic labor and capital as well as of foreign exchange—if this is deemed appropriate. If acceptable forecasts of (actual) relative price changes become available, these can be incorporated into its projections, and if serviceable estimates of the price elasticities of the demand for particular products also become available, there can be consequent adjustments in the real composition of the projections. In short, the planning-backward approach can encompass all of these refinements or—at worst—none of them. But meanwhile, whatever its degree of sophistication in these respects, it is the one approach that provides the working planner with a way of getting on with his principal, immediate job—which is to come up quickly, and to keep coming up, with comprehensive, presumptively consistent, sets of program numbers that are sufficiently detailed to supply firing-line decision makers with serviceable operating instructions....

planners have shown great initiative in assembling the empirical information they need. However, there still are surprising gaps in the national income estimates when one considers that national income accounting and national-income-oriented economic planning both are more than ten years old in India. The country at this writing still has no official historical series on final demand. Even the available estimates of investment are exceptionally weak and sketchy. And planners have been led into the very risky practice of working out their whole quantitative program in a net-national-income rather than a gross-national-product frame (thereby submerging the problem of replacement investment) by Indian national income accounting's perverse failure yet to supply any regular series of historical estimates of the gross national product. There are a good many comparable examples, outside the national income field, of serious deficiencies in the current economic series. There is no reason, for example, for the between-censuses manpower data to be as generally weak as they are — even after allowance is made for the conceptual difficulties encountered in measuring labor idleness. All in all, it is fair to say that the development of statistics in India has fallen well short of the potential in view of the fact that, in terms of advanced theoretical statistical competence, India may well be the most richly endowed country in the world.

Moreover, these gaps and soft spots in the published economic series are paralleled by a failure on the part of Indian planners generally to marshal as much solid *ad hoc* empirical detail as they readily could use. Many of the top officials, while competent and diligent themselves, seem to be insufficiently aggressive in driving their own staffs, or the staffs in the operating ministries, to prepare needed pieces of information and analysis in time to gear into the general planning exercise.

Instead of forcing determined and imaginative assaults on the informational barriers, many key officials spend long hours reasoning and speculating their way around them.

Furthermore, the arrangements for injecting technological expertise into the planning process are less than ideal. Some, but not much, of this difficulty may be the one, usual in an underdeveloped economy, of simply not having enough technically-trained people. Most of India's problem in this regard has been instead first, a failure to distinguish clearly those issues in development design that should be left essentially to decision by professionally trained specialists instead of being submitted for independent decision (and not just authentication) to the bureaucratic-political process; and second, a failure to seat cadres of the best available specialists within the government, or to attach them to it, in such fashion that when appropriate matters of development design are referred to them, they can make themselves heard through the muffling of administrative layers and channels.

Conclusions The Indian system of planning and plan-implementation is an admirable, indeed a remarkably good, one for any country with a per capita income of less than one hundred dollars a year. It is an experienced, sophisticated system of high average integrity. But it is also highly susceptible of improvement. In the realm of programming techniques, the Indian planners (encumbered no little by inappropriate economic theories learned mostly from the West) have been groping their way toward a serviceable set of procedures for spelling out a comprehensive, internally consistent production program that is well enough articulated both cross-sectionally and chronologically to be truly implementable. But there are still a number of statistical gaps to be filled, analytical techniques and administrative practices to be sharpened up, and political reinforcements to be provided before the battle for cohesive planning will have been clearly won.

Of the battle for vital planning and administration, much more yet remains to be fought. Indian planning as a whole has tended to be too cautious, too afraid of making mistakes, too little animated with an uncompromising determination to activate idle resources. It still looks too much like what it is — the progeny of an administrative system dedicated to the prevention of wrongdoing rather than to the marshalling and energizing of "rightdoing."

From the viewpoint of American policymaking toward India, there need be nothing fundamentally discouraging about these conclusions, to which many Indian planners candidly agree, off the record. The diagnosis should be essentially encouraging because it not only finds the system improvable—and improving—but probably effective enough as it stands to manage much of the development tasks it has set itself. However, it would be foolish policy for the United States to expect the present Indian system to economize perfectly either resources or time. And it would be irresponsible policy on the part of the United States government—or any other concerned outsider—not to do whatever it appropriately can to assist and encourage specific improvements in Indian planning and plan-implementing procedures.

3.6 THE STRATEGY OF INDIAN PLANNED DEVELOPMENT *

In spite of poverty and malnutrition, severe underemployment, and the gathering threat of open urban unemployment,

* From I. M. D. Little, "The Third Five Year Plan and the Strategy of Indian Development," *The Economic Weekly,* Bombay, Special Number, June 1960, pp. 885-92. Reprinted by permission.

it cannot be easily assumed that the overriding objective of the Third Five Year Plan should be to increase consumption, or employment. India's growth in the past few years has been heavily dependent on foreign aid (and reduced reserves). This will continue to be true for at least the next 10 years, but it cannot go on forever. Consequently, India must also plan to develop and strengthen her economy in such a way that she can both rectify her severe foreign exchange deficit, and at the same time either make or buy the much larger quantities of capital goods which will undeniably be required to sustain a continued process of expansion.... So the Third Plan must be seen in the context of the Fourth Plan at least. Theoretically, indeed, there is no time horizon beyond which the planner does not need to try to peer; but the end of the Fourth Plan will do to be getting on with.

The more or less official aims of the Government, and its implied choice between the conflicting demands of the present and the future, are known. It is hoped to balance foreign payments without aid by 1970, with a rate of net investment of around 16 per cent of net national income. At present the rate of investment is probably only 10 per cent, with only $7\frac{1}{2}$ per cent financed from domestic savings. By 1965–66 it is hoped that investment may have risen to 14 per cent, about 12 per cent being domestically financed. These figures are thought to be consistent with investment of Rs.9,950 crores in the Third Plan, and of Rs.15,000 crores in the Fourth Plan [1 crore is approximately equal to $2 million]. Thus it is hoped that the proportion of national income invested and financed by domestic savings can double in the next ten years.

The strain which this achievement would impose depends greatly on the rate of growth of output and income. Provided that income grows at 5 per cent or more, these targets can be attained or surpassed if consumption grows by one percentage point less than income. Put like that, the task appears manageable—for consumption per head would be growing at least as fast as in the past. In effect the idea is to invest most of the proceeds of the hoped for increase in the growth rate. To achieve this the marginal rate at which current income is ploughed back would need to be high— about 25 per cent. There is no possibility of this being achieved without increases in taxation which would be remarkable in the light of the recent past, although the resultant rates still need not be high by the standards of many other countries. But if output fails to rise by 5 per cent per annum it would be difficult to increase investment to the extent indicated, and the hope of an adequate, self-sufficient, and soundly based, growth by 1970 would probably have to be abandoned.

The above ideas have changed little since the beginning of the Second Plan. But success to date has been less than anticipated. Thus real National Income has been rising at only about 3 per cent per annum, or a little more. As a result, the development envisaged in 1955–56 in terms of 1952–53 rupees remains roughly the same in terms of 1957–58 rupees. This means that the anticipated levels of income and investment, while bearing approximately the same relation to each other, are really lower by 10–15 per cent.

Allowing for the change in prices (and an apparent change in the coverage of private investment included) the Third Plan is probably less than 50 per cent larger than the actual achievement of the Second Plan, and is about 20 per cent smaller than was originally envisaged. It is certainly inadequate to the needs of the situation. Even if as successful as hoped, the standard of living will rise only slowly from its desperately low level, and it can make no great impact on the problem of underemployment. Moreover, if much more attention were successfully paid to consumption and employment within the framework of a Plan of this size, then India would probably remain relatively as heavily dependent on foreign assistance as before. The question naturally arises as to whether the Third Plan could not be bigger, and aim at larger increase in all the three key magnitudes, investment, consumption, and employment....

It is sometimes thought that there is no potential inflation barrier in the way of putting idle hands to work, because agricultural production (and well over half India's personal consumption comes from agriculture) would quickly increase. But this is a mistake, for the men employed on land improvement schemes must be paid and any extra output, however quickly it materializes (and in fact there must be a lag) will add to agricultural incomes as well as to output, so that the extra output is an offset only to the extent that farmers save more of their higher incomes. Thus the ability or willingness to tax provides a limit, not merely to the size of the Plan, but to the amount of extra employment it can create. A larger Plan with less employment may put less strain on the fiscal system and on a politician's courage than a smaller, more labour intensive Plan.

To put it in another way, if the future growth path of consumption is as planned, then greater employment than at present planned will mean that this consumption must be more evenly spread. The limitation on possible employment results from unwillingness or inability to redistribute consumption sufficiently in favour of the newly or more intensively employed men. This is the barrier round which many believe that China has found a way.

To turn to organization, this can also provide a limitation which might bite before the fiscal difficulty referred to above. My impression is that it is the latter that is now operative. Some disagreement has been reported between the Ministry of Agriculture and the Planning Commission over the agricultural allocation for the Third Plan. This may suggest that the former believes that it could usefully spend more. India has many monuments to the power of unassisted labour in the shape not only of vast forts and palaces, but also canals and railways. Of course, more is needed than merely recruiting large numbers of men, and setting them to work, if the result is to be as productive as it might be. But I guess that agricultural and other departments have the skill to organize more work than is planned....

Owing to the present very small size of the capital goods industry, and of the production of intermediate goods, programmes of industrial development result in a rapidly rising level of imports. More domestic savings can help to finance such programmes only to the extent that consumption good imports can be reduced, or exports expanded as a result of lower consumption at home. Analysis of the pattern of Indian imports and exports suggests that the possibilities of this are very limited....

More savings and less consumption at home could therefore have only a slight impact on India's balance of payments in the next five years, provided that there is no greater tendency to excess demand than in recent years. This would be false only if deflation were carried so far that output in Indian industry was reduced, with a fall in the need for imported materials and semi-manufactures. Obviously this is an absurdity which must be avoided.

Thus foreign aid is an effective limitation on the size of the Plan, except insofar as it is possible to reshape the Plan to use fewer imports of capital equipment for every rupee spent....

What part must foreign savings play in the Third Plan? It appears that the planners expect to need Rs.2,100 crores of aid, inclusive of private capital, but excluding any refinancing and PL 480. The latter two items may each add about Rs.500 crores making a total gross call on foreign resources of Rs.3,100 crores and a net call of Rs.2,600 crores. If realized, this would imply that foreign savings would be financing rather over one quarter of Indian investment as compared with rather less than one third last time.

Taking the Third Plan for granted, the foreign aid requirements can be estimated only from realistic predictions of imports and exports. I think the estimates are likely to be much nearer the mark this time. But imports in particular are extremely hard to predict, depending as they do not only on the import content of new projects but also on the whole development of Indian output (the more successful the output growth the greater the import saving). The above figures for aid imply an average deficit on current account, including interest on loans already contracted, of about Rs.500 crores. This compares with figures of 352, 509, 380 for 1956–57, 1957–58 and 1958–59. . . .

Turning to the developing pattern of demand, first consider consumption goods. Well over half of consumption (in 1952 it was probably about 60 per cent) is food. Food-grains are about two-thirds of food consumption, and I gather that the target will probably end up as 100–105 million tons (around 5 per cent per annum) against 73½ million tons in 1958–59—an increase of 36–43 per cent compared with an expected increase in total consumption of about 30 per cent (4 per cent per annum for seven years). PL 480 imports will continue, but even if they are 1–2 million tons less, it is difficult to see that people will eat so much—for, assuming other food production goes up at least *pari passu*, it would mean increasing the proportion of food eaten as income rises, contrary to all observation. This could come about only as a result of a large relative fall in food prices; or a large redistribution of consumption to the very poor or both. Both may happen to some extent—but my guess would be that the price shift, to get so much food eaten, would need to be disturbingly large, unless there is a much greater increase in non-farm employment than seems to be planned.

This is the corollary of the point made earlier; i.e., that greater employment requires a more even spread of consumption. Since the poor spend more of their incomes on food, the present target for food production is reconcilable with the implied target for total consumption only if consumption is more evenly spread; and this could best be brought about by greater employment, and higher taxation of those who spend a relatively high proportion of their incomes on non-food items....

The determination of the planned output-shape of the Second, Third and Fourth Plans can be summed up as follows. First, there is the aim to produce enough food, together with sufficient other agricultural output to provide those raw materials and exports which can be produced in India (tea, cotton, jute, coffee, etc.). No one doubts the importance of this; and no one could possibly argue that the targets are generally inadequate.

Secondly, there is the need to produce sufficient of the "non-importables," electricity, transport, and communications. These three will have accounted for almost half the public investment achieved in the Second Plan, in spite of which the supply has been inadequate. Expenditure on them is planned to rise by 35 per cent in the Third Plan, though the proportion will fall—due probably to the completion of some of the most expensive parts of the railway programme.

Thirdly, the remainder of the available investment (and this remainder is limited by the foreign aid to be received) is and will be primarily devoted to import substitution. In the Second Plan the three steel plants will have formed much the largest element of import-substitution (about 15 per cent of public investment) so that steel imports will be much lower in the Third Plan period. The major emphasis in industrial expansion will shift to fertilizers and machinery making in the Third Plan. So that the forthcoming rapid rise in machinery imports will level off or might actually fall by the end of the Fourth Plan period (towards 1970).

There is also an increasing realization of the need for building up exports. But little public investment goes into it. It seems to me that this is perfectly correct, and that it would be folly not to put the main emphasis on non-importables and import substitution, if only because there is no doubt about the demand being there.

The most common criticism of Indian planning is that it has been, and will be, too much orientated towards heavy industry. It is true that agricultural production failed to rise fast enough in the Second Plan period. But it is being wise after the event to say that therefore more attention should have been paid to it. Also it does not follow from the relative failure of output that there should have been more direct investment in it. Probably the surest way to have increased output more would have been to have more heavy industry in the shape of more fertilizer plants. The argument for more direct investment in agriculture should be more solidly based on the possibility of mobilizing the surplus labour potential.

Apart from food and agricultural materials, it has been seen above that what India most needs is the products of mining and heavy industry—steel, electricity, coal, heavy chemicals, cement, oil, etc. Who can seriously suggest that she ought to import these things — especially when in some of them at least (coal, steel) she has a marked comparative advantage in the cheapness of the raw materials? Yet she cannot plan to produce all she needs of everything. There is some choice within the field of import substitution: and here the argument in favour of low capital intensity should probably be kept more to the forefront than it has been.

The broad strategy of Indian planned development seems eminently sound. The Third Plan is part of a series designed to raise the proportion of investment in a rising National Income, and reduce and eventually eliminate that part financed by foreign savings. One cannot quarrel with this aim, and scarcely anyone who has studied the problem doubts that it involves a rapid increase in industrialization, involving the building up of heavy industry roughly on the scale planned. There is room for argument only at the margin.

The chief doubt is whether India uses enough of her own resources, and whether she gets enough out of her investment. There seems to have been insufficient effort to solve the problem of putting idle hands to work. Naturally this is a difficult administrative as well as a more narrowly economic problem. Speaking only of the latter, I believe that fear of inflation has been a barrier to greater employment, and hence more output, and that greater willingness to tax (and also to stop wage increases for those already employed) would pave the way for significantly more employment and higher output. India should certainly use all the foreign resources she can get: so that a more full utilization of Indian resources would require a larger Plan than the Third Plan if the aid now hoped for is forthcoming. This, I believe, to be not merely within the real limitations of the Indian economy, but also, with sufficient determination, to be possible of achievement without inflation. If India gets less foreign aid than she

expects, then the industrial part of the Plan would probably have to be cut: but I believe the Plan could be enlarged in other directions to provide at least a partial offset to the loss.

Getting more out of any given investment programme is largely a matter of commercial skill and good administration at all levels. On this I have nothing to say. But economic coherence is also important. It is important to have a sensible pricing policy. It is important to produce enough non-importables, so that production is not held up by bottlenecks. It is important to select the right things to produce more of in India, and not to produce too much of them, and so on. All of this requires difficult and interlocking estimates of demand, but also, if output is to be maximized with limited capital, it requires close attention to problems of phasing and to the problem of optimum resource allocation. Since economic decisions have to be, in practice, largely guided by actual costs and returns, this latter suggests an enquiry into how prices can be made to reflect scarcities whenever possible—and where not, how some rational and consistent bias can be introduced at planning levels. Although some attention is paid to these problems I doubt whether it is sufficient—and certainly adequate attention is not paid to the information required for good coherent planning. Lack of good statistics is not an altogether minor limitation on the detailed soundness of Indian Plans.

But, whatever criticism may be made, it is reasonable to hope for better results from the Third Plan than the Second. Experience of planning and economic administration has increased: and I believe that more realistic and better work has gone into the formulation of the Third Plan. There is a good chance that an urgently needed increase in the tempo of development will be achieved.

4. THE STATE OF DEVELOPMENT PLANNING—NOTE

Although it is readily understandable that national economic planning should appeal to the governments of newly developing countries, the actual accomplishments of development planning have, with a rare exception, failed to fulfill original expectations. The difficulties of planning have only too often been underestimated, and the anticipated results have been overestimated. Development planning in practice has clearly revealed a need to improve upon its formulation and implementation.

During the first plan-period in many countries, the so-called "plan" was simply a list of projects on which the government proposed to spend its financial resources—at most, a public capital expenditure program. Subsequent planning efforts in many countries, however, have given increasing attention to the consistency and coordination of decisions, to the indirect effects on the economy of the proposed projects, and to projections and targets for the private sector as well as the public sector. As a result, the formulation of development plans has certainly improved. And yet major shortcomings remain at the level of formulation—and even more so at the level of implementation.

Formulation of a plan is bound to be difficult in so far as there is no theory of development that can be readily translated into a development program. In few, if any, areas of economic policy does the distance between theory and policy tend to be as great as it is for development problems. All the theories of development —classical, Marxian, Schumpeterian, neo-Keynesian—are simply ways of looking systematically at the general development process. They relate to the "economics *about* development"—the way one looks at development in the abstract and from the outside. But this is far different from the "economics *for* development"—the economics that the development practitioner needs in formulating and administering an actual program. Unfortunately, however, development theories have only too often been interpreted as if they provided recipes for successful development, and access to the teachings of modern economics has been thought to have some new magical quality. The delusions of such a naïve approach have been exposed, and the local practitioner of practical programming now realizes that a planning model—if it is to serve as a basis for assessing policy alternatives—must be far more complex and comprehensive than any development theory.[1]

The ability to formulate a development plan has also been severely limited by the lack of requisite data and the imperfect character of such statistics as are available. Economic policy measures necessarily assume quantitative estimation for their formulation and for the evaluation of their effects. The illumination of policy choices is therefore handicapped when the existence of historical statistics is negligible and the measurement of key variables is deficient. Errors may be large when the data are inadequate to calculate such strategic variables as total savings, capital coefficients, the extent of underemployment, or the value of an investment project.[2]

While there has been progress in overcoming the deficiencies in empirical infor-

1. For a list of technical criticisms of various mathematical models of development programming, see Jan Tinbergen and Hendricus C. Bos, *Mathematical Models of Economic Growth*, New York, 1962, pp. 113-16.

2. For a discussion of data needed for econometric models of development programming, ranging from the simplest to the more complex types of models, see United Nations, Economic Commission for Asia and the Far East, *Programming Techniques for Economic Development*, Bangkok, 1961, chapters IV, VI.

mation and in improving planning methods, there is still a tendency to expect too much from a planning model. It is sometimes thought that a planning model can remove or simplify the hard choices of development policy and provide a definitive set of "decision rules" that can serve as specific guides to action for the policymaker. In formulating a development plan, however, the policy-maker cannot expect to find through the exercise of economic techniques, no matter how refined, a complete set of unambiguous answers that absolve him from the ultimate responsibility of choice. Regardless of improvements in the evolution of planning models, the policy-maker cannot escape from the making of value judgments, and political decisions are still required. This is true for both establishing objectives and for selecting policy instruments. A conflict among multiple objectives is frequently encountered in development programming, and it is then necessary to decide which objective should receive precedence in planning. Instead of a single development program, there are in fact any number of alternative programs according to the values given to diverse objectives and to various policy instruments. For each criterion of a policy action there is also likely to be a non-economic criterion, and while a planning model might point up the economic and non-economic consequences of different policy decisions, the ultimate decision is political. Thus, although development economists can contribute some illumination to the ultimate choice of policy by determining a range of alternative feasible programs and by showing the consequences for each alternative, nonetheless the economist alone cannot determine an optimum program.

Further, it is necessary to realize that in formulating a development plan, the mere act of co-ordination does not guarantee in any way the merit of the particular decisions that are being taken. A program, as Professor Cairncross remarks, "is a focus, not a substitute for decision-making ... it is nonsense to think that a programme settles everything and that no sensible decisions can be taken without one. It furnishes no more than a systematic way of trying to co-ordinate decisions and improve on unco-ordinated decisions. Although unco-ordinated decisions may be bad or costly so also may co-ordinated decisions: there is no magic about a programme that transforms the quality of decisions beyond the virtue that coordination lends." [3]

The record of development policies in many emerging countries makes it clear that problems of implementing a development plan now need to receive even more attention than problems of formulation. The better performance of planning in an advanced country is not to be attributed so much to a more incisive understanding of economic policy, but to the greater ability to execute policies effectively. The governments of many newly developing nations have fairly rapidly attained an understanding of what development measures might be taken, but the capacity to implement these policies has remained limited.

The fact that a development plan may meet the tests of efficiency and consistency on paper, only to fail in practice is due in large measure to deficiencies in political and administrative requirements. Without sufficient political leadership and authority, a government is unwilling and unable to act upon the plan. Political interests may also run counter to the economic rationale of the development plan if the political party in power is concerned with only short-run policies, is willing to settle for "showcase" projects and public symbols, is

3. A. K. Cairncross, "Programmes as Instruments of Co-ordination," *Scottish Journal of Political Economy*, June 1961, p. 90.

influenced by sectional interests, or is unwilling to allow a loss in social status or political power for certain groups upon which it depends for political support.

Deficiencies in the executive and administrative machinery severely handicap the implementation of a plan. The organization of public administration in many poor countries still tends to be limited to simply the "law and order" kind of administration. But this is not suited for the more subtle administration of economic controls or for the complex operation of economic enterprises. For more effective implementation of a development plan, a specialized economic civil service is essential. It is also necessary for the planning agency to have executive functions and to be able to influence the planning activities of individual government departments. There must also be a clear delineation of the responsibility for framing and carrying out economic policy, so that the relative bureaucratic strengths of the respective agencies are not allowed to determine the outcome of the plan. And since planning is a continuous process, there must be provision for the necessary revisions of the original plan and some guidance on when the several departments and agencies ought to deviate from the originally established policies.

The implementation of a development plan also tends to be extremely difficult when its formulation has been based upon the most advanced economics. Too frequently there has been an attraction to the most refined model, the newest technique, the latest element of expertise. But when policy-makers borrow and imitate at too high a level, the development plan is then likely to become too refined for practical implementation. Given their present circumstances, most poor countries might benefit more from the sound application of fundamental elementary principles of economics than from attempts to use the

highest style theory. Indeed, the meeting of immediate needs may be lost through the overreaching for more complex techniques of analysis and highly formalized models. In this connection, much of the effort devoted to the use of econometric models and the technique of linear programming in framing a development program might be considered premature. These models and techniques have tended to focus too exclusively on investment; they have made the economic analysis overly refined for practical applicability in most poor countries; and they have also intensified the problem of communication between economics and the other social sciences which is so necessary for a full understanding of development issues.

The temptation to use the highest level of analysis also reinforces the tendency to neglect the non-economic components of the development process. The more rigorous is the economic analysis, the less is it able to incorporate non-economic elements. Yet the implementation of development programming is very much a matter of how much political change and cultural change the society can absorb and how quickly. For a country that is still in only an early phase of development, it is especially important that attention first be given to whether the total environment is favorable for development, before concentrating on the purely economic factors. Unless this is done, there is little likelihood of effective implementation of policies designed to remove the economic barriers to development. For, regardless of the economic logic of the development plan, its success in gaining popular support and participation will depend on cultural elements, values, attitudes. As Professor Galbraith observes, "on even the most preliminary view of the problem, effective government, education, and social justice emerge as critically important. In many countries, in diagnosing the barriers to advance, it is lack of these that is of critical importance. And it follows that until these barriers are removed little will come from capital investment and technical assistance. While plans may be big on paper they will be small in result." [4]

From considerations such as the foregoing, the conclusion is becoming more widespread that a comprehensive, heavy type of planning is likely to be premature for most poor countries at their present level of development. Although a few countries may have already laid the administrative, social, and educational groundwork that is necessary for a complex development plan, and a few governments may have the necessary political and administrative powers, most of the poor countries are not yet capable of undertaking the comprehensive type of planning that involves the government in numerous decisions of a direct specific character.

In recent years there has been some retrenchment from comprehensive planning as certain undesirable results have become apparent. In practice, this type of planning has tended to be too investment-centered and biased toward heavy industry; has accentuated inflationary pressures; neglected the problems of allocation and distribution; reacted on the supply of private entrepreneurship and hindered the full realization of investment potentials in the private sector; led to inefficient industrialization with projects that are handicapped by technical difficulties and excess capacity; and has slighted the strategic importance of agricultural growth and export expansion.

In contrast with their earlier enthusiasm

4. J. K. Galbraith, *Economic Development in Perspective,* Cambridge, 1962, pp. 9-10.

for comprehensive centralized planning, a number of countries are now attempting to place more reliance on decentralized regulation and are giving more emphasis to the improvement and guidance of the market mechanism. In this lighter-type of planning, the initial objectives may be to achieve the maximum utilization of existing resources, increase investment in the areas of social overhead and economic overhead, and effect agrarian reforms—rather than to concentrate on a forced take-off and high speed development, with a large amount of public investment and deliberate industrialization constituting the core of the plan. The special recognition of the need to increase the marketable surplus of agriculture is of fundamental importance. Government policies are emphasizing more the strengthening of the general conditions for development by providing social and economic overhead capital, establishing markets by institutional arrangements, and improving the efficiency of markets. While light industry may be promoted, the development of capital-intensive heavy industry awaits the more gradual inducement from the progress of agriculture. As development proceeds, the economy may also be expected to use capital more effectively, and capital formation should result from the increase in income.

It may be submitted that this type of planning conforms better to the present needs and capabilities of most poor countries. It is predicated upon policy requirements that should prove possible to implement. And it should avoid the too easy notion that the problems of development are solved—and the costs of development are avoided—merely by engaging in national development planning.

5. BIBLIOGRAPHICAL NOTE

1. For a general introduction to development programming techniques, the following are especially noteworthy: G. Colm and T. Geiger, "Country Programming as a Guide to Development," in R. E. Asher (editor), *Development of the Emerging Countries*, Washington, D.C., 1962; International Development Agency, *Organization, Planning and Programming for Economic Development*, United Nations Conference on the Application of Science and Technology for the Benefit of the Less Developed Areas, Vol. VIII, Washington, 1962; Gustav F. Papanek, *Framing a Development Program, International Conciliation*, March 1960; Dudley Seers, "Economic Programming in a Country Newly Independent," *Social and Economic Studies*, March 1962; Jan Tinbergen, *The Design of Development*, Baltimore, 1958; Tinbergen, "Problems of Economic Policy," *International Social Science Journal*, Vol. XI, No. 3, 1959; United Nations, Department of Economic and Social Affairs, *Analyses and Projections of Economic Development: I. An Introduction to the Technique of Programming*, New York, 1955; United Nations, ECAFE, *Programming Techniques for Economic Development*, Bangkok, 1960, and *Formulating Industrial Development Programmes*, Bangkok, 1961.

2. Mathematical models of development and the techniques of mathematical programming of development may be examined more intensively in the following references: Russell Ackoff, "Operations Research and National Planning, *Operations Research*, August 1957; Charles Hitch, "A Dissent," *Operations Research*, October 1957; M. Bronfenbrenner, "A Simplified Mahalanobis Development Model," *Economic Development and Cultural Change*, October 1960; S. Chakravarty, "The Existence of an Optimum Savings Program," *Econometrica*, Vol. 30, 1962; Chakravarty, "The Mahalanobis Model of Development Planning," *Arthaniti*, November 1957; H. B. Chenery, "The Role of Industrialization in Development Programs," *American Economic Review, Papers and Proceedings*, May 1955; Chenery and K. S. Kretschmer, "Resources Allocation for Economic Development," *Econometrica*, October 1956; Chenery and P. C. Clark, *Interindustry Economics*, New York, 1959; R. Dorfman, P. A. Samuelson, and R. M. Solow, *Linear Programming and Economic Analysis*, New York, 1958; O. Eckstein, "Capital Theory and Some Theoretical Problems in Development Planning," *American Economic Review*, May 1951; R. F. Findlay, "Capital Theory and Development Planning," *Review of Economic Studies*, February 1962; T. Haavelmo, *A Study in the Theory of Economic Evolution*, Amsterdam, 1954; L. Johansen, *A Multisectoral Model of Economic Growth*, Amsterdam, 1960; R. Komiya, "A Note on Professor Mahalanobis' Model of Indian Economic Policy," *Review of Economics and Statistics*, February 1959; P. C. Mahalanobis, "The Approach of Operational Research to Planning in India," *Sankhya*, December 1955; E. Malinvaud, "Capital Accumulation and Efficient Allocation of Resources," *Econometrica*, Vol. 21, 1953; Roy Radner, *Notes on the Theory of Economic Planning*, Center of Economic Research, Athens, 1963; J. Sandee, *A Demonstration Planning Model for India*, Calcutta, 1960; I. J. Sattinger, "System Analysis in Development Programs," *International Development Review*, September 1963; J. K. Sengupta and G. Tintner, "On Some Economic Models of Development Planning," *Economia Internazionale*, February 1963; T. N. Srinivasan, "Investment Criteria and Choice of Techniques of Production,"

Yale Economic Essays, Spring 1962; Jan Tinbergen and Hendricus C. Bos, *Mathematical Models of Economic Growth,* New York, 1962; P. J. Verdoorn, "Complementarity and Long-Range Projections," *Econometrica,* October 1956.

3. The following references consider quantitative aspects of development programming: R. A. Bishop, "Input-Output Work as a Basis for Development Planning," *Monthly Bulletin of Agricultural Economics and Statistics,* May 1956; Michael Bruno, *Interdependence, Resource Use and Structural Change in Israel,* Jerusalem, 1962; Phyllis Deane, *Colonial Social Accounting,* Cambridge, 1953; A. T. Peacock and Douglas Dosser, "Input-Output Analysis in an Underdeveloped Country: A Case Study," *Review of Economic Studies,* Vol. 25 (1), No. 66, October 1957; A. R. Prest, *The Investigation of National Income in British Tropical Dependencies,* London, 1957; Dudley Seers, "The Role of National Income Estimates in the Statistical Policy of an Underdeveloped Area," *Review of Economic Studies,* Vol. 20 (3), No. 53, 1952–53; United Nations, ECAFE, "Statistics Required for Planning in the ECAFE Region," *Economic Bulletin for Asia and the Far East,* November 1955, and Statistical Office, *Statistical Series for the Use of Less Developed Countries in Programmes of Economic and Social Development,* New York, 1959.

4. A large number of case studies are now available for an appraisal of development planning in practice. A selected list of readings follows: Peter Bauer, *Indian Economic Policy and Development,* London, 1961; Werner Baer, "Puerto Rico: An Evaluation of a Successful Development Program," *Quarterly Journal of Economics,* November 1959; David E. Bell, "Allocating Development Resources: Some Observations Based on Pakistan Experience," in *Public Policy,* Vol. IX, Cambridge, 1959; Bell, "Planning for Development in Pakistan," *Pakistan Economic Journal,* March 1962; V. V. Bhatt, "A Decade of Planned Development: The Indian Experience," *Economia Internazionale,* Vol. XV, No. 2, 1962; R. Braibanti and J. J. Spengler (editors), *Administration and Economic Development in India,* Durham, 1963; Douglas Dosser, "The Formulation of Development Plans in the British Colonies," *Economic Journal,* June 1954; G. R. Gadgil, *Planning and Economic Policy in India,* New York, 1961; B. Glassburner, "Economic Policy-Making in Indonesia, 1950–57," *Economic Development and Cultural Change,* January 1962; Frank H. Golay, *The Philippines: Public Policy and National Economic Development,* Ithaca, 1961; U. K. Hicks, "The Integration of the Budget and the Development Plan with Special Reference to the Spanish Situation," *Public Finance,* Vol. XVII, No. 2, 1962; A. O. Hirschman, *Journeys Toward Progress—Studies of Economic Policy-Making in Latin America,* New York, 1963; J. P. Lewis, *Quiet Crisis in India,* Washington, 1962; I. M. D. Little, "The Strategy of Indian Development," *National Institute Economic Review,* May 1960; Little, "Indian Third Five-Year Plan," *Oxford Economic Papers,* February 1962; W. Malenbaum, *Prospects for Indian Development,* London, 1962; S. M. Mark, "Chinese Economic Growth Under the Five Year Plans," *Malayan Economic Review,* April 1962; R. S. Milne (editor), *Planning for Progress,* Manila, 1960; Ragnar Nurkse, "Reflections on India's Development Plan," *Quarterly Journal of Economics,* May 1957; M. Narasimham, "India's Third Five Year Plan," *IMF Staff Papers,* November 1962; Barba Niculescu, *Colonial Planning: A Comparative Study,* London, 1958; A. T. Peacock and Douglas Dosser, "Stabilization and Economic Planning in African Countries," *Public Finance,* Vol. XVII, No. 3, 1962;

J. H. Power, "Industrialization in Pakistan: A Case of Frustrated Take-off," *Pakistan Development Review*, Summer 1963; K. N. Raj, "Growth Models and Indian Planning," *Indian Economic Review*, February 1961; Sayre P. Schatz, "Influence of Planning on Development: The Nigerian Experience, *Social Research,* Winter 1960; F. C. Shorter, "Planning Procedures in Pakistan," *Pakistan Development Review*, Autumn 1961; United Nations, ECAFE, "Economic Growth of ECAFE Countries," *Economic Survey of Asia and the Far East, 1961,* Bankok, 1962, and "Economic Development and Planning in Asia and the Far East," *Economic Bulletin for Asia and the Far East,* December 1961; Raymond Vernon, *The Dilemma of Mexico's Development*, Cambridge, 1963.

Absorptive capacity, 93, 135, 270; *see also* Capital formation

Accounting prices, 235, 238, 487, 490-91, 510-12, 520-21; *see also* Programming

Adler, J. H., 98, 439, 500

Administration, 548f., 554-6, 560, 563

Africa, 7, 137-8, 529-32

Aggregate models, 467-71, 493-4, 508

Agrarian reform, 218, 420, 488

Agriculture, 263, 289f., 419-20; and capital formation, 294-7, 309-10; and industry, 44, 253-4; and inflation, 214-15; cash crops, 50; exports, 293-4; in Colombia, 318-22; in Japan, 292, 304-15; in Latin America, 315f.; in traditional society, 15; underemployment in, 74-88; investment in, 334-5; productivity in, 263-4, 289; surplus, 127, 324; taxation of, 127f., 295-6; *see also* Agrarian reform, Food supply

Akerman, J., 277-8

Anderson, C. Arnold, 276

Autonomous development, 354

Backwardness, degrees of, 39-41

Balance of payments, 155, 328, 331-5, 362, 364, 404, 406, 539; *see also* Debt servicing, Foreign exchange

Balanced growth, 250f., 254f., 265, 277-8; critique of, 254f.

Baran, P. A., 120

Barber, W., 87

Bauer, P. T., 359

Benham, Frederic, 131

"Big push," 92, 416, 431-40

Bloomfield, A. I., 189

Boeke, J. H., 48, 53, 55

Bos, H. C., 476

Bowman, Mary Jean, 276

Budget, *see* Public expenditures, Taxation

Buffer pools, 395

Cairncross, A. K., 4, 33, 98, 104, 363, 562

Campos, Roberto de Oliveira, 210

Capital accumulation, 16f., 86, 88, 90f., 331-2; and taxation, 115-31; contribution of, 104f., 110-12; in take-off, 35f.; process of, 112f.; requirements, 92f., 103, 485-7; sources, 91, 112-15; *see also* Foreign aid, Taxation

Capital coefficient, *see* Capital-output ratio

Capital-output ratio, 17, 90, 93-5, 98-104, 231-2; criticisms of, 101-4

Capital transfer, 356-7

Capitalist sector, 85f.; *see also* Dual economy

Ceylon, 120, 327-32, 460-62

Chelliah, R. J., 119

Chenery, H. B., 232, 234, 241, 503, 520

Chile, 219f.

China, 16, 20, 37, 296, 312

Colonialism, 55

Commercial policy, *see* Customs union, Protection

Commodity stabilization, 393f., 403

Comparative cost, 234, 293, 344, 354, 357, 411, 522-3, 560

Compensatory financing, 391, 392, 399f., 404f.

Complementarity, 258-9

Cultural change, *see* Social change, Value system

Customs union, 408f.

Deane, Phyllis, 5

Debt servicing, 141-2, 148, 155-6

Deficit financing, 174-83

Demonstration effect, 62-3, 371-2

Development blocks, 236

Development insurance fund, 401-2

Disguised unemployment, 49, 70, 77-85, 287, 420

Distribution of income, 216

Diversification, 294, 353, 394

Dorrance, G. S., 184

Dosser, Douglas, 247

Dual economy, 48-54, 90; and technological dualism, 68-70; Boeke's theory, 53-64; employment problem, 71f.; exchange sector, 50f.; in Africa, 49-53; Lewis's model of, 85-8, 294-7; Social systems, 53-5

Eckaus, R. S., 68, 243

Eckstein, O., 233

Economic infrastructure, 489

Economic surplus, 120-21

Education, 15, 137-8, 270f., 276f., 526

Ellis, H. S., 436

Enclaves, 7

Entrepreneurship, 11, 98-9

Exchange rate, 205, 218, 293, 357; *see also* Foreign exchange, Balance of payments

Exports, 291, 338f., 374-5; and inflation, 183-4; cash crops, 50-51; of manufactures, 352, 371, 375-6, 378f.; proceeds, 385f.; prospects, 299; taxes, 124-6; *see also* Trade-induced development

External economies, 94, 257, 259-60, 302, 432-4, 437-8, 446

Factor movements, *see* Foreign investment, International trade, Labor
Factor proportions problem, 68
Finance, 19, 20, 21, 40, 113, 543
Food supply, 82, 291f., 324-5, 328, 332, 370
Foreign aid, 46, 91, 114, 131f., 389, 558; and India, 142-5; requirements, 131-8; types and conditions of, 138-42; utilization of, 145f.; *see also* Balance of payments, Capital formation, Foreign capital
Foreign capital, 21, 421
Foreign enterprises, 69
Foreign exchange, 143-5, 293, 294, 333, 399, 422, 484, 534; shortage of, 165-6, 205, 234, 421-2, 540; *see also* Exchange rate, Foreign capital, Balance of payments
Foreign trade, *see* International trade
Frankel, S. H., 110
Free trade areas, 408f.
Friedmann, W. G., 159
Furnivall, J. S., 64

Gains from trade, 340, 349, 409; *see also* Comparative cost, Protection, Import-substitution
Galbraith, J. K., 563-4
Galenson, W., 232, 239
Gerschenkron, A., 4, 31, 38, 43
Ghana, 322-5, 524
Goode, R., 117, 122
Growth rates, measurement of, 5-11
Grunwald, J., 213

Habakkuk, H. J., 4, 36
Haberler, G., 77, 352, 361
Hagen, E, E., 10
Harbison, F. H., 272
Harrod-Domar analysis, 101-2, 466-9, 538
Heckscher, Eli F., 344
Heller, W. W., 115
Hicks, J. R., 327, 348, 361
Higgins, B. H., 48, 55
Hilgert, Folke, 344
Hirschman, A. O., 254, 260, 262, 522
Hoffman, Paul G., 133
Human investment, *see* Human resources
Human resources, 266f., 448-9; *see also* Education, Entrepreneurship, Population

Imperialism, 359
Import substitution, 205, 216, 265, 288, 293, 297f., 300, 351, 370, 376-7, 409, 437
Imports, 299, 329, 391-2; *see also* Commercial policy, Import substitution
Income distribution, 119-20
Increasing returns, 349-50
India, 6-7, 20, 94, 121, 142-5, 542-60; Third Plan, 129-30, 542-60
Indivisibilities, 417, 434
Industrial centers, 340f.
Industrialization, 276f.; and employment, 300f.; and production, 297f.; in Argentina, 287; in Ceylon, 327-32; in Europe, 5-6, 38-41; in Ghana, 322-5; in Pakistan, 381; in West Indies, 325-6, 379
Infant industry, 302-3, 357; *see also* Comparative cost, Protection
Inflation, 20, 266, 292, 357, 421, 485, 557; and capital formation, 169f.; causes of, 174f., 203f.; control of, 184-9; effects, 170-74, 183-4; in Chile, 213f.; in Latin America, 203f., 224f.; monetarist view, 210f.; structuralist view, 207f., 210f., 217-19
Innovations, 11, 13, 16, 34, 37, 106
Input-output, 245-6, 473-6, 552-3; *see also* Inter-industry models
Interest rates, 194f.
Inter-industry models, 473-6, 494-5; *see also* Input-output
I. M. F., 404-8
International trade, and capital formation, 348-51, 356-7; and dynamic benefits, 352f.; and innovations, 355-6; back-setting effects of, 345-8; classical theory of, 344-5, 352-7; pattern of, 350-52, 355, 360-61, 368-70
Investible surplus, 253; *see also* Agriculture, Capital formation, Labor surplus
Investment, *see* Capital accumulation
Investment criteria, 148, 231f., 488-9, 516-20, 522, 550
Investment in human capital, 266f.; *see also* Human resources
Investment insurance, 157

Japan, 9, 16, 20, 94, 120, 304-15, 441
Johnson, H. G., 425
Johnston, B. F., 291
Joint ventures, 135, 158, 159-63, 164-5

Kahn, A. E., 232
Kindleberger, C. P., 360
Koestner, N., 81
Krishnaswamy, K. S., 98
Kuznets, S., 4, 5, 25, 43, 120, 268, 439

Labor surplus, 233-4, 327, 333
Lange, Oskar, 487
Lary, H. B., 376
Latin America, 7, 8, 97, 137, 224, 287-9
Leading sectors, 3, 12, 22-3, 28-9, 35-6
Leibenstein, H., 70, 232, 239
Lewis, J. P., 547
Lewis, W. A., 80, 85, 95, 163, 265, 297, 322, 325, 378, 418, 523
Linear programming, 475-6, 520-22, 551, 563
Linkages, 72, 262, 373
Little, I. M. D., 556
Lovasy, Gertrude, 183

Management, 451-2
Manoilesco, Mihail, 78
Manpower shortages, 271f.
Marginal-productivity criterion, 236-8
Market mechanism, defects, 416-18, 427-30, 505; functions, 252, 427; merits, 415, 425-31, 564
Marketable surplus, 253; see also Agriculture, Capital formation, Labor surplus
Marketing board, 296, 389, 396
Marshall, Alfred, 358
Marx, Karl, 4, 23-4, 38, 69
Mayne, A., 496
Mellor, John W., 291
Migrant labor, 87
Mill, J. S., 356
Mobilization of capital, see Capital accumulation, Foreign investment, Taxation
Monetarists, see Inflation
Monetary policy, 189-93, 207f., 224
Money markets, 193-203
Myint, H., 280, 371
Myrdal, G., 344, 354, 389

Narasimham, M., 129
Nigeria, 452-6
Nurkse, R., 74, 81, 233, 250, 358

Ohkawa, K., 304
Ohlin, Bertil, 344
Optimum population theory, 76-7

Pakistan, 380-85
Papanek, G. F., 289
Patel, S. J., 119
Patterson, Gardner, 174
Periphery, 286f., 339
Planning, 418f., 423-6, 440-45; assessment, 523f.; country studies, 523-61; implementation, 548, 563; in Asia, 532-42; in India, 456-60, 542-60; period, 536-8; phasing, 554; premature, 563-4; priorities, 526-8; problems, 492-5, 496-500, 561-4

Plural society, 64-8
Polak, J. J., 231, 234
Policy instruments, 503f.
Population, 12, 44, 64, 76-7, 292, 327, 347
Prebisch, R., 207, 286, 339
Preconditions, 4, 14-16, 29-30, 33-4, 37
Price system, see Market mechanism
Private foreign capital, 91, 114; contribution of, 149-59; in Ghana, 163-6; protection of, 156-7; see also Capital accumulation
Production functions, 49, 68-71, 373
Production theory, 11f.
Programming, 417, 449, 508; aim, 417-18, 449-51, 466-7, 476f., 493, 529, 533-5, 562; mathematical, 476-83 (see also Linear programming); models, 465-76, 479-83; techniques, 438, 529f., 547-54 (see also Planning)
Project evaluation, 512-16
Project loans, 140-41
Protection, 237, 287, 298, 300-303, 353, 411, 430, 506; see also Comparative cost, Customs union
Public expenditure, 419, 500-502, 530-32
Public finance, see Inflation, Public expenditure, Taxation
Public sector, 96, 416, 440-45, 448-9, 456-8, 460, 491, 501, 535, 543f.
Puerto Rico, 497-500
Purchase contracts, 395

Quotas, 395

Rao, V. K. R. V., 5, 42
Reddaway, W. B., 103
Regional integration, 157-8, 408f.
Resource immobility, 181-2
Robertson, D. H., 358
Robinson, Joan, 77
Rosenstein-Rodan, P. N., 98, 255, 416, 431
Rosovsky, H., 304
Rostow, W. W., 3f., 11, 13, 23f.
Rural development, 291

School leavers, 84, 275
Schott, F. H., 219
Schultz, T. W., 267f., 361
Scitovsky, T., 255-7
Sectoral allocations, 539
Sectoral growth, 12-13, 21-2
Sectoral integration, 408
Sectoral models, 471-3, 509
Seers, Dudley, 224, 483
Self-sustained growth, 31-2
Sen, A. K., 83
Shadow prices, see Accounting prices
Singer, H. W., 179, 263

Social change, 16, 24, 44, 66, 112; *see also* Human resources, Social infrastructure, Value system
Social dualism, 54
Social infrastructure, 280f.
Social marginal productivity, 232
Soviet Union, 96, 278, 296
Stages of growth, 3f.; characteristics of, 25-6; criticisms of, 23-41; empirical evidence, 25-33; Marxian analysis, 23-5; Rostow's analysis, 3-23; *see also* Preconditions, Self-sustained growth, Take-off, Traditional society
Staple exports, 389
Stolper, W. F., 491
Streeten, P., 259
Structural changes, 290, 311
Structural disequilibrium, 388
Structural equilibrium, 210
Structural transformation, 277
Structural unemployment, 68
Structuralists, 210f.; *see also* Inflation
Subsistence sector, 75, 85f.
Surplus labor, 74-7, 114, 272, 289, 300; *see also* Underemployment
Swerling, B. C., 385

Take-off, 3, 13, 16-23, 33f., 132; conditions of, 17; dates, 18; empirical evidence, 26-8; historical cases, 42-3; in future, 42-7; *see also* Stages of growth
Tariff factories, 303

Taxation, 91, 97, 113, 115f., 180, 290; concessions, 157; consumption taxes, 126; income taxes, 122-3, 129; land tax, 118, 128, 309-10; machinery, 389; of agriculture, 127-9
Technological dualism, 49, 68-71, 90
Technological progress, 10, 13, 15, 59, 70-71, 100, 106-7, 109, 267-8
Technology, 243-7, 516f.
Terms of trade, 114, 154-5, 340-43, 360, 362, 372-3, 387-8, 410
Tinbergen, J., 232, 476
Trade creation, 409-10
Trade diversion, 409-11
Trade-induced development, 20-21, 264-5, 354f., 358f., 363f., 371f.; *see also* Exports
Traditional society, 13-14

Unbalanced growth, 259f.
Underemployment, 49, 58, 74-85
"Unit multiplier," 114

Value system, 16, 24, 44-5, 59
Viner, J., 79

Wage differential, 300-302
Wai, U Tun, 185, 193
Wald, H. P., 295
Wallich, H. C., 393
West Africa, 97, 270-71
West Indies, 325-7, 378-80

Young, Allyn, 433-4